Communication engineering principl

Communication engineering principles

Ifiok Otung

palgrave

Published by
PALGRAVE
Houndmills, Basingstoke, Hampshire RG21 6XS and
175 Fifth Avenue, New York, N. Y. 10010
Companies and representatives throughout the world

PALGRAVE is the new global academic imprint of
St. Martin's Press LLC Scholarly and Reference Division and
Palgrave Publishers Ltd (formerly Macmillan Press Ltd).

ISBN 0–333–77522–8 paperback

This book is printed on paper suitable for recycling and made from fully managed and sustained forest sources.

A catalogue record for this book is available from the British Library.

Typeset by Ian Kingston Editorial Services, Nottingham, UK

10 9 8 7 6 5 4 3 2 1
10 09 08 07 06 05 04 03 02 01

Printed and bound in Great Britain by
Antony Rowe Ltd, Chippenham, Wiltshire

Contents

Preface

A new approach to teaching communication engineering

Communication Engineering Principles is aimed at undergraduate courses in communication engineering, and may be used successfully as supplementary reading for MSc students or for short courses in telecommunications for practising engineers. Although many current textbooks purport to do this effectively, the innovative approach adopted in *Communication Engineering Principles* has been shown in my experience to be preferred by all students when first encountering the subject.

Minimal mathematics

The essential approach taken is to impart a thorough grounding in the fundamental concepts and design issues involved in communication engineering using minimal mathematics. Most of the existing textbooks on communication engineering take a mathematical systems approach that requires the student to jump over a mathematical high-hurdle before being able to enjoy what is a thoroughly exciting subject and a highly rewarding career. Such a needlessly mathematical approach may deter potentially successful engineers or cloud their insight into the underlying *engineering* concepts. At the other end of the scale are those textbooks that are unsuitable to the intended readership of *Communication Engineering Principles* because they are written to educate non-technical and non-mathematical readers on the terminology and basic concepts of communication engineering.

Engineering first, mathematics second

The presentation throughout the book emphasises the underlying engineering considerations. Mathematics is used only to the extent and at a level that is absolutely necessary. A good demonstration of this philosophy is the novel derivation of the matched filter in Chapter 6. Furthermore, lucid graphs and diagrams are employed to facilitate understanding and assimilation. The reader is coached in solving a wide range of practical problems, all of which have a direct bearing on current applications in communication engineering.

A thorough grounding in the principles

After studying the material presented in *Communication Engineering Principles* or completing a course based on the book, the reader will have a thorough understanding of the principles of telecommunications, and a sound knowledge of the interplay of various systems parameters and the trade-offs involved in the design of communications systems. The reader will also be very well equipped and sufficiently motivated to deal with more specialised telecommunications topics and applications.

Lecturer support

Lecturer support is available in the form of a Solutions Manual, available from the publisher. In addition, all the figures from the book are available as PowerPoint slides, accessible from the Publisher's Web site.

Chapter by chapter overview

Chapter 1 gives a comprehensive and non-mathematical *overview of communication systems*. The treatment erects crucial pegs on which to hang further knowledge and is sufficiently detailed to serve as the material for a short course that presents a survey of modern telecommunications. The presentation includes *non-electrical telecommunications*, *key developments* in modern telecommunications, *elements* and *classifications* of a communication system, *signal processing* in communication systems, and an introduction to *digital communications*.

Chapter 2 provides a carefully gauged and step-by-step discussion of *telecommunication signals* and how they are manipulated in telecommunication systems. The *sinusoidal signal* is introduced as the basic building block of all types of signal waveforms and an indicator of system characteristics. This allows us to deal with important concepts such as *signal spectrum*, *system transfer function* and *signal transmission* and *distortions*. *Logarithmic measures* and *calibration* of signal transmission paths are also discussed.

Chapter 3 is a comprehensive treatment of *amplitude modulation* and all its variants, which include *vestigial sideband*, *independent sideband*, *single sideband* and *double sideband*. The presentation emphasises key principles and design considerations, and includes *modulation* and *demodulation circuits*, the *AM transmitter*, the *superheterodyne* receiver and various applications.

Chapter 4 on *angle modulation* brings a fresh approach to the teaching of *frequency* and *phase modulations*. Emphasis is placed on a thorough understanding of the fundamental concepts, the relationships between the two modulation techniques, the design considerations, and circuits for modulation and demodulation.

Chapter 5 presents a lucid and comprehensive discussion of *sampling* and lays an important foundation for the introduction of digital transmission techniques. Topics treated include the sampling of *low pass* and *bandpass* signals, *anti-alias filter design*, *natural* and *flat-top sampling*, and *aperture distortion*.

Chapter 6 covers *digital baseband transmission*, and includes a wide range of techniques for the digital representation of analogue signals, *line coding*, *pulse shaping* to combat *intersymbol interference*, *digital baseband receiver* operations and the *matched filter*. In particular, the chapter features a detailed discussion of *A-law* and *μ-law pulse code modulation* (PCM) and a review of *low bit rate speech coding* techniques.

Chapter 7 on *digital modulated transmission* continues the discussion of digital communication with a detailed treatment of the major digital modulation techniques. An important feature is the use of a simple geometrical approach to obtain the *bit error rate* (BER) of an arbitrary binary transmission system, which is then extended to various *M-ary transmissions*. Crucial information is provided to guide the systems designer on the choice of *modulation technique, bit rate, transmission bandwidth, signal power* and *bit error rate*.

Chapter 8 deals with *multiplexing strategies* for multi-user communication systems and includes up-to-date information on various international telecommunications standards. Topics discussed in detail include *frequency division multiplexing* (FDM), *time division multiplexing* (TDM), the *plesiochronous* and *synchronous digital hierarchies, SONET, ATM* and *code division multiplexing* (CDM).

Chapter 9 is the final chapter of the book and covers the evaluation of the impact of noise in digital and analogue communication systems, with several illustrative examples from *satellite communications*. The chapter also includes a discussion of *signal attenuation* in various transmission media and a lucid treatment of *white* and *narrowband random noise*.

Acknowledgements

I would like to thank Dr John Brush (University of Dundee), Mr Henry Green (Manchester Metropolitan University) and Dr Noel Evans (University of Ulster) for painstakingly reviewing the entire book and making many constructive suggestions for improvement. Their positive comments were an important source of inspiration. I wish to express my gratitude to my editor Christopher Glennie for his professional support throughout the writing of the book, and to Jacqueline Harbor for her enthusiastic editorial work and encouragement during the crucial early stages of the project.

I would also like to thank my wife Buchi for her unflinching and selfless support. She patiently engaged in countless discussions of different renderings of some sections of the book and made useful suggestions from her literary arsenal. My thanks also go to our children, Ifiok (12), Andikan (11), Yama (11), Iniekem (9) and Sara (6) for their keen interest in seeing the completion of 'this story'. They uncomplainingly accepted the ubiquitous presence of a laptop computer even at some of their sporting and school events.

Finally, I am grateful to God for the privilege to make this contribution to the education, training, career and reading pleasure of many.

Ifiok Otung
July 2000

About the author

Ifiok Otung holds BSc (first class honours) and MSc degrees in Electronic and Electrical Engineering from the University of Ife, and a PhD degree from the University of Surrey. A chartered engineer and member of the IEE, Dr Otung has been involved in telecommunications teaching and research since 1986 at Universities in Nigeria, England and Wales. He is currently with the University of Glamorgan.

Overview of communication systems

IN THIS CHAPTER

- A quick overview of non-electrical telecommunication techniques, highlighting their gross inadequacies for today's communication needs. You will find, however, that these ancient techniques are still indispensable in certain situations.

- A brief review of the developments in modern (electrical) telecommunication from telegraphy to the Internet. Key developments in binary codes for data transmission, electronic components, transmission media, signal processing and telecommunication services are highlighted.

- A discussion of the elements of a communication system. Modern telecommunication systems may vary widely in complexity and applications, but they are all accurately represented by one block diagram. You will become thoroughly conversant with the elements of this generic diagram and the roles and signal processing tasks that they perform. Information sources, information sinks, transmitters, receivers and transmission media are all introduced.

- A detailed overview of the classification of communication systems. Every system is *simplex* or *duplex*, *analogue* or *digital*, *baseband* or *modulated*. You will learn the features of each of these systems and find out just why we have undergone a *digital revolution*.

1.1 Introduction

This first chapter provides a panoramic view of communication systems. It is intended to give a lucid and comprehensive introduction to the subject of Communication Engineering. We follow a non-mathematical approach and attempt to show you how each telecommunication concept fits into the overall picture. Armed with this knowledge, it is hoped that you will have sufficient inspiration and motivation to go on to the remaining chapters, where the principles and terminology are treated in more detail. In the event that you do not have the time to study the entire book, it is advised that you work carefully through this chapter and the introductory sections of the remaining chapters. The material thus covered is suitable for a short course that presents a survey of modern telecommunications.

To drive home the fact that telecommunication generally means communication at a distance, we begin with a quick overview of various non-electrical means of 'telecommunicating'. The use of the word *telecommunication* is then narrowed to apply exclusively to the electrical techniques. After a quick review of the significant historical developments, we present a block diagram that adequately describes all communication systems. Each component and the processes that it contributes to the overall performance of the system are discussed in a non-mathematical way.

Different types and classifications of communication systems are discussed. Digital and analogue communication systems are compared and analogue baseband systems are discussed in detail. The features of digital baseband transmission are introduced. We show that modulated systems are essential to exploit the radio spectrum and the optical fibre medium, and discuss the features of this class of systems. Our discussion includes brief references to some of the main modern applications of telecommunications, namely television systems, communication networks, telephony, satellite communications, optical fibre communication systems and mobile communication systems.

On completing this chapter, you will be well equipped to make informed decisions regarding the suitability of different types of system blocks (including transmission media) and various classes of communication systems for different applications. You will also have a clear overall picture of telecommunication and a good foundation on which you can build a more detailed knowledge of the subject. I hope that working through this chapter will inspire you towards a career in telecommunication or a very enjoyable further study of this exciting field.

1.2 Non-electrical telecommunication

This book is concerned with modern telecommunication or *communication over a distance*, which relies principally on electrical means to convey information from one point S, the sending end, to another point R, the receiving end. After this section, we will use telecommunication, communication systems and other similar terms to refer exclusively to these modern technologies. However, before the advent of telegraphy, the forerunner of modern telecommunications in 1837, many forms of non-electrical 'telecommunications' existed. We will briefly introduce these non-electrical communication systems and discuss their demerits, before turning our attention to various types and classifications of modern communication systems.

1.2.1 Verbal non-electrical telecommunication

The most basic non-electrical telecommunication was verbal, in which for example a town crier used a combination of a gong and their voice to broadcast information in an African village. Trumpets were also blown to summon to war, call a truce or announce victory, depending on the distinctive sounds made. The transmitter in this case is the human vocal system and other suitable instrumental sound sources such as the gong, drum and trumpet. The signal is a pressure wave called an *acoustic signal*, the transmission medium is air and the receivers are every human ear within range of hearing. This form of 'telecommunication' is fraught with problems, which include the following.

- *Interference*: The ear also receives other *unwanted* sound signals in the environment, which serves as a common transmission medium. These sounds, which may be artificial or natural background noise, or the intelligible communication of other people, interfere with and hence corrupt the wanted signal. In the town crier example, an African woman would have to hush her chattering children, bleating goats and barking dogs, or move away from the noisy zone in order to minimise interference with the town crier's message.

- *Nuisance*: The signal is received by those who do not want it. If you had to use this verbal means to 'telecommunicate' with a friend a few blocks away, your neighbours would not be pleased.

- *Huge losses*: The signal suffers a lot of *attenuation*, or reduction in the *amplitude* of the pressure wave as it is reflected back at material boundaries and as it spreads out with distance over a wider wave front. For this reason, it is difficult to hear the town crier from within a closed room or from afar.

- *Limited range*: Communication can only take place over small distances (i.e. small separations between S and R). To overcome the above losses, sound signals of high SPL (sound pressure level) must be used to extend communication range. However, this increases the nuisance effect and endangers the hearing of those close to the sound source. Besides, the human vocal system and other practical sound sources are severely limited in the SPL that they can generate.

- *Masking effect*: The wanted signal can be easily *masked* by louder signals in the medium. This makes hearing (i.e. *detection*) of the wanted signal impossible. The threshold of hearing increases with ambient noise. This means that the ear–brain system will be completely oblivious to the presence of one sound if there is another louder sound of about the same frequency.

- *Lack of privacy*: Privacy is an important requirement that this means of communication is incapable of providing. Everyone (within range) hears your message and is potentially able to understand and react to it. Therefore this means of communication is only suitable for the broad-cast of public information and would not be suitable for the communi-cation of private, military, commercial or classified information.

- *Delay*: Even if we could overcome all the problems discussed above, *propagation delay*, the time it takes for the signal to travel from S to R, would still make this type of telecommunication unacceptable. Sound travels at a speed $v = 330$ m/s in standard air. Over very short distances, it seems as though we hear at the same instant as the sound is produced. However, imagine that S and R are separated by a distance of say $d = 2376$ km, a realistic international (and in some cases national) distance. The propagation delay is

$$t = \frac{d}{v} = \frac{2376000 \text{ m}}{330 \text{ m/s}} = 7200 \text{ seconds} = 2 \text{ hours}$$

Thus, if you made an acoustic 'phone call' over this distance, the person would hear each utterance a staggering two hours after it was made. And if the person said 'pardon', you would complete your call and hang up without knowing they wanted you to say it again. Real-time interactive communication would only be possible over short distances. This is in sharp contrast to the case of modern telecommunications using *electromag-netic waves*, which travel at the speed of light ($v \equiv c = 3 \times 10^8$ m/s). The prop-agation delay for the distance $d = 2376$ km is $t = 8$ ms. Barring other delays, you would hear each other practically instantaneously.

1.2.2 Visual non-electrical telecommunication

Various methods of non-verbal telecommunication were developed as a vast improvement on the basic technique discussed above. Here, the infor-mation to be conveyed is coded in the form of visually observable events. The transmitter generates these events. Light signals convey the informa-tion through a transmission medium that is ideally a vacuum, but is in prac-tice air. The receiver is a human eye within visibility range along an unobstructed line-of-sight path. The problems of interference, nuisance, propagation delay and masking by other signals are negligible compared to the verbal technique. Furthermore, the communication range is extended, especially in clear non-foggy weather. However, the receiver must have an unobstructed view of the signalling event and the major problem of lack of privacy remains. Visual non-electrical telecommunication systems were identical in transmission medium and receiver, differing only in the type of transmitter. The most common techniques are now discussed.

1.2.2.1 *Flags, smoke and bonfires*

The practice of raising a highly visible object, or performing complex coded motions with the object, has had universal application in warfare and ordi-nary social interactions over the centuries. Hand signals remain an indispensable means of communication in modern society. For example, hand signals are used by traffic wardens to control traffic. Hoisting a red flag or red light is still used to warn of danger, and raising a white flag in warfare communicates a message of surrender over distances that would be difficult to reach by verbal means.

An interesting record of a military application of this method of visual non-electrical telecommunication around 1405 BC is given in the Bible. Hebrew soldiers divide into two parties to attack a city. One party waits in ambush outside the city gates while the other attacks the city and fakes defeat in order to draw the city guards away in pursuit. At a good distance from the city, the fleeing party raises a javelin from a vantage point, thus *signalling* to the ambush party to take the now defenceless city. This party takes the city and quickly starts a bonfire, which 'telecommunicates' their success to the retreating party and *signals* the beginning of a bidirectional attack on the guards, who are in shock at the sight of their burning city.

1.2.2.2 *Heliography*

Heliography was a system of communication developed in the 19th century in which the rays of the Sun were directed using movable mirrors on to distant points. Some links for heliograph communication were set up and the technique was reliably used, for example in 1880 by General Stewart to give a battle account over some distance. Reading a *heliogram* (a message sent by heliography) was said to cause eye fatigue.

A technique for transmitting information using variations in the pattern of light had been developed by the Greeks as far back as the 2nd century BC. Different combinations and positions of torch light signals were employed to represent the letters of the Greek alphabet. In this way messages could be coded and transmitted.

1.2.2.3 *Semaphore*

A semaphore consists of an upright post with one or more arms moving in a vertical plane. Beginning with the 18th century, different positions of the arms or flags were used to represent letters. Table 1.1 gives the conventional alphanumeric semaphore codes. The semaphore codes for letters A, Q and V are illustrated in Fig. 1.1. Note that some of the letters of the alphabet are shared with numerals 0 to 9. A numerical message is distinguished by being preceded with the code (0°, 45°). Code AR is used to indicate end of signal and code *R* to acknowledge reception. In Table 1.1, the arm positions are given in degrees measured clockwise from vertical.

Some governments built large semaphore towers on hilltops along strategic routes. For example, during the Napoleonic wars (1792–1815) a relay

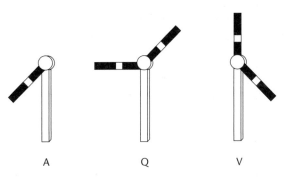

Figure 1.1 Semaphore codes for letters A, Q and V.

Table 1.1 Semaphore codes.

Symbol		Positions of semaphore flags	Symbol	Positions of semaphore flags
A	1	225°	N	(135°, 225°)
B	2	270°	O	(270°, 315°)
C	3	315°	P	(270°, 0°)
D	4	0°	Q	(270°, 45°)
E	5	45°	R	(270°, 90°)
F	6	90°	S	(270°, 135°)
G	7	135°	T	(315°, 0°)
H	8	(225°, 270°)	U	(315°, 45°)
I	9	(225°, 315°)	V	(0°, 135°)
	J	(0°, 90°)	W	(45°, 90°)
K	0 (zero)	(0°, 225°)	X	(45°, 135°)
	L	(45°, 225°)	Y	(90°, 315°)
	M	(90°, 225°)	Z	(90°, 135°)

of semaphore towers was built in England from London to Portsmouth. By the year 1886, semaphore had been almost universally adopted for signalling on railways. Semaphore is still used today at sea by warships preferring radio silence and for mechanical railway signalling.

1.2.2.4 Demerits of visual non-electrical telecommunication

The major disadvantages of visual non-electrical telecommunication include the following.

- *Low signalling speed*: The rates of signal generation at the transmitter and detection at the receiver are extremely low by modern standards. For example, if the torchlight or semaphore flag patterns are manipulated quickly enough to complete the representation of one letter every second, we have a maximum data rate of one character (or *byte*) per second. In modern systems, a *modem* that operates at 1000 times this speed is considered slow. Note, however, that propagation delay is negligible and the signal is received at almost the same instant as it is generated at the transmitter.

- *Manual operation*: A trained signaller is required at the transmitter to code the information and at the distant receiver to view and decode the signal patterns as they are transmitted. Automation of both transmission and reception is impractical.

- *Limited range*: The maximum separation that allows visibility between transmission and reception points may range from less than 50 m in thick fog to a few miles in obstruction-free terrain under very clear weather. However, this range is very low compared with the distances involved in modern communications.

- *Lack of privacy*: Even with the use of encrypted codes, the communication process is carried out in full view of all within the communication range.

- *Limited application*: A combination of the above factors means that visual non-electrical telecommunication remained a system that could only accommodate a very few users (*low capacity*) for very limited applications. This is grossly inadequate to meet the modern requirements of a high-capacity integrated services communication system.

1.3 Modern telecommunication

Modern telecommunication began in 1837 with the invention of telegraphy in the USA by Samuel Morse, a painter. Various coding schemes were developed to represent characters, namely letters of the alphabet, numbers (0 to 9), symbols and control characters. These codes are introduced below in chronological order. We then discuss some of the most significant developments in telecommunication since the advent of telegraphy.

1.3.1 Developments in binary codes for data transmission

1.3.1.1 Morse code

Transmission of textual information by telegraphy was carried out using 39 characters (26 letters of the alphabet, 10 numerals and 3 punctuation marks), which were represented in Morse code. An extended version of the Morse code is shown in Table 1.2. This is a variable-length code which is adequate for manual keying and is built from an alphabet of four symbols, namely a dot, a dash, a short pause (between characters) and a long pause (between words). Characters that occur frequently are represented using shorter codes, while less frequent characters are assigned longer codes. For example, the Morse code for letter E is a single dot · and the code for the letter Q is — — · —.

A simple telegraph circuit consisted of a key or switch that was pressed to close a circuit consisting of a battery connected by a single pair of wires to a distant lamp. The key and battery constitute the transmitter, the pair of wires the transmission medium and the lamp the receiver. The basic timing unit is the duration T of a dot. A dash is of duration $3T$. Dots and dashes within a Morse code are separated by a time interval T; characters are separated by $3T$; and words are separated by $7T$. A dot in a code is represented by an electrical pulse generated by pressing down on the key for a time T and a dash is represented by a pulse of duration $3T$. Thus the statement (excluding quotes) "THANK GOD." would be conveyed by the voltage pulse sequence shown in Fig. 1.2.

Figure 1.2 Morse code's sequence of voltage pulses for the words "THANK GOD.".

Table 1.2 Morse code.

Character	Morse code	Character	Morse code
A	· —	2	· · — — —
B	— · · ·	3	· · · — —
C	— · — ·	4	· · · · —
D	— · ·	5	· · · · ·
E	·	6	— · · · ·
F	· · — ·	7	— — · · ·
G	— — ·	8	— — — · ·
H	· · · ·	9	— — — — ·
I	· ·	:	— — — · · ·
J	· — — —	,	— — · · — —
K	— · —	;	— · — · — ·
L	· — · ·	?	· · — — · ·
M	— —	.	· — · — · —
N	— ·	'	· — — — — ·
O	— — —	"	· — · · — ·
P	· — · —	/	· · · ·
Q	— — · —	-	— · · · · —
R	· — ·	0	— · · · —
S	· · ·	) or (	— · — — · —
T	—	Attention	— · — · —
U	· · —	Break	— · · · — · —
V	· · · —	End of Message	· — · — ·
W	· — —	Error	· · · · · · · ·
X	— · · —	Go ahead	— · —
Y	— · — —	OK	· — ·
Z	— — · ·	SOS	· · · — — — · · ·
0	— — — — —	Understand	· · · — ·
1	· — — — —	Wait	· — · · ·

1.3.1.2 *Baudot code*

In 1875 Emile Baudot developed a fixed-length code that is more suitable
for automatic transmission and reception. The Baudot code (now known as
International Alphabet IA2) is shown in Table 1.3. Each character is represented by five symbols drawn from a binary alphabet, namely a mark
(voltage pulse) and a space (no voltage pulse), corresponding to binary

Table 1.3 Baudot code.

Character		Baudot code	Character		Baudot code
Letters	Figures		Letters	Figures	
A	-	11000	Q	1	11101
B	?	10011	R	4	01010
C	:	01110	S	bel	10100
D	$	10010	T	5	00001
E	3	10000	U	7	11100
F	!	10110	V	;	01111
G	&	01011	W	2	11001
H	#	00101	X	/	10111
I	8	01100	Y	6	10101
J	'	11010	Z	"	10001
K	(	11110	Letter shift		11111
L	)	01001	Figure shift		11011
M	.	00111	Space		00100
N	,	00110	Carriage Return		00010
O	9	00011	Line Feed		01000
P	0	01101	Blank (Null)		00000

digits or *bits* 1 and 0 respectively. With fixed-length codes like this, there is no need for the short pause (between characters) and long pause (between words) as in Morse code. Rather, a code 00100 for the space character is used to separate words. However, only $2^5 = 32$ different characters can be represented using 5-bit codes, which is insufficient to cover the 52 upper-case and lower-case letters of the alphabet, 10 numbers and various punctuation and control characters. To alleviate this, two 'shift codes' are used. A letter shift code 11111 is transmitted to indicate that all subsequent characters are upper-case letters until a figure shift code 11011 is encountered, which causes all following characters to be interpreted as numbers or punctuation marks. Note that lower-case letters are not represented.

Each character is framed before transmission by preceding the 5-bit character code with a start bit (usually a space) and terminating with a stop bit (usually a mark), giving seven transmitted bits per character. The Baudot code is still used in Telex networks operating at a transmission rate of 50 symbols/second (called *baud*). However, in other data communication systems this code has been replaced by ASCII and EBCDIC codes, which can represent a larger number of characters.

1.3.1.3 ASCII code

The American Standard Code for Information Interchange (ASCII) is currently the most widely used code for computer characters. It is also known as International Alphabet Number 5 (IA5). ASCII was first adopted in 1963 and updated in 1967. It uses 7 bits, which allows the representation of $2^7 = 128$ characters covering 26 lower-case letters, 26 upper-case letters, 10 numbers, punctuation marks and mathematical symbols and a wide range of control characters, as shown in Table 1.4. An 8th bit (b_8) may be added as a parity bit for error detection in asynchronous data transmission systems (discussed further in Appendix B). However, asynchronous data transmission is seldom used today. The 8th bit is therefore usually employed to extend the number of codewords to cover $2^8 = 256$ characters. In this case, the most significant bit (MSB) b_8 is set to zero for the conventional characters listed in Table 1.4 and $b_8 = 1$ for graphic and foreign language characters.

Table 1.4 ASCII code.

$b_7b_6b_5 \rightarrow$ $b_4b_3b_2b_1$ ↓	000	001	010	011	100	101	110	111
0000	NUL	DLE	SP	0	@	P	`	p
0001	SOH	DC1	!	1	A	Q	a	q
0010	STX	DC2	"	2	B	R	b	r
0011	ETX	DC3	#	3	C	S	c	s
0100	EOT	DC4	$	4	D	T	d	t
0101	ENQ	NAK	%	5	E	U	e	u
0110	ACK	SYN	&	6	F	V	f	v
0111	BEL	ETB	'	7	G	W	g	w
1000	BS	CAN	(	8	H	X	h	x
1001	HT	EM	)	9	I	Y	i	y
1010	LF	SUB	0	:	J	Z	j	z
1011	VT	ESC	0	;	K	[	k	{
1100	FF	FS	,	<	L	\	l		
1101	CR	GS	-	0	M	]	m	}
1110	SO	RS	.	>	N	^	n	~
1111	SI	US	/	?	O	_	o	DEL

ACK = acknowledge; BEL = bell or alarm; BS = backspace; CAN = cancel; CR = carriage return; DC1...4 = device control 1...4; DEL = delete; DLE = data link escape; EM = end of medium; ENQ = enquiry; EOT = end of transmission; ESC = escape; ETB = end of transmission block; ETX = end of text; FF = form feed; FS = file separator; GS = group separator; HT = horizontal tab; LF = line feed; NAK = negative acknowledge; NUL = Null or all zeros; RS = record separator; SI = shift in; SO = shift out; SOH = start of heading; SP = space; STX = start of text; SUB = substitute; SYN = synchronous idle; US = unit separator; VT = vertical tab

The following features of the ASCII coding scheme may be observed in Table 1.4.

- The three most significant bits indicate the type of character. For example, $b_7b_6b_5 = 000$ or 001 specifies a control character.
- The allocation of codewords to numbers (0 to 9) and letters of the alphabet (A to Z and a to z) follows a binary progression. For example, the codewords for the numbers 0, 1 and 2 are respectively 0110000, 0110001 and 0110010, the last 4 bits being the binary equivalent of the decimal numbers. The codewords for the letters R, S and T are 1010010, 1010011 and 1010100, respectively. Mathematical operations can therefore be performed on the codewords that represent numbers and alphabetisation can be achieved through binary mathematical operations on the codewords for letters. For this reason, ASCII codes are described as *computable* codes.
- For ease of generation on a keyboard, lower-case and upper-case letters differ only at the sixth bit position (b_6). For example, the ASCII codes for letter 'A' and 'a' are 1000001 and 1100001, respectively. This bit position (b_6) is changed on the keyboard by holding down the shift key.

Data are transmitted serially (i.e. one bit at a time) starting from the least significant bit (LSB) b_1, using either asynchronous or synchronous transmission methods, which are summarised in Appendix B.

1.3.1.4 EBCDIC code

The *extended binary-coded decimal interchange code* (EBCDIC — pronounced ebb-sea-dick) is a proprietary 8-bit alphanumeric code used mostly in IBM mainframes. It provides $2^8 = 256$ codewords for the representation of 256 different characters and has a wider range of control characters than the ASCII scheme. An ASCII terminal such as a personal computer (PC) therefore requires code conversion to be able to communicate with an IBM mainframe computer. Table 1.5 gives a list of EBCDIC codewords. Note the following features.

- As in ASCII, the codewords for upper-case and corresponding lower-case letters differ in only one bit position, bit 7 in this case. For example the codewords for letters 'm' and 'M' are 10010100 and 11010100 respectively.
- Like ASCII, the codes are computable. However, unlike ASCII, codewords of larger decimal value are assigned to upper-case letters and codewords of smaller decimal value are assigned to lower-case letters. Thus, a desktop computer program that manipulates letters of the alphabet by the relative decimal values of their ASCII codewords would not run properly on an IBM machine, which uses EBCDIC codes.
- Codewords for numbers and letters are restricted to those whose lowest four bits (i.e. first hexadecimal digit) have decimal values in the range 0

Table 1.5 EBCDIC code.

First hexadecimal digit (= $b_4b_3b_2b_1$)

Second hexadecimal digit (= $b_8b_7b_6b_5$)

	0	1	2	3	4	5	6	7	8	9	A	B	C	D	E	F
0 (= 0000)	NUL	DLE	DS		SP	&	-						(	)	\	0
1 (= 0001)	SOH	DC1	SOS		RSP		/		a	j	-		A	J	NSP	1
2 (= 0010)	STX	DC2	FS	SYN					b	k	s		B	K	S	2
3 (= 0011)	ETX	DC3	WUS	IR					c	l	t		C	L	T	3
4 (= 0100)	SEL	RES	BYP	PP					d	m	u		D	M	U	4
5 (= 0101)	HT	NL	LF	TRN					e	n	v		E	N	V	5
6 (= 0110)	RNL	BS	ETB	NBS					f	o	w		F	O	W	6
7 (= 0111)	DEL	POC	ESC	BOT					g	p	x		G	P	X	7
8 (= 1000)	GE	CAN	SA	SBS					h	q	y		H	Q	Y	8
9 (= 1001)	SPS	EM	SPE	IT					i	r	z		I	R	Z	9
A (= 1010)	RPT	UBS	SM	RFF	¢	!	^	:								
B (= 1011)	VT	CU1	CSP	CU3	.	$	,	#								
C (= 1100)	FF	IFS	MFA	DC4	<	0	%	@								
D (= 1101)	CR	IGS	ENQ	NAK	(	)	-	'								
E (= 1110)	SO	IRS	ACK		0	;	>	0								
F (= 1111)	SI	IUS	BEL	SUB	|	¬	?	"								

to 9. It is for this reason that the term 'binary-coded decimal (BCD)' features in the name of the coding scheme.

1.3.2 Historical systems and developments in modern telecommunication

Data transmission by telegraphy was soon followed by voice transmission with the invention of the telephone by Alexander Graham Bell in 1876. Initially, communication was only possible over short distances between two people using permanently linked telephone sets. The novelty of switching made it possible for two subscriber terminals connected to the same switching office or local exchange to be manually linked by an operator. In 1897, an undertaker, A. B. Strowger, developed a step-by-step electromechanical switch that made automatic switching possible. The technology was thus in place for the communication of voice and data over wire line connections, although the speed and quality of transmission left much to be desired by today's standards.

In 1894, Oliver Lodge demonstrated radio communication over a distance of 150 yards. Seven years later, Guglielmo Marconi received a radio signal transmitted 1700 miles across the Atlantic from Cornwall in the UK to Newfoundland in the USA. The way was thus open for *wireless* communication of voice and data. James Maxwell made a noteworthy contribution to this significant breakthrough in telecommunication. In 1864, he made a theoretical prediction of the existence of radio waves. 23 years later in 1887, Heinrich Hertz provided an experimental verification of Maxwell's electromagnetic wave theory.

The demonstration of the first all-electronic television system by Philo Farnsworth in 1928 was a major development that extended telecommunication capability to include the transmission of still and moving images. This was however preceded by the pioneering and tireless work of John Logie Baird, who invented mechanical television and successfully demonstrated a working prototype on 26 January 1926 to members of the Royal Institution in London. In 1936, the British Broadcasting Corporation (BBC) became the first to start a television broadcast. Thus, by the late 1930s, people could, for the first time in history, efficiently transmit by electrical means a wide range of information (including speech, music, text, data, graphics and moving pictures) between two points that might not even be physically connected together. The ensuing years have witnessed revolutionary developments in telecommunication systems and services, which have reduced cost and size, increased capacity and capability, improved reliability and convenience, and extended the range of telecommunication services far beyond what could have been contemplated by the pioneers of telegraphy, telephony and television. Developments have taken place in four key areas.

1.3.2.1 Development of new components

The invention of the vacuum-tube diode in 1904 by John Fleming, and Lee de Forest's innovative extension of the device to produce a vacuum-tube triode in 1906, made electronic signal amplification possible. In 1948 Walter Brattain, John Bardeen and William Shockley of Bell Laboratories invented a semiconductor device known as the *transistor*, which became an instant success for electronic circuit design. The transistor could perform almost all the functions of vacuum tubes with less bulk, less power consumption and greater reliability. It therefore began to replace the vacuum tube for signal amplification and switching.

In 1958, Robert Noyce of Fairchild produced the first silicon integrated circuit (IC). This eventually led to the development of very large-scale integrated circuits (VLSI). By 1971, Intel Corporation had developed the first single-chip microprocessor. Today's revolutions in computing and digital signal processing have been driven by the availability of microprocessor chips of rapidly increasing computational capability.

1.3.2.2 Development of new signal processing

Numerous forms of communication signal processing have been devised to serve various purposes, such as modulation, digital representation and transmission of analogue signals, data compression, bandwidth reduction, simultaneous accommodation of multiple users in one transmission link, better noise performance and error correction. Notable early developments that still hold sway today include the *superheterodyne* principle for radio reception and *frequency modulation* (FM), both devised by Edwin Armstrong in 1918 and 1933 respectively. The pulse code modulation (PCM) technique was developed in 1937 by Alec Reeves and applied to convert speech to a digital signal. The *matched filter* technique was devised by D. O. North in 1947 for the optimum detection of a known signal in additive white noise.

1.3.2.3 *Development of new transmission media*

The completion of the first transatlantic coaxial cable in 1954 provided a better medium for transoceanic telephony than HF radio, which had been used for commercial telephone services between the UK and the USA since 1927.

Global television relay became possible with the advent of satellite communication in 1962. The first spacecraft (*Sputnik I*) had been launched by the USSR in 1957, but it was *Telstar I*, built by Bell Laboratories and launched in 1962, that relayed the first television signals between the USA and Europe.

The use of optical fibre as a transmission medium was first proposed in 1966 by K. C. Kao and G. A. Hockham of STC Technology Ltd, Essex, UK. The company installed a 140 Mbit/s optical fibre system between Hitchin and Stevenage in 1977 and this marked the beginning of an *optical fibre revolution*. The first international submarine optical fibre system was installed in 1986 between the UK and Belgium, a link length of 113 km with three repeaters. In 1988, the first transoceanic optical fibre system was installed between Europe and the USA. Known as the transatlantic telephone cable No. 8 (TAT-8), it is 9360 km long and is served by about 140 repeaters. Today, all new long-haul line systems are optical fibre. As costs decrease, this transmission medium is penetrating closer to subscriber premises, with *fibre to the curb* (FTTC), *fibre to the building* (FTTB) and, ultimately, *fibre to the home* (FTTH) implementations.

The *local access network* — the connection between a telephone subscriber terminal and the local exchange — was dominated by copper wire pairs for nearly 100 years. However, the installation of a wire-based connection is a labour-intensive and expensive exercise, often involving digging up the ground to lay cables. This cost is a major obstacle to the provision of telecommunication access in developing countries, remote locations and areas with geographically inhospitable terrains. A very economical alternative access medium, known as the *wireless local loop* (WLL), was developed in the 1990s, spurred by a wave of telecommunications deregulation which started in the 1980s. WLL employs a radio link operating at a frequency around 3.5 GHz to give the subscriber fixed access to a local exchange and hence the global telecommunications network (at transmission speeds up to 128 kbit/s). The first WLL system in the UK was launched in May 1996 by

Ionica, with an initial capacity of 125 000 lines. Ionica's network grew rapidly, covering about 3 million UK homes within two years. WLL is now being deployed in a growing number of countries around the world.

1.3.2.4 Development of new services

The last three decades have witnessed a plethora of new telecommunication services. The advent of computer networking in 1971, with the Advanced Research Project Agency Network (ARPANET), evolved into the *Internet revolution* of the 1990s.

The cellular telephone concept, first demonstrated by Motorola in 1972, developed into the *mobile communication revolution* of the 1990s. Pocket-sized mobile units capable of voice, text and video communication on a global scale, and of speech recognition, will soon become commonplace.

Digital exchanges and time division multiplexing (TDM) began effectively to replace analogue technology — i.e. analogue exchanges and frequency division multiplexing (FDM) — in the public switched telephone network (PSTN) during the 1970s, although the first TDM telephony system had been installed as far back as 1962 by Bell Laboratories in the USA. The momentum of digitalisation grew into a *digital revolution* in the 1990s: the telecommunication networks of some countries are now nearly 100% digital. Digital audio broadcasting began in September 1995 with some field trials by the British Broadcasting Corporation (BBC). This signalled the end of the long reign of FM radio as the best in broadcast sound quality. Furthermore, terrestrial digital television broadcast started in the UK in 1998.

The invention of the compact disc (CD) by Philips and Sony in 1980 has not only made a profound impact on the digital recording of audio and video, but has also made possible the creation of software for multimedia training and entertainment on the PC. At the beginning of the 1990s, the multimedia PC came into being, but by the end of that decade the description of a PC as 'multimedia' had become superfluous — virtually all PCs had multimedia capability. By the end of the 1990s, the convergence of communication and computing had become a reality. A few examples will suffice. Television programs can be watched on a PC equipped with a TV card. Radio broadcasts can be received over the Internet (a global network of computers). Telephone calls can be made over the Internet. Access to the Internet can be gained via WebTV, which involves a television set, a set-top box and a standard telephone line. Finally, a laptop computer equipped with a suitable modem allows mobile computing and communication.

In view of the rapid pace of development and diverse range of services, a detailed study of all telecommunication applications is an extremely challenging and perhaps inadvisable task. Fortunately, the underlying principles do not change and the best way to approach the exciting field of telecommunications is first to acquire a thorough grounding in these principles. We begin this study with a presentation of the major elements of a modern telecommunication system, before embarking on a detailed discussion of the different classes of communication systems.

1.4 Communication system elements

Modern communication systems vary widely in their applications and complexity, but they are all accurately represented by the block diagram shown in Fig. 1.3. A variety of information sources feed a transmitter with the message signal to be transmitted. The transmitter transforms the message signal into a form that is compatible with the type of communication system and that is suitable for passage through the particular transmission medium with acceptable distortion. The output of the transmitter, known as the transmitted signal, is placed into the transmission medium, which conveys it to a receiver located at the intended destination. The received signal at the output of the transmission medium and input of the receiver is a distorted version of the transmitted signal. Noise, distortion and reduction in strength have been introduced by the medium. The receiver has the task of removing (as far as possible) the transmission impairments and undoing each operation performed by the transmitter. It then delivers an exact or close copy of the original message to a user or information sink. The receiver is also selected to match the characteristics of the transmission medium and to be compatible with the type of communication system.

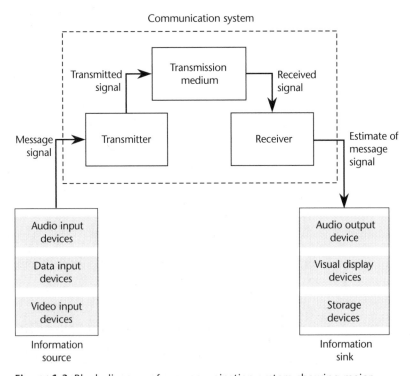

Figure 1.3 Block diagram of a communication system showing major elements.

1.4.1 Information source

The information source or input device acts as an interface between the communication system and the outside world and provides the message signal that is processed by the transmitter. There are four main classes, namely audio, video and data input devices and sensors.

1.4.1.1 Audio input devices

The *microphone* is the most basic audio input device. It converts *acoustic* (sound) pressure wave into an electrical signal (current or voltage) of similar variations, which serves as the message signal input of the communication system. A voltage supply is often required for the operation of the microphone, or for the amplification of the weak electrical signal that it generates. Other audio input devices may include a music keyboard, musical instruments digital interface (MIDI), cassette deck and compact disc (CD) player. There are different types of microphones based on the principle of their operation.

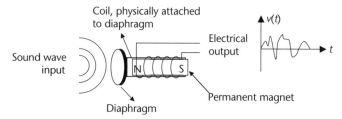

Figure 1.4 Moving coil dynamic microphone.

Dynamic microphone The dynamic or electromagnetic microphone is based on a natural law (named Faraday's law), which basically states that a changing magnetic field induces voltage in a conductor lying within the field. In the *moving-coil* dynamic microphone shown in Fig. 1.4, a wire coil enclosing a fixed permanent magnet is physically attached to a diaphragm. Pressure waves from a sound source fall on the diaphragm, causing it to vibrate along with the coil. The motion of the coil in the field of the permanent magnet induces an electromotive force (electrical output) in the coil, which varies in synchrony with the sound pressure waves. A *moving-magnet* dynamic microphone is also possible in which the coil is fixed and the magnet is attached to the diaphragm. Sound waves moving the diaphragm also move the magnet causing a change in the magnetic field in which the coil lies and hence inducing electromotive force in the coil. A type of dynamic microphone with much better fidelity at high frequencies is the *ribbon* microphone. Here a light (low-inertia) aluminium ribbon is suspended edgewise between the poles of a magnet. Electromotive force is induced in the ribbon when it is moved in the magnetic field by air particles flowing past it from sound waves.

Piezoelectric microphone When a piezoelectric material is subjected to mechanical strain, voltage is induced between its ends. The operation of a *piezoelectric microphone* is based on this important property. If one end of such a material is fixed and the other end is attached to a diaphragm, sound waves falling on the diaphragm will cause a strain in the material. This induces a voltage that varies according to the strain and hence according to the sound pressure.

Carbon microphone In a *variable-resistance* or *carbon microphone*, carbon granules are packed in a chamber formed by one fixed and one movable electrode. The movable electrode is attached to a diaphragm. Sound waves falling on the diaphragm vary the packing density of the granules and hence the resistance of the chamber. The variable resistance R is converted to a varying current I by connecting a constant voltage V across the chamber since, by Ohm's law, $I = V/R$.

Electret microphone An *electret microphone* is of variable capacitance design. A capacitor is formed using two metallic plates, one fixed and the other movable. The movable plate is a thin metallic layer diaphragm. The fixed plate is a metal plate covered with a film of teflon-like plastic that has a permanent electric charge Q; hence the name *electret*. Air pockets are trapped between the electret and the fixed electrode due to irregularities on the surface of the electret. When sound waves fall on the movable diaphragm the size of the air pockets and hence the capacitance C of the capacitor is varied. This produces a variable voltage V according to the relation $V = Q/C$. An alternative variable capacitance design is the *condenser microphone* in which the charge Q is maintained by an external voltage source.

1.4.1.2 Video input devices

A video input device presents a video message signal to the communication system. The video signal is a variable voltage that originates from a visual signal, which consists of light intensity (or luminance) and colour (or chrominance) information. The most basic video input devices are the *video camera* (e.g. digital or analogue camcorder) for movable three-dimensional images and the *scanner* for still two-dimensional images. Secondary input devices include those that read pre-recorded video signals such as the video cassette recorder (VCR), which reads analogue video signals stored on magnetic tape in two-reel cassettes.

1.4.1.3 Data input devices

There is a wide variety of data input devices, which generate data serving as the message signal input of a communication system. Many of these devices work in conjunction with a computer system or other suitable *data terminal equipment* (DTE). A few examples of data input devices are given below.

- A *keyboard* generates the ASCII (or EBCDIC) code corresponding to the key pressed.
- A number of devices are used to convert finger and hand movement into computer commands, which may involve data generation under

the control of a computer program. Examples of such devices include the *mouse*, *trackball* (an upside down mouse), *joystick* and *touch screen*.

- There are different types of devices that read stored data and present these to the communication system for processing and/or transmission. A *barcode reader* or *laser scanner* scans a barcode, which encodes information (e.g. the price of an item) in black lines of varying width. A *magnetic ink character reader* reads information written on a document using magnetic ink characters. A *magnetic strip reader* reads data stored magnetically on magnetic strips such as those found in credit cards and security access cards. *Optical character readers* and *optical mark readers* are used (in conjunction with software) to read printed characters and to detect and decode marks on paper. *Punched card readers* read information stored as an array of small holes and spaces on paper. Other data-reading input devices include the *optical disc drive* for reading data from an optical disc, the *disk drive* for reading data from a floppy or hard disk and the *tape reader* for reading data from a magnetic tape.

- A *digitising tablet* is used to convert graphics information (drawn on the tablet) into computer data. The drawing is displayed on a computer screen and the associated data may be processed by a communication system.

1.4.1.4 Sensors

Sensors measure physical quantities, such as temperature, pressure and mass, and convert the measurements into an electrical signal that serves as the message signal input for the communication system. Sensors are used in telemetry systems to obtain information from remote or inaccessible locations, e.g. monitoring the status of equipment on satellites or detecting the accumulation of ice on the wings of an aircraft. They are also used in numerous systems including automatic data-logging systems, security systems, safety systems, traffic control systems, manufacturing systems and process control systems. For example, a tipping-bucket rain gauge generates a voltage pulse each time a standard-size cup tips after filling with rain water. The irregular sequence of voltage pulses serves as the message signal, which may be transmitted and analysed to obtain the rainfall rate. A security system may use a sensor to detect movement. An alarm (or message) signal is then generated and transmitted to a console and used to initiate appropriate action, such as the ringing of a bell.

In the most general sense, every input device can be described as a sensor of some sort. The camera senses reflected light, the microphone senses sound pressure, the keyboard senses key presses, the mouse senses hand movements, etc. However, the classification of input devices presented here is useful in identifying the type of information provided by the device to the communication system, whether audio, video, data or a more general measurement of a physical quantity.

1.4.2 Information sink

The information sink is the final destination of the transmitted signal. It may serve as an interface between human users and the communication system, making the transmitted information understandable through sight or sound. It may also serve as a repository, storing the transmitted information for later processing, retransmission or display. There are therefore three types of information sink, namely audio output devices, visual display devices and storage devices.

1.4.2.1 *Audio output devices*

Generation of sound   The audio output device converts the electrical signal output of the communication system to mechanical vibrations at the same frequencies. Figure 1.5 shows the basic operation of a moving-coil loudspeaker. A cone is physically attached to a wire coil, which encloses a permanent magnet lying along its axis. The electrical signal is fed as current into the coil. This current sets up a magnetic field that varies proportionately with the current and has maximum strength along the coil axis. The interaction of the field of this electromagnet with the field of the permanent magnet results in a force that varies in synchrony with the field strength of the electromagnet and hence with the input current. This varying force causes the coil to vibrate along with the attached cone, thereby producing sound waves that follow the input current variations. The vibrations also generate sound waves travelling in the backward direction, which are reflected by the loudspeaker casing, and may interfere in a destructive manner with the forward waves. To prevent this, the casing is padded with sound-absorbent material. It is usual to have separate loudspeakers: a *woofer* for the low frequencies and a *tweeter* (with a smaller cone) for the high frequencies.

Sound pressure level (SPL)   A sound signal or sound wave is an oscillation in pressure, stress, particle displacement or particle velocity in an elastic medium such as air. When this sound wave is received and processed by the ear–brain mechanism the sensation of hearing is produced, provided two conditions are met: (1) the oscillation or vibration frequency must be within the audible range; and (2) the *sound pressure level* (SPL) produced by the vibrations must be high enough, i.e. above the threshold of hearing.

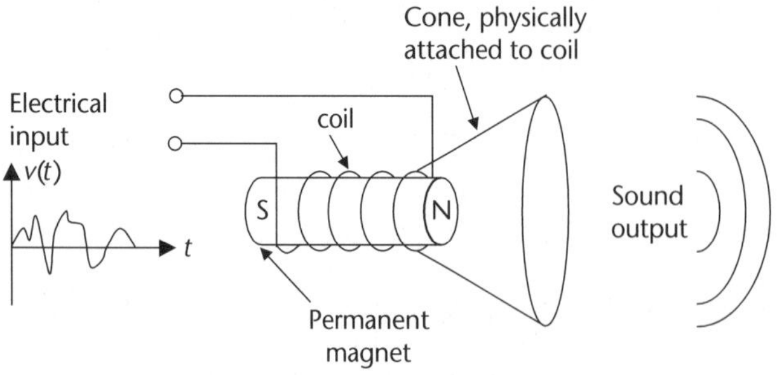

The ear only perceives sound signals of frequency in the range 20 Hz to 20 kHz. This is the theoretical audible range of frequencies. However, in practice most people have a narrower hearing range, with the top end decreasing with age above about 30 years. Sound pressure may be expressed in dyne/cm^2, microbar, or Newton/m^2, where

Figure 1.5 Audio output device: a loudspeaker.

$$1 \text{ dyne/cm}^2 = 1 \text{ microbar} = 0.1 \text{ N/m}^2 \tag{1.1}$$

The threshold of hearing for an average person below age 30 when the sound signal is at a frequency of 1 kHz is 0.0002 dyne/cm^2. That is, sound of 1 kHz in frequency will be heard (by this standard listener) only if the vibrations produce (in the ears) a sound pressure of at least 0.0002 dyne/cm^2. This value has been adopted as a reference P_{REF} for expressing *sound pressure level* (SPL) in decibels (dB). Thus, the SPL of a sound of pressure P dyne/cm^2 is expressed in dB above P_{REF} as

$$\text{SPL} = 20 \log_{10}\left(\frac{P}{P_{REF}}\right) \quad \text{dB} \tag{1.2}$$

where P_{REF} = 0.0002 dyne/cm^2.

The SPL of ambient noise in a quiet home is about 26 dB; that of formal conversation is about 62 dB, while that of jet planes at takeoff is about 195 dB. The threshold of hearing increases irreversibly with age above 30 and is raised to a higher level in the presence of ambient noise. The second effect is transient and is referred to as *noise masking*. The *dynamic range* of the ear is typically 120 dB, bounded at the bottom by the threshold of hearing and at the top by the threshold of pain. Sounds of SPL < 0 dB are inaudible, while sounds of SPL ≥ 120 dB will cause pain and may result in an immediate and irreversible loss of hearing.

Frequency response of the ear While SPL is an objective measure of the amplitude of sound vibrations, another closely related term, *loudness*, is not. Loudness is the response of the human ear to the amplitude of sound waves. It is a subjective attribute that allows us to place a given sound at a point on a scale from soft to loud. The loudness level of a sound is expressed in *phon*, which is numerically equal to the SPL (in dB) of a 1 kHz reference tone. The sensitivity or response of the human ear to sound varies markedly with frequency. While a 1 kHz sound at an SPL of 130 dB is deafeningly loud, a 22 kHz sound at the same SPL is not loud at all. In fact you would not hear the latter (because it is outside your audible range), although both vibrations cause the same high level of sound pressure.

The ear acts like a bandpass filter, shutting out all frequencies outside the audible band. Within the audible band itself, the response of the ear is far from uniform. Figure 1.6 shows the ISO 226 standard curves of the SPL that maintain constant loudness at various frequencies. It shows, for example, that sound of SPL 70 dB is 70 phon loud at 1 kHz, but only 40 phon loud at 40 Hz. We observe also that the ear's frequency response is more variable when dealing with softer sound, but reasonably flat with loud sounds (> 100 phon).

1.4.2.2 *Visual display devices*

Three broad classes of visual display devices are common as information sinks in communication systems. Cathode-ray tube (CRT) and flat-panel displays present what is usually called a *soft copy* of the received message signal, while printers produce a *hard copy* of the message.

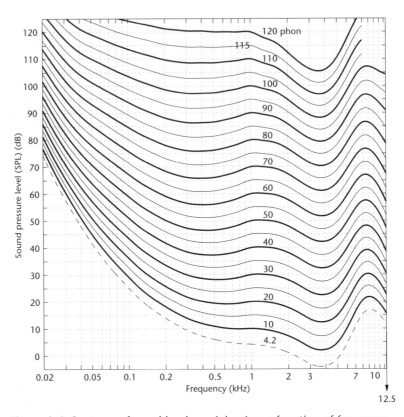

Figure 1.6 Contours of equal loudness (phon) as a function of frequency (kHz) and sound pressure level (dB).

Cathode-ray tube (CRT) Cathode ray tubes display information (pictures, text, graphics etc.) by using an accelerated beam of electrons to excite electrons in phosphor atoms, which emit visible energy as they return to their unexcited state. The basic parts of a CRT are shown in Fig. 1.7. The CRT consists of an electron gun, a focusing system, a deflection system and a phosphor-coated screen. Electrons are boiled off a hot cathode surface, a process called *thermionic emission*. The number of electrons emitted by the gun, and hence the brightness of the display, is controlled by a negative voltage on the control grid. A focusing system is needed to prevent beam spreading due to mutual repulsion among the electrons and to focus the electron beam to a small point on the screen. The system may be an electrostatic lens formed by the electric field of a positively charged metal cylinder, or a magnetic lens formed by the magnetic field of a current carrying coil mounted around the outside of the CRT envelope.

The deflection system is used to direct the beam to any spot on screen. Figure 1.7 shows an electrostatic deflection system. Magnetic deflection may be obtained by using current in a pair of coils mounted on the top and bottom of the neck of the CRT envelope for horizontal deflection and another pair of current-carrying coils mounted left and right for vertical deflection.

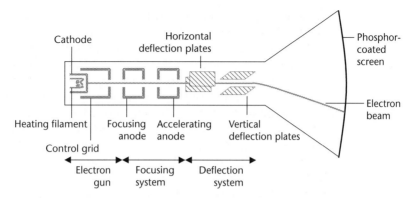

Figure 1.7 Basic components of a CRT.

The phosphor atoms on the screen at the spot impacted by the accelerated electron beam will glow for a short time. The duration or persistence of the glow and its colour depend on the type of phosphor. To maintain an image without flicker, the entire screen is refreshed at a regular rate by repeatedly moving the electron beam along rows of the screen from top to bottom, while simultaneously varying the beam intensity to reproduce the desired image.

For a colour display, each spot has three phosphor dots that glow with a red, green or blue colour. Three electron guns are used, one for each colour dot. Any desired colour can be produced at each spot by (additive) mixing of these three primary colours at the right intensity. For example, a yellow colour is obtained by exciting the green and red phosphor dots equally without exciting the blue phosphor dot — that is, the electron gun aligned with the blue phosphor dot is switched off.

In spite of its excellent display quality, the weight, bulk and power consumption of a CRT make it unsuitable for portable devices (e.g. pocket calculators) and the large displays required for example in high-definition television (HDTV).

Flat-panel displays Flat-panel displays have smaller volume, weight and power consumption than a CRT. They are increasingly used in a wide range of applications requiring portable monitors, such as small TV monitors, laptop computers, mobile telephone units etc. There are two main classes of flat panel display. One class, called *emissive display*, works by converting electrical energy into light. The other class, called *non-emissive display*, uses an arrangement that modulates (i.e. blocks or passes to varying degrees) light from an external or internal source, thereby creating a graphics pattern.

Examples of an emissive flat-panel display include a *light-emitting diode* (LED) display, *plasma-panel* (or gas-discharge) display and *thin-film electroluminescent* display.

In an LED display, a matrix of diodes is arranged to form the screen spots or picture elements (called *pixels*) and a picture is displayed by applying a voltage to light the diode at each required location.

In plasma-panel and electroluminescent displays, the volume between two glass panels is filled with a suitable substance — a mixture of neon and some other gases for the former, and a manganese-doped phosphor for the latter. One panel carries a series of vertical conducting ribbons and the other carries a series of horizontal ribbons. The intersection between a vertical ribbon and a horizontal ribbon defines a display pixel. To light a particular pixel, firing voltages are applied to the pair of ribbons that intersect at that point. This breaks down the gas at the pixel to form glowing plasma, or, in the case of the electroluminescent display, causes the manganese atoms at the pixel to absorb electrical energy, which makes them glow. The firing is refreshed at a regular rate (e.g. 60 Hz) using the picture definition stored in a refresh buffer.

A *liquid crystal display* is non-emissive. In this case, the volume between two glass plates is filled with a liquid crystal compound (LCC), a substance that has a crystalline arrangement of molecules but flows like a liquid. One of the glass plates contains rows of transparent conductors and a light polariser. The other plate contains columns of transparent conductors and a light polariser at right angles to the polariser in the other plate. The intersection of a row conductor with a column conductor defines a pixel. A pixel is turned on when the LCC molecules at its location are unaligned and is turned off when these molecules are forced to align by the application of a voltage. This happens because the unaligned molecules at the pixel twist the polarised light, causing it to pass through both polarisers. On the other hand, if a voltage is applied to two conductors it aligns the LCC molecules at their intersection and prevents the twisting of the light so that it cannot pass through both polarisers, thereby being blocked.

Printers Impact printers produce hard copies by pressing the face of formed characters against an inked ribbon onto the paper. The characters are usually formed using a dot-matrix print head, which has a rectangular array of protruding pins, by retracting appropriate pins. The quality of the print depends on the dot size and on the number of dots per inch (or lines per inch) that can be displayed.

Various non-impact printing techniques have been devised. Laser printers create a charge distribution on a rotating drum using a laser beam. Ink-like toner particles are then emitted from a toner cartridge onto the drum. These particles adhere only to the charged parts of the drum. The particles are then attracted from the drum to paper and pressed into the paper by heated rollers. Inkjet printers use an electric field to deflect an electrically charged ink stream to produce dot-matrix patterns on paper. Electrostatic printers charge the paper negatively at the right spots. These spots then attract a positively charged toner to create the required picture or text. Electrothermal printers apply heat in a dot-matrix print head to create the required pattern on a heat-sensitive paper.

Colour printing is obtained by mixing the right quantity of the colour pigments cyan, magenta and yellow. For example, an equal mixture of magenta and cyan gives blue, and an equal mixture of all three pigments gives black. Laser colour printers deposit the three pigments on separate passes to produce a range of colour patterns, while inkjet colour printers shoot the three colours simultaneously.

1.4.2.3 Storage devices

Many communication services are designed to store the received message signal for visual or audio display at a later time. In electronic mail (email) the text message signal is stored at the recipient's email server machine or 'post office' until the recipient accesses the server to obtain a soft copy (screen display) or hard copy (printout) of the message. Voicemail service provides for the storage of a digitised speech message signal, which is played back later to the authorised recipient at their request. In these services, the information sink (in Fig. 1.3) is an appropriate storage medium.

The desirable characteristics of a storage medium include large storage capacity, high access and data-reading speeds, portability, durability, low cost, data integrity and reusability. Three types of storage medium are most commonly used as information sinks in communication systems.

Magnetic tape   This is made of a thin coating of a film of magnetic metal or ferromagnetic particles (embedded in a binding material) on a plastic strip of width 6 to 50 mm and length up to 1.5 km. The overall thickness of the tape (magnetic coating and substrate strip) is about 15 to 60 μm. The tape is contained in a two-reel *cassette* and is read from and written to in a tape drive or deck. The drive winds the tape from one reel to the other, causing it to move past a read–write head. Magnetic tapes offer large storage capacity (up to 700 Mbyte for a typical cassette and several gigabytes for an *exabyte* tape); they are reusable and easy to edit, compact and portable, cheap and available in a variety of formats. However, they have several demerits, which limit their use mostly to data archiving and hard disk backup. They are easily damaged through breaking or deterioration if exposed to heat or humidity. Recorded information degrades with continuous use, due to tape wear. Information can also be ruined by strong magnetic interference. Furthermore, access to data on the tape is slow and sequential.

Magnetic disks   Magnetic disks may be fixed or removable. A flat disk substrate is coated with a thin film of magnetic material. The disk is either a floppy disk, with a flexible substrate, or a hard disk, with a rigid substrate. The surface of the disk is divided into a number of evenly spaced concentric tracks and each track is divided into sectors. Data are stored in these sectors. During a read–write operation, the disk is rotated at constant speed and the read–write head is moved in a radial direction to position it at the desired track. This radial movement is referred to as seeking. Floppy disks are magnetically coated on both sides and contained within a plastic with a spring-loaded door that is forced open when the disk is inserted in its drive. A hard disk drive, including the disk and read–write head, is hermetically sealed to prevent contamination by dust particles, and the head glides on a thin film of air without making actual contact with the disk. A PC hard drive usually consists of several disks (with a head for each disk) mounted on the same rotating axle. In this case, the set of tracks at the same radius on all the disks is called a cylinder. The total storage capacity of such multiple-disk hard drives may reach tens of Gbytes. Magnetic disks have a number of advantages. Access time is very short: less than 28 ms in high-speed drives. Random data access is possible using an index or directory (stored at a specific location on the disk) that lists the physical location of all data objects. Magnetic disks are reusable, cheap and easy to write to, read from or edit. Removable hard disks and floppy disks are also portable. However, magnetic disks can fail, data on the disk becoming unreadable if certain critical sectors are damaged or otherwise corrupted. Floppy disk drives are slower than hard drives and have very limited storage, although *floptical* discs are available with storage capacity of up to 120 MB. These use an optical tracking mechanism to improve head positioning and hence the data storage density on the disc.

Optical discs Optical discs include CD-R, magneto-optical, DVD-R and DVD-RAM, discussed below. The compact disc (CD) is based on a 12 cm plastic disc that stores data in the variation of the reflectivity of densely packed spots on the disc surface. The disc is read by bouncing a laser beam off the surface. Both the *compact disc recordable* (CD-R) and the *digital versatile disc recordable* (DVD-R) are write once, read many media. On the other hand, the *magneto-optical disc* and the *DVD random-access memory* (DVD-RAM) can be erased and rewritten. CDs and DVDs have numerous advantages. They provide a very large storage capacity: 650 Mbyte for a CD and up to 17 Gbyte for a double-sided dual-layer DVD. Data stored on a CD-R cannot be altered later, which ensures the integrity of archived information. Optical discs are very durable as the reading process is without physical contact with the disc and so does not cause any mechanical wear. Stored information can be read countless times with practically no degradation. There is ample provision for error correction and the error rate is below 10^{-15}. The disc is cheap, portable, compact and not easily damaged, and the recording technique is immune to electric and magnetic fields. The main disadvantages of optical discs are that most of them, except magneto-optical discs and DVD-RAM, are not reusable. Once data has been written, it cannot be changed. Secondly, unlike magnetic disks that use the same head for reading and writing, a special disc writer is required to write information onto an optical disc. Thirdly, CD access times are about 10 to 20 times longer than those of magnetic hard disks.

1.4.3 Transmitter

The transmitter is essentially a signal processor. Its primary role is to transform the message signal into a form that best suits the transmission medium, complies with any regulations governing the particular communication service and meets the system design objectives. How the transmitter does this depends on the type of information source, the type of transmission medium and the type of communication system. For example, if the transmission medium is radio then the signal-processing tasks of the transmitter would necessarily include modulation and radiation. The transmitter would process the signal in such a way as to ensure that it is transmitted in the authorised frequency band and at the permitted transmitted power level. If the main design objective is to minimise the cost of receivers, then a simple amplitude modulation would be preferred to, say, digital radio processing.

Subject to the above considerations, the signal processing performed by the transmitter may include one or more of the following processes. A detailed discussion of most of these processes can be found in later sections of the book.

1.4.3.1 Source coding

Source coding (also called source encoding) deals with the efficient representation of the message signal. A number of processes may be involved, depending on the type of communication system. The following are examples of source coding.

1. *Low-pass filtering* to limit the bandwidth of the message signal.
2. *Multiplexing* to combine several message signals for simultaneous transmission.
3. *Analogue-to-digital conversion* (ADC) to represent an analogue signal in digital format.
4. *Data compaction* to minimise the number of symbols or bits that represent the message. Examples of data compaction include variable-length codes (e.g. Morse code and Huffman code), which assign shorter codewords to more frequent source symbols, and the Lempel–Ziv algorithm, which uses a codebook built from the message.

1.4.3.2 Encryption

Here, the transmitter processes the message signal in order to disguise it in some way to ensure security. An example is the scrambling employed in analogue pay TV to prevent unauthorised viewing.

1.4.3.3 Channel coding

This process (also called channel encoding) is necessary to ensure that the message signal is compatible with the transmission medium (or channel). It attempts to protect the message signal against channel distortion and transmission errors. It may add some redundancy to the transmitted symbols. Examples of channel coding include pre-emphasis/de-emphasis in analogue systems (e.g. FM), line coding in digital baseband systems, and provision for error detection and correction at the receiver. In fact, the process of carrier modulation introduced next is actually a form of channel coding, which is required for some transmission media, such as radio.

1.4.3.4   Carrier modulation

This process translates the message signal frequencies from baseband into a frequency band that is suitable for and allows efficient exploitation of the transmission medium.

1.4.3.5   Spread spectrum modulation

Spread spectrum modulation involves the transmitted signal being deliberately spread out over a very wide frequency band. This technique was previously designed for military communications to protect against frequency-selective fading, interference and intentional jamming; but is now also employed as a multiplexing strategy in non-military communications.

1.4.3.6   Radiation

In a wireless communication system, the message signal must be processed and radiated as electromagnetic waves in the desired direction. The radiating element required depends on the type of wireless system. In general, *antennas* of various designs are used for radio systems and *light-emitting diodes* are employed in infrared systems.

1.4.4   Receiver

A receiver is required at the other end of the transmission medium (i.e. destination of the transmitted signal) to process the received signal to obtain a close estimate of the message signal and deliver this to the information sink. Note that the receiver's input comes from the original message signal after it has been processed by two blocks of the communication system, purposely in the transmitter and undesirably in the transmission medium. The receiver undoes the processing of the transmitter in a series of steps performed in reverse order to that of the transmitter. This may include one or more of the following tasks.

1. Radio *reception* using a receive-antenna to convert the received electromagnetic waves back to a voltage signal.
2. Spread spectrum *demodulation* to remove the carrier spreading.
3. Carrier demodulation to translate the signal back to baseband frequencies.
4. *Clock extraction* and *synchronisation* to recover the clock signal (if any) used at the transmitter in order to use the same timing intervals for operations at transmitter and receiver.
5. Channel *decoding* to correct errors, remove redundancy etc.
6. *Decryption* to recover the plain and undisguised symbol sequence.
7. Source decoding to recover the original message signal from the symbol sequence. This may involve *demultiplexing* (which breaks up a composite (multiplexed) signal into the components belonging to each

of the multiple users), digital-to-analogue conversion (DAC), low-pass filtering etc.

1.4.5 Transmission medium

The transmission medium provides a link between the transmitter and the receiver in a communication system. One important note on terminology should be made here. We will sometimes use the term 'communication channel' to mean transmission medium, but will use the word 'channel' on its own to mean the bandwidth or other system resource devoted to one user in a multiple-user communication system. For example, we can refer to a 30-channel TDM, which means a system that can simultaneously convey 30 independent user-signals in one transmission medium using TDM.

There are two broad classifications of transmission media, namely *closed* and *open* media. Closed media enable communication between a transmitter and a specific physically connected receiver. They include *twisted wire pair* (also called *paired cable*), *coaxial cable*, *optical fibre* and *metallic waveguide*. Open media provide *broadcast* (point-to-area communication) and *mobility* capabilities in telecommunication, which are not possible with closed media. It includes all forms of electromagnetic wave (e.g. radio and infrared) propagation, not only in the Earth's atmosphere, but also in empty space and sea water.

A metallic waveguide is preferred to coaxial cables above about 3 GHz for very short links, for example to link an antenna to its transmitter or receiver. It is a metallic tube of rectangular or circular cross-section. An electromagnetic wave is launched into the waveguide using a wire loop or probe. The wave travels down the guide by repeated reflections between the walls of the guide. Ideally, energy is totally reflected at the walls and there are no losses. In practice, although the guide walls are polished to enhance reflection, some absorption takes place, leading to losses which, however, are small compared with cable losses at these frequencies.

1.4.5.1 *Twisted wire pairs*

Wire pairs are made from copper in a number of standardised diameters, e.g. 0.32, 0.4, 0.5, 0.63, 0.9 and 1.1 mm. The conductors were paper-insulated in older networks, but are now insulated with plastic, which provides better insulation as well as protection against humidity effects. A pair of insulated conductors may be twisted together and the pair contained in plastic insulation to provide the 'go' and 'return' paths for one circuit connection (see Fig. 1.8(a)). Four insulated conductors may be grouped together in a star-quad arrangement with diagonally opposite conductors forming a pair, as shown in Fig. 1.8(b). This arrangement reduces capacitance imbalance between pairs and increases packing density in multi-pair cable cores when compared with the twisted-pair arrangement of Fig. 1.8(a). Often, for example in a local telephone link, many wire pairs are required between two points. This is realised by making a cable with tens or even hundreds of insulated wire pairs carried in the cable core. A sheath

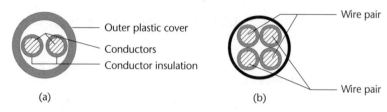

Figure 1.8 Wire pairs: (a) single pair; (b) star-quad arrangement of two wire pairs.

surrounds the cable core to give mechanical protection. If the sheath is made from a combination of plastic and aluminium foil, it also shields the wires from electrical and magnetic interference. The wire pairs are colour coded for pair identification.

Limiting factors   Limiting factors in the use of wire pairs include:

1. Crosstalk between pairs
2. Interference noise from power lines, radio transmission and lightning strikes
3. Severe bandwidth limitation

The attenuation of wire pairs increases as the square root of frequency, as shown in Fig. 1.9 for a 0.63 mm diameter copper wire pair. Wire pairs make a good transmission medium for low-bandwidth applications. Underground cable cores represent a massive global investment and the challenge is to devise ways of using them in modern high-bandwidth applications.

Applications of wire pairs

1. A wire pair is used to carry a single voice channel in telephone circuits, where the frequency band of interest is 300 to 3400 Hz. It is important to maintain a constant attenuation in this band to avoid distortion. This is achieved through inductive loading, a technique invented by Oliver Heaviside in 1885 but which took several years to be appreciated and actually used. Here, extra inductance is inserted in the wire pair at a regular spacing. For example, a loading of 88 mH per 1.83 km is used in 0.63 mm audio cables to obtain a constant attenuation of ~0.47 dB/km up to 3.5 kHz. This should be compared with the attenuation of an unloaded wire pair (Fig. 1.9), which is about 0.9 dB/km at 3.5 kHz. Thus loading reduces the attenuation of the wire pair at voice frequencies. However, the bandwidth of a loaded cable is much more restricted, with attenuation increasing very rapidly beyond 3.5 kHz.

2. Extensive growth in the use of digital communication made it necessary to explore ways of transmitting digitised speech signals over these audio cables. This could not be done as long as the cable bandwidth was restricted to 3.5 kHz by inductive loading that was designed to support analogue speech transmission. A solution was found by removing the loading coils (called *de-loading* the cables) and installing regenerative

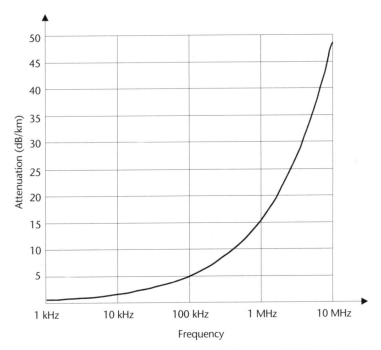

Figure 1.9 Attenuation of (unloaded) 0.63 mm paired cable at 20 °C.

repeaters at the old loading coil sites. The de-loaded cables are used to carry 24-channel and 30-channel TDM signals operating at bit rates of 1.5 Mbit/s and 2 Mbit/s respectively.

3. Wire pairs have also been specified for carrying 12 to 120 voice channels in FDM systems, necessitating operation at bandwidths up to 550 kHz. The wires are of conductor diameter 1.2 mm and have an attenuation of about 2 dB/km at 120 kHz. The same type of wire pair has also been used for digital communication systems operating at bit rates 6 Mbit/s and 34 Mbit/s.

4. With careful installation, wire pairs have been successfully deployed within buildings for some local area network (LAN) connections. Unscreened twisted pair (UTP) can be used for data rates up to 10 Mbit/s (e.g. 10Base-T Ethernet), with cable lengths up to 100 m. Screened twisted pair (STP) can support data rates up to 100 Mbit/s (e.g. 100Base-T Ethernet), with cable lengths of a few hundred metres.

xDSL technologies The *digital subscriber line* (DSL) is an emerging application of twisted wire pairs, the deployment of which began in the late 1990s, allowing multimedia information (including voice, text, graphics and video) to be transmitted on the existing copper wire installation of the local loop. The *local loop*, sometimes called the *last mile* of the PSTN, is the wire pair that connects between equipment at a customer site (e.g. a telephone handset) and the *local exchange* — called *central office* in North America — of a *network service provider* (NSP). DSL technologies provide access to a number of fixed (i.e. non-mobile) communication services for both home and business users, which, depending on the standard, may include voice transmission, video telephony, high bit-rate Internet access, video-on-demand, interactive television and HDTV.

The abbreviation xDSL is often used, where 'x' is a placeholder for specifying different DSL standards. The *asymmetric digital subscriber line* (ADSL) standard provides higher transmission bit rates (32 kbit/s to 8.192 Mbit/s) *downstream* — from NSP to subscriber — and lower bit rates (16 to 640 kbit/s) *upstream* — from subscriber to NSP. This efficiently supports such services as video-on-demand and Internet access, since users typically download much more information than they send.

ADSL allows simultaneous transmission of three independent services on one wire-pair of maximum length ranging from 3.5 to 5.5 km (depending on transmission speed): (1) analogue voice — called *plain old telephone service* (POTS); (2) *downstream* data; and (3) *upstream* data. Figure 1.10 shows an FDM-based ADSL system, which requires a *splitter* and an *ADSL modem* to place the three services into separate frequency bands in the wire pair — POTS in the lower band from 0 to 4 kHz, and data in the higher band up to about 2.2 MHz.

Other xDSL standards include SDSL (*single-line DSL*), which provides equal, and therefore symmetric, transmission rates of 1.544 or 2.048 Mbit/s in both directions using a single wire-pair of maximum length 3 km. It is suitable for certain high-bandwidth applications such as video conferencing, which require identical upstream and downstream transmission speeds. VDSL (*very high-speed DSL*) supports downstream transmission at 12.9 to 52.8 Mbit/s and upstream transmission at rates between 1.5 and 2.3 Mbit/s using a single wire-pair. Such a high downstream speed potentially allows a subscriber to receive all types of services, including HDTV, from an NSP. However, the wire-pair is limited to a maximum length of about 1.4 km. Another xDSL standard, known simply as *DSL*, allows (only) data transmissions at (symmetric) speeds up to 144 kbit/s in either direction on a single wire-pair of maximum length 5.5 km.

An important note of caution is in order here. The xDSL technologies discussed above must not be confused with ISDN (*integrated services digital*

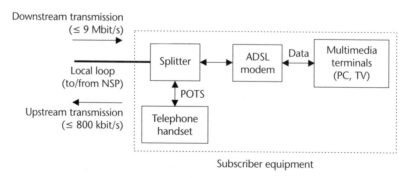

Figure 1.10 ADSL system components.

network), which is a TDM-based service (discussed in Chapter 8) that allows voice, data and video signals to be carried simultaneously on one transmission link, e.g. a wire-pair. The following differences are worth mentioning at this point.

1. ISDN converts voice to a digital signal before transmission (see Section 1.5.2), whereas xDSL transmits voice in its original analogue format, i.e. POTS.

2. ISDN is a switched service that requires the two communicating ends to support the same ISDN standard if transmission at optimum speed (e.g. a basic rate of 144 kbit/s) is to be realised. xDSL, on the other hand, is a point-to-point access technology. In simple terms, there is a permanent wire-pair connection between your equipment and your NSP, which allows a faster flow of information. At the NSP premises, a splitter separates the voice (i.e. POTS) and data (e.g. email) components of your transmission, connecting the former to the PSTN and the latter to a high-speed digital line. Importantly, the addressee at the other end does not require an xDSL connection to receive your voice or email message.

3. ISDN requires external electrical power supply for operation, whereas xDSL carries power on the same wire-pair. In the event of a power failure, xDSL POTS service is sustained, although the data service is interrupted.

4. ISDN is currently more widely adopted than xDSL.

1.4.5.2 Coaxial cable

A coaxial cable (or *coax* for short) consists of a plastic-covered tube-shaped outer conductor (sometimes of braided design) with a second conductor fixed into the centre of the tube and separated from it by air and/or plastic insulation (see Fig. 1.11). The ITU-T has standardised three coaxial cable sizes, specified by the diameter of the inner conductor followed by the inner diameter of the outer conductor. Normal core coaxial cable has dimensions of 2.6/9.5 mm. It has sufficient bandwidth to support digital transmission at bit rates up to 565 Mbit/s, or to carry up to 10 800 speech channels in FDM systems. Small core coax has dimensions of 1.2/4.4 mm. It can be used for digital transmission at bit rates up to 140 Mbit/s. The micro coax (of dimensions 0.7/2.9 mm) is recommended for transmission at bit rates up to 34 Mbit/s. In normal core coax, the inner conductor is kept centred using polyethylene discs spaced at 30 mm. This arrangement also protects the outer conductor from being squashed.

Features The outer conductor of a coax is usually earthed. As a result, it neither interferes with nor is interfered with by nearby

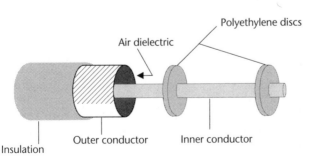

Figure 1.11 Structure of coaxial cable with air dielectric.

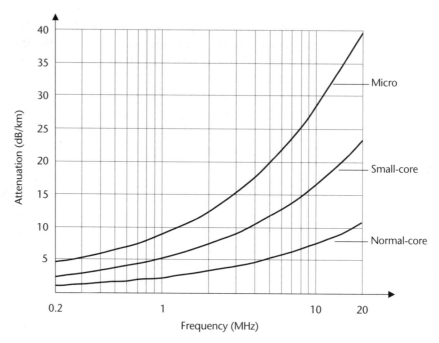

Figure 1.12 Attenuation of coaxial cables: micro-coax (0.7/2.9 mm), small-core coax (1.2/4.4 mm) and normal-core coax (2.6/9.5 mm).

cables, but provides screening against interference for the inner conductor. This greatly reduces radiation loss, interference and crosstalk compared with twisted pair cables. The attenuation of coaxial cables increases with frequency, but is lower than the attenuation encountered in twisted pairs (see Fig. 1.12). At 10 MHz the attenuation of the standard coaxial cables are 7.5, 16.4 and 28.5 dB/km, in order of decreasing conductor size. This should be compared with Fig. 1.9, which gives an attenuation value of 49 dB/km for the 0.63 mm twisted pair cable at the same frequency.

Applications

1. In addition to the digital transmission systems mentioned above, coaxial cables are also used as the transmission medium in high-bandwidth analogue systems. They are commonly used in the inter-exchange network where the number of voice channels is high and are carried in a cable core containing 2, 4, 6, 8, 12, 18 or 40 coaxial cables.

2. Normal-core cable is used to carry FDM telephony at bandwidths of 4 MHz (960 voice channels), 12 MHz (2700 voice channels), 18 MHz (3600 voice channels) and 60 MHz (10 800 voice channels). Repeaters have to be more closely spaced in the higher bandwidth systems due to increased attenuation at higher frequencies. The recommended repeater spacing ranges from 1.5 km for the 10 800-channel FDM system to 9.1 km for the 960-channel system. Multichannel cable TV

(CATV), comprising audio, data and television signals, is also distributed to home subscribers via normal-core coax.

3. Small core coax is also used for FDM telephony transmission at bandwidths of 4, 12 and 18 MHz, but with closer repeater spacing (necessitated by higher attenuation) compared with normal core coax. For example, the 960-channel 4 MHz FDM system is carried in the small core coax with a repeater spacing of 4 km.

4. Coaxial cables are also used for data terminal equipment interconnection within buildings. They can operate at higher bit rates with better immunity to noise and crosstalk than twisted wire pairs. Thicker coaxial cables (e.g. 9.3/37.3 mm) with a solid dielectric insulation are used for submarine lines.

The development of optical fibre has led to a sharp decline in the deployment of coax for long-distance transmission. All new installations of long-distance line systems are optical fibre.

1.4.5.3 *Optical fibre*

The metallic waveguide is suitable only for very short links, due to its cost, rigid structure and bulk. The optical fibre is a much cheaper and more suitable form of waveguide, which may be used for long-distance links. Signals are carried by light waves in the fibre. Optical fibre is now common in metropolitan area networks (MAN) and inter-exchange networks.

An optical fibre is a dielectric waveguide about 125 μm in diameter made from high-purity silica glass. It consists of a glass core surrounded by a glass cladding of lower refractive index. A plastic sheath covers the cladding to give mechanical protection. An optical cable contains a number of fibres, used in pairs — one for each transmission direction. Light waves propagate within the inner core over long distances. The dimension of an optical fibre is usually stated as a pair of numbers in microns (μm), which gives the diameters of the core and cladding. For example, a 50/125 fibre has a core diameter of 50 μm and a cladding diameter of 125 μm. Three types of optical fibre have been developed (see Fig. 1.13). The differentiation is according to the refractive index profile of the core and cladding and the mode of propagation of the optical signal. The surface diameter of the cladding in all three types is about 125 μm.

Multimode step index fibre   This has a core of diameter 50 μm, which has a uniform refractive index n_2. There is a step drop in refractive index by about 1% at the core–cladding boundary. The cladding has a uniform refractive index n_1, which is about $0.99n_2$.

The larger core diameter allows *splicing* (joining two pieces) and *coupling* to an optical source to be done with only a small loss penalty. Light is launched into the core from an optical source and the rays propagate within the core by total internal reflection at the core–cladding interface. The light source is usually an infrared *light-emitting diode* (LED) or an *injection laser diode* (ILD) and the wavelengths of practical operation are nominally 820, 1330 and

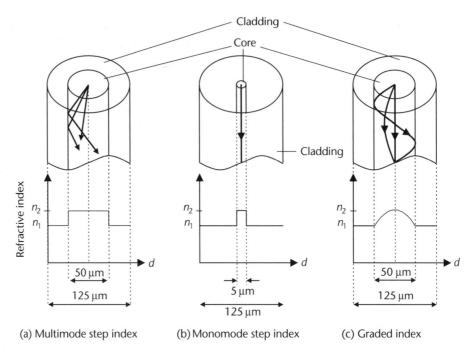

Figure 1.13 Structure, ray path and refractive index profile of optical fibres.

1550 nm. Bandwidth is limited by *modal dispersion* (also called *multipath dispersion*), which arises because rays launched at small angles of incidence into the core travel through a shorter path and hence arrive earlier at the receiver than rays with larger incidence angles. The effect of multipath dispersion is to broaden narrow pulses and therefore limit the bit rate that can be used without adjacent pulses overlapping in time.

Monomode step index   This has a very small core with a diameter of about 5 μm and a uniform refractive index n_2. The refractive index n_1 of the cladding is smaller than that of the core by about 0.4% and there is a step change in refractive index at the core–cladding boundary. Rays are launched into the core from an optical source but only the central ray can propagate in the core. This corresponds to one half-cycle of standing waves across the core. The problem of multipath encountered in multimode fibre propagation and its consequent bandwidth restriction do not arise. This type of fibre therefore has the largest bandwidths, limited only by *material dispersion* arising from the variation of the speed of light with wavelength. However, its tiny core diameter makes splicing and coupling to an optical source extremely difficult. An optical source generating coherent light of very narrow wavelength spread is required for the proper operation of the single-mode fibre. This is provided by an injection laser diode (ILD) such as the Fabry–Perot laser diode.

Multimode graded index   This fibre type was devised to take advantage of the convenience afforded by the larger core of the multimode fibre, while at the same time alleviating the multipath propagation problem. The core is about 50 μm in diameter, but its refractive index is not uniform. Rather it decreases according to a parabolic law, from a maximum n_2 at the core axis to a minimum n_1 ($\approx 0.99n_2$) at the core–cladding interface. By careful selection of the refractive index profile, the wave can be made to propagate within the core by continuous refraction along helical paths at nearly the same axial speed irrespective of incident angle. Rays that travel through longer paths do so in the lower index region, where they have greater speed. On the other hand, those rays that travel through shorter distances have smaller average speed since they spend most of their time near the fibre axis where the refractive index is maximum. All rays, irrespective of their path, arrive at the other end of the fibre at roughly the same time. Modal dispersion is therefore reduced. This feature can increase the bandwidth of this type of fibre by up to an order of magnitude (a factor of 10) above that obtainable with multimode step index fibres. Graded index fibres also give the practical benefit of a larger core diameter.

Advantages of optical fibre medium

1.   Optical fibre conveys an optical carrier of very high frequency — about 200 000 GHz. Assuming a transmission bandwidth of only 1% of the supported carrier frequency, we see that optical fibre offers an enormous potential bandwidth of about 2000 GHz. This is practically a limitless bandwidth when one considers the bandwidth requirement of foreseeable multimedia communication services. However, the realisable bandwidth in the optical communication systems that are currently in operation is restricted to less than about 2 GHz by the limitations of the electronic interface devices.

2.   Intensive research into optical fibre over the last 30 years has led to the development of optical fibre with attenuation reduced from a figure of about 20 dB/km to around 0.2 to 0.5 dB/km within transmission windows at 1550 nm and 1330 nm. Recall that the least lossy (standardised land-line) coaxial cable has attenuation of about 7.5 dB/km at 10 MHz. The much lower attenuation offered by optical fibre means that repeaters can be more widely spaced. This yields a significant reduction in initial and maintenance costs of the communication system. Transmission systems at 140 Mbit/s can be operated with a repeater spacing of 90 km, an order of magnitude better than the largest repeater spacing used in normal-core coax (for a transmission bandwidth of only 4 MHz). Some long-haul communication systems and metropolitan area networks can be implemented using optical fibre without the need for intermediate repeaters.

3.   The fibre carries an optical signal, which is immune to electrical interference. Optical fibre can therefore be deployed in electrically noisy environments without the need for the expensive measures that must be adopted for wire pairs and coax.

4. The problem of crosstalk is completely eliminated. The optical signal in one fibre is confined entirely within that fibre. It does not cause any direct or indirect effects on adjacent fibres in the same or other cable core.

5. The fibre (an electrical insulator) presents infinite resistance to the transmitter and receiver that it connects together. Current and voltage levels at the transmitter and receiver are therefore kept apart. The electrical isolation (of DC bias levels) of different parts of a communication system is desirable to simplify design. Optical fibre provides this isolation naturally and no further measures like transformer or capacitor coupling need to be taken.

6. Fibre is made from a cheap and abundant raw material and advances in the manufacturing process have reached a stage where the finished fibre is now cheaper than copper cable.

7. Fibres are small in dimension (about the thickness of a human hair), low in weight and flexible. They take up much less space than copper cables and can therefore be easily accommodated in existing cable conduits.

Disadvantages of optical fibre

1. Special and costly connectors are required to join together two fibres and to couple a fibre to an optical source. Losses are always incurred, even in the best splices or connectors. A good splice introduces a loss < 0.1 dB, whereas a connector is considered good if its loss is below 0.5 dB. The interconnection of copper cables is easier, cheaper and less lossy. Furthermore, because of its small dimension great care is required to avoid subjecting fibre to mechanical stress.

2. Electric power, needed for example to drive electronic components at repeaters, cannot be sent over the fibre since it is not a conductor. Consider the local telephone loop as an example. The electric current needed to operate the subscriber terminal is sent from the local exchange along the same wire pair that carries the message signal. If fibre is to penetrate the telecommunication network sufficiently to make its huge bandwidth available for multimedia communication to the home, then an alternative means of supplying electric power to the home subscriber unit has to be found at extra cost.

3. It is more difficult to locate faults on a fibre than it is on a metallic conductor. However, pulse reflectometers have been developed that can locate a fibre break to within 0.1% of a repeater section, which could be an uncertainty of up to 90 m (for systems that use 90 km repeater spacing).

1.4.5.4 Radio

Radio is a small part of the wider electromagnetic spectrum shown in Fig. 1.14. An electromagnetic wave consists of a changing electric field, which

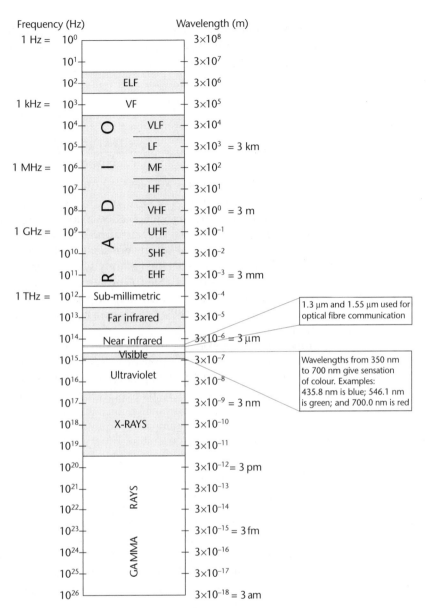

Figure 1.14 The electromagnetic spectrum. ELF = extremely low frequencies (30–300 Hz); VF = voice frequencies (300–3000 Hz). For the abbreviations in the radio band see Table 1.6.

generates a changing magnetic field in the surrounding region, which in turn generates a changing electric field in the surrounding region and so on. The coupled electric and magnetic fields therefore travel out in space. The speed of propagation in air can be shown to be $c = 3 \times 10^8$ m/s, which is the speed of light. At any given point in the region of space covered by the wave, the electric (or magnetic) field goes through a cycle of values, completing one cycle in a time T seconds. That is, the wave makes $f = 1/T$

oscillations per second. The wave is said to have a period T, frequency f and wavelength λ (defined as the distance travelled by the wave during a time of one period). These quantities are related by

$$\lambda = cT = c/f \qquad (1.3)$$

or, in words,

$$\text{Radio wavelength (m)} = \frac{\text{Speed of light } (= 3 \times 10^8 \text{m/s})}{\text{Frequency (Hz)}}$$

Radio waves have been extensively used for information transmission. The basic steps are simple. An information signal in the form of a varying high-frequency current signal is passed into a wire or antenna. This sets up a varying magnetic field in the surrounding region, which in turn sets up a varying electric field, and so on. We say that the antenna radiates electromagnetic waves. Remembering Faraday's law of electromagnetic induction, we know that this wave is able to induce a similarly varying current signal in a distant wire or receive-antenna. In this way the information signal is recovered, having travelled from transmitter to receiver at the terrific speed of light.

How the wave makes this journey, or its *mode of propagation*, depends on the wave frequency. The modes of radio wave propagation in the atmosphere are depicted in Fig. 1.15, which shows how a radio wave travels from a transmitter to a receiver in five different ways, namely

- Ground wave
- Sky wave
- Line-of-sight (LOS)
- Ionospheric scatter
- Tropospheric scatter

For radio communication application, an appropriate frequency band is usually chosen that gives the required coverage and propagation characteristics. Before discussing these propagation modes, it is useful first to review the vertical structure of the atmosphere.

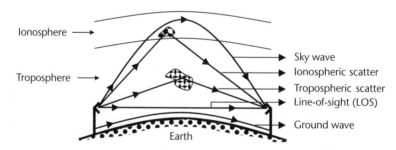

Figure 1.15 Different radio wave propagation modes in the atmosphere.

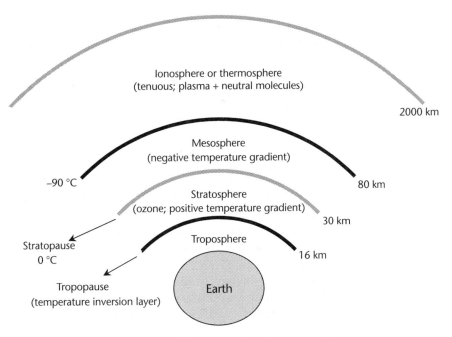

Figure 1.16 Vertical structure of the atmosphere (not to scale).

Vertical structure of Earth's atmosphere Figure 1.16 shows the division of the Earth's atmosphere into four shells. The *troposphere* is the lowest layer of the atmosphere, extending to a height of about 16 km at the equator and about 8 km at the poles. It contains 75% of total gaseous mass and virtually all water vapour and aerosols. It has a negative temperature gradient of about −6.5 °C/km and terminates in most places with a temperature inversion layer called the *tropopause*, which effectively limits convection.

Above the tropopause lies the *stratosphere*, a region that contains most of the atmospheric ozone and extends to about 30 km. Temperature increases with height to a maximum of about 0 °C at the *stratopause*. The heating of the stratopause is caused by the absorption of the Sun's ultraviolet radiation by the ozone.

The *mesosphere* is a region of negative temperature gradient that lies above the stratopause. It extends to about 80 km, where temperatures reach a minimum of about −90 °C.

The *thermosphere* or *ionosphere* is a region of plasma (electrons and positive ions) and large quantities of neutral molecules extending from about 80 km to 2000 km above the Earth's surface. In this region, the Sun's radiation is strong enough to cause the ionisation of gas molecules. Since at this height the atmosphere is rare, the rate of recombination (of electron and ion back to neutral molecule) is very low. Thus, electrons, ions and neutral molecules coexist. The amount of ionisation is usually given in terms of the number of free electrons per cubic metre.

The term *homosphere* is sometimes used to refer to the first 80 km of the atmosphere, where atmospheric gases are well mixed, and *heterosphere* is used to refer to the rest of the atmosphere beyond this height, where the gases tend to stratify according to weight. About 99.9998% of the atmosphere is contained in the homosphere, of which 75% lies in the comparatively small tropospheric volume. The ionosphere is therefore very tenuous.

Ground wave Ground wave propagation is the dominant mode of propagation below about 2 MHz. The wave follows the contour of the Earth by diffraction. This is the propagation mode used in AM broadcasting. Reliable intercontinental communication can be achieved by ground wave communication using high transmit power (> 1 MW). The *minimum usable frequency* is determined by the condition that for efficient radiation the antenna should be longer than one-tenth of the signal wavelength. For example, a 1 kHz wave has a wavelength of 300 km — from Eq. (1.3) — and therefore requires an antenna at least 30 km long to radiate it efficiently. Energy in the surface waves is expended in setting up displacement and conduction currents in the Earth. The resulting wave attenuation increases with frequency, and depends on the salinity (salt content) of the Earth's surface. This attenuation is what sets the *maximum usable frequency*.

Sky wave In the sky wave propagation mode, the atmosphere behaves like a massive waveguide that is bounded below by the Earth's surface and above by a layer of the ionosphere. The wave travels by repeated reflections from these two layers. In reality, what appears to be a reflection from the ionosphere actually results from continuous refraction as the wave travels through a decreasing refractive index profile. Sky wave is the dominant mode of propagation for frequencies about 2 to 30 MHz.

Line-of-sight (LOS) This is the dominant mode of propagation for frequencies above about 30 MHz. The wave propagates in a straight line from transmitter to receiver. The signal path has to be above the radio horizon, which differs from the geographical horizon due to atmospheric refraction. If the two antennas are located on the Earth, then the maximum distance d between the transmit antenna of height h_t and the receive antenna of height h_r for LOS to be achieved (i.e. for the receiver to 'see' the transmitter) is given by

$$d = \sqrt{2R}(\sqrt{h_t} + \sqrt{h_r}) \tag{1.4}$$

Here, $R = 8.5 \times 10^6$ m is the effective radius of the Earth, which is higher than the true Earth radius of ~6.4×10^6 m. Using an effective Earth radius gives correct results with the radio path treated as a straight line from the transmitter to the receiver, whereas in reality radio waves are bent due to refraction. We see from Eq. (1.4) that to increase d we must increase the transmitter and/or receiver height. This explains why the antennas used for *radio relay* links are usually located on raised towers.

LOS is also the mode of propagation employed in (unobstructed) *mobile communications* and *satellite communications*, although Eq. (1.4) is clearly not applicable to the latter.

Satellite communication In satellite communications, one end of the link is a transmitting and/or receiving *Earth station* and the other end is a *spacecraft* or *satellite* equipped with signal reception and transmission facilities. If the satellite is placed in an eastward orbit directly above the equator at an altitude of 35 874 km, then it circles this orbit in synchrony with the Earth's rotation and therefore remains above the same spot on the Earth. This special orbit is described as *geostationary*, and its use allows signal transmission to and reception from the satellite by an Earth station antenna that is pointed in a fixed direction (towards the satellite). Tracking is not required for continuous communication, which is a significant reduction in Earth station complexity and costs.

A unique advantage offered by satellite communication is *broad-area coverage*. One geostationary satellite can 'see' most of half the Earth's surface, allowing reliable communications to take place between any two points within this large coverage area. In its simplest design, the satellite acts as a *repeater* located in the sky. It receives a weak signal from an Earth station transmitter, boosts the signal strength and retransmits it back to Earth on a different frequency. The original signal can then be received by one or more Earth stations. In this way, a live television broadcast of an important event can be provided to many countries using one satellite (and of course many receiving Earth stations). A relay of just three geostationary satellites allows the entire world to be covered.

The main drawback of the geostationary orbit is that the large distance between the Earth station and the satellite gives rise to large propagation delays ($\geq$ 120 ms one way) and extremely weak received signal strengths. These problems are alleviated by using low Earth orbits (LEO), at an altitude ~1000 km, and medium Earth orbits (MEO), at an altitude ~10 000 km. However, tracking is required for communication using one LEO or MEO satellite. Furthermore, communication from a given spot on the Earth is limited to a few hours each day when the satellite is visible. The use of a constellation of many such satellites, equipped with inter-satellite links (to permit a seamless *handoff* from one satellite that is disappearing over the horizon to another visible satellite), allows continuous communication using non-tracking portable units. This is the basis of many proposed mobile satellite communication systems, such as *IRIDIUM*, *GLOBALSTAR*, *ODYSSEY* and *ARIES*.

Mobile communications A mobile communication link consists of a mobile unit, which is capable of large-scale motion, at one end and a fixed base station at the other end, both equipped with radio transmission and reception facilities. An important difference between the mobile link and a fixed satellite or radio relay link is the increased significance of *multipath* propagation. The transmitted radio signal reaches the other end of the link through various paths due to reflections from nearby buildings and/or terrain features and diffraction around obstacles. In fact, the line-of-sight path is often blocked altogether at some locations of the mobile unit. As the mobile unit moves, the received signal strength will therefore vary rapidly in a very complicated manner since the multipath components add destructively in some locations and constructively in others. The phenomenon of multipath propagation is discussed further in Chapter 2.

Ionospheric scatter   Radio waves are scattered by refractive index irregularities in the lower ionosphere. This mode occurs for frequencies between about 30 and 60 MHz and can provide communication (beyond LOS) up to distances of several thousand kilometres.

Tropospheric scatter   Radio waves at frequencies about 40 MHz to 4 GHz are scattered by refractive index irregularities in the troposphere. This scattering can provide communication over distances up to many hundred kilometres. An important area of application of tropospheric scatter is to provide multichannel (e.g. 12 to 240 voice channels) communication over large distances spanning large bodies of water or other inhospitable terrain. Reliable communication with annual availability up to 99.9% is readily achieved over distances up to 650 km on a single hop, or thousands of kilometres using several hops in tandem.

Radio frequency allocation   In order to avoid interference, and for the efficient exploitation of the radio spectrum, it is necessary for appropriate frequency bands to be allocated and agreed for different services. Not all frequency bands are suitable for certain services. For example, low frequencies cannot be used for portable mobile telephony because they require bulky antennas. We have seen that, depending on the frequency band and hence mode of propagation, radio waves can travel over a range of distances. Without some regulation and control over the frequencies used for radio communication, there would be both national and international chaos in the utilisation of radio.

On a global scale, frequency allocation and technical standards are recommended by the International Telecommunications Union (ITU), which is a specialised agency of the United Nations with administrative headquarters in Geneva, Switzerland. The ITU is divided into three sectors. The radio communication sector (ITU-R) is responsible for frequency allocation; the telecommunications standardisation sector (ITU-T) recommends global standards for telecommunication; and the telecommunication development sector (ITU-D) provides technical assistance (especially to developing countries).

Inaugurated on 1 January 1866 by 16 European countries, the ITU now has 188 member nations covering every part of the world. The newest member nation is Saint Lucia, which joined on 4 September 1997. Member nations retain autonomy over the telecommunication standards and frequency allocation adopted in their territories. They are, however, expected to abide by the recommendations of the ITU. It is heartening to note that in a world of political, cultural and religious diversity and (at times) confrontation, ITU member nations have always voluntarily abided by ITU recommendations.

The administration of radio frequency assignments in each nation is usually the responsibility of a specially designated agency — e.g. the

Table 1.6 Typical services in various radio frequency bands.

Frequency band	Typical services
VLF (3–30 kHz) Very low frequency	1. Long-range navigation 2. Submarine communication
LF (30–300 kHz) Low frequency	1. Long-range navigation 2. Marine communication 3. Radio beacons
MF (300–3000 kHz) Medium frequency	1. AM broadcast (550 kHz–1.6 MHz) 2. Direction finding 3. Maritime radio
HF (3–30 MHz) High frequency	1. Amateur radio 2. International broadcasting 3. Long distance aircraft and ship communication 4. Military communication 5. Telephone, telegraph and fax
VHF (30–300 MHz) Very high frequency	1 Aircraft navigational aid 2 AM aircraft communication 3. FM radio broadcast (88–108 MHz) 4. VHF Television (54–88 MHz for channels 2–6; and 174–216MHz for channels 7–13)
UHF (0.3–3 GHz) Ultra high frequency *Sub-bands*: L band = 1–2 GHz S band = 2–4 GHz	1. Cellular telephone 2. Microwave links 3. Navigational aids 4. Personal communication systems (PCS) 5. Radar 6. UHF TV (470–890 MHz for channels 14–83)
SHF (3-30 GHz) Super high frequency *Sub-bands*: C = 4–8; X = 8–12; Ku = 12–18; K = 18–27GHz	1. Satellite communication 2. Radar 3. Microwave links
EHF (30–300 GHz) Extra high frequency *Sub-bands*: Ka = 27– 40; V = 40–75 GHz	1. Experimental 2. Radar 3. Satellite communication

Sub-bands above 300 GHz: Sub-millimetric (300 GHz–3 THz); far-infrared (3–30 THz); near-infrared (30–430 THz) used for optical fibre communication; and visible light (430–860) THz

Federal Communications Commission (FCC) in the USA. Table 1.6 gives a list of the radio services assigned to various frequency bands.

1.5 Classification of modern communication systems

There are three major ways of classifying the wide variety of communication systems in operation today. If we consider the direction of transmission, then the communication system will be either *simplex* or *duplex*. If we consider the type of signal transmitted by the system, then we have either an *analogue communication system* or a *digital communication system*. Comparing the frequency content of the transmitted signal to that of the original signal leads to a classification of the system as either a *baseband communication system* or a *modulated (or passband) communication system*.

1.5.1 Simplex or duplex?

1.5.1.1 Simplex communication system

If information flows in only one direction, the communication system is referred to as *simplex* (SX). Typically, information originates from one transmitter and has one (or more) receiver as its destination. These receivers do not have the capability of responding through the *same* communication link.

By the above explanation, interactive digital television broadcast is a simplex communication system. Although a customer is able to respond (via a telephone link), information transmission from the television house to the customer and from the customer to the television house are carried out on two different links. *Radar*, a system that measures electromagnetic signals reflected off objects (such as ship, aircraft, missile, storm, hydrometeor etc.) in order to determine their range and velocity is also a simplex system. In this case, although the signal may be reflected by the object back towards the transmitter *S*, giving an appearance of bidirectional information flow, there is strictly speaking only one transmitter, which is co-located with one receiver. The reflecting object is neither a transmitter nor a receiver.

Other examples of simplex systems include audio broadcast (AM radio, FM radio, music services and digital radio), television broadcast (satellite, cable and terrestrial), paging services, telemetry and remote control.

1.5.1.2 Duplex communication system

When information can flow in both directions on the same link, the communication system is referred to as *duplex*. The communication equipment at both locations *S* and *R* are equipped with transmission and reception capabilities and is therefore referred to as a *transceiver*. The system may be designed in such a way that simultaneous communication in both directions is possible. This is a *full duplex* (FDX) system and requires a separate channel (e.g. a different band of frequencies, a different time slot or a different wire pair) being allocated for each direction of communication. If, on the other hand, information can only flow in one direction at a time, then the system is referred to as *half duplex* (HDX).

The most common example of a full duplex system is public telephony (both fixed and mobile). Data communication via modems in the PSTN is also full duplex (although some older modem standards are half duplex), as is computer interconnection in local area networks (LAN). An example of a half duplex system is the *walkie-talkie* used for wireless voice communication between two locations. Transmission in either direction uses the same radio frequency band. The handset at each location can be switched between transmit and receive modes, so that at any given time one location transmits while the other receives.

1.5.1.3 *Number of communicating transceivers*

In both simplex and duplex systems, if communication takes place between only two transceivers, then the system may be further described as a *point-to-point* communication system. If there is one transmitter or transceiver communicating with several receivers or transceivers, we have a *point-to-multipoint* system. If there are many intercommunicating transceivers (as in a LAN, or a video conference system linking more than two locations), then we have what is called a *multipoint-to-multipoint* communication system. In this last case, information flow between two transceivers or *nodes* is essentially bidirectional and therefore a simplex multipoint-to-multipoint system is not possible. The Internet is a global network of computers and has become the most popular multipoint-to-multipoint communication system. A radio or television broadcast system is a good example of a point-to-multipoint simplex system (see Fig. 1.17).

1.5.1.4 *Error correction*

An important limitation of simplex systems is that there is no return path for the receiver to automatically request retransmission in the event of an error. Thus, there are two options to deal with the problem of errors: (1) ignore them in non-critical systems or (2) include sufficient redundancy in the transmitted signal so that, in the event of an error, the receiver is able to make a reliable guess of the transmitted information. The guess will occasionally be wrong. This system of error correction is called *forward error correction* (FEC). Duplex systems are not under this limitation and can also use the more reliable technique of error correction called *automatic repeat request* (ARQ), in which the receiver automatically requests retransmission once an error is detected.

1.5.2 Analogue or digital?

An important classification of a communication system, from the point of view of the technology involved in its implementation, is based on the type of information signals conveyed, whether *analogue* or *digital*. Analogue

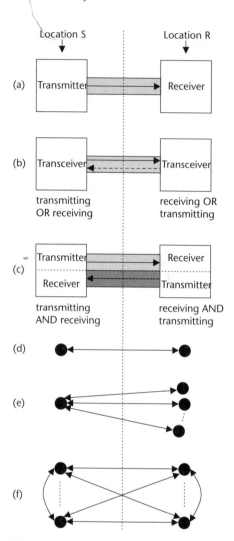

Figure 1.17 Communication systems: (a) simplex; (b) half duplex; (c) full duplex; (d) point-to-point; (e) point-to-multipoint; (f) multipoint-to-multipoint.

communication systems convey analogue signals, while digital systems convey digital signals. However, note that a digital communication system may employ an analogue waveform called a *carrier signal* to convey the digital signal, as in the use of modems for data transmission over public telephone networks, which were originally designed for analogue speech signals.

1.5.2.1 *Analogue signals*

An analogue signal is a *continuous-value* and *continuous-time* physical quantity. Examples include the voltage or current output signal of a microphone (called an audio signal, or more specifically a speech signal in the case of a voice input), acoustic pressure, ambient temperature and the video output

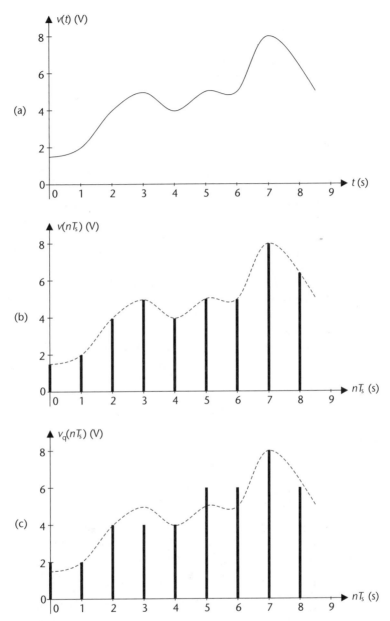

Figure 1.18 (a) Analogue signal; (b) sampled signal; (c) quaternary digital signal.

signal of a television camera. Figure 1.18(a) shows the waveform of an analogue signal $v(t)$ that is defined for the duration $t_{min} = 0$ s to $t_{max} = 8.5$ s, with a range of values from $V_{min} = 1.5$ V to $V_{max} = 8.0$ V. There is an infinite number of time instants between t_{min} and t_{max} and $v(t)$ is defined at every instant. Furthermore, $v(t)$ can take on any of the infinite number of values between V_{min} and V_{max}. Therefore the defining feature of an analogue signal is that it can take on a continuum of values at a continuum of time instants. That is, an analogue signal $v(t)$ is continuous in both value and time.

1.5.2.2 Digital signals

A digital signal, on the other hand, can only take on a set of values at a set of time instants. A digital signal is therefore *discrete* in value and time. If at each time instant there are only two possible values (e.g. 0 and 1, or $+V$ and $-V$), the signal is referred to as a *binary* digital signal. This is by far the most commonly used digital signal in digital communication, but a *ternary* digital signal with three possible values is also used for *line coding* (to represent data as voltage levels in a *baseband* transmission system).

The time instants are usually regularly spaced at t = 0, T_s, $2T_s$, $3T_s$, ..., where T_s is called the *sampling period*. We may therefore denote a digital signal as $v_q(nT_s)$, where the subscript q indicates that the values of the signal are quantised (i.e. restricted to a discrete set of values); $n = 0$, 1, 2, 3, ... and nT_s specifies the sampling instant. Figure 1.18(c) shows how the analogue voltage $v(t)$ has been reduced to a *quaternary* digital signal that can take on one of four possible values 2, 4, 6 and 8 volts, at the sampling instants nT_s = 0, 1, ..., 8 s.

Some signals may be discrete in time but continuous in value, or discrete in value but continuous in time. Note that such signals are *not* digital. An example of the former is the sampled signal $v(nT_s)$ shown in Fig. 1.18(b), which results from taking the instantaneous values of the analogue signal $v(t)$ at a sampling interval T_s = 1 s, starting from $t = 0$. An example of the latter is the voltage signal shown in Fig. 1.19 and defined by

$$s(t) = \begin{cases} -V & t \leq 0 \\ V & t > 0 \end{cases} \tag{1.5}$$

Two features of digital signals make them more suitable for representing information in practical and impairment-prone communication systems. Firstly, unlike an analogue signal, the precise value of a digital signal is not important. Rather, what matters is the interval in which the signal value lies. For example, if a binary digital signal is transmitted using +12 volts to represent binary 1 and −12 volts to represent binary 0, then any received signal value above 0 volts would be interpreted as binary 1 and any below zero as binary 0. It would then take an impairment effect exceeding 12 volts to cause any bit error.

Secondly, unlike analogue signals, only the sampling instants are significant. This means that the detected value of a digital signal is not impaired by any distortions or noise outside the decision instants. Thus a careful choice of sampling instants allows the digital signal to be

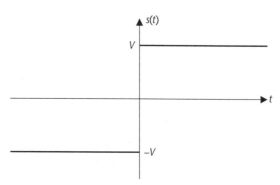

Figure 1.19 Discrete-value continuous-time signal $s(t)$.

detected at the instants of minimum distortion to its values.

Digital signals are therefore extensively used in modern telecommunication systems. Telegraphy, the beginning of modern telecommunication, made use of digital signals to represent the Morse coding of characters. Computer data are today transmitted using digital signals to represent the ASCII, EBCDIC or other coding of the characters. The advantages of digital communication over analogue communication are so great that even analogue signals such as speech and video are nowadays mostly transmitted digitally by first converting them to a digital format at the transmitter. This *analogue-to-digital conversion* (ADC) at the transmitter is followed at the receiver by the reverse process of *digital-to-analogue conversion* (DAC).

1.5.2.3 *Advantages of digital over analogue communication*

- *Low cost*: Inexpensive digital circuits may be used to implement the signal processing tasks required in digital communication. With continuing advances in semiconductor technology, the cost of *very large-scale integrated* (VLSI) circuits will drop even further, making digital communication systems cheaper than their analogue counterparts in spite of the simplicity of the latter. Cost is an important factor that determines whether a new technology is successfully assimilated into society. The digital revolution of the 1990s, which we referred to earlier, was driven to a large extent by the falling costs of digital circuits of increasing computational power.

- *Privacy and security*: Increased reliance on telecommunication systems for private, business and military communications and the sale of entertainment and information services calls for *secrecy*, *authenticity* and *integrity*. The first requirement ensures that the information is received only by an authorised user, while the last two requirements assure the receiver that there has not been any impersonation of the sender and that the information has not been deliberately or accidentally altered in transit. Digital communication permits data encryption to be easily implemented on the information bit stream in order to satisfy these requirements.

- *Dynamic range*: The dynamic range of a communication system refers to the amplitude ratio between the strongest and weakest signals that the system can process with an acceptable level of impairment. Signals of a wider range of values (from very small to very large) than is possible with analogue systems can be accurately represented and transmitted with negligible distortion in digital communication systems. The dynamic range may be increased as much as desired by increasing the number of bits used to represent each sample of the analogue signal during the ADC process. The penalty, of course, is increased bandwidth requirements; see the discussion of disadvantages in Section 1.5.2.4.

- *Noise immunity*: The number of errors in the received data, or the bit error rate, may be very small even in the presence of a significant amount of noise in the received signal. Although the precise value of the received signal will be changed by additive noise, the change will only rarely be large enough to force the signal value beyond the range that represents the transmitted bit.

- *Regeneration*: Digital communication systems allow the possibility of regenerating (at sufficiently closely spaced regenerative repeaters) clean new symbols or pulses, which are free from all impairment effects and are (ideally) an exact replica of the original transmission. Thus, unlike analogue systems, noise does not accumulate from repeater to repeater and no further signal distortion occurs beyond that which was introduced at the analogue-to-digital conversion stage. Digital signals may also be stored in various storage media (e.g. optical or magnetic disks) and processed or retransmitted later without loss of fidelity.

- *Error correction*: It is possible to detect and even correct errors in the received data by the use of various coding techniques, which generally insert some redundancy in the transmitted data.

- *Flexibility*: The signal processing tasks of a digital communication system may be readily reconfigured simply by changing the software program, without any need to change the hardware. Modification of system functions can therefore be implemented more cheaply and speedily.

- *Integrated services*: Voice, video and data can all be represented in a common bit stream format and transmitted simultaneously in a common communication system. Multimedia communication is only possible via digital communication.

1.5.2.4 *Disadvantages of digital communication*

Digital communication also has a number of important disadvantages. However, in most cases these disadvantages are under the system designer's control and their effects may be reduced as much as desired by making a suitable trade-off. It should therefore be noted that the following disadvantages are far outweighed by the advantages discussed above. Thus, the trend in telecommunication has been towards an all-digital network.

- *Large bandwidth*: Digital communication systems generally require more bandwidth than analogue systems. For example, a 4 kHz bandwidth is adequate for analogue speech transmission, whereas digital speech transmission using standard (64 kbit/s) PCM requires a minimum bandwidth of 32 kHz. The spectrum of all transmission media, especially radio, is very limited. Transmission techniques that minimise required bandwidth are therefore preferred in order to increase the number of users and services that can be accommodated. Various low bit rate speech coding and data compression techniques have been devised to reduce the bandwidth requirements of digital audio and video transmission and storage, at the price of reduced signal quality.

- *Complexity*: Digital communication systems generally perform more complex processing operations on the input signal and require more sophisticated circuitry. Synchronisation usually has to be maintained between receiver and transmitter. However, advances in semiconductor technology make circuit complexity a less significant disadvantage. Most of the signal processing tasks may be performed in a single highly reliable and affordable VLSI unit, which can be easily replaced in the unlikely event of a malfunction. Furthermore, some digital transmission techniques such as the asynchronous transfer mode (ATM) — discussed in Chapter 8 — make synchronisation a less difficult problem.

- *Quantisation distortion*: Analogue signals such as speech must be converted to digital form prior to transmission or processing in a digital communication system. This conversion introduces an irreversible quantisation distortion — see Fig. 1.18(c), where the quantised value at each sampling instant clearly differs from the value of the original signal. However, this distortion may be made as small as the system designer wishes by increasing the number of quantisation levels. The price for this improvement is increased bandwidth requirements.

1.5.3 Baseband or modulated?

Communication systems may also be classified as either *baseband* or *modulated*, depending on how the information signal is prepared for the transmission medium.

1.5.3.1 Baseband communication systems

When the transmission medium can pass signals of frequency around 0 Hz and upwards it is described as a *low pass* medium. The original information signal (called the *baseband* signal since it usually contains frequencies near 0 Hz) may be conveyed to the receiver by being placed directly into the low pass medium without any frequency translation. Such a communication system is referred to as a baseband communication system.

The only practical low pass media are wire pairs and coaxial cable. Thus, baseband systems are *always* wire line connected systems. Although the radio spectrum stretches all the way down to frequencies near 0 Hz and it is theoretically possible to convey a baseband signal (e.g. speech signal) by radio, this is impossible in practice. Because it contains low-frequency components, the baseband signal cannot be efficiently placed into the radio medium at the transmitter or extracted from it at the receiver. We will have more to say on this later.

Analogue baseband communication system The simplest example of baseband transmission is the voice intercom system. The baseband voice output signal of a microphone is conducted along a wire pair to a loudspeaker at some distance. Other examples of analogue baseband communication system include the fixed (i.e. non-mobile) telephone connection between two local subscriber terminals in the PSTN and a closed circuit television (CCTV) system.

It could be argued that the communication system block diagram of Fig. 1.3 does not apply in this case, since there is neither transmitter nor receiver and the transmission medium connects the message signal directly from information source to information sink. However, in most cases a transmitter is incorporated that performs very basic signal processing such as frequency-dependent *amplification* to compensate for attenuation and distortion in the transmission medium. The identifying feature of a baseband system is that any type of frequency translation is specifically excluded. The system usually includes a receiver that performs *low-pass filtering* to minimise the effect of noise and *amplification* to provide for output volume control.

A block diagram of the CCTV system is shown in Fig. 1.20. A lens in the video camera forms an image of the scene on a light-sensitive camera sensor, which converts the light intensity into an electrical signal called the video signal. This has a peak-to-peak value of 1 volt and contains frequencies in the range 0 to 10 MHz, depending on the horizontal resolution of the camera. It is obvious that the video signal is a baseband signal. For a large distance between camera and console sites, a video amplifier is inserted to boost the video signal level. If there is only one camera then its output is connected directly via coaxial cable to a monitor. Otherwise, the outputs of several cameras are connected to a video switcher. This is an electronic device that selects different cameras automatically or manually for

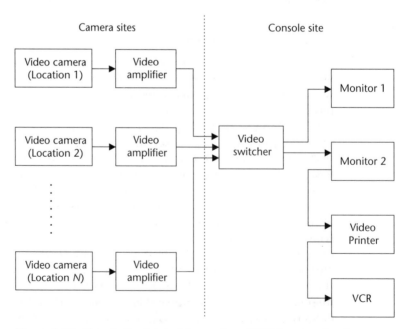

Figure 1.20 Closed-circuit television system (CCTV), example of an analogue baseband transmission system.

display on one or more monitors. The monitor is similar to a television set but has no tuning/demodulation circuits and therefore cannot receive a television broadcast off air. The monitor is simply a CRT or other type of visual display device that converts the baseband video signal into a visible display on its screen. A VCR may also be used for a permanent record of the video signal, and a printer to obtain a hard copy of a selected scene.

Note particularly that in the above example there is no frequency translation, which is why this is a baseband system. This is the most common type of CCTV system. However, there are some implementations that use radio, infrared or optical fibre connection between camera and monitor. There must necessarily be some modulation in these other CCTV types, and therefore they are not baseband systems.

One of the main difficulties with analogue baseband transmission is that a separate transmission medium (wire pair or coaxial cable) is required for each signal. One medium cannot be shared simultaneously by multiple users without interference, since each user's signal is continuous in time and occupies (or at least partly overlaps) the same frequency band. The cost would be prohibitive to provide a separate wire pair for all anticipated simultaneous telephone calls between two exchanges in the PSTN. If the analogue signal is transformed into a discrete-time function then an analogue baseband transmission system can be implemented that has the capability to accommodate multiple users.

Discrete baseband communication system   If we take regular samples of an analogue signal $v(t)$ at intervals of T_s to obtain a sequence of continuous-value samples $v(nT_s)$, then we can perfectly reconstruct the original signal $v(t)$ from the samples $v(nT_s)$ by passing these samples through a suitable low-pass filter, provided that T_s is at most half the period of the highest frequency component of $v(t)$. This is a statement of the *sampling theorem*. A discrete baseband communication system transmits $v(t)$ by sending one voltage pulse at the instance of each sample $v(nT_s)$. The value of each sample may be conveyed in the amplitude, duration or position of the pulse.

If the pulses are sent with equal width at regular intervals T_s but the *height* of the nth pulse (occurring at time $t = nT_s$) is varied in proportion to the sample value $v(nT_s)$, then we have what is referred to as *pulse amplitude modulation* (PAM). If the pulses are sent with equal height at regular intervals T_s but the *duration* or *width* of the nth pulse is varied in proportion to $v(nT_s)$, we refer to this as *pulse duration modulation* (PDM), also called *pulse width modulation* (PWM). Finally, sending the pulses with equal height and width but at irregular intervals such that the time of occurrence or *position* of the nth pulse is delayed relative to the nth sampling instant by an amount that is proportional to $v(nT_s)$ gives rise to *pulse position modulation* (PPM). Figure 1.21 illustrates these waveforms. In Fig. 1.21(d), the sampling instants are indicated by dotted lines. Note from this figure that the longest delay τ_{max} occurs at the third pulse where the sample value is maximum. The first pulse corresponds to the smallest sample value and has the

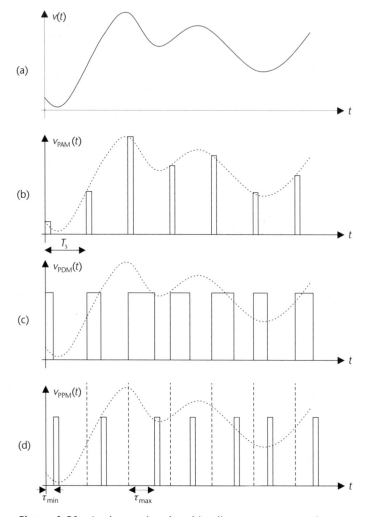

Figure 1.21 Analogue signal and its discrete representation as PAM, PDM and PPM.

shortest delay τ_{min}. The remaining pulses have delays ranging between τ_{min} and τ_{max}. In this way, information regarding the sample values is correctly conveyed by the positions of transmitted pulses.

The block diagram of a PAM generator and receiver is shown in Fig. 1.22 and a suitable arrangement for generating PDM and PPM waveforms is given in Fig. 1.23. Signal waveforms have been sketched at various points of these block diagrams in order to clarify the function of each element. The effect of the transmission medium is not shown. Note the simplicity of the discrete baseband system, in particular the PAM receiver, which is simply a low-pass filter. This filter, often referred to as a *reconstruction filter*, may have a frequency response that is shaped in such a way as to correct for a small distortion due to the action of the sample-and-hold circuit. PWM and PPM signals can be received (i.e. converted back to original analogue signal)

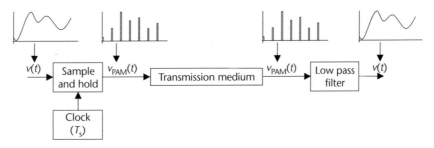

Figure 1.22 Block diagram of a PAM generator and receiver.

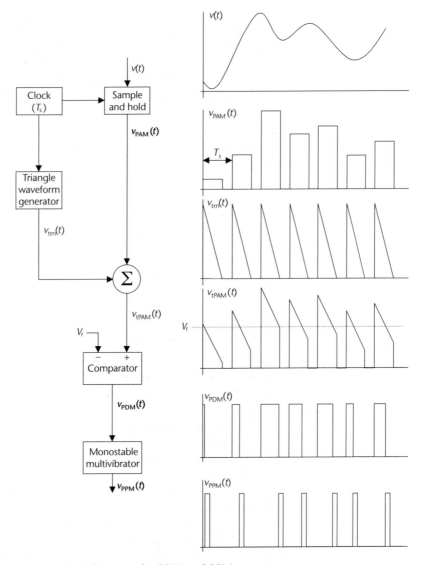

Figure 1.23 Block diagram of a PDM and PPM generator.

by using an integrator to convert pulse width or pulse position to voltage level. This process essentially converts PWM and PPM to a PAM waveform, which is then processed in a low-pass filter to recover the original signal.

Salient features

- Although it is sometimes erroneously viewed as a form of modulation employing a pulse train as the carrier, a discrete baseband communication system is actually a baseband transmission because the spectra of PAM, PDM and PPM signals contain frequencies down to 0 Hz. In fact, the spectrum of an instantaneously sampled PAM signal is the spectrum of the original (baseband) signal plus exact duplications at regular intervals along the frequency axis.

- A discrete baseband system is an analogue communication system, since the parameter of the pulse train that is varied may take on a continuum of values in a specified range. For example, the precise value of the pulse height is significant in a PAM system and any variation due to noise will distort the received signals.

- The bandwidth required to transmit a discrete baseband signal (PAM, PDM or PPM) far exceeds the bandwidth of the original analogue signal. Actually, an instantaneously sampled PAM signal has infinite bandwidth. A discrete baseband signal fills up all the bandwidth available on the transmission medium. To share the medium among multiple signals, each must be sent in a separate time slot.

- PAM is very susceptible to noise. PDM and PPM have a better noise performance that is similar to that of frequency modulation (FM) systems, but is inferior to the noise immunity obtainable with digital baseband transmission systems. If the pulses were perfectly rectangular, then PDM and PPM would be completely immune to additive noise as this would only alter the unused height parameter, without affecting the zero crossings of the pulse which determine pulse width or pulse location. Unfortunately, perfectly rectangular pulses, with zero rise time, are not only impossible to generate, they are also impossible to maintain in a low pass transmission medium.

- PDM is wasteful of power compared to PPM. Long pulses in PDM expend more power but carry no additional information. PPM on the other hand transmits pulses of equal energy.

- The main *advantage* of a discrete baseband system is that transmission medium sharing by multiple users, known as *multiplexing*, is possible. The intervals between the samples of one signal are used to transmit samples of other signals. This type of multiplexing is known as *time division multiplexing*.

Time division multiplexing of several PAM signals   Figure 1.24 shows the block diagram of an *N*-channel TDM system that allows simultaneous transmission of several independent PAM signals over a single transmission medium. The commutator is drawn as a rotating arm. It is actually an

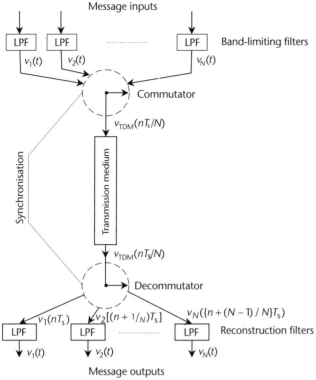

Figure 1.24 Block diagram of an analogue TDM system.

electronic switching circuit that samples each input at a rate $f_s = 1/T_s$ and interleaves the N samples inside the sampling interval T_s. Low-pass filters remove insignificant high-frequency components of the input signals and limit their bandwidth to at most $f_s/2$. These bandlimited analogue waveforms can then be correctly reconstructed at the receiver by passing their respective sequence of samples through low-pass filters, as shown in Fig. 1.24. The waveforms referred to in Fig. 1.24 are sketched in Fig. 1.25 for $N = 3$. It must be emphasised that this is an analogue system. Its main advantage of simplicity is outweighed by its susceptibility to noise and distortion and therefore the analogue TDM system shown in Figs. 1.24 and 1.25 is rarely used in practice. However, this system forms the basis for the time division multiplexing of digital signals, which has now become a ubiquitous technique in telecommunication systems. Some of the features of time division multiplexing, whether of PAM or digital signals, include:

- The bandwidth requirement of an N-channel TDM signal expands by a factor N, the number of multiplexed signals or channels. This is the case since N samples are squeezed into one sampling interval, reducing the sampling pulse period by a factor N and hence increasing its frequency by the same factor. In practice, the bandwidth increase will be even more, since some time slots must be reserved for system management and synchronisation.

- The transmitter and receiver must be synchronised in order that the interleaved samples in the TDM signal are correctly distributed by the decommutator to their respective channels.

- TDM is sensitive to transmission medium dispersion, which arises because the transmission medium differently attenuates or delays various frequency components of the transmitted pulse. As a result, the pulse may broaden out sufficiently to overlap adjacent time slots, an undesirable situation known as *intersymbol interference* (ISI).

- However, TDM is immune to system non-linearity as a source of crosstalk between independent signals, since at any given time instant only one signal is present. This feature is an important advantage that allows amplifiers to be operated near their maximum rating, a typically non-linear region.

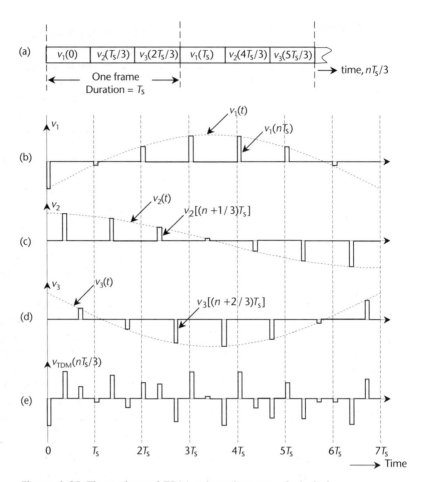

Figure 1.25 Three-channel TDM. n is an integer = 0, 1, 2, 3, ...

Digital baseband communication system Digital signals, originating from coded textual information or from digitised analogue signals, may also be transmitted at baseband. This is by far the most common type of baseband transmission, as it has all the advantages of digital communication systems discussed earlier. The baseband transmitter performs line coding on the input bit stream, while the baseband receiver has the task of decoding the received (and channel-distorted) coded waveforms back into the original bit stream with minimum error. Before looking at these two operations, let us first consider how an analogue signal is converted into a digital bit stream.

Analogue-to-digital conversion (ADC) Various techniques have been devised to convert analogue signals to digital. The earliest and still widespread technique is *pulse code modulation* (PCM).

Figure 1.26 shows four signal-processing steps involved in converting an analogue signal to a PCM signal. The low-pass filter removes non-essential

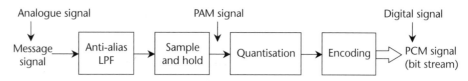

Figure 1.26 Digitisation of an analogue signal: PCM signal generation.

frequency components in the message signal and limits the highest frequency component to f_{max}. This serves to reduce transmission bandwidth and to ensure that the sampling theorem is satisfied when the message signal is sampled (in the sample-and-hold circuit block) at a manageable rate $f_s \geq 2f_{max}$. Next, the continuous-value sample sequence (PAM signal) is converted to a discrete-value sequence. This process is known as *quantisation*. It introduces irrecoverable errors as each sample is approximated to the nearest of a set of quantisation levels. In a practical system with a large number of quantisation levels, the errors are referred to as quantisation noise, since their effect is similar to that of white noise. If quantisation levels are uniformly spaced, we refer to this as *uniform* or *linear* quantisation and to the signal conversion process as *uniform ADC* or *linear PCM*. *Non-linear PCM* results from the use of a non-uniform quantisation, which spaces the quantiser levels non-uniformly in such a way as to make the *signal-to-quantisation-noise ratio* (SQNR) approximately constant over all analogue signal values. Finally, the encoder converts each quantised signal level to a unique binary word of length k bits. Note that k bits can be used to uniquely represent $N = 2^k$ quantisation levels. Taking f_s samples of the signal per second and representing each sample with k bits, the number of bits generated each second, or *bit rate*, is given by

$$\text{bit rate} = kf_s \text{ bits/s} \tag{1.6}$$

In PCM telephony, $f_s = 8000$ samples per second (or Hz) and $k = 8$ bits/sample, yielding a bit rate of 64 kbit/s. In certain bandwidth-limited communication services such as *multimedia mobile communication*, or storage-limited applications such as *voicemail*, the bit rate requirement of PCM is excessive.

    Reducing the redundancy inherent in a PCM signal allows the bit rate and hence bandwidth and storage requirements to be significantly reduced. In a technique called *differential pulse code modulation* (DPCM), it is the difference $e(nT_s)$ between the actual sample and a predicted value that is quantised and encoded, rather than the sample itself. If the predictor is properly designed and an adequate sampling rate ($f_s = 1/T_s$) is used, then the range of $e(nT_s)$ will be very small, allowing fewer quantisation levels and hence a smaller k (bits/sample) to be used to achieve a SQNR comparable to that of a PCM system. Assuming the same sampling rate as in PCM, we see from Eq. (1.6) that the bit rate of a DPCM system will be lower than that of a PCM system of comparable SQNR. The ITU-T has adopted for voice telephony a 32 kbit/s DPCM system, obtained by using only $k = 4$ bits to code each sample taken at the rate $f_s = 8$ kHz. A 64 kbit/s DPCM system has also been adopted for wideband audio (of 7 kHz bandwidth). This uses $k = 4$ and $f_s = 16$ kHz.

Further bit rate reduction can be achieved by using sophisticated *data compression* algorithms and, for the digitisation of speech, a range of methods known as *low bit rate speech coding*. These techniques are inherently lossy. They exploit the features of the message signal, and the characteristics of human hearing and vision, to eliminate redundant as well as insignificant information and produce a modified signal of greatly reduced bit rate. After this signal has been decompressed or otherwise processed at the receiver, a human observer finds it acceptably close to the original.

Operations of a digital baseband transmission system Line coding: So whatever its origin, whether from ASCII-coded textual information or from a digitised analogue signal, we have a bit stream to be transmitted. A digital baseband transmitter chooses suitable voltage symbols (e.g. rectangular or shaped pulses) to represent the string of 1s and 0s, a process known as *line coding*, and places these symbols directly into a transmission line system. Figure 1.27 shows the line codes used in Europe for connections between equipment (often within one exchange building) in the interfaces of the digital transmission hierarchy. Line codes are designed to have certain desirable characteristics and to fulfil a number of important functions.

- The spectral characteristics of coded data must be matched to the characteristics or frequency response of the transmission medium. A mismatch may result in significant distortion of the transmitted voltage pulses. In particular, the code should have no DC offset. Line transmission systems are easier to design when different parts of the system are capacitor or transformer coupled to separate their DC bias voltage levels. These coupling elements pass higher frequency (AC) voltages but block zero frequency (DC) voltages. The coded data must therefore be void of DC content to prevent *droop* and *baseline wander*,

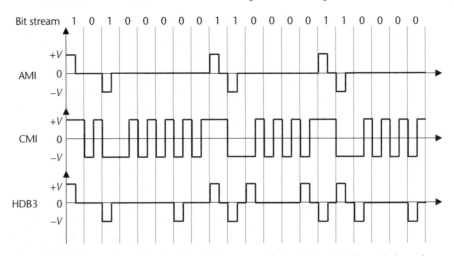

Figure 1.27 Examples of line codes: alternate mark inversion (AMI), coded mark inversion (CMI) and high density bipolar with three zero maximum (HDB3).

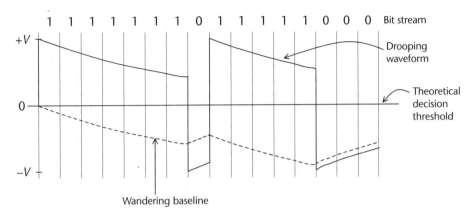

Figure 1.28 Illustration of droop and baseline wander in a binary code.

whereby the received waveform drifts significantly relative to the decision threshold, which is 0 V for the case of a bipolar binary code (see Fig. 1.28).

- The line code must combine data and timing information in one signal. It would be very expensive if a separate wire pair or coaxial cable had to be employed to carry the timing information needed at the receiver for setting decision or sampling instants. Furthermore, the line code must have a reasonable amount of clock content: the *timing content* of a code is the maximum number of symbols that can occur together without a level transition — a small number indicating high timing content. Ideally, there should be at least one transition in every symbol, but the major penalty is an increased bandwidth requirement.

- Vulnerability of the data to noise and inter-symbol interference (ISI) must be minimised. Sudden changes in a signal imply high frequencies in its spectrum. A rectangular pulse (with sharp transitions) transmitted through a low pass transmission medium will spread out, with a potential for ISI. Thus pulse shaping is frequently employed to reduce high-frequency components, which also reduces crosstalk since higher frequencies are more readily radiated. Pulse shaping also reduces the bandwidth necessary to correctly transmit the coded waveforms. The larger this bandwidth, the larger will be the amount of noise power that the receiver inevitably 'admits' in the process of receiving these waveforms.

- The line code should allow some amount of error detection. This usually involves the use of redundancy in which some codewords or symbol patterns are forbidden. A received codeword that violates the coding rule in force would then indicate some error.

- The line code should maximise code efficiency to allow a lower symbol rate to be used for a given bit rate. In long-distance cable systems, a lower symbol rate allows increased repeater spacing and reduces overall system cost. It turns out, however, that codes of high efficiency may lack certain other desirable characteristics. The code selected in prac-tice will involve some compromise and will depend on the priorities of the particular system. Code efficiency is the ratio of actual information content (or bits) per code symbol to potential information content per code symbol. Potential information content per code symbol being given by $\log_2$(code radix), where *code radix* is the number of signalling levels or voltage levels used by the code symbols. For example, the potential information content per code symbol of a binary code (radix = 2) is $\log_2(2) = 1$ bit; that of a ternary code (radix = 3) is $\log_2(3) = 1.585$ bits; and that of a quaternary code (radix = 4) is $\log_2(4) = 2$ bits; etc. Codes with higher radix can therefore convey more information per symbol, but there is increased codec complexity and a higher proba-bility of error. Although multilevel codes (of radix ≥ 4) are very common in modulated communication systems to cope with restricted bandwidth, only codes with radix ≤ 4 are employed in baseband systems.

One example of a quaternary code is the 2B1Q line code, which was adopted by ANSI (American National Standards Institute) in 1986 for use on basic ISDN lines. It is also the line code used on DSL local loops. As the name suggests, the 2B1Q code represents two binary digits using one quaternary symbol, i.e. one of four voltage levels. More specifi-cally, the *dibits* 00, 01, 11 and 10 are represented by the voltage levels $-3A$, $-A$, $+A$ and $+3A$, respectively, where A is a constant.

● Finally, the complexity of the encoder and decoder circuits (codec) should be kept to a minimum in order to reduce costs. In general, line codes that can be implemented by simple codecs are used for short links, whereas more efficient but complex and costly codecs are used for long-distance links because they can work with fewer repeaters and hence reduce the overall system cost.

Line decoding: The transmission medium distorts the transmitted pulses by adding noise and by differently attenuating and delaying various frequency components of the pulses. A baseband receiver or repeater takes the distorted pulses as input and produces the original clean pulses at its output. It does this through three 'R' operations. First, a *reshaping* circuit comprising an equaliser and a low-pass filter is used to reshape the pulse and ensure that its spectrum has a raised cosine shape. This operation is important to minimise ISI. Next, a *retiming* circuit recovers the clock signal from the stream of reshaped pulses. Level transitions within the pulse stream carry the clock information. Finally, a *regenerating* circuit detects the pulses at the sampling instants provided by the recovered clock signal. Occasionally an error will occur when a noise voltage causes the pulse amplitude to cross the detection threshold. The frequency of occurrence of such errors, or bit error rate (BER), can be maintained at an acceptable level by ensuring that the noisy pulses are detected before the ratio of pulse energy to noise power density falls below a specified threshold. Figure 1.29 is a block diagram of a digital baseband system showing the basic opera-tions discussed here.

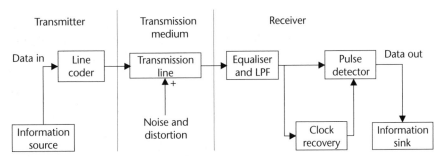

Figure 1.29 Digital baseband transmission system.

1.5.3.2 Modulated communication systems

In very many situations it is necessary to translate the baseband signal (without distorting its information content) to a frequency band centred at a frequency f_c that is well above 0 Hz. A communication system in which the information signal undergoes this *modulation* process before being placed into the transmission medium is referred to as a *modulated communication system*. There are numerous examples of modulated systems. All satellite communication systems, mobile communication systems, radio and TV broadcast systems, radio relay systems and optical communication systems are modulated systems.

Formally, we define modulation as the process of imposing the variations (or information) in a lower-frequency electrical signal (called the *modulating* or *baseband* or *message* signal) onto a higher frequency signal (called the *carrier*). The carrier signal is usually a sinusoidal signal of frequency f_c. It effectively gives the message signal a 'ride' through the transmission medium because, for a number of reasons, it is impossible or undesirable for the message signal to make the 'journey' on its own.

Role of modulation There are a number of reasons why modulation is extensively used in modern communication.

1. Modulation is used to obtain a more efficient exploitation of the transmission medium by accommodating more than one user in the same medium at the same time. In most cases, the bandwidth that is available in the medium is much larger than is required by one user or message signal. For example, the bandwidth available on a coaxial cable is more than 10 000 times the bandwidth of one telephone speech channel. The bandwidth of an optical fibre medium exceeds that of an analogue TV signal by a factor of up to one million; and the radio spectrum is much wider than the bandwidth required by one radio station for its broadcasts. Modulation allows the implementation of FDM in which each user's signal is placed in a separate frequency band by modulating an appropriate carrier. As long as the carrier frequencies are sufficiently far apart, the different signals do not interfere with each other. A particular signal can be recovered at the receiver

by filtering (to exclude the unwanted channels) and demodulation (to detect the message signal in the carrier signal). Providers of radio services are able to transmit and receive within the bands allocated to them (Table 1.6) by using a suitable modulation technique.

2. Modulation allows us to select a frequency that is high enough to be efficiently radiated by an antenna in radio systems. The power radiated by an antenna may be expressed as $P = I^2R_r$, where I is the root mean square (rms) value of the current signal fed into the antenna and R_r is the antenna's radiation resistance. It turns out that R_r depends on the size of the antenna measured in wavelength units. In general, the size of the antenna must be at least one-tenth of the signal wavelength if the antenna is to radiate an appreciable amount of power. Consider the minimum size of antennas required to radiate signals at three different frequencies: 3 kHz, 3 MHz and 3 GHz. The wavelengths of these signals, obtained using Eq. (1.3), are 100 km, 100 m and 10 cm, respectively. Thus, if we attempted to radiate a 3 kHz speech signal, we would need an antenna that is at least 10 km long. Not only is such an antenna prohibitively expensive, it is hardly suited to portable applications such as in handheld mobile telephone units. If on the other hand we use our 3 kHz speech signal to modulate a 3 GHz carrier signal, it can be efficiently radiated using very small and hence affordable antennas of minimum size 1 cm.

3. The use of modulation to transmit at higher frequencies also provides a further important advantage. It allows us to exploit the higher bandwidths available at the top end of the radio spectrum in order to accommodate more users or to transmit signals of large bandwidth. For example, an AM radio signal has a bandwidth of 10 kHz. Thus the maximum number of AM radio stations that can be operated at LF (30–300 kHz) in one locality is given by

$$\text{Maximum number of AM stations at LF} = \frac{300 - 30}{10} = 27$$

Observe that there is a ten-fold increase in the number of AM radio stations when we move up by just one band to MF (300–3000 kHz):

$$\text{Maximum number of AM stations at MF} = \frac{3000 - 300}{10} = 270$$

The NTSC television signal requires a radio frequency bandwidth of 6 MHz. Frequency bands at MF and below cannot therefore be used for TV transmission because they do not have sufficient bandwidth to accommodate the signal. The HF band (3–30 MHz) can accommodate a maximum of only four such TV channels. However, as we move to higher bands we can accommodate 45 TV channels at VHF, 450 at UHF, 4500 at SHF and 45 000 at EHF; and the optical fibre medium can accommodate literally millions of TV channels.

4. Another important function of modulation is that it allows us to transmit at a frequency that is best suited to the transmission medium.

The behaviour of all practical transmission media is frequency-dependent. Some frequency bands are passed with minimum distortion, some are heavily distorted and some others are blocked altogether. Modulation provides us with the means of placing the signal within a band of frequencies where noise, signal distortion and attenuation are at an acceptable level within the transmission medium. Satellite communication was pioneered in the C-band inside the 1–10 GHz window, where both noise (celestial and atmospheric) and propagation impairments are minimum. Ionospheric reflection and absorption become increasingly significant the lower you go below this band, until at about 12 MHz the signal is completely blocked by the ionosphere. Furthermore, attenuation by tropospheric constituents, such as rain, atmospheric gases, fog and cloud water droplets, becomes significant and eventually very severe at higher frequency bands. For this reason, modulation must be used in satellite communication to translate the baseband signal to a congenial higher frequency band.

Another example of a bandpass transmission medium is the optical fibre medium. This blocks signals at radio wave frequencies, but passes signals in the near-infrared band, particularly the frequencies around 194 and 231 THz. Thus, the only way to use this valuable medium for information transmission is to modulate an optical carrier signal with the baseband information signal.

Types of modulation There are three basic methods of modulation depending on which parameter of the carrier signal is varied (or modulated) by the message signal. Consider the general expression for a sinusoidal carrier signal

$$v_C(t) = A_c \cos(2\pi f_c t + \phi) \tag{1.7}$$

There are three parameters of the carrier, which may be varied in sympathy with the message signal. The (unmodulated) carrier signal $v_C(t)$ has a constant amplitude A_c, a constant frequency f_c and a constant initial phase ϕ. Varying the amplitude according to the variations of the message signal, while maintaining the other parameters constant, gives what is known as *amplitude modulation* (AM). *Frequency modulation* is obtained by varying the frequency f_c of a constant-amplitude carrier and *phase modulation* is the result of varying only the phase ϕ of the carrier signal.

An analogue modulating signal will cause a continuous variation of the carrier parameter, the precise value of the varied parameter being significant at all times. It is obvious that this is then an analogue modulation and the resulting system is an *analogue modulated communication system*.

A digital modulating signal (consisting of a string of binary 1s and 0s) will on the other hand cause the carrier parameter to change (or shift) in discrete steps. Information is then conveyed not in the precise value of the parameter at all times, but rather in the interval of the parameter value at discrete decision (or sampling) instants. This is therefore digital modulation and the resulting system is a *digital modulated communication system* having all the advantages of digital communication. In this case, the three modulation methods are given the special names *amplitude shift keying* (ASK), *frequency shift keying* (FSK) and *phase shift keying* (PSK) to emphasise that the parameters are varied in discrete steps. The number of steps of the parameter generally determines the complexity of the digital modulation scheme. The simplest situation, and the one most robust to noise, is *binary modulation* (or binary shift keying), where the carrier parameter can take on one of two values (or steps). This is shown in Fig. 1.30.

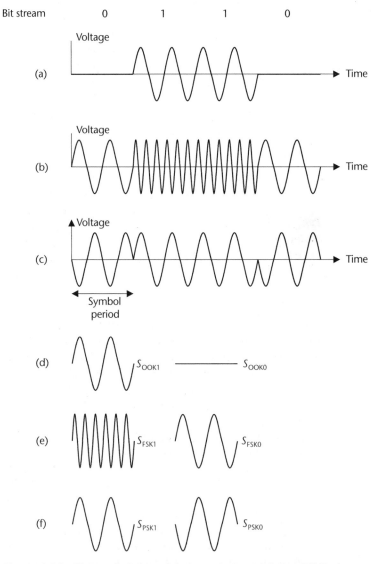

Figure 1.30 Binary digital modulation schemes: (a) On–Off Keying (OOK), a special type of ASK; (b) Frequency Shift Keying (FSK); (c) Phase Shift Keying (PSK); (d) OOK symbols; (e) FSK symbols; (f) PSK symbols.

To transmit a bit stream using binary ASK, we take one bit at each clock instant and transmit a sinusoidal carrier of frequency f_c for the duration of the bit. The carrier frequency f_c is chosen to suit the transmission medium. The carrier amplitude is set to A_1 for bit '1' and to A_0 for bit '0'. If either A_1 or A_0 is zero, we have a special type of binary ASK known as *On–Off Keying* (OOK), which is the digital modulation scheme used in optical fibre communication. In binary FSK, same-amplitude and same-phase carriers of frequencies f_1 and f_0 are transmitted for bit 1 and bit 0, respectively. In binary PSK, the carrier amplitude and frequency are fixed, but the carrier is transmitted with a phase ϕ_1 for bit 1 and ϕ_0 for bit 0. Usually one phase is 0° and the other is 180° in order to use the maximum spacing between the two carrier phases.

A useful way to look at digital modulation is to treat each transmitted carrier state as a code symbol. Thus, OOK represents bits 1 and 0 with the symbols S_{OOK1} and S_{OOK0} shown in Fig. 1.30(d); FSK uses the symbols S_{FSK1} and S_{FSK0} shown in Fig. 1.30(e); and PSK uses the symbols S_{PSK1} and S_{PSK0} shown in Fig. 1.30(f). The symbol rate (or signalling rate) is limited by the bandwidth available on the transmission medium. The theoretical maximum symbol rate is twice the medium bandwidth. In a telephone channel with a bandwidth of about 3.1 kHz, the maximum possible symbol rate is therefore 6200 symbols per second.

The main drawback of binary shift keying is that bit rate and symbol rate are equal, since each symbol represents one bit. In many applications, a much higher bit rate is desired than can be obtained by increasing the symbol rate, which is limited by the available bandwidth. A higher bit rate can be achieved by using multi-level (also called M-ary) digital modulation, in which M distinct carrier states are transmitted. Binary modulation is the special case $M = 2$. To do this, we take a group of k bits at a time and represent them with a unique carrier state or code symbol, where $k = \log_2 M$, or $M = 2^k$. For example, taking $k = 3$ bits at a time, we have $M = 2^3 = 8$ possible states, namely 000, 001, 010, 011, 100, 101, 110 and 111, which must each be represented by a unique carrier state. Each symbol now carries three bits of information and the bit rate is therefore three times the symbol rate. In general, M-ary modulation increases the bit rate according to the relation

$$\text{bit rate} = \log_2 M \times (\text{symbol rate}) \tag{1.8}$$

However, the symbol states are closer together than in binary modulation, making it easier for noise effects to shift one state sufficiently close to an adjacent state to cause a symbol error. For example, the phase difference between adjacent states in an M-ary PSK is $(360/M)°$, which for $M = 16$ is only 22.5°. Bearing in mind that these PSK states all have the same energy, carrier amplitude being constant, we see that there is great potential for error if the transmission medium is prone to phase distortion. A combination of *amplitude and phase keying* (APK), also called *quadrature amplitude modulation* (QAM), is often used which increases the phase difference between symbol states. For example, the minimum phase difference between states of equal energy is 90° in 16-APK, compared to only 22.5° in 16-PSK.

TYPES OF SYSTEM: A SUMMARY

In summary, from a signal processing perspective, there are four major types of communication system.

1. Analogue baseband communication systems, e.g. voice intercom systems.

2. Analogue modulated communication systems, e.g. AM radio broadcasts.

3. Digital baseband communication systems, e.g. some computer networks via coaxial cables.

4. Digital modulated communication systems, e.g. data communication via modems on public switched telephone networks.

The above systems may be implemented as simplex or duplex and they may be point-to-point, point-to-multipoint or multipoint-to-multipoint. In many instances, a complete communication system involves the interfacing of several of the above types of system. For example, the public switched telephone network may be an analogue baseband system from the local subscriber to the local exchange, then a digital baseband system for connections between local exchanges and a digital modulated system for international connection via satellite or optical fibre line.

This now completes our overview of communication systems. In the next chapter, we begin a more in-depth study of the subject with a detailed consideration of telecommunication signals.

REVIEW QUESTIONS

1.1 (a) Discuss the drawbacks of verbal and visual non-electrical telecommunications.

(b) In spite of its many drawbacks, non-electrical telecommunication remains indispensable in society. Discuss various situations in which non-electrical telecommunication has some important advantage over (modern) electrical telecommunications. In your discussion, identify the type of non-electrical telecommunication and the advantage it provides in each situation.

1.2 Sketch the flags that represent the following messages in semaphore code. Remember to include an end of signal code in each case.

(a) NO
(b) TAKE 5

1.3 Sketch the voltage pulse sequence for the Morse code representation of each of the following complete messages.

(a) WE WON 2-0
(b) I LOVE YOU

1.4 Baudot code (Table 1.3) requires seven transmitted bits per character, which includes a start bit (binary 0) and a stop bit (binary 1). Write out the complete bit sequence for the transmission (LSB first) of the following messages using Baudot code.

(a) DON'T GIVE UP

(b) 7E;Q8

1.5 Repeat Question 1.4 for asynchronous transmission of the same messages using ASCII code. Compare the number of bits required by Baudot and ASCII codes in each case and comment on your results. In particular, calculate the transmission efficiency of both coding schemes in (a) and (b). [*Note*: The framing of an ASCII character for asynchronous transmission and the definition of transmission efficiency are given in Appendix B.].

1.6 The 20th century witnessed revolutionary developments in telecommunications far beyond what could have been contemplated by the pioneers of telegraphy. Discuss four key areas of these developments.

1.7 Draw a clearly labelled block diagram that is representative of all modern communication systems. List 12 different devices that could serve as the information source of a communication system. Identify a suitable information sink that may be used at the receiver in conjunction with each of these sources.

1.8 With the aid of a suitable diagram, discuss the operation of the following information sources or sinks.

(a) Dynamic microphone

(b) Loudspeaker

(c) CRT

(d) Plasma-panel display

(e) Liquid crystal display

1.9 Fig. 1.6 shows the ISO standard 226 contours of equal loudness as a function of frequency and SPL.

(a) What is the loudness of sound of frequency 200 Hz and SPL 40 dB?

(b) If a tone of SPL 55 dB is perceived at a loudness 50 phon, what are the possible frequencies of the tone?

(c) Determine the amount by which the vibration (i.e. SPL in dB) of a 50 Hz tone would have to be increased above that of a 1 kHz tone in order that both tones have equal loudness 10 phon.

1.10 Discuss the signal processing tasks performed by the transmitter in a communication system. Indicate why each process is required and how it is reversed at the receiver to recover the original message signal.

1.11 Discuss the importance and limiting factors of a copper wire-pair as a transmission medium in modern communication systems. List current applications of this transmission medium and the practical measures taken to minimise the effects of its limitations.

1.12 Discuss the features and applications of coaxial cable as a transmission medium. Which of these applications do you expect to continue into the future? Give reasons for your answer.

1.13 (a) Carry out a detailed review of the structure and features of the three standard types of coaxial fibre.
(b) Discuss the advantages and disadvantages of the optical fibre transmission medium.
(c) Give your opinion on the future role of optical fibre in the local access network taking into account the emerging telecommunication services, competing local access technologies and costs.

1.14 Give a brief review of the five modes of radio wave propagation in the atmosphere. Identify the major applications and frequency range of each mode and state the factors that set the limits of the usable frequency.

1.15 The 1990s witnessed what has been described as a digital revolution, with the introduction of digital audio and television broadcasting, in addition to a virtually complete digitalisation of the telecommunication networks of many countries. Examine the reasons for this trend of digitalisation by presenting a *detailed* discussion, with examples where possible, of the advantages and disadvantages of digital communication. Indicate in your discussion how the impact of each of the disadvantages can be minimised in practical systems.

1.16 Give *two* examples of each of the following types of communication systems:
(a) Simplex system
(b) Half duplex system
(c) Duplex system
(d) Analogue baseband
(e) Analogue modulated
(f) Digital baseband
(g) Digital modulated

1.17 (a) With the aid of suitable block diagrams, discuss the operation of *any two* examples of an analogue baseband communication system.
(b) What are the most significant disadvantages of an analogue baseband communication system?

1.18 With the aid of suitable block diagrams, discuss the generation of the following discrete baseband signals starting from an analogue message signal.
(a) PAM
(b) PDM
(c) PPM

1.19 Compare the discrete baseband systems of Question 1.18 in terms of noise performance, bandwidth requirement, power consumption and circuit complexity.

1.20 Explain how three independent user signals can be simultaneously carried on one transmission link using discrete baseband techniques. What are the major drawbacks of this system?

1.21 Using a suitable block diagram, discuss the steps involved in the analogue to digital conversion (ADC) process. Identify the major parameters that must be specified by the ADC system designer and explain the considerations involved.

1.22 Give a detailed discussion of the desirable characteristics of line codes, which are used to electrically represent bit streams in digital baseband communication systems.

1.23 Discuss the three 'R' operations of a digital baseband receiver.

1.24 Discuss the roles of modulation in communication systems. Hence identify the transmission media that can be used for voice communication in the absence of modulation.

1.25 Sketch the resulting waveform when the bit stream 1 0 1 1 1 0 0 1 modulates a suitable carrier using

   (a) OOK
   (b) Binary FSK
   (c) Binary PSK

Assume that the carrier frequency is always an integer multiple of $1/T_b$, where T_b is the bit interval.

1.26 If the following digital communication systems operate at the same symbol rate of 4 kbaud, determine the bit rate of each system.

   (a) OOK
   (b) 2B1Q
   (c) Binary FSK
   (d) 16-APK

Telecommunication signals

IN THIS CHAPTER

- Forms and classification of telecommunication signals
- Sinusoidal signals
- Frequency content of signals
- Power content of signals
- Logarithmic measures of signal and power
- Calibration of a signal transmission path
- Transmission through linear systems
- Signal distortion

2.1 Introduction

The field of telecommunication deals with the transfer or movement of information from one point to another by electronic or electromagnetic means. The information to be transferred has first to be represented as a telecommunication signal. In approaching this important field of study, one must therefore have a thorough understanding of telecommunication signals and how they are manipulated in telecommunication systems. The following presentation has been carefully designed to help you acquire this crucial grounding using a minimal-mathematics approach that emphasises applications and a graphical appreciation of concepts. It will pay you rich dividends to work diligently through this chapter, *skipping nothing*. You will gain important insights into crucial fundamental principles and acquire versatile telecommunications systems analysis skills, which will serve you very well in your studies and career.

We discuss the representation of signals and channels in Communication Engineering and introduce the basic concepts of *frequency*, *power* content of signals and its common logarithmic measures, *spectrum* (of phase, amplitude and power), *bandwidth*, *linear time-invariant systems*, *filters* and *signal distortion*. We introduce the sinusoidal signal as the basic building block of all periodic signals, and a non-periodic signal as a special case of the periodic signal when the period tends to infinity. In this way, we introduce the Fourier transform as essentially a mathematical expression of our ability to synthesise any arbitrary signal using a large number of harmonically related sinusoids. You will then see why a certain minimum bandwidth is required to faithfully transmit a signal and how signal distortion is the result of some of the component sinusoids of the signal being differently attenuated or delayed by a system.

You will not be required to delve into the computation of the Fourier transform of signals, which in any case is nowadays done using readily available software packages. For reference purposes, a table of Fourier Transforms for various standard waveforms is given in the Appendix.

2.2 Forms and classification of telecommunication signals

A telecommunication signal is a time-varying event used to convey aural and visual information, or for performing system control functions. Of the five senses used by human beings, only two, namely sight and hearing, can be readily conveyed as a telecommunication signal. Smell may however be indirectly telecommunicated using a technique that analyses gas mixtures and represents their constituent parts as a coded signal. This signal can be transmitted in the usual manner. A suitable receiver will receive and interpret the coded signal and release a mixture of the constituent gases in the right proportion, thereby reproducing the original smell.

An important feature of information-bearing signals is that one or more parameters of the signal must *vary with time*. Although a constant signal may be useful in conveying *energy*, such a signal carries little or no information. Signals can exist in different forms and media. Table 2.1 lists five different forms of signal, the media in which they can exist and the signal parameter that varies to convey information. Where a signal exists in acoustic or visual form, the first operation of a telecommunication system is to convert the signal into electrical form (using a suitable *transducer*) for ease of processing and transmission or further conversions before transmission.

Figure 2.1 shows various examples of transducers often employed to convert a telecommunication signal from one form to another.

● The *microphone* converts an acoustic (or sound) signal such as music and speech into an electrical signal, while the *loudspeaker* performs a reverse process to that of the microphone and converts electrical signals into sound. See Section 1.4.1 for further discussion.

● The *scanner* or *television camera* converts a visual signal into an electrical signal. The scanner works only on printed (two-dimensional and

Table 2.1 Forms of signals.

Form	Medium	Varying parameter
Electrical	Wire, e.g. twisted wire pair in local subscriber loop and coaxial cable in CATV	Current or voltage level
Electromagnetic	Space, e.g. broadcast TV and radio	Electric and magnetic fields
Acoustic	Air, e.g. interpersonal communication	Air pressure
Light	Optical fibre	On–off switching of light from injection laser diode (ILD) or light-emitting diode (LED)
Visual	Paper, e.g. print image	Reflected light intensity

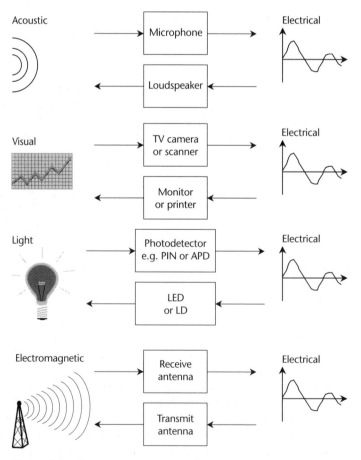

Figure 2.1 Signal conversions in telecommunication.

still) images, whereas the television camera is able to handle physical scenes (three-dimensional and movable) as well. The reverse process of converting from electrical to a visual signal is performed using a suitable display device, e.g. the cathode-ray tube in a TV receiver or a printer attached to a computer terminal.

● A light detector or *photodetector* converts light energy into electric current. Examples include the PIN diode and the avalanche photodiode (APD). In both cases, the diode consists of an intrinsic (I) semiconductor layer sandwiched between heavily doped layers of p-type and n-type semiconductors. The diode is reverse-biased and this creates a charge-depleted layer in the intrinsic region. Light falling on this layer creates electron–hole pairs that drift in opposite directions to the diode terminals (electrons towards the positive voltage terminal and holes towards the negative), where they register as current flowing in the same direction. The APD uses a large reverse-bias voltage so that the photo-induced electrons acquire sufficient kinetic energy to ionise other atoms, leading to an avalanche effect.

A *light-emitting diode* (LED) and a *laser diode* (LD) perform the reverse process of converting electric current to light. The optical radiation results from the recombination of electron–hole pairs in a forward-biased diode. In the laser diode, there is a threshold current above which the stimulated emission of light of very narrow spectral width ensues.

● An *antenna* may be regarded as a type of transducer. Used as a transmitter, it converts electrical signals to electromagnetic waves launched out into space in the desired direction. When used as a receiver, it converts an incoming electromagnetic radiation into a current signal.

Signals may be classified subjectively according to the type of information they convey, or objectively depending on their waveform structure. The waveform or wave shape of a signal is a plot of the values of the signal as a function of time. Note that the following discussion employs terms such as *frequency* and *bandwidth* which will be explained fully in later sections.

2.2.1 Subjective classification

2.2.1.1 *Speech*

Speech sound is the response of the human ear–brain system to the sound pressure wave emitted through the lips or nose of a speaker. The elements involved in speech production are illustrated in Fig. 2.2. Air is forced from the lungs by a muscular action that is equivalent to pushing the piston. The air stream passes through the *glottis*, the opening between the *vocal cords* or *folds*. For voiced sounds, the vocal chords are set into vibration as the air stream flows by, and this provides a pulse-like and periodic excitation to the *vocal tract*. For unvoiced (or voiceless) sounds, there is no vibration of the vocal chords. The vocal tract, comprising the oral and nasal cavities, is a tube of non-uniform cross-section beginning at the glottis and ending at

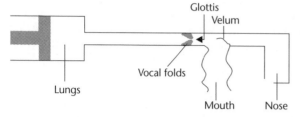

Figure 2.2 Elements involved in human speech production.

the lips and nose. The nasal cavity is shut off from the vocal tract by raising the *velum* and coupled by lowering the velum. The vocal tract acts as a sound modifier. Its shape is changed to determine the type of sound that is produced. Different vowel sounds are generated by the resonance of the vocal tract under different shapes. Vowels have strong periodic structures and higher amplitudes. On the other hand, different consonant sounds are produced by constriction of the vocal tract at different points. The air stream from the lungs flows through this point of constriction at a high velocity, giving rise to turbulence. Consonants have weaker amplitude and a noise-like spectrum. Some sounds, such as the non-vowel part of 'zee', are generated by mixed excitation. In this case the turbulent airflow at a point of constriction is switched on and off by the closing and opening of the glottis due to the vibration of the vocal chords.

A microphone converts acoustic signal into an electrical signal referred to as *speech signal*. Knowledge of the time-domain and frequency domain characteristics of speech signals is very useful in the design of speech transmission systems. Note that the exact details of these characteristics will vary significantly depending on the speaker's sex, age, emotion, accent etc. The following summary is therefore intended as a rough guide.

A typical speech waveform is the sum of a noise-like part and a periodic part. Figure 2.3 shows 100 ms segments of the voiced sound 'o' in 'over', the unvoiced sound 'k' in 'kid' and the mixed sound 'z' in 'zee'. The voiced sound is strongly periodic and of large amplitude. On the other hand, the unvoiced sound is noise-like and of small amplitudes. Even for a single speaker, speech signals tend to have a large *dynamic range* of about 55 dB. The dynamic range is given by the ratio of the largest amplitude during intervals of, say, shouting or syllabic stress to the smallest amplitude in soft intervals, observed over a period of 10 minutes or more. The ratio of the peak value to the root mean square (rms) value, known as the *peak factor*, is about 12 dB. Compared to a sinusoidal signal that has a peak factor of 3 dB, we see therefore that speech signals have a preponderance of small values. It is evident from Fig. 2.3 that most of these small values would represent consonants and they must be faithfully transmitted to safeguard intelligibility. Over a long period of time the large amplitudes of a speech signal follow what is close to an *exponential* distribution, whereas the small amplitudes follow a roughly *Gaussian* distribution.

The short-term spectrum of speech is highly variable, but a typical long-term spectrum is shown in Fig. 2.4. This spectrum has a low-pass filter shape with about 80% of the energy below 800 Hz. The low-frequency components (50–200 Hz) enhance speaker recognition and naturalness, while the high-frequency components (3.5–7 kHz) enhance intelligibility, such as being able to distinguish between the sounds 's' and 'f'. Good subjective speech quality is, however, obtained in telephone systems with the baseband spectrum limited to the range 300 to 3400 Hz. This

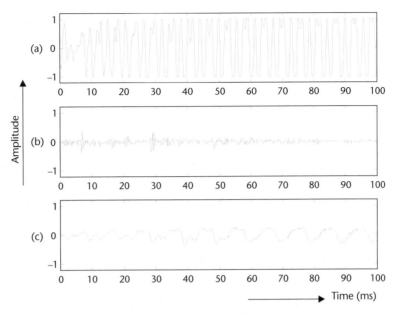

Figure 2.3 Speech waveforms of (a) voiced sound 'o' in 'over', (b) unvoiced sound 'k' in 'kid', and (c) mixed sound 'z' in 'zee'.

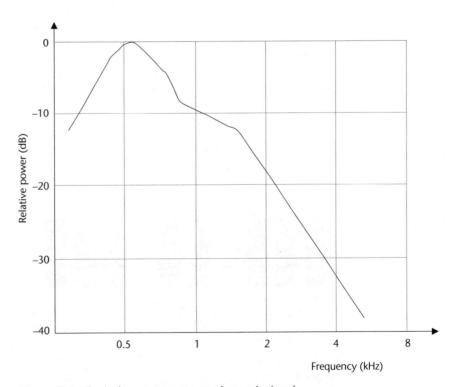

Figure 2.4 Typical power spectrum of speech signal.

bandwidth is the ITU-T standard for telephony, although a smaller bandwidth (500–2600 Hz) has been used in the past on some international networks to increase capacity.

2.2.1.2 Music

Music is a pleasant sound resulting from an appropriate combination of notes. A *note* is sound at a specific frequency, usually referred to as the *pitch* of the note. Pitch may be expressed in Hz or using a notation based on a musical scale. Western musical scale consists of notes spaced apart in frequency at the ratio of $2^{1/12}$ (= 1.059463). For example, if the middle A of a piano is of frequency 440 Hz, then subsequent notes up to the next A, one *octave* higher, are 466, 494, 523, 554, 587, 622, 659, 698, 740, 784, 831 and 880 Hz. You will observe that there is a doubling of frequency in one octave, the space of 12 notes; see Fig. 2.5.

Sounds of the same note played on different instruments are distinguishable because they differ in a characteristic known as *timbre*. The note of each musical instrument comes from a peculiar combination of a fundamental frequency, certain harmonics and some otherwise related frequencies, and perhaps amplitude and frequency variations of some of the components. Although sounds from different musical instruments can be differentiated over a small bandwidth of say 5 kHz, a much larger bandwidth is required to reproduce music that faithfully portrays the timbre. High-fidelity music systems must provide for the transmission of all frequencies in the audible range from 20 Hz to 20 kHz. Note therefore the significant difference in bandwidth requirements for speech and music transmission. The maximum bandwidth required for speech transmission is 7 kHz for audio conference and loudspeaking telephones. This is referred to as *wideband audio* to distinguish it from the normal speech transmission using the baseband frequencies 300–3400 Hz.

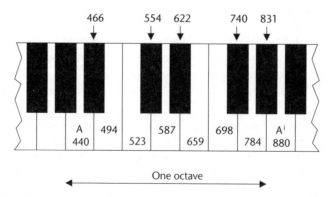

Figure 2.5 Fundamental frequency (in Hz) of various notes on a piano keyboard.

2.2.1.3 Video

The video signal is in general the electrical representation of movable three-dimensional scenes as transmitted in television systems. A special case called *image* signal arises when the scene is a still two-dimensional picture. Information conveyed by video signals include the following:

- *Motion*: Video signals must contain the information required for the display system to be able to create the illusion of continuous motion (if any) when pictures of the scene are displayed. To do this the camera must take snapshots of the scene at a high enough rate. Each snapshot is called a *frame*. Observations show that a frame rate of about 30 (or a little less) per second is adequate. In motion pictures (or movies) a frame rate of 24 frames/s is used, but at the display each frame is projected twice to avoid flicker. This means a refresh rate of 48 Hz. Increasing the frame rate increases the amount of information and hence the required transmission bandwidth.

- *Luminance*: Information about the brightness of the scene is contained in a luminance signal, which is a weighted combination of the red, green and blue colour contents of the scene. The weighting emphasises green, followed by red and lastly blue, in a way that reflects the variation of perceived brightness with the colour of light. For example, given red, green and blue electric bulbs of the same wattage, the green light appears brightest, followed by the red; the blue light appears dullest.

- *Chrominance*: The colour content of the scene must be conveyed. There is an infinite range of shades of colours, just as there is an infinite range of shades of grey, or an infinite set of real numbers between, say, 0 and 1. However, (almost) any colour can be produced by adding suitable proportions of the three primary additive colours: red, green and blue. Colour information is conveyed by chrominance signals from which the display device extracts the proportion of each of the primary colours contained in the scene. Because the eye is not very sensitive to changes in colour, the fine details of colour changes are usually omitted to allow the use of a smaller bandwidth for the chrominance signals.

- *Audio*: The sound content of the recorded scene or other superimposed sound information is conveyed in a bandwidth of 15 kHz. This allows high-fidelity sound reproduction.

- *Control signals*: The television receiver or display device needs information to correctly construct a two-dimensional picture of the scene from the one-dimensional (time function) video signal. Thus synchronisation pulses are included that control the rate at which the display device 'draws' the scene line by line in step with the image scanning operation of the camera.

How the above signals are combined to form the composite baseband video signal depends on the type of television system. However, it is obvious that video signals contain much more information than music or speech signals and will therefore require a larger transmission bandwidth. The 625/50 TV standard requires a bandwidth of 8 MHz.

2.2.1.4 *Digital data*

Digital data originates mostly from textual information generated by PCs or other data terminal equipment and encoded using the American Standard Code for Information Interchange (ASCII) in Table 1.4. Coding transforms the message text into a stream of binary digits. For example, the message 'Take $1' is coded in 8-bit ASCII as

$$01010100011000010110101101100101001000000010010000110001$$

An important consideration in the transmission of textual information is that there are no insignificant details that may be ignored or modified. For example, changing even just one bit can have far-reaching consequences. To verify this, check the effect of changing the 53rd bit in the above 56-bit digital data. Elaborate schemes have been devised to detect and in some cases correct transmission errors in digital data by adding extra bits to the message bits. Any data compression techniques adopted to reduce the message bit stream must be *lossless*. That is, the receiver must be able to expand the compressed data back to the original uncompressed bit stream.

Increasingly, speech, music and video signals are being converted to a digital representation in order to exploit the numerous advantages of digital transmission and storage. Although the resulting digital signal is again a bit stream similar to digital data, there is an added flexibility that both lossless and lossy compressions can be applied to reduce the number of bits required to represent these analogue signals. Lossy compression eliminates some (insignificant) details in order to save bandwidth. For example, barring other distortions, speech can be accurately transmitted (with intelligibility and speaker recognition) by using nearly lossless representation at 128 kbit/s, or using lossy compression to reduce the bit rate to 16 kbit/s or lower. There is a loss of subjective quality in the latter, but the consequences are not catastrophic as would be the case if digital data were lossily compressed.

2.2.1.5 *Facsimile*

A facsimile signal, usually abbreviated to *fax*, conveys the visual information recorded on paper, whether printed or handwritten documents, drawings or photographs. The transmission medium is in most cases a telephone line or sometimes radio. The popularity of fax for business communication is now being challenged by the *electronic mail* (email) system. Email is particularly convenient for sending documents that are in electronic (word-processed) form, as it can be done without the sender leaving their desk or feeding any paper into a machine. However, fax remains popular for transmitting hard copies and documents that must be supported by a signature, headed paper etc.

There are several fax standards. The Group 3 (G3) standard is the most common in use today and can transmit an A4 page in less than one minute, typically 15–30 s. A new standard, the Group 4 (G4) requires a dedicated wideband digital-grade telephone line and can transmit an A4 page in less than 5 s with a resolution of 400 *lines per inch* (lpi). In the G3 standard, the resolution is 200 lpi, meaning that the paper is divided into a rectangular grid of picture elements (pixels), with 200 pixels per inch along the vertical and horizontal directions. That is, there are 62 pixels per square millimetre. Starting from the top left-hand corner, the (A4) paper is scanned from left to right, one grid line at a time, until the bottom right-hand corner of the paper is reached. For black-and-white only reproduction, each pixel is coded as either white or black using one binary digit (0 or 1). For better quality reproduction in G3 Fax, up to 5 bits per pixel may be used to represent up to $2^5 =$ 32 shades of grey. The resulting bit stream is compressed at the transmitter and decompressed at the receiver in order to increase the effective transmission bit rate. At the receiver, each pixel on a blank (A4) paper is printed black, white or a shade of grey according to the value of the bit(s) for the pixel location. In this way the transmitted picture pattern is reproduced.

Early fax machines used a drum scanner to scan the paper directly, but modern machines form an image of the paper on a matrix of charge-coupled devices (CCD), which build up a charge proportional to incident light intensity.

2.2.1.6 *Ancillary and control signals*

Ancillary and control signals perform system control functions and carry no user-consumable information. There are numerous examples. Synchronising pulses are transmitted along with a video signal to control the start of each line and field scan. Pilot signals are transmitted along copper line systems to monitor variation in attenuation. Extra symbols or bits are inserted in digital signals for error detection/correction, synchronisation and other system management functions.

2.2.2 Objective classification

2.2.2.1 *Analogue or digital*

Analogue signals can take on any value at any time within a specified range; i.e. an analogue signal is *continuous* in both value and time. Most naturally occurring signals are analogue, e.g. speech or outside temperature. *Digital* signals, on the other hand, can only take on a set of values (e.g. 0 and 1, or V and $-V$ for binary signals) at a set of time instants (e.g. $t = 0$, Δ, 2Δ, 3Δ, ..., where Δ is called the *sampling period*). That is, a digital signal is *discrete* in value and time.

2.2.2.2 *Periodic or non-periodic*

A *periodic* signal has a basic or *fundamental shape* that repeats over and over in time. The length in time (or duration) of the shortest fundamental shape is called the *period*, *T*, of the waveform. Mathematically, if $v(t)$ is a periodic signal of period T, then

$$v(t) = v(t \pm nT); \quad n = 0,1,2,3,... \tag{2.1}$$

The smallest duration of time T for which Eq. (2.1) is satisfied is the period of $v(t)$. It means, for example, that the signal has the same value at the time instants $t = 0$, T, $2T$, $3T$, ..., which we may write as

$$v(0) = v(T) = v(2T) = v(3T) = ...$$

Strictly speaking, a periodic signal is *eternal*, having neither a beginning nor an end. It exists from $t = -\infty$ to $+\infty$. In this respect, it would seem impossible to generate a truly periodic signal. However, in practical systems, the duration of interest is always limited. Thus, if a signal has a fundamental shape that repeats over and over within the finite interval of interest, then the signal is said to be periodic.

A *non-periodic* (sometimes called *aperiodic*) signal has no repetitive pattern and hence does not satisfy Eq. (2.1) for any T. Some signals (e.g. some speech waveforms) may have a *slowly changing* repetitive pattern. They are referred to as *quasi-periodic* signals. Figure 2.6 shows examples of periodic, non-periodic and quasi-periodic waveforms. The fundamental shape of the periodic waveform is emphasised.

The *fundamental frequency* f_0 of a periodic signal is the rate at which the fundamental shape repeats itself. This is the number of cycles per second, which is usually expressed in hertz (Hz). Since one cycle or fundamental

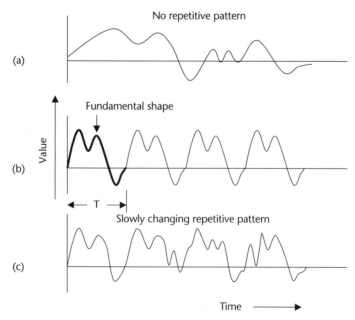

Figure 2.6 Waveforms: (a) non-periodic; (b) periodic with period T; (c) quasiperiodic.

shape has a duration T (the period), it follows that the fundamental frequency is given by

$$f_0 = \frac{1}{T} \tag{2.2}$$

In Eq. (2.2), if the period T is in seconds, the frequency is in Hz; when T is in milliseconds (ms), the frequency is in kHz; when T is in microseconds (μs), the frequency is in MHz; etc.

In addition to the fundamental frequency, every periodic signal (except sine waves, which we discuss later) contains other frequencies, called *harmonic frequencies*, at integer multiples of the fundamental frequency. The nth harmonic frequency is

$$f_n = nf_0; \; n = 1, 2, 3, \ldots \tag{2.3}$$

Note that the first harmonic frequency, $f_1 = 1 \times f_0 = f_0$, is the same as the fundamental frequency f_0. This is different from conventional usage in *music*, where the first harmonic is twice the fundamental frequency.

2.2.2.3 *Deterministic or random*

A *deterministic* signal can be expressed as a completely specified function of time. A random signal, on the other hand, can only be described in terms of the *probability* that its instantaneous value will lie in a given range. While there is always some *uncertainty* about the value of a random signal before it actually occurs, there is no uncertainty whatsoever about the value of a deterministic signal at any time past, present or future.

2.2.2.4 *Power or energy*

If the signal has a finite non-zero energy E (i.e. $0 < E < \infty$), it is said to be an energy signal. If on the other hand the signal has a finite non-zero power P (i.e. $0 < P < \infty$), it is described as a power signal. Every signal will be either an energy signal or a power signal, but not both. A deterministic non-periodic signal is always an energy signal. A periodic signal is always a power signal, and a random signal is always a power signal. The meanings of power and energy are discussed later.

2.2.2.5 *Waveform examples*

Figure 2.7 shows some popular waveforms in telecommunication systems. Both the *pulse train* and the *square* wave are *rectangular* waveforms; but while the former has a *duty cycle* other than 50%, the latter has a duty cycle of exactly 50%. The duty cycle of a rectangular waveform (often expressed as a percentage) is defined by

$$\text{Duty cycle} = \frac{\text{Duration of pulse}}{\text{Period of waveform}} = \frac{\tau}{T} \tag{2.4}$$

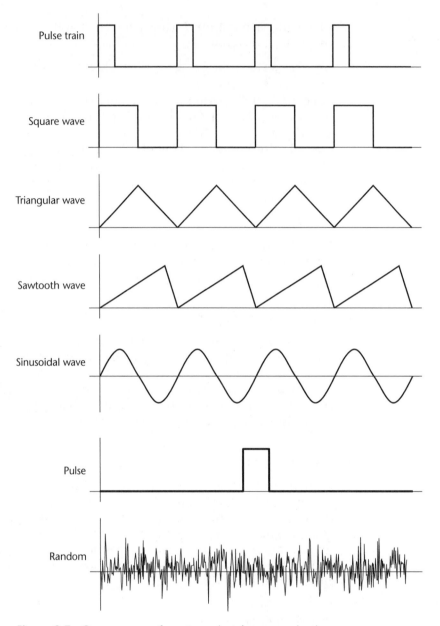

Figure 2.7 Common waveform types in telecommunications.

Observe also in Fig. 2.7 the difference between the *triangular* and *sawtooth* waveforms. The triangular waveform has equal rise and fall times, whereas the sawtooth waveform has a rise time that is much longer than its fall time. Sawtooth signals are used, for example, in *television receivers* and *oscilloscopes* to sweep an electron beam across the face of the cathode ray tube (CRT) during the rising portion of the waveform and to provide a quick *flyback* of the beam during the falling portion of the waveform.

WORKED EXAMPLE   2.1

Sketch a rectangular waveform of amplitude 5 V that has a duty cycle 20% and a 3rd harmonic frequency 6 kHz.

We are given $f_3 = 6$ kHz and duty cycle = 0.2. To sketch the waveform, the period T and pulse duration τ must first be determined. Equation (2.3) gives the fundamental frequency,

$$f_0 = \frac{f_3}{3} = \frac{6 \text{ kHz}}{3} = 2 \text{ kHz}$$

The period is then obtained using Eq. (2.2):

$$T = 1/f_0 = 1/(2 \text{ kHz}) = 0.5 \text{ ms}$$

Eq. (2.4) then gives the pulse duration

$$\tau = T \times \text{Duty cycle} = 0.5 \times 0.2 = 0.1 \text{ ms}$$

A sketch of the rectangular waveform is shown in Fig. 2.8.

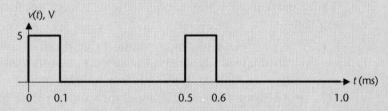

Figure 2.8   Two periods of the rectangular waveform of Example 2.1

WORKED EXAMPLE   2.2

Determine the first three harmonic frequencies of the periodic waveform shown in Fig. 2.9(a) (overleaf).

The crucial first step here is to identify the fundamental shape or cycle of the waveform. This is done in Fig. 2.9(b), and the fundamental shape is emphasised. We see that there are three repetitions of the shape in a time of 6 μs, giving a period $T = 2$μs. Equation (2.2) yields the fundamental frequency of the waveform,

$$f_0 = 1/T = 1/(2 \text{ μs}) = 0.5 \text{ MHz}$$

Therefore,

First harmonic frequency $f_1 = 1 \times f_0 = 0.5$ MHz

Second harmonic frequency $f_2 = 2 \times f_0 = 1.0$ MHz

Third harmonic frequency $f_3 = 3 \times f_0 = 1.5$ MHz

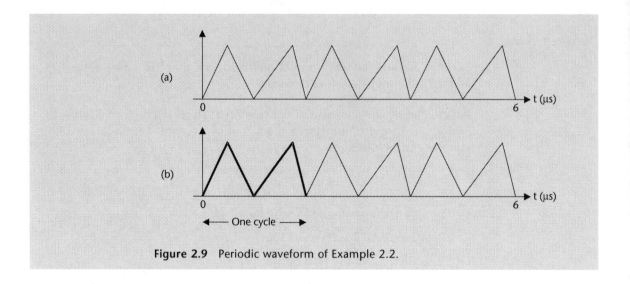

Figure 2.9 Periodic waveform of Example 2.2.

2.3 Sinusoidal signals

Sinusoidal signals play a major role in telecommunications for two main reasons:

1. Every type of telecommunication signal can be obtained as the sum of sinusoidal signals. This is the subject of Fourier analysis and synthesis, which we address briefly in this chapter.

2. If we input a sinusoidal signal into a linear time-invariant system, the output will be another sinusoidal signal of the same frequency, although there may be a change in amplitude and initial phase. These parameters are discussed shortly.

A thorough understanding of basic telecommunication concepts like frequency, signal bandwidth, frequency response of a system, distortion, dispersion, modulation etc. requires a sound knowledge of sinusoidal signals. It is therefore suggested that you study this section carefully, even if just to refresh your memory.

2.3.1 Qualitative introduction

A sine waveform is generated by oscillatory motion without energy losses. A good example is the displacement of a pendulum swinging in vacuum through small angles, e.g. in the range ±2° or less as shown in Fig. 2.10(a). Figure 2.10(b) is obtained by plotting the displacement $d(t)$ of the pendulum from its rest position as a function of time. The pendulum starts at the rest position (displacement $d = 0$) at time $t = 0$, i.e., the initial displacement $d(0) = 0$. The standard convention is to treat displacements to the right of the rest position as positive and displacements to the left as negative. The pendulum first swings right and reaches a maximum displacement (called *amplitude*) d_m at time T_1. It then swings leftward,

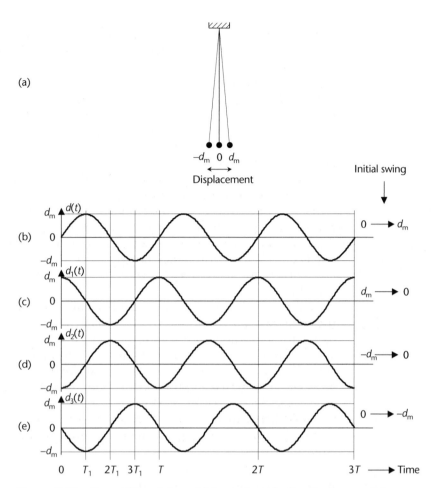

Figure 2.10 Generation of sinusoidal waveform by a swinging pendulum.

reaching the rest position ($d = 0$) at time $2T_1$ and a minimum displacement ($-d_m$) at time $3T_1$. It reverses direction yet again and swings rightward to reach the rest position ($d = 0$) at time $4T_1$. This completes one cycle of oscillation. Therefore the period of the displacement waveform is $T = 4T_1$. Subsequent oscillation cycles continue and the pendulum repeats the above sequence over and over, but with time constantly increasing in equal amounts such that the second cycle is completed at time $t = 2T$, the third cycle at $t = 3T$ etc. The displacement $d(t)$ is a sinusoidal waveform, also referred to simply as a *sinusoid*.

The oscillation of a pendulum with period T and amplitude d_m can differ in the *initial phase*, which reflects both the initial displacement and the initial direction of swing. Three different situations $d_1(t)$, $d_2(t)$ and $d_3(t)$ will be discussed. In Fig. 2.10(c) the pendulum starts at the maximum displacement, i.e. $d_1(0) = d_m$, and swings leftward. It reaches the rest position ($d_1 = 0$) at $t = T_1$ and the minimum displacement ($d_1 = -d_m$) at $t = 2T_1$. At this point, it changes direction and swings rightward to reach $d_1 = 0$ at $t = 3T_1$

and $d_1 = d_m$ at $t = 4T_1 = T$, thereby completing one cycle of oscillation. Using the waveform $d(t)$ of Fig. 2.10(b) as the reference and noting that there it took ¼ period (or cycle) for $d(t)$ to reach d_m — the starting point of $d_1(t)$, we say that the waveform $d_1(t)$ has a ¼ cycle head start compared with the waveform $d(t)$. In conventional terminology, we say that $d_1(t)$ has an *initial phase* of ¼ cycle or 90° — since there are 360 degrees in one cycle. Equivalently, we say that $d_1(t)$ *leads* $d(t)$ by 90°. It should be emphasised that, when talking about the initial phase of a sinusoidal waveform, there must always be a reference waveform of the same period. In this discussion our reference waveform is $d(t)$ in Fig. 2.10(b). The initial phase of the reference waveform is always taken as 0°.

In Fig. 2.10(d) the pendulum starts at minimum displacement $d_2(0) = -d_m$ and swings rightward (of course). It passes through the points $d_2 = -d_m$, 0, d_m, 0 and $-d_m$ at times $t = 0$, T_1, $2T_1$, $3T_1$ and $4T_1$, respectively, to complete one cycle of oscillation. Since it takes $d_2(t)$ ¼ period to reach the starting point of $d(t)$, we say that $d_2(t)$ *lags* $d(t)$ by 90°, or that it has an initial phase of –90°.

Finally, Fig. 2.10(e) shows the displacement waveform generated when the pendulum starts at $d_3 = 0$ and swings leftward. To complete one cycle, it passes through the points $d_3 = 0$, $-d_m$, 0, d_m, 0 at times $t = 0$, T_1, $2T_1$, $3T_1$ and $4T_1$, respectively. The initial phase of $d_3(t)$ may be stated in one of two equivalent ways. Considering that it takes $d_3(t)$ a time of ½ period (or a move of ½ cycle) to reach the starting point of $d(t)$, which is *rightward-going* $d = 0$, we say that $d_3(t)$ lags $d(t)$ by 180°. On the other hand, considering that it takes $d(t)$ a move of ½ cycle to reach the starting point of $d_3(t)$, it follows that $d_3(t)$ leads $d(t)$ by 180°. That is, $d_3(t)$ has an initial phase of +180° or, equivalently, –180°.

2.3.2 Parameters of a sinusoidal signal

For a quantitative discussion, let us consider the sine waveforms generated by the projections, onto the x- and y-axes, of a radial line OP that rotates anticlockwise about the origin O at constant speed; see Fig. 2.11. OP sustains the angle θ with the positive direction of the x-axis. This angle may be expressed in the three units shown in Table 2.2. If OP starts from the $+x$-axis direction and rotates to the $-x$-axis direction, then θ has increased from 0° to 180°. Alternatively, we may say that θ has increased by half a *cycle*; or that it has increased by half the circumference of the circle swept by OP, which is

$$½ \times 2\pi \times \text{Radius} = \pi \times \text{Radius}$$

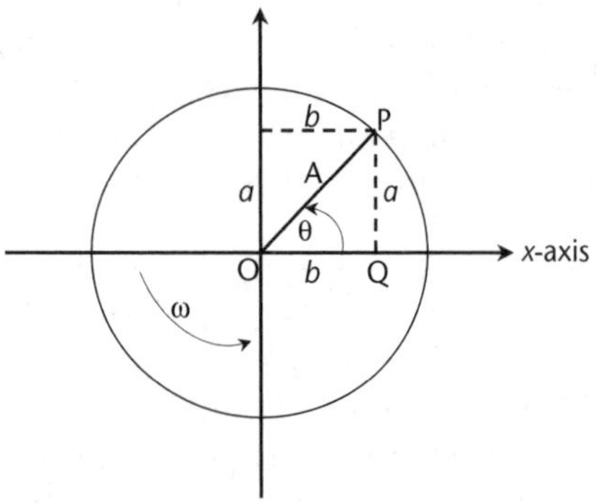

In the special case where the radius is unity, then the unit of angle measured as the length of the arc swept by $\bar{O}P$ is called a *radian*. Thus, we have the following relationships between the three units:

Figure 2.11 Generation of sinusoidal waveform by a rotating radial line OP.

$$180° = ½ \text{ cycle} = \pi \text{ radian} \tag{2.5}$$

Table 2.2 Different units of angle.

Degrees	Cycles	Radians
360°	1	2π
0°	0	0
45°	1/8	$\pi/4$
90°	1/4	$\pi/2$
180°	1/2	π
720°	2	4π

If angle is expressed in cycles, then the rate of change of angle gives the *frequency f* of the oscillation in cycles per second or hertz (Hz). On the other hand, expressing θ in radians leads to a rate of change of angle given in radians per second (rad/s), which is called the *angular frequency* ω of the oscillation. Since, from Eq. (2.5), 1 cycle = 2π rad, it follows that angular frequency and frequency are related by

$$\omega = 2\pi f \tag{2.6}$$

The radian is the SI unit of angle and will be used subsequently unless some other unit is explicitly indicated.

If in Fig. 2.11 the line OP starts initially at an angle ϕ and rotates at a constant rate ω rad/s, then at any time t the angle θ is given by

$$\theta = \omega t + \phi \tag{2.7}$$

As θ changes with time, the projection a of OP on the y-axis and the projection b of OP on the x-axis become functions of time denoted $a(t)$ and $b(t)$, respectively. Consider the right-angled triangle OPQ. By Eq. (2.7) and the definitions of the sine and cosine functions we have

$$\begin{aligned} a(t) &= A\sin(\omega t + \phi) \\ b(t) &= A\cos(\omega t + \phi) \end{aligned} \tag{2.8}$$

Figure 2.12 shows the plot of $a(t)$ and $b(t)$ as functions of time for $\phi = 0$. It is obvious that the two periodic functions have the same overall shape and differ only in the initial point at which oscillation begins. Therefore $a(t)$ as well as $b(t)$ is called a *sinusoidal signal*, but $b(t)$ leads $a(t)$ by ¼ cycle = 90°.

We are now in a position to define the parameters of sinusoidal signals with references to Eq. (2.8) and Figs. 2.11 and 2.12.

● The *phase angle* θ (= $\omega t + \phi$) is the value of the argument of the sine function at any time instant t. It is usually expressed in radian.

● The *amplitude A* is the maximum value of the signal.

● *Angular frequency* ω is the rate of change of phase angle, in rad/s.

● The *frequency f* is the number of cycles (of values) completed by the signal each second. It is expressed in Hz and is related to ω by Eq. (2.6).

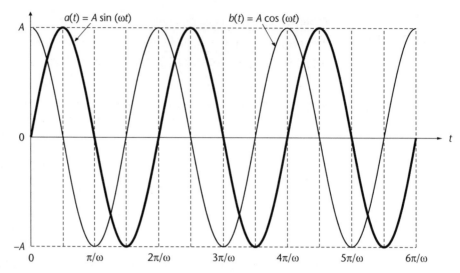

Figure 2.12 Relationship between the sine and cosine functions.

The angular frequency ω is sometimes simply referred to as the frequency, it being assumed that the reader knows that the actual signal frequency is $f = \omega/2\pi$.

- The *period T* is the time taken by the signal to complete one cycle and is therefore the reciprocal of frequency, as in Eq. (2.2)

- The *wavelength* λ is the distance (in metres) travelled by the sine wave during a time of one period. Thus $\lambda = vT = v/f$, where v is the speed of the wave (in m/s). For example, if the sinewave is an acoustic signal, then $v \sim 330$ m/s in air, 1460 m/s in water and 5000 m/s in steel. If the wave is an electromagnetic signal then $v = 3 \times 10^8$ m/s in air or vacuum.

- The *initial phase* ϕ of a sinusoidal signal is the value of phase angle θ at time $t = 0$. The reference waveform is therefore $\sin(\omega t)$, with an initial phase angle of zero.

- *Phase difference* is the difference between the initial phases of two sinusoidal signals that have the same frequency (or same period). Phase difference can be compared to the distance or gap between two cars travelling on a motorway. Unless the two cars travel at the same velocity, the gap between them changes with time. If two sinusoidal signals have different frequencies then their phase relationship changes continuously. The higher frequency sinusoid 'overtakes' the lower frequency sinusoid repeatedly along the 'circular motorway' and phase difference is therefore not defined.

WORKED EXAMPLE   2.3

Given the voltage signal $v(t) = 20\cos(314.2t - 30°)$ volts, determine

(a) The period of $v(t)$
(b) The instantaneous value of $v(t)$ at $t = 10$ ms
(c) The phase difference between $v(t)$ and the current signal $i(t) = 200\sin(314.2t + 70°)$ mA

(a) Comparing $v(t)$ with the standard sinusoidal expression,

$$v(t) = 20\cos(314.2t - 30° \equiv A\cos(\omega t + \phi)$$

we see that $\omega = 314.2$ rad/s. Therefore,

$$T = 1/f = 2\pi/\omega = \textbf{20 ms}$$

(b) Before evaluating the cosine function to obtain the instantaneous value of voltage, we need to express t in seconds and the argument of the cosine function in radian.

$$t = 10 \text{ ms} = 0.01 \text{ s}; \quad 30° = 30 \times \pi/180 \text{ rad} = \pi/6 \text{ rad}$$

Therefore,

$$v(0.01) = 20 \times \cos(314.2 \times 0.01 - \pi/6)$$
$$= 20 \times \cos(2.618) = 20 \times (-0.866)$$
$$= \textbf{-17.32 V}$$

(c) To determine the phase difference between $v(t)$ and $i(t)$, we first obtain their initial phases with respect to a common reference waveform, which of course must have the same frequency. Choosing $\sin(314.2t)$ as a reference, we must convert $v(t)$ from cosine to a sine function using the fact that the cosine function is simply a sine function with a phase lead of 90°. Thus,

$$i(t) = 200\sin(314.2t + 70°)$$
$$v(t) = 20\cos(314.2t - 30°) = 20\sin(314.2t + 90° - 30°)$$

That is,

Initial phase of $i(t) = 70°$

Initial phase of $v(t) = 60°$

Phase difference = 10°, with $v(t)$ lagging $i(t)$.

WORKED EXAMPLE   2.4

Sketch three cycles of the sinusoidal waveforms

(a) $v_1(t) = 10\sin(2\pi t - \pi/2)$
(b) $v_2(t) = 20\sin(4\pi t + 30°)$

We can sketch the waveforms without evaluating the sine functions by making the following observations.

$v_1(t)$ has amplitude 10 V, period $T_1 = 1$ s and an initial phase $-\pi/2 = -90°$. This means that $v_1(t)$ starts (from 0 towards +10) late by 90°, which, expressed in time, is (90/360) of T_1, or 0.25 s.

Similarly, $v_2(t)$ has amplitude 20 V, period $T_2 = 0.5$ s and a head start of 30°, which is equivalent to $30/360 \times T_2$, or 0.0417 s.

The value of a sine function is zero at angle 0, maximum at angle 90°, zero at angle 180°, minimum (i.e. negative amplitude) at angle 270°, zero at angle 360°, and so on. Alternatively, we say that the sine function takes on these values in time intervals of ¼ period.

Using these observations, we first sketch the waveforms shown in Fig. 2.13(a). To obtain a final sketch of three cycles (Fig. 2.13(b)) that starts at $t = 0$, we delete the left end of $v_2(t)$ that lies beyond $t = 0$ and extend the right end of $v_2(t)$ by the same amount. Note that $v_2(t)$ has a value of 20sin(30°) = 10 V at $t = 0$. Similarly, we extend the left end of $v_1(t)$ to the point $t = 0$ and reduce its right end by the same amount. Note also that, when extended properly, $v_1(t)$ has a value 10sin(–90°) = –10 V at $t = 0$.

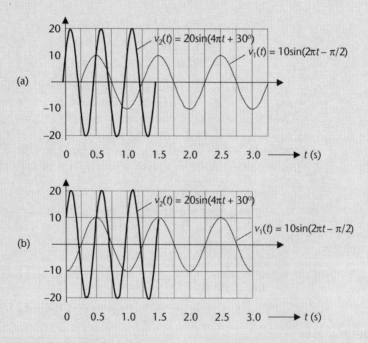

Figure 2.13 Worked example 2.4.

2.3.3 Addition of sinusoids

The addition of two or more signals (in a summing device or from interference) occurs very often in telecommunication. We consider three possibilities that may arise in the addition of sinusoidal signals:

1. The signals have the same frequency and phase.
2. The signals have the same frequency but different phases.
3. The signals have different frequencies.

2.3.3.1 *Same frequency and initial phase*

When two or more sinusoids of the same frequency and phase are added together, the result is another sinusoid of the same frequency and phase, but of amplitude equal to the sum of the amplitudes of the added sinusoids. This is by far the simplest, and in fact trivial, situation. Mathematically,

$$A_1 \sin(\omega t + \phi) + A_2 \sin(\omega t + \phi) + \cdots = [A_1 + A_2 + \cdots]\sin(\omega t + \phi)$$

It is important to avoid a common mistake and note that

$$A_1 \sin(\omega t + \phi) + A_2 \cos(\omega t + \phi) \neq [A_1 + A_2]\sin(\omega t + \phi)$$

since the sinusoids on the left-hand side clearly differ in phase by 90°.

2.3.3.2 *Same frequency but different phases*

The result of adding two or more sinusoids of the same frequency but different phases is another sinusoid of the same frequency. Thus,

$$A_1 \sin(\omega t + \phi_1) + A_2 \sin(\omega t + \phi_2) + \cdots = A\sin(\omega t + \phi)$$

The amplitude A and phase ϕ of the resultant sinusoid are obtained by the method of phasors described below in Worked example 2.5, for the case of two sinusoids. More than two sinusoids can be added by following the same procedure and taking two sinusoids at a time. If the signals are a mixture of sine and cosine functions then it is advisable to first convert to an all-sine or all-cosine form in order to make their relative phases more obvious. Sinusoids may also be subtracted by first incrementing by 180° the phase of each sinusoid that is to be subtracted and then proceeding exactly as for the case of addition. Adding 180° has the effect of maintaining the direction of the phasor representation of the sinusoid but reversing its sense (e.g. leftward pointing becomes rightward pointing).

WORKED EXAMPLE   2.5

Obtain the sum of the sinusoidal voltages $v_1(t) = 3\sin(\omega t)$ and $v_2(t) = 4\sin(\omega t - \pi/3)$ volts.

The sum voltage is

$$v(t) = 3\sin(\omega t) + 4\sin(\omega t - \pi/3)$$
$$= A\sin(\omega t \pm \phi)$$

To determine A and ϕ, we represent $v_1(t)$ as a phasor $A_1\angle\phi_1$. This is a straight line of length equal (or scaled) to the amplitude A_1 of $v_1(t)$ and of orientation equal to the initial phase ϕ_1 of $v_1(t)$. Next, we draw the phasor representation $A_2\angle\phi_2$ of $v_2(t)$ starting at the end point of $A_1\angle\phi_1$. The phasor $A\angle\phi$ obtained by joining the starting point of $A_1\angle\phi_1$ to the end point of $A_2\angle\phi_2$ gives the resultant voltage $v(t)$ in both amplitude A and phase ϕ. The phasor diagram is shown in Fig. 2.14. Note that the orientation of $A_2\angle\phi_2$ is 60° *below* the 0° direction (the +x-axis) since ϕ_2 is negative (= $-\pi/3$ rad = $-60°$).

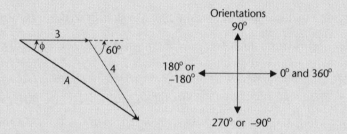

Figure 2.14 Worked example 2.5.

To solve the triangle for A and ϕ, we first use the cosine rule to obtain A and then the sine rule to obtain ϕ. The cosine rule is used to solve a triangle (as in this case) where two sides and an included angle are known. The sine rule is simpler and is applicable in all other situations where up to three parameters of the triangle are known, including at least one side and at least one angle. In terms of the naming convention shown in Fig. 2.15, we have

$$\text{Cosine rule:} \quad d^2 = b^2 + c^2 - 2cb\cos(D)$$
$$\text{Sine rule:} \quad \frac{\sin(B)}{b} = \frac{\sin(C)}{c} = \frac{\sin(D)}{d} \qquad (2.9)$$

Thus,

$$A^2 = 3^2 + 4^2 - 2 \times 3 \times 4 \times \cos(120°)$$
$$= 37$$
$$A = 6.08 \text{ volts}$$

and

$$\frac{\sin\phi}{4} = \frac{\sin(120°)}{6.08}$$

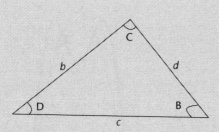

Figure 2.15 Naming convention for angles and sides in Eq. 2.9.

which evaluates to $\phi = 34.73°$.

Hence the resultant voltage is the sinusoid

$$v(t) = 6.08\sin(\omega t - 34.73°) \text{ volts}$$

The initial phase is correctly indicated as negative since ϕ lies below the $0°$ direction.

2.3.3.3 Sinusoids of different frequencies

When two or more sinusoids of different frequencies are added together, the resulting waveform is no longer a single sinusoid as in the previous cases. There is no general analytic method for obtaining the resultant waveform in this case. The sinusoids may be added graphically by plotting them over the desired time interval and adding the instantaneous values of the sinusoids at each point to obtain the value of the resultant waveform at that point. There are, however, two special cases worth identifying.

1. If the sinusoidal signals are harmonically related (i.e. all the other sinusoids are integer multiples of one of the sinusoids), then the resultant waveform is a periodic signal. Figure 2.16 shows an example of adding two sinusoids at frequencies f_1 and $3f_1$ and respective amplitudes $A_1 > A_2$. The case of $A_1 < A_2$ would also produce a periodic waveform, albeit of a different shape.

2. The other special case is when a large-amplitude high-frequency sinusoid is added to a small-amplitude low-frequency sinusoid. The resultant waveform is a high-frequency sinusoid with a slowly varying short-term mean level. The resultant waveform wiggles with time according to the variation of the lower-frequency sinusoid and should not be confused with amplitude modulation. An example is shown in Fig. 2.17.

2.3.4 Multiplication of sinusoids

Multiplication of sinusoids finds numerous applications in telecommunication and takes place, for example, in a mixer circuit that translates a

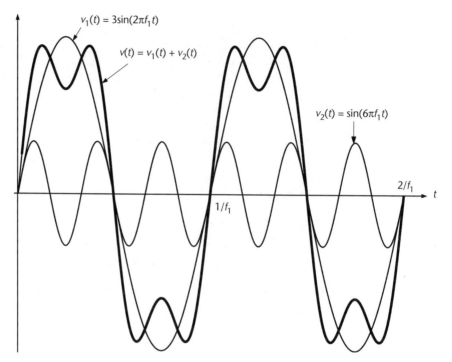

Figure 2.16 Sum of harmonically related sinusoids.

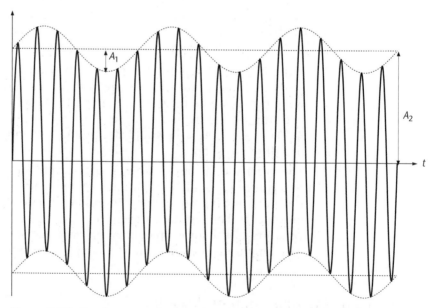

Figure 2.17 Resultant waveform when a sinusoid of lower frequency $3f_0$ and smaller amplitude A_1 is added to another sinusoid of higher frequency $19f_0$ and larger amplitude A_2.

signal from one radio frequency to another. It is important to become thoroughly familiar with the trigonometric identities presented in Appendix A, since they will feature prominently in our subsequent study. Note in particular the identities (A.5)–(A.7) for the product of two sinusoids. Therefore, consider two sinusoidal signals at frequencies f_1 and f_2:

$$v_1(t) = A_1 \cos(2\pi f_1 t)$$
$$v_2(t) = A_2 \cos(2\pi f_2 t)$$

Their product follows from Eq. (A.6) with $A = 2\pi f_1 t$ and $B = 2\pi f_2 t$:

$$v(t) = v_1(t)v_2(t) = \frac{A_1 A_2}{2}\cos[2\pi(f_2 - f_1)t] + \frac{A_1 A_2}{2}\cos[2\pi(f_2 + f_1)t]$$

The principle in the above result finds extensive application in telecommunications. It shows that multiplying two sinusoids generates two new frequencies at the sum and difference of the original frequencies. Chapter 3 is devoted to the study of some of the applications of this principle.

Note further that Eq. (A.15) confirms the result obtained earlier by graphical means, showing that the cosine function leads the sine function by 90°. We also see from Eqs. (A.13) and (A.14) that advancing or delaying the phase of a signal by 180° is equivalent to multiplying the signal by –1. What then is the effect of advancing the phase by 90°? Let us say that it is equivalent to multiplying the signal by a number denoted j. Since increasing the phase twice by 90° equals a 180° increase, it follows that

$$j \times j = -1; \text{ or } j = \sqrt{-1} \tag{2.10}$$

Thus, multiplication of a signal by the imaginary number $\sqrt{-1}$ causes a phase change of 90°. Note the following peculiar but correct identities involving j.

$$j^2 = -1$$
$$\frac{1}{j} = \frac{1}{j} \times \frac{j}{j} = \frac{j}{j^2} = -j$$
$$j^3 = j^2 \times j = -j \tag{2.11}$$
$$j^4 = j^2 \times j^2 = -1 \times -1 = 1$$
$$j^5 = j^4 \times j = j$$

Returning to Fig. 2.11, the relevant portion of which is repeated in Fig 2.18, and treating lines OQ and QP as phasor representations of sinusoids, it follows that

$$OP = b + ja$$
$$= A(\cos\theta + j\sin\theta) \tag{2.12}$$
$$= A\exp(j\theta)$$

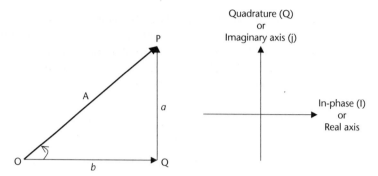

Figure 2.18 In-phase and quadrature components.

The second line above indicates that OP has a 0°-phase (or *in-phase*) compo-nent $A\cos\theta$ and a 90°-phase (or *quadrature*) component $A\sin\theta$. The exponen-tial expression specifies that OP is of magnitude A and phase θ, given by

$$A = \sqrt{a^2 + b^2} \qquad \text{(Pythagoras' theorem)}$$

$$\theta = \tan^{-1}\left(\frac{a}{b}\right) \qquad \left(\tan\theta = \frac{\text{opposite side}}{\text{adjacent side}}\right) \qquad (2.13)$$

2.4 Frequency content of signals

2.4.1 Fourier theorem

We have seen that adding together harmonically related sinusoids yields a periodic signal. By appropriately selecting the amplitude, frequency and phase of such sinusoids, any arbitrary periodic signal can be realised as the sum of these harmonically related sinusoids. This is in fact the *Fourier theorem*, which states:

> Any periodic function or waveform can be expressed as the sum of sinewaves with frequencies at integer multiples (called harmonics) of the fundamental frequency, and with appropriate amplitudes and phases.

Mathematically,

$$v(t) = A_0 + A_1 \cos(2\pi f_1 t + \phi_1) + A_2 \cos(2\pi f_2 t + \phi_2) + \dots$$

$$= A_0 + \sum_{n=1}^{\infty} A_n \cos(2\pi f_n t + \phi_n) \qquad (2.14)$$

where

A_0 = DC or average value of $v(t)$
A_n = Amplitude of the sinusoidal component of frequency f_n
f_n = nf_0 is the nth harmonic frequency; $n = 1, 2, 3, \dots$

f_0 = $1/T$ is the fundamental frequency

T = Period of $v(t)$

ϕ_n = Initial phase of the sinusoidal component of frequency f_n. As is obvious from Eq. (2.14), the reference waveform is $\cos(\omega t)$ and not $\sin(\omega t)$. This choice allows us to specify phase relative to the in-phase axis (Fig. 2.18).

Figure 2.19 shows the building (called *Fourier synthesis*) of some standard waveforms using a few harmonic sinusoids. Figure 2.19(a) shows how

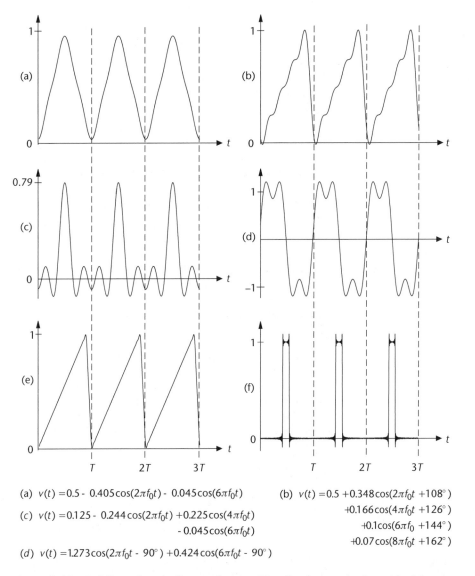

(a) $v(t) = 0.5 - 0.405\cos(2\pi f_0 t) - 0.045\cos(6\pi f_0 t)$

(b) $v(t) = 0.5 + 0.348\cos(2\pi f_0 t + 108°)$
$+0.166\cos(4\pi f_0 t + 126°)$
$+0.1\cos(6\pi f_0 + 144°)$
$+0.07\cos(8\pi f_0 t + 162°)$

(c) $v(t) = 0.125 - 0.244\cos(2\pi f_0 t) + 0.225\cos(4\pi f_0 t)$
$- 0.045\cos(6\pi f_0 t)$

(d) $v(t) = 1.273\cos(2\pi f_0 t - 90°) + 0.424\cos(6\pi f_0 t - 90°)$

Figure 2.19 Building of periodic waveforms with a few harmonic sinusoids: (a) triangular; (b) sawtooth; (c) pulse train of 12.5% duty cycle; (d) bipolar square wave; (e) sawtooth using 0.5 volts DC + 18 harmonic sinusoids; (f) pulse train using 0.125 volts DC + 88 harmonic sinusoids. Note that $T = 1/f_0$.

closely a triangular waveform is approximated by just a DC component and two harmonic sinusoids. Syntheses of sawtooth, rectangular pulse train and bipolar square waveforms are also shown in (b)–(d). The bipolar square wave has a zero average value and therefore a DC component is not involved in the synthesis, i.e. $A_0 = 0$ in Eq. (2.14). The approximation improves as more harmonic sinusoids of the correct frequencies, amplitudes and phases are added. An almost perfect synthesis of a sawtooth waveform using a DC component and 18 harmonic sinusoids is shown in Fig. 2.19(e).

The rectangular pulse train in (c) is re-synthesised in (f) using a DC component and 88 harmonic sinusoids. Ripples have been markedly reduced in the synthesised waveform, but overshoots persist at the points of discontinuity or sharp transition where an ideal rectangular pulse train changes level instantaneously between 0 V and 1 V. The problem is known as *Gibbs' phenomenon* and will be present even if an infinite number of harmonic sinusoids of the correct amplitudes and phases were added. By comparing the two sawtooth waveforms in Fig. 2.19(b) and (e), you can see that a sawtooth waveform (or any other periodic waveform for that matter) transmitted through a low pass transmission medium will be noticeably distorted unless there is sufficient bandwidth to pass all significant higher-frequency harmonic components.

The frequency f_n of each of the harmonic sine waves present in a periodic signal $v(t)$ is determined straightforwardly as the reciprocal of the period of $v(t)$, but determining the amplitude A_n and phase ϕ_n in general requires Fourier analysis. A plot of the sine wave amplitudes A_n against their frequencies nf_0 is called the *magnitude* or *amplitude spectrum*. A plot of $\frac{1}{2}A_n^2$ versus nf_0 is the *power spectrum*, while a plot of ϕ_n versus nf_0 is called the *phase spectrum*. The amplitude spectrum is frequently referred to simply as the spectrum. Figure 2.20 shows the waveform, amplitude spectrum and phase spectrum of the signal

$$v(t) = 10 \cos(2000\pi t) + 17.32 \sin(2000\pi t)$$

The amplitude spectrum is a single vertical line of height 20 V located at frequency $f = 1$ kHz. The phase spectrum is also a single line of height –60° at frequency $f = 1$ kHz. The spectral information shows that the frequency content of $v(t)$ is a single sinusoid of frequency 1 kHz, amplitude 20 V and phase –60° and therefore

$$v(t) = 20 \cos(2\pi \times 10^3 t - 60°)$$

In this simple example, the spectral information could have been obtained without spectral analysis, since it can be seen that $v(t)$ is the result of adding two sinusoids that have the same frequency (1 kHz) but different phases.

Figure 2.21 shows the spectrum of a rectangular pulse train that is centred at $t = 0$. It has amplitude $A = 1$ V and duty cycle $d = \tau/T$. Except for the DC component, which has the value $A_0 = d$, the amplitude spectrum A_n follows the envelope

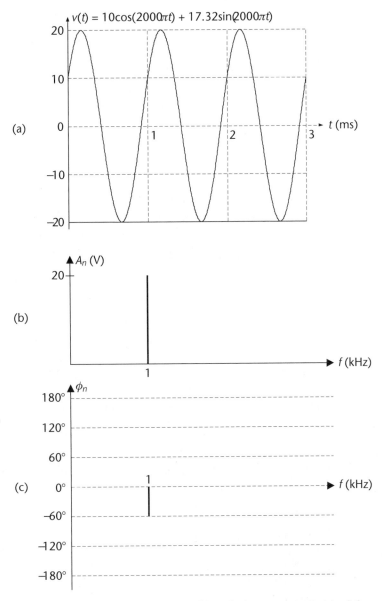

Figure 2.20 Amplitude spectrum (b) and phase spectrum (c) of the waveform shown in (a).

$$2d\frac{\sin(\pi nd)}{\pi nd} \equiv 2d\,\mathrm{sinc}(nd)$$

The *sinc* function introduced above occurs very often in telecommunications because of the important role of pulses and pulse trains. It is worthwhile to take a moment to become familiar with its features and with the significance of the spectrum in Fig. 2.21(b). You may verify using your calculator that the sine of very small angles (2° or less) is approximately

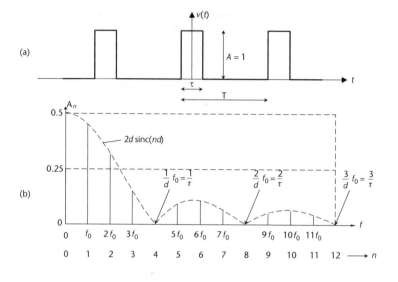

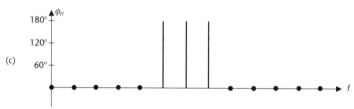

Figure 2.21   Spectrum of pulse train of duty cycle $d = 1/4$.

equal to the value of the angle (in rad), the approximation becoming exact at 0°. That is,

$$\sin\theta \to \theta \ \text{ as } \ \theta \to 0$$

So we may write

$$\frac{\sin(\pi x)}{\pi x} \to \frac{\pi x}{\pi x} = 1 \ \text{ as } \ \pi x \to 0$$

It then follows that

$$\frac{\sin(\pi x)}{\pi x} \equiv \mathrm{sinc}(x) = 1 \ \text{ at } \ x = 0$$

Secondly, recall that the sine of integer multiples of π is zero. Therefore,

$$\frac{\sin(\pi x)}{\pi x} \equiv \mathrm{sinc}(x) = 0 \ \text{ at } \ x = 1, 2, 3, \dots$$

In summary,

$$\text{sinc}(x) = \begin{cases} 1 & x = 0 \\ 0 & x = 1, 2, 3, \ldots \\ \sin(\pi x)/\pi x & x \neq 0 \end{cases} \tag{2.15}$$

We can now make some important observations regarding the amplitude and phase spectra of a rectangular pulse train.

- Spectral lines occur at frequencies $f = 0$, f_0, $2f_0$, $3f_0$, ..., where $f = 0$ is the DC component, $f = f_0 = 1/T$ is the fundamental frequency component, $f = nf_0$ is the nth harmonic frequency component and T is the period of the pulse train.

- The amplitude of the nth harmonic frequency component is $A_n = 2d\,\text{sinc}(nd)$, for $n = 1, 2, 3, \ldots$, where d is the duty cycle of the unit-amplitude pulse train. A bipolar rectangular pulse train has no DC component, while a unipolar rectangular pulse train (as in Fig. 2.21) has a DC component $A_0 = d$. If the rectangular pulse train has amplitude $A \neq 1$, then all components in the spectrum (including A_0) are increased by the factor A.

- In the light of Eq. (2.15), harmonic frequencies corresponding to $nd = 1, 2, 3, \ldots$, will have zero amplitude. In other words, every $(1/d)$th harmonic frequency will be missing. For example, a square wave is a rectangular pulse train with $d = 0.5$ and therefore will not contain frequencies $2f_0$, $4f_0$, $6f_0$ etc. Figure 2.21 shows a rectangular pulse train of duty cycle $d = 0.25$. Therefore every $(1/0.25)$th or 4th harmonic frequency (i.e. $4f_0$, $8f_0$, $12f_0$ etc.) is missing.

- One *lobe* (between adjacent zero points) of the spectral envelope has width $f = 1/\tau$. The number of spectral lines contained in one lobe depends only on the duty cycle:

$$\text{Number of spectral lines in one lobe} = \frac{1}{d} - 1 \tag{2.16}$$

Fixing the pulse width τ fixes the lobe width and if the period T of the rectangular pulse train is increased then $d\ (= \tau/T)$ decreases and hence the density of spectral lines increases. This can also be seen by noting that the spectral line spacing $f_0 = 1/T$ decreases as T increases. We will have more to say about this later.

- The rectangular pulse train in Fig. 2.21(a) has even symmetry – i.e. $v(t) = v(-t)$. It can therefore be synthesised using cosine functions only, since the cosine function also has even symmetry. This means that all frequency components lie along the in-phase axis (Fig. 2.18) and therefore have a phase of either $0°$ or $180°$. The phase spectrum in Fig. 2.21(c) confirms this argument. Phases of the spectral components are $0°$ and $180°$, respectively, in alternate lobes.

- The spectral effect of delaying a signal by some amount t_0 is shown in Fig. 2.22. If the rectangular pulse train in Fig. 2.21(a) is $v(t)$, then that of Fig. 2.22(a) is $v_1(t) = v(t - t_0)$, where $t_0 = \tau/2$ for the purpose of this discussion. The amplitude spectra of $v(t)$ and $v(t - t_0)$ are the same, indi-

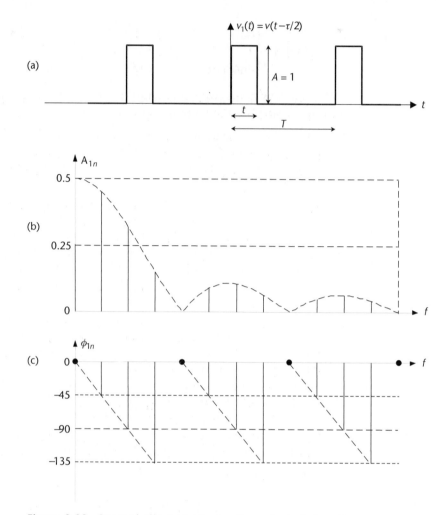

Figure 2.22 Spectral effect of delaying the pulse train by $\tau/2$.

cating that a delay does not alter the amplitude of the frequency components of a signal. However, recall that the phase of a sinusoid of angular frequency $\omega = 2\pi f$ changes at the rate of ω rad/s. Thus, a time delay t_0 corresponds to a phase delay of $2\pi n f_0 t_0$ for the nth harmonic frequency component. Therefore the phase spectrum ϕ_{1n} of $v(t - t_0)$ is related to the phase spectrum ϕ_n of $v(t)$ by

$$\phi_{1n} = \phi_n - 2\pi n f_0 t_0 \qquad (2.17)$$

We see that the effect of a time delay is to cause a change in phase that is a linear function of frequency (nf_0). The requirement for distortionless transmission of signals is that the received signal should be a (propagation) delayed but otherwise exact version of the transmitted signal. We see here that this requires that the transmission medium changes the shape of the phase spectrum of the signal linearly with frequency as given in Eq. (2.17) without altering the shape of the amplitude spectrum. You may wish to verify using Eq. (2.17) and $t_0 = \tau/2$ that the phase spectral plot in Fig. 2.22(c) is correct.

- The width of the main lobe in the amplitude spectrum (from $f = 0$ to $f = 1/\tau$), sometimes taken as the bandwidth of the pulse train, is inversely proportional to the pulse width. Narrower pulses are often required, for example, in time division multiplexing to pack several independent (information-bearing) pulses into a fixed sampling period T. We see therefore that such capacity increase is achieved at the expense of (at least) a proportionate increase in bandwidth requirements.

2.4.2 Types of spectrum

2.4.2.1 Single-sided spectrum

A single-sided spectrum contains only positive frequencies, as shown in Fig. 2.23. Some of the frequency components may have zero amplitude and therefore be missing from both the amplitude and phase spectra. Our discussion so far has featured only single-sided spectra. Figure 2.20 shows that the single-sided amplitude spectrum of a sinusoidal signal of amplitude A, frequency f and phase ϕ is a single vertical line of height A located along the frequency axis at f. The phase spectrum is also a single vertical line of height ϕ located at f.

2.4.2.2 Double-sided spectrum

When dealing with passband transmission systems in which a signal is translated to a different frequency band, a lot of mathematical simplification results if a double-sided spectral representation of signals is adopted. A double-sided spectrum contains pairs of positive and negative frequencies. To see how

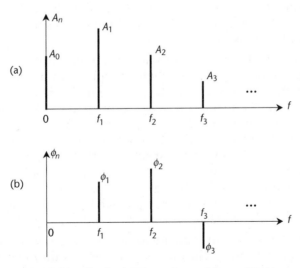

Figure 2.23 Single-sided spectrum: (a) amplitude; (b) phase.

this may be obtained, observe from Eq. (A.18) that the nth harmonic component of a signal may be written as the sum of a pair of sinusoids:

$$A_n \cos\theta_n = A_n\left(\frac{1}{2}\cos\theta_n + \frac{1}{2}\cos\theta_n\right)$$

$$= A_n\left[\frac{1}{2}\cos\theta_n + \frac{1}{2}\cos(-\theta_n)\right] \tag{2.18}$$

$$= \frac{A_n}{2}\cos\theta_n + \frac{A_n}{2}\cos(-\theta_n)$$

Equation (2.14) represents $v(t)$ as the sum of positive-frequency sinusoids from which the single-sided spectrum of $v(t)$ is obtained. Now using Eq. (2.18) the same signal may be represented as the sum of pairs of positive- and negative-frequency sinusoids as follows:

$$v(t) = A_0 + \frac{A_1}{2}\cos(2\pi f_1 t + \phi_1) + \frac{A_1}{2}\cos(-2\pi f_1 t - \phi_1)$$
$$+ \frac{A_2}{2}\cos(2\pi f_2 t + \phi_2) + \frac{A_2}{2}\cos(-2\pi f_2 t - \phi_2)$$
$$+ \frac{A_3}{2}\cos(2\pi f_3 t + \phi_3) + \frac{A_3}{2}\cos(-2\pi f_3 t - \phi_3) \tag{2.19}$$
$$+ \cdots$$

This may be written as

$$v(t) = \sum_{n=-\infty}^{\infty} D_n \cos(2\pi n f_0 t + \alpha_n) \tag{2.20}$$

Let us take a moment to understand Eq. (2.20):

- The double-sided spectrum (DSS) extends from $f = -\infty$ to $+\infty$, i.e. $-nf_0$ to $+nf_0$ for $n \to \infty$.

- The DC component in a DSS, corresponding to the $n = 0$ harmonic, has the same amplitude as in the single-sided spectrum (SSS), i.e. $D_0 = A_0$, and we must define $\alpha_0 \equiv 0$.

- The nth harmonic sinusoidal component of $v(t)$ (with amplitude A_n and phase ϕ_n) is now divided equally to a pair of locations on the frequency axis, one at the positive frequency $f = nf_0$ having amplitude $D_n = A_n/2$ and phase $\alpha_n = \phi_n$; the other at the negative frequency $f = -nf_0$ having amplitude $D_{-n} = A_n/2$ and phase $\alpha_{-n} = -\phi_n$. Figure 2.24 is the double-sided spectrum corresponding to the single-sided spectrum of Fig. 2.23. Double-sided spectral components always occur in pairs, at $f = \pm nf_0$ with equal amplitude $A_n/2$ and phases $\pm\phi_n$. In fact, the DC component A_0 may be viewed as a pair of components $A_0/2$ at $f = +0$ and $A_0/2$ at $f = -0$. For an example, see Fig. 2.25, which gives a plot of the DSS of the voltage $v(t) = 5 + 20\cos(4000\pi t + 75°)$.

- It follows that the amplitude spectrum has *even* symmetry, which means that its value at frequency $f = +nf_0$ is exactly the same as its value at $f = -nf_0$. The phase spectrum on the other hand has *odd* symmetry, meaning that its values at $f = +nf_0$ and $f = -nf_0$ are the same magnitude but of opposite sign.

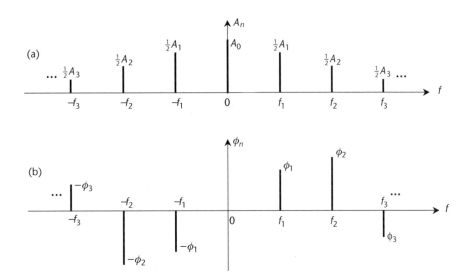

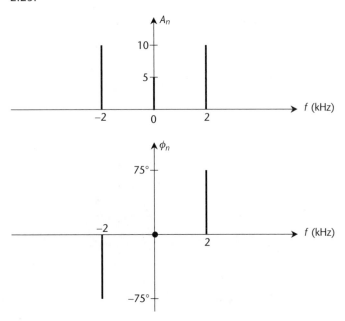

Figure 2.24 Double-sided amplitude and phase spectra corresponding to Fig. 2.23.

Figure 2.25 Double-sided spectrum of the signal $v(t) = 5 + 20\cos(4000\pi t + 75°)$ volts.

2.4.2.3 Line spectrum

We have so far been dealing with line spectra. A line spectrum consists of harmonic sinusoids at discrete frequencies $f_0, 2f_0, 3f_0, ...$, each of which is represented on the spectral plot by a vertical line, hence the name *line* or *discrete spectrum*. All periodic signals have a discrete spectrum with frequencies spaced $f_0 = 1/T$ apart, where T is the period of the signal.

2.4.2.4 *Continuous spectrum*

A continuous spectrum consists of spectral components at all frequencies in a given range. All non-periodic signals have a continuous spectrum. To see that this is indeed the case, consider Fig. 2.26. The (non-periodic) rectangular pulse signal $v(t)$ in (a) is the limiting case of the (periodic) rectangular pulse train $v_T(t)$ in (b) as the period T tends to infinity. Since $f_0 = 1/T$, it follows that

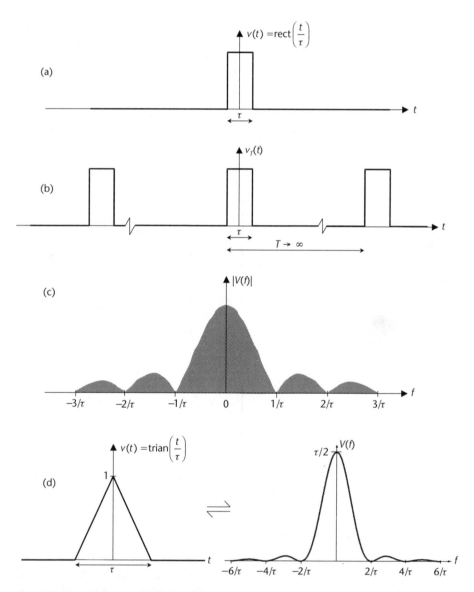

Figure 2.26 (a)–(c): A non-periodic signal $v(t)$ as a limiting case of the periodic signal $v_T(t)$, and the resulting continuous spectrum $V(f)$; (d) triangular pulse and its spectrum.

$$f_0 \to 0 \quad \text{as} \quad T \to \infty$$

Therefore, as $v_T(t)$ is being transformed to $v(t)$ by increasing T towards infinity, an important transformation also takes place in the (discrete) spectrum of $v_T(t)$. The spacing f_0 of the spectral components tends to zero, giving rise to the continuous (double-sided) spectrum $V(f)$ of $v(t)$ in Fig. 2.26(c). This function of frequency $V(f)$ is called the *Fourier transform* of the time waveform $v(t)$, while $v(t)$ is referred to as the *inverse Fourier transform* of $V(f)$. Both $v(t)$ and $V(f)$ are said to form a Fourier transform pair. These transform relations are often expressed, respectively, in the following shorthand notations:

$$V(f) = F[v(t)]$$
$$v(t) = F^{-1}[V(f)] \tag{2.21}$$
$$v(t) \rightleftharpoons V(f)$$

In general, $V(f)$ has magnitude and phase, both of which are functions of frequency and may be written as follows using Eq. (2.12):

$$V(f) = |V(f)| \exp[j\phi_V(f)]$$

where $|V(f)|$ is the amplitude spectrum and $\phi_V(f)$ is the phase spectrum.

The inverse Fourier transform is a generalisation of the Fourier series representation in Eq. (2.20). The Fourier series specifies the absolute amplitude A_n of the nth harmonic sinusoidal component of frequency nf_0, whereas the Fourier transform $V(f)$ gives the relative amplitude of a sinusoidal component of frequency f. While Eq. (2.20) shows that $v_T(t)$ may be synthesised by a discrete sum of sinusoidal signals, it is clear that the synthesis of $v(t)$ from $V(f)$ involves a continuous summation or *integration* process. A measure of the energy E_Δ of $v(t)$ carried by sinusoidal components in the infinitesimally small frequency band f to $f + \Delta f$ is given by the Fourier transform of $v(t)$ as

$$E_\Delta = |V(f)|^2 \, \Delta f$$

where $|V(f)|$ denotes the absolute value of $V(f)$. Thus, $V(nf_0)$ gives a direct measure of the significance of the frequency component $f = nf_0$, but is not the amplitude of that sinusoidal component.

2.4.3 Fourier transform examples

2.4.3.1 *Unit impulse or Dirac delta function $\delta(t)$*

This is a signal that is zero at all times except at $t = 0$, where its value is infinite such that the total area under the curve of the signal is unity. Mathematically, we write

$$\delta(t) = 0, \quad t \neq 0$$

$$\int_{-\infty}^{\infty} \delta(t)dt = 1 \tag{2.22}$$

The waveform of $\delta(t)$ is an upward pointing vertical arrow at $t = 0$. This strange signal turns out to be an extremely useful idealisation in systems analysis. For example, (1) instantaneous sampling of an analogue signal is readily analysed when viewed as the product of the analogue signal and a train of unit impulses, (2) the Fourier transform of periodic signals can be specified if impulse functions are introduced, and (3) an arbitrary signal $x(t)$ can be represented as the (continuous) sum of variously weighted and delayed impulse functions. An important outcome of the last application is that the output waveform of a linear time-invariant system is realised as the *convolution* (Section 6.7.6) of the input waveform and the system's impulse response. It can be shown that

$$\delta(t) \rightleftharpoons 1 \tag{2.23}$$

That is, the Fourier transform of $\delta(t)$ is unity. The implication is that $\delta(t)$ contains sinusoids of equal amplitude at all frequencies from $f = 0$ to $f = \infty$. Thus, this zero duration signal has, expectedly, an infinite bandwidth.

2.4.3.2 *Rectangular pulse*

The unit rectangular pulse, shown in Fig. 2.26(a), is zero everywhere except in the interval $-\tau/2 \leq t \leq \tau/2$, where it has unit amplitude. Let us denote this signal as $\mathrm{rect}(t/\tau)$. Then

$$\mathrm{rect}\left(\frac{t}{\tau}\right) = \begin{cases} 1, & -\tau/2 \leq t \leq \tau/2 \\ 0, & |t| > \tau/2 \end{cases} \tag{2.24}$$

It can be shown that

$$\mathrm{rect}\left(\frac{t}{\tau}\right) \rightleftharpoons \tau\,\mathrm{sinc}(f\tau) \tag{2.25}$$

That is, the Fourier transform of a unit rectangular pulse of duration τ is a sinc waveform of amplitude τ, having zeros at intervals of $f = 1/\tau$; see Fig. 2.26(c).

2.4.3.3 *Triangular pulse*

The unit triangular pulse, shown in Fig. 2.26(d), is zero everywhere except in the interval $-\tau/2 \leq t \leq \tau/2$ where it increases linearly from zero at $|t| = \tau/2$ to unity at $t = 0$. Denoting this signal as $\mathrm{trian}(t/\tau)$, we may write

$$\mathrm{trian}\left(\frac{t}{\tau}\right) = \begin{cases} 1 - |2/\tau|t, & -\tau/2 \leq t \leq \tau/2 \\ 0, & |t| > \tau/2 \end{cases} \tag{2.26}$$

It can be shown that

$$\mathrm{trian}\left(\frac{t}{\tau}\right) \rightleftharpoons \frac{\tau}{2}\mathrm{sinc}^2\left(f\frac{\tau}{2}\right) \tag{2.27}$$

That is, the Fourier transform of a unit triangular pulse of duration τ is a squared sinc function of amplitude $\tau/2$, having zeros at frequency intervals $f = 2/\tau$.

2.4.4 Bandwidth and frequency response

Equation (2.14) suggests that periodic signals contain an infinite number of harmonic frequencies. In practice, however, A_n becomes very small for large n and these high-frequency components may be neglected with negligible effect on the signal $v(t)$. For example, the sawtooth waveform in Fig. 2.19(e) shows negligible distortion, although all frequency components above $25f_0$ were excluded. The width of the significant band of *positive* frequencies of a signal is its *bandwidth* in Hz. The word 'significant' is imprecise and a more clear-cut definition is required. Two commonly used definitions are the *null-bandwidth* and the *3 dB bandwidth*.

- *Null bandwidth*: If the double-sided spectrum of the signal has a main lobe bounded by one *null* (zero amplitude spectrum) at a positive frequency f_2 and another null at a lower frequency f_1, then the bandwidth of the signal is usually specified as the null bandwidth:

$$\mathrm{Null\ bandwidth} = \begin{cases} f_2, & f_1 < 0 \quad \text{(low-pass signal)} \\ f_2 - f_1, & f_1 > 0 \quad \text{(bandpass signal)} \end{cases} \tag{2.28}$$

  Figure 2.27 illustrates each of the cases in Eq. (2.28). A low-pass or baseband signal contains significant positive frequency components down to or near $f = 0$, while a bandpass signal has its significant positive frequencies centred at a non-zero frequency f_c.

- *3 dB bandwidth*: The spectra of most signals do not have well-defined nulls. In such cases the most common specification of bandwidth is in terms of a positive frequency point f_2 and the next lower frequency point f_1 at which the double-sided amplitude spectrum reduces to $1/\sqrt{2}$ of its peak value. A drop in amplitude spectrum by this factor is equivalent to a 3 dB reduction, hence the name. Using the new definition of f_2 and f_1 given here, the 3dB bandwidth is again obtained from Eq. (2.28). Figure 2.28 shows various examples of 3dB bandwidth.

In order to maximise capacity and radio spectrum exploitation, it is frequently necessary in telecommunication for the bandwidth of a signal to be limited by international agreement to the minimum value that gives a subjectively acceptable quality. For example, the following bandwidths have been standardised:

- Analogue telephone speech = 3100 Hz
- AM broadcast signal = 10 kHz

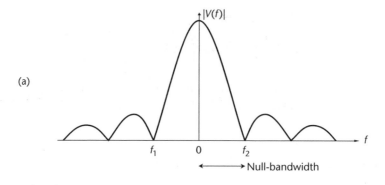

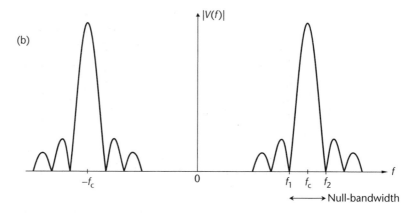

Figure 2.27 Null bandwidth: (a) Low-pass signal; (b) bandpass signal.

- FM broadcast signal = 200 kHz
- Analogue TV broadcast signal = 6 or 8 MHz (depending on standard)

The term *bandwidth* is not restricted to signals only, but is also used in connection with transmission media and electronic devices. The bandwidth of a transmission medium or an electronic device is the width of the band of positive frequencies that it passes with little or no distortion. The bandwidth may be specified in terms of the null- or 3dB-points of the *frequency response* of the device.

The *frequency response* or *transfer function*, denoted $H(f)$, is an important characterisation of a transmission medium or communication device. It indicates how the system alters the amplitude and phase of each sinusoidal signal that is passed through it. Written in exponential form

$$H(f) = |H(f)| \exp[j\phi_H(f)] \tag{2.29}$$

it shows that when a sinusoidal signal of frequency f is transmitted through the system the amplitude of the signal will be increased by the factor $|H(f)|$ and the phase incremented by an amount $\phi_H(f)$. In other words, $|H(f)|$, also termed the *amplitude response*, specifies *gain* as a function of frequency,

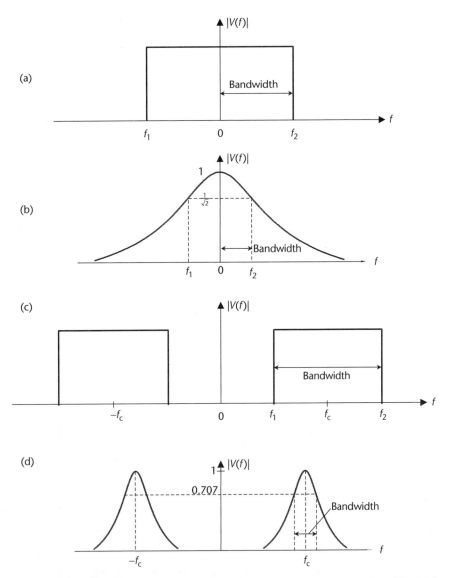

Figure 2.28 3 dB bandwidths: (a) strictly band-limited and (b) non-band-limited low-pass signals; (c) bandlimited and (d) non-band-limited band-pass signals.

while $\phi_H(f)$, also called the *phase response*, specifies *phase shift* as a function of frequency.

A *filter* is designed to have a non-flat frequency response in order to pass a specified band of frequencies with little or no attenuation while heavily attenuating (ideally blocking) all frequencies outside the *pass band*. In most cases, it is desired that the filter's gain is constant within the pass band. There is, however, a class of filters, known as *equalisers*, that are designed not only to exclude signals in the stop band but also to compensate for the distortion effects introduced into the pass band by, for example, the

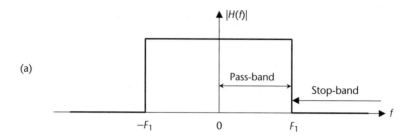

(a)

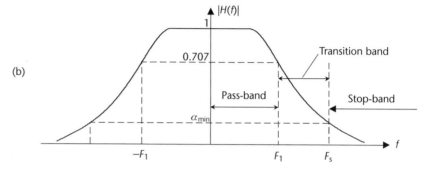

(b)

Figure 2.29 Frequency response of (a) ideal low-pass filter; (b) practical filter.

transmission medium. An equaliser has a non-flat frequency response, which when combined with the response of the transmission medium gives the desired overall flat response. Examples of filters include the *low-pass filter* (LPF), which passes only frequencies below a cut-off frequency F_1. A *high-pass filter* (HPF) passes only frequencies above a cut-off frequency F_2. A *bandpass filter* (BPF) passes only those frequencies in the range from F_1 to F_2. A *band stop filter* (BSF) passes all frequencies except those in the range from F_1 to F_2. The normalised frequency response of an ideal low-pass filter is shown in Fig. 2.29(a). The gain of the filter drops from unity to zero at the cut-off frequency F_1. Such a *brick wall* filter is impossible to obtain in practice. A realisable filter, shown in Fig. 2.29(b), requires a finite frequency interval to change from pass-band, where the minimum gain is $1/\sqrt{2} = 0.707$, to stop band, where the maximum gain is α_{min}. The interval from F_1 to F_s, the start of the stop band, is known as the *transition band*.

2.4.5 Inverse relationship between time and frequency

Signals may be fully specified in either the *time domain* or the *frequency domain*. The former gives the instantaneous values of the signal as a function of time, e.g. $v(t)$, whereas the latter specifies the spectrum of the signal. In general the spectrum is given by the Fourier transform $V(f)$ of the signal, but in the special case of a periodic signal the spectrum is specified as the amplitude A_n and phase ϕ_n of each sine wave (of frequency nf_0) that adds to make up the signal. Once we specify $v(t)$ then $V(f)$ can be determined by

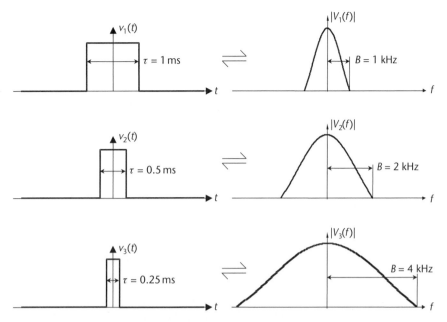

Figure 2.30 Spectra (up to null bandwidth) of rectangular pulses of duration 1, 0.5 and 0.25 ms. Note that $B\tau$ = constant.

Fourier analysis. If $V(f)$ is specified then $v(t)$ follows from *Fourier synthesis.* Thus, the time and frequency domains provide alternative methods of describing the same signal. There are important general relationships between the shape of a signal waveform $v(t)$ and the shape of its spectrum $V(f)$.

The shorter the time duration of a signal, the broader its spectrum. Observe in Fig. 2.26 that the bandwidth B (i.e. significant spectrum) of the rectangular pulse of duration τ is

$$B = \frac{1}{\tau} \tag{2.30}$$

Thus, as demonstrated in Fig. 2.30, if we expand the duration of a signal then its spectrum contracts by the same factor and vice versa, in such a way that the product of signal duration and signal bandwidth, called the *time-bandwidth product*, remains constant. In the special case of a rectangular pulse, Eq. (2.30), the constant is unity.

A signal cannot be both strictly band-limited and strictly duration-limited. If the spectrum of a signal is precisely zero outside a finite frequency band, then the time waveform $v(t)$ will have infinite duration although $v(t)$ may tend to zero as $t \to \infty$. Conversely, if $v(t)$ is precisely zero outside a finite time duration, then the spectrum $V(f)$ will carry on and on, although $|V(f)|$ will tend to zero as $f \to \infty$. For example, a (duration-limited) rectangular pulse has a sinc spectrum, which carries on and on; and a (band-limited) rectangular spectrum belongs to a sinc pulse.

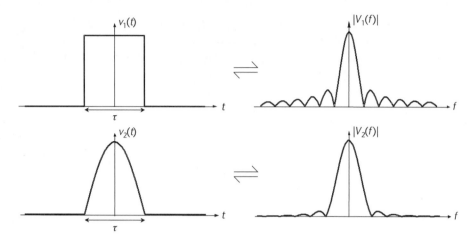

Figure 2.31 Comparing the effect of sudden transitions in signals. There are more significant higher frequency components in $v_1(t)$ than in $v_2(t)$.

Sudden changes in a signal imply high frequencies in its spectrum. Figure 2.31 shows the spectra of two pulses of the same duration, but of different shapes. One pulse is rectangular and has sharp transitions between zero and maximum value, while the other pulse is cosine-shaped with no sharp transitions. It can be observed that the amplitudes of the higher frequency components decay less rapidly in the rectangular pulse.

2.5 Power content of signals

Figure 2.32 shows a voltage signal $v(t)$ (volts) developed across a resistor element of resistance R (ohms). This causes a current signal $i(t)$ (ampere) to flow through the resistor. The relationship between $i(t)$, $v(t)$ and R is given by Ohm's law:

$$v(t) = Ri(t) \qquad (2.31)$$

The *instantaneous power* (measured in watts) dissipated (as heat) in the resistor is given by

$$p(t) = \frac{|v(t)|^2}{R} \qquad (2.32)$$

Using, Eq. (2.31), this is equivalent to

$$p(t) = R|i(t)|^2 \qquad (2.33)$$

Figure 2.32 Voltage and current in an equivalent circuit of resistance R.

It is convenient to work with normalised power, which is the power dissipated in a 1 Ω resistor. In this case, irrespective of whether the signal $s(t)$ is a current or a voltage, the instantaneous power is given by the same expression:

$$\text{Normalised instantaneous power } p(t) = |s(t)|^2 \tag{2.34}$$

We will subsequently work with normalised power except when otherwise indicated. The peak power P_{max} of a signal $s(t)$ is defined as the square of the maximum absolute value of the signal:

$$P_{max} = |s(t)|^2_{max} \tag{2.35}$$

The average power P in a periodic signal $s(t)$ is defined as the average of the squares of the signal values in one period T of the signal. This means that P is the *mean square value* of the signal. Taking the square root of the mean square value gives what is usually called the *root mean square* (and abbreviated *rms*) value of the signal. P is the amount of heat that would be dissipated per second if the signal $s(t)$ were a current or voltage in a 1 Ω load resistance. It is obtained by averaging the square of the signal, say $v(t)$, over one period T:

$$P = \frac{1}{T} \int_{-T/2}^{T/2} v^2(t)dt = V^2_{rms} \tag{2.36}$$

where V_{rms} is the rms value of $v(t)$. The average power of non-periodic signals is obtained by evaluating Eq. (2.36) in the limit $T \rightarrow \infty$. For the special and important case of a sinusoidal signal

$$v(t) = A \cos(\omega t + \phi)$$

Equation (2.36) gives (see Worked example 2.7)

$$P = \frac{1}{2} A^2 \tag{2.37}$$

That is, the average power of a sinusoidal signal equals half the square of its amplitude. The rms value of the sinusoid is

$$V_{rms} = \sqrt{P} = \frac{A}{\sqrt{2}} = \frac{\text{Signal amplitude}}{\sqrt{2}} \tag{2.38}$$

We can show (Worked example 2.8) that the average power of any periodic signal can be obtained from the single-sided magnitude spectrum as

$$P = A_0^2 + \frac{A_1^2}{2} + \frac{A_2^2}{2} + \frac{A_3^2}{2} + \cdots \tag{2.39}$$

where A_0 is the DC value and A_n is the amplitude of the component at frequency nf_0. For a non-periodic signal, the spectrum is continuous and the summation of Eq. (2.39) becomes an integration operation over the band of significant frequencies. Note that the instantaneous power of a signal cannot be obtained directly from the spectrum of the signal. Eqs. (2.37) and (2.39) apply only to average power P.

WORKED EXAMPLE   **2.6**

Sketch the single-sided and double-sided amplitude spectra of the signal (in volts)

$$v(t) = 5 + 20\cos(2000\pi t + 30°) - 10\cos(6000\pi t) + 15\cos(12000\pi t + 60°)$$

and determine its average power.

The signal contains the following components:

1. DC value = 5 V.

2. A sinusoid of amplitude 20 V and angular frequency $\omega = 2000\pi$, or frequency $f = \omega/2\pi = 1$ kHz.

3. A sinusoid of amplitude 10 V and frequency $f = 3$ kHz.

4. A sinusoid of amplitude 15 V and frequency $f = 6$ kHz.

The single-sided spectrum summarises the above information, as shown in Fig. 2.33(a). The double-sided spectrum is also sketched in Fig. 2.33(b). Using Eq. (2.39) and the single-sided spectrum, the average power of $v(t)$ is

$$P = 5^2 + \frac{20^2}{2} + \frac{10^2}{2} + \frac{15^2}{2}$$
$$= 387.5 \text{ W}$$

(a)

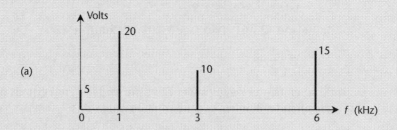

(b)

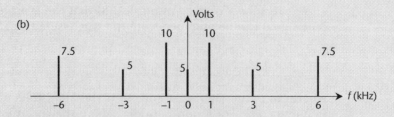

Figure 2.33 Worked example 2.6: (a) single-sided and (b) double-sided spectra of $v(t)$.

Using the above result, you may wish to verify that signal power P can also be computed from the double-sided spectrum of the signal according to the formula

$$P = \sum_{i=-\infty}^{\infty} D_i^2 \qquad (2.40)$$

where D_i is the amplitude of the ith frequency component and the summation is over all the frequency components — positive, negative and DC.

WORKED EXAMPLE   **2.7**

This and the next worked example require familiarity with the integral operation. We want to show that the average power of a sinusoidal signal $v(t) = A\cos(\omega t + \phi)$ is equal to half the square of its amplitude.

Using Eq. (2.36),

$$P = \frac{1}{T} \int_{-T/2}^{T/2} [A\cos(\omega t + \phi)]^2 \, dt$$

Substituting $T = 2\pi/\omega$,

$$P = \frac{\omega}{2\pi} \int_{-\pi/\omega}^{\pi/\omega} A^2 \cos^2(\omega t + \phi) dt$$

$$= \frac{\omega}{2\pi} A^2 \int_{-\pi/\omega}^{\pi/\omega} \tfrac{1}{2}[1 + \cos 2(\omega t + \phi)] dt$$

$$= \frac{\omega A^2}{4\pi} \left[t + \frac{\sin 2(\omega t + \phi)}{2\omega} \right]_{-\pi/\omega}^{\pi/\omega}$$

$$= \frac{\omega A^2}{4\pi} \left[\left\{ \pi/\omega + \frac{\sin(2\omega \frac{\pi}{\omega} + 2\phi)}{2\omega} \right\} - \left\{ -\pi/\omega + \frac{\sin(-2\omega \frac{\pi}{\omega} + 2\phi)}{2\omega} \right\} \right]$$

$$= \frac{\omega A^2}{4\pi} \left[\frac{2\pi}{\omega} + \frac{\sin(2\phi) - \sin(2\phi)}{2\omega} \right] = \frac{\omega A^2}{4\pi} \times \frac{2\pi}{\omega}$$

$$= \frac{A^2}{2}$$

In the above, we used (1) Eq. (A.11) to re-express $\cos^2(\omega t + \phi)$ and (2) $\cos(\phi \pm 2\pi) = \cos(\phi)$.

WORKED EXAMPLE   **2.8**

We want to obtain Eq. (2.39), an expression for the power in a periodic signal $v(t)$.

We may express $v(t)$ in terms of the Fourier series, Eq. (2.14),

$$v(t) = A_0 + A_1 \cos(2\pi f_0 t + \phi_1) + A_2 \cos(2\pi 2 f_0 t + \phi_2) + \cdots$$

Substituting this expression for $v(t)$ in Eq. (2.36):

$$P = \frac{1}{T} \int_{-T/2}^{T/2} [A_0 + A_1 \cos(2\pi f_0 t + \phi_1) + A_2 \cos(2\pi 2 f_0 t + \phi_2) + \cdots]^2 dt$$

$$= \frac{1}{T} \int_{-T/2}^{T/2} [A_0{}^2 + A_1^2 \cos^2(2\pi f_0 t + \phi_1) + A_2^2 \cos^2(2\pi 2 f_0 t + \phi_2) + \cdots] dt$$

$$+ \frac{2}{T} A_0 \int_{-T/2}^{T/2} [A_1 \cos(2\pi f_0 t + \phi_1) + A_2 \cos(2\pi 2 f_0 t + \phi_2) + \cdots] dt$$

$$+ \frac{2}{T} A_1 \int_{-T/2}^{T/2} [A_2 \cos(2\pi f_0 t + \phi_1) \cos(2\pi 2 f_0 t + \phi_2) + \cdots] dt$$

$$+ \cdots$$

Consider the three lines in the expanded expression for P. The first line reduces to

$$A_0^2 + \frac{A_1^2}{2} + \frac{A_2^2}{2} + \cdots$$

following the steps in Worked example 2.7.

The second line reduces to zero because each term in that line is the integral of a sinusoid over an interval of one period or an integer multiple of a period. This integral covers an equal amount of positive and negative areas and is therefore zero.

Now the third and subsequent (...) lines also reduce to zero, since they consist entirely of the sum of the terms

$$I_{mn} = \frac{2}{T} A_m A_n \int_{-T/2}^{T/2} \cos(2\pi m f_0 t + \phi_m) \cos(2\pi n f_0 t + \phi_n) dt \qquad m \neq n$$

$$= \frac{A_m A_n}{T} \int_{-T/2}^{T/2} \{\cos[2\pi(m-n)f_0 t + \phi_m - \phi_n]\} dt$$

$$+ \frac{A_m A_n}{T} \int_{-T/2}^{T/2} \cos[2\pi(m+n)f_0 t + \phi_m + \phi_n] dt$$

$$= 0$$

In the above, we used Eq. (A.6) to re-express I_{mn} as the sum of the integrals of sinusoidal signals over integer multiples of their periods. These integrals reduce to zero. The harmonic sinusoids (of frequencies,

$f_0, 2f_0, 3f_0, ...$) are said to be *orthogonal* over the interval $T = 1/f_0$, since the integral of the product of any two of them over the interval T is zero.

Thus, we obtain the result

$$P = A_0^2 + \frac{A_1^2}{2} + \frac{A_2^2}{2} + \cdots$$

2.6 Logarithmic measures of signal and power

A signal is subject to gains and losses at various stages of transmission through a communication system. To determine the signal power at a given point in the system, one multiplies the input signal power by all the power gains and divides by all the power losses experienced by the signal up to that point. This is a linear-units procedure involving multiplication and division. Signal power is in watts (W) and gains and losses are dimensionless numbers greater than unity. In Fig. 2.34, an input power P_{in} = 3.16 mW enters the transmission system. The power at various points in the system is

$$P_A = 3.16 \text{ mW} \times 10 = 31.6 \text{ mW}$$
$$P_B = 3.16 \text{ mW} \times 10 \div 63.1 = 0.50 \text{ mW}$$
$$P_{out} = 3.16 \text{ mW} \times 10 \div 63.1 \times 10 = 5.01 \text{ mW}$$

We can simplify the process of signal power computation in a transmission system by adopting units of measure of power, gains and losses that transform a complex series of multiplication and division into additions and subtractions. *Logarithmic* units furnish this transformation.

The logarithm of a number (to base 10), denoted $\log_{10}$, is by definition the power to which 10 is raised to obtain that number. For example, because $10^2 = 100$, we say that the logarithm of 100 is 2 and because $10^0 = 1$, we say that the logarithm of 1 is zero, which we write as

$$\log_{10}100 = 2; \text{ and } \log_{10}1 = 0$$

Consider two positive numbers A and B whose logarithms (to base 10) are x and y, respectively. We may write

$$\log_{10}(A) = x \qquad \text{(a)}$$
$$\log_{10}(B) = y \qquad \text{(b)}$$

$$(2.41)$$

Figure 2.34 Gain and loss in transmission system: linear-units procedure.

It follows that

$$10^x = A \qquad \text{(a)}$$
$$10^y = B \qquad \text{(b)}$$

(2.42)

Multiplying Eqs. (2.42) (a) and (b) together

$$10^x 10^y = 10^{x+y} = AB$$

And it follows by the above definition that

$$\log_{10}(AB) = x + y = \log_{10}(A) + \log_{10}(B)$$

Note that we have made use of Eq. (2.41).
  Now dividing Eq. (2.42) (a) by (b)

$$\frac{10^x}{10^y} = 10^{x-y} = \frac{A}{B}$$

It similarly follows that

$$\log_{10}\left(\frac{A}{B}\right) = x - y = \log_{10}(A) - \log_{10}(B)$$

To summarise, the following relations hold for logarithms to any base:

$$\log(AB) = \log(A) + \log(B)$$
$$\log\left(\frac{A}{B}\right) = \log(A) - \log(B)$$

(2.43)

Putting $A = 1$,

$$\log\left(\frac{1}{B}\right) = \log(1) - \log(B) = 0 - \log(B)$$
$$= -\log(B)$$

(2.44)

Observe that multiplication $(A \times B)$ is replaced by the addition of logarithms, division (A/B) by subtraction of logarithms and inversion $(1/B)$ by changing the sign of the logarithm. For example,

$$\log_{10}(10^3) = \log_{10}(10 \times 10 \times 10) = \log_{10}(10) + \log_{10}(10) + \log_{10}(10)$$
$$= 3 \times \log_{10}(10) = 3$$

In general

$$\log(A^b) = b \log(A)$$

(2.45)

where b is any real number.
  In logarithmic units therefore, the output signal power of a transmission system is obtained by adding the system gains to the input power and subtracting the system losses. Of course every quantity, including both the input and output powers, must be expressed in logarithmic units. The most commonly used logarithmic unit in the field of engineering is the *decibel* (dB).

It is common to use gain as a generic term for both a boost in signal strength — actual gain and a reduction in signal strength — a loss. In logarithmic units such as the decibel, a positive gain then indicates an increase in signal strength, while a negative value for gain indicates a loss or reduction in signal strength. So one may, for example, refer to a gain of 18 dB, or a gain of –10 dB (meaning a loss of 10 dB), but one would not normally refer to the former as a loss of –18 dB, even though this would be mathematically correct.

2.6.1 Logarithmic units for system gain

Figure 2.35 represents an arbitrary system of total gain G and input power P_1, input current I_1, input voltage V_1, output power P_2, output current I_2 and output voltage V_2. The input and output resistances of the system are Z_1 and Z_2, respectively.

Various gains of the system, expressed as dimensionless ratios are:

$$\text{Power gain} = \frac{P_2}{P_1}$$
$$\text{Current gain} = \frac{I_2}{I_1} \tag{2.46}$$
$$\text{Voltage gain} = \frac{V_2}{V_1}$$

The power gain of the system in *decibel* (dB) is defined as

$$G = 10\log_{10}\left(\frac{P_2}{P_1}\right)\text{dB} \tag{2.47}$$

If dealing with normalised power, or if the input and output resistances of the system are equal (i.e. $Z_1 = Z_2$), then

$$\frac{P_2}{P_1} = \frac{V_2^2}{V_1^2} = \frac{I_2^2}{I_1^2}$$

Substituting in Eq. (2.47), we obtain

$$G = 10\log_{10}\left(\frac{V_2^2}{V_1^2}\right) = 10\log_{10}\left(\frac{V_2}{V_1}\right)^2$$
$$= 20\log_{10}\left(\frac{V_2}{V_1}\right) \tag{2.48}$$
$$= 20\log_{10}\left(\frac{I_2}{I_1}\right)$$

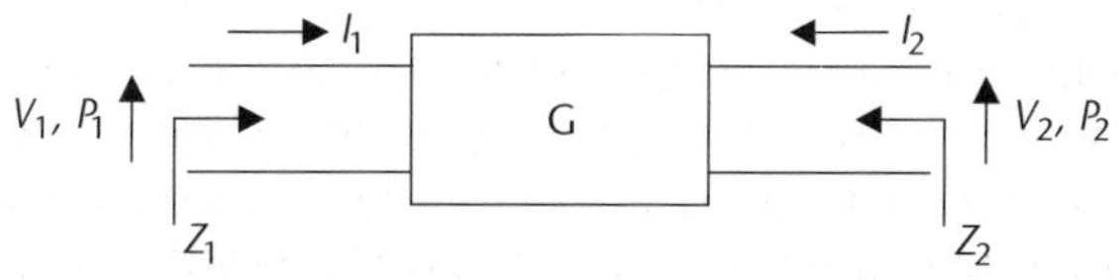

Figure 2.35 System gain.

Eqs. (2.47) and (2.48) show that for power gain in dB, the constant of multiplication is 10, whereas for current and voltage gains in dB, the constant of multiplication is 20. This difference is extremely important and must always be remembered to avoid errors. It is worth emphasising that Eq. (2.47) for power gain does not depend on the values of system resistances, whereas Eq. (2.48) for voltage and current gains holds only if the system's input and output resistances are equal.

A less commonly used logarithmic unit of gain is the *neper* (Np) defined as the natural logarithm of the ratio of output to input. This is logarithm to base e = 2.718281828459..., denoted ln. It follows that for the system in Fig. 2.35,

$$\text{Gain in } neper \text{ (Np)} = \ln\left(\frac{V_2}{V_1}\right) = \ln\left(\frac{I_2}{I_1}\right) = \frac{1}{2}\ln\left(\frac{P_2}{P_1}\right) \tag{2.49}$$

To obtain the relationship between Np and dB, note in Eq. (2.49) that a current or voltage gain of 1 Np, implies that

$$\log_e\left(\frac{V_2}{V_1}\right) = 1; \quad \text{or} \quad \frac{V_2}{V_1} = e^1 = e$$

From Eq. (2.48), the corresponding dB gain is

$$20\log_{10}\left(\frac{V_2}{V_1}\right) = 20\log_{10}(e) = 8.686 \text{ dB}$$

Similarly, a power gain of 1 Np means that

$$\frac{1}{2}\log_e\left(\frac{P_2}{P_1}\right) = 1, \text{ or } \frac{P_2}{P_1} = e^2$$

The corresponding dB gain follows from Eq. (2.47):

$$10\log_{10}\left(\frac{P_2}{P_1}\right) = 10\log_{10}(e^2) = 20\log_{10}(e) = 8.686 \text{ dB}$$

The logarithmic units, *neper* (Np) and *decibel* (dB) are therefore related as follows

$$\text{Voltage, current or power gain of 1 Np} = 8.686 \text{ dB} \tag{2.50}$$

2.6.2 Logarithmic units for voltage and power

The *decibel* and *neper* are actually units of relative measure. For example, in Eq. (2.47) the decibel value gives a measure of P_2 relative to P_1. By selecting a universally agreed reference level, we can express any signal power or voltage in dB relative to the agreed reference. In this way, absolute power level can be measured in dB and Np. Standard power reference levels are 1 W and 1 mW. Power expressed in dB relative to 1 W is said to be measured in dBW, while power expressed in dB relative to 1 mW is said to be measured in dBm.

Logarithmic units for voltage measurement are designated dBV for a 1 V reference and dBu for a 775 mV reference. The 775 mV reference, often used in telephony, is the voltage that gives a power dissipation of 1 mW across a 600 Ω resistance. Thus,

$$P \text{ (watt)} = 10 \log_{10} \left(\frac{P}{1W} \right) \text{ dBW} = 10 \log_{10} P \text{ dBW}$$

$$= 10 \log_{10} \left(\frac{P}{1 \times 10^{-3} W} \right) \text{ dBm} = 30 + 10 \log_{10} P \text{ dBm}$$

(2.51)

and

$$V \text{ (volt)} = 20 \log_{10} (V) \text{ dBV}$$

$$= 20 \log_{10} \left(\frac{V}{775 \times 10^{-3}} \right) \text{ dBu} = 2.214 + 20 \log_{10} V \text{ dBu}$$

(2.52)

Note, for example, that to convert power expressed in dBW to dBm, you simply add 30 to the dBW value.

2.6.3 Logarithmic unit for noise power

A *psophometer* is often used in speech telephony to measure power in noise and crosstalk. Although the noise spectrum spans the entire receiver bandwidth, the human ear is less sensitive to some of the spectral components, which will therefore have a less annoying effect. Human ear sensitivity is greatest between about 500 and 2000 Hz. The *psophometer* weights the noise spectrum to take account of the non-flat frequency response of the ear and the receiving equipment. It reduces noise power at each spectral frequency point in proportion to the reduced sensitivity of the ear at that point. The weighting has a peak at 800 Hz and gives a noise measurement that is smaller than would be the case in the absence of weighting, but which gives a better indication of how a human recipient perceives the noise. When the psophometer is used, a suffix 'p' is added to whatever unit is employed. Thus, we have dBmp, pWp, etc. Psophometrically weighted noise power is less than unweighted white noise power by 2.5 dB over a 3.1 kHz bandwidth and by 3.6 dB over a 4 kHz bandwidth. White noise is discussed in Section 9.5.

In summary, the following relations apply to the logarithmic units for voltage and power:

$$\begin{aligned}
\text{dBm} &= \text{dBW} + 30 \\
\text{dBu} &= \text{dBV} + 2.214 \\
\text{dBmp} &= \text{dBm} - 2.5, \quad \text{over 3.1 kHz} \\
\text{dBmp} &= \text{dBm} - 3.6, \quad \text{over 4 kHz}
\end{aligned}$$

(2.53)

Based on Eqs. (2.51) and (2.52), we can convert a power value *dBW* (in dBW) to *W* (in watt); a power value *dBm* (in dBm) to *mW* (in mW), and a voltage value *dBV* (in dBV) to *V* (in volt), using the following relations:

$$W = 10^{(dBW/10)}$$
$$mW = 10^{(dBm/10)}$$
$$V = 10^{(dBV/20)}$$

(2.54)

WORKED EXAMPLE 2.9 _____

Let us now apply logarithmic units to the transmission system of Fig. 2.34 to determine power levels at various points in the system.

$$P_{in} = 3.16 \text{ mW} = 10\log_{10}\left(\frac{3.16\text{mW}}{1\text{mW}}\right) = 5.0 \text{ dBm}$$

Gain of 1st element = 10 (ratio) = $10\log_{10}(10)$ = 10 dB
Loss of 2nd element = 63.1 (ratio) = $10\log_{10}(63.1)$ = 18 dB
Gain of 3rd element = 10 (ratio) = $10\log_{10}(10)$ = 10 dB

The power levels P_A, P_B and P_{out} now follow by simple addition (subtraction) of the gains (losses) of the relevant elements; see Fig. 2.36.

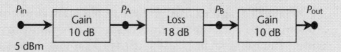

Figure 2.36 Gain and loss in transmission system: logarithmic-units procedure.

$$P_A = 5 \text{ dBm} + 10 = 15 \text{ dBm}$$
$$P_B = 5 \text{ dBm} + 10 - 18 = -3 \text{ dBm}$$
$$P_{out} = 5 \text{ dBm} + 10 - 18 + 10 = 7 \text{ dBm}$$

You may verify that these results agree with those obtained earlier using the linear-units procedure. For example, using Eq. (2.54), $P_B = -3$ dBm = $10^{(-3/10)}$ mW = 0.5 mW, as obtained earlier. Note that we could have converted –3 dBm to mW without using a calculator by observing that –3 dBm means 3 dB below 1 mW, which means a factor of 2 below 1 mW, which means 0.5 mW.

2.7 Calibration of a signal transmission path

A transmission path imposes continual attenuation on a signal, which necessitates the placement of amplifiers (called *repeaters* in analogue systems) at regular intervals along the path to boost the signal strength. To trace the power level of a signal from its source through various points along a transmission path, we can exploit the computational advantage offered by logarithmic units by calibrating the transmission path relative to a chosen reference point. This point is called the *zero-level reference point* (ZRP) and is usually set around the input to the link. For a four-wire circuit, the ZRP is usually the two-wire input to the hybrid transformer.

The transmission path is calibrated by assigning to every point on the link a transmission level (in dB) *relative* to the ZRP, hence the unit dBr. As illustrated in Fig. 2.37, the assigned dBr value is the algebraic sum of the dB gains (a loss being accounted as negative gain) from the ZRP to that point. This applies to points lying beyond the ZRP in the forward path direction. The ZRP is usually chosen at the input and therefore all points would normally fall into this category. However, if for reasons of accessibility the ZRP is located other than at the input, then the dBr of each point lying before the ZRP is obtained by negating the algebraic sum of all gains from that point to the ZRP. For example, a point lying beyond the ZRP and separated from it by a 10 dB gain amplifier is assigned 10 dBr. A point lying beyond the ZRP and separated from it by 18 dB loss ($G = -18$dB) and 15 dB gain ($G = +15$ dB) is marked $-18 + 15 = -3$ dBr. A point located before the ZRP and separated from it by 10 dB loss ($G = -10$ dB) and 25 dB gain is marked $-(-10 + 25) = -15$ dBr. The ZRP itself is marked 0 dBr, since it is the reference. Absolute signal power measured in dBm or dBW at the ZRP is expressed as dBm0 or dBW0, respectively.

The absolute power level (dBm) of a signal at any point on the link is determined by adding the link's dBr mark at that point to the signal's dBm0 value – the value of the signal at ZRP. That is,

$$dBm = dBm0 + dBr \tag{2.55}$$

where

dBm = Signal power at the given point
dBm0 = Signal power at the ZRP
dBr = Relative transmission level of the given point

Equation (2.55) may also be used to determine the power of a signal at the entry point into the link (i.e. dBm0). This is given by the difference between the signal power at an arbitrary point along the link (i.e. dBm) and the dBr value of the point. For example, in Fig. 2.37, if we measure the signal level at the –8 dBr point and find that it is –3 dBm, then we know that the level of the signal at the entry (i.e. ZRP) point is $-3 - (-8) = 5$ dBm0.

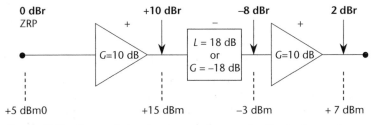

Figure 2.37 Transmission levels and the zero-level reference point (ZRP).

WORKED EXAMPLE 2.10 _____

A transmission system consists of the following gain and loss components in the listed order:

1. Loss = 30dB
2. Gain = 50 dB
3. Loss = 8 dB
4. Loss = 12 dB
5. Gain = 25 dB

Draw a block diagram of the transmission system and calibrate it in dBr with the ZRP located at

(a) The input of the 1st component
(b) The input of the 4th component

A block diagram of the system is shown in Fig. 2.38. Note that we entered loss as negative gain in order to simplify the algebraic summation involved in the calibration. The calibration for ZRP at the input of the 1st component is shown on the upper part of the block diagram and that for ZRP at the input of the 4th component is shown on the lower part. The procedure used is as earlier described. Points lying beyond the ZRP have a dBr value equal to the algebraic sum of the gains up to that point. Points lying before the ZRP (in this case, the first three components in (b)) have a dBr value equal to the negated algebraic sum of the gains from the ZRP to the point.

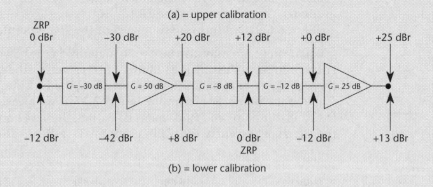

Figure 2.38 Worked example 2.10.

2.8 ## Transmission through linear systems

Consider the *linear time-invariant* (LTI) system in Fig. 2.39. The input signal is $x(t)$ and the corresponding output signal is $y(t)$, which is also called the

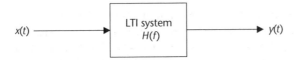

Figure 2.39 Transmission through a linear time-invariant (LTI) system.

response of the system to the input $x(t)$. Let us denote this relationship as follows:

$$x(t)\xrightarrow{R} y(t)$$

which is read, '$x(t)$ yields response $y(t)$'.

A *linear time-invariant* system is one that obeys the following rules:

Given that

$$x_1(t)\xrightarrow{R} y_1(t)$$

and

$$x_2(t)\xrightarrow{R} y_2(t) \qquad (2.56)$$

then

$$a_1 x_1(t) + a_2 x_2(t)\xrightarrow{R} a_1 y_1(t) + a_2 y_2(t) \qquad (a)$$

$$x_1(t - t_0)\xrightarrow{R} y_1(t - t_0) \qquad (b)$$

where a_1 and a_2 are arbitrary constants. Equation (2.56a) is known as the *principle of superposition*. According to Eq. (2.56b), the response of the system does not depend on the time of application of the input. That is, the response to a delayed input is simply the output shape delayed by the same amount. Equation (2.56) allows us to characterise a linear time-invariant system in the time-domain by its impulse response $h(t)$ and in the frequency domain by its transfer function or frequency response $H(f)$. The impulse response $h(t)$ is defined as the response of an LTI system with zero initial conditions to a unit impulse function $\delta(t)$ applied at its input:

$$\delta(t)\xrightarrow{R} h(t) \qquad (2.57)$$

The frequency response $H(f)$ of an LTI system is defined as the ratio of output to input when the input is a sinusoidal signal of frequency f. Using Eq. (2.29) we may write

$$\cos(2\pi ft + \phi)\xrightarrow{R} |H(f)|\cos[2\pi ft + \phi + \phi_H(f)] \qquad (2.58)$$

Since any arbitrary signal $x(t)$ can be written as a (discrete or continuous) sum of sinusoidal signals represented by its Fourier transform $X(f)$, it follows by the principle of superposition that the Fourier transform $Y(f)$ of the output signal $y(t)$ is given by

$$Y(f) = H(f)X(f) \qquad (2.59)$$

The output spectrum for a transmission through an LTI system is therefore the product of the input spectrum and the system's frequency response. The output waveform $y(t)$ is obtained by taking the inverse Fourier transform of $Y(f)$. It can be shown that the impulse response $h(t)$ and the frequency response $H(f)$ form a Fourier transform pair:

$$h(t) \rightleftharpoons H(f)$$

(2.60)

WORKED EXAMPLE 2.11

Determine the transfer function $H(f)$ of the simple RC low-pass filter shown in Fig. 2.40. For $R = 1$ kΩ and $C = 79.58$ nF,

(a) Obtain the output spectrum when the input signal is an impulse function $\delta(t)$.
(b) Determine the output voltage $v_2(t)$ for an input voltage $v_1(t) = 10\cos(2000\pi t + 30°)$.
(c) Determine the bandwidth of the filter.

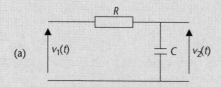

(a)

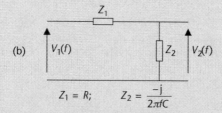

(b)

$Z_1 = R;$ $Z_2 = \dfrac{-j}{2\pi f C}$

Figure 2.40   (a) RC Low-pass filter; (b) equivalent circuit for sinusoidal input signal of amplitude V_1 and frequency f.

(a) The equivalent RC circuit for a sinusoidal input signal of frequency f is shown in Fig. 2.40(b). The input voltage $V_1(f)$ is divided between the resistance R and the capacitance C according to the ratio of their impedances Z_1 and Z_2, respectively. The voltage drop across C is the required output voltage. Thus,

$$H(f) \equiv V_2(f)/V_1(f) = Z_2/(Z_1 + Z_2)$$

Since $Z_1 = R$ and $Z_2 = -j/2\pi f C$, we obtain

$$H(f) = \frac{-j/2\pi fC}{R - j/2\pi fC}$$

$$= \frac{1}{1 + j2\pi fCR}$$

$$= \frac{1}{1 + j2\pi fCR} \times \frac{1 - j2\pi fCR}{1 - j2\pi fCR}$$

$$= \frac{1}{1 + 4\pi^2 f^2 C^2 R^2} - j\frac{2\pi fCR}{1 + 4\pi^2 f^2 C^2 R^2}$$

$$= |H(f)| \exp[j\beta(f)]$$

where $|H(f)| = \dfrac{1}{\sqrt{1 + 4\pi^2 f^2 C^2 R^2}} \equiv$ Amplitude response

$$\beta(f) = \tan^{-1}(-2\pi fCR) \equiv \text{Phase response}$$

Eqs. (2.11) and (2.13) were used in the above steps.

The output spectrum $Y(f)$ is the product of the frequency response $H(f)$ and the input spectrum $F[\delta(t)] \equiv \Delta(f)$. From Eq. (2.23), $\Delta(f) = 1$. Thus,

$$Y(f) = H(f)\Delta(f) = H(f)$$

We already know by definition that when the input is the impulse function $\delta(t)$, the output is the impulse response $h(t)$. We observe here that the spectrum of this output is the frequency response $H(f)$, thus verifying that the frequency response $H(f)$ is the Fourier transform of the impulse response $h(t)$. Substituting the values of R and C in the amplitude and phase expressions for $H(f)$ yields the output spectrum

$$|H(f)| = \frac{1}{\sqrt{1 + 4\pi^2 f^2 (79.58 \times 10^{-9})^2 (1000)^2}}$$

$$= \frac{1}{\sqrt{1 + [f/(2 \times 10^3)]^2}}$$

$$\phi_H(f) = \tan^{-1}[-2\pi fCR]$$

$$= \tan^{-1}(-5 \times 10^{-4} f)$$

Fig. 2.41 illustrates the effect of the RC low-pass filter.

(b) $v_1(t)$ is a sinusoid of frequency $f = 1000$ Hz. The output is a sinusoid of the same frequency but with amplitude reduced by the factor $|H(f)|$ and phase increased by $\phi_H(f)$. Thus,

$$v_2(t) = 10 |H(f)| \cos[2000\pi t + 30° + \phi_H(f)]\big|_{f=1000}$$

$$= \frac{10}{\sqrt{1 + (1000/2000)^2}} \cos[2000\pi t + 30° + \tan^{-1}(-5 \times 10^{-4} \times 10^3)]$$

$$= 8.94 \cos[2000\pi t + 30° - 26.6°]$$

$$= \mathbf{8.94\cos(2000\pi t + 3.4°)}$$

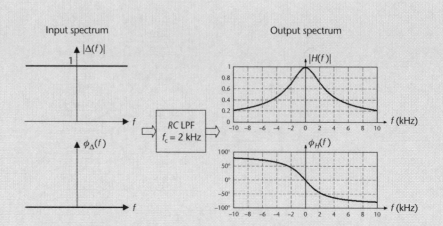

Figure 2.41 Transmission of impulse function through simple *RC* low-pass filter of cut-off frequency $f_c = 2$ kHz.

(c) By definition, see Eq. (2.28), the (3dB) bandwidth is the frequency f_2 at which $|H(f)|$ is $1/\sqrt{2}$ of its peak value, which in this case is 1. We may therefore write

$$|H(f_2)| = \frac{1}{\sqrt{1 + (f_2/2 \times 10^3)^2}} = \frac{1}{\sqrt{2}}$$

This reduces to

$$1 + \left(\frac{f_2}{2 \times 10^3}\right)^2 = 2$$

and

$$f_2 = 2 \text{ kHz}$$

2.9 Signal distortion

2.9.1 Distortionless transmission

When a signal is transmitted through a medium, it is desirable that the received signal be an exact copy of the transmitted signal except for some propagation delay, which causes the signal to be received at a later time than it was transmitted. This ideal is known as *distortionless transmission*. We have observed that a transmission medium can be characterised by its transfer function, which completely specifies how the medium modifies the amplitudes and phases of frequency components in an information signal. We are interested in determining the specification of a transfer function that would support distortionless transmission.

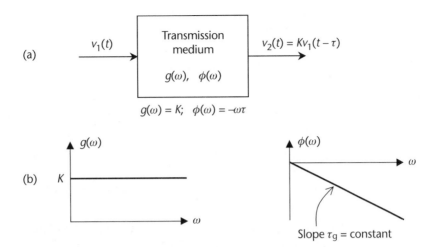

$g(\omega) = K; \quad \phi(\omega) = -\omega\tau$

Figure 2.42 Conditions for distortionless transmission.

Consider, in Fig. 2.42, a transmission medium of amplitude response $g(\omega)$ and phase response $\phi(\omega)$, where $\omega = 2\pi f$. Let us determine the dependence of g and ϕ on ω in order for the output signal $v_2(t)$ to be an exact copy of the input signal $v_1(t)$, except for some propagation delay. We may write $v_1(t)$ in terms of its frequency components

$$v_1(t) = A_1 \cos(\omega_1 t + \phi_1) + A_2 \cos(\omega_2 t + \phi_2) + \cdots$$

The effect of the transmission medium is to change the amplitude of each frequency component in $v_1(t)$ by a factor equal to the value of $g(\omega)$ at that frequency. The medium also shifts the phase of each frequency component by an amount equal to the value of $\phi(\omega)$ at that frequency. Therefore

$$A_1 \rightarrow A_1 g(\omega_1); \quad \phi_1 \rightarrow \phi_1 + \phi(\omega_1)$$
$$A_2 \rightarrow A_2 g(\omega_2); \quad \phi_2 \rightarrow \phi_2 + \phi(\omega_2)$$
$$\vdots$$

and the output signal $v_2(t)$ is given by

$$\begin{aligned}
v_2(t) &= A_1 g(\omega_1) \cos[\omega_1 t + \phi_1 + \phi(\omega_1)] \\
&\quad + A_2 g(\omega_2) \cos[\omega_2 t + \phi_2 + \phi(\omega_2)] + \cdots \\
&= A_1 g(\omega_1) \cos[\omega_1(t + \phi(\omega_1)/\omega_1) + \phi_1] \\
&\quad + A_2 g(\omega_2) \cos[\omega_2(t + \phi(\omega_2)/\omega_2) + \phi_2] + \cdots
\end{aligned}$$

For a distortionless transmission, $v_2(t)$ is a scaled and delayed version of $v_1(t)$. We must have

$$g(\omega_1) = g(\omega_2) = \cdots = K \quad \text{(a constant)}$$
$$\frac{\phi(\omega_1)}{\omega_1} = \frac{\phi(\omega_2)}{\omega_2} = \cdots = -\tau \quad \text{(another constant)} \tag{2.61}$$

so that we can write

$$
\begin{aligned}
v_2(t) &= KA_1\cos[\omega_1(t-\tau)+\phi_1]\\
&\quad +KA_2\cos[\omega_2(t-\tau)+\phi_2]+\cdots\\
&= Kv_1(t-\tau)
\end{aligned}
\tag{2.62}
$$

There are therefore two conditions for distortionless transmission, as specified in Eq. (2.61):

1. The amplitude response of the transmission medium must be constant, i.e. $g(\omega) = K$.

2. The phase response of the transmission medium must be linear, i.e. $\phi(\omega) = -\omega\tau$.

See also Fig. 2.42(b). The transfer function of a distortionless transmission medium is therefore given by the expression

$$
H(\omega) = K\exp(-j\omega\tau)
\tag{2.63}
$$

2.9.2 Attenuation and delay distortions

Any departure of the amplitude response of a transmission medium from a constant value K over the frequency band of interest gives rise to *attenuation distortion*. Similarly, any departure of the phase response from a linear law gives rise to *phase distortion*, also called *delay distortion*. The slope of the phase response is called the *group delay* τ_g. Mathematically,

$$
\tau_g = -\frac{d\phi(\omega)}{d\omega}
\tag{2.64}
$$

A distortionless transmission medium has a linear phase response and hence the group delay is constant, as shown in Fig. 2.42(b). If the phase response is non-linear then group delay will vary over the frequency band of interest. That is, the delay becomes a function of frequency. A measure of the resulting delay distortion is usually specified by the *differential delay*, which is the difference between the maximum and minimum values of group delay within the frequency band of interest.

An important cause of attenuation and delay distortions is *multipath propagation*, which arises when the signal arrives at the receiver having travelled over more than one path with different delays. Such a situation arises, for example, when a radio signal is received both by direct transmission and by reflection from an obstacle. If we consider two paths that differ in propagation time by $\Delta\tau$, this translates to a phase difference of $\omega\Delta\tau$ between two signals $x_1(t)$ and $x_2(t)$ of frequency ω arriving over the two paths. If the phase difference is an integer multiple of 2π then $x_1(t)$ and $x_2(t)$ add constructively to give a received signal $x(t)$ that has an enhanced amplitude. However, if the phase difference is an odd integer multiple of π then the two components add destructively and the received signal is severely attenuated. If $x_1(t)$ and $x_2(t)$ have equal amplitude, then $x(t)$ is zero under this situation. In practice, the direct signal (termed the *primary signal*) has a larger amplitude than the reflected signal (termed the *secondary signal*). The received signal amplitude therefore varies from a non-zero minimum under destructive interference to a maximum value under constructive interference. For values of phase difference other than integer multiples of π, the amplitude and phase of $x(t)$ are determined according to the method of phasor addition studied earlier. There are three important consequences:

1. Because the phase difference between the two paths is a function of frequency, the amplitude and phase of the received (resultant) signal depends on frequency. Some frequencies are severely attenuated, while some are enhanced. This results in attenuation and phase distortion.

2. The propagation delay difference between the two paths depends on the location of the receiver. This gives rise to *fast fading* in mobile communication systems where the receiver is not stationary.

3. In digital communications, multipath propagation over two or more differently delayed paths gives rise to pulse broadening or *dispersion*. One transmitted narrow pulse becomes a sequence of two or more narrow pulses at the receiver and this is received as one broadened pulse. Broader pulses place a limit on the bit rate that can be used without the overlap of adjacent pulses.

An *equaliser* may be used, as shown in Fig. 2.43, to compensate for amplitude and phase distortions over a desired frequency range. Ideally, the equaliser, which you may recall (Section 2.4.4) is just a filter, should satisfy two requirements:

1. The amplitude response of the equaliser should be the inverse of the amplitude response of the transmission medium.

2. The sum of the phase response of the equaliser and the phase response of the transmission medium should be a linear function of frequency.

That is,

$$g_e(\omega)g(\omega) = K$$
$$\phi_e(\omega) + \phi(\omega) = -\omega\tau \tag{2.65}$$

The equaliser in Fig. 2.43 provides both attenuation and phase equalisation. However, the ear is insensitive to phase differences and therefore only attenuation equalisation is required in speech transmission. For example, the attenuation (in dB) of audio telephone lines increases as the square root

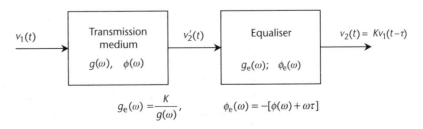

$$g_e(\omega) = \frac{K}{g(\omega)}, \qquad \phi_e(\omega) = -[\phi(\omega) + \omega\tau]$$

Figure 2.43 Compensating for attenuation and phase distortions.

of frequency. The amplitude response of the transmission medium in this case is

$$g(\omega) = K_1 \exp(-a\sqrt{f})$$

where K_1 and a are constants. That is, the gain decreases exponentially – so that dB attenuation increases linearly – with the square root of frequency. An equaliser can be used to compensate for the distortion that this will cause to the spectrum and hence waveform, of transmitted audio signals. The gain of the equaliser $g_e(\omega)$ must increase with the square root of frequency at the same rate as that at which the gain of the transmission medium decreases. Thus,

$$g_e(\omega) = K_2 \exp(+a\sqrt{f})$$

The overall amplitude response of the combination of transmission medium and equaliser in tandem is flat and independent of frequency:

$$g(\omega)g_e(\omega) = K_1 \exp(-a\sqrt{f})K_2 \exp(+a\sqrt{f})$$
$$= K_1 K_2 = K \text{ (a constant)}$$

2.9.3 Non-linear distortions

Our discussion of attenuation distortion was concerned with the modification of the shape of a signal's amplitude spectrum by a transmission medium. The amplitudes of existing frequency components were modified, but no new frequency components were created. When the transmission medium or communication system is non-linear then the output signal is subject to a non-linear distortion, which is characterised by the following:

1. The output signal is no longer directly proportional to the input signal.
2. The output signal contains frequency components not present in the input signal.

An example of non-linear distortion termed *clipping distortion* is demonstrated in Fig. 2.44. The input signal is

$$x(t) = \sin(2000\pi t) + \sin(22000\pi t)$$

The non-linear device clips the output signal $y(t)$ at 60% of the input amplitude, but otherwise passes the input signal unchanged. The output signal and its line spectrum up to 19 kHz are shown. It can be observed that new frequency components have been generated in the output signal due to this clipping distortion.

Analysis of non-linear distortion can be very complex for an information signal, which contains a band of frequencies, and for a transmission system having a non-linearity that may require a high-order polynomial for accurate representation. However, to demonstrate how the new frequency components are created, let us take a simple signal $x(t)$ consisting of only two sinusoids of zero initial phase at frequencies ω_1 and ω_2:

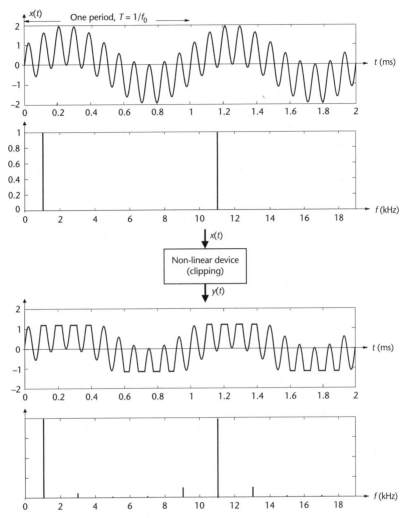

Figure 2.44 Non-linear distortion showing that clipping generates new frequency components in the spectrum of the output signal.

$$x(t) = A_1 \cos(\omega_1 t) + A_2 \cos(\omega_2 t) \tag{2.66}$$

Let this signal be transmitted through a non-linear medium whose output $y(t)$ is a non-linear function of the input, represented by a third-order polynomial:

$$y(t) = g[x(t)] = a_1 x(t) + a_2 x^2(t) + a_3 x^3(t) \tag{2.67}$$

Equation (2.67) specifies what is known as the *transfer characteristic* of the non-linear medium. You may verify that using Eq. (2.66) in Eq. (2.67) gives the output of this non-linear medium as

$$y(t) = \tfrac{1}{2}a_2(A_1^2 + A_2^2)$$
$$+\left[a_1A_1 + \tfrac{1}{4}a_3(3A_1^3 + 6A_2^2A_1)\right]\cos\omega_1 t$$
$$+\left[a_1A_2 + \tfrac{1}{4}a_3(3A_2^3 + 6A_1^2A_2)\right]\cos\omega_2 t$$
$$+\tfrac{1}{2}a_2A_1^2\cos 2\omega_1 t + \tfrac{1}{2}a_2A_2^2\cos 2\omega_2 t$$
$$+\tfrac{1}{4}a_3A_1^3\cos 3\omega_1 t + \tfrac{1}{4}a_3A_2^3\cos 3\omega_2 t \qquad (2.68)$$
$$+a_2A_1A_2\cos(\omega_1 + \omega_2)t + a_2A_1A_2\cos(\omega_1 - \omega_2)t$$
$$+\tfrac{3}{4}a_3A_1^2A_2\cos(2\omega_1 + \omega_2)t + \tfrac{3}{4}a_3A_2^2A_1\cos(2\omega_2 + \omega_1)t$$
$$+\tfrac{3}{4}a_3A_1^2A_2\cos(2\omega_1 - \omega_2)t + \tfrac{3}{4}a_3A_2^2A_1\cos(2\omega_2 - \omega_1)t$$

Let us take a moment to examine Eq. (2.68). Note first of all that the non-linear distortion is caused by the coefficients a_2, a_3, ... If these coefficients were identically zero, the transmission medium would be linear and $y(t)$ would be an exact replica of $x(t)$ except for a gain/delay factor a_1. Now observe the following distortions:

- There is a DC component (i.e. $f = 0$), which was not present in the input. This happens whenever any of the even coefficients a_2, a_4, ... in Eq. (2.67) is non-zero.

- The output amplitude of a frequency component present in the input signal no longer depends exclusively on the system gain, but also on the amplitude of the other frequency component.

- For each input frequency component ω_k, there appear new frequency components in the output signal at $m\omega_k$, $m = 2, 3, ..., N$, where N is the order of the non-linearity ($= 3$ in the Eq. (2.67) illustration). Since these new frequencies are harmonics of the input frequency, this type of distortion is termed *harmonic distortion*.

- For any two input frequencies ω_1 and ω_2, there appear new components at $m\omega_1 \pm n\omega_2$, $|m|+|n| = 2, 3, ..., N$. These are the sum and difference of the harmonic frequencies. This type of distortion is termed *intermodulation distortion*. The frequency component at $m\omega_1 \pm n\omega_2$ is called an *intermodulation product* (IMP) of order $|m|+|n|$. The power in an IMP decreases with its order.

Some of the above new frequencies may fall in adjacent channel bands in frequency division multiplex (FDM) or radio systems and appear as unwanted noise. Increasing signal power to boost the signal-to-noise ratio (e.g. by increasing A_1 and A_2 in Eq. (2.66)) also increases the harmonic and intermodulation products. The practical way to minimise this type of distortion is to ensure that amplifiers and other system components operate in their *linear region*.

In some applications, such as amplitude modulation, non-linearity is actually put to good use. For example, a carrier signal (of frequency say ω_1) may be added to a message signal (of frequency say ω_2) and this sum signal is then transmitted through a non-linear device such as a diode. Equation

(2.68) shows that the output signal would contain the carrier ω_1 and side frequencies $\omega_1 - \omega_2$ and $\omega_1 + \omega_2$, which can be readily separated from the other frequency components using a bandpass filter. We will have more to say on this in the next chapter.

SUMMARY

After a detailed study of various types of telecommunication signals and their properties, we focused on the sinusoidal signal as a building block for all signals. We were then able to introduce two concepts that play a pivotal role in telecommunications, namely

1. The *spectrum* of a signal, which specifies the relative amplitude and phase of each member (called frequency component) of the assemblage of sinusoids that constitute the signal.

2. The *frequency response* of a communication system, which specifies how the system will change the amplitude and phase of a sinusoidal input signal at a given frequency.

The signal spectrum gives a complete specification of the signal from which important signal parameters such as *bandwidth, power* and *signal duration* can be computed. The frequency response of a *linear time-invariant system* gives a full description of the system, allowing us to determine the output signal spectrum corresponding to an arbitrary input signal by virtue of the *principle of superposition*. Other important transmission parameters can then be obtained, such as *system gain*, output signal power, and *attenuation* and *phase distortions*. Our discussion included *logarithmic measures* for voltage, current, power and system gain as well as the *dBr calibration* of a transmission path.

For a non-linear system or device, the superposition principle does not hold. In this case, we may employ the device's *transfer characteristic*, which specifies the output signal as a polynomial function of the input. By doing this, we find that the effect of a non-linearity is to introduce new frequency components (known as *harmonic* and *intermodulation products*) into the output signal, which were not present in the input signal. Non-linearity is undesirable in transmission media and *repeaters*, but is exploited in transmitters and receivers to achieve important signal processing tasks, such as frequency translation, modulation and demodulation.

At this point, it is worth summarising the major issues in communication system design that we address in this book.

1. The message signal must be transformed into a transmitted signal that requires a minimum transmission bandwidth and experiences minimum attenuation and distortion in the transmission medium. Furthermore, those transformation techniques are preferred in which the information contained in the transmitted signal is insensitive to small distortions in the spectrum of the transmitted signal.

2. The system should approach as closely as possible distortionless transmission. This may require the use of equalisers to shape the overall frequency response of the system and the implementation of measures to minimise noise and interference.

3. The original information should be recovered – at the intended destination only – using a received signal that is in general a weak, noise-corrupted and somewhat distorted version of the transmitted signal.

4. We must be able to evaluate the performance of a communication system and to fully appreciate the significance of various design parameters and the trade-offs involved.

In this chapter we have introduced important concepts and tools which will be used and gradually extended in the remaining chapters to develop the above systems design and analysis skills. The next two chapters are devoted to a comprehensive study of modulation – a signal processing scheme that is indispensable to the design of all types of communication systems, except baseband transmission systems operating on metallic lines.

REVIEW QUESTIONS

2.1 (a) Determine the fundamental frequency and first three harmonics of the periodic voltage waveforms shown in Fig. 2.45.

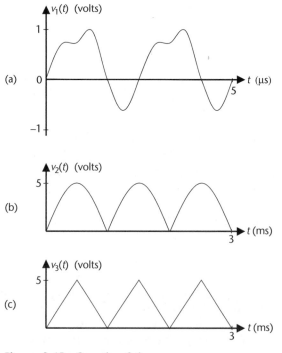

Figure 2.45 Question 2.1.

(b) Does $v_2(t)$ have the same amplitude spectrum as $v_3(t)$? If not, which of the two waveforms has a more significant content of higher frequency components? Give reasons for your answers.

2.2 Given the voltage signals

$$v_1(t) = 20\sin(t)$$
$$v_2(t) = -5\cos(t - 60°)$$
$$v_3(t) = \sin(2\pi \times 10^3 t)$$
$$v_4(t) = 2\sin(4\pi \times 10^3 t - 60°)$$

(a) Determine the period of each signal.
(b) Determine the phase difference between $v_1(t)$ and $v_2(t)$.
(c) Make clearly labelled sketches of $v_3(t)$ and $v_4(t)$ over three cycles starting at $t = 0$ and hence explain why there is no defined phase difference between sinusoids of unequal frequencies.
(d) If $v_3(t)$ is applied as input to a loudspeaker, what is the wavelength (in air) of the resulting audible sound?

2.3 Determine the output signal $v(t)$ of each of the summing devices shown in Fig. 2.46, expressed in the form

$$v(t) = A \sin(\omega t + \phi)$$

The amplitude A and initial phase ϕ of $v(t)$ must be specified.

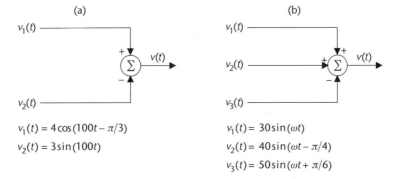

(a)

$v_1(t)$

$v(t)$

$v_2(t)$

$v_1(t) = 4\cos(100t - \pi/3)$
$v_2(t) = 3\sin(100t)$

(b)

$v_1(t)$

$v_2(t)$

$v(t)$

$v_3(t)$

$v_1(t) = 30\sin(\omega t)$
$v_2(t) = 40\sin(\omega t - \pi/4)$
$v_3(t) = 50\sin(\omega t + \pi/6)$

Figure 2.46 Question 2.3.

2.4 Fig. 2.47 is a sketch of a voltage waveform $v(t)$ that consists of a DC component and two sinusoids. Write out the full expression for $v(t)$ in the form

$$v(t) = A_0 + A_1 \sin(\omega_1 t + \phi_1) + A_2 \sin(\omega_2 t + \phi_2)$$

Explain clearly how you arrive at the values of A_0, A_1, A_2, ω_1, ω_2, ϕ_1 and ϕ_2.

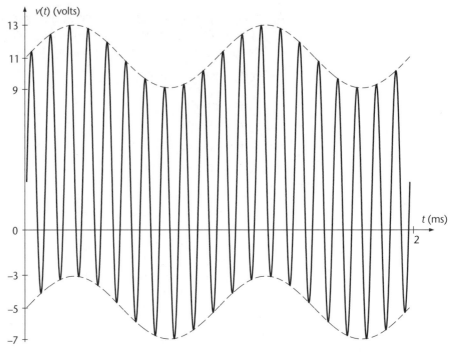

Figure 2.47 Question 2.4.

2.5 Two sinusoidal voltages

$$v_1(t) = 10 + 4\sin(2\pi \times 10^3 t) \text{ volts}$$

and

$$v_2(t) = 25\sin(4\pi \times 10^4 t) \text{ volts}$$

are multiplied together.

(a) Sketch the waveform of the product signal.
(b) Sketch the single-sided line spectrum of the product signal and hence calculate its normalised average power.
(c) Sketch the double-sided line spectrum of the product signal.
(d) What is the power dissipated when the product signal is applied across a 50 Ω resistor?

2.6 Given the voltage waveform

$$v(t) = 10 - 20\cos(100\pi t) + 10\cos(200\pi t + \pi/3)$$
$$-5\cos(500\pi t - \pi/2) \text{ volts}$$

sketch the single-sided *and* double-sided

(a) amplitude spectrum
(b) power spectrum
(c) phase spectrum

2.7 A periodic voltage signal in the form of a rectangular pulse train of period T, amplitude A and pulse duration τ is shown in Fig. 2.48.

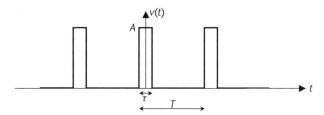

Figure 2.48 Question 2.7.

(a) Obtain an expression for the normalised power of the waveform in terms of A, T and τ.

(b) Based on the discussion in Section 2.4.1, obtain an expression in the form of Eq. (2.20) for the double-sided Fourier series of the rectangular pulse train in terms of A, T and τ.

(c) Hence sketch the double-sided amplitude spectrum of $v(t)$ for $A = 10$ V, $\tau = 20$ μs and $T = 100$ μs and determine the (null) bandwidth of the pulse train.

(d) Write out the Fourier series of the pulse train in (c), including up to the first seven non-zero sinusoidal components.

(e) What percentage of the total power of the pulse train in (c) lies in the main lobe?

(f) Give a detailed explanation of the effect on the spectrum when the duty cycle of the pulse train in (c) is reduced to 10% by (i) reducing τ to 10 μs, with T unchanged at 100 μs; (ii) increasing T to 200 μs, with τ unchanged at 20 μs.

2.8 Show that the phase spectrum of the pulse train in Fig. 2.22(a) is as plotted in Fig. 2.22(c).

2.9 Consider a rectangular pulse $x(t)$ of amplitude A and width τ.

(a) Write an expression for the Fourier transform $X(f)$ of the pulse.

(b) Sketch $|X(f)|$ versus frequency f.

(c) For $\tau = 5$ μs, determine (i) the bandwidth of the pulse and (ii) the phases of the components at frequencies $f = 5$ kHz and 300 kHz.

(d) What is the bandwidth if the pulse in (c) is made narrower by a factor of 4?

(e) What would you do to the pulse in order to reduce the amplitudes of its frequency components outside the main lobe?

2.10 Fig. 2.49(a) shows a triangular waveform $v(t)$ of amplitude A and period T.

(a) Obtain an expression for the normalised power of the waveform in terms of A and T.

(b) Starting from Eq. (2.27), show that the double-sided Fourier series of $v(t)$ is given by

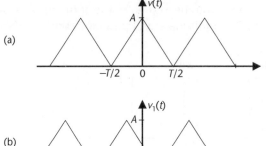

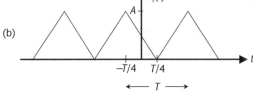

Figure 2.49 Question 2.10.

$$v(t) = \frac{A}{2} \sum_{n=-\infty}^{\infty} \text{sinc}^2(n/2)\cos(2\pi n f_0 t)$$

where $f_0 = 1/T$

(c) Hence sketch the single-sided amplitude spectrum of the triangular waveform.

(d) Determine the null bandwidth of $v(t)$ and the fraction of total power contained therein.

(e) The triangular waveform $v_1(t)$ shown in Fig. 2.49(b) is identical to $v(t)$ in every respect, except that $v_1(t)$ leads $v(t)$ by one-quarter of a period. Sketch the phase spectrum of $v_1(t)$.

2.11 Fill in the blank cells in Table 2.3. Assume that the input and output resistances of the system are equal to 1 Ω, which also means that we are dealing with *normalised power*.

Table 2.3 Question 2.11.

Power (W)	Power (dBm)	Power (dBW)	Power (dBmp, 3.1 kHz)	Volts (dBV)	Volts (dBu)
100					
	20				
		30			
			10		
					10

2.12 A transmission system consists of the following gain and loss components in the listed order:

1. Gain = 20 dB
2. Gain = 50 dB
3. Loss = 95 dB

4. Gain = 30 dB
5. Loss = 12 dB

(a) Draw a block diagram of the transmission system and calibrate it in dBr with the ZRP located at the input of the second component.
(b) A signal monitored at the ZRP has a level of 60 dBm0. What will be the absolute power level of this signal at the output of the transmission system?

2.13 Consider the transmission of a signal through the simple LTI system shown in Fig. 2.50.

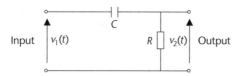

Input $v_1(t)$ R $v_2(t)$ Output

Figure 2.50 Question 2.13.

For $R = 200 \ \Omega$ and $C = 39.79$ nF:

(a) Obtain the transfer function $H(f)$ of the system.
(b) Determine the output voltage $v_2(t)$ for the following input voltages

   (i) $v_1(t) = 10\cos(1000\pi t)$
   (ii) $v_1(t) = 10\cos(8 \times 10^4 \pi t)$

   Comment on your results by discussing the action of the circuit.
(c) Obtain and sketch the amplitude and phase spectra of the output when the input signal is the rectangular pulse train of Question 2.7, with $A = 10$ V, $\tau = 20$ μs and $T = 100$ μs. Discuss the manner in which the pulse train has been distorted by the system.

2.14 Fig. 2.51 shows a parallel LC circuit, usually referred to as a *tank circuit*.

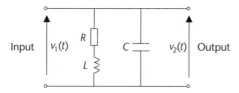

Input $v_1(t)$ R C $v_2(t)$ Output
       L

Figure 2.51 Question 2.14.

(a) Obtain an expression for the transfer function $H(f)$ of the circuit and hence plot the amplitude and phase response of the filter as a function of frequency for $C = 0.5$ nF, $L = 240$ μH and $R = 15 \ \Omega$.
(b) Show that the circuit has maximum gain at the frequency (known as *resonant frequency*)

$$f_r = \frac{1}{2\pi\sqrt{LC}}$$

and (3 dB) bandwidth

$$B = \frac{R}{2\pi L}$$

(c) A filter's *quality factor* is defined as the ratio $Q = f_r/B$. It gives a measure of the selectivity of the filter — how narrow the filter's passband is compared to its centre frequency. What is the Q of this filter for the component values in (a)?

(d) The *shape factor* of a filter is defined as the ratio between its 60-dB bandwidth and 6 dB bandwidth. It gives a measure of how steeply the filter's attenuation increases beyond the passband. An ideal bandpass filter has a shape factor of unity. Determine the shape factor of this filter for the component values in (a).

Amplitude modulation

IN THIS CHAPTER

- Time domain discussion of amplitude modulation (AM) signals.

- Spectrum and power of AM signals.

- AM modulators and demodulators, including the superheterodyne receiver.

- Waveform description, spectrum, modulators, demodulators, and applications for double sideband suppressed carrier AM (DSB). You will particularly benefit from the presentation on balanced modulators.

- Single sideband suppressed carrier amplitude modulation (SSB) — spectrum, modulators, demodulators and applications.

- Independent sideband suppressed carrier amplitude modulation (ISB) — spectrum, modulators, demodulators, and applications.

- Vestigial sideband suppressed carrier amplitude modulation (VSB) — spectrum, modulators, demodulators, and applications

3.1 Introduction

The roles of modulation in telecommunication were discussed in detail in Section 1.5.3. Modulation allows us to

1. Accommodate multiple users on the same communication link.
2. Achieve efficient radiation in radio systems.
3. Exploit the larger bandwidths available at higher radio frequencies.

4. Use a frequency band best suited to the transmission medium.

We also defined modulation as the process of imposing the variations (or information) in a lower-frequency electrical signal (called *modulating* or *baseband* or *message* signal) onto a higher-frequency sinusoidal signal (called the *carrier*), and pointed out there are three parameters of the sinusoidal carrier signal that may be varied, namely:

1. The carrier amplitude, leading to what is termed *amplitude modulation*.
2. The carrier frequency, resulting in *frequency modulation*.
3. The carrier phase, giving rise to *phase modulation*.

This chapter is devoted to amplitude modulation, while frequency and phase modulation are treated in the next chapter. We apply the skills acquired in Chapter 2 to build on the introduction to modulation that was presented in Section 1.5.3. First, there is an introduction to amplitude modulation (AM), and the definition of common terms such as *modulation depth* and *modulation sensitivity* based on a simple staircase message signal. Next, we obtain the spectrum of an AM signal, since signal spectra must be known in every communication situation to determine the required transmission bandwidth and the type of transmission medium. To do this, a sinusoidal message signal is used, and it is shown that the AM process generates three frequency components, namely the *lower side frequency* (LSF), the *carrier* and the *upper side frequency* (USF). You will then see that for an information signal consisting of a band of sinusoids, a *lower sideband* (LSB) replaces the LSF, and an *upper sideband* replaces the USF.

We discuss the power content of an AM signal and highlight AM's demerits in power and spectral usage, but emphasise its great advantage in transmitter and receiver circuit simplicity. Alternative AM schemes that save power and/or bandwidth at the cost of increased circuit complexity are then introduced, including *double sideband suppressed carrier* amplitude modulation (DSB), *single sideband* amplitude modulation (SSB), *independent sideband* amplitude modulation (ISB) and *vestigial sideband* amplitude modulation (VSB). The modulator and demodulator circuits that implement the above AM schemes are discussed in block diagram format.

The chapter includes a discussion of the applications of AM and its variants and the factors that dictate these applications. However, a detailed discussion of noise effects is postponed until Chapter 9, which gives a comprehensive treatment of noise and its impact on analogue and digital communication systems.

3.2 AM signals — time domain description

In amplitude modulation (AM), the amplitude of a sinusoidal carrier signal is varied in proportion to the instantaneous value of a message signal, which is the modulating signal. The change in carrier amplitude per volt of modulating signal is called the *modulation sensitivity k*, expressed in volt/ volt. The modulation sensitivity is usually 1 volt/volt, and this value should be assumed except where otherwise indicated. The information contained in the variations of the message signal is perfectly preserved in the variations of the carrier amplitude, and this information is recovered at the receiver by tracking the carrier amplitude. The main benefit is that while the frequency content of the message signal is relatively fixed, there is a great deal of freedom in the choice of the frequency of a carrier onto which the information is impressed, the choice being guided by the four roles of modulation stated earlier. In this way, a variety of message signals can be transmitted using a variety of transmission media and communication systems. For example, voice signals with frequency content in the range ~50–7000 Hz can be transmitted by various means, such as

1. Via satellite by impressing the voice information onto a carrier of frequency in the SHF band (3–30 GHz).
2. Via optical fibre by modulating an optical carrier (frequency ~194 THz) with a digitised version of the voice signal.
3. Via AM radio by modulating a carrier of frequency between 540 kHz and 1.64 MHz.

3.2.1 AM waveform

Consider the simple staircase message signal $v_m(t)$ shown in Fig. 3.1(a), which is used to amplitude modulate the sinusoidal carrier $v_c(t)$ shown in Fig. 3.1(b). Observe that $v_c(t)$ has a constant amplitude $V_c = 3$ V, and completes three cycles in every 1 ms interval. That is, the *unmodulated* carrier oscillates between the fixed levels $\pm V_c$ at a frequency $f_c = 3$ kHz. Amplitude modulation of $v_c(t)$ by the message signal $v_m(t)$ is achieved by changing the amplitude of $v_c(t)$ from the constant value V_c to the value

$$V_{am} = V_c + kv_m(t) \tag{3.1}$$

The result is the amplitude-modulated (AM) signal $v_{am}(t)$ shown in Fig. 3.1(c) for modulation sensitivity $k = 1$. Note that the AM signal $v_{am}(t)$ maintains the same rate of three oscillations per ms as the carrier $v_c(t)$, but its amplitude V_{am} is now a function of time depending on the instantaneous value of the message signal $v_m(t)$, and has the following values

$$V_{am}(t) = V_c + kv_m(t) = 3 + v_m(t) = \begin{cases} 3 \text{ V}, & 0 \leq t < 1 \text{ ms} \\ 5 \text{ V}, & 1 \leq t < 2 \text{ ms} \\ 4 \text{ V}, & 2 \leq t < 3 \text{ ms} \\ 2 \text{ V}, & 3 \leq t < 4 \text{ ms} \\ 1 \text{ V}, & 4 \leq t < 5 \text{ ms} \\ 3 \text{ V}, & 5 \leq t \leq 6 \text{ ms} \end{cases}$$

$V_{am}(t)$ defines the envelope of the AM waveform, which is indicated in dotted lines in Fig. 3.1(c). The dotted lines are not part of the AM waveform — they would not appear in an oscilloscope display of the waveform — but are very useful as guides for sketching the AM waveform.

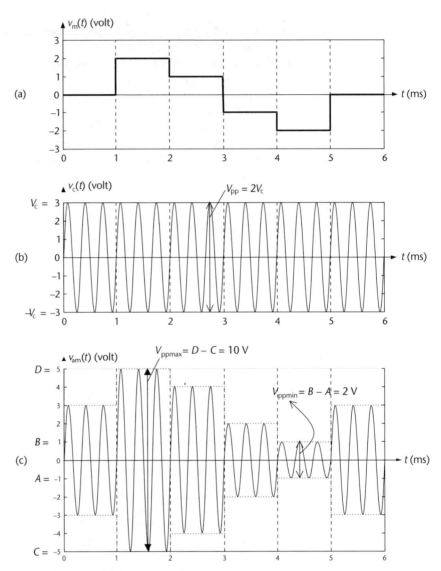

Figure 3.1 (a) Message signal; (b) carrier signal; (c) AM signal, with modulation sensitivity k = 1 volt/volt.

3.2.2 Sketching AM waveforms

The following steps, shown in Fig. 3.2, were involved in drawing the AM waveform shown in Fig. 3.1(c), and can be followed in sketching any AM waveform.

1. Draw two dotted horizontal lines at $\pm V_C$, where V_C is the carrier amplitude. In the absence of modulation, the carrier oscillates between these two levels, implying constant amplitude V_C.

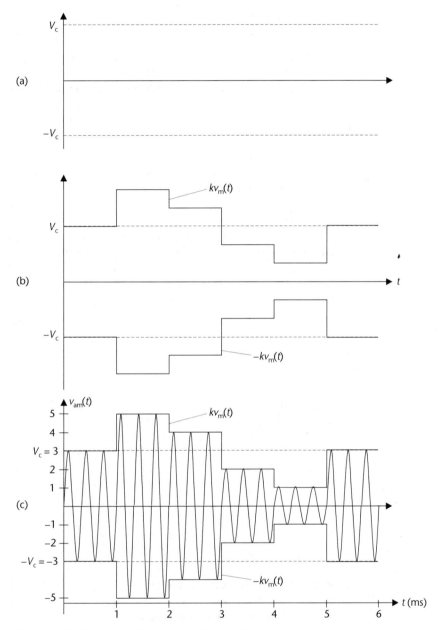

Figure 3.2 Steps in sketching an AM waveform.

2. Sketch the waveform $kv_m(t)$ at the level $+V_c$, and the (inverted) waveform $-kv_m(t)$ at the level $-V_c$. The envelope of the AM waveform is now defined.

3. Insert the sinusoidal carrier centred within the envelope defined above, ensuring that its positive and negative peaks are stretched or reduced as necessary to touch the envelope at all times, and that its rate of

oscillation is unchanged. Significant points on the voltage and time axis should be clearly labelled as shown. If the carrier frequency is so high that it is impractical to sketch individual cycles, then it is acceptable to represent the AM waveform as a set of closely packed vertical lines or shading that completely fills the area within the envelope.

3.2.3 Modulation factor

The peak value or amplitude of a sinusoidal signal does not change, and hence its peak-to-peak value V_{pp} is constant. In Fig. 3.1(b), we see that for a sinusoidal signal of amplitude V_c,

$$V_{pp} = 2V_c$$

The peak value of an AM signal is not constant, but varies according to the modulating signal between a minimum V_{ppmin} and a maximum V_{ppmax}. A parameter called the *modulation factor* (denoted m) provides a measure of the extent of carrier amplitude variation caused by the modulating signal. It is defined by the expression

$$m = \frac{\text{Maximum peak to peak} - \text{Minimum peak to peak}}{\text{Maximum peak to peak} + \text{Minimum peak to peak}}$$
$$= \frac{V_{ppmax} - V_{ppmin}}{V_{ppmax} + V_{ppmin}} \tag{3.2}$$

Equation (3.2) applies to all AM signals regardless of modulation sensitivity k and type of modulating signal $v_m(t)$, and is particularly convenient to use when the AM waveform has been sketched on paper or displayed on an oscilloscope. For the AM waveform shown in Fig. 3.1(c), $V_{ppmax} = 10$ V and $V_{ppmin} = 2$ V, and it follows from Eq. (3.2) that

$$m = \frac{10 - 2}{10 + 2} = 0.667$$

Note carefully that here and in all cases,

$$V_{ppmin} = B - A \tag{3.3}$$

where B is the lowest level of the top envelope, and A is the highest level of the bottom envelope. In this case $B = 1$, $A = -1$, and $V_{ppmin} = 1 - (-1) = 2$ V. The maximum peak-to-peak value is given by

$$V_{ppmax} = D - C \tag{3.4}$$

where D is the highest level of the top envelope and C is the lowest level of the bottom envelope. In this case, $D = 5$ V and $C = -5$ V so that $V_{ppmax} = 5 - (-5) = 10$ V.

When expressed as a percentage, m is referred to as the *modulation index*, or *percentage modulation*, or *depth of modulation*. Therefore in the above example, the modulation index is $m = 66.7\%$. When the modulation factor has a value between 0 and less than unity, as in this case, the AM signal is said to be *undermodulated*.

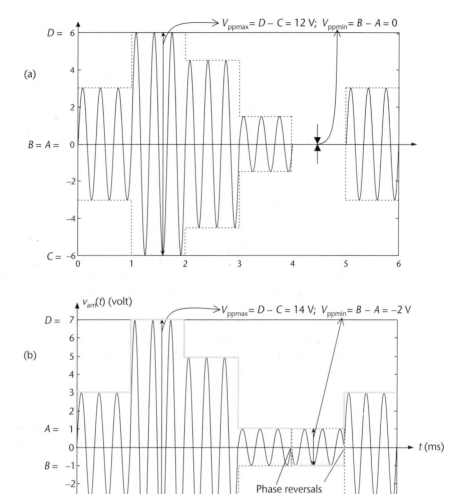

Figure 3.3 AM signal with (a) 100% modulation; (b) over-modulation.

Figure 3.3(a) shows an AM waveform obtained using the same message signal and carrier as in Fig. 3.1, but with the modulation sensitivity increased to $k = 1.5$. The carrier amplitude has been varied until the minimum peak-to-peak value V_{ppmin} of the AM signal is zero, since $B = A = 0$. In this case it follows from Eq. (3.2) that $m = 1$. The AM signal is said to be *100% modulated*. We shall show later that the most (power) efficient AM transmission is obtained when operation is as close as possible to 100% modulation.

Let us consider the result of varying the carrier amplitude beyond the 100% modulation limit. This may be done by sufficiently increasing the modulation sensitivity or by using a sufficiently large modulating signal. An example of this is shown in Fig. 3.3(b) for the same staircase modulating signal and carrier as before, but with $k = 2$. Observe that the lowest level of the top envelope (light solid line) is $B = -1$; and the highest level of the bottom envelope (dotted line) is $A = 1$. Therefore V_{ppmin} ($= B - A$) is negative. It then follows from Eq. (3.2) that the modulation factor $m > 1$. In this case,

$$m = \frac{14 - (-2)}{14 + (-2)} = 1.33$$

The AM signal is said to be *overmodulated*. There is then a portion of the AM waveform at which the amplitude $V_{am} = V_c + kv_m(t)$ is negative. This is equivalent to a phase change of 180°, or phase reversal. There is a carrier phase reversal at every point where the top envelope crosses the x-axis. The top and bottom envelopes cross each other at these points. You will also observe that the envelope of the AM signal is no longer a replica of the message signal. This *envelope distortion* makes it impossible to recover the original message signal from the AM waveform envelope. Overmodulation must be avoided by ensuring that the message signal $v_m(t)$ satisfies the following condition:

$$V_m \leq \frac{V_c}{k} \tag{3.5}$$

where V_m is a positive voltage equal to the maximum excursion of the message signal below 0 V, V_c is the carrier amplitude, and k is the modulation sensitivity (usually $k = 1$).

WORKED EXAMPLE   3.1

An audio signal $v_m (t) = 30\sin(5000\pi t)$ volts modulates the amplitude of a carrier $v_c(t) = 65\sin(50000\pi t)$ volts.

(a) Sketch the AM waveform.
(b) What is the modulation factor?
(c) Determine the modulation sensitivity that would give a modulation index of 80%.
(d) If the message signal amplitude is changed to a new value that is 6 dB below the carrier amplitude, determine the resulting modulation factor.

(a) We will sketch the AM waveform over two cycles of the audio signal $v_m(t)$. The audio signal frequency f_m and the carrier frequency f_c must be known in order to determine how many carrier cycles are completed in one cycle of $v_m(t)$:

$$v_m(t) = 30\sin(5000\pi t) \equiv V_m \sin(2\pi f_m t), \quad \Rightarrow f_m = 2.5 \text{ kHz}$$
$$v_c(t) = 65\sin(50000\pi t) \equiv V_c \sin(2\pi f_c t), \quad \Rightarrow f_c = 25 \text{ kHz}$$

Thus, $f_c = 10f_m$, meaning that the carrier completes 10 cycles in the time it takes the audio signal to complete one cycle. Following the steps outlined in Section 3.2.1 for sketching AM waveforms, we sketch two cycles of $v_m(t)$ — a sinusoid of amplitude 30 V at level V_c = 65 V, and two cycles of $-v_m(t)$ at level –65 V. This defines the envelope of the AM waveform. We then sketch in the carrier, stretching its amplitude to always touch the envelope, and ensuring that there are exactly 10 cycles of this carrier in one cycle of the envelope. This completes the required sketch of the AM waveform $v_{am}(t)$, which is shown properly labelled in Fig. 3.4. Note that we assumed modulation sensitivity $k = 1$. This is always the case except where specifically otherwise indicated as in (c) below.

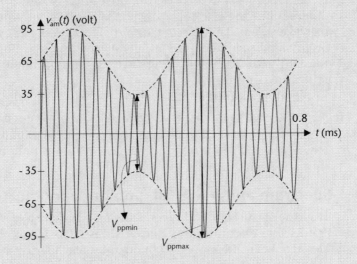

Figure 3.4 AM waveform in Worked example 3.1.

(b) From Fig. 3.4 and Eq. (3.2)

$$V_{pp\,max} = 2 \times 95 = 190\,\text{V}$$
$$V_{pp\,min} = 2 \times 35 = 70\,\text{V}$$
$$m = \frac{190 - 70}{190 + 70} = 0.462$$

(c) The expression for $V_{pp\,max}$ and $V_{pp\,min}$ taking account of a non-unity modulation sensitivity k is

$$V_{pp\,max} = 2(V_c + kV_m); \quad V_{pp\,min} = 2(V_c - kV_m)$$

Using Eq. (3.2),

$$m = \frac{2(V_c + kV_m) - 2(V_c - kV_m)}{2(V_c + kV_m) + 2(V_c - kV_m)} = \frac{kV_m}{V_c}$$

Therefore,

$$k = \frac{mV_c}{V_m} = \frac{0.8 \times 65}{30} = 1.73$$

(d) Assuming $k = 1$, we have from (c) above

$$m = \frac{V_m}{V_c}$$

Given that V_m is 6 dB below V_c, we have

$$20 \log_{10}\left(\frac{V_m}{V_c}\right) = -6$$

or,

$$\frac{V_m}{V_c} = 10^{(-6/20)} = 0.5$$

Therefore, $m = 0.5$.

Observe that m is simply the dB value converted to a ratio.

3.3 Spectrum and power of amplitude-modulated signals

By virtue of the Fourier theorem, any message signal $v_m(t)$ can be realised as the discrete or continuous sum of sinusoidal signals. The spectrum of an AM signal can therefore be obtained by considering a sinusoidal message signal and extending the result to information signals, which in general consist of a band of frequencies (or sinusoids).

3.3.1 Sinusoidal modulating signal

Consider a carrier signal of amplitude V_c and frequency f_c:

$$v_c(t) = V_c \cos(2\pi f_c t) \tag{3.6}$$

and a sinusoidal modulating signal of amplitude V_m and frequency f_m:

$$v_m(t) = V_m \cos(2\pi f_m t) \tag{3.7}$$

Usually

$$V_m \leq V_c; \quad f_m \ll f_c \tag{3.8}$$

An expression for the AM signal $v_{am}(t)$ is obtained by replacing the constant carrier amplitude V_c in Eq. (3.6) with the expression for the modulated amplitude V_{am} given in Eq. (3.1):

$$v_{am}(t) = [V_c + kv_m(t)]\cos(2\pi f_c t)$$
$$= [V_c + V_m \cos(2\pi f_m t)]\cos(2\pi f_c t), \qquad \text{for } k = 1 \tag{3.9}$$

where we have set $k = 1$ (as is usually the case), and substituted the expression for $v_m(t)$ from Eq. (3.7). Following the steps outlined in Section 3.2, the AM waveform given by Eq. (3.9) is sketched in Fig. 3.5. It is obvious from Fig. 3.5 that the maximum and minimum peak-to-peak amplitudes of $v_{am}(t)$ are given respectively by

$$V_{pp\,max} = (V_c + V_m) - (-V_c - V_m) = 2(V_c + V_m)$$
$$V_{pp\,min} = (V_c - V_m) - (-V_c + V_m) = 2(V_c - V_m)$$

From Eq. (3.2), we obtain a simple expression for the modulation factor m in the special case of a sinusoidal message signal and the usual case of unity modulation sensitivity:

$$m = \frac{2(V_c + V_m) - 2(V_c - V_m)}{2(V_c + V_m) + 2(V_c - V_m)}$$
$$= \frac{V_m}{V_c} \tag{3.10}$$

The modulation factor is given by the ratio of sinusoidal message signal amplitude to carrier amplitude. The ideal modulation factor $m = 1$ is obtained when $V_m = V_c$, and overmodulation occurs whenever $V_m > V_c$.

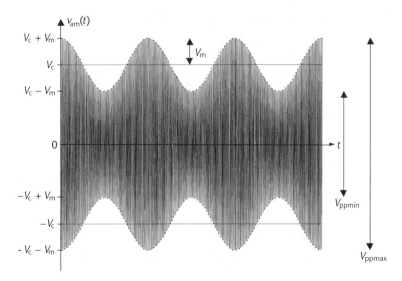

Figure 3.5 AM waveform for a sinusoidal message message signal of frequency f_m and amplitude V_m. The plot is for carrier frequency $f_c = 100\,f_m$, and carrier amplitude $V_c = 3V_m$.

Returning to Eq. (3.9) and expanding it with the trigonometric identity

$$\cos A \cos B = \tfrac{1}{2}\cos(A - B) + \tfrac{1}{2}\cos(A + B)$$

we obtain

$$v_{am}(t) = V_c \cos(2\pi f_c t)$$
$$+ \frac{V_m}{2}\cos[2\pi(f_c - f_m)t]$$
$$+ \frac{V_m}{2}\cos[2\pi(f_c + f_m)t]$$

(3.11)

The AM signal therefore contains three frequency components, namely:

1. The carrier frequency f_c with amplitude V_c.
2. A frequency component $f_c - f_m$ with amplitude $\tfrac{1}{2}V_m$. This frequency component is called the *lower side frequency* (LSF), since it lies below the carrier frequency.
3. A frequency component $f_c + f_m$ with amplitude $\tfrac{1}{2}V_m$. This frequency component is called the *upper side frequency* (USF), since it lies above the carrier frequency.

Note in particular that the AM signal does not contain any component at the message signal frequency f_m. Figure 3.6 shows the single-sided spectra

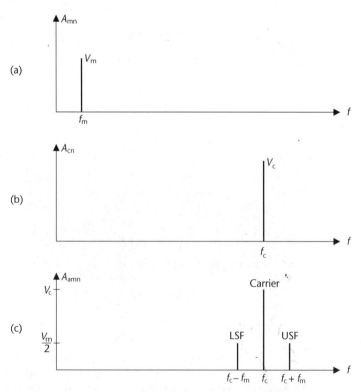

Figure 3.6 Single-sided amplitude spectrum of (a) sinusoidal modulating signal; (b) carrier signal; and (c) AM signal.

of $v_m(t)$, $v_c(t)$, and $v_{am}(t)$. You will observe by studying this figure along with Eq. (3.11) that amplitude modulation translates the message frequency f_m of amplitude V_m to two side frequencies $f_c - f_m$ and $f_c + f_m$, each of amplitude $0.5V_m$. Let us denote this process as follows

$$f_m|_{V_m} \xrightarrow[f_c]{AM} (f_c - f_m)|_{\frac{1}{2}V_m} + (f_c + f_m)|_{\frac{1}{2}V_m} \tag{3.12}$$

Equation (3.12) states that a frequency component f_m of amplitude v_m is translated by an AM process (that uses a carrier of frequency f_c) to two new frequency components at $f_c - f_m$ and $f_c + f_m$ each of amplitude $\frac{1}{2}V_m$. From Eq. (3.10), this amplitude can be expressed in terms of the carrier amplitude V_c and the modulation factor m:

$$\frac{V_m}{2} = \frac{mV_c}{2} \tag{3.13}$$

Treating the sinusoidal message signal as a low-pass signal and the AM signal as a bandpass signal, it follows (see Section 2.4.4) that they have the following bandwidths

$$\text{Message signal bandwidth} = f_m$$
$$\text{AM signal bandwidth} = (f_c + f_m) - (f_c - f_m) = 2f_m$$

Thus the AM bandwidth is twice the message bandwidth. It should be noted that regarding $v_m(t)$ as a bandpass signal would give it zero bandwidth, the width of the significant frequency components being $f_m - f_1 = f_m - f_m = 0$. This would lead to incorrect results.

WORKED EXAMPLE   3.2

For the AM waveform $v_{am}(t)$ obtained in Worked example 3.1:

(a) Determine the frequency components present in the AM waveform and the amplitude of each component.
(b) Sketch the double-sided amplitude spectrum of $v_{am}(t)$.

(a) The sinusoidal message signal $v_m(t)$ of amplitude 30 V and frequency $f_m = 2.5$ kHz is translated by the AM process with carrier frequency $f_c = 25$ kHz in the manner given by Eq. (3.12):

$$2.5\,\text{kHz}|_{30\,V} \xrightarrow[25\,\text{kHz}]{AM} (25 - 2.5\,\text{kHz})|_{15\,V} + (25 + 2.5\,\text{kHz})|_{15\,V}$$

The carrier of amplitude 65 V is also a component of $v_{am}(t)$. So there are three components as follows:

(i)   LSF of frequency 22.5 kHz and amplitude 15 V
(ii) Carrier of frequency 25 kHz and amplitude 65 V
(iii) USF of frequency 27.5 kHz and amplitude 15 V

(b) The double-sided amplitude spectrum showing each of the above components as a positive and negative frequency pair is sketched in Fig. 3.7.

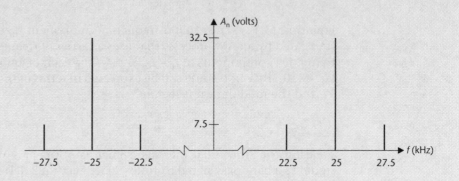

Figure 3.7 Double-sided spectrum of AM waveform in Worked example 3.2.

3.3.2 Arbitrary message signal

In practice, a message signal consists of a band of frequencies from f_1 to f_m, where f_1 may be zero and f_m is finite. We will represent this band of frequencies symbolically by the trapezoidal spectrum shown in Fig. 3.8. If this message signal is used to modulate a carrier of frequency f_c, then following Eq. (3.12)

$$f_1|_{V_1} \xrightarrow[f_c]{\text{AM}} (f_c - f_1)|_{\frac{1}{2}V_1} + (f_c + f_1)|_{\frac{1}{2}V_1}$$

$$f_m|_{V_m} \xrightarrow[f_c]{\text{AM}} (f_c - f_m)|_{\frac{1}{2}V_m} + (f_c + f_m)|_{\frac{1}{2}V_m}$$

The above frequency translation is shown in Fig. 3.9. Each of the remaining frequency components of the message signal is translated to an upper side frequency in the range $f_c + f_1$ to $f_c + f_m$, and a lower side frequency lying between $f_c - f_m$ and $f_c - f_1$. The result is that the message signal spectrum is translated to an upper sideband (USB) and a lower sideband (LSB) as shown in Fig. 3.10. The shape of the message spectrum is preserved in the sidebands, although the LSB is mirror-inverted while the USB is erect. However, the amplitude of each sideband is reduced by a factor of 2 compared to the message spectrum. The condition $f_c > f_m$ ensures that the LSB lies entirely along the positive frequency axis and does not overlap with the negative-frequency LSB in a

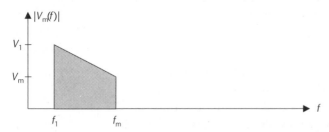

Figure 3.8 Symbolic representation of the amplitude spectrum of a message signal.

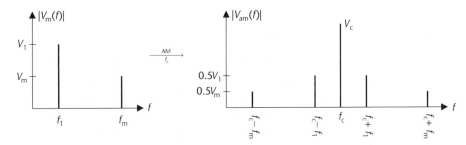

Figure 3.9 Translation of the maximum and minimum frequency components of a message signal in AM.

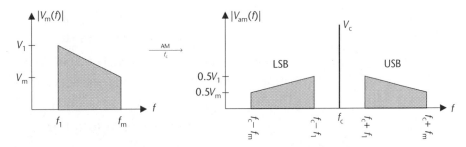

Figure 3.10 Production of lower and upper sidebands in AM.

double-sided spectrum. We will see that for the AM waveform to have an envelope that can be easily detected at the receiver, the carrier frequency must be much larger than the highest frequency component f_m in the message signal. That is,

$$f_c \gg f_m \tag{3.14}$$

A message signal (also called baseband signal) is always regarded as a low-pass signal, since it usually contains positive frequency components near zero. Its bandwidth is therefore equal to the highest significant frequency component f_m. Thus, the message signal whose spectrum is represented by Fig. 3.8 has bandwidth f_m, rather than $f_m - f_1$, which would be the case if the signal were treated as bandpass. The AM signal, on the other hand, results from the frequency translation of a baseband signal, and is therefore a bandpass signal with a bandwidth equal to the width of the band of significant positive frequencies. It follows that for an arbitrary message signal of bandwidth f_m, the AM bandwidth (see Fig. 3.10) is given by

$$(f_c + f_m) - (f_c - f_m) = 2f_m$$

In general,

$$\text{AM bandwidth} = 2 \times \text{Message bandwidth} \tag{3.15}$$

WORKED EXAMPLE   3.3

A 1 MHz carrier is amplitude modulated by a music signal that contains frequency components from 20 Hz to 15 kHz. Determine

(a) The frequencies in the AM signal and sketch its double-sided amplitude spectrum.

(b) The transmission bandwidth of the AM signal.

(a) Carrier frequency $f_c = 1$ MHz and the message frequency band is from $f_1 = 20$ Hz to $f_m = 15$ kHz. The AM signal therefore contains the following frequencies:

(i) Lower sideband (LSB) in the frequency range

$$f_c - (f_1 \rightarrow f_m) = 1\,\text{MHz} - (20\,\text{Hz} \rightarrow 15\,\text{kHz})$$
$$= \textbf{985 kHz} \rightarrow \textbf{999.98 kHz}$$

(ii) Carrier frequency at $f_c = 1$ MHz = **1000 kHz**.

(iii) Upper sideband (LSB) in the frequency range

$$f_c + (f_1 \rightarrow f_m) = 1\,\text{MHz} + (20\,\text{Hz} \rightarrow 15\,\text{kHz})$$
$$= \textbf{1000.02 kHz} \rightarrow \textbf{1015 kHz}$$

The double-sided spectrum is shown in Fig. 3.11. Note that this plot is a mixture of a discrete spectrum (for the carrier) with the y-axis in volts, and a continuous spectrum (for the sidebands) with the y-axis in volt/Hz.

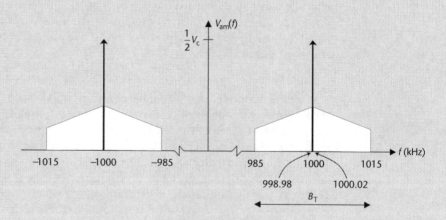

Figure 3.11   AM spectrum in Worked example 3.3.

(b) The transmission bandwidth B_T is given by Eq. (3.15):

$$B_T = 2f_m = 2 \times 15\,\text{kHz} = \textbf{30 kHz}$$

Note that B_T is the width of the positive frequency band in Fig. 3.11.

3.3.3 Power

The distribution of power in AM between the carrier and sidebands is easier to determine using the spectrum of a carrier modulated by a sinusoidal message signal. This spectrum is shown in Fig. 3.6(c), from which we obtain the following (normalised) power distribution:

Power in carrier:

$$P_c = \frac{V_c^2}{2} \tag{3.16}$$

Power in upper side frequency (USF):

$$P_{USF} = \frac{(V_m/2)^2}{2} = \frac{V_m^2}{8} = \frac{(mV_c)^2}{8}$$
$$= \frac{m^2 P_c}{4} \tag{3.17}$$

Power in lower side frequency (LSF):

$$P_{LSF} = P_{USF} = \frac{m^2 P_c}{4} \tag{3.18}$$

Power in side frequencies (SF):

$$P_{SF} = P_{LSF} + P_{USF} = \frac{m^2 P_c}{2} \tag{3.19}$$

Total power in AM waveform:

$$P_t = P_c + P_{SF} = P_c + \frac{m^2 P_c}{2}$$
$$= P_c\left(1 + \frac{m^2}{2}\right) \tag{3.20}$$

Equation (3.19) states that the total power P_{SF} in the side frequencies is a fraction $m^2/2$ of the power in the carrier. Thus, P_{SF} increases with modulation factor. The maximum total side frequency power P_{SFmax} is 50% of the carrier power, and this is obtained when $m = 1$, i.e. at 100% modulation. We may use Eq. (3.20) to express P_c in terms of P_t,

$$P_c = \frac{P_t}{1 + m^2/2} = \frac{2}{2 + m^2} P_t \tag{3.21}$$

This allows us to determine P_{SF} as a fraction of the total power in the AM waveform as follows

$$P_{SF} = P_t - P_c = P_t - \left(\frac{2}{2 + m^2}\right)P_t = P_t\left(1 - \frac{2}{2 + m^2}\right)$$
$$= \frac{m^2}{2 + m^2} P_t \tag{3.22}$$

Therefore the maximum power in side frequencies, obtained at 100% modulation ($m = 1$), is

$$P_{SF\,max} = \frac{1}{2+1}P_t = \frac{1}{3}P_t \tag{3.23}$$

This corresponds to a minimum carrier power

$$P_{c\,min} = \frac{2}{3}P_t \tag{3.24}$$

Equation (3.24) may also be obtained by putting $m = 1$ in Eq. (3.21). It shows that at least 2/3 of the transmitted AM power is contained in the carrier, which carries no information. The side bands, which contain all the transmitted information, are only fed with at most one-third of the transmitted power. This is a serious demerit of AM.

Eqs. (3.16)–(3.24) were derived assuming a sinusoidal modulating signal, but they are equally applicable to all AM signals involving arbitrary message signals. The only change is that LSF, USF and SF are replaced by LSB, USB and SB (sideband), respectively. The frequency domain representation of the arbitrary message and AM signals was presented in Fig. 3.10. The above equations are applicable to this general case provided we define the modulation factor m in terms of the total sideband power P_{SB} and carrier power P_c as follows (based on Eq. (3.19)):

$$m = \sqrt{\frac{2P_{SB}}{P_c}} \tag{3.25}$$

WORKED EXAMPLE 3.4 _____

An AM broadcast station operates at a modulation index of 95%.

(a) Determine what percentage of the total transmitted power is in the sidebands.

(b) If the transmitted power is 40 kW when the modulating signal is switched off, determine the total transmitted power at 95% modulation.

(a) Using Eq. (3.22), the ratio of sideband power P_{SF} to total power P_t is

$$\frac{P_{SF}}{P_t} = \frac{m^2}{2+m^2} = \frac{0.95^2}{2+0.95^2} = 0.311$$

Therefore 31.1% of the total power is in the sidebands.

(b) The unmodulated carrier power $P_c = 40$ kW. Using Eq. (3.21), the total transmitted power P_t is given by

$$P_t = P_c\left(1 + \frac{m^2}{2}\right) = 40\left(1 + \frac{0.95^2}{2}\right)$$
$$= 40(1 + 0.45) = 58 \text{ kW}$$

WORKED EXAMPLE   **3.5**

The carrier $v_c(t) = 100\sin(3 \times 10^6 \pi t)$ V is amplitude modulated by the signal $v_m(t) = 60\sin(80 \times 10^3 \pi t) + 30\sin(100 \times 10^3 \pi t)$ V.

(a) Determine the total power in the AM wave.
(b) Determine the modulation index.

(a) Carrier amplitude $V_c = 100$ V, and carrier frequency $f_c = 1.5$ MHz. The message signal contains two frequencies $f_1 = 40$ kHz with amplitude 60 V, and $f_2 = 50$ kHz with amplitude 30 V. From Eq. (3.12), the AM wave has the following frequency components, which are shown in the single-sided spectrum of Fig. 3.12:

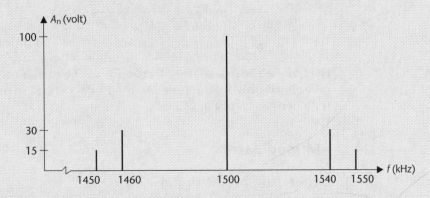

Figure 3.12   AM spectrum in Worked example 3.5.

(i) $f_c - f_2 = 1450$ kHz with amplitude 15 V.
(ii) $f_c - f_1 = 1460$ kHz with amplitude 30 V.
(iii) $f_c = 1500$ kHz with amplitude 100 V.
(iv) $f_c + f_1 = 1540$ kHz with amplitude 30 V.
(v) $f_c + f_2 = 1550$ kHz with amplitude 15 V.

The total power P_t in the AM wave is the sum of the power of each of these components; see Section 2.5. Therefore,

$$P_t = \frac{15^2}{2} + \frac{30^2}{2} + \frac{100^2}{2} + \frac{30^2}{2} + \frac{15^2}{2}$$
$$= 6125 \text{ W}$$

(b) The modulation index can be determined from Eq. (3.25). The carrier power P_c, i.e. the power in the frequency component f_c, and the total sideband power P_{SF} are given by

$$P_c = \frac{100^2}{2} = 5000 \text{ W}$$
$$P_{SF} = P_t - P_c = 6125 - 5000 \text{ W} = 1125 \text{ W}$$

Therefore the modulation index is

$$\sqrt{\frac{2P_{SB}}{P_c}} \times 100\% = \sqrt{\frac{2250}{5000}} \times 100\%$$

$$= 67\%$$

You may wish to verify, using the last result of the above worked example, that in the case of a message signal consisting of multiple tones (i.e. sinusoids) of amplitudes V_1, V_2, V_3, ..., the modulation factor m can be obtained from the following formula:

$$m = \sqrt{(V_1/V_c)^2 + (V_2/V_c)^2 + (V_3/V_c)^2 + \cdots}$$
$$= \sqrt{m_1^2 + m_2^2 + m_3^2 + \cdots} \tag{3.26}$$

Here, m_1 is the modulation factor due to the carrier of amplitude V_c being modulated only by the tone of amplitude V_1, and so on. See Question 3.5 for a derivation of Eq. (3.26).

3.4 AM modulators

3.4.1 Generation of AM signals

AM signals can be generated using two different methods. In one, the carrier is passed through a device that has its gain varied linearly by the modulating signal, and in the other, both the carrier and modulating signal are passed through a non-linear device.

3.4.1.1 Linearly varied gain modulator

The first method is illustrated in Fig. 3.13. The carrier signal is transmitted through a device whose gain G is varied linearly by the modulating signal according to the relation

$$G = 1 + k_1 v_m(t) \tag{3.27}$$

The output of the device is given by

$$\begin{aligned} v_o(t) &= Gv_i(t) \\ &= [1 + k_1 v_m(t)]V_c \cos(2\pi f_c t) \\ &= [V_c + kv_m(t)]\cos(2\pi f_c t), \qquad k = k_1 V_c \\ &\equiv v_{am}(t) \end{aligned} \tag{3.28}$$

The output is therefore an AM signal. This modulator has a modulation sensitivity $k = k_1 v_c$, where k_1 is a constant that determines the sensitivity of the gain G to the value of the modulating signal. The *operational amplifier* (opamp) configuration shown in Fig. 3.13(b) has the gain variation given

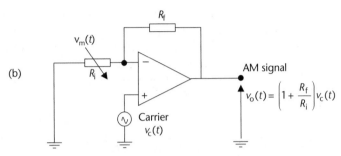

Figure 3.13 (a) AM generation using a variable gain device; (b) opamp implementation.

by Eq. (3.27), and therefore will implement this method of amplitude modulation. The variable input resistance R_i is provided by a field-effect transistor (FET), which is biased (using a fixed DC voltage) to operate at the centre of its linear characteristic. A modulating signal $v_m(t)$ connected to its gate then causes the FET to be more conducting as $v_m(t)$ increases. In effect, the source-to-drain conductance G_i (= $1/R_i$) of the FET is made to vary linearly with the modulating signal:

$$G_i = av_m(t) = \frac{1}{R_i}$$

or

$$R_i = \frac{1}{av_m(t)} \tag{3.29}$$

Two important characteristics of an opamp, in the configuration shown, are that both the inverting (labelled –) and non-inverting (labelled +) terminals are forced to the same potential, and negligible current flows into either of these terminals. There are two implications:

1. The absence of current flow into the inverting terminal implies that the same current flows through R_f and R_i, which are therefore in series. Thus, the voltage v_0 is shared between R_f and R_i according to the ratio of their resistance. In particular, the voltage drop across R_i, which is the voltage at the inverting terminal is given by

$$v_- = \frac{R_i}{R_f + R_i} v_o$$

2.   The voltage $v_- = v_c$, since the two terminals are at the same potential. Therefore the output voltage v_o and the carrier voltage v_c are related by

$$v_o = \frac{R_i + R_f}{R_i} v_c = \left[1 + \frac{R_f}{R_i} \right] v_c \qquad (3.30)$$

Substituting Eq. (3.29) for R_i gives the gain of the opamp circuit:

$$G = \frac{v_o}{v_c} = 1 + R_f a v_m(t) = 1 + k_1 v_m(t)$$

We see that the amplifier has a gain that varies linearly with modulating signal as specified by Eq. (3.27), with $k_1 = R_f a$, and therefore v_o is the AM signal given by Eq. (3.28).

3.4.1.2   Switching and square-law modulators

The second method for generating an AM signal is by adding together the carrier and modulating signals, and then passing the sum signal through a non-linear device. Diodes and suitably biased transistors provide the required non-linear characteristic. Transistors are, however, preferred because they also provide signal amplification. The summation can be realised by connecting the carrier and message voltages in series at the input of the non-linear device, so that the device input is

$$v_i(t) = v_m(t) + v_c(t) \qquad (3.31)$$

Switching modulator   The device is called a *switching modulator* if the principle of operation is by the device being switched on and off (at the carrier frequency) during the positive half of the carrier signal cycle. This requires that the carrier amplitude be much greater than the peak value of the message signal so that switching action is controlled entirely by the carrier signal. The output voltage $v_o(t)$ equals input voltage $v_i(t)$ during one half of the carrier frequency (when the device is on), and equals zero during the remaining half cycle (when the device is off). Therefore the output is effectively the product of input signal and a periodic square wave $v_s(t)$, which has amplitude 1 during half the carrier cycle (when the device is on), and amplitude 0 during the other half cycle (when the device is off). Note then that $v_s(t)$ has period $T = 1/f_c$. We may write

$$v_o(t) = v_i(t) v_s(t) = [v_m(t) + v_c(t)] v_s(t) \qquad (3.32)$$

Recall from Chapter 2 that $v_s(t)$ can be written as a Fourier series

$$v_s(t) = A_o + A_1 \cos(2\pi f_c t) + \cdots$$

Substituting this expression in Eq. (3.32) and assuming for simplicity a sinusoidal message signal, we obtain the output signal

$$v_o(t) = [V_m \cos(2\pi f_m t) + V_c \cos(2\pi f_c t)][A_o + A_1 \cos(2\pi f_c t) + \cdots]$$

$$= A_o V_m \cos(2\pi f_m t)$$

$$+ A_o V_c \cos(2\pi f_c t) + A_1 V_m \cos(2\pi f_m t) A_1 \cos(2\pi f_c t)$$

$$+ A_1 V_c \cos^2(2\pi f_c t) + \cdots \tag{3.33}$$

$$= A_o V_c \cos(2\pi f_c t) + \frac{A_1 V_m}{2} \cos 2\pi(f_c - f_m)t + \frac{A_1 V_m}{2} \cos 2\pi(f_c + f_m)t$$

$$+ \frac{A_1 V_c}{2} + A_o V_m \cos(2\pi f_m t) + \frac{A_1 V_c}{2} \cos(4\pi f_c t) + \cdots$$

The output $v_o(t)$ therefore contains the three frequency components that constitute an AM signal, namely the carrier at f_c, the LSF at $f_c - f_m$, and the USF at $f_c + f_m$. However, it also contains other components at DC (i.e. $f = 0$), the message frequency f_m, even harmonics of the carrier frequency (i.e. $2f_c$, $4f_c$, $6f_c$, ...), and side frequencies around odd harmonics of the carrier frequency (i.e. $3f_c \pm f_m$, $5f_c \pm f_m$, ...). You may verify this by including more terms in the Fourier series representation of $v_s(t)$, bearing in mind that it contains only odd harmonics of f_c. To obtain the required AM signal $v_{am}(t)$, we pass $v_o(t)$ through a bandpass filter centred on f_c and having a bandwidth equal to twice the message bandwidth. This filter passes the carrier frequency and the two side bands, and blocks all the other frequency components in $v_o(t)$ including f_m, the maximum frequency component in the message signal. The lowest frequency in the LSB is $f_c - f_m$, and this frequency must be larger than f_m for the message signal to be excluded by the filter. Thus, the following condition must be satisfied,

$$f_c > 2f_m \tag{3.34}$$

Square-law modulator The non-linear circuit is called a *square-law modulator* if the device is continuously on, but with a variable resistance that depends on the input voltage. In this case, the output voltage is a non-linear function of input voltage, which may be approximated by the quadratic expression

$$v_o(t) = a v_i(t) + b v_i^2(t) \tag{3.35}$$

Substituting Eq. (3.31) for $v_i(t)$, and again assuming a sinusoidal message signal for simplicity,

$$v_o(t) = a[V_m \cos(2\pi f_m t) + V_c \cos(2\pi f_c t)]$$

$$+ b[V_m \cos(2\pi f_m t) + V_c \cos(2\pi f_c t)]^2 \tag{3.36}$$

Expanding and simplifying the above equation, using the trigonometric identities in Appendix A, we obtain

$$v_o(t) = \tfrac{1}{2} b(V_c^2 + V_m^2) + a V_m \cos(2\pi f_m t) + \tfrac{1}{2} b V_m^2 \cos(4\pi f_m t)$$

$$+ a V_c \cos(2\pi f_c t) + b V_c V_m \cos 2\pi(f_c - f_m)t$$

$$+ b V_c V_m \cos 2\pi(f_c + f_m)t \tag{3.37}$$

$$+ \tfrac{1}{2} b V_c^2 \cos(4\pi f_c t)$$

Notice that $v_o(t)$ contains the AM signal comprising the carrier f_c and sidebands $f_c \pm f_m$. However, there are also other components at DC, f_m, $2f_m$ and

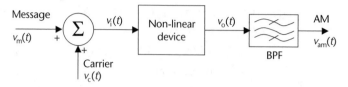

Figure 3.14 Square-law and switching (AM) modulator.

$2f_c$. These extra components can be excluded using a bandpass filter as discussed above for the switching modulator. Because there is a component at twice the message frequency $2f_m$, which must be excluded by the filter while still passing the LSB, it means that if f_m is the maximum frequency component of the message signal, then the following condition must be satisfied:

$$f_c > 3f_m \tag{3.38}$$

In Eq. (3.35), the non-linear characteristic was approximated by a polynomial of order $N = 2$. In practice, a higher-order polynomial may be required to represent the input–output relationship of the non-linear device. But the AM signal can still be obtained as discussed above using a bandpass filter, provided the carrier frequency is sufficiently higher than the maximum frequency component f_m of the message signal. There will in this general case be a component in $v_o(t)$ at Nf_m, and therefore the carrier frequency must satisfy the condition

$$f_c > (N+1)f_m \tag{3.39}$$

Figure 3.14 shows a block diagram of the AM modulator based on the non-linear principle — switching or square-law. The bandpass filter is usually realised using an LC tuned circuit, which has a resonance frequency f_c, and a bandwidth that is just large enough to pass the sidebands.

3.4.2 AM transmitters

The AM transmitter is used to launch electromagnetic waves that carry information in their amplitude variations. It can be implemented using either low-level or high-level modulation.

3.4.2.1 Low-level transmitter

Low-level modulation uses a non-linear device, such as diode, bipolar junction transistor (BJT), or field-effect transistor (FET), to generate a weak AM signal. This signal is then amplified in one or more linear amplifiers to bring it to the required high power level before radiation by an antenna. A low-level modulation system is shown in Fig. 3.15, where the amplitude modulator block consists of a non-linear device followed by a bandpass filter.

The radio frequency (RF) power amplifiers must be linear in order to preserve the AM signal envelope, avoiding the non-linear distortions

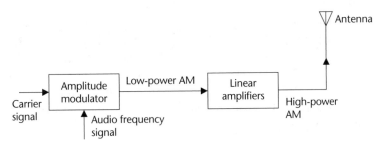

Figure 3.15 Low-level AM transmitter.

discussed in Section 2.9.3. The main disadvantage of these linear amplifiers is that they are highly inefficient in converting DC power to RF power. Transmitters for AM broadcasting rarely use low-level operation. The method is however widely used on international HF links for radio-telephony.

3.4.2.2 *High-level transmitter*

In high-level modulation, the message signal directly varies the carrier amplitude in the final RF amplifier stage of the transmitter. Figure 3.16 shows the block diagram of a standard high-level broadcast transmitter. The carrier is generated by a crystal-controlled oscillator and amplified by a number of Class C tuned RF amplifiers. Some of these amplifiers may be operated as frequency multipliers to give the desired carrier frequency f_c. The audio input is linearly amplified, and this may be by a Class A audio amplifier followed by a high-power Class B audio amplifier. This raises the audio signal to a level required to sufficiently modulate the carrier. The high-power audio is then connected (via transformer coupling) to a final (non-linear) Class C tuned RF amplifier of passband $f_c - 5$ kHz to $f_c + 5$ kHz, where it amplitude modulates the high-power carrier signal. This gives a high-power AM signal that is launched by the antenna. High-power transmitters that radiate several kilowatts of power still use thermionic valves, at least in the last stage of amplification. However, low-power transmitters such as used in mobile units may be fully implemented using solid state components.

The main advantage of the high-level transmitter is that it allows the use of the highly efficient, albeit non-linear, Class C tuned amplifiers throughout the RF section. Unlike the audio signal, the single-frequency carrier can be non-linearly amplified since the tuned section can be readily

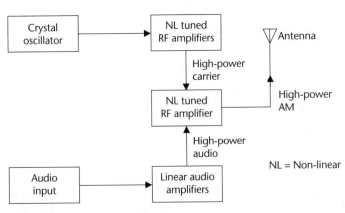

Figure 3.16 High-level AM transmitter.

designed to eliminate the resulting harmonic products. The main drawback of a high-level transmitter is that it requires a high-power audio signal, which can only be achieved by using expensive high-power linear amplifiers. Nevertheless, almost all AM transmitters use high-level operation due to the above-mentioned overriding advantage.

3.5 AM demodulators

Demodulation is the process of recovering the message signal from the received modulated carrier. If the message signal is digital the demodulation process is more specifically called *detection* since the receiver detects the range of the modulated parameter and is not concerned with determining its precise value. However, beware! The most common usage treats demodulation and detection as synonymous terms.

A simple yet highly efficient circuit for demodulating an AM signal is commonly called an *envelope* or *diode detector*, although a more appropriate name is *envelope* or *diode demodulator*. This is a non-coherent demodulation technique, which does not require a locally generated carrier. *Coherent demodulation* is also possible, involving mixing the AM signal with a reference carrier (extracted from the incoming AM signal), but this a much more complex circuit and therefore is not commonly used.

The input signal at a receiver usually consists of several weak carriers and their associated sidebands. A complete receiver system must therefore include an arrangement for isolating and amplifying the desired carrier before demodulation. A very efficient technique for achieving this goal is based on the *superheterodyne* principle, which we also discuss in this section.

3.5.1 Diode demodulator

A simple diode demodulator circuit is shown in Fig. 3.17(a). The circuit consists of a diode, which has the ideal characteristic shown in Fig. 3.17(b), in series with an RC filter. The AM signal $v_{am}(t)$ is fed from a source with internal resistance R_s.

When the diode is reverse-biased, i.e. v_D is negative, no current flows. That is, the diode has an infinite resistance ($R_r = \infty$) when reverse-biased. Under a forward bias (i.e. v_D positive), the diode has a small and constant resistance R_f equal to the ratio of forward-bias voltage v_D to diode current i_D. To understand the operation of the demodulator, let the AM signal $v_{am}(t)$ be as shown in Fig. 3.17(c). This consists of a 50 kHz carrier that is 80% modulated by a 1 kHz sinusoidal message signal. Thus,

$$v_{am}(t) = V_c[1 + m\sin(2\pi f_m t)]\sin(2\pi f_c t)$$
$$= V_{am}(t)\sin(2\pi f_c t) \tag{3.40}$$

with $m = 0.8$, and the envelope $V_{am}(t) = V_c[1 + m\sin(2\pi f_m t)]$. During the first positive cycle of $v_{am}(t)$, the diode is forward-biased (i.e. $v_D \geq 0$) and has a small resistance R_f. The capacitor C then charges rapidly from 0 V towards $V_{am}(1/4f_c)$, which is the value of the envelope v_{am} at $t = 1/4f_c$. At the instant

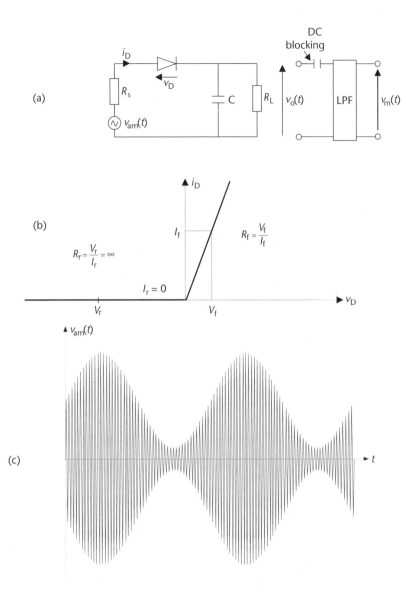

Figure 3.17 Diode demodulator: (a) circuit; (b) ideal diode characteristic; (c) input AM signal (*continues overleaf*).

$t = 1/4f_c$, the AM signal $v_{am}(t)$ begins to drop in value below $V_{am}(1/4f_c)$, which causes the diode to be reverse-biased, since its positive terminal is now at a lower potential than its negative terminal. With the diode effectively an open circuit, the capacitor discharges slowly towards 0 V through the load resistance R_L, and this continues for the remaining half of the first positive cycle and for the entire duration of the first negative cycle of $v_{am}(t)$.

During the second positive cycle of $v_{am}(t)$, the diode becomes forward-biased again at the instant that $v_{am}(t)$ exceeds the (remaining) capacitor

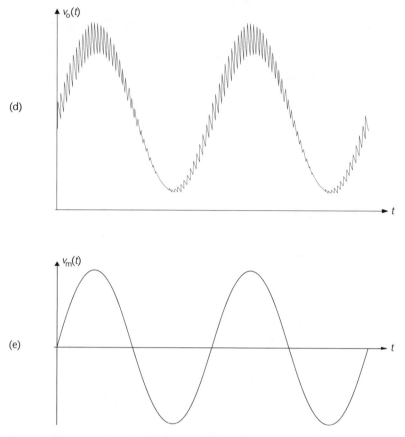

Figure 3.17 (*continued*)   (d) Output signal; (e) message signal.

voltage. The capacitor then rapidly charges towards $V_{am}(5/4f_c)$. At the instant $t = 5/4f_c$, the input $v_{am}(t)$ begins to drop below $V_{am}(5/4f_c)$, the diode becomes reverse-biased, and the capacitor again begins to discharge slowly towards 0 V.

The process just described is repeated over and over, and this gives rise to the output signal $v_0(t)$ shown in Fig. 3.17(d). The output signal contains two large frequency components — one at DC and the other at the message frequency(s) f_m, and several small (unwanted) components or *ripples* at frequencies $f = nf_c$, and $nf_c \pm f_m$, where $n = 1, 2, 3, \ldots$. The DC component is often used for *automatic gain control*. It can be removed by passing $v_0(t)$ through a large DC-blocking capacitor. The ripples are usually ignored — being outside the audible range of frequencies — but can be easily removed by low-pass filtering. If both DC and ripples are removed it leaves a smooth message signal $v_m(t)$ shown in Fig. 3.17(e).

For the diode demodulator to work properly as described above, a number of important conditions must be satisfied. Before stating these conditions it is important to note that when a capacitor C charges or discharges through a resistor R from an initial voltage V_i (at $t = 0$) towards a final voltage V_f (at $t = \infty$),

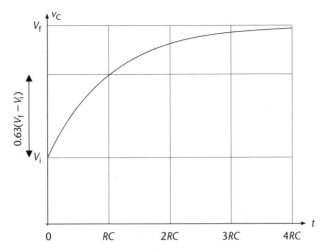

Figure 3.18 Exponential rise in voltage across a capacitor *C* that is charging through resistor *R* from an initial voltage V_i towards a final voltage V_f.

the voltage drop v_C across the capacitor changes exponentially according to the expression

$$v_C(t) = V_f - (V_f - V_i)\exp\left(-\frac{t}{RC}\right) \tag{3.41}$$

The capacitor is charging if $V_f > V_i$, and discharging if $V_f < V_i$. Figure 3.18 shows the voltage across a charging capacitor. The maximum change in capacitor voltage from its initial value at $t = 0$ to its final value at t = ∞ is $V_f - V_i$. After a time $t = RC$, the voltage has changed to

$$v_c(RC) = V_f - (V_f - V_i)\exp(-1)$$
$$= V_f - 0.368(V_f - V_i)$$

and the amount of voltage change in the time from $t = 0$ to $t = RC$ is

$$v_c(RC) - v_c(0) = V_f - 0.368(V_f - V_i) - V_i$$
$$= 0.632(V_f - V_i)$$

This is 63.2% of the maximum change. This time interval is called the *time constant* of the series *RC* circuit. That is, the capacitor voltage undergoes 63.2% of its total change within the initial time of one time constant. The rate of voltage change slows down continuously with time, so that in fact the capacitor only approaches but never actually reaches 100% of its maximum possible change, except until $t = ∞$. The smaller the time constant, the more rapidly the capacitor charges or discharges, and the larger the time constant the longer it takes the capacitor to charge or discharge. We may now state the conditions that must be satisfied in the design of the envelope demodulator:

1. The charging time constant must be short enough to allow the capacitor to charge rapidly and track the AM signal up to its peak value before

the onset of the negative-going portion of the oscillation when charging is cut off by the diode. Since charging is done through resistor $R = R_f + R_s$, and the AM signal oscillates with period $T_c = 1/f_c$, this requires that

$$(R_f + R_s)C \ll \frac{1}{f_c} \qquad (3.42)$$

2. The discharging time constant must be long compared with T_c so that the capacitor voltage does not follow the AM signal to fall significantly towards 0 V during its negative-going oscillation. At the same time, the discharging time constant must be short enough for the capacitor voltage to be able to track the fastest changing component of the AM signal envelope. Knowing that this component is the maximum frequency f_m in the message signal, and that the capacitor charges through the load resistor R_L, it follows that the condition that must be satisfied is

$$\frac{1}{f_m} \gg R_L C \gg \frac{1}{f_c} \qquad (3.43)$$

3. The third condition is implied in Eq. (3.43), but is so important that it is separately stated here for emphasis. The carrier frequency f_c must be much larger than the maximum frequency component f_m of the message signal. In practice, f_c is greater than f_m by a factor of about 100 or more.

4. In the above discussions, we assumed an ideal diode characteristic (see Fig. 3.17(b)). In reality a diode has a non-linear characteristic for small values of forward-bias voltage v_D, followed by a linear characteristic (as shown in Fig. 3.17(b)) for large values of v_D. The effect of the non-linear characteristic is that diode resistance R_f becomes a function of bias voltage, and this causes the output $v_0(t)$ to be distorted in the region of small carrier amplitudes. To avoid this distortion the modulated carrier amplitude must always be above the non-linear region, which imposes the additional condition that 100% modulation cannot be employed.

Figs. 3.17 (c)–(e) were obtained using the following values:

$$
\begin{aligned}
f_c &= 50 \text{ kHz} && \text{(Carrier frequency)} \\
f_m &= 1 \text{ kHz} && \text{(Message signal frequency)} \\
R_s &= 50\ \Omega && \text{(AM signal source resistance)} \\
R_f &= 20\ \Omega && \text{(Forward-biased diode resistance)} \\
C &= 10 \text{ nF} && \text{(Charging/discharging capacitor)} \\
R_L &= 10 \text{ k}\Omega && \text{(Load resistance)} \\
m &= 0.8 && \text{(Modulation factor)}
\end{aligned}
\qquad (3.44)
$$

Note that all four conditions are satisfied by the above selection of values:

● *Condition 1*: The charging time constant = $(R_f + R_s)C = 0.7$ μs. This is much less than the carrier period $1/f_c = 20$ μs as required.

- *Condition 2*: The discharging time constant $R_LC = 100$ µs. As required, this is much less than the period of the maximum frequency component in the message signal $1/f_m = 1000$ µs and much larger (although by a factor of 5 only) than the carrier period (20 µs). A choice of carrier frequency $f_c = 100$ kHz would have satisfied this condition better, while at the same time still satisfying condition 1. However, $f_c = 50$ kHz was chosen in order to produce clearer illustrative plots for our discussion.

- *Condition 3*: The carrier frequency $f_c = 50$ kHz is much larger than the maximum frequency component ($f_m = 1$ kHz) in the message signal as required.

- *Condition 4*: The modulation depth is 80%, which is less than 100% as required.

Figure 3.19 shows the envelope demodulator output using the same values in Eq. (3.44), except that the carrier frequency is changed to $f_c = 4$ kHz. Observe that the fluctuations in the output are more than just small ripples. You should work out which of the four conditions have been flouted and explain why the capacitor discharges significantly towards zero before being recharged.

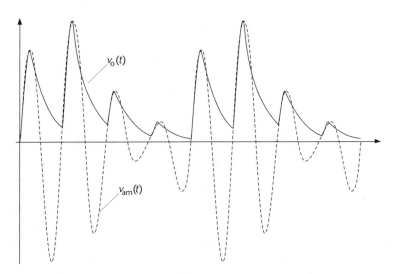

Figure 3.19 Effect on envelope demodulator output $v_o(t)$ when f_c is set to 4 kHz in Eq. (3.41). The input AM waveform $v_{am}(t)$ is also shown.

3.5.2 Coherent demodulator

Figure 3.20(a) shows the block diagram of a coherent demodulator. It consists of a multiplier and a low-pass filter. This excludes the arrangement for obtaining the carrier frequency, which is discussed later. The multiplier is also called product modulator, and its implementation will be discussed in Section 3.7. Assuming a sinusoidal message signal, the output of the multiplier is given by

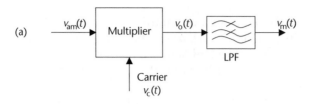

(a)

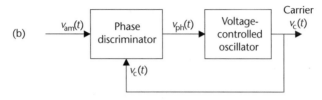

(b)

Figure 3.20 (a) Coherent AM demodulator; (b) phase-locked loop (PLL).

$$v_{\mathrm{o}}(t) = v_{\mathrm{am}}(t) \times v_{\mathrm{c}}(t) = GV_{\mathrm{c}}[1 + m\cos(2\pi f_{\mathrm{m}}t)]\cos(2\pi f_{\mathrm{c}}t) \times \cos(2\pi f_{\mathrm{c}}t)$$
$$= GV_{\mathrm{c}}\cos^2(2\pi f_{\mathrm{c}}t) + mGV_{\mathrm{c}}\cos(2\pi f_{\mathrm{m}}t)\cos^2(2\pi f_{\mathrm{c}}t)$$
$$= \frac{GV_{\mathrm{c}}}{2} + \frac{GmV_{\mathrm{c}}}{2}\cos(2\pi f_{\mathrm{m}}t)$$
$$+ \frac{GmV_{\mathrm{c}}}{4}\cos[2\pi(2f_{\mathrm{c}} - f_{\mathrm{m}})t] + \frac{GmV_{\mathrm{c}}}{4}\cos[2\pi(2f_{\mathrm{c}})t]$$
$$+ \frac{GmV_{\mathrm{c}}}{4}\cos[2\pi(2f_{\mathrm{c}} + f_{\mathrm{m}})t]$$

The constant G is a scaling factor that represents the total gain of the transmission link from transmitter output to demodulator input. The signal $v_0(t)$ contains the wanted message signal (at frequency f_{m}) and other (unwanted) components at $f = 0$, $2f_{\mathrm{c}} - f_{\mathrm{m}}$, $2f_{\mathrm{c}}$ and $2f_{\mathrm{c}} + f_{\mathrm{m}}$. The DC component ($f = 0$) is removed by a series capacitor, and the higher frequency components are filtered out by a low-pass filter that has a bandwidth just sufficient to pass the highest frequency component of the message signal.

The technique of coherent demodulation is very different from that of envelope demodulation. You will recall that amplitude modulation translates the message spectrum from baseband (centred at $f = 0$) to bandpass (centred at $-f_{\mathrm{c}}$ and $+f_{\mathrm{c}}$), without any further change to the spectrum except for a scaling factor. Coherent demodulation performs a further translation of the (bandpass) AM spectrum by $\pm f_{\mathrm{c}}$. When this is done, the band at $-f_{\mathrm{c}}$ is translated to locations $f = -2f_{\mathrm{c}}$ and 0, while the band at $+f_{\mathrm{c}}$ is translated to locations $f = 0$ and $+2f_{\mathrm{c}}$. The band of frequencies at $f = 0$ has exactly the same shape as the original message spectrum. It has twice the magnitude of the bands at $\pm 2f_{\mathrm{c}}$, being the superposition of two identical bands originally located at $\pm f_{\mathrm{c}}$. This baseband is extracted by a low-pass filter and provides the message signal $v_{\mathrm{m}}(t)$ at the output of Fig. 3.20.

The use of coherent demodulation requires that the receiver have a local carrier that is at the same frequency and phase as the transmitted carrier. Since the received AM signal already contains such a carrier, what is needed is a circuit that can extract this carrier from the AM signal. One way of achieving this is to use the *phase-locked loop* (PLL), a block diagram of which is shown in Fig. 3.20(b). This consists of a voltage-controlled oscillator (VCO), which generates a sinusoidal signal that is fed into a phase discriminator along with the incoming AM signal. The VCO is designed to have an output at the carrier frequency f_c when its input is zero. The phase discriminator includes a low-pass filter (not explicitly shown). It produces an output voltage $V_{ph}(t)$ that is proportional to the phase difference between its two inputs. If $V_{ph}(t)$ is fed as input to the VCO, then it will be proportional to the phase difference between the VCO output signal and the carrier component in the AM signal, and will cause the VCO frequency to change in order to minimise this difference. When $V_{ph}(t) = 0$, the loop is said to be locked and the output of the VCO is the required carrier.

3.5.3 AM receivers

A radio receiver performs a number of important tasks.

1. It selects one signal from the many reaching the antenna, and rejects all others. The receiver could be more easily designed to receive only one particular carrier frequency, but in most cases it is required to be able to select any one of several carrier signals (e.g. from different broadcast stations) spaced over a wide frequency range. The receiver must therefore be capable of both *tuning* (to select any desired signal) and *filtering* (to exclude the unwanted signals).

2. It provides signal *amplification* at the RF stage to boost the signal to a level sufficient to properly operate the demodulator circuit and at the baseband frequency stage to operate the information sink — a loudspeaker in the case of audio broadcast.

3. It extracts the message signal through the process of *demodulation*, which we have already discussed for the case of AM signals.

3.5.3.1 Tuned RF receiver

Figure 3.21 shows one simple design, which performs the above tasks. This design was used in the first broadcast AM receivers. It consists of a tunable RF amplifier that amplifies and passes only the desired carrier and its associated sidebands, an envelope demodulator that extracts the audio signal,

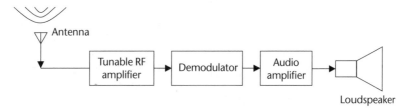

Figure 3.21 Tunable radio frequency (TRF) receiver.

and an audio amplifier that drives a loudspeaker. Called the *tuned radio frequency* (TRF) receiver, this implementation has serious drawbacks.

It is difficult to design the RF amplifier with the required level of selectivity, since the bandwidth needs to be as small as 10 kHz to separate adjacent AM broadcast carriers. Several stages of tuned circuits are required, and this poses problems with stray capacitance and inductance, which give rise to unwanted feedback and possible oscillations. Furthermore, each circuit stage is tuned by a separate variable capacitor, and *gang-tuning* these stages (i.e. arranging for all the variable capacitors to be adjusted by a single control knob) is no small mechanical challenge.

The bandwidth of a TRF receiver varies depending on the resonance frequency f_c to which the above stages have been tuned. The Q of a tuned circuit (i.e. a bandpass filter) is defined as the ratio of its centre frequency f_c to its bandwidth B. This ratio remains roughly the same as the capacitance is varied (to change f_c). The bandwidth of a TRF receiver therefore changes roughly proportionately with f_c. For example, a receiver that has a bandwidth $B = 10$ kHz at the centre (1090 kHz) of the medium wave band (540–1640 kHz), will have a narrower bandwidth $B = 4.95$ kHz when tuned to a carrier frequency at the bottom end of the band. This is a reduction by a factor of 1090/540. If this receiver is tuned to a carrier at the top end of the band, its bandwidth will be about 15.05 kHz, representing an increase by a factor of 1640/1090. Thus, at one end we have impaired fidelity due to reduced bandwidth, and at the other end we have increased noise and interference from adjacent channels due to excessive bandwidth.

3.5.3.2 Superheterodyne receiver

The superheterodyne receiver (or *superhet* for short) is an elegant solution that performs all the required receiver functions without the drawbacks of the TRF receiver discussed above. The desired RF carrier is translated to a fixed intermediate frequency (IF), which is the same irrespective of the carrier frequency selected. The bulk of required amplification and selectivity is performed at the IF stage. This IF amplifier can be more easily designed since it is required to amplify a fixed band of frequencies. All commercial receivers for analogue radio and TV are superhet. Figure 3.22

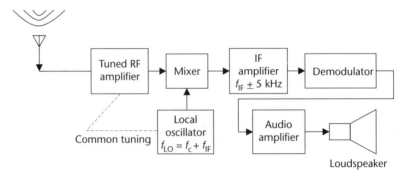

Figure 3.22 The superheterodyne AM receiver.

shows the block diagram of an AM superhet receiver. The operation of the superhet receiver is as discussed below.

Frequency translation To select the desired transmission at carrier frequency f_c, the local oscillator and the RF amplifier are tuned together so that the local oscillator frequency is always at a fixed frequency f_{IF} above f_c. This frequency f_{IF} is called the intermediate frequency (IF) — being lower than the incoming RF carrier frequency and higher than the message baseband frequencies. For AM radio with RF carrier in the frequency range 540–1640 kHz, f_{IF} = 470 kHz (or 455 kHz in North America), and for FM radio with RF carrier in the range 88–108 MHz, f_{IF} is typically 10.7 MHz. Thus,

$$f_{LO} = f_c + f_{IF} \tag{3.45}$$

The required frequency translation could also be achieved with the local oscillator maintained at frequency f_{IF} below the incoming carrier, rather than *above* the carrier frequency as specified in Eq. (3.45). However, this is not done in practice because it would lead to a much larger ratio between the highest oscillator frequency (needed to receive a transmission at the top end of the band) and the lowest oscillator frequency (needed to receive a transmission at the bottom end of the band). Take the example of an AM radio receiver that covers the RF carrier range 540 to 1640 kHz with f_{IF} = 470 kHz. For f_{LO} above f_c,

$$f_{LOmin} = f_{cmin} + f_{IF} = 540 + 470 = 1010 \text{ kHz}$$
$$f_{LOmax} = f_{cmax} + f_{IF} = 1640 + 470 = 2110 \text{ kHz}$$

This gives a ratio f_{LOmax}/f_{LOmin} = 2.1, whereas for f_{LO} below f_c,

$$f_{LOmin} = f_{cmin} - f_{IF} = 540 - 470 = 70 \text{ kHz}$$
$$f_{LOmax} = f_{cmax} - f_{IF} = 1640 - 470 = 1170 \text{ kHz}$$

This is a ratio f_{LOmax}/f_{LOmin} = 16.7, which is more difficult to achieve using a variable capacitor in the LO circuit.

The mixer is a non-linear device that multiplies the modulated carrier at f_c with the sinusoidal signal generated by the local oscillator at frequency f_{LO}. The result is that the message signal, carried by the carrier at f_c, is translated to new frequency locations at the sum and difference frequencies

$$f_{LO} \pm f_c = f_c + f_{IF} \pm f_c$$
$$= 2f_c + f_{IF} \quad \text{and} \quad f_{IF}$$

Intermediate frequency (IF) amplifier The IF stage provides tuned amplification with a pass band of 10 kHz (for AM radio) centred at f_{IF}. This amplifier therefore performs the following functions.

1. It rejects the sum-frequency signal at $2f_c + f_{IF}$, since this is outside its pass band.

2. It amplifies the difference-frequency signal at f_{IF} to a level required for the correct operation of the demodulator. Note that this signal carries

the exact sidebands of the original RF carrier. The mixer merely translated this carrier along with its sidebands without any distortion.

3. It removes any adjacent channels since these also lie outside its pass band.

Image interference The superhet receiver has the disadvantageous possibility for simultaneous reception of two different transmissions, one at the desired frequency f_c, and the other at a frequency f_i equal to twice the intermediate frequency above the desired frequency. The frequency f_i is referred to as the *image frequency* of f_c. To see how this happens, note that the unwanted transmission at a carrier frequency $f_i = f_c + 2f_{IF}$ would be translated by the mixer to the sum and difference frequencies

$$f_i \pm f_{LO} = f_c + 2f_{IF} \pm f_{LO}$$
$$= f_c + 2f_{IF} \pm (f_c + f_{IF})$$
$$= 2f_c + 3f_{IF} \quad \text{and} \quad f_{IF}$$

While the sum frequency at $2f_c + 3f_{IF}$ is of course rejected at the IF stage, the difference frequency equals f_{IF} and is not rejected. The transmission at f_i is therefore also received. It interferes with the wanted transmission at f_c. This problem is known as *image interference*. A practical solution to this undesirable simultaneous reception of two transmissions is to use selective stages in the RF section that discriminate against the undesired image signal. However, the image frequency is located far away from the wanted carrier — a separation of $2f_{IF}$. Thus, the pass band of the RF section does not need to be as narrow as in the case of the TRF receiver, which is required to pass only the wanted carrier and its side bands.

WORKED EXAMPLE **3.6**

(a) Describe how an incoming AM radio transmission at a carrier frequency of 1 MHz would be processed. Assume an intermediate frequency $f_{IF} = 470$ kHz.

(b) What is the image frequency of this transmission?

(a) The action of using a control knob to tune to the transmission at $f_c = 1000$ kHz also sets the local oscillator frequency to

$$f_{LO} = f_c + f_{IF} = 1000 + 470 = 1470 \text{ kHz}$$

The RF amplifier is thus adjusted to have a passband centred on f_c. It boosts the carrier at f_c and its sidebands, but heavily attenuates other transmissions at frequencies far from f_c, including the image frequency. The amplified carrier and its sidebands are passed to the mixer, which translates f_c (along with the message signal carried by f_c in its sidebands) to two new frequencies, one at $f_{LO} + f_c = 2470$ kHz, and the other at $f_{LO} - f_c = 470$ kHz. The copy of the signal at 2470 kHz is rejected by the IF bandpass filters, while the other copy at the IF frequency of 470 kHz is amplified and applied to an envelope demodulator, which extracts the message signal. The message signal is amplified in a linear audio amplifier, which drives a loudspeaker that converts the message signal to audible sound.

(b) The image frequency f_i is given by

$$f_i = f_c + 2f_{IF} = 1000 + 2 \times 470 = 1940 \text{ kHz}$$

To confirm that this is correct, we check that f_i is translated by the mixer to a difference frequency equal to the intermediate frequency:

$$f_i - f_{LO} = 1940 - 1470 = 470 \text{ kHz}$$

3.6 Merits, demerits and applications of AM

The most important advantage of amplitude modulation over other modulation techniques is its circuit simplicity. Specifically,

- AM signals are easy to generate using simple circuits such as a switching or square-law modulator.
- AM signals can also be easily demodulated using the simple envelope demodulator discussed earlier, or a simple *square-law demodulator* discussed in Question 3.11.

However, AM has the following drawbacks.

- It is wasteful of power. It was shown in Eq. (3.24) that at least two-thirds of the power is in the transmitted carrier, which carries no information. Only a maximum of one-third of the transmitted power is actually used to support the information signal (in the sidebands). For example, to transmit a total sideband power of 20 kW, one must transmit a total power above 60 kW, since 100% modulation is never used in practice. In this case, more than 40 kW of power is wasted.
- Amplitude modulation is also wasteful of bandwidth. We saw in Eq. (3.15) that AM requires twice the bandwidth of the message signal. Two sidebands, one a mirror image of the other, are transmitted even though any one of them is sufficient to reproduce the message signal at the receiver.

AM is suitable for the transmission of low-bandwidth message signals in telecommunication applications that have low-cost receiver implementation as a major design consideration. Its main application is therefore in audio broadcasting where it is economical to have one expensive high-power transmitter and numerous inexpensive receivers.

3.7 Variants of AM

So far, we have discussed what may be fully described as *double sideband transmitted carrier amplitude modulation (DSB-TC-AM)*. You may also wish to describe it as *double sideband large carrier amplitude modulation (DSB-LC-AM)*, to emphasise the presence of a large carrier component in the transmitted signal. Various modifications of this basic AM technique have been devised to save power and/or bandwidth, at the cost of increased transmitter and receiver complexity.

3.7.1 DSB

The *double sideband suppressed carrier amplitude modulation (DSB-SC-AM)*, usually simply abbreviated *DSB*, is generated by directly multiplying the message signal with the carrier signal using a balanced modulator. The carrier is not transmitted (i.e. the carrier is *suppressed*) and this saves a lot of power, which can be put into the two sidebands that carry the message signal.

3.7.1.1 *Waveform and spectrum of DSB*

The DSB waveform is given by

$$v_{dsb}(t) = v_m(t) \times v_c(t) = v_m(t)V_c \cos(2\pi f_c t) \tag{3.46}$$

And for a sinusoidal message signal $v_m(t) = V_m \cos(2\pi f_m t)$,

$$v_{dsb}(t) = V_m \cos(2\pi f_m t) \times V_c \cos(2\pi f_c t)$$
$$= \underbrace{\tfrac{1}{2} V_m V_c \cos 2\pi(f_c - f_m)t}_{\text{LSF}} + \underbrace{\tfrac{1}{2} V_m V_c \cos 2\pi(f_c + f_m)t}_{\text{USF}} \tag{3.47}$$

The DSB consists of a lower side frequency (LSF) of amplitude $0.5 V_m V_c$, and an upper side frequency (USF) of the same amplitude. There is no carrier component. Figure 3.23 shows the waveform of a DSB signal for the case $f_c = 20 f_m$ and $V_c = 2V_m$. Note that the envelope of the DSB is not the same as the message signal, and therefore a simple envelope demodulator cannot be used to extract the message signal as was done in basic AM. Compared to basic AM, we see that a simple (and hence low-cost) receiver circuit has been traded for a saving in transmitted power.

Figure 3.24(a) shows the spectrum of the DSB signal in Eq. (3.47). For an arbitrary message signal consisting of a band of sinusoids in the frequency range from f_1 to f_m, each component sinusoid is translated to a lower side frequency and an upper side frequency. This results in the lower sideband (LSB) and upper sideband (USB) shown in Fig. 3.24(b). DSB therefore has the same bandwidth as AM, which is twice the message bandwidth.

3.7.1.2 *DSB modulator*

A circuit that generates a DSB waveform must be able to prevent the carrier signal from getting to its output while at the same time passing the side

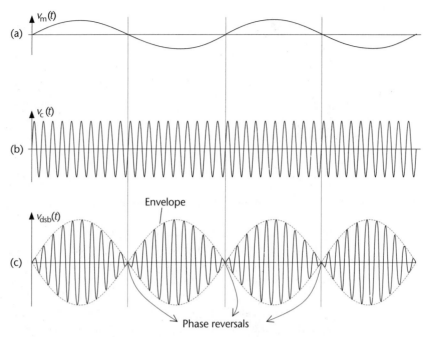

Figure 3.23 DSB signal waveform: (a) sinusoidal message; (b) carrier; (c) DSB.

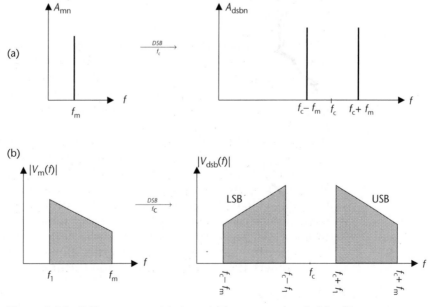

Figure 3.24 DSB spectrum: (a) sinusoidal message signal; (b) arbitrary message signal.

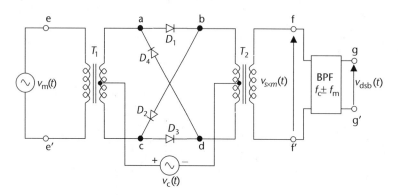

Figure 3.25   Ring or lattice implementation of a balanced modulator.

frequencies. This cannot be easily achieved by filtering since the side frequencies are very close to the carrier. A *balanced modulator* is able to generate a DSB waveform, suppressing the carrier and passing only the side frequencies to the output. It is also called a *product modulator*.

A realisation of balanced modulation using a diode ring is shown in Fig. 3.25. The diode ring or lattice modulator consists of an input transformer T_1, an output transformer T_2, and four diodes connected to form a ring (a–b–c–d–a) in which each diode is traversed in the same direction (from its positive terminal to its negative terminal). The carrier signal $v_c(t)$ is connected between the exact centre taps of T_1 and T_2; the message signal $v_m(t)$ is connected to the primary terminals e–e' of T_1; and the output signal $v_{s \times m}(t)$ is taken from the secondary terminals f–f' of T_2.

It is easy to understand the operation of this popular circuit if we take the discussion in parts. We first look at the effect of the carrier signal and then at how the message signal is transferred from the input terminals e–e' to the output terminals f–f'.

Carrier suppression   Ignore the message signal for the moment and concentrate on the carrier. Let the polarity of the carrier source be as shown in Fig. 3.25 during the positive cycle of the carrier. The polarity will be reversed during the negative half of the carrier cycle. Now consider what happens during the positive half of the carrier cycle. There is a positive voltage at node a, which forward-biases diode D_1 so that it is effectively a small resistance R_{fD1}, and reverse-biases diode D_4 so that it is effectively an open circuit. There is also a positive voltage at node c, which forward-biases diode D_3 so that it is effectively a small resistance R_{fD3}, and reverse-biases diode D_2 so that it is effectively an open circuit. The circuit (ignoring the message signal) therefore reduces to what is shown in Fig. 3.26(a). We cut out diodes D_2 and D_4 (since they are open circuits) and rotated the remaining circuit clockwise through 90° to obtain this figure. Z_1 is the impedance of the lower half of the secondary coil of T_1; Z_2 is the impedance of the upper half of this coil. Similarly, Z_3 is the impedance of the lower half of the primary coil of T_2 and Z_2 is the impedance of the upper half of this primary coil. The carrier voltage produces current I_t, which divides into I_a that flows through Z_2–R_{fD1}–Z_4, and I_c that flows through Z_1–R_{fD3}–Z_3. If the transformers are perfectly balanced and the diodes are identical, then

$$Z_1 = Z_2$$
$$Z_3 = Z_4$$
$$R_{fD1} = R_{fD4}$$

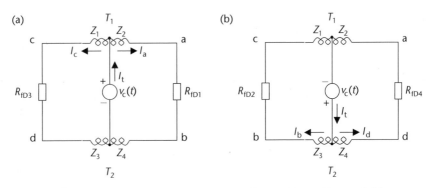

Figure 3.26 Currents due to carrier voltage during (a) positive and (b) negative cycles of carrier.

Under this condition, I_t divides equally into the two paths and

$$I_a = I_c$$

The result is that the carrier causes two equal currents to flow in opposite directions in the primary of T_2. These currents induce opposite magnetic fields that cancel out exactly so that no current is induced in the secondary winding of T_2. Thus, the carrier has been suppressed or balanced out and does not reach the output terminals f–f' during the positive half cycle of the carrier.

Now consider what happens during the negative half cycle of the carrier. There is a positive voltage at node b, which forward-biases diode D_2 so that it is effectively a small resistance R_{fD2}, and reverse-biases diode D_1 so that it is effectively an open circuit. There is also a positive voltage at node d, which forward-biases diode D_4 so that it is effectively a small resistance R_{fD4}, and reverse-biases diode D_3 so that it is effectively an open circuit. The circuit (again ignoring the message signal) therefore reduces to what is shown in Fig. 3.26(b). To obtain this figure, we cut out diodes D_1 and D_3 (since they are open circuits), twist the circuit through 180° so that paths b–c and a–d no longer cross, and rotate the remaining circuit clockwise through 90°. By a similar argument as for the positive cycle, it follows that the carrier is also prevented from reaching the output terminals f–f' during the negative half of the cycle. Thus the function of the carrier is to switch the diodes rapidly (at carrier frequency) providing different paths for the message signal to reach the output as we now discuss, but the carrier itself is prevented from reaching the output. This is a notable achievement.

Message signal transfer   We have seen that during the positive cycle diodes D_1 and D_3 are forward-biased, while D_2 and D_4 are reverse-biased. Ignoring the carrier, since it has no further effect on the circuit beyond this switching action, we obtain the circuit of Fig. 3.27(a) for the positive cycle. The message signal is coupled from e–e' to a–c by transformer T_1 action. It is then applied across b–d, with a small drop across R_{fD1} and R_{fD3} (which we

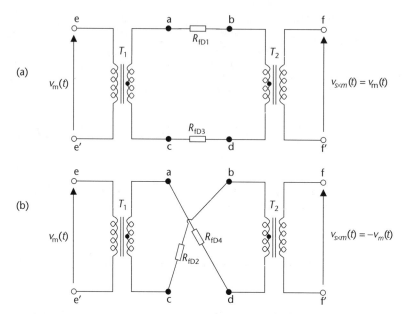

Figure 3.27 Transfer of message signal $v_m(t)$ from input terminals e–e′ to output terminals f–f′ during (a) positive and (b) negative cycles of carrier.

ignore). The message signal is coupled from b–d to the output terminal f–f′ by transformer T_2 action. Thus, during the positive half of a carrier cycle,

$$v_{s \times m}(t) = v_m(t)$$

Now consider what happens during a negative half of the cycle. The effective circuit is as shown in Fig. 3.27(b). The message signal is coupled to terminal a–c as before. The paths to terminal b–d have been reversed causing the message signal to be applied to b–d with a reversed polarity. That is, signal $-v_m(t)$ is applied to b–d. The small drop across R_{fD2} and R_{fD4} is again ignored. From b–d this signal is coupled to the output terminal f–f′. Thus,

$$v_{s \times m}(t) = -v_m(t)$$

DSB signal From the foregoing, we see that the signal $v_{s \times m}(t)$ is the product of the message signal $v_m(t)$ and a bipolar unit-amplitude square wave $v_s(t)$ of period equal to the carrier period. This is demonstrated in Fig. 3.28 for a sinusoidal message signal. The bipolar square wave has amplitude +1 during the positive half of the carrier cycle and amplitude –1 during the negative half of the cycle. Being a square wave, it contains only odd harmonic frequencies. Furthermore, since its average value is zero, it does not contain a DC component A_0 in its Fourier series. So we may write

$$\begin{aligned}
v_{s \times m}(t) &= v_m(t) \times v_s(t) \\
&= v_m(t)\{A_1 \cos[2\pi f_c t] + A_3 \cos[2\pi(3f_c)t] + \cdots\} \\
&= v_m(t) A_1 \cos[2\pi f_c t] + v_m(t) A_3 \cos[2\pi(3f_c)t] + \cdots
\end{aligned} \tag{3.48}$$

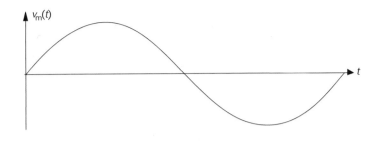

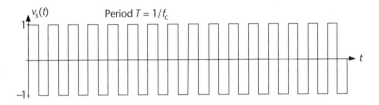

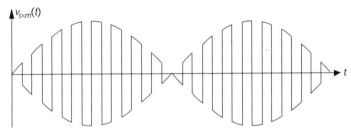

Figure 3.28 Output $v_{s \times m}(t)$ of a diode ring modulator is the product of the message signal $v_m(t)$ and bipolar unit-amplitude square wave $v_s(t)$.

The first term is the required DSB signal — being a direct multiplication of the message signal and the carrier. Subsequent terms are the sidebands of the message signal centred at odd harmonics of the carrier frequency, namely, $3f_c$, $5f_c$, ...

Therefore, as shown in Fig. 3.25, the DSB signal $v_{dsb}(t)$ is obtained by passing $v_{s \times m}(t)$ through a bandpass filter of centre frequency f_c and bandwidth $2f_m$, where f_m is the maximum frequency component of the message signal. For this to work, adjacent sidebands in Eq. (3.48) must not overlap. This requires that the lowest lying frequency $3f_c - f_m$ in the LSB located just below $3f_c$ must be higher than the highest frequency $f_c + f_m$ in the USB located just above f_c. That is,

$$3f_c - f_m > f_c + f_m$$
$$\text{or} \quad f_c > f_m \tag{3.49}$$

Subsequently, a balanced modulator or product modulator will be treated as comprising a diode ring modulator and an appropriate bandpass filter. This leads to the block diagram of Fig. 3.29 in which the product modulator

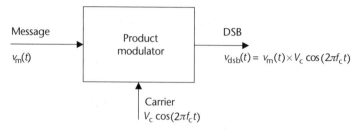

Figure 3.29 The product modulator consisting of a ring modulator followed by a bandpass filter of centre frequency f_c and bandwidth $2f_m$.

receives two inputs, namely, the message signal and the carrier, and produces the DSB signal as output.

3.7.1.3 *DSB demodulator*

The original message signal $v_m(t)$ can be extracted from a received DSB signal $v_{dsb}(t)$ by a product modulator followed by a low-pass filter, as shown in Fig. 3.30. However, this requires that the locally generated carrier should have exactly the same frequency and phase as the carrier used at the transmitter including the phase perturbations imposed by the transmission medium. This demodulation scheme is therefore referred to as coherent (or *synchronous*) demodulation.

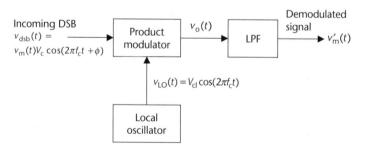

Figure 3.30 Coherent demodulation of DSB.

Effect of phase error To see why phase synchronisation is important, let us assume in Fig. 3.30 that variations in the transmission medium have perturbed the phase of the missing DSB carrier by ϕ relative to the locally generated carrier, which is matched in frequency. The incoming DSB signal $v_{dsb}(t)$ and the locally generated carrier $v_{LO}(t)$ are therefore given by

$$v_{dsb}(t) = v_m(t) \times V_c \cos(2\pi f_c t + \phi)$$
$$v_{LO}(t) = V_{cl} \cos(2\pi f_c t)$$

The output of the product modulator is therefore

$$
\begin{aligned}
v_o(t) &= v_{DSB}(t) \times v_{LO}(t) \\
&= [v_m(t)V_c\cos(2\pi f_c t + \phi)][V_{cl}\cos(2\pi f_c t)] \\
&= v_m(t)V_cV_{cl}\cos(2\pi f_c t)\cos(2\pi f_c t + \phi) \\
&= Kv_m(t)\cos(\phi) + Kv_m(t)\cos(4\pi f_c t + \phi)
\end{aligned}
\tag{3.50}
$$

where we have used the trigonometric identity of Eq. (A.6) (Appendix A), and set the constant $K = \frac{1}{2}V_cV_{cl}$. The last term in Eq. (3.50) is a bandpass signal centred at frequency $2f_c$, and is rejected by the low-pass filter, which therefore yields the demodulated signal

$$
v'_m(t) = K\cos(\phi)v_m(t)
\tag{3.51}
$$

Thus the received message signal is proportional to the cosine of the phase error ϕ. If ϕ has a constant value other than $\pm 90°$, then the message signal is simply scaled by a constant factor and is not distorted. However, in practice the phase error will vary randomly leading to random variations (i.e. distortions) in the received signal. The received signal is maximum when $\phi = 0$, and is zero when $\phi = \pm 90°$. This means that a DSB signal carried by a cosine carrier cannot be demodulated by a sine carrier, and vice versa — the so called *quadrature null effect*.

Phase synchronisation The *Costas loop* shown in Fig. 3.31 is an arrangement that keeps the locally generated carrier synchronised in phase and frequency with the missing carrier of the incoming DSB signal. It employs two coherent demodulators. A coherent demodulator consists of a product modulator fed with the incoming DSB and a locally generated carrier, and a low-pass filter. Check that you can identify the two coherent demodulators in Fig. 3.31. Both demodulators are fed with a carrier generated by the same

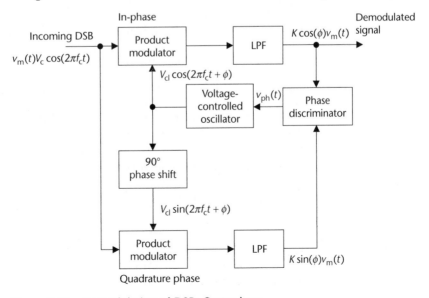

Figure 3.31 Demodulation of DSB: Costas loop.

voltage-controlled oscillator (VCO). However, one of the demodulators — referred to as the quadrature-phase demodulator has its carrier phase reduced by 90° (to make it a sine carrier), while the other (in-phase) demodulator is fed with the VCO-generated cosine carrier that is ideally in-phase with the missing carrier of the DSB signal. The demodulated signal is taken at the output of the in-phase demodulator. When there is no phase error, the quadrature demodulator output is zero — recall the quadrature null effect — and the in-phase demodulator provides the correct demodulated signal.

Now consider what happens when there is a phase difference or error ϕ between the VCO output and the missing carrier in the DSB signal. Treating this missing carrier as the reference, its initial phase is zero and the incoming DSB signal is

$$v_{dsb}(t) = v_m(t)V_c \cos(2\pi f_c t)$$

The carrier fed to the in-phase and quadrature demodulators are therefore respectively $V_{cl} \cos(2\pi f_c t + \phi)$ and $V_{cl} \sin(2\pi f_c t + \phi)$. The in-phase demodulator output is then $K \cos(\phi)v_m(t)$ as earlier derived, while the quadrature demodulator output is $K \sin(\phi)v_m(t)$. Thus, a phase error causes the in-phase demodulator output to drop, and the quadrature demodulator output to increase from zero.

Phase synchronisation, which maintains the value of the phase error ϕ around zero is achieved by the combined action of the phase discriminator and the VCO. The two demodulator outputs are fed into the phase discriminator, which produces an output voltage $v_{ph}(t)$ proportional to ϕ and causes the VCO output frequency to change slightly in such a way that the phase error is reduced towards zero.

3.7.1.4 DSB applications

The advent of integrated circuits made it possible for the problem of phase synchronisation in DSB reception to be overcome using affordable receivers, and paved the way for the use of DSB in a number of areas.

- The most popular analogue television systems, namely, NTSC (in North America) and PAL (in Europe) employ DSB to transmit colour (or chrominance) information. Two colour-difference signals are transmitted on two sub-carriers that have the same frequency but differ in phase by 90°. You may wish to view it this way: one signal is carried on an *in-phase* cosine carrier of frequency f_c, and the other on a (*quadrature-phase*) sine carrier of the same frequency. It can be shown (Question 3.12) by virtue of the quadrature null effect that the two signals will be separated at the receiver without mutual interference. This particular modulation strategy may be described in full as *double sideband suppressed carrier quadrature amplitude modulation*.

- DSB is also used for transmitting *stereo information* in FM sound broadcast at VHF. Sending two different audio signals $v_L(t)$ and $v_R(t)$ termed the left and right channels respectively, representing, for example, sound from different directions entering two sufficiently spaced micro-phones at a live musical program, greatly enriches the reproduction of the (musical) program at a receiver. However, this stereo transmission must be on a single carrier in order not to exceed the bandwidth already allocated to FM. Furthermore, it must be sent in such a way that non-stereo receivers can give normal mono-aural reproduction. These stringent conditions are satisfied as follows.

At the FM stereo transmitter (Fig. 3.32(a)):

1. Sum signal $v_{L+R}(t)$ and difference signal $v_{L-R}(t)$ are generated by summing and subtracting the two channels respectively.

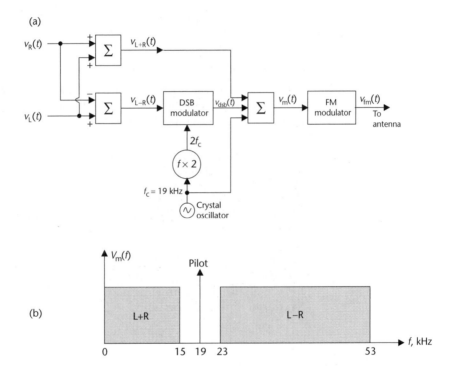

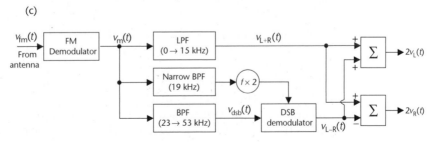

Figure 3.32 FM stereo: (a) transmitter; (b) spectrum $V_m(f)$ of composite signal $v_m(t)$; (c) receiver.

2. $v_{L-R}(t)$ is DSB modulated using a 38 kHz carrier obtained by doubling the frequency of a 19 kHz crystal oscillator. Let's denote this DSB signal $v_{dsb}(t)$.

3. The signals $v_{L+R}(t)$, $v_{dsb}(t)$ and the 19 kHz oscillator frequency are summed to give a composite signal $v_m(t)$. The spectrum $v_m(f)$ of the composite signal $v_m(t)$ is shown in Fig. 3.32(b). Clearly there is no mutual interference between the three signals that are summed since each lies in a separate frequency band, $v_{L+R}(t)$ in the baseband from 0 to 15 kHz, $v_{dsb}(t)$ in the pass band from 23 to 53 kHz and of course the pilot carrier at 19 kHz. This is an application of *frequency division multiplexing*, which is discussed in detail in Chapter 8.

4. The composite signal $v_m(t)$ is transmitted as $v_{fm}(t)$ using *frequency modulation* — the subject of the next chapter.

At the receiver (Fig. 3.32(c)):

1. $v_m(t)$ is extracted from $v_{fm}(t)$ by frequency demodulation.

2. A LPF of 15 kHz bandwidth extracts $v_{L+R}(t)$ from $v_m(t)$. A non-stereo receiver plays $v_{L+R}(t)$ on a loudspeaker and that completes its signal processing. A stereo receiver however goes further through steps $3 \rightarrow 5$ below.

3. The 19 kHz pilot is extracted using a narrow bandpass filter (BPF), and $v_{dsb}(t)$ is extracted using a BPF of bandwidth 30 kHz centred on 38 kHz.

4. The 19 kHz pilot is doubled in frequency. This provides a phase synchronised 38 kHz carrier that is used to demodulate $v_{dsb}(t)$ to yield $v_{L-R}(t)$. In this way, the sum and difference signals have been recovered.

5. The left and right channels are obtained by taking the sum and difference of $v_{L+R}(t)$ and $v_{L-R}(t)$. You may wish to check that this is the case. The two channels can now be played back on separate loudspeakers to give stereo reproduction.

3.7.2 SSB

DSB provides a power saving improvement over basic AM. However, it still requires twice the bandwidth of the message signal since both the lower and upper sidebands are transmitted. It is obvious in Fig. 3.24(b) that these sidebands (LSB and USB) are mirror images of each other about the carrier frequency f_c. That is, measuring outward from f_c, the LSB contains exactly the same frequencies at the same amplitudes as the USB. They therefore represent the same information — that contained in the message signal, and it is wasteful of bandwidth to send two copies of the same information.

Single sideband suppressed carrier amplitude modulation — abbreviated SSB — transmits only one sideband. As in DSB, the carrier is also not transmitted. Figure 3.33 shows the spectrum of an SSB signal.

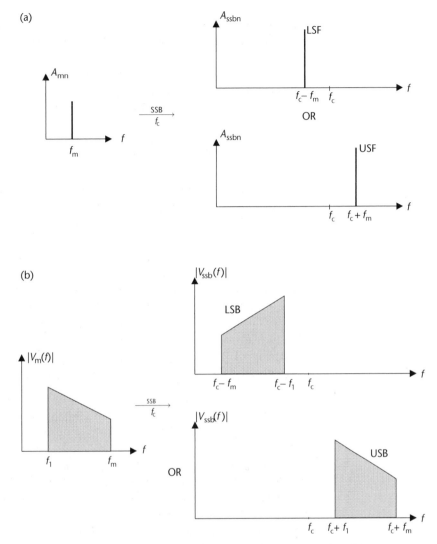

Figure 3.33 SSB spectrum: (a) sinusoidal message signal; (b) arbitrary message signal.

3.7.2.1 Merits and demerits of SSB

SSB provides numerous benefits.

1. The bandwidth of an SSB signal is exactly the same as that of the original message signal, and is therefore half the bandwidth that would be required to transmit the same message by DSB or basic AM. Thus, SSB doubles spectrum utilisation in that it allows twice as many signals to be packed into the same frequency range as could be done with DSB or AM.

2. The pass band of an SSB receiver is half that of AM and DSB receivers. As a result, noise power — proportional to bandwidth — is reduced by a factor of two. This yields a 3 dB improvement in signal-to-noise ratio.

3. Power that was spread out over two sidebands (and a carrier in the case of AM) is now concentrated into one sideband. So for the same output power, the SSB signal can be received with a higher signal power per unit message bandwidth than AM and DSB. For the same reason, SSB transmission can be received at greater distances than AM and DSB transmission of the same power.

4. The SSB transmitter produces a non-zero power output only when a message signal is present, unlike an AM transmitter, which continues to radiate a high-power carrier during those time intervals when there is a pause in the message signal. The SSB (and DSB) transmitter is therefore more efficient.

5. SSB transmission is less susceptible to the phenomenon of selective fading than AM and DSB. Under selective fading, different frequency components of a signal will arrive at the receiver having undergone different amounts of propagation delay. This may arise in the case of sky wave propagation because these frequencies have been effectively reflected from different layers of the ionosphere. It can be shown (see Question 3.13) that for AM and DSB transmission to be correctly received the LSB, USB, and carrier must have the same initial phases. Selective fading causes the phases of these three components to be altered by amounts that are not proportional to their frequency. As a result, they appear at the receiver to have different initial phases, which causes distortion in the received signal.

   Fig. 3.34(a) demonstrates an example of the potential effect of selective fading on AM signals. The (undistorted) AM signal results from 80% modulation of a 1 MHz carrier by a 25 kHz sinusoidal message signal. We assume that selective fading causes the side frequencies to be shifted in phase by 60° relative to the carrier frequency. The received AM signal will have the waveform shown in Fig. 3.34(a). An envelope demodulator would then produce the output shown in Fig. 3.34(b), which is compared with the original message signal on the same plot. It is apparent that signal distortion occurs when carrier and side frequencies have unequal initial phases.

   In exceptional circumstances, complete signal cancellation may occur at certain time instants.

   SSB transmission has only one sideband, which is demodulated using a locally generated carrier. The effect of selective fading is therefore greatly reduced.

6. The SSB technique reduces the effect of amplifier non-linearity in frequency division multiplex (FDM) systems. We saw in Chapter 2 that the effect of a non-linear transmission medium is to generate intermodulation products, the amplitudes of which increase with signal power. In FDM systems where many independent signals (or channels) are transmitted in adjacent frequency bands on the same

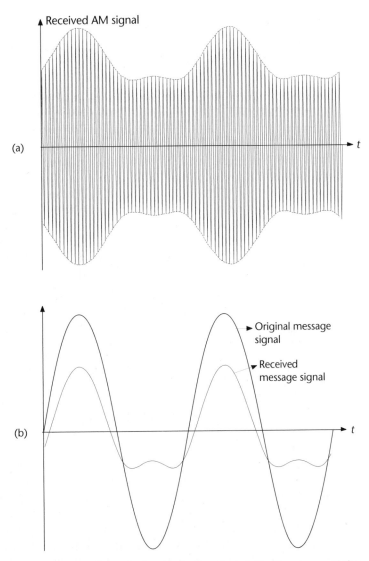

Figure 3.34 Effect of selective fading that shifts the phases of the side frequencies by 60° relative to the carrier. The original AM signal is an 80% modulation of a 1 MHz carrier by a 25 kHz sinusoidal message signal. (a) Received AM signal; (b) original and received message signals compared.

link, some of these products will fall in bands occupied by other signals, giving rise to crosstalk. Carrier suppression allows the use of a smaller signal power in SSB (and to a lesser extent in DSB), and therefore minimises the effect of non-linearity.

The main disadvantage of SSB is that it requires complex and expensive circuits since a local carrier signal must be generated that is synchronised in frequency and phase with the missing carrier in the incoming SSB signal.

3.7.2.2   SSB modulators

SSB can be generated in two different ways, namely *filtering* (i.e. frequency discrimination) and *phase discrimination*.

Frequency discrimination method [The most obvious method of generating an SSB signal is to first generate a DSB signal using a product modulator and then to filter out one of the sidebands.]This *filtering method* is shown in Fig. 3.35. [The main difficulty with this method is that the required selectivity of the bandpass filters may be very high, making the filters expensive and uneconomical.]

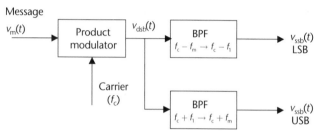

Figure 3.35 SSB generation: filtering method.

If f_1 is the lowest frequency component of the message signal, then the frequency gap between the two sidebands that must be separated by the filter is $2f_1$. In telephony with voice baseband standardised at 300 to 3400 Hz, this gap is 600 Hz; while in TV with $f_1 = 0$, there is no gap between the sidebands. Obviously therefore this method cannot be employed with TV signals. Even for voice telephony, a bandpass filter that has a transition width of only about 600 Hz is uneconomical at RF frequencies. For example, if the carrier frequency is say 3 MHz, the filter would require a steep enough frequency response slope within the transition band so that it goes from pass band at 3 000 300 Hz to stop band at 2 999 700 Hz. The transition width in this case would be only about 0.02% of the centre frequency.

If, however, a lower-frequency carrier is used, say f_c = 100 kHz, the required transition width becomes 0.6% of the centre frequency and the filter can be realised more cheaply. Generation of a high-frequency carrier SSB is therefore usually done in two stages. First, a lower frequency carrier f_{c1} is employed to generate the SSB. The gap between the sidebands is only $2f_1$, where f_1 is the lowest frequency component of the message signal. However, because f_{c1} is small, an affordable bandpass filter can be used to separate the sidebands. The output of this filter enters a second product modulator that operates at a higher carrier frequency f_{c2}. This again generates two sidebands. However, the gap between the sidebands is now $2(f_{c1} - f_m)$, where f_m is the maximum frequency component of the message signal. Since f_{c1} is much larger than f_m, the gap between the sidebands in this second stage is large enough for an affordable BPF to separate the two sidebands. The overall result of this two-stage procedure is the generation of an SSB signal at a carrier frequency $f_{c1} + f_{c2}$.

To transmit the LSB, which occupies the frequency interval from $f_{c2} + f_{c1} - f_m$ to $f_{c2} + f_{c1} - f_1$, one selects the LSB in the first stage and the USB in the second stage. On the other hand, the USB, which occupies the frequency interval from $f_{c2} + f_{c1} + f_1$ to $f_{c2} + f_{c1} + f_m$, is transmitted by selecting the USB in both stages.

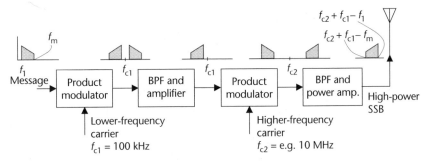

Figure 3.36 SSB transmitter.

Figure 3.36 shows a block diagram of an SSB transmitter that uses the method just described. Follow the spectrum sketches in the diagram and you will observe how the LSB is transmitted at carrier frequency $f_{c2} + f_{c1}$ by selecting the LSB in the first DSB modulation, and the USB in the second. Most high-power SSB transmission in the HF band (3–30 MHz) employs the filter method.

Phase discrimination method A different scheme for SSB generation is based on *phase discrimination*. Two signals are summed whose phase relationship is such that one of the sidebands is eliminated. It is easier to demonstrate how this method works by using a sinusoidal message signal

$$v_m(t) = V_m \cos(2\pi f_m t) \tag{3.52}$$

With a carrier of frequency f_c, the SSB signal is given by

$$v_{ssb}(t) = \begin{cases} A\cos[2\pi(f_c - f_m)t], & \text{LSB} \\ A\cos[2\pi(f_c + f_m)t], & \text{USB} \end{cases} \tag{3.53}$$

where A represents the amplitude of the SSB signal. Using the trigonometric identities (A.3) and (A.4) in Appendix A, the expressions for the SSB signals can be expanded as follows:

$$v_{ssb}(t) = \begin{cases} A\cos(2\pi f_c t)\cos(2\pi f_m t) + A\sin(2\pi f_c t)\sin(2\pi f_m t), & \text{LSB} \\ A\cos(2\pi f_c t)\cos(2\pi f_m t) - A\sin(2\pi f_c t)\sin(2\pi f_m t), & \text{USB} \end{cases} \tag{3.54}$$

Equation (3.54) is very important. It shows that we may obtain a single sideband signal by adding together two double sideband signals. Consider first the expression for the LSB. The first term is the output of a product modulator that takes the carrier and the message signal as inputs. The second term is the output of another product modulator whose inputs are (i) the same carrier delayed in phase by 90° (to change it from cosine to sine), and (ii) the message signal delayed in phase by 90°. The sum of the outputs of these two product modulators yields the lower sideband SSB signal, while the difference yields the upper sideband SSB signal. Equation (3.54) therefore suggests the block diagram shown in Fig. 3.37 for the generation of SSB.

A transformation that changes the phase of every positive frequency component of a signal by –90°, and the phase of every negative frequency

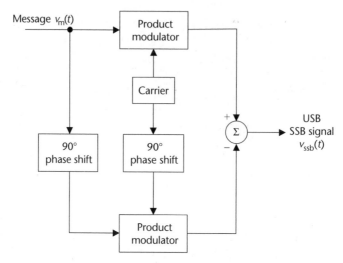

Figure 3.37 SSB generation by phase discrimination: Hartley modulator. USB output is shown. For an LSB output, change subtraction to addition in the summing device.

component of the signal by +90°, but does not alter the amplitude of any of these components is known as the *Hilbert transform*. Thus the inputs to the second product modulator are the Hilbert transform of the carrier signal, and the Hilbert transform of the message signal. It is easy to obtain the Hilbert transform of the carrier signal — a circuit that changes the phase of this single frequency by exactly −90° is readily available. However, an accurate hardware implementation of the Hilbert transform of the message signal is more difficult because of the wide range of frequency components that must each be shifted in phase by exactly 90°.

The SSB generator based on phase discrimination implemented as shown in Fig. 3.37 is known as the *Hartley modulator*. It has several advantages over the frequency discrimination or filtering technique of Fig. 3.36.

1. The SSB signal is generated directly at the required RF frequency without the need for an intermediate lower frequency stage.

2. Bulky and expensive bandpass filters have been eliminated.

3. It is very easy to switch from a lower sideband to an upper sideband SSB output. The former is obtained by adding the outputs of the two product modulators, while the latter results by subtraction.

The main disadvantage of the Hartley modulator is that it requires the Hilbert transform of the message signal. This transform changes the phase of each positive frequency component in the message signal by exactly −90°. If the wideband phase shifting network shifts the phase of any frequency component in the message signal by an amount not equal to −90°, it causes a small amplitude of the unwanted side frequency of this component to appear at the output. Complete suppression of the unwanted sideband is achieved only with a phase difference of exactly −90° between corresponding frequency components at the inputs of the two product modulators. In practice, it is easier to achieve this by using two phase-shifting networks. One network shifts the message signal input to one modulator by ϕ_1, and the other shifts the message signal input to the other modulator by ϕ_2, with

$$\phi_1 - \phi_2 = 90° \tag{3.55}$$

3.7.2.3 SSB demodulator

Just as for DSB reception, coherent demodulation is necessary to extract the original message signal from an incoming SSB signal. Figure 3.38 shows the block diagram of an SSB demodulator. To understand the operation of this circuit we assume for simplicity a sinusoidal message signal — Eq. (3.52). Then for upper sideband transmission, the SSB signal at the input of the demodulator is

$$v_{ssb}(t) = V_{ssb} \cos[2\pi(f_c + f_m)t] \tag{3.56}$$

Let us assume that the locally generated carrier $v_c(t)$ has a phase error ϕ compared to the missing carrier in $v_{ssb}(t)$. The output of the product modulator is then given by

$$
\begin{aligned}
v_o(t) &= v_{ssb}(t) \times v_c(t) \\
&= V_{ssb} \cos[2\pi(f_c + f_m)t] \times V_c \cos(2\pi f_c t + \phi) \\
&= K \cos(2\pi f_m t - \phi) + K \cos[2\pi(2f_c + f_m)t + \phi]
\end{aligned} \tag{3.57}
$$

where we have set $K = 0.5 V_{ssb} V_c$. The last term in Eq. (3.57) is a high-frequency component at $2f_c + f_m$. This component is eliminated by passing $v_o(t)$ through an LPF. The output of this filter gives the demodulated signal

$$v'_m(t) = K \cos(2\pi f_m t - \phi) \tag{3.58}$$

Comparing this with the original message signal in Eq. (3.52), we see that apart from a constant gain factor, which is not a distortion, the demodulated signal differs from the original message signal by a phase distortion equal to the phase error in the local oscillator. The receiver changes the phase of each frequency component in the original message signal by a constant amount ϕ. From our discussion in Section 2.9.1, this causes a phase distortion, which is unacceptable in data and video transmission as well as in music, where some harmonic relationships could be destroyed by a small shift in the demodulated frequency components from their original frequency values. However, it may be tolerated in speech transmission because the human ear is relatively insensitive to phase distortion.

Older systems minimised the phase error by inserting a low-level pilot carrier into the transmitted SSB signal, which is then used to periodically lock

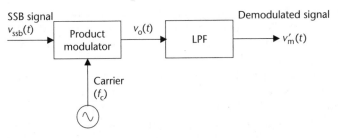

Figure 3.38 SSB demodulator.

the local oscillator at the receiver. Modern systems use a crystal-controlled oscillator along with a frequency synthesiser to generate a local carrier with good frequency stability, e.g. 1 part in 10^6. The need to generate a carrier of highly stable frequency is the main factor in the complexity and cost of SSB receivers.

3.7.2.4 *Applications of SSB*

SSB has numerous applications.

1. It is employed for two-way radio communication to conserve spectrum and transmitted power requirements. Thus more users can be accommodated in a given bandwidth, and battery life can be prolonged. SSB is used for marine and military communication, and is very popular with radio amateurs, allowing them to maximise signal range with a minimum of transmitted signal power.

2. SSB is universally employed in the implementation of frequency division multiplexing. It allows twice as many independent channels to be packed into a given frequency band as can be done with say DSB.

3. Although not usually identified as such, SSB is the technique of frequency *up-conversion* in numerous telecommunication systems. For example, in satellite communications, the message signal modulates a lower-frequency carrier signal using, for example, phase modulation. The phase-modulated carrier is then translated or up-converted to the required up-link frequency using what is essentially the filter method of SSB modulation. At the satellite, the signal is amplified (but not phase-demodulated), translated to a different down-link frequency, and transmitted back towards the Earth.

4. It is important to point out that the ubiquitous non-linear device, termed a *mixer*, is realised as the SSB demodulator shown in Fig. 3.38. The mixer is found in all receivers based on the superheterodyne principle (see Fig. 3.22) and employed for frequency *down-conversion* to translate a bandpass RF signal to a lower centre frequency.

3.7.3 ISB

Independent sideband amplitude modulation, abbreviated ISB, and sometimes called *twin sideband suppressed carrier amplitude modulation*, is a type of SSB. Two different message signals are transmitted on the two sidebands of a single carrier, with one message carried in the lower sideband, and the other carried in the upper sideband.

Figure 3.39 shows the spectrum of an ISB signal that carries two arbitrary and independent message signals on a single carrier of frequency f_c. Each message signal contains a band of sinusoids (or spectrum) in the frequency range from f_1 to f_m. The spectrum of one message signal has been translated to form a lower sideband below the carrier frequency, while the spectrum of the other signal forms the upper sideband. There are therefore two

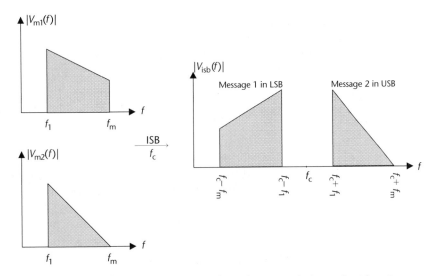

Figure 3.39 ISB spectrum $V_{isb}(f)$ resulting from two independent input signals with spectra $V_{m1}(f)$ and $V_{m2}(f)$.

sidebands around the carrier, but each corresponds to a different message signal.

3.7.3.1 ISB modulator

Figure 3.40 shows the block diagram of an ISB modulator. It consists of two SSB modulators (filter method) fed with the same carrier signal of frequency f_c. One modulator generates a lower sideband SSB signal $v_{lsb}(t)$ of one message signal, while the other generates an upper sideband SSB signal $v_{usb}(t)$ of the other message signal. The sum of these two signals gives the

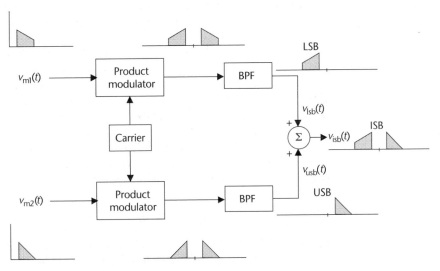

Figure 3.40 ISB modulator.

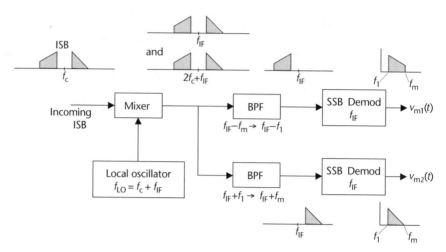

Figure 3.41 ISB demodulator.

ISB signal. A reduced level of the carrier (termed *pilot carrier*) may be inserted for use in coherent demodulation at the receiver.

3.7.3.2 ISB demodulator

One way to demodulate an ISB signal is shown in block diagram form in Fig. 3.41. The incoming ISB signal (centred on an RF carrier f_c) is translated down to a lower intermediate frequency f_{IF} = say 100 kHz, where affordable bandpass filters can be used to separately extract the two sidebands. The frequency translation is accomplished in a mixer that uses an oscillator frequency $f_{LO} = f_c + f_{IF}$ and generates the sum frequency $f_{LO} + f_c = 2f_c + f_{IF}$ and the difference frequency $f_{LO} - f_c = f_{IF}$.

The output of the mixer is fed into two bandpass filters with pass bands $f_{IF} - f_m \rightarrow f_{IF} - f_1$ and $f_{IF} + f_1 \rightarrow f_{IF} + f_m$ respectively. The first BPF passes the lower sideband of the frequency-translated ISB signal. This sideband contains one message signal. The other BPF passes the upper sideband that contains the other message signal. Both filters reject the sum frequency output of the mixer. The output of each BPF is passed through an SSB demodulator, which extracts the original message signal. The operation of the SSB demodulator was discussed earlier using Fig. 3.38. The only point that needs to be added in this case is that two sinusoidal signals are used at the receiver, namely f_{LO} (at the mixer) and f_{IF} (at the SSB demodulator). It is important for the sum of these two signals to be matched in frequency and phase with the missing carrier of the incoming ISB signal. A low-level pilot carrier f_c may be inserted at the transmitter and used at the receiver to maintain this synchronisation.

3.7.3.3 ISB Merits, demerits and application

ISB offers all the advantages of SSB. In addition, it allows closer packing of sidebands than is possible with SSB. A more efficient spectrum utilisation can therefore be achieved in transmitting multiple signals.

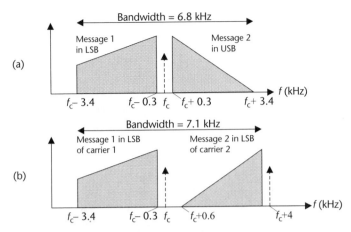

Figure 3.42 Bandwidth required to transmit two voice channels of baseband frequency from $f_1 = 300$ Hz to $f_m = 3400$ Hz: (a) using ISB and (b) using SSB with carrier spacing 4 kHz.

As an example, let us consider speech communication. The baseband frequency is in the range $f_1 = 300$ Hz to $f_m = 3400$ Hz. The DSB bandwidth is therefore 6800 Hz, and with ISB two independent channels can therefore be transmitted within a bandwidth of 6800 Hz, as shown in Fig. 3.42(a). The separation between the two sidebands is twice the minimum frequency component of the baseband speech signal, or 600 Hz. In SSB modulation, each channel is carried on a separate carrier, and two carriers would be required to transmit two independent channels. These carriers have to be allowed sufficient guard band to avoid mutual interference between the two channels since realisable filters of non-zero transition width will be employed to separate them. A carrier spacing of 4 kHz (in FDM telephony) would be a realistic minimum. Thus, as shown in Fig. 3.42(b), the two channels would occupy a bandwidth of 7.1 kHz in SSB. This is larger than the bandwidth requirement of ISB by 300 Hz. A spectrum saving of 150 Hz/channel is therefore achieved with ISB. It is important to emphasise that this saving in bandwidth has resulted simply from the closer spacing of sidebands that is possible with ISB. It can be seen in Fig. 3.42 that the sideband spacing is 600 Hz with ISB and 900 Hz with SSB. The modulated spectrum of each of the two signals remains the same (3.1 kHz) for both SSB and ISB.

The main demerit of ISB is that its per-channel circuit requirement for transmission is about the same as that of SSB, but its receiver circuit is more extensive, and therefore more expensive. The ISB technique would only be considered in situations where two or more independent signals must be transmitted on a link of very limited bandwidth. ISB has only a few applications, mostly in military communication.

3.7.4 VSB

Vestigial sideband modulation, abbreviated VSB, is used mainly in analogue television for the transmission of the luminance signal. The baseband signal contains frequency components down to DC. This makes SSB impractical since there is no frequency separation between the upper and lower sidebands to allow the use of a realisable filter for separating them. At the same time, the bandwidth requirement of DSB is rather excessive. For example, the bandwidth of a luminance signal is 4.2 MHz in the NTSC (CCIR M) TV standard used in North America, and 5.5 MHz in the PAL standard used in Western Europe. Double sideband transmission would require bandwidths of 8.4 MHz and 11 MHz respectively for these standards. This is

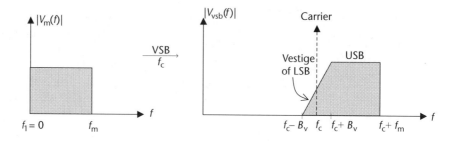

Figure 3.43 VSB spectrum for a message signal of bandwidth f_m. B_v is the width of the remaining portion (or vestige) of the LSB.

well above the total RF bandwidth of 6 and 8 MHz, respectively, allocated in the two standards for transmitting one complete television channel (including audio and colour signals).

VSB provides a compromise in which one almost complete sideband and a portion or *vestige* of the other sideband are transmitted. The bandwidth requirement of VSB is typically about 1.25 times the message signal bandwidth. This is larger than that of SSB, but a significant saving on DSB and AM requirements.

Figure 3.43 shows the spectrum of a VSB signal. A rectangular message spectrum has been adopted in order to demonstrate the filtering of sidebands more clearly. The USB is retained in full except for a small portion that has been filtered off. A vestige of the LSB equal to an inverted mirror image of the missing USB portion is retained. The width of this vestigial LSB has been denoted B_v. It can be seen, measuring outward from the carrier frequency, that all components in the LSB from B_v to f_m have been totally eliminated. Compare this with SSB, where all LSB components would be removed — not just a portion — and with DSB where all LSB components would be retained. The bandwidth of a VSB signal is therefore

$$\text{VSB bandwidth} = f_m + B_v \tag{3.59}$$

where f_m is the bandwidth of the message signal and B_v is the width of the vestigial sideband. Note that although Fig. 3.43 shows a linear-slope clipping of the sidebands, all that is required is that the vestigial LSB be an inverted mirror image of the missing portion in the USB. This allows a lot of flexibility in the choice of a suitable filter to generate the VSB signal.

3.7.4.1 VSB modulator

The discussion of VSB thus far suggests the simple modulator shown in Fig. 3.44(a). A product modulator generates a DSB signal, which is passed through a bandpass filter that has an appropriate frequency response to attenuate one of the sidebands and reduce it to a vestige, while passing the other sideband with only a small attenuation of a portion of the frequency band. This filter is known as the VSB filter, and its normalised frequency response (with maximum gain equal to unity) is shown in Fig. 3.44(b). It is

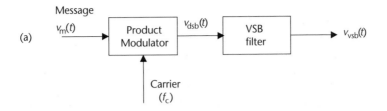

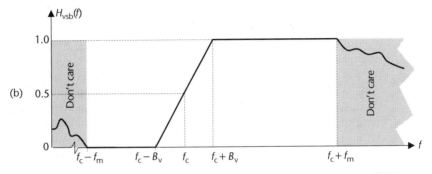

Figure 3.44 (a) VSB modulator; (b) normalised frequency response of VSB filter.

assumed in our discussion that it is the lower sideband that is reduced to a vestige.

The frequency response of the VSB filter must be such that it allows the original message signal to be recovered at the receiver using coherent demodulation. It will be shown later that a filter with the normalised frequency response $H_{vsb}(f)$ shown in Fig. 3.44b satisfies this requirement. The response of this filter is asymmetric about the carrier frequency. However, the filter can have any arbitrary response outside the interval $f = f_c \pm f_m$, where the DSB signal is zero. These 'don't care' regions are shown shaded in Fig. 3.44(b), and the filter response is continued within these regions in a completely arbitrary manner. Actually, the requirement of asymmetry about f_c is satisfied by filters with a variety of response slopes. A linear-slope filter is shown in Fig. 3.44(b) for simplicity, but this is not required.

If the width of the vestigial sideband is B_v, the filter response must be zero in the frequency range $f_c - f_m \rightarrow f_c - B_v$ in order to eliminate this portion of the LSB. It follows from the asymmetry condition that the response must be unity in the interval $f_c + B_v \rightarrow f_c + f_m$ so that this portion of the USB is passed with no attenuation. Thus,

$$H_{vsb}(f) = \begin{cases} 1 & f_c + B_v \leq f \leq f_c + f_m \\ 0 & f_c - f_m \leq f \leq f_c - B_v \\ 0.5 & f = f_c \\ \text{Asymmetric} & f_c - B_v \leq f \leq f_c + B_v \\ \text{Arbitrary} & \text{Otherwise} \end{cases} \qquad (3.60)$$

3.7.4.2 VSB demodulator

If the normalised frequency response of the VSB filter used in the modulator satisfies Eq. (3.60), then a VSB signal can be extracted by coherent demodulation as shown in Fig. 3.45. The operation of a coherent demodulator has been discussed in previous sections and will not be repeated here, except to remind that the sum frequency output of the product modulator is rejected by the LPF. We therefore concentrate on the difference frequency, which is the output of the low-pass filter. Our concern here will be to demonstrate how the vestigial LSB compensates perfectly for the attenuated portion of the USB, resulting in the recovery of the original message spectrum.

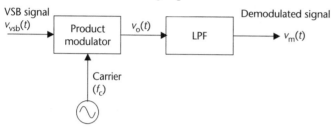

Figure 3.45 Coherent demodulation of VSB.

We need to use the double-sided VSB spectrum shown in Fig. 3.46(a). The difference frequency output is the result of the band of positive frequencies in the VSB signal being translated downwards by f_c, and the band of negative frequencies being translated upwards by f_c. You will recall from Chapter 2 that the amplitude spectrum of a real signal has even symmetry. Thus, if a positive frequency component is shifted to the left (i.e. downwards in frequency), then the corresponding negative frequency component is shifted to the right (i.e. upwards in frequency) by the same amount. Figure 3.46(b) shows the double-sided spectrum of the LPF output. The negative band of frequencies $-f_c - f_m \rightarrow -f_c + B_v$ in the VSB signal $v_{vsb}(t)$ has been translated to $-f_m \rightarrow B_v$, while the corresponding positive band $f_c - B_v \rightarrow f_c + f_m$ has been translated to $-B_v \rightarrow f_m$. These bands

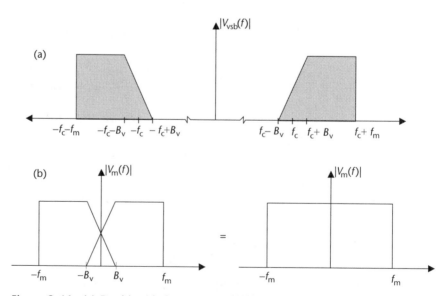

Figure 3.46 (a) Double-sided spectrum of VSB signal; (b) output of LPF.

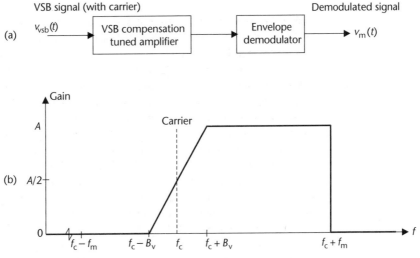

Figure 3.47 (a) Envelope demodulation of VSB; (b) gain response of VSB compensation-tuned amplifier.

overlap as shown and the resultant spectrum, which is the spectrum of the LPF output, is the double-sided equivalent of the original message spectrum shown earlier in Fig. 3.43. The condition of asymmetry about f_c is required so that the sum of the bands in the region of overlap equals a constant — normalised to unity.

In commercial television receivers, where the cost of the receiver is an important design consideration, the use of envelope demodulation (as in AM) is preferred to coherent demodulation. To accomplish this the carrier signal is added to the VSB signal before transmission. A cheap diode demodulator (discussed in Section 3.5.1) can then be used to recover the message signal. However, the recovered signal is distorted in that frequency components (from DC to B_v) that appear in both sidebands are doubled in amplitude compared to components in only one sideband (from B_v to f_m). To compensate for this the diode demodulator is preceded with a tuned amplifier, the gain of which varies asymmetrically about the carrier frequency. Figure 3.47(a) shows a basic block diagram of an envelope demodulator for a VSB signal, with the frequency response of the VSB compensation amplifier shown in Fig. 3.47(b).

SUMMARY

In this chapter we have studied amplitude modulation and its four variants in detail. The basic scheme, *double sideband transmitted carrier amplitude modulation*, is referred to simply as amplitude modulation (AM). The amplitude of a sinusoidal carrier signal is varied proportionately with the message signal between a non-negative minimum value and a maximum value. The result is that the AM signal consists of the carrier signal and two sidebands. The carrier signal does not carry any information, but its presence allows a simple envelope demodulation scheme to be employed at the receiver to recover the message signal. The main advantage of AM is the simplicity of the circuits required for transmission and reception. AM can be generated using a non-linear device followed by a suitable filter. It can be demodulated using an envelope demodulation circuit that consists of a diode, capacitor and load resistor. However, AM is very wasteful of power. At least two thirds of the transmitted power is in the carrier. To put, say, 10 kW of power in the information-bearing sidebands, one must generate a total power of at least 30 kW. AM is therefore employed mainly in sound broadcasting where it is advantageous to have numerous cheap receivers and one expensive high-power transmitter.

To save power the AM carrier may be suppressed, leading to the first variant of AM that is called *double sideband suppressed carrier amplitude modulation*, abbreviated simply as DSB. There is, however, a penalty. The simple envelope modulator can no longer be used at the receiver because the envelope of the missing carrier does not correspond with the message signal. Coherent demodulation is required, which introduces increased circuit complexity. The *Costas loop* was discussed, which allows the locally generated carrier to be synchronised in phase and frequency with the missing carrier in the incoming DSB signal. Another way of achieving synchronisation is to insert a low-level pilot carrier at the transmitter, which is extracted at the receiver and scaled in frequency to generate the required carrier. DSB is used in those radio communication applications involving low-bandwidth message signals that must be transmitted over a long range with a minimum of power.

It was noted that AM and DSB both transmit two sidebands, one a mirror image of the other, which carry identically the same information. The bandwidth requirement can be halved, with a further reduction in the required transmitted power level, if both the carrier and one sideband are removed. This leads to what is known as *single sideband suppressed carrier amplitude modulation*, abbreviated simply as SSB. Telecommunication applications that favour SSB are those with significant bandwidth constraints, limited transmit power capability and comparable numbers of transmitters and receivers.

Independent sideband modulation (ISB) places two message signals onto one carrier, with one message in each of the sidebands. We showed that it makes extra spectrum saving by allowing the two sidebands to be more closely packed than is possible with SSB. However, it requires more extensive circuitry than SSB, and is therefore less commonly used.

When a message signal has a combination of a large bandwidth and significant frequency components near DC, then neither DSB nor SSB is suitable. DSB would involve excessive bandwidth, and SSB would require impractical filters to separate the sidebands. A compromise technique, called *vestigial sideband amplitude modulation* (VSB) sends one nearly complete sideband plus a vestige of the other sideband. This is achieved at the transmitter by filtering the DSB signal with a filter whose response is asymmetric about the carrier frequency. The original message signal can be recovered at the receiver by straightforward coherent demodulation. A cheaper envelope demodulator is used in TV receivers. To do this the carrier must be inserted into the VSB signal at the transmitter, and the incoming VSB signal must first be passed through a tuned amplifier that compensates for those frequency components appearing in only one sideband.

This completes our study of amplitude modulation applied to analogue message signals. We shall briefly return to amplitude modulation in Chapter 7 when we apply it to digital signals. In the next chapter, we take another important step in our study of communication systems by looking at the terminology, waveform, spectrum, power, operation and applications of angle modulation.

REVIEW QUESTIONS

3.1 A carrier signal $v_c(t) = 5\sin(2\pi \times 10^6 t)$ V is modulated in amplitude by the message signal $v_m(t)$ shown in Fig. 3.48.

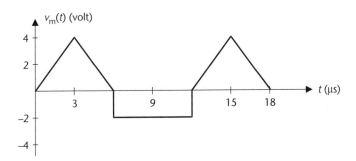

Figure 3.48 Figure for Question 3.1.

(a) Sketch the waveform of the AM signal that is obtained.
(b) What is the modulation factor?
(c) Determine the modulation sensitivity that would give 100% modulation.

3.2 An oscilloscope display of an AM waveform involving a sinusoidal message signal shows a maximum peak-to-peak value 10 V and a minimum peak-to-peak value 2 V. Calculate

(a) Carrier signal amplitude
(b) Message signal amplitude
(c) Modulation index

3.3 An AM signal is analysed by a spectrum analyser, which shows that there are the following frequency components:

(i) 998 kHz of amplitude 10 V

(ii) 1 MHz of amplitude 50 V

(iii) 1.002 MHz of amplitude 10 V

(a) Specify the carrier and message signals as functions of time, assuming that the initial phase of each is zero.

(b) Determine the depth of modulation.

(c) What power would be dissipated by this AM signal in a 50 Ω load?

3.4 An engineering student wishing to improve AM power utilisation generates an AM signal in which the carrier and each sideband have equal power. By calculating the modulation factor, determine whether a conventional (non-coherent) AM receiver would be able to demodulate this AM signal.

3.5 A carrier of amplitude V_c is modulated by a multi-tone message signal, which is made up of sinusoids of amplitudes V_1, V_2, V_3, ... Starting from Eq. (3.25), show that the modulation factor is given by

$$m = \sqrt{m_1^2 + m_2^2 + m_3^2 + \cdots}$$

where $m_1 = V_1/V_c$, $m_2 = V_2/V_c$, $m_3 = V_3/V_c$, ...

3.6 The carrier $v_c(t) = 120\sin(4 \times 10^6 \pi t)$ V is amplitude modulated by the message signal

$$v_m(t) = 80\sin(40 \times 10^3 \pi t) + 50\sin(80 \times 10^3 \pi t)$$
$$+ 30\sin(100 \times 10^3 \pi t) \text{ V}$$

(a) Sketch the AM signal spectrum.

(b) Determine the fraction of power in the sidebands.

(c) Determine the modulation index.

3.7 A 75% modulated AM signal has 1 kW of power in the lower sideband. The carrier component is attenuated by 4 dB before transmission but the sideband components are unchanged. Calculate:

(a) The total transmitted power.

(b) The new modulation index.

3.8 A 1.2 MHz carrier of amplitude 10 V is amplitude modulated by a message signal containing two frequency components at 1 kHz and 3 kHz, each having amplitude 5 V. Determine

(a) The bandwidth of the message signal.

(b) The width of each of the sidebands of the AM signal.

(c) The condition under which the bandwidth of the AM signal is twice the width of each sideband.

(d) The modulation index.

(e) The total power in the AM signal.

3.9 The output voltage v_o and input voltage v_i of a non-linear device are related by

$$v_o = v_i + 0.2v_i^2$$

A series connection of a carrier signal source of amplitude 20 V and frequency 100 kHz, and a message signal source of amplitude 10 V and frequency 5 kHz provides the input to this device.

(a) Sketch the amplitude spectrum of the output signal v_o.

(b) Specify the frequency response of a filter required to extract the AM signal component of v_o without distortion.

(c) Determine the modulation index of the AM signal.

3.10 The envelope demodulator in an AM superheterodyne receiver consists of the diode demodulator circuit shown in Fig. 3.17(a). Determine suitable values of load resistance R_L and capacitance C, assuming a forward-bias diode resistance $R_f = 20\ \Omega$, and IF amplifier output impedance $R_s = 50\ \Omega$. Note that carrier frequency is $f_{IF} = 470$ kHz and the message signal is audio of frequencies 50 Hz to 5 kHz.

3.11 A *square-law demodulator* is shown in Fig. 3.49, where the input voltage $v_{am}(t)$ is the incoming AM signal. For small input voltage levels, the diode current is a non-linear function of $v_{am}(t)$ so that the output voltage $v_o(t)$ is given approximately by

$$v_o = a_1 v_{am} + a_2 v_{am}^2$$

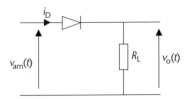

Figure 3.49 Figure for Question 3.11.

(a) Evaluate the output voltage $v_o(t)$ and show that it contains the original message signal.

(b) Discuss how the message signal may be extracted from $v_o(t)$ and the conditions that must be satisfied to minimise distortion.

3.12 *Quadrature amplitude modulation* (QAM) is used to transmit two DSB signals within the same bandwidth that would be occupied by one DSB signal. One message signal $v_{m1}(t)$ is carried on a carrier of frequency f_c, while the other (independent) message signal $v_{m2}(t)$ is carried on a carrier of the same frequency but with a 90° phase difference. The QAM signal is therefore given by

$$v_{qam}(t) = v_{m1}(t)V_c \cos(2\pi f_c t) + v_{m2}(t)V_c \sin(2\pi f_c t)$$

(a) Draw the block diagram of a QAM modulator that generates $v_{qam}(t)$.

(b) Show that the message signal $v_{m1}(t)$ can be extracted at the receiver by passing $v_{qam}(t)$ through a coherent demodulator that uses an oscillator generating a synchronised carrier $V'_c \cos(2\pi f_c t)$, and that another coherent demodulator operating with carrier signal $V'_c \sin(2\pi f_c t)$ extracts $v_{m2}(t)$.

(c) Draw the block diagram of a QAM demodulator.

3.13 Let a sinusoidal message signal of frequency f_m be transmitted on a carrier of frequency f_c. Assume that, due to selective fading, the lower side frequency reaches the receiver with a phase ϕ_1 relative to the carrier, while the upper side frequency has a phase ϕ_2 relative to the carrier.

(a) Obtain an expression for the coherently demodulated signal, given that the transmission is DSB and the local carrier is perfectly synchronised with the missing carrier in the incoming signal. Discuss the distortion effects of ϕ_1 and ϕ_2, and specify the condition under which there is complete cancellation so that the demodulated signal is zero.

(b) Sketch the AM waveform for $\phi_1 = 60°$, and $\phi_2 = 0°$. How does the selective fading affect the output of an envelope demodulator?

(c) Use a sketch of the AM waveform to examine the effect on the AM envelope when selective fading attenuates the carrier signal by 3 dB more than the attenuation of the side frequencies. Assume that the side frequencies remain in phase with the carrier.

Angle modulation

IN THIS CHAPTER

- Basic concepts of FM and PM: a fresh and lucid approach to the theory of angle modulation, which gives you a very confident start to the study of FM and PM systems.

- FM and PM waveforms: a detailed discussion of all types of angle-modulated waveforms. You will be able to sketch these waveforms and to identify them by visual inspection.

- Spectrum and power of FM and PM: you will be able to solve various problems on the spectrum, bandwidth and power of FM and PM signals. You will particularly benefit from the lucid treatment of *narrowband* FM and PM, with comparisons to AM.

- FM and PM modulators: a detailed discussion of various methods of applying the theory of previous Sections to generate FM and PM signals.

- FM and PM demodulators: a discussion of how to track the frequency variations in received angle-modulated signals and to convert these frequency variations to voltage variations.

- FM transmitters and receivers: a discussion of the building blocks and signal processing in a complete FM communication system, including the tasks of *pre-emphasis* and *de-emphasis*. A simplified treatment of the trade-off between transmission bandwidth and signal-to-noise power ratio (SNR) is also presented.

- Features overview: a discussion of the merits, demerits and applications of angle modulation.

4.1 Introduction

Modulation plays very significant roles in telecommunication, as discussed in Section 1.5.3. Amplitude modulation was treated in detail in Chapter 3. It is the oldest modulation technique, obtained by varying the amplitude of a high-frequency sinusoidal carrier in synchrony with the message signal. One of the problems with amplitude modulation is that additive noise in the transmission medium will also impose variations on the amplitude of the modulated carrier in a manner that is impossible for the receiver to separate from the legitimate variations caused by the message signal. The received message signal will therefore be corrupted to some extent by noise.

An alternative modulation technique that is less susceptible to additive noise was first proposed in 1931. In this technique, which is given the generic name *angle modulation*, the amplitude V_c of the sinusoidal carrier is kept constant, but the angle θ_c of the carrier is varied in synchrony with the message signal. The angle θ_c of a sinusoidal carrier at any instant of time t depends on the frequency f_c and *initial phase* ϕ_c of the carrier, according to the relation

$$\theta_c(t) = 2\pi f_c t + \phi_c \tag{4.1}$$

Thus, the angle of the carrier may be varied in one of two ways:

1. By varying the frequency f_c of the carrier, giving rise to what is known as *frequency modulation*, or
2. By varying the initial phase ϕ_c of the carrier, resulting in *phase modulation*. Some textbooks refer to ϕ_c as the *phase shift*.

This chapter is devoted to the study of the related techniques of frequency modulation (FM) and phase modulation (PM). First, we introduce FM and PM using a simple staircase signal, and define common terms such as *frequency sensitivity*, *phase sensitivity*, *frequency deviation* and *percent modulation*. Next, we study the angle modulation of a carrier by a sinusoidal message signal. It is shown that FM and PM are implicitly related in that FM transmission of a message signal is equivalent to the PM transmission of a suitably low-pass filtered version of the message signal. Narrowband and wideband angle modulations are discussed in detail, including two of the most common definitions of the bandwidth of FM and PM.

The modulator and demodulator circuits that implement FM and PM schemes are discussed in block diagram format. The presentation also includes FM transmitter and receiver systems, and concludes with a discussion of the applications of angle modulation and its merits and demerits compared to AM.

4.2 Basic concepts of FM and PM

Angle modulation (FM or PM) represents a message signal using non-linear variations in the angle of a sinusoidal carrier signal. The amplitude of the carrier signal is not varied, and therefore any noise-imposed fluctuations in carrier amplitude are simply ignored at the receiver. This gives FM and PM a greater robustness against noise and interference than is possible with AM.

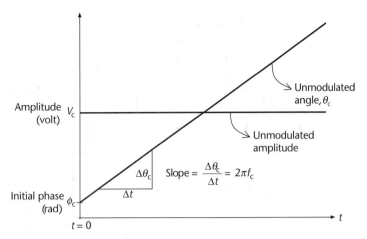

Figure 4.1 Amplitude and angle of an unmodulated carrier as functions of time.

The information contained in the variations of the message signal is perfectly preserved in the variations of the carrier angle, and this information is recovered at the receiver by tracking the carrier angle. As with AM, there is a great deal of freedom in the choice of the frequency of the unmodulated carrier signal, allowing information transmission through a variety of transmission media and communication systems.

The angle θ_c of an unmodulated sinusoidal carrier of frequency f_c is given by Eq. (4.1), which shows that θ_c increases linearly with time at the constant rate $2\pi f_c$ radian per second. The amplitude of this carrier remains constant at V_c. Figure 4.1 is a plot of both parameters (the angle and amplitude) of an unmodulated carrier as functions of time. We saw in Chapter 3 that the effect of amplitude modulation is to cause the amplitude to deviate from the constant value V_c in accordance with the instantaneous value of the message signal. The angle of an amplitude-modulated carrier is not varied by the message signal, so it continues to be a linear function of time. What happens in the case of angle modulation is that the carrier amplitude remains constant with time, but the carrier angle is caused to deviate from being a linear function of time by variations of the message signal. The carrier angle has two components, namely frequency f_c and initial phase ϕ_c, and the manner of the deviation depends on which of these two components is varied by the message signal.

As an example, Fig. 4.2(a) shows a simple staircase message signal that has the following values

$$v_m(t) = \begin{cases} 0\ \text{V}, & 0 \le t < 1\ \text{ms} \\ 2\ \text{V}, & 1 \le t < 2\ \text{ms} \\ 1\ \text{V}, & 2 \le t < 3\ \text{ms} \\ -1\ \text{V}, & 3 \le t < 4\ \text{ms} \\ -2\ \text{V}, & 4 \le t < 5\ \text{ms} \\ 0\ \text{V}, & 5 \le t \le 6\ \text{ms} \end{cases} \tag{4.2}$$

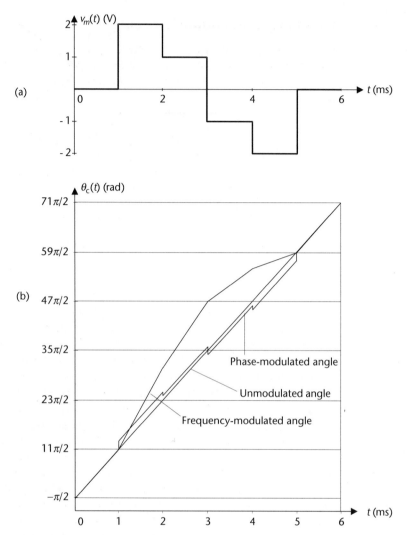

Figure 4.2 (a) Staircase message signal; (b) angle of sinusoidal carrier. Frequency sensitivity k_f = 1 kHz/volt; phase sensitivity k_p = $\pi/2$ rad/volt.

Let this signal modulate the angle of the carrier

$$\begin{aligned} v_c(t) &= V_c \cos[\theta_c(t)] \\ &= V_c \cos(2\pi f_c t + \phi_c) \end{aligned} \tag{4.3}$$

In the following discussion we will use the values, amplitude v_c = 2 V, frequency f_c = 3 kHz, and initial phase ϕ_c = $-\pi/2$ to demonstrate the angle modulation process. Of course, any other set of values could have been selected. The modulation can be performed either by varying the frequency or the initial phase of the carrier, as discussed below.

4.2.1 Frequency modulation concepts

In frequency modulation, the frequency of the carrier at any given time is changed from its unmodulated value f_c by an amount that depends on the value of the message signal at that time. The *instantaneous frequency f_i* of the carrier is given by

$$f_i = f_c + k_f v_m(t) \tag{4.4}$$

where k_f is the change in carrier frequency per volt of modulating signal, called *frequency sensitivity* and expressed in units of Hz/volt. In our example, with $k_f = 1$ kHz/volt and the message and carrier signals specified in Eqs. (4.2) and (4.3), the instantaneous frequency of the frequency-modulated carrier is as follows

$$f_i = f_c + k_f v_m(t) = \begin{cases} 3 \text{ kHz,} & 0 \le t < 1 \text{ ms} \\ 5 \text{ kHz,} & 1 \le t < 2 \text{ ms} \\ 4 \text{ kHz,} & 2 \le t < 3 \text{ ms} \\ 2 \text{ kHz,} & 3 \le t < 4 \text{ ms} \\ 1 \text{ kHz,} & 4 \le t < 5 \text{ ms} \\ 3 \text{ kHz,} & 5 \le t \le 6 \text{ ms} \end{cases} \tag{4.5}$$

In the interval $0 \le t < 1$ ms the message signal is 0 V, so the carrier frequency is unchanged from its unmodulated value $f_c = 3$ kHz. However, in the interval $1 \le t < 2$ ms the message signal is 2 V, and the carrier frequency is changed from f_c by an amount $k_f \times v_m(t) = (1 \text{ kHz/V}) \times 2 \text{ V} = 2$ kHz. The instantaneous carrier frequency during this interval is therefore $f_i = 5$ kHz. The values of f_i in other time intervals are similarly determined.

Now consider the effect of this variable carrier frequency on the angle $\theta_c(t)$ of the carrier. The carrier angle θ_c starts at the initial value ϕ_c ($= -\pi/2$ in this example). During the first 1 ms interval when the modulating signal $v_m(t) = 0$ V, $f_i = f_c$ ($= 3$ kHz in this example), and θ_c increases at the rate of $2\pi f_i$ rad/s $= 6\pi$ rad/ms, reaching the value $\theta_c = 11\pi/2$ at $t = 1$ ms. At this time instant $v_m(t)$ increases to 2 V, so the instantaneous carrier frequency is increased to $f_i = 5$ kHz as already shown, and the carrier angle then increases at a faster rate $2\pi f_i$ rad/s or 10π rad/ms, reaching the value $\theta_c = 31\pi/2$ at $t = 2$ ms. During the third 1 ms interval the instantaneous frequency $f_i = 4$ kHz, and θ_c increases from $31\pi/2$ at the rate 8π rad/ms to reach $\theta_c = 47\pi/2$ at $t = 3$ ms.

Following the above reasoning, the values of carrier angle at all time instants are obtained. This is plotted in Fig. 4.2(b). It can be seen that the carrier angle is constantly increasing. This is the same as saying that the carrier is constantly oscillating, since it will have the same value at angles that differ by integer multiples of 2π. However, unlike the unmodulated carrier, the rate of carrier angle increase ($= 2\pi f_i$) is not constant but changes in synchrony with the message signal. The carrier oscillates faster (than f_c) for positive message values, and more slowly for negative message values. If, as in this example, the message signal has zero average value (i.e. equal amounts of negative and positive values), then the carrier oscillation (or increase in angle) is slowed down by as much as it is speeded up at various times. The final value of θ_c is then the same as that of the unmodulated carrier. However, the modulated carrier has increased from its initial angle value (ϕ_c) to its final angle value using a variable rate of increase, which is what conveys information. On the other hand, the unmodulated carrier maintains a constant rate of increase of angle in going between the same endpoints and therefore conveys no information.

Let us now introduce a number of important terms that are associated with frequency modulation. We show later that these terms are also applicable to phase modulation. It is obvious from Eq. (4.4) that the instantaneous frequency f_i increases as the modulating signal $v_m(t)$ increases. The minimum instantaneous frequency f_{imin} occurs at the instant that $v_m(t)$ has its minimum value V_{min}, and the maximum instantaneous frequency f_{imax} occurs when $v_m(t)$ has its maximum value V_{max}:

$$f_{imin} = f_c + k_f V_{min}$$
$$f_{imax} = f_c + k_f V_{max} \tag{4.6}$$

The difference between f_{imax} and f_{imin} gives the range within which the carrier frequency is varied, and is known as the *frequency swing* $f_{p\text{-}p}$

$$\begin{aligned} f_{p\text{-}p} &= f_{imax} - f_{imin} \\ &= k_f(V_{max} - V_{min}) \\ &= k_f V_{mp\text{-}p} \end{aligned} \tag{4.7}$$

where $V_{mp\text{-}p}$ is the peak-to-peak value of the modulating signal $v_m(t)$.

The maximum amount by which the carrier frequency deviates from its unmodulated value f_c is known as the *frequency deviation* f_d. It depends on the frequency sensitivity k_f of the modulator, and the maximum absolute value of the modulating signal. Thus,

$$f_d = k_f |v_m(t)|_{max} \tag{4.8}$$

A maximum allowed frequency deviation is usually set by the relevant telecommunication regulatory body (e.g. the FCC in the USA), in order to limit bandwidth utilisation. This maximum allowed frequency deviation is called the *rated system deviation* F_D:

$$F_D = \begin{cases} 75 \text{ kHz}, & \text{FM radio (88–108 MHz band)} \\ 25 \text{ kHz}, & \text{TV sound broadcast} \\ 5 \text{ kHz}, & \text{2-way mobile radio (25 kHz bandwidth)} \\ 2.5 \text{ kHz}, & \text{2-way mobile radio (12.5 kHz bandwidth)} \end{cases} \tag{4.9}$$

The ratio (expressed as a percentage) of actual frequency deviation f_d in a particular FM implementation to the maximum allowed deviation is known as the *percent modulation m*:

$$m = \frac{f_d}{F_D} \times 100\% \tag{4.10}$$

Note that this concept of percent modulation is different from that associated with amplitude modulation, where there is no regulatory upper limit on the deviation of the carrier amplitude from its unmodulated value v_c.

The ratio of frequency deviation f_d of the carrier to the frequency f_m of the modulating signal is known as the *modulation index* β:

$$\beta = \frac{f_d}{f_m} \tag{4.11}$$

The modulation index has a single value only in those impractical situations where the modulating signal is a sinusoidal signal — this contains a single frequency f_m. For the practical case of an information-bearing message signal, a band of modulating frequencies from f_1 to f_m is involved. The modulation index then ranges in value from a minimum β_{min} to a maximum β_{max}, where

$$\beta_{min} = \frac{f_d}{f_m}; \qquad \beta_{max} = \frac{f_d}{f_1} \tag{4.12}$$

In this case, the more useful design parameter is β_{min}, which is also called the *deviation ratio D*. It is the ratio between frequency deviation and the maximum frequency component of the message signal. Deviation ratio replaces modulation index when dealing with non-sinusoidal message signals. It corresponds to a worst-case situation where the maximum frequency component f_m of the message signal has the largest amplitude and therefore causes the maximum deviation of the carrier from its unmodulated frequency f_c. Thus, if an arbitrary message signal of maximum frequency component f_m modulates a carrier and causes a frequency deviation f_d, then

$$\text{Deviation ratio } D = \frac{f_d}{f_m} \tag{4.13}$$

WORKED EXAMPLE 4.1

A message signal $v_m(t) = 2\sin(30 \times 10^3 \pi t)$ volt is used to frequency modulate the carrier $v_c(t) = 10\sin(200 \times 10^6 \pi t)$ V. The frequency sensitivity of the modulating circuit is $k_f = 25$ kHz/V. Determine

(a) The frequency swing of the carrier
(b) The modulation index
(c) The percent modulation

(a) The message signal has amplitude $V_m = 2$ V, and peak-to-peak value $V_{mp\text{-}p} = 2V_m = 4$ V. From Eq. (4.7), the frequency swing is given by

$$f_{p\text{-}p} = k_f V_{mp\text{-}p}$$
$$= (25\,\text{kHz/V}) \times 4\,\text{V} = 100\,\text{kHz}$$

(b) The maximum absolute value $|v_m(t)|_{max}$ of this (sinusoidal) message signal is its amplitude $V_m = 2$ V. Multiplying this by the frequency sensitivity gives the frequency deviation $f_d = 50$ kHz. From the expression for $v_m(t)$, the modulating signal frequency $f_m = 15$ kHz. Thus, modulation index

$$\beta = \frac{f_d}{f_m} = \frac{50}{15} = 3.33$$

(c) Since the carrier frequency is 100 MHz, we may safely assume that the application is FM radio with a rated system deviation of 75 kHz. The percent modulation is then

$$m = \frac{f_d}{F_D} \times 100\% = \frac{50}{75} \times 100\% = 66.7\%$$

4.2.2 Phase modulation concepts

In phase modulation, the phase of the carrier at any given time is changed from its unmodulated value ϕ_c by an amount that depends on the value of the message signal at that time. Recall the expression for the unmodulated carrier given in Eq. (4.3):

$$v_c(t) = V_c \cos[\theta_c(t)]$$
$$= V_c \cos(2\pi f_c t + \phi_c)$$

With the variations in phase imposed in sympathy with the message signal, we can now refer to the *instantaneous phase* ϕ_i of the carrier, given by

$$\phi_i = \phi_c + k_p v_m(t) \tag{4.14}$$

where k_p is the change in carrier phase per volt of modulating signal, called *phase sensitivity* and expressed in units of rad/volt. The unmodulated carrier phase ϕ_c is usually set to zero without any loss of generality, since the message signal is carried in the variation of the carrier phase rather than its absolute magnitude. Then

$$\phi_i = k_p v_m(t) \tag{4.15}$$

Let us now examine the variation of the angle of the carrier in Eq. (4.3) when it is phase-modulated by the staircase message signal $v_m(t)$ in Eq. (4.2). We assume a phase modulator sensitivity $k_p = \pi/2$ rad/V. The unmodulated phase of the carrier is $\phi_c = -\pi/2$, and Eq. (4.14) gives the instantaneous phase of the phase-modulated carrier:

$$\phi_i = \phi_c + k_p v_m(t) = \begin{cases} -\pi/2 \text{ rad,} & 0 \le t < 1 \text{ ms} \\ \pi/2 \text{ rad,} & 1 \le t < 2 \text{ ms} \\ 0 \text{ rad,} & 2 \le t < 3 \text{ ms} \\ -\pi \text{ rad,} & 3 \le t < 4 \text{ ms} \\ -3\pi/2 \text{ rad,} & 4 \le t < 5 \text{ ms} \\ -\pi/2 \text{ rad,} & 5 \le t \le 6 \text{ ms} \end{cases} \tag{4.16}$$

It would pay to check that you agree with the above values. The carrier angle θ_c is given at any time t by the sum of two terms,

$$\theta_c(t) = 2\pi f_c t + \phi_i \qquad (4.17)$$

The first term is a component that increases at the *constant* rate $2\pi f_c$ rad/s or 6π rad/ms — since the frequency f_c (= 3 kHz) is not altered in phase modulation. It has the values 0, 6π, 12π, 18π, 24π, 30π and 36π, at $t = 0, 1, 2, 3, 4, 5$ and 6 ms, respectively. The second term is the instantaneous phase, which varies according to the modulating signal, and has the values given in Eq. (4.16). The sum of these two terms gives the phase-modulated angle $\theta_c(t)$ plotted against time in Fig. 4.2(b). Observe that in those intervals where the modulating signal is constant, the phase-modulated carrier angle increases at the same constant rate (= $2\pi f_c$) as the unmodulated carrier angle. Then at the instant that $v_m(t)$ changes by say ΔV V, the phase-modulated angle undergoes a step change equal to $k_p \Delta V$. Herein lies an important difference between FM and PM. In PM, the carrier angle deviates from the unmodulated rate of change (= $2\pi f_c$) only when the modulating signal is changing; whereas in FM the carrier angle changes at a different rate than $2\pi f_c$ whenever the message signal is non-zero.

It should be observed that phase modulation does indirectly produce frequency modulation. For example, phase modulation may cause the angle of a carrier to jump from a lower to a higher value, which is equivalent to the carrier oscillating at a faster rate, i.e. with a higher frequency. Similarly, a drop in carrier angle is equivalent to a reduction in oscillation frequency. FM and PM are therefore very closely related. In Fig. 4.2(b), the phase-modulated angle deviates by discrete jumps from the constant rate of increase that is followed by unmodulated angles. This is because the modulating signal is a staircase and changes in steps. If a smoothly varying (analogue) signal phase-modulates a carrier, the deviations of the rate of change of carrier angle from $2\pi f_c$ will also be smooth, and FM and PM will differ only in the value and time of occurrence of the carrier frequency variations. We will explore the relationship between FM and PM further in the next section.

We could define the terms *phase swing, phase deviation* and so on for phase modulation by analogy with the corresponding definitions for frequency modulation. But these terms are rarely used since it is conventional to treat phase modulation in terms of frequency variations, making the frequency modulation terms applicable to phase modulation. However, the term *phase deviation*, denoted ϕ_d, merits some discussion. It is defined as the maximum amount by which the carrier phase — or the carrier angle — deviates from its unmodulated value. Thus,

$$\phi_d = k_p |v_m(t)|_{max} \qquad (4.18)$$

Remember that a sinusoidal signal completes one full cycle of oscillation when its angle advances through 2π rad. Any further advance in angle merely causes the carrier to repeat a portion or more of a cycle. Using the standard convention of specifying positive angles as anticlockwise rotation from the $+x$-axis direction and negative angles as clockwise rotation from the

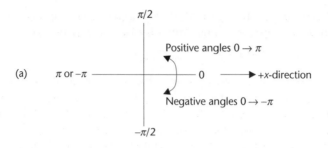

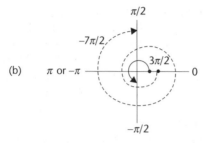

Figure 4.3 (a) Positive and negative angles; (b) examples of equivalent angles; $3\pi/2$ is equivalent to $-\pi/2$; and $-7\pi/2$ is equivalent to $\pi/2$.

same direction, the range of angles that covers a complete cycle is $-\pi$ to $+\pi$; see Fig. 4.3(a). Any phase change by an amount Φ that is outside this range can be shown to be equivalent to some value ϕ within this range, where

$$\phi = \Phi + 2n\pi, \quad n = \ldots, -3, -2, -1, 1, 2, 3, \ldots \tag{4.19}$$

That is, ϕ is obtained by adding to or subtracting from Φ an integer number of 2π in order to place it within the interval $-\pi$ to $+\pi$. For example, Fig. 4.3(b) shows that the phase change $\Phi = 3\pi/2$ is equivalent to

$$\phi = \Phi - 2\pi = 3\pi/2 - 2\pi = -\pi/2$$

and the phase change $\Phi = -7\pi/2$ is equivalent to

$$\phi = \Phi + 4\pi = -7\pi/2 + 4\pi = \pi/2$$

It therefore follows that the maximum possible value of phase deviation ϕ_d is π rad. A value of ϕ_d in excess of π rad is equivalent to a smaller value in the interval $-\pi$ to $+\pi$, according to Eq. (4.19), and would lead to an error at a PM demodulator that tracks the carrier phase. A large message value (that gives a phase deviation $> \pi$) would be mistaken for a smaller message value that would cause an equivalent phase deviation between $-\pi$ and π. Note that this problem only applies in direct wideband phase demodulation, which is never used in analogue communication systems. We define the *phase modulation factor m* as the ratio of actual phase deviation in a particular phase modulation implementation to the maximum possible deviation:

$$m = \frac{\phi_d}{\pi} \tag{4.20}$$

WORKED EXAMPLE 4.2

A message signal $v_m(t) = 5\sin(30 \times 10^3 \pi t)$ volt is used to phase modulate the carrier $v_c(t) = 10\sin(200 \times 10^6 \pi t)$ volt, causing a phase deviation of 2.5 rad. Determine

(a) The phase sensitivity of the modulator.
(b) The phase modulation factor.

(a) The maximum absolute value $|v_m(t)|_{max}$ of the message signal is its amplitude $V_m = 5$ V. From Eq. (4.18), phase sensitivity is

$$k_p = \frac{\phi_d}{|v_m(t)|_{max}} = \frac{2.5\,rad}{5\,V} = 0.5\,rad/V$$

(b) Phase modulation factor:

$$m = \frac{\phi_d}{\pi} = \frac{2.5}{\pi} = 0.796$$

4.2.3 Relationship between FM and PM

Let us now obtain a quantitative indication of the relationship between frequency and phase modulations. We first explore the type of carrier frequency variation that occurs in PM and then consider phase variations in FM signals.

4.2.3.1 Frequency variations in PM

Any message signal $v_m(t)$ can be approximated by a staircase signal $v_{st}(t)$, as shown in Fig. 4.4(a). Time is divided into small intervals Δt, and the curve of $v_m(t)$ in each interval is approximated by two line segments. One segment is horizontal and has a length Δt. The other is vertical and of length Δv_m, which gives the change undergone by $v_m(t)$ during the time interval Δt. In the limit when Δt is infinitesimally small the approximation becomes exact — i.e. $v_{st}(t)$ and $v_m(t)$ become identical.

Consider the result of phase-modulating a carrier of frequency f_c by the signal $v_{st}(t)$. The variation of the carrier angle θ_c during one time interval Δt is shown in Fig. 4.4(b). $v_{st}(t)$ has a constant value until just before the end of the interval, so the carrier angle increases at the unmodulated rate of $2\pi f_c$ from point A to point B. When $v_{st}(t)$ makes a step change of Δv_m at the end of the interval, this causes the carrier phase, and hence its angle, to increase by $k_p \Delta v_m$ from point B to C. The result

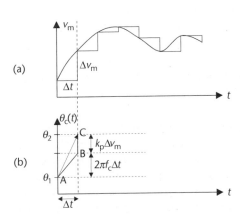

(a)

(b)

Figure 4.4 (a) Staircase approximation of an arbitrary message signal; (b) increase in carrier angle during time interval Δt.

is that the carrier angle has increased from θ_1 to θ_2 in a time Δt. The average rate of change of carrier angle is therefore

$$2\pi f_a = \frac{\theta_2 - \theta_1}{\Delta t} = \frac{2\pi f_c \Delta t + k_p \Delta v_m}{\Delta t}$$

$$= 2\pi f_c + k_p \frac{\Delta v_m}{\Delta t}$$

where f_a is the average carrier frequency during the interval Δt. By making the time interval Δt infinitesimally small, $v_{st}(t)$ becomes the message signal $v_m(t)$; the ratio of Δv_m to Δt becomes the derivative or slope of the message signal; and f_a becomes the instantaneous carrier frequency f_i. Thus

$$f_i = f_c + \frac{1}{2\pi} k_p \frac{dv_m(t)}{dt} \tag{4.21}$$

Equation (4.21) is a remarkable result that reveals how phase modulation varies the carrier frequency. Compare it with Eq. (4.4), repeated below for convenience, which gives the instantaneous frequency of this carrier when frequency-modulated by the same message signal $v_m(t)$ in a modulator of frequency sensitivity k_f:

$$f_i = f_c + k_f v_m(t)$$

Phase modulation (PM) and frequency modulation (FM) are therefore related as follows.

1. Both PM and FM vary the carrier frequency — but not the carrier amplitude of course. FM's frequency variation is achieved directly as expressed in Eq. (4.4). However, PM's frequency variation is indirect and occurs because a (direct) change in the carrier phase causes the carrier's angle to change at a different rate. In other words, it alters the carrier's angular frequency, and hence frequency.

2. PM varies the carrier frequency from its unmodulated value f_c only at those instants when the message signal is changing. The carrier frequency is unchanged whenever the message signal has a constant value, say V_1. During this time the phase of the carrier is simply held at a level $k_p V_1$ above its unmodulated value ϕ_c. FM causes the carrier frequency to deviate from its unmodulated value whenever the message signal has a non-zero value, irrespective of whether that value is constant or changing.

3. In PM, the maximum instantaneous carrier frequency f_{imax} occurs at the instant where the message signal is changing most rapidly, i.e. at the point where the derivative of the message signal is at a maximum. An FM carrier has its maximum instantaneous frequency at the instant that the message signal is at a maximum value. This feature provides a sure way of distinguishing between FM and PM waveforms when the message signal is a smoothly varying analogue signal. This is discussed further in Section 4.3.2.

4. Frequency deviation f_d in PM depends on both the amplitude and frequency of the message signal, whereas in FM it depends only on the message signal amplitude. To see that this is the case, assume a sinusoidal message signal $v_m(t) = V_m \sin(2\pi f_m t)$ in Eqs. (4.4) and (4.21). It follows that

$$f_i = \begin{cases} f_c + k_f V_m \sin(2\pi f_m t), & \text{FM} \\ f_c + k_p f_m V_m \cos(2\pi f_m t) & \text{PM} \end{cases}$$

$$f_{imax} = \begin{cases} f_c + k_f V_m, & \text{FM} \\ f_c + k_p f_m V_m, & \text{PM} \end{cases} \qquad (4.22)$$

The frequency deviation is therefore

$$f_d = f_{imax} - f_c = \begin{cases} k_f V_m, & \text{FM} \\ k_p f_m V_m, & \text{PM} \end{cases} \qquad (4.23)$$

which agrees with the previous statement. Thus, given two frequency components of the same amplitude in a modulating signal, the higher frequency component produces a larger carrier frequency deviation than the deviation caused by the lower frequency component if PM is used; whereas in FM both frequency components produce exactly the same frequency deviation. For this reason, FM has a more efficient bandwidth utilisation than PM in analogue communication.

5. PM can be obtained using an FM modulator. A block diagram of the arrangement is shown in Fig. 4.5. The operation of the FM modulator results in the signal $v_o(t)$ frequency-modulating a carrier of frequency f_c. This produces an FM signal with instantaneous frequency f_i given by Eq. (4.4) as

$$f_i = f_c + k_f v_o(t)$$

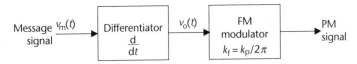

Figure 4.5 PM generation using FM modulator.

Since $v_o(t)$ is the output of the differentiator circuit whose input is the message signal $v_m(t)$, we have

$$v_o(t) = \frac{dv_m(t)}{dt}$$

Substituting this identity for $v_o(t)$ in the expression for f_i, and using a modulator of frequency sensitivity $k_f = k_p/2\pi$, we have the following result for the instantaneous frequency at the output of the FM modulator:

$$f_i = f_c + \frac{k_p}{2\pi} \frac{dv_m(t)}{dt}$$

You will recognise this as Eq. (4.21) — the instantaneous frequency of a PM signal. That is, the message signal has phase-modulated the carrier, and this was achieved by passing the message signal through a differentiator and then using the differentiator output to frequency-modulate a carrier. The differentiator essentially performs high-pass filtering that boosts high-frequency components of $v_m(t)$ relative to the lower frequency components. When this filtered signal $v_o(t)$ is fed into an FM modulator (whose frequency deviation, you will recall, is proportional to modulating signal amplitude), the (boosted) higher frequency components will produce a larger frequency deviation than the deviation produced by lower frequency components of originally similar amplitude. This is a PM characteristic, and therefore the overall result is that the carrier has been phase-modulated by $v_m(t)$.

4.2.3.2 *Phase variations in FM*

We have explored in detail the relationship between FM and PM by looking at the frequency variations in both signals. An alternative approach that concentrates on phase variations is also very illuminating. We already know that PM varies the phase of a carrier signal. Let us show that FM does also vary the carrier phase, albeit indirectly, and explore the relationships between the phase variations in both techniques.

Figure 4.6(a) shows an arbitrary message signal $v_m(t)$ approximated by a staircase signal. We want to determine the instantaneous phase ϕ_i of the carrier signal $v_c(t) = V_c \cos(2\pi f_c t + \phi_i)$ when it is frequency-modulated by $v_m(t)$. The angle of the modulated carrier at any time is given by Eq. (4.17), where ϕ_i is the required instantaneous phase of the carrier. We already know from Eq. (4.14) that PM gives $\phi_i = \phi_c + k_p v_m(t)$. To determine ϕ_i in the case of FM, consider how the modulated carrier angle increases in the time from 0 to t. We have divided this duration into N infinitesimal intervals, numbered from 0 to $N-1$, each of width Δt. The message signal, approximated by the staircase signal $v_{st}(t)$, has a constant value during each interval Δt, which leads to a constant instantaneous frequency of the carrier during that interval. Let us denote the instantaneous frequency of the jth infinitesimal interval as f_j, so that the carrier frequency is f_0 during the interval numbered 0, f_1 during the interval numbered 1, and so on. The carrier angle increases by $2\pi f_j \Delta t$ inside the jth interval, so that the angle of the carrier after time $t = N\Delta t$ is

$$\theta_c(t) = \phi_c + 2\pi f_0 \Delta t + 2\pi f_1 \Delta t + 2\pi f_2 \Delta t + \cdots$$

$$= \phi_c + 2\pi \sum_{j=0}^{N-1} f_j \Delta t \tag{4.24}$$

Observe in Fig. 4.6(b) that the modulating signal has a constant value $v_m(j\Delta t)$ during the jth interval. Thus, Eq. (4.4) gives the instantaneous frequency f_j in this interval as

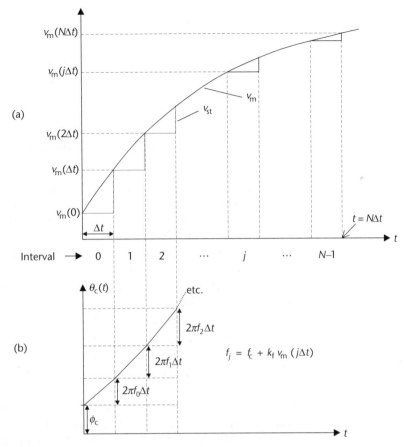

Figure 4.6 (a) Message signal $v_m(t)$ and staircase approximation $v_{st}(t)$; (b) increase in angle of carrier of unmodulated frequency f_c, when modulated in frequency by $v_{st}(t)$.

$$f_j = f_c + k_f v_m(j\Delta t)$$

Substituting this expression in Eq. (4.24) yields

$$\theta_c(t) = \phi_c + 2\pi \sum_{j=0}^{N-1} [f_c + k_f v_m(j\Delta t)]\Delta t$$

$$= \phi_c + 2\pi f_c t + 2\pi k_f \sum_{j=0}^{N-1} v_m(j\Delta t)\Delta t \tag{4.25}$$

In the limit $\Delta t \to 0$, the staircase approximation becomes exact, and the above summation becomes an integration from 0 to t, so that

$$\theta_c(t) = 2\pi f_c t + \phi_c + 2\pi k_f \int_0^t v_m(t)dt \tag{4.26}$$

It follows from Eq. (4.17) that the instantaneous phase of the frequency-modulated carrier is

$$\phi_i = \phi_c + 2\pi k_f \int_0^t v_m(t)dt \tag{4.27}$$

Now compare Eq. (4.27) with Eq. (4.14), repeated below for convenience, which gives the instantaneous phase of the same carrier when it is phase-modulated by the same message signal $v_m(t)$:

$$\phi_i = \phi_c + k_p v_m(t)$$

Therefore, the relationships between FM and PM stated in terms of carrier phase variation are as follows:

1. Both PM and FM vary the carrier phase from its unmodulated value ϕ_c, which is usually set to zero. Phase variation in FM is, however, indirect and results from the fact that a change in the carrier frequency causes the carrier angle to rise to a level that is different from its unmodulated value, and this difference in angle can be accounted as a phase change.

2. PM changes the carrier phase anytime that the message signal is non-zero, whereas FM changes the carrier phase at a given instant only if the average of all previous values of the signal is non-zero.

3. The maximum instantaneous carrier phase occurs in PM at the instant that the modulating signal has its maximum value, whereas in FM it occurs at the instant that the average of all previous values of the signal is at a maximum.

4. Phase deviation ϕ_d in FM depends on both the amplitude and frequency of the message signal, increasing with amplitude but decreasing with frequency. In PM, on the other hand, phase deviation depends only on the amplitude of the message signal. It can be shown that this is the case by substituting a sinusoidal message signal $v_m(t) = v_m \cos(2\pi f_m t)$ in Eqs. (4.14) and (4.27). This yields the result

$$\phi_i = \begin{cases} \phi_c + k_p V_m \cos(2\pi f_m t), & \text{PM} \\ \phi_c + k_f \dfrac{V_m}{f_m} \sin(2\pi f_m t), & \text{FM} \end{cases}$$

and hence

$$\phi_d = \begin{cases} k_p V_m, & \text{PM} \\ k_f \dfrac{V_m}{f_m}, & \text{FM} \end{cases} \tag{4.28}$$

Higher frequency components therefore produce smaller phase deviations in FM.

5. FM can be generated from a PM modulator using the arrangement shown in Fig. 4.7. The PM modulator causes the signal $v_o(t)$ to phase-modulate a carrier. This produces a PM signal with instantaneous phase

$$\phi_i = \phi_c + k_p v_o(t)$$

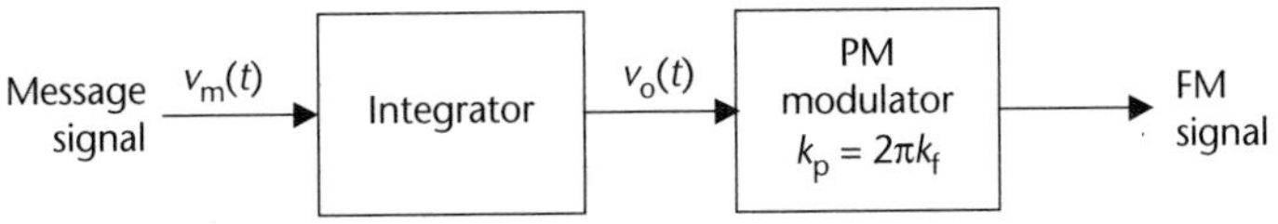

Figure 4.7 FM generation using PM modulator.

However,

$$v_0(t) = \int_0^t v_m(t)dt$$

so that

$$\phi_i = \phi_c + k_p \int_0^t v_m(t)dt = \phi_c + 2\pi k_f \int_0^t v_m(t)dt$$

where we have used a modulator of phase sensitivity $k_p = 2\pi k_f$. You will no doubt recognise this as Eq. (4.27) — the instantaneous phase of an FM signal. That is, the overall result of the arrangement in Fig. 4.7 is that the message signal $v_m(t)$ has frequency-modulated the carrier. FM has been achieved by passing the message signal through an integrator and then using the integrator output to phase-modulate a carrier. In more practical terms, the integrator performs low-pass filtering that attenuates high-frequency components of $v_m(t)$ relative to the lower frequency components. When this filtered signal $v_0(t)$ is fed into a PM modulator (whose phase deviation, you will recall, is proportional to modulating signal amplitude), the (attenuated) higher frequency components will produce a smaller phase deviation than the deviation produced by lower frequency components of (originally) similar amplitude. We showed above that this is a feature of FM, and therefore the overall result is that the carrier has been frequency-modulated by $v_m(t)$.

WORKED EXAMPLE 4.3

Determine
(a) The phase deviation that arises in the FM implementation in Worked example 4.1
(b) The frequency deviation experienced by the PM carrier in Worked example 4.2

(a) What is required here is the maximum amount ϕ_d by which the phase of the frequency-modulated carrier deviates from the phase ϕ_c of the unmodulated carrier. By Eq. (4.28),

$$\phi_d = \frac{k_f V_m}{f_m} = \frac{f_d}{f_m} = \beta \qquad (4.29)$$

This is an important result, which shows that the phase deviation (in rad) of an FM carrier equals its modulation index. Therefore, from Worked example 4.1, $\phi_d = 3.33$ rad.

Note that in this example ϕ_d exceeds π rad. There will however be no error at the receiver as discussed earlier for PM, because an FM demodulator will be used, which only responds to the rate of change of carrier phase, and not the phase magnitude.

(b) We wish to determine the maximum amount f_d by which the frequency of the phase-modulated carrier deviates from the frequency f_c of the unmodulated carrier. By Eq. (4.23),

$$f_d = k_p V_m f_m = \phi_d f_m = 2.5 \times 15\,\text{kHz} = \textbf{37.5\,kHz}$$

We see that the frequency deviation of a PM carrier is given by the product of the carrier phase deviation and the message signal frequency.

4.3 FM and PM waveforms

We studied AM waveforms in Chapter 3 and saw that it was very easy to sketch them — you simply draw a sinusoid with the same number of cycles per second as the carrier but with its amplitude varied to match the message signal waveform. FM and PM waveforms are not as easy to sketch by hand except for the simple cases involving staircase message signals. However, armed with the basic concepts of angle modulation discussed above you can easily distinguish between the oscilloscope displays of FM and PM waveforms. You can also readily plot the FM and PM waveforms for an arbitrary message signal with the aid of a calculator or computer.

4.3.1 Sketching simple waveforms

When the message signal has a staircase shape the FM and PM waveforms can be easily sketched, following the procedure discussed below through a specific example. It should be emphasised that the following approach is only valid for staircase message waveforms. However, this condition is not as restrictive as may first appear. A large number of message signals, including all digital signals — binary, ternary, quarternary etc. — belong in this category.

Consider then the simple staircase message signal $v_m(t)$ and carrier $v_c(t) = V_c \cos(2\pi f_c t + \phi_c)$ introduced in Eqs. (4.2) and (4.3). The carrier signal has amplitude $V_c = 2$ V, frequency $f_c = 3$ kHz, and initial phase $\phi_c = -\pi/2$. We wish to sketch the FM and PM waveforms obtained when $v_m(t)$ modulates the frequency and phase of $v_c(t)$ respectively. We assume frequency sensitivity $k_f = 1$ kHz/V, and phase sensitivity $k_p = \pi/2$ rad/V. Figure 4.8 shows the waveforms involved. The message signal is sketched at the top in (a). The

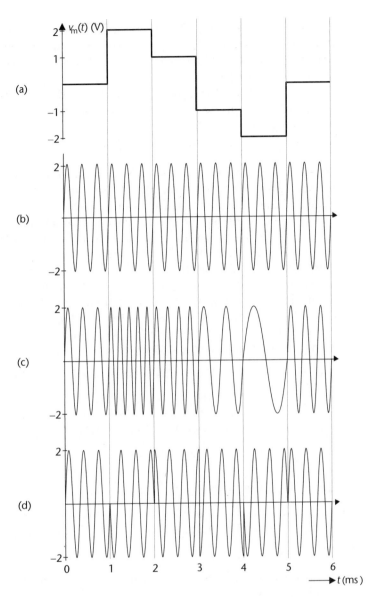

Figure 4.8 (a) Staircase-modulating signal; (b) carrier; (c) frequency modulated carrier; (d) phase-modulated carrier.

unmodulated carrier is sketched in (b) over the duration of the message signal from $t = 0$ to $t = 6$ ms. This is easily done by noting that a frequency of 3 kHz means that the sinusoid completes three cycles in each 1 ms interval, and that an initial phase of $-\pi/2$ rad simply converts the cosine sinusoid to a sine.

The FM signal is sketched in (c). To do this, we determine, using Eq. (4.4), the instantaneous frequency f_i of the modulated carrier within each interval over which the message signal has a constant value. The simplification made possible by the staircase nature of the message signal is that we can treat the FM signal as having constant amplitude and phase over all intervals, and having a single value of instantaneous frequency in each interval. During the first 1 ms, $v_m(t) = 0$ and $f_i = f_c = 3$ kHz. So we sketch three cycles of a cosine sinusoid of amplitude 2 V, and phase $-\pi/2$. The amplitude and phase remain unchanged throughout. In the next 1ms interval, $v_m(t) = 2$ V and

$$f_i = f_c + k_f \times 2 \text{ V} = 3 \text{ kHz} + 1 \text{ kHz/V} \times 2 \text{ V} = 5 \text{ kHz}$$

Therefore we sketch five cycles of the sinusoid. Proceeding in this manner the sketch shown in (c) is completed. Equation (4.5) gives a complete list of values of the instantaneous frequency.

The staircase nature of the message signal again greatly simplifies the procedure for sketching the PM waveform shown in (d). We can treat not only the amplitude but also the frequency of the carrier as constant throughout. So we sketch in each 1 ms interval three cycles (because $f_c = 3$ kHz) of a sinusoid of amplitude 2 V, but the phase ϕ_i in each interval is determined by the message signal value during that interval, according to Eq. (4.14). During the first 1 ms, $v_m(t) = 0$ and $\phi_i = \phi_c = -\pi/2$ rad. So we sketch three cycles of a cosine sinusoid of amplitude 2 V and phase $-\pi/2$. In the next 1 ms interval, $v_m(t) = 2$ V and

$$\phi_i = \phi_c + k_p \times 2 \text{ V} = -\pi/2 + \pi/2 \text{ rad/V} \times 2 \text{ V} = \pi/2 \text{ rad}$$

So we sketch the (cosine) sinusoid with a phase $\pi/2$ rad. Proceeding in this manner we complete the sketch shown in (d) using the complete list of values of ϕ_i given in Eq. (4.16). You may wish to review much of Section 2.3 if you have any difficulty with sketching sinusoids of different phases.

4.3.2 General waveform

Let an arbitrary message signal $v_m(t)$ modulate the angle of the sinusoidal carrier, given by Eq. (4.3), of amplitude V_c, frequency f_c and initial phase ϕ_c:

$$v_c(t) = V_c \cos(2\pi f_c t + \phi_c)$$

Based on the basic concepts discussed earlier, the resulting angle-modulated signal is

$$v(t) = V_c \cos(2\pi f_c t + \phi_i) \tag{4.30}$$

where ϕ_i is the instantaneous phase given by Eqs. (4.14) and (4.27). Specifically,

$$\phi_i = \begin{cases} \phi_c + 2\pi k_f \int_0^t v_m(t)dt, & \text{FM} \\ \phi_c + k_p v_m(t), & \text{PM} \end{cases} \tag{4.31}$$

Substituting Eq. (4.31) in Eq. (4.30) yields the following general expressions for the waveforms of a frequency-modulated signal $v_{fm}(t)$ and a phase-modulated signal $v_{pm}(t)$:

$$v_{fm}(t) = V_c \cos\left[2\pi f_c t + \phi_c + 2\pi k_f \int_0^t v_m(t)\mathrm{d}t\right]$$

$$v_{pm}(t) = V_c \cos[2\pi f_c t + \phi_c + k_p v_m(t)] \tag{4.32}$$

Equation (4.32) gives a complete specification of FM and PM signals in the time domain. It shows that they have the same constant amplitude V_c as the unmodulated carrier, but a variable rate of completing each cycle, caused by the dependence of instantaneous phase on modulating signal. The unmodulated carrier, on the other hand, completes each cycle at a constant rate f_c.

Given a specification of the carrier and message signals, a reliable hand-sketch of $v_{fm}(t)$ and $v_{pm}(t)$ is generally not possible. However, an accurate waveform can be displayed by using Eq. (4.32) to calculate the values of $v_{fm}(t)$ and $v_{pm}(t)$ at a sufficient number of time instants and plotting these points on a graph. We will examine the result of this procedure applied to four different message signals, namely bipolar, sinusoidal, triangular and arbitrary. The same carrier signal is used in the first three examples, with amplitude $V_c = 2$ V, frequency $f_c = 10$ kHz and initial phase $\phi_c = 0$ rad. The bipolar signal has a staircase waveform. It is used here to demonstrate that Eq. (4.32) is applicable to all types of message signals — including the simple staircase waveforms discussed earlier. One of our aims is to show that although FM and PM both involve carrier frequency variation, the difference between their waveforms can be spotted by visual inspection.

Figure 4.9 shows the plots for a bipolar message signal $v_m(t)$ of duration 2 ms and amplitude 1 V using modulations of frequency sensitivity $k_f = 5$ kHz/V, and phase sensitivity $k_p = -\pi/2$ rad/V. A plot of $v_m(t)$ computed at a large number N of time instants ranging from $t = 0$ to 2 ms is shown in (a). The phase-modulated signal $v_{pm}(t)$ is easily calculated at each time instant using Eq. (4.32), and this is plotted in (c), with the unmodulated carrier plotted in (b) for comparison. Calculating the frequency-modulated signal $v_{fm}(t)$ is a little more involved. Specifically, to determine the value of $v_{fm}(t)$ at the time instant $t = \tau$, one numerically integrates $v_m(t)$ from $t = 0$ to $t = \tau$, obtaining a value say $V(\tau)$, and then determines $v_{fm}(\tau)$ as

$$v_{fm}(\tau) = V_c \cos[2\pi f_c \tau + \phi_c + 2\pi k_f V(\tau)]$$

The computation is done for all the N time instants in the range from 0 to 2 ms, where N must be large to make the numerical integration accurate. The signal $v_{fm}(t)$ computed as described here is plotted in Fig. 4.9(d). A detailed discussion of numerical integration is outside our scope. But if you have access to MATLAB version 5, then you can perform the entire computation for $v_{fm}(t)$ using the following single line of code:

```
vfm = Vc*cos(2*pi*fc*t + phic + 2*pi*kf*cumtrapz(t,vm));   (4.33)
```

To use Eq. (4.33), you must first create a vector of time instants t and a vector of corresponding message values vm, and assign values to the following variables: carrier amplitude Vc, carrier frequency fc, carrier initial

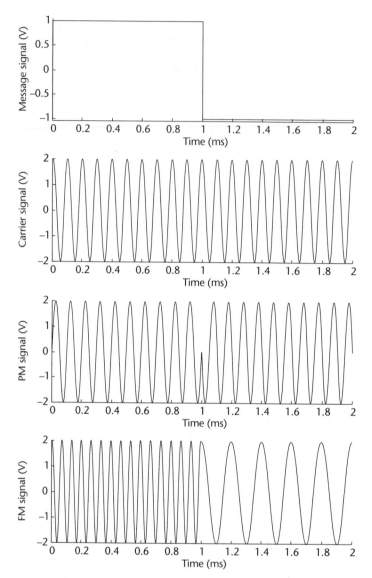

Figure 4.9 Angle modulation by bipolar message signal. Waveforms of (a) message signal; (b) sinusoidal carrier; (c) PM signal; (d) FM signal.

phase phic and frequency sensitivity kf. Typical code that would precede Eq. (4.33) could be

```
N = 4096; t = linspace(0,2,N)'; % N time instants in ms
vm = [ones(N/2,1);-ones(N/2,1)]; % Values of bipolar signal
Vc = 2; fc = 10; % Carrier amplitude (volts) and frequency (kHz)
phic = 0; kf = 5; % Initial phase (rad) and frequency
                  % sensitivity (kHz/V)
```
(4.34)

Observe in Fig. 4.9 that the unmodulated carrier completes 10 cycles per ms, as expected of a 10 kHz sinusoidal signal. The difference between the waveforms of the phase-modulated signal $v_{pm}(t)$ and the frequency-modulated signal $v_{fm}(t)$ is very obvious. The frequency of $v_{pm}(t)$ is the same (f_c = 10 kHz) in each interval where $v_m(t)$ is constant, while that of $v_{fm}(t)$ is different from f_c wherever $v_m(t)$ is non-zero, which in this case is at all time instants.

Following the procedure discussed above, angle-modulated waveforms are plotted in Figs. 4.10, 4.11 and 4.12 for different message signals. The carrier is the same as in Fig. 4.9(b), so its plot is omitted. Figure 4.10 shows a sinusoidal message signal of amplitude v_m = 2 V and frequency f_m = 1 kHz in (a). The PM waveform is shown in (b) for phase sensitivity k_p = 4 rad/V, which according to Eq. (4.23) gives a frequency deviation of 8 kHz. The FM waveform shown in (c) was calculated with frequency sensitivity k_f = 4 kHz/V, which also yields a frequency deviation of 8 kHz. These values of k_f and k_p were chosen specifically to achieve a large and equal frequency deviation in both FM and PM. This gives a pronounced variation in instantaneous frequency that aids our discussion, and allows us to demonstrate that the two waveforms have distinguishing features even when their frequency deviations are equal. However, the value of k_p here is larger than would be used in practice, since it leads to a phase deviation ϕ_d = 8 rad, and hence a phase modulation factor m larger than unity ($m = \phi_d/\pi$ = 2.55). You may

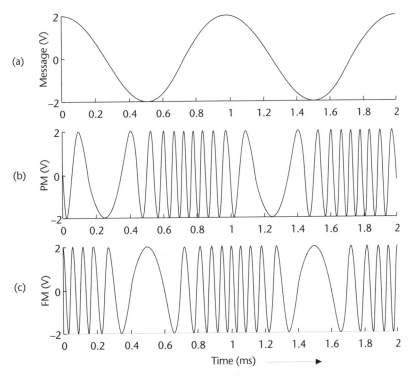

Figure 4.10 Angle modulation by sinusoidal message signal. Waveforms of (a) message signal; (b) PM signal; (c) FM signal.

wish to verify that when FM and PM signals are obtained using the same carrier and the same message signal (of frequency f_m), the condition for their frequency deviations to be equal is given by

$$k_f = k_p f_m \qquad (4.35)$$

It is interesting to observe how the instantaneous frequency of both the PM and FM waveforms in Fig. 4.10 changes smoothly, because the modulating signal is non-staircase. The question then arises, how to identify which waveform is PM and which is FM. The identification can be done very straightforwardly using any one of several tests, all based on the discussion in Section 4.2.3.1. The simplest of these tests are as follows.

1. If the instantaneous frequency f_i of the modulated waveform is maximum at the same instants in which the message signal is maximum, then it is FM. Otherwise, it is PM. In Fig. 4.10, the message signal is maximum at $t = 0$, 1 and 2 ms. The waveform in (b) is *not* oscillating most rapidly at these instants, making it PM; whereas the waveform in (c) has a maximum oscillation rate at these instants, making it definitely FM.

2. If f_i is minimum wherever the modulating signal $v_m(t)$ is minimum, then the waveform is FM; otherwise it is PM. Looking again at Fig. 4.10 we see that $v_m(t)$ is minimum at $t = 0.5$ and 1.5 ms. The waveform in (c) has the lowest rate of oscillation at these instants, making it FM, while waveform (b) does not, and is therefore PM.

3. If f_i is maximum wherever $v_m(t)$ is increasing most rapidly, then the waveform is PM; otherwise it is FM. Note that in Fig. 4.10 waveform (b) has the largest oscillation rate at the time instants $t = 0.75$ and 1.75 ms when the modulating signal is increasing most rapidly.

4. Finally, if f_i is minimum wherever $v_m(t)$ is decreasing most rapidly, then the waveform is PM; otherwise it is FM. Again note that waveform (b) in Fig. 4.10 has a minimum oscillation rate at $t = 0.25$ and 1.25 ms when $v_m(t)$ has the largest negative slope.

Another interesting observation in Fig. 4.10 is that both modulated waveforms complete the same number of cycles as the unmodulated carrier in any 1ms interval. This is not a coincidence. As a general rule, the average frequency of an FM signal is equal to the unmodulated carrier frequency f_c in any time interval over which the modulating signal has a zero *mean value*. A PM signal, on the other hand, has an average frequency equal to f_c in any interval in which the modulating signal has a zero *mean slope*.

Figure 4.11 shows the results for a triangular modulating signal. It is recommended that you verify that each of the waveform identification tests discussed above is valid in this case. Can you explain why the PM waveform has the same number of cycles as the unmodulated carrier over the interval $t = 0$ to 1 ms, whereas the FM waveform has a larger number of cycles?

Figure 4.12 shows the modulated waveforms for an arbitrary and non-staircase modulating signal obtained with modulation parameters $k_f =$

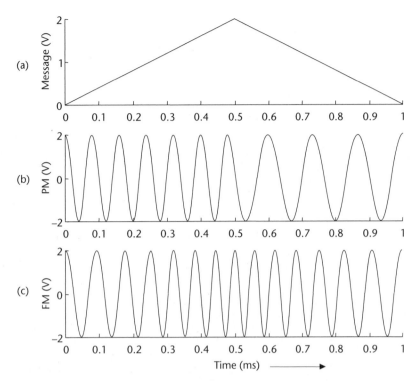

Figure 4.11 Angle modulation by triangular message signal. Waveforms of (a) message signal; (b) PM signal; (c) FM signal.

8kHz/V, $k_p = \pi/2$ rad/V, $f_c = 20$ kHz, and $\phi_c = 0$. You may wish to verify that the waveform identification tests are again valid. Neither the PM nor FM waveform has the same number of cycles (= 20) as the unmodulated carrier over the time interval from 0 to 1 ms. Can you explain why?

The carrier frequency in the above modulation examples was selected to be low enough to allow clear illustrations of the cycles, but high enough to be sufficiently larger than the highest significant frequency component f_m of the message signal. The latter condition is important to avoid distortion, as explained in the next section.

4.4 Spectrum and power of FM and PM

We are now in a position to discuss the important issues of spectrum and power in angle-modulated signals, which leads naturally to bandwidth considerations. To simplify the discussion, let us assume a sinusoidal modulating signal $v_m(t) = V_m \cos(2\pi f_m t)$, and a carrier of initial phase $\phi_c = 0$. Substituting these expressions in Eq. (4.32) gives

$$v_{fm}(t) = V_c \cos\left[2\pi f_c t + \frac{k_f V_m}{f_m} \sin(2\pi f_m t)\right]$$

$$v_{pm}(t) = V_c \cos\left[2\pi f_c t + k_p V_m \cos(2\pi f_m t)\right]$$

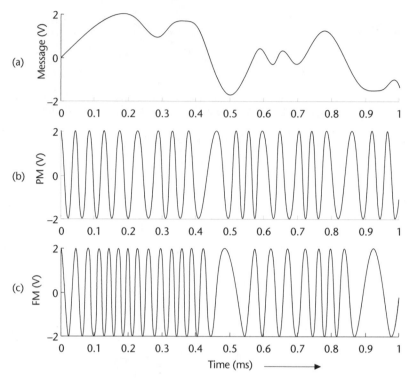

Figure 4.12 Angle modulation by an arbitrary non-staircase message signal. Waveforms of (a) message signal; (b) PM signal; (c) FM signal.

But, from Eq.(4.29), the term $k_f V_m/f_m$ is the FM modulation index β; and, from Eq. (4.28), the term $k_p V_m$ is the PM phase deviation ϕ_d. Therefore,

$$v_{fm}(t) = V_c \cos\left[2\pi f_c t + \beta\sin(2\pi f_m t)\right]$$
$$v_{pm}(t) = V_c \cos\left[2\pi f_c t + \phi_d \cos(2\pi f_m t)\right] \tag{4.36}$$

The time domain relationships between FM and PM have been discussed at length already. This and the striking similarity of the two expressions in Eq. (4.36) suggest that FM and PM will also be strongly related in the frequency domain. Let us explore this further by first assuming that the modulation index β and phase deviation ϕ_d are small, which leads us to what is known as *narrowband angle modulation*. When the restriction on the size of β and ϕ_d is removed, we have what is termed *wideband angle modulation*.

4.4.1 Narrowband FM and PM

4.4.1.1 Frequency components

Let us expand the right-hand side (RHS) of Eq. (4.36) using the compound angle identity of Eq. (A.3) (Appendix A):

Table 4.1 Errors in the approximations $\cos(\theta) \approx 1$, $\sin(\theta) \approx \theta$ and $\tan(\theta) \approx \theta$ for small values of θ (rad).

θ (rad)	0	0.05	0.1	0.15	0.2	0.25	0.3	0.35	0.4
$\cos\theta$	1	0.999	0.995	0.989	0.980	0.969	0.955	0.939	0.921
Approximation (x)	1	1	1	1	1	1	1	1	1
% error = $100(x - \cos\theta)/\cos\theta$	0	0.125	0.502	1.136	2.034	3.209	4.675	6.454	8.570
$\sin\theta$	0	0.050	0.010	0.149	0.199	0.247	0.296	0.343	0.389
Approximation (y)	0	0.05	0.1	0.15	0.2	0.25	0.3	0.35	0.4
% error = $100(y - \sin\theta)/\sin\theta$	0	0.042	0.167	0.376	0.670	1.049	1.516	2.071	2.717
$\tan\theta$	0	0.050	0.100	0.151	0.203	0.255	0.309	0.365	0.423
Approximation (z)	0	0.05	0.1	0.15	0.2	0.25	0.3	0.35	0.4
% error = $\lvert 100(z - \tan\theta)/\tan\theta \rvert$	0	0.083	0.334	0.751	1.337	2.092	3.018	4.117	5.391

$$
\begin{aligned}
v_{\mathrm{fm}}(t) &= V_{\mathrm{c}}\cos(2\pi f_{\mathrm{c}}t)\cos[\beta\sin(2\pi f_{\mathrm{m}}t)] \\
&\quad - V_{\mathrm{c}}\sin(2\pi f_{\mathrm{c}}t)\sin[\beta\sin(2\pi f_{\mathrm{m}}t)] \\
v_{\mathrm{pm}}(t) &= V_{\mathrm{c}}\cos(2\pi f_{\mathrm{c}}t)\cos[\phi_{\mathrm{d}}\cos(2\pi f_{\mathrm{m}}t)] \\
&\quad - V_{\mathrm{c}}\sin(2\pi f_{\mathrm{c}}t)\sin[\phi_{\mathrm{d}}\cos(2\pi f_{\mathrm{m}}t)]
\end{aligned}
\tag{4.37}
$$

For sufficiently small angles θ (in rad), we may use the approximation

$$
\begin{aligned}
\cos(\theta) &\approx 1 \\
\sin(\theta) &\approx \theta \\
\tan(\theta) &\approx \theta
\end{aligned}
\tag{4.38}
$$

Table 4.1 shows the error involved in this approximation for a number of small angles $\theta = 0$ to 0.4 rad.

The error increases as θ increases, and the cut-off point for using the approximations in Eq. (4.38) is usually taken as $\theta = 0.25$ rad. At this point the approximation $\cos(\theta) \approx 1$ introduces an error of 3.209%, $\sin(\theta) \approx \theta$ produces a 1.049% error, while $\tan(\theta) \approx \theta$ causes an error of 2.092%.

It follows that in Eq. (4.37) when the conditions

$$
\begin{aligned}
\beta &\le 0.25, \quad \text{FM} \\
\phi_{\mathrm{d}} &\le 0.25, \quad \text{PM}
\end{aligned}
\tag{4.39}
$$

are satisfied, then we may use the substitutions

$$
\begin{aligned}
\cos[\beta\sin(2\pi f_{\mathrm{m}}t)] &\approx 1 \\
\sin[\beta\sin(2\pi f_{\mathrm{m}}t)] &\approx \beta\sin(2\pi f_{\mathrm{m}}t) \\
\cos[\phi_{\mathrm{d}}\cos(2\pi f_{\mathrm{m}}t)] &\approx 1 \\
\sin[\phi_{\mathrm{d}}\cos(2\pi f_{\mathrm{m}}t)] &\approx \phi_{\mathrm{d}}\cos(2\pi f_{\mathrm{m}}t)
\end{aligned}
\tag{4.40}
$$

to realise

$$v_{fm}(t) \approx V_c \cos(2\pi f_c t) - \beta V_c \sin(2\pi f_c t)\sin(2\pi f_m t)$$
$$\equiv v_{nbfm}(t) \tag{4.41}$$

$$v_{pm}(t) \approx V_c \cos(2\pi f_c t) - \phi_d V_c \sin(2\pi f_c t)\cos(2\pi f_m t)$$
$$\equiv v_{nbpm}(t) \tag{4.42}$$

Using the trigonometric identities of Appendix A to expand the product terms on the RHS of Eq. (4.41) and (4.42), replacing the sine terms in the resulting expression for $v_{nbpm}(t)$ with cosine according to the identity $\sin(\theta) = \cos(\theta - \pi/2)$, and then absorbing any negative sign that precedes a cosine term by using the identity $-\cos(\theta) = \cos(\theta + \pi)$, we finally obtain

$$v_{nbfm}(t) = V_c \cos(2\pi f_c t) + \frac{\beta V_c}{2}\cos[2\pi(f_c - f_m)t + \pi]$$
$$+ \frac{\beta V_c}{2}\cos[2\pi(f_c + f_m)t] \tag{4.43}$$

$$v_{nbpm}(t) = V_c \cos(2\pi f_c t) + \frac{\phi_d V_c}{2}\cos[2\pi(f_c - f_m)t + \pi/2]$$
$$+ \frac{\phi_d V_c}{2}\cos[2\pi(f_c + f_m)t + \pi/2] \tag{4.44}$$

The above signals are referred to as narrowband FM (NBFM) and narrowband PM (NBPM), and result from angle modulation using a small modulation index β (for FM), and a small phase deviation ϕ_d (for PM), as specified by Eq. (4.39). Under this condition, and for a sinusoidal modulating signal, the resulting angle-modulated signal has only three frequency components, namely the carrier at f_c, a lower side frequency (LSF) at $f_c - f_m$, and an upper side frequency (USF) at $f_c + f_m$. You will recall from Chapter 3 that an AM signal $v_{am}(t)$ consists precisely of these same components:

$$v_{am}(t) = V_c \cos(2\pi f_c t)$$
$$+ \frac{mV_c}{2}\cos[2\pi(f_c - f_m)t] + \frac{mV_c}{2}\cos[2\pi(f_c + f_m)t] \tag{4.45}$$

It is worthwhile to take a moment to examine Eqs. (4.43), (4.44) and (4.45) in order to have a thorough understanding of narrowband angle modulation and their relationship with AM.

4.4.1.2 Comparing AM, NBFM and NBPM

Amplitude spectra Figure 4.13 shows the amplitude spectrum of AM, NBFM, and NBPM. We see that they have the same bandwidth,

$$B_{AM} = B_{NBFM} = B_{NBPM} = 2f_m \tag{4.46}$$

where f_m is the frequency of the message signal. The amplitude of side frequencies in each spectrum is

$$V_{SF} = \begin{cases} mV_c/2, & \text{AM} \\ \beta V_c/2, & \text{NBFM} \\ \phi_d V_c/2, & \text{NBPM} \end{cases} \tag{4.47}$$

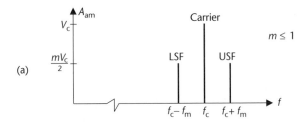

(a)

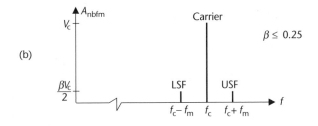

(b)

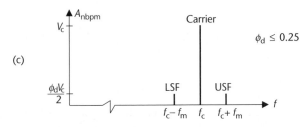

(c)

Figure 4.13 Single-sided amplitude spectrum of (a) AM, (b) NBFM and (c) NBPM.

The goal in AM design is to make modulation factor m close to but not exceeding unity. However, the maximum value of modulation index β (for NBFM) and phase deviation ϕ_d (for NBPM) is 0.25. Therefore the maximum amplitude of each side frequency is

$$V_{\text{SFmax}} = \begin{cases} V_c/2, & \text{AM} \\ V_c/8, & \text{NBFM} \\ V_c/8, & \text{NBPM} \end{cases} \tag{4.48}$$

Waveforms The waveforms of AM, NBFM and NBPM signals obtained with parameter values $m = \beta = \phi_d = 0.25$, $V_c = 1$ V, $f_c = 40$ kHz, and $f_m = 2$ kHz are shown in Fig. 4.14. It is interesting to note how very different the AM waveform $v_{\text{am}}(t)$ is from the angle modulated waveforms even though all three waveforms contain the same frequency components of the same amplitude. The amplitude of $v_{\text{am}}(t)$ varies markedly between $(1 \pm m)V_c$, whereas the angle-modulated waveforms exhibit only a slight amplitude variation. This peculiar behaviour is due to differences in the phase relationships of the frequency components in each signal, which can be readily understood using phasors.

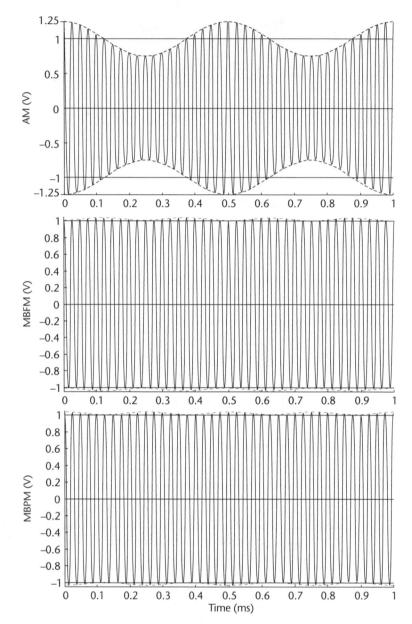

Figure 4.14 Waveforms of AM, NBFM, and NBPM. Parameters: $m = \beta = \phi_d = 0.25$; $f_c = 40$ kHz; $f_m = 2$ kHz; $V_c = 1$ V.

Phase considerations Eqs. (4.43)–(4.45) reveal that at the initial time ($t = 0$), AM has both the LSF and USF in phase with the carrier. NBFM has its USF in phase with the carrier, but its LSF is 180° out of phase. NBPM on the other hand has both its LSF and USF leading the carrier by 90°. This information is summarised in the phase spectra of Fig. 4.15, which gives the initial phases (i.e. angle at $t = 0$) of all frequency components in the modulated signals.

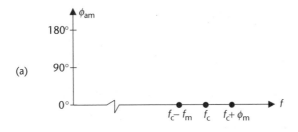

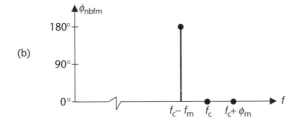

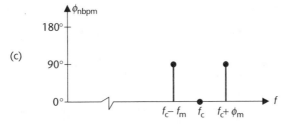

Figure 4.15 Single-sided phase spectrum of (a) AM, (b) NBFM and (c) NBPM.

The implication of these phase relationships on the instantaneous amplitude of each signal is very significant. The best way to illustrate this is by the method of phasors introduced in Chapter 2.

Figure 4.16 uses phasor addition of the carrier, LSF, and USF to obtain the AM, NBFM, and NBPM signals in both amplitude and phase at various time instants. At $t = 0$, the LSF and USF of the AM signal both have zero phase, so their phasors point in the 0° direction. In the NBFM signal, the phase of the LSF is π rad, and that of the USF is 0 rad, so their phasors point in the 180° and 0° directions, respectively. Similarly, the LSF and USF phasors of the NBPM signal both point in the 90° direction at $t = 0$. Phasor addition in each diagram involves drawing the phasors of the carrier, LSF and USF in turn, one phasor starting from the end-point of the previous one. The resultant signal is the phasor obtained by joining the start point of the first-drawn phasor to the end-point of the last-drawn phasor. Note that phasors that would lie on top of each other in Fig. 4.16 have been displaced to keep each one distinct for the purpose of illustration.

To better understand Fig. 4.16, you may wish to consider a useful analogy of three cars L, C and U starting at the same time ($t = 0$) and travelling

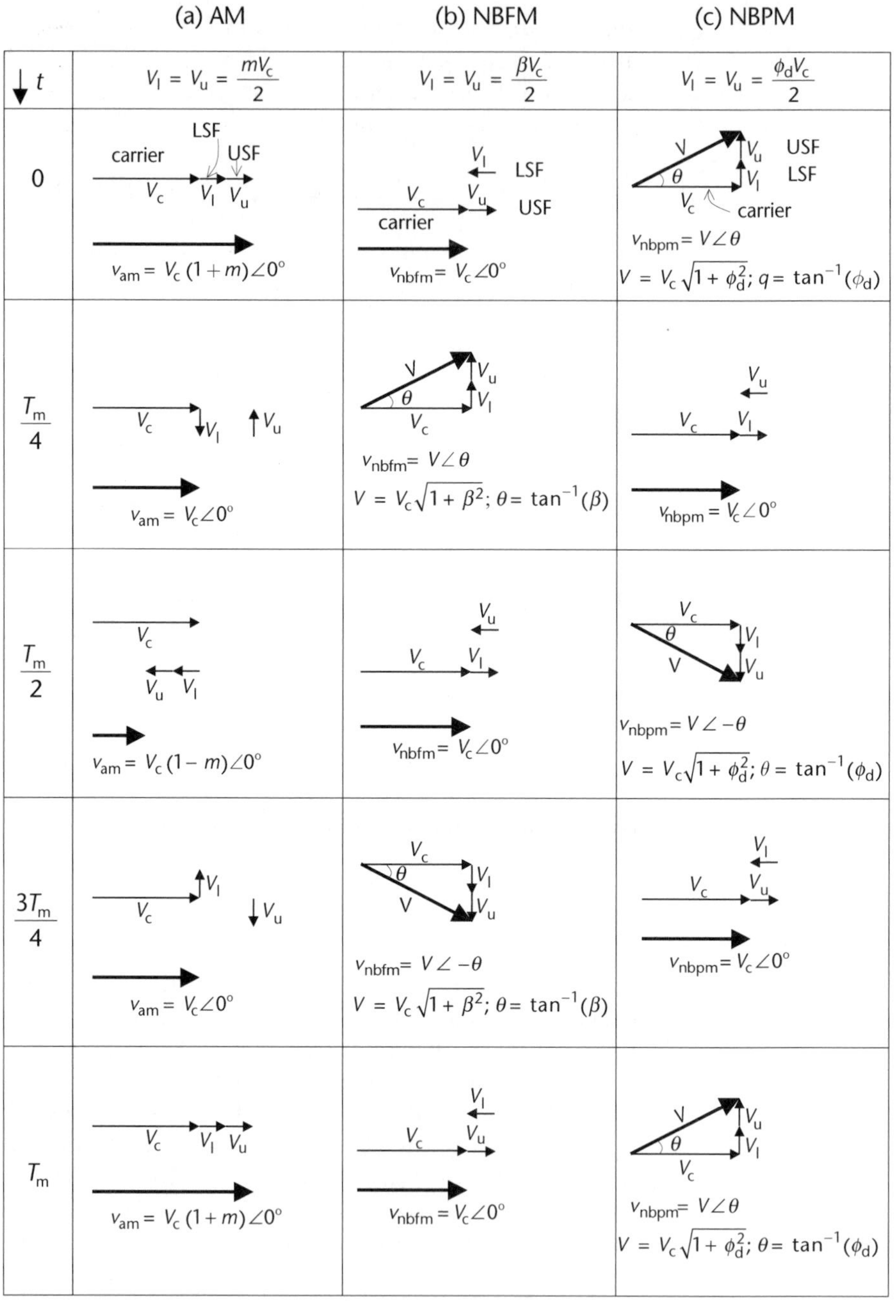
(a) AM
(b) NBFM
(c) NBPM
t
$V_l = V_u = \frac{mV_c}{2}$
$V_l = V_u = \frac{\beta V_c}{2}$
$V_l = V_u = \frac{\phi_d V_c}{2}$
0
LSF
carrier
USF
V_c V_l V_u
$v_{am} = V_c(1+m)\angle 0°$
V_l LSF
V_c V_u USF
carrier
$v_{nbfm} = V_c \angle 0°$
V V_u USF
θ V_l LSF
V_c carrier
$v_{nbpm} = V\angle\theta$
$V = V_c\sqrt{1+\phi_d^2}$; $q = \tan^{-1}(\phi_d)$
$\frac{T_m}{4}$
V_c V_l V_u
$v_{am} = V_c\angle 0°$
V V_u θ V_l V_c
$v_{nbfm} = V\angle\theta$
$V = V_c\sqrt{1+\beta^2}$; $\theta = \tan^{-1}(\beta)$
V_u V_c V_l
$v_{nbpm} = V_c\angle 0°$
$\frac{T_m}{2}$
V_c V_u V_l
$v_{am} = V_c(1-m)\angle 0°$
V_u V_c V_l
$v_{nbfm} = V_c\angle 0°$
V_c θ V_l V V_u
$v_{nbpm} = V\angle -\theta$
$V = V_c\sqrt{1+\phi_d^2}$; $\theta = \tan^{-1}(\phi_d)$
$\frac{3T_m}{4}$
V_l V_c V_u
$v_{am} = V_c\angle 0°$
V_c θ V_l V V_u
$v_{nbfm} = V\angle -\theta$
$V = V_c\sqrt{1+\beta^2}$; $\theta = \tan^{-1}(\beta)$
V_l V_c V_u
$v_{nbpm} = V_c\angle 0°$
T_m
V_c V_l V_u
$v_{am} = V_c(1+m)\angle 0°$
V_l V_c V_u
$v_{nbfm} = V_c\angle 0°$
V V_u θ V_l V_c
$v_{nbpm} = V\angle\theta$
$V = V_c\sqrt{1+\phi_d^2}$; $\theta = \tan^{-1}(\phi_d)$

Figure 4.16 Phasor diagrams at intervals of $0.25T_m$ for (a) AM, (b) NBFM and (c) NBPM signals, with parameters: message signal frequency f_m ($= 1/T_m$); carrier amplitude V_c; AM modulation factor m; FM modulation index β; and PM phase deviation ϕ_d.

anticlockwise on a circular road at different speeds. Speed is specified in units of cycles per second, i.e. how many laps of the circular road a car completes in one second. Assume that car L travels at speed $f_c - f_m$, car C at speed f_c and car U at speed $f_c + f_m$. Let car C be chosen as a reference point from which the other two cars are observed. The result will be that C appears stationary, L appears to be travelling *clockwise* at speed f_m, and U appears to be travelling anticlockwise at the same speed f_m. That is, L is falling behind at the same speed that U is edging ahead. One final point in our analogy is to imagine that there are three different starting position scenarios, with car C always starting (at $t = 0$) from the starting point, called the 0-radian point. In what we may call the AM scenario, all three cars start together from the starting point. In the NBFM scenario, car L starts from half cycle ahead — at the π-radian point; and in the NBPM case, both cars L and U start at the $\pi/2$-radian point, which is one-quarter cycle ahead of the starting point.

Returning then to the three frequency components — LSF, carrier and USF — of the modulated signals, we choose the carrier (of frequency f_c) as reference, which allows the carrier to be represented at all times as a zero-phase sinusoid. This means that its phasor will always point horizontally to the right. On the other hand, the phasor of the USF (of frequency $f_c + f_m$) will change its direction with time as though it were rotating anticlockwise at the rate of f_m cycles per second. The phasor of the LSF (of frequency $f_c - f_m$) will also change its direction with time, only that the change occurs as though the LSF were rotating clockwise at the rate of f_m cycles per second.

It takes the USF a time $T_m = 1/f_m$ to complete one cycle or 2π rad — relative to the carrier of course. An arbitrary angle θ is therefore traversed in a time

$$t = \frac{\theta}{2\pi} T_m = \frac{\theta}{2\pi f_m} \tag{4.49}$$

Figure 4.16 shows the phasor diagrams and resultant amplitudes for the three modulated waveforms at intervals of $\frac{1}{4}T_m$ starting at $t = 0$. It follows from Eq. (4.49) that the USF advances (anticlockwise) by $\pi/2$ rad relative to the carrier during this interval, while the LSF retards (clockwise) by the same angle. By studying Fig. 4.16 carefully, you can see why AM has a significant amplitude variation, whereas both NBFM and NBPM have a much smaller amplitude variation.

In AM, the initial phases of the LSF and USF relative to the carrier are such that, they add constructively in phase with the carrier at $t = nT_m$, and in *opposition* to the carrier at $t = (n + \frac{1}{2})T_m$, for $n = 0, 1, 2, ...$, giving the AM signal a maximum amplitude V_{ammax}, and minimum amplitude V_{ammin}, respectively, where

$$
\begin{aligned}
V_{ammax} &= V_c + V_l + V_u = V_c + \frac{mV_c}{2} + \frac{mV_c}{2} \\
&= V_c(1 + m) \\
V_{ammin} &= V_c - (V_l + V_u) \\
&= V_c(1 - m)
\end{aligned}
\tag{4.50}
$$

Furthermore, the AM signal is in phase with the carrier at all times because the initial phases of the LSF and USF are such that their quadrature components are always equal and opposite.

In NBFM and NBPM, on the other hand, whenever one side frequency is in phase with the carrier, the other is exactly in opposition. The minimum amplitude of the resultant signal is therefore equal to the carrier amplitude V_c. The maximum amplitude occurs when the LSF and USF add constructively at 90° to the carrier. Therefore,

$$V_{nbfmmin} = V_{nbpmmin} = V_c$$

$$V_{nbfmmax} = \sqrt{V_c^2 + \left(\frac{\beta V_c}{2} + \frac{\beta V_c}{2}\right)^2} = V_c\sqrt{1 + \beta^2} \tag{4.51}$$

$$V_{nbpmmax} = V_c\sqrt{1 + \phi_d^2}$$

Note in Fig. 4.16 that the NBFM and NBPM waveforms do not attain maximum or minimum together, but at different time instants separated by $\frac{1}{4}T_m$.

We see that the maximum peak-to-peak amplitude variation in NBFM or NBPM is only 3% of the carrier amplitude when the modulation index or phase deviation are at their maximum value of 0.25. This should be compared with AM, which has a peak-to-peak amplitude variation given by $(200 \times m)\%$ of the carrier. This is 50% at $m = 0.25$, and 200% when m has its maximum allowed value of unity, at which point the modulated carrier amplitude varies between 0 and $2V_c$. Thus, the effect of the above differences in phase relationships is to cause the amplitude variation in an AM waveform to be at least 16 times greater than in NBFM and NBPM, even when the three signals have identical amplitude spectra.

4.4.1.3 Amplitude variations in NBFM and NBPM

General expressions for the envelope of the three modulated waveforms can be obtained through phasor addition. Considering Fig. 4.17, we see that the resultant phasor representing each modulated waveform at a time t when each side frequency has rotated through angle θ (relative to the carrier) is given by

$$V_{am} = (V_c + 2x)\angle 0 = V_c[1 + m\cos\theta]\angle 0$$

$$V_{nbfm} = \left[\sqrt{V_c^2 + (2y)^2}\right]\angle\phi_{fm}$$

$$= \left[V_c\sqrt{1 + \beta^2\sin^2\theta}\right]\angle\tan^{-1}(\beta\sin\theta)$$

$$V_{nbpm} = \left[\sqrt{V_c^2 + (2z)^2}\right]\angle\phi_{pm}$$

$$= \left[V_c\sqrt{1 + \phi_d^2\cos^2\theta}\right]\angle\tan^{-1}(\phi_d\cos\theta)$$

Using Eq. (4.49) to express θ as a function of time, and employing the approximation $\theta \approx \tan^{-1}(\theta)$ suggested in Eq. (4.38), we obtain

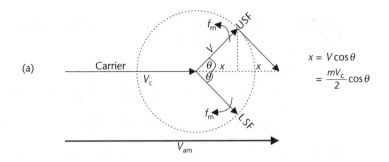

$$x = V\cos\theta$$
$$= \frac{mV_c}{2}\cos\theta$$

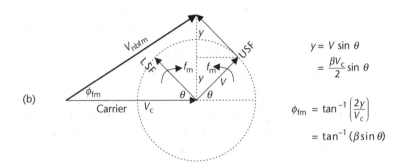

$$y = V\sin\theta$$
$$= \frac{\beta V_c}{2}\sin\theta$$

$$\phi_{fm} = \tan^{-1}\left(\frac{2y}{V_c}\right)$$
$$= \tan^{-1}(\beta\sin\theta)$$

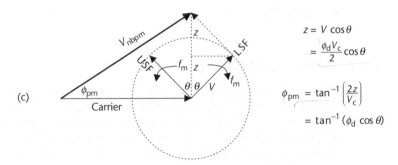

$$z = V\cos\theta$$
$$= \frac{\phi_d V_c}{2}\cos\theta$$

$$\phi_{pm} = \tan^{-1}\left(\frac{2z}{V_c}\right)$$
$$= \tan^{-1}(\phi_d\cos\theta)$$

Figure 4.17 LSF, carrier, and USF phasors at $t = 1/(8f_m)$ for (a) AM, (b) NBFM and (c) NBPM. The carrier remains fixed (as reference), while the LSF and USF phasors rotate at the same speed but in opposite directions as indicated.

$$V_{am} = V_c[1 + m\cos(2\pi f_m t)]\angle 0$$
$$V_{nbfm} = \left[V_c\sqrt{1 + \beta^2\sin^2(2\pi f_m t)}\right]\angle\beta\sin(2\pi f_m t) \tag{4.52}$$
$$V_{nbpm} = \left[V_c\sqrt{1 + \phi_d^2\cos^2(2\pi f_m t)}\right]\angle\phi_d\cos(2\pi f_m t)$$

Equation (4.52) gives the AM, NBFM and NBPM signals in phasor form. It states, for example, that $v_{nbfm}(t)$ has amplitude $V_c[1 + \beta^2\sin^2(2\pi f_m t)]^{1/2}$, and phase $\beta \sin(2\pi f_m t)$ relative to the carrier signal used as reference in Fig. 4.17. We may therefore write

$$v_{am}(t) = V_c[1 + m\cos(2\pi f_m t)]\cos(2\pi f_c t)$$

$$v_{nbfm}(t) = \left[V_c\sqrt{1 + \beta^2 \sin^2(2\pi f_m t)}\right]\cos[2\pi f_c t + \beta \sin(2\pi f_m t)]$$

$$v_{nbpm}(t) = \left[V_c\sqrt{1 + \phi_d^2 \cos^2(2\pi f_m t)}\right]\cos[2\pi f_c t + \phi_d \cos(2\pi f_m t)]$$

(4.53)

Equation (4.53) reveals that in AM only the carrier amplitude is varied by the modulating signal, with up to 200% peak-to-peak variation possible. NBFM and NBPM involve up to a maximum of about 3% peak-to-peak amplitude variation, as well as angle modulation in which the instantaneous phase ϕ_i of the carrier is a function of modulating signal given by

$$\phi_i = \begin{cases} \beta \sin(2\pi f_m t), & \text{NBFM} \\ \phi_d \cos(2\pi f_m t), & \text{NBPM} \end{cases}$$

(4.54)

You may wish to verify that Eqs. (4.43)–(4.45) are equivalent to Eq. (4.53) by evaluating them at selected time instants. However, Eq. (4.53) explicitly gives the envelope and phase of the modulated waveforms at any given instant. The AM signal conveys information in its envelope, whereas NBFM and NBPM convey information in the variation of their angles beyond the linear increase of unmodulated carriers. Note that the variation in NBFM and NBPM amplitudes is due to the error introduced by the approximations of Eq. (4.40).

4.4.2 Wideband FM and PM

When the modulation index β (in FM) and phase deviation ϕ_d (in PM) exceed about 0.25, the narrowband angle-modulation approximations are no longer valid. To determine the bandwidth requirements of a carrier that is angle-modulated by a sinusoidal message signal, we must know the frequency, amplitude and phase of each sinusoidal component contained in the angle-modulated signals $v_{fm}(t)$ and $v_{pm}(t)$ in Eq. (4.36). It turns out by Fourier analysis (see Question 4.9), that $v_{fm}(t)$ and $v_{pm}(t)$ can be written as a sum of sinusoids as follows:

$$\begin{aligned} v_{fm}(t) = {}& V_c J_0(\beta)\cos(2\pi f_c t) \\ &+ V_c J_1(\beta)\{\cos[2\pi(f_c + f_m)t] + \cos[2\pi(f_c - f_m)t + \pi]\} \\ &+ V_c J_2(\beta)\{\cos[2\pi(f_c + 2f_m)t] + \cos[2\pi(f_c - 2f_m)t]\} \\ &+ V_c J_3(\beta)\{\cos[2\pi(f_c + 3f_m)t] + \cos[2\pi(f_c - 3f_m)t + \pi]\} \\ &+ V_c J_4(\beta)\{\cos[2\pi(f_c + 4f_m)t] + \cos[2\pi(f_c - 4f_m)t]\} \\ &+ V_c J_5(\beta)\{\cos[2\pi(f_c + 5f_m)t] + \cos[2\pi(f_c - 5f_m)t + \pi]\} \\ &+ \cdots \end{aligned}$$

(4.55)

$$v_{pm}(t) = V_cJ_0(\phi_d)\cos(2\pi f_c t)$$
$$+ V_cJ_1(\phi_d)\{\cos[2\pi(f_c + f_m)t + \pi/2] + \cos[2\pi(f_c - f_m)t + \pi/2]\}$$
$$+ V_cJ_2(\phi_d)\{\cos[2\pi(f_c + 2f_m)t + \pi] + \cos[2\pi(f_c - 2f_m)t + \pi]\}$$
$$+ V_cJ_3(\phi_d)\{\cos[2\pi(f_c + 3f_m)t - \pi/2] + \cos[2\pi(f_c - 3f_m)t - \pi/2]\} \quad (4.56)$$
$$+ V_cJ_4(\phi_d)\{\cos[2\pi(f_c + 4f_m)t] + \cos[2\pi(f_c - 4f_m)t]\}$$
$$+ V_cJ_5(\phi_d)\{\cos[2\pi(f_c + 5f_m)t + \pi/2] + \cos[2\pi(f_c - 5f_m)t + \pi/2]\}$$
$$+ \cdots$$

Eqs. (4.55) and (4.56) are applicable to both narrowband (β and $\phi_d \leq 0.25$) and wideband angle-modulation (β and $\phi_d > 0.25$). They provide a complete insight into the spectrum of FM and PM signals involving a sinusoidal modulating signal. It is worthwhile to examine in some detail their implications.

The expressions for $v_{fm}(t)$ and $v_{pm}(t)$ reveal that FM and PM have the same amplitude spectrum, with phase deviation ϕ_d playing the same role in PM that modulation index β does in FM. If PM and FM are implemented with $\phi_d = \beta$, and with the same values of carrier amplitude V_c and modulating frequency f_m, then their amplitude spectra are identical.

However, PM differs from FM in its phase spectrum, which accounts for the waveform differences discussed earlier. Ignore for the moment the sign of the amplitude of each frequency component — this will introduce a phase shift of π rad if negative. We see from Eq. (4.55) that in FM, the upper side frequencies (USF), namely $f_c + f_m$, $f_c + 2f_m$, ... and the even-numbered lower side frequencies (LSF), e.g. $f_c - 2f_m$, all have zero initial phase, and only the odd-numbered LSF differ in phase by π rad. In PM, Eq. (4.56) shows that each USF and the corresponding LSF (e.g. $f_c + 2f_m$ and $f_c - 2f_m$) have the same phase, which increases in steps of $\pi/2$ rad starting from zero phase at the carrier. That is, the phase of the nth pair of side frequencies is $n\pi/2$. For example, the phase of the 4th pair of side frequencies is $4 \times \pi/2 = 2\pi \equiv 0$ rad, and the phase of the 3rd pair of side frequencies is $3 \times \pi/2 = 3\pi/2 \equiv -\pi/2$ rad.

In view of the above similarities, the following discussion will be focused entirely on FM. The results on spectrum, bandwidth, and power are applicable to PM, with phase deviation ϕ_d replacing modulation index β. Recall, however, that to avoid distortion in phase demodulators that track absolute phase, ϕ_d is limited to values not exceeding π rad, whereas β has no theoretical restriction on its values, except that transmission bandwidth requirement increases as β is increased. Phase spectrum will not be discussed further, but this can be easily obtained where desired by following the above comments.

4.4.2.1 *Spectrum*

It follows from Eq. (4.55) that an FM signal $v_{fm}(t)$ contains the carrier frequency f_c and an infinite set of side frequencies, which occur in pairs on either side of f_c. The spectral components are spaced apart by the modulating signal frequency f_m, and the nth pair of side frequencies consists of the nth LSF at $f_c - nf_m$, and the nth USF at $f_c + nf_m$, both of which have the

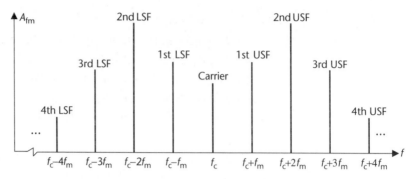

Figure 4.18 Example of single-sided amplitude spectrum of FM signal.

same amplitude. Figure 4.18 gives an example of an FM spectrum, which should be compared with the spectrum in amplitude modulation. AM contains only the carrier and the 1st pair of side frequencies, whereas FM contains an infinite set of side frequencies in addition to the carrier.

It would appear that FM has infinite bandwidth. However, it will become obvious in the following discussion that the amplitude of the side frequencies $f_c \pm nf_m$ at sufficiently high n is negligible, so that FM bandwidth is indeed finite. In fact, an FM signal can be realised with little distortion if only the first few side frequencies are retained. For example, Fig. 4.19 shows the synthesis of an FM signal of modulation index $\beta = 3$, using only the carrier and the first few side frequencies. Observe that the distortion is significant when only the first two pairs of side frequencies are included, but negligible when up to the first five pairs are retained. Note that the number of side frequencies required for negligible distortion increases as β is increased.

The amplitude of the nth pair of side frequencies is given by the unmodulated carrier amplitude v_c scaled by the factor $J_n(\beta)$, which is the nth-order Bessel function of the first kind evaluated with argument β. That is, an FM signal generated with modulation index β will contain a number of frequency components, namely:

1. The unmodulated carrier frequency f_c, which may be viewed as the 0th (zeroth) side frequency ($f_c \pm 0f_m$), of amplitude $V_c J_0(\beta)$.
2. The 1st pair of side frequencies ($f_c + f_m$ and $f_c - f_m$) of amplitude $V_c J_1(\beta)$.
3. The 2nd pair of side frequencies ($f_c + 2f_m$ and $f_c - 2f_m$) of amplitude $V_c J_2(\beta)$.
4. Etc.

It is therefore important to understand the characteristic of the Bessel function. Figure 4.20 shows a plot of $J_n(\beta)$ as a function of β for various integer values of n. To understand this diagram, assume a normalised carrier of unit amplitude ($V_c = 1$). Then the curve labelled $J_0(\beta)$ gives the amplitude of the carrier component (0th side frequency) in the FM signal as a function of the modulation index β. If you follow this curve through the plot, you will observe that $J_0(\beta) = 0$ at modulation index $\beta = 2.4048, 5.5201, 8.6537, 11.7915, 14.9309$ etc. At these values of modulation index the FM spectrum

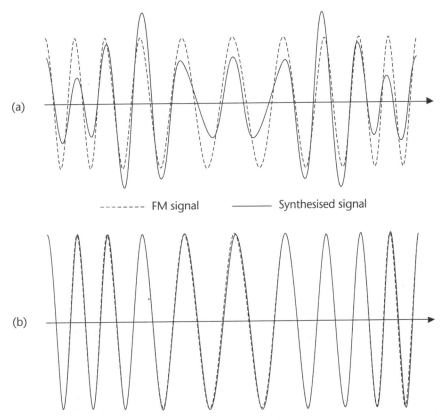

Figure 4.19 Synthesis of FM waveform using carrier plus (a) first two pairs of side-frequencies, and (b) first five pairs of side-frequencies. The FM waveform has parameters $\beta = 3.0$, $f_c = 10$ kHz, and $f_m = 1$ kHz.

does not contain a component at the unmodulated carrier frequency f_c. Energy in the unmodulated carrier has been entirely distributed to the side frequencies. We will have more to say about this later. Note also that $J_0(\beta)$ is negative for certain values of modulation index, e.g. for β between 2.4048 and 5.5201. The effect of a negative value of $J_n(\beta)$ is that the phase of the nth pair of side frequencies is advanced by π rad from that indicated in Eq. (4.55). Therefore when dealing with the amplitude spectrum, only the absolute magnitude of $J_n(\beta)$ is considered, and its sign is ignored since that only affects the phase spectrum.

Considering the other $J_n(\beta)$ curves in Fig. 4.20, a trend can be observed that as n increases, the curves remain near zero until a larger value of β is reached. For example, the value of $J_4(\beta)$ is negligible until β has increased to about 1.1, whereas $J_{10}(\beta)$ is negligible up to $\beta \approx 5.5$. This is an important characteristic of $J_n(\beta)$, which signifies that the higher side frequencies (n large) are insignificant in the FM spectrum when the modulation index is low. As modulation index increases, more side frequencies become significant. In other words, FM bandwidth increases with modulation index β. In fact Fig. 4.20 shows that when $\beta \leq 0.25$, then only $J_0(\beta)$ and $J_1(\beta)$ have

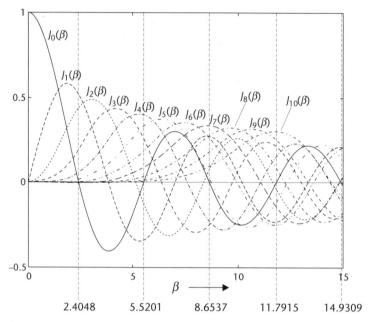

Figure 4.20 Graph of Bessel functions $J_n(\beta)$ versus β for various values of n.

significant values. This means that only the carrier and the first pair of side frequencies $f_c \pm f_m$ are noticeably present in the spectrum. You should recognise this as the special case of narrowband FM discussed earlier.

Values of $J_n(\beta)$ can be more easily read from tables such as Table 4.2, which is given accurate to four decimal places, although an accuracy of two decimal places is sufficient for practical calculations.

4.4.2.2 Power

Equation (4.30) gives the general expression for an FM signal, and shows that it is a sinusoidal signal of constant amplitude V_c but variable or modulated instantaneous phase. Bearing in mind that the power in a sinusoidal signal depends only on its amplitude, and is independent of frequency and phase, it follows that power in an FM signal equals the power in the unmodulated carrier. Working with normalised power, we may write

$$P_{fm} = \frac{1}{2}V_c^2 \tag{4.57}$$

Total power in an FM signal can also be obtained by summing the power in all spectral components in the FM spectrum. Thus,

$$\begin{aligned}
P_{fm} &= \frac{1}{2}V_c^2 J_0^2(\beta) + V_c^2 J_1^2(\beta) + V_c^2 J_2^2(\beta) + V_c^2 J_3^2(\beta) + \cdots \\
&= V_c^2 \left[\frac{1}{2} J_0^2(\beta) + J_1^2(\beta) + J_2^2(\beta) + J_3^2(\beta) + \cdots \right]
\end{aligned} \tag{4.58}$$

Table 4.2 Bessel functions to four decimal places (continued overleaf).

β	$J_0(\beta)$	$J_1(\beta)$	$J_2(\beta)$	$J_3(\beta)$	$J_4(\beta)$	$J_5(\beta)$	$J_6(\beta)$	$J_7(\beta)$	$J_8(\beta)$	$J_9(\beta)$	$J_{10}(\beta)$	$J_{11}(\beta)$	$J_{12}(\beta)$	$J_{13}(\beta)$	$J_{14}(\beta)$	$J_{15}(\beta)$	$J_{16}(\beta)$
0	1.0000	–	–	–	–	–	–	–	–	–	–	–	–	–	–	–	–
0.10	0.9975	0.0499	0.0012	–	–	–	–	–	–	–	–	–	–	–	–	–	–
0.20	0.9900	0.0995	0.0050	0.0002	–	–	–	–	–	–	–	–	–	–	–	–	–
0.25	0.9844	0.1240	0.0078	0.0003	–	–	–	–	–	–	–	–	–	–	–	–	–
0.50	0.9385	0.2423	0.0306	0.0026	0.0002	–	–	–	–	–	–	–	–	–	–	–	–
1.0	0.7652	0.4401	0.1149	0.0196	0.0025	0.0002	–	–	–	–	–	–	–	–	–	–	–
1.5	0.5118	0.5579	0.2321	0.0610	0.0118	0.0018	0.0002	–	–	–	–	–	–	–	–	–	–
2.0	0.2239	0.5767	0.3528	0.1289	0.0340	0.0070	0.0012	0.0002	–	–	–	–	–	–	–	–	–
2.4048	–	0.5192	0.4318	0.1990	0.0647	0.0164	0.0034	0.0006	0.0001	–	–	–	–	–	–	–	–
3.0	-0.2601	0.3391	0.4861	0.3091	0.1320	0.0430	0.0114	0.0025	0.0005	0.0001	–	–	–	–	–	–	–
4.0	-0.3971	-0.0660	0.3641	0.4302	0.2811	0.1321	0.0491	0.0152	0.0040	0.0009	0.0002	–	–	–	–	–	–
5.0	-0.1776	-0.3276	0.0466	0.3648	0.3912	0.2611	0.1310	0.0534	0.0184	0.0055	0.0015	0.0004	–	–	–	–	–
5.5201	–	-0.3403	-0.1233	0.2509	0.3960	0.3230	0.1891	0.0881	0.0344	0.0116	0.0035	0.0009	0.0002	–	–	–	–
6.0	0.1506	-0.2767	-0.2429	0.1148	0.3576	0.3621	0.2458	0.1296	0.0565	0.0212	0.0070	0.0020	0.0005	0.0001	–	–	–
7.0	0.3001	-0.0047	-0.3014	-0.1676	0.1578	0.3479	0.3392	0.2336	0.1280	0.0589	0.0235	0.0083	0.0027	0.0008	0.0002	0.0001	–
8.0	0.1717	0.2346	-0.1130	-0.2911	-0.1054	0.1858	0.3376	0.3206	0.2235	0.1263	0.0608	0.0256	0.0096	0.0033	0.0010	0.0003	0.0001
9.0	-0.0903	0.2453	0.1448	-0.1809	-0.2655	-0.0550	0.2043	0.3275	0.3051	0.2149	0.1247	0.0622	0.0274	0.0108	0.0039	0.0013	0.0004
10	-0.2459	0.0435	0.2546	0.0584	-0.2196	-0.2341	-0.0145	0.2167	0.3179	0.2919	0.2075	0.1231	0.0634	0.0290	0.0120	0.0045	0.0016
11	-0.1712	-0.1768	0.1390	0.2273	-0.0150	-0.2383	-0.2016	0.0184	0.2250	0.3089	0.2804	0.2010	0.1216	0.0643	0.0304	0.0130	0.0051
12	0.0477	-0.2234	-0.0849	0.1951	0.1825	-0.0735	-0.2437	-0.1703	0.0451	0.2304	0.3005	0.2704	0.1953	0.1201	0.0650	0.0316	0.0140
13	0.2069	-0.0703	-0.2177	0.0033	0.2193	0.1316	-0.1180	-0.2406	-0.1410	0.0670	0.2338	0.2927	0.2615	0.1901	0.1188	0.0656	0.0327
14	0.1711	0.1334	-0.1520	-0.1768	0.0762	0.2204	0.0812	-0.1508	-0.2320	-0.1143	0.0850	0.2357	0.2855	0.2536	0.1855	0.1174	0.0661
15	-0.0142	0.2051	0.0416	-0.1940	-0.1192	0.1305	0.2061	0.0345	-0.1740	-0.2200	-0.0901	0.1000	0.2367	0.2787	0.2464	0.1813	0.1162
16	-0.1749	0.0904	0.1862	-0.0438	-0.2026	-0.0575	0.1667	0.1825	-0.0070	-0.1895	-0.2062	-0.0682	0.1124	0.2368	0.2724	0.2399	0.1775
17	-0.1699	-0.0977	0.1584	0.1349	-0.1107	-0.1870	0.0007	0.1875	0.1537	-0.0429	-0.1991	-0.1914	-0.0486	0.1228	0.2364	0.2666	0.2340
18	-0.0134	-0.1880	-0.0075	0.1863	0.0696	-0.1554	-0.1560	0.0514	0.1959	0.1228	-0.0732	-0.2041	-0.1762	-0.0309	0.1316	0.2356	0.2611
19	0.1466	-0.1057	-0.1578	0.0725	0.1806	0.0036	-0.1788	-0.1165	0.0929	0.1947	0.0916	-0.0984	-0.2055	-0.1612	-0.0151	0.1389	0.2345
20	0.1670	0.0668	-0.1603	-0.0989	0.1307	0.1512	-0.0551	-0.1842	-0.0739	0.1251	0.1865	0.0614	-0.1190	-0.2041	-0.1464	-0.0008	0.1452
21	0.0366	0.1711	-0.0203	-0.1750	-0.0297	0.1637	0.1076	-0.1022	-0.1757	-0.0318	0.1485	0.1732	0.0329	-0.1356	-0.2008	-0.1321	0.0120
22	-0.1207	0.1172	0.1313	-0.0933	-0.1568	0.0363	0.1733	0.0582	-0.1362	-0.1573	0.0075	0.1641	0.1566	0.0067	-0.1487	-0.1959	-0.1185
23	-0.1624	-0.0395	0.1590	0.0672	-0.1415	-0.1164	0.0909	0.1638	0.0088	-0.1576	-0.1322	0.0427	0.1730	0.1379	-0.0172	-0.1588	-0.1899
24	-0.0562	-0.1540	0.0434	0.1613	-0.0031	-0.1623	-0.0645	0.1300	0.1404	-0.0364	-0.1677	-0.1033	0.0730	0.1763	0.1180	-0.0386	-0.1663
25	0.0963	-0.1254	-0.1063	0.1083	0.1323	-0.0660	-0.1587	-0.0102	0.1530	0.1081	-0.0752	-0.1682	-0.0729	0.0983	0.1751	0.0978	-0.0577

Table 4.2 (continued)

β	$J_{17}(\beta)$	$J_{18}(\beta)$	$J_{19}(\beta)$	$J_{20}(\beta)$	$J_{21}(\beta)$	$J_{22}(\beta)$	$J_{23}(\beta)$	$J_{24}(\beta)$	$J_{25}(\beta)$	$J_{26}(\beta)$	$J_{27}(\beta)$	$J_{28}(\beta)$	$J_{29}(\beta)$	$J_{30}(\beta)$
0	—	—	—	—	—	—	—	—	—	—	—	—	—	—
0.10	—	—	—	—	—	—	—	—	—	—	—	—	—	—
0.20	—	—	—	—	—	—	—	—	—	—	—	—	—	—
0.25	—	—	—	—	—	—	—	—	—	—	—	—	—	—
0.50	—	—	—	—	—	—	—	—	—	—	—	—	—	—
1.0	—	—	—	—	—	—	—	—	—	—	—	—	—	—
1.5	—	—	—	—	—	—	—	—	—	—	—	—	—	—
2.0	—	—	—	—	—	—	—	—	—	—	—	—	—	—
2.4048	—	—	—	—	—	—	—	—	—	—	—	—	—	—
3.0	—	—	—	—	—	—	—	—	—	—	—	—	—	—
4.0	—	—	—	—	—	—	—	—	—	—	—	—	—	—
5.0	—	—	—	—	—	—	—	—	—	—	—	—	—	—
5.5201	—	—	—	—	—	—	—	—	—	—	—	—	—	—
6.0	—	—	—	—	—	—	—	—	—	—	—	—	—	—
7.0	—	—	—	—	—	—	—	—	—	—	—	—	—	—
8.0	—	—	—	—	—	—	—	—	—	—	—	—	—	—
9.0	0.0001	—	—	—	—	—	—	—	—	—	—	—	—	—
10	0.0005	0.0002	—	—	—	—	—	—	—	—	—	—	—	—
11	0.0019	0.0006	0.0002	0.0001	—	—	—	—	—	—	—	—	—	—
12	0.0057	0.0022	0.0008	0.0003	0.0001	—	—	—	—	—	—	—	—	—
13	0.0149	0.0063	0.0025	0.0009	0.0003	0.0001	—	—	—	—	—	—	—	—
14	0.0337	0.0158	0.0068	0.0028	0.0010	0.0004	0.0001	—	—	—	—	—	—	—
15	0.0665	0.0346	0.0166	0.0074	0.0031	0.0012	0.0004	0.0002	0.0001	—	—	—	—	—
16	0.1150	0.0668	0.0354	0.0173	0.0079	0.0034	0.0013	0.0005	0.0002	0.0001	—	—	—	—
17	0.1739	0.1138	0.0671	0.0362	0.0180	0.0084	0.0037	0.0015	0.0006	0.0002	0.0001	—	—	—
18	0.2286	0.1706	0.1127	0.0673	0.0369	0.0187	0.0089	0.0039	0.0017	0.0007	0.0003	0.0001	—	—
19	0.2559	0.2235	0.1676	0.1116	0.0675	0.0375	0.0193	0.0093	0.0042	0.0018	0.0007	0.0003	0.0001	—
20	0.2331	0.2511	0.2189	0.1647	0.1106	0.0676	0.0380	0.0199	0.0098	0.0045	0.0020	0.0008	0.0003	0.0001
21	0.1505	0.2316	0.2465	0.2145	0.1621	0.1097	0.0677	0.0386	0.0205	0.0102	0.0048	0.0021	0.0009	0.0004
22	0.0236	0.1549	0.2299	0.2422	0.2105	0.1596	0.1087	0.0677	0.0391	0.0210	0.0106	0.0051	0.0023	0.0010
23	−0.1055	0.0340	0.1587	0.2282	0.2381	0.2067	0.1573	0.1078	0.0678	0.0395	0.0215	0.0110	0.0054	0.0025
24	−0.1831	−0.0931	0.0435	0.1619	0.2264	0.2343	0.2031	0.1550	0.1070	0.0678	0.0399	0.0220	0.0114	0.0056
25	−0.1717	−0.1758	−0.0814	0.0520	0.1646	0.2246	0.2306	0.1998	0.1529	0.1061	0.0678	0.0403	0.0225	0.0118

Obviously, the power in the side frequencies is obtained only at the expense of the carrier power. Equating the two expressions for P_{fm} in Eq. (4.57) and Eq. (4.58), we obtain the mathematical identity

$$J_0^2(\beta) + 2 \sum_{n=1}^{n=\infty} J_n^2(\beta) = 1 \tag{4.59}$$

It follows that the fraction of power r_N contained in the carrier frequency and the first N pairs of side frequencies is given by

$$r_N = J_0^2(\beta) + 2 \sum_{n=1}^{n=N} J_n^2(\beta) \tag{4.60}$$

4.4.2.3 Bandwidth

Two different definitions of FM bandwidth are in common use, namely *Carson's bandwidth* and *1% bandwidth*. Carson's bandwidth is an empirical definition, which gives the width of the band of frequencies centred at f_c that contains at least 98% of the power in the FM signal. The 1% bandwidth is defined as the separation between the pair of side frequencies of order n_{max} beyond which there is no spectral component with amplitude up to 1% of the unmodulated carrier amplitude V_c.

In Fig. 4.21, we employ Eq. (4.60) to show, at various integer values of modulation index β, the fraction of power r_N carried by spectral components that include f_c and N pairs of side frequencies. It can be observed that with $N = \beta + 1$ the minimum fraction of power is $r_N = 0.9844$. With $N = \beta$, r_N

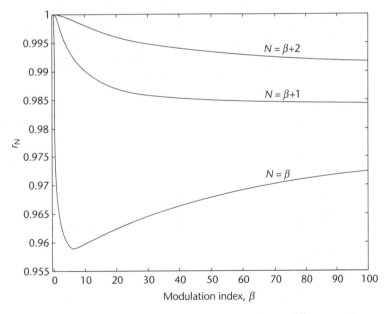

Figure 4.21 Fraction r_N of power in FM signal carried by spectral components at the unmodulated carrier frequency f_c and N pairs of side frequencies, as a function of integer values of modulation index β.

= 0.9590 minimum (at $\beta = 6$). With $N = \beta + 2$, $r_N = 0.9905$ (at $\beta = 361$, a point not reached on the plot). Thus, $N = \beta + 1$ is the minimum number of pairs of side frequencies that, along with f_c, account for at least 98% of the total FM power. Therefore Carson's bandwidth B_C of an FM signal is given by the frequency interval from the $(\beta + 1)$th LSF to the $(\beta + 1)$th USF. Since the spacing of the spectral components is f_m, it follows that

$$\text{Carson's bandwidth, } B_C = 2(\beta + 1)f_m$$
$$= 2(f_d + f_m) \qquad (4.61)$$

where we have used the definition of modulation index given in Eq. (4.11). Note that in the limit $\beta \ll 1$, Eq. (4.61) yields $B_C = 2f_m$. Thus, the definition of Carson's bandwidth is consistent with our earlier discussion of narrowband FM, which also has a bandwidth of $2f_m$.

The 1% bandwidth B_P is given by the width of the frequency interval from the (n_{max})th LSF to the (n_{max})th USF beyond which the amplitude of every spectral component is less than 1% of the unmodulated carrier amplitude v_c. Thus,

$$\text{1\% bandwidth, } B_P = 2n_{max}f_m \qquad (4.62)$$

The value of n_{max} is usually read from a table of Bessel functions such as Table 4.2 by looking along the row specified by the modulation index β for the furthest column (or side frequency n) with the smallest value ≥ 0.01. For example, if $\beta = 5.0$ we look in Table 4.2 along the row $\beta = 5.0$ and find that the highest column with the smallest entry ≥ 0.01 is the $J_8(\beta)$ column. Therefore $n_{max} = 8$ in this case and $B_P = 16f_m$.

At practical values of modulation index $\beta \leq 100$, B_P accounts for at least 99.97% of the total FM power, compared to a minimum of 98.44% in Carson's bandwidth B_C. Figure 4.22 shows the *normalised* (i.e. $f_m = 1$Hz) Carson's and 1% bandwidths as functions of modulation index β. It can be observed that B_P exceeds B_C for $\beta > 0.5$. However, as $\beta \to \infty$, the two

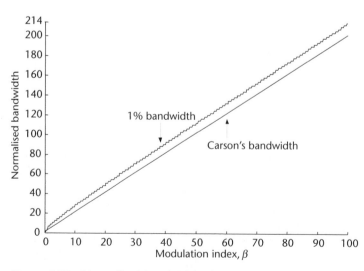

Figure 4.22 Normalised bandwidth ($f_m = 1$).

bandwidths become equal (at $\beta \approx 78{,}474$), and eventually B_C exceeds B_P, since the carrier power is increasingly distributed in smaller fractions to a larger number of side frequencies.

One disadvantage of the 1% bandwidth definition is that, unlike Carson's bandwidth, it is not equal to the narrowband FM bandwidth of $2f_m$ in the limit $\beta \to 0$. Rather, $B_P = 0$ for $\beta \le 0.02$).

The above discussion of FM bandwidth assumed a sinusoidal modulating signal. However, the bandwidth definitions in Eq. (4.61) and Eq. (4.62) can be applied to the more general case in which the modulating signal consists of frequencies up to a maximum f_m. To do this, the modulation index β is replaced by the deviation ratio D defined in Eq. (4.13).

WORKED EXAMPLE   4.4

An audio signal that contains frequencies in the range 30 Hz to 15 kHz is used to frequency modulate a 100 MHz carrier causing a frequency deviation of 45 kHz. Determine the Carson's and 1% transmission bandwidths.

This is an example of a non-sinusoidal modulating signal, in which deviation ratio D plays the role that modulation index β plays in sinusoidal modulating signals. The maximum frequency component of the message signal is $f_m = 15$ kHz and the frequency deviation $f_d = 45$ kHz, giving

$$D = f_d/f_m = 3.0$$

Thus, Carson's bandwidth:

$$B_C = 2(D+1)f_m = 2(4)(15) = 120 \text{ kHz}$$

To determine the 1% bandwidth B_P we look in Table 4.2 along the row $\beta = 3.0$ (since $D = 3.0$) where we find that all entries beyond $J_6(\beta)$ are less than 0.01. Thus $n_{max} = 6$ and

$$B_P = 2n_{max}f_m = 2(6)(15) = 180 \text{ kHz}$$

Observe that $B_P > B_C$ as discussed earlier.

WORKED EXAMPLE   4.5

A sinusoidal signal of frequency 15 kHz modulates the frequency of a 10 V 100 MHz carrier, causing a frequency deviation of 75 kHz.

(a) Sketch the amplitude spectrum of the FM signal, including all spectral components of amplitude larger than 1% the amplitude of the unmodulated carrier frequency.

(b) Determine the fraction of the total power contained in the frequency band 99.93 MHz to 100.07 MHz.

(a) Modulation index $\beta = f_d/f_m$; $f_c = 100$ MHz; and $V_c = 10$ V. Using row β = 5.0 in Table 4.2 we obtain the amplitudes of the frequency components in the FM spectrum as follows:

Carrier frequency $f_c = 100$ MHz, of amplitude $V_c|J_0| = 10(0.1776) = 1.78$ V.

1st pair of side frequencies $f_c \pm f_m = 99985$ and 100015 kHz, of amplitude $V_c|J_1| = 10(0.3276) = 3.28$ V.

2nd pair of side frequencies $f_c \pm 2f_m = 99970$ and 100030 kHz, of amplitude $V_c|J_2| = 10(0.0466) = 0.47$ V.

3rd pair of side frequencies $f_c \pm 3f_m = 99955$ and 100045 kHz, of amplitude $V_c|J_3| = 10(0.3648) = 3.65$ V.

4th pair of side frequencies $f_c \pm 4f_m = 99940$ and 100060 kHz, of amplitude $V_c|J_4| = 10(0.3912) = 3.91$ V.

5th pair of side frequencies $f_c \pm 5f_m = 99925$ and 100075 kHz, of amplitude $V_c|J_5| = 10(0.2611) = 2.61$ V.

6th pair of side frequencies $f_c \pm 6f_m = 99910$ and 100090 kHz, of amplitude $V_c|J_6| = 10(0.1310) = 1.31$ V.

7th pair of side frequencies $f_c \pm 7f_m = 99895$ and 100105 kHz, of amplitude $V_c|J_7| = 10(0.0534) = 0.53$ V.

8th pair of side frequencies $f_c \pm 8f_m = 99880$ and 100120 kHz, of amplitude $V_c|J_8| = 10(0.0184) = 0.18$ V.

The 9th and higher side frequencies are ignored since they correspond to Table entries < 0.01, and therefore have amplitudes less than 1% of V_c. The required amplitude spectrum simply provides a graphical presentation of the above results; see Fig. 4.23.

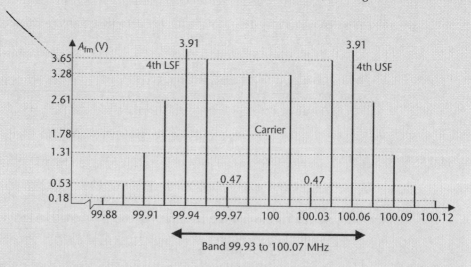

Figure 4.23 Single-sided amplitude spectrum of FM signal in Worked example 4.5.

(b) The specified band encompasses the carrier and the first four pairs of side frequencies, as indicated in Fig. 4.23. Therefore the fraction of power in this band is obtained using Eq. (4.60) as follows:

$$r_4 = 0.1776^2 + 2(0.3276^2 + 0.0466^2 + 0.3648^2 + 0.3912^2)$$
$$= 0.8228$$

This means that of the total (normalised) power in the FM signal $(P_c = V_c^2 / 2 = 50 \text{ W})$, 82.3% or 41.14 W is in the carrier and first four pairs of side frequencies – a bandwidth of 120 kHz. For comparison, you may wish to verify that in this case the Carson's bandwidth $B_C = 180$ kHz contains 99.34% of the total power; while the 1% bandwidth $B_P = 240$ kHz contains 99.98% of the power.

WORKED EXAMPLE 4.6

A 5 kHz tone of amplitude 5 V serves as the modulating signal for two modulator circuits, one an FM modulator of sensitivity 15 kHz/V, and the other a PM modulator of sensitivity 0.6 rad/V.

(a) Determine the Carson's bandwidth of each angle-modulated signal.
(b) Repeat (a) with tone frequency increased to 15 kHz.

(a) Given $f_m = 5$ kHz; $v_m = 5$ V; $k_f = 15$ kHz/V; $k_p = 0.6$ rad/V.

$$\text{FM modulation index, } \beta = \frac{k_f V_m}{f_m} = 15$$
$$\text{PM phase deviation, } \phi_d = k_p V_m = 3$$

It follows that

$$\text{FM Carson's bandwidth, } B_{CFM} = 2(\beta + 1)f_m = 160 \text{ kHz}$$
$$\text{PM Carson's bandwidth, } B_{CPM} = 2(\phi_d + 1)f_m = 40 \text{ kHz}$$

(b) With f_m increased to 15 kHz, the FM modulation index reduces to $\beta = k_f V_m/f_m = 15 \times 5/15 = 5$, but the phase deviation does not depend on frequency and so remains at $\phi_d = k_p V_m = 3$ rad. Hence

$$\text{FM Carson's bandwidth, } B_{CFM} = 2(\beta + 1)f_m = 180 \text{ kHz}$$
$$\text{PM Carson's bandwidth, } B_{CPM} = 2(\phi_d + 1)f_m = 120 \text{ kHz}$$

4.4.2.4 FM or PM?

It is noteworthy in Worked example 4.6 that the PM bandwidth increased from 40 kHz to 120 kHz in direct proportion to the increase in the message signal frequency, compared with a less dramatic increase in FM bandwidth from 160 kHz to 180 kHz. The reason for this is that frequency deviation in PM is proportional to both amplitude and frequency of the modulating signal, whereas in FM it depends only on modulating signal amplitude; see Eq. (4.23). PM therefore requires a wider transmission bandwidth for higher frequency components of a message signal. Because receiver noise is directly proportional to transmission bandwidth, it is apparent that the noise performance of PM will be inferior to that of FM. For this reason, and because phase deviation in PM is limited to $\phi_d \leq \pi$ rad, allowing less scope to trade bandwidth for noise performance improvement, FM is preferred to PM for analogue communication. However, in digital communication, the staircase nature of the modulating signals gives PM an important advantage over FM in bandwidth efficiency. Because there is no carrier frequency deviation in PM when the modulating signal is constant, the bandwidth requirement of PM for digital transmission is less than that of FM. PM is therefore widely used in digital communication. This is the subject of Chapter 7.

4.5 FM and PM modulators

A detailed discussion of narrowband angle modulation was presented in Section 4.4.1. We will now show how narrowband PM may be generated using the product modulator that was introduced in Chapter 3. Armed with a NBPM modulator, it is an easy step to obtain a NBFM modulator based on the inherent relationship between FM and PM. Wideband FM and PM may be obtained in two ways. In the indirect method, frequency multiplication is applied to a narrowband angle-modulated signal. The direct method of wideband angle modulation uses the modulating signal to vary the output frequency of a voltage-controlled oscillator.

4.5.1 Narrowband modulators

Consider Eq. (4.42), which gives the expression for a NBPM signal that is obtained when a carrier signal $v_c(t) = V_c \cos(2\pi f_c t)$ is weakly phase-modulated by the message signal $v'_m(t) = V_m \cos(2\pi f_m t)$, such that the phase deviation $\phi_d \leq 0.25$. Let us rewrite this equation as follows.

$$v_{nbpm}(t) = V_c \cos(2\pi f_c t) - \phi_d \cos(2\pi f_m t) V_c \sin(2\pi f_c t)$$
$$= v_c(t) - v_m(t) v'_c(t) \tag{4.63}$$

The modulating signal $v_m(t)$ has maximum absolute value

$$|v_m(t)|_{max} = \phi_d \leq 0.25 \tag{4.64}$$

and is obtained by attenuating the original message signal $v'_m(t)$ of maximum absolute value V_m by the factor V_m/ϕ_d. From earlier discussions, you will recognise the importance of Eq. (4.64). It is the condition that must be satisfied to ensure that $v_{nbpm}(t)$ is an NBPM signal.

The form of Eq. (4.63) suggests that a narrowband phase-modulated signal $v_{nbpm}(t)$ may be generated by the circuit shown in block diagram form in Fig. 4.24. A stable crystal oscillator generates the carrier signal $v_c(t)$, and hence provides the first term on the RHS of Eq. (4.63). The oscillator output is also fed through a phase-shifting network, which produces the

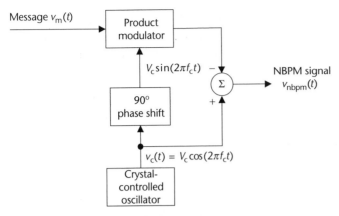

Figure 4.24 Narrowband phase modulator.

signal $v_c'(t) = V_c \sin(2\pi f_c t)$ at its output by imposing a phase delay of 90° on the carrier signal at its input. The second term in the expression for $v_{nbpm}(t)$ requires the use of a product modulator (see Chapter 3) that has the signals $v_m(t)$ and $v_c'(t)$ at its inputs. A summing device subtracts the output of the product modulator from the carrier signal to give the required NBPM signal.

We showed in our discussion of the relationships between FM and PM that if a message signal is first integrated before being applied to phase-modulate a carrier, then the result is an FM signal. You may wish to review Section 4.2.3.2 at this point. Therefore the block diagram of a narrowband frequency modulator is as shown in Fig. 4.25(a). The message signal is integrated and fed through the narrowband phase modulator discussed above.

The basic requirement is for the integrator to perform a specific type of low-pass filtering in which the gain is inversely proportional to frequency. We saw that frequency deviation in phase modulation is directly proportional to both the frequency and amplitude of the modulating signal. Therefore if the integrator output phase-modulates a carrier, the frequency dependence will cancel out, and we have an angle-modulated signal whose frequency deviation depends only on amplitude. We learned earlier that this is an FM signal. Thus the output of the narrowband phase modulator is the desired NBFM signal.

A typical integrator circuit is the opamp circuit shown in Fig. 4.25(b). The gain of the circuit is proportional to the impedance of the element in the

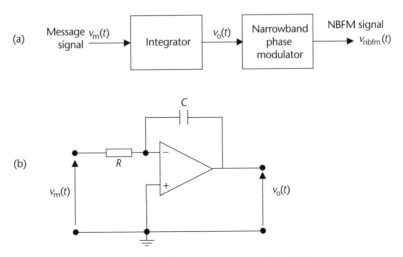

Figure 4.25 (a) Narrowband frequency modulator; (b) Integrator circuit.

feedback path. So placing in the feedback path an element whose impedance is inversely proportional to signal frequency leads to the low-pass filtering action described above. A capacitor is such an element. It blocks DC (i.e. it has infinite impedance at zero frequency) and it passes AC, with impedance that reduces as frequency increases.

To show more quantitatively how the circuit of Fig. 4.25(b) works in conjunction with the NBPM modulator to generate a NBFM signal, let us assume a sinusoidal message signal $v_m(t) = V_m\cos(2\pi f_m t)$. Then the impedance of the capacitor in Fig. 4.25(b) is

$$Z = \frac{1}{j2\pi f_m C}$$

The non-inverting terminal of the opamp is grounded, so the inverting terminal is forced to the same zero potential, which means that the input voltage $v_m(t)$ is dropped entirely across resistor R, and the output voltage $v_o(t)$ is dropped entirely across impedance Z of capacitor C. Furthermore, the currents through R and C are equal and opposite, since, by a property of opamps, negligible current flows into their input terminals. We may therefore write

$$\frac{V_m\cos(2\pi f_m t)}{R} = -\frac{v_o(t)}{Z}$$
$$= -v_o(t)[j2\pi f_m C]$$

From which it follows that

$$v_o(t) = j\frac{V_m\cos(2\pi f_m t)}{2\pi f_m CR} = \frac{V_m\sin(2\pi f_m t)}{2\pi f_m CR}$$
$$= \frac{k_f V_m}{f_m}\sin(2\pi f_m t) \tag{4.65}$$
$$= \beta\sin(2\pi f_m t)$$

where k_f is the frequency sensitivity given by

$$k_f = \frac{1}{2\pi RC} \tag{4.66}$$

and we have used the fact (discussed in Chapter 2) that the factor j represents a phase shift of 90°. Component values and the amplitude of $v_m(t)$ are chosen to ensure that the modulation index $\beta \leq 0.25$.

When the integrator output $v_o(t)$, given by Eq. (4.65), is fed as input into the NBPM modulator shown in Fig. 4.24, you should verify that the output signal will be

$$v_{nbfm}(t) = v_c(t) - v_o(t)v_c'(t)$$
$$= V_c\cos(2\pi f_c t) - \beta V_c\sin(2\pi f_c t)\sin(2\pi f_m t) \tag{4.67}$$

This is exactly the same expression as Eq. (4.41), derived for NBFM. The opamp circuit of Fig. 4.25(b) therefore works as an integrator in conjunction with a NBPM modulator to generate a NBFM signal.

4.5.2 Indirect wideband modulators

Indirect wideband modulators generate wideband angle modulation by frequency multiplication of a narrowband angle-modulated signal. The indirect wideband modulator was first proposed by Armstrong in 1936. For this reason, it is also called the *Armstrong modulator*. The following discussion assumes FM. However, it is equally applicable to PM by substituting PM and ϕ_d for FM and β, respectively, wherever they occur.

Figure 4.26 shows the block diagram of a basic Armstrong modulator. It consists of a NBFM modulator, which generates an NBFM signal $v_{nbfm}(t)$ of carrier frequency f_{c1} and modulation index $\beta \leq 0.25$. A completely general expression for $v_{nbfm}(t)$ is given by Eq. (4.30)

$$v_{nbfm}(t) = V_c \cos(2\pi f_{c1}t + \phi_i)$$

where ϕ_i is the instantaneous phase. To increase the modulation index to the level required for wideband FM, this NBFM signal is fed into a frequency multiplier, which multiplies the angle of $v_{nbfm}(t)$ by a factor n. The output of the frequency multiplier is therefore

$$v'_{wbfm}(t) = V_c \cos(2\pi n f_{c1}t + n\phi_i)$$

Since the instantaneous phase is proportional to modulation index, it follows that $v'_{wbfm}(t)$ is a wideband FM signal of (unmodulated) carrier frequency nf_{c1}, and modulation index $n\beta$. With the new modulation index ($n\beta$) at the desired wideband value, the frequency nf_{c1} is usually much higher than desired. A downconverter is therefore used to downconvert to the desired carrier frequency f_c. The downconverter consists of a mixer followed by a BPF of bandwidth equal to the bandwidth of $v'_{wbfm}(t)$ and centre frequency chosen to pass only the difference frequency output of the mixer. A crystal-controlled oscillator supplies the downconverter with a sinusoid of frequency

$$f_{LO} = f_c + nf_{c1}$$

The output of the frequency multiplier is the desired wideband FM signal $v_{wbfm}(t)$ of unmodulated carrier frequency f_c and modulation index $n\beta$.

The frequency multiplier in Fig. 4.26 is a non-linear device of order n followed by a BPF of centre frequency nf_{c1}, and bandwidth equal to n times the bandwidth of $v_{nbfm}(t)$. You may recall from Section 2.9.3 that when a

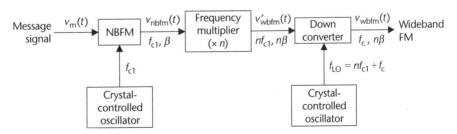

Figure 4.26 Armstrong wideband frequency modulator: basic elements.

sinusoidal signal of angle $\theta(t) = 2\pi f_m t + \phi_m$ is passed through a non-linear device of order n, then new sinusoids are created in the output, including one with angle $\theta_n(t) = 2\pi n f_m t + n\phi_m$, which of course has frequency $n f_m$. Thus, if a signal containing sinusoids of frequencies in the range f_1 to f_m is passed through this non-linear device, the output will contain, among others, frequencies $n f_1$ to $n f_m$. A BPF of passband $n f_1$ to $n f_m$, hence bandwidth $n(f_m - f_1)$, may be used to extract this band of frequencies, and in this way frequency multiplication has been accomplished. In practice, the frequency multiplier block consists of several cascaded stages to achieve the required frequency multiplication factor. For example, multiplication by the factor 81 may be achieved using four multiply-by-3 stages.

It is important to note the difference between frequency downconversion and frequency multiplication. The former process merely shifts a signal to a lower centre frequency. It does not change the modulation index or the bandwidth of the shifted signal. The latter process alters all three parameters, namely centre frequency, modulation index and bandwidth, by the factor n.

4.5.3 Direct wideband modulators

Oscillators are widely used in electronics to generate periodic waveforms for applications as a carrier or a control signal that directs various repetitive system actions. The basic output of the oscillator is usually a non-sinusoidal waveform (e.g. sawtooth or rectangular) from which a sinusoidal

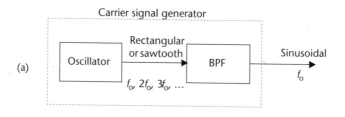

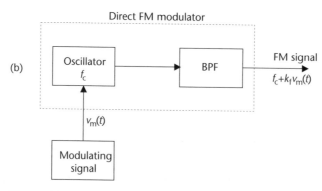

Figure 4.27 (a) Carrier signal source; (b) direct FM modulator.

signal may be obtained, especially for application as a carrier signal, by extracting the fundamental frequency or other harmonic frequency using a BPF. This is shown in Fig. 4.27(a).

FM generation by the direct method works by a modulating signal directly varying the frequency of the oscillator output signal. This yields the desired FM signal. The basic block diagram is shown in Fig. 4.27(b). How the oscillator frequency is varied depends on the type of oscillator, and this is briefly discussed below. To obtain phase modulation, the signal is first passed through a differentiator circuit before entering the FM modulator. The basis of this method of obtaining PM was discussed in Section 4.2.3 and shown in Fig. 4.5. The differentiator is a special type of high-pass filter with gain that is directly proportional to signal frequency.

Two types of oscillator are in common use for FM generation. The simplest is the LC oscillator (LCO), which has the capacitance of its tank circuit varied somehow by the modulating signal. This has the effect of varying the resonant frequency of the oscillator. The second type is the *voltage-controlled oscillator* (VCO) in which the modulating signal varies the voltage limits between which a timing capacitor charges/discharges. In this way the period, and hence fundamental frequency, of the capacitor voltage is varied to yield the desired FM signal.

An important disadvantage of the direct method of angle modulation is that the carrier signal is not generated by a stable crystal oscillator, and will therefore tend to drift in frequency due to, for example, the effect of temperature changes on component values. Some arrangement, called *automatic frequency control* (AFC), must be put in place to ensure frequency stability. A common AFC method is shown in Fig. 4.28. The mixer is fed with the direct modulator output signal $v_{fm}(t)$ — of average frequency f_c — and a reference signal $v_{ref}(t)$ of frequency f_c generated using a stable crystal oscillator. The difference-frequency signal output of the mixer serves as the input to a frequency discriminator, the output of which is proportional to the frequency of the signal at its input. The discriminator output $v_e(t)$ is zero when the modulator carrier frequency is at precisely the right value f_c. Any carrier frequency error leads to a non-zero voltage of the correct sign, which is applied to adjust the direct modulator in order to eliminate the deviation of the modulator carrier frequency from its allotted value.

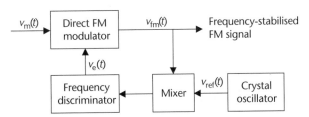

Figure 4.28 Automatic frequency control (AFC) of a direct FM modulator.

4.5.3.1 LCO modulator

In the LCO modulator, the capacitance of the LC oscillator tank circuit is varied by the modulating signal. Figure 4.29(a) shows a tank circuit with a parallel arrangement of inductance and capacitance. The total capacitance C_i at any instant is contributed by two capacitors, one with a fixed capacitance C_o, and the other with a capacitance C_v that is varied by the modulating voltage $v_m(t)$. The resonant (or oscillation) frequency of the LC oscillator circuit, that is the frequency of the oscillator's output signal, at any instant is given by

$$f_i = \frac{1}{2\pi(LC_i)^{1/2}} \tag{4.68}$$

Let the total capacitance of the tank circuit in the absence of a modulating signal be C_c. Then we may write

$$
\begin{aligned}
C_i &= C_c + \Delta C \\
&= C_c - kv_m(t)
\end{aligned} \tag{4.69}
$$

where k is a constant known as the *capacitance sensitivity*, which gives the increase in capacitance per voltage decrease in modulating signal; ΔC is the change in capacitance due to the modulating signal; it is assumed that operation is restricted to the region of linear change of variable capacitance with modulating signal.

The oscillator's output frequency in the absence of a modulating signal gives the unmodulated carrier frequency

$$f_c = \frac{1}{2\pi(LC_c)^{1/2}} \tag{4.70}$$

Substituting Eq. (4.69) into Eq. (4.68) leads to the following expression for the instantaneous frequency f_i of the oscillator's output signal.

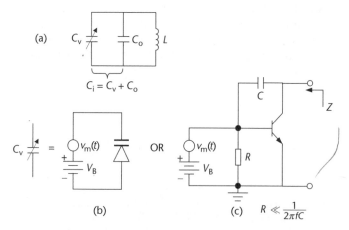

Figure 4.29 (a) Tank circuit of an LC oscillator; variable-capacitance C_v obtained using (b) a varactor and (c) a transistor.

$$f_i = \frac{1}{2\pi[L(C_c + \Delta C)]^{1/2}}$$

$$= \frac{1}{2\pi(LC_c)^{1/2}[1 + (\Delta C/C_c)]^{1/2}} = f_c[1 + (\Delta C/C_c)]^{-1/2}$$

$$\approx f_c\left(1 - \frac{1}{2}\frac{\Delta C}{C_c}\right) = f_c + \frac{kf_c}{2C_c}v_m(t)$$

where we used the approximation

$$(1 + x)^n \approx 1 + nx, \quad \text{for } |x| \ll 1 \tag{4.71}$$

Equation (4.71) is applicable in this case, with $x = \Delta C/C_c$ and $n = -\frac{1}{2}$, the change in capacitance ΔC being a small fraction of the unmodulated capacitance value C_c. The error in the above approximation is less than 0.4% for $x \leq 0.1$. Note that f_i has the form

$$f_i = f_c + k_f v_m(t) \tag{4.72}$$

where

$$k_f = \frac{kf_c}{2C_c} = \frac{k}{4\pi\sqrt{LC_c^3}} \tag{4.73}$$

The LC oscillator output is therefore the desired FM signal, with instantaneous frequency given by Eq. (4.72), and frequency sensitivity k_f given by Eq. (4.73). It is obvious that the variable capacitance must be operated in its linear region, otherwise k and hence k_f become functions of the modulating signal, leading to distortion when the signal is demodulated at the receiver. This requirement, and the need to keep $\Delta C/C_c \ll 1$ in order for approximation (4.71) — that leads to Eq. (4.72) — to be valid, means that the frequency deviation may not be sufficient for wideband FM operation. In such situations, it is a straightforward matter to obtain wideband FM with the required frequency deviation by passing the oscillator output (FM) signal through a frequency multiplier and downconverter as discussed in Section 4.5.2 and Question 4.14.

Figure 4.29(b) shows two popular arrangements for obtaining the voltage-variable capacitance C_v. One arrangement uses a special variable-capacitance diode known as a *varactor*, while the other employs a transistor that is set up in such a way that it has a reactive output impedance, which is varied by a modulating signal at the input. The transistor is equivalent to a capacitor, with capacitance set by the bias voltage plus modulating signal.

Variable capacitance diode All pn diodes exhibit junction capacitance under reverse bias. A varactor is a pn diode that is specially constructed to increase the sensitivity of its junction capacitance to reverse-bias voltage and extend the linear region of the capacitance variation. The nominal capacitance of a varactor diode may be in the range from about 2 to 400 pF depending on type. In all cases, the capacitance decreases as the reverse bias voltage increases. A DC bias voltage V_B sets the varactor capacitance at the value

$$C_{vo} = C_c - C_o$$

needed to fix the unmodulated carrier frequency as given by Eq. (4.70). The modulating signal $v_m(t)$ causes the total reverse bias voltage to vary about V_B, which changes the varactor capacitance and hence the instantaneous capacitance C_i of the oscillator tank circuit according to Eq. (4.69). An LCO modulator that uses a varactor diode in its tank circuit is sometimes referred to as a *varactor diode modulator*.

UHF two-way radios generate NBFM by using a varactor diode modulator followed by frequency multiplication of ×36 (typical) to maintain linearity.

Variable reactance transistor Figure 4.29(c) shows the basic transistor connection needed to provide a voltage-variable capacitance C_v seen looking into the collector of the transistor. For simplicity, the usual transistor biasing components that provide the indicated DC bias voltage V_B and those that perform decoupling functions have been omitted. The impedance Z looking into the collector terminal is given by

$$Z = \frac{1}{j2\pi f g_m RC} \equiv \frac{1}{j2\pi f C_v} \tag{4.74}$$

where g_m is the transconductance of the transistor. The transistor therefore appears as a capacitor of equivalent capacitance

$$C_v = g_m RC \tag{4.75}$$

A modulating signal applied to the base of the transistor varies g_m and hence the capacitance C_v. An LCO modulator that obtains its variable capacitance in this way is sometimes referred to as a *transistor reactance modulator*.

4.5.3.2 VCO modulator

A voltage-controlled oscillator (VCO) modulator generates an FM signal that has a highly linear relationship between frequency and modulating signal, which is applied as the control voltage. Practical VCO modulators are available in integrated circuit (IC) form, the most popular of which is the 566 VCO used for frequencies below 1 MHz. Figure 4.30 shows the block diagram and external connections to a 566 VCO IC.

The control terminal (5) is biased to V_B using the supply voltage V_{cc} and the voltage divider formed with resistors R_1 and R_2. This bias voltage, along with the timing resistor R, determines the constant charging (discharge) current I_c that the timing capacitor C receives (sends) from (to) the current source (sink):

$$I_c = \frac{V_{cc} - V_B}{R} \tag{4.76}$$

The repetitive charging and discharging of capacitor C makes available at terminal (4) a periodic triangular waveform of fundamental frequency

$$f_c = \frac{2(V_{cc} - V_B)}{RCV_{cc}} \tag{4.77}$$

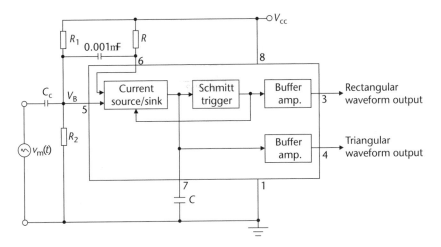

Figure 4.30 The 566 VCO.

This voltage is fed into a Schmitt trigger to generate a rectangular waveform of the same fundamental frequency, available at terminal (3). The Schmitt trigger output also serves to switch the operating mode of the current source/sink each time the trigger output changes level.

When a modulating signal is applied to terminal (5) via a coupling capacitor C_C, it varies the effective bias voltage V_B, and hence the output frequency, according to Eq. (4.77). Connecting either terminal (3) or (4) to a BPF of centre frequency f_c then produces an FM signal based on a sinusoidal carrier signal. The bandwidth of the BPF is required to be just enough to pass the fundamental frequency f_c, and all significant side frequencies associated with f_c, but not any of the side frequencies associated with $2f_c$, $3f_c$ etc.

The 566 has had a long history as an instrumentation VCO and is also used in FM telemetry.

4.6 FM and PM demodulators

The practical implementation of angle modulation has been discussed above. Let us now turn our attention to the reverse process of angle demodulation. Given a PM or FM signal, how do we recover the original message signal from the angle variations of the carrier? We first discuss frequency demodulation systems, and then show how they may be extended to perform phase demodulation. There are two broad classes of frequency demodulator, namely the direct demodulator, which uses frequency discriminators or zero crossing detectors, and the indirect demodulator, which employs a phase-locked loop (PLL).

4.6.1 Direct demodulator

FM represents a message signal using a sinusoid of frequency proportional to the message signal value. A direct demodulator somehow detects the instantaneous frequency of the incoming FM signal and produces an output voltage of proportionate value. There are two ways of achieving this.

4.6.1.1 Filter-based demodulator

The message signal can be recovered at a receiver by passing the incoming FM signal through a filter with a linear frequency response, i.e. with a gain that is proportional to frequency. Thus the filter takes in a constant amplitude FM signal and produces an output signal whose amplitude varies in synchrony with the instantaneous frequency of the FM signal, and hence with the original message signal. Thus this filter changes the envelope of the FM signal from a constant value v_c to a value that varies exactly as the original message signal — a sort of AM–FM hybrid signal. An envelope demodulator (discussed in Chapter 3) will ignore the frequency variations and recover the original message signal. The filter just described is known as a *frequency discriminator*, and the combination of a frequency discriminator followed by an envelope demodulator gives direct FM demodulation.

Note that the frequency response of the discriminator need only be linear in the frequency band that contains all possible instantaneous frequency values of the FM signal. This is the band $f_c \pm f_d$. Furthermore, there may be amplitude variations in the incoming FM signal due to the effect of noise and distortion in the transmission medium, or due to the small amplitude variations that are inherent in NBFM generation. To prevent these unwanted variations getting into the recovered message signal, the incoming FM signal is first passed through a circuit known as a *limiter*, which clips the FM signal to eliminate fluctuations in its envelope. To exclude the new frequency components associated with the clipping action (Section 2.9.3), the limiter usually includes a tuned tank circuit that passes only the wanted frequency components around f_c. Furthermore, a transistor circuit is usually employed, which provides signal amplification as well, all carrier amplitudes above a certain minimum or *threshold* level being boosted to the same output level. The output of the limiter is then the desired constant-amplitude FM signal. A block diagram of the direct FM demodulator is shown in Fig. 4.31, which also shows the waveform at each stage of the demodulation process.

4.6.1.2 Digital demodulator

Direct FM demodulation can also be accomplished using a digital technique. The number of zero-crossings in the FM signal within fixed time intervals of duration T is gated into a binary counter, which feeds a digital-to-analogue converter (DAC). The DAC output gives a direct measure of the instantaneous frequency of the FM signal, and hence of the original message signal during the interval. The interval T over which the number of positive-going zero crossings is counted should satisfy the condition

$$\frac{1}{f_c} \ll T \ll \frac{1}{f_m} \tag{4.78}$$

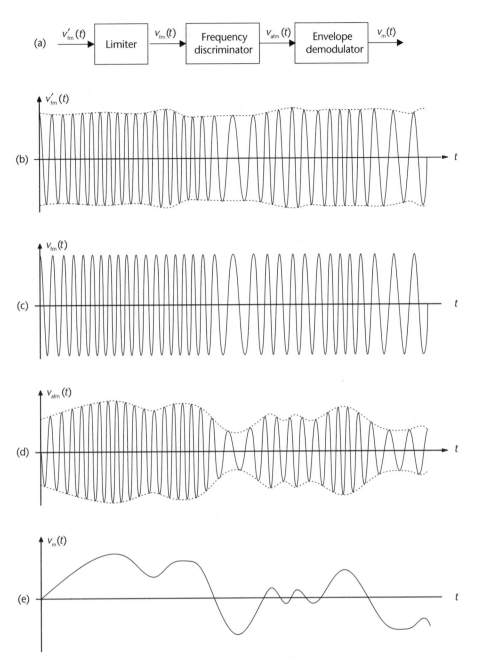

Figure 4.31 Direct FM demodulator using frequency discriminator: (a) block diagram; (b)–(e) waveforms.

where f_m is the maximum frequency component of the message signal. The first condition $T \gg 1/f_c$ ensures that there are zero crossings within the interval T, while the second condition $T \ll 1/f_m$ avoids excessive averaging of the message signal.

4.6.2 Indirect demodulator

The indirect method of FM demodulation uses a phase-locked loop (PLL, introduced in Chapter 3) to match the frequency of a VCO to the frequency variations in the FM signal. When the VCO correctly tracks the FM signal in frequency, then it follows that its control voltage corresponds exactly to the original message signal. Figure 4.32(a) shows a block diagram of the PLL (FM) demodulator.

The PLL consists of a phase discriminator with a VCO in its feedback path, which is arranged such that the output $v_v(t)$ of the VCO tends towards the same frequency as the FM signal input to the phase discriminator. The phase discriminator consists of a multiplier or product modulator followed by a low-pass filter (LPF). The LPF rejects the sum-frequency output of the multiplier but passes the difference-frequency output, denoted $v_p(t)$, which serves as the control voltage of the VCO. The VCO is set so that when its input or control voltage is zero then its output $v_v(t)$ has the same frequency as the unmodulated carrier, but with a phase difference of $\pi/2$ rad. Thus, if the (normalised) unmodulated carrier is

$$v_c(t) = \cos(2\pi f_c t)$$

then, from Eq. (4.32), the VCO output at any time is given by

$$v_v(t) = \cos(2\pi f_c t + \pi/2 + \phi_v)$$

(4.79)

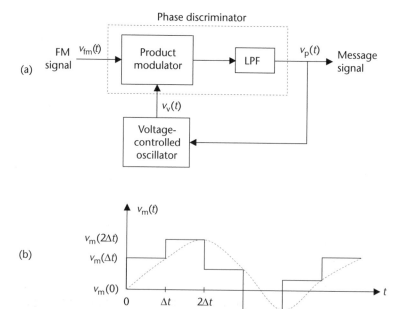

Figure 4.32 (a) Indirect frequency demodulator using phase-locked loop (PLL); (b) staircase approximation of original message signal $v_m(t)$.

where

$$\phi_v = 2\pi k_v \int_0^t v_p(t)dt \tag{4.80}$$

k_v is the frequency sensitivity of the VCO, and $\phi_v = 0$ when the VCO is free-running.

4.6.2.1 PLL demodulation process

For a simplified view of how the PLL demodulates the input FM signal $v_{fm}(t)$, let us assume a staircase approximation of the original message signal $v_m(t)$ as shown in Fig. 4.32(b) and reckon time from the instant when the VCO is free-running and v_{fm} has frequency f_c. That is, the original message signal is zero at this instant ($t = 0$), and we may write $v_m(0) = 0$. Furthermore, let us assume that the VCO output only changes at the discrete time instants $t = \Delta t, 2\Delta t, \ldots$.

The phase discriminator output $v_p(t)$ at $t = 0$ is the difference-frequency product of $v_c(t)$ and $v_v(t)$ with $\phi_v = 0$:

$$v_p(0) = \cos(\pi/2) = 0$$

Now consider the situation at $t = \Delta t$. The message signal made a step increase to the value $v_m(\Delta t)$ at time $t = 0$, and therefore just before this time ($t = \Delta t$) the phase of $v_{fm}(t)$ has gained on the phase of the VCO output $v_v(t)$, which is still free-running, by a small amount ϕ_{fm1} given by

$$\phi_{fm1} = [2\pi k_f v_m(\Delta t)]\Delta t \tag{4.81}$$

At the instant $t = \Delta t$, the VCO re-establishes tracking by making a step change of $\phi_{v1} = \phi_{fm1}$ in its phase. From Eq. (4.80), this requires a control voltage of average value v_{pa1} during the interval $t = 0$ to Δt given by the relation

$$\phi_{v1} = 2\pi k_v v_{pa1}\Delta t \tag{4.82}$$

Equating the RHS of Eq. (4.81) and Eq. (4.82) yields the result

$$v_{pa1} = \frac{k_f}{k_v} v_m(\Delta t) \tag{4.83}$$

By the next time instant $t = 2\Delta t$, the FM signal phase has increased to

$$\phi_{fm2} = \phi_{fm1} + [2\pi k_f v_m(2\Delta t)]\Delta t$$

and the VCO again makes a step change in the phase of $v_v(t)$ to the new value

$$\phi_{v2} = \phi_{v1} + 2\pi k_v v_{pa2}\Delta t$$

where v_{pa2} is the average value of $v_p(t)$ in the interval $t = \Delta t$ to $2\Delta t$. Equating the expressions for ϕ_{v2} and ϕ_{fm2}, and noting that $\phi_{v1} = \phi_{fm1}$, we obtain

$$v_{pa2} = \frac{k_f}{k_v} v_m(2\Delta t)$$

It follows by a similar argument that the average value of $v_p(t)$ in the nth time interval is related to the original message signal by

$$v_{pa,n} = \frac{k_f}{k_v} v_m(n\Delta t), \quad n = 1, 2, 3, \ldots \tag{4.84}$$

In the limit $\Delta t \to 0$, tracking becomes continuous, and the average values $v_{pa1}, v_{pa2}, \ldots$, become the instantaneous values of $v_p(t)$, and we may write

$$v_p(t) = \frac{k_f}{k_v} v_m(t) \tag{4.85}$$

The above equation shows that when the PLL is in the tracking or phase-locked state, its output gives the original message signal $v_m(t)$, with a scaling factor k_f/k_v. FM demodulation has therefore been achieved. The LPF is designed with a bandwidth that is just sufficient to pass the original message signal, e.g. up to 15 kHz for audio signals.

4.6.2.2 PLL states

The PLL can operate in three different states. It is in the *free-running* state when the VCO control voltage is zero, or when the input and VCO frequencies are too far apart. In this state the VCO output $v_v(t)$ oscillates at a frequency determined by an external timing capacitor (in the usual IC implementation of PLLs). The *tracking* or *locked* state has been discussed above. Once locked to an input signal $v_{fm}(t)$, the PLL is able to vary the frequency of $v_v(t)$ to keep step with the frequency variations of $v_{fm}(t)$ over a wide but finite band, referred to as the *lock range*. The PLL is said to be in the *capture state* when it is in the process of continuously changing the frequency of $v_v(t)$ until it is equal to the frequency of the input signal $v_{fm}(t)$, i.e. until lock is achieved and the tracking state ensues. However, lock will not be achieved if the initial separation between the input frequency and the VCO frequency is too large. The band of input signal frequencies over which the PLL will capture the signal is known as the *capture range*. This is usually much narrower than the lock range. Both the capture and lock ranges are centred at the free-running frequency.

4.6.2.3 PLL features

The PLL is an extremely versatile device with numerous applications in electronics. It provides excellent FM demodulation with a number of advantages over discriminator-based direct demodulation. For example, it is not sensitive to amplitude variations in the FM signal, so a limiting circuit is not required. Since its circuit does not include inductors, the PLL is more easily implemented in IC form. It also obviates the need for complicated coil adjustments. The PLL is also very linear, giving accurate recovery of the original message signal. Furthermore, the PLL's feature of capturing or passing only signals that are within a small band makes it very effective at rejecting noise and interference, and gives it a superior signal-to-noise-ratio.

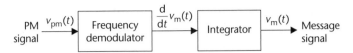

Figure 4.33 Phase demodulator.

4.6.3 Phase demodulator

A phase demodulator can be easily derived from the frequency demodulators discussed above, based on the theoretical relationships between PM and FM. To see how this may be achieved, consider Eq. (4.21), which gives the instantaneous frequency f_i of a PM signal. Note that the frequency variation in a PM signal is proportional to the derivative of the message signal. We were able to use the above FM demodulator schemes because frequency variation in FM is proportional to the message signal; see Eq. (4.4). Thus, if a PM signal is the input to any of the above FM demodulators, the output signal will be the derivative of the original message signal. The original message signal can then be obtained by following the FM demodulator with an integrator. A PM demodulator is therefore as shown in Fig. 4.33.

4.6.4 Frequency discriminators

Frequency discriminators can be implemented using various circuits. The main requirements are that the frequency response $H(f)$ of the circuit should be linear in the frequency band of interest, and should change rapidly with frequency to give acceptable demodulation sensitivity. Thus, any circuit whose amplitude response can be represented by the following linear function of frequency f will function properly as a discriminator:

$$|H(f)| = k_1 + k_2 f \tag{4.86}$$

Here k_1 is a constant, which may be zero, but k_2 is a non-zero constant that determines the sensitivity with which frequency variation in the FM signal at the discriminator input is converted to amplitude variation in the AM–FM hybrid signal at the output. A few examples of discriminators are discussed below.

4.6.4.1 Differentiators

We want to show that a differentiator satisfies Eq. (4.86), which means that it can be used as a frequency discriminator. Let the input to the differentiator in Fig. 4.34 be a sinusoidal signal of frequency f:

$$x(t) = \cos(2\pi f t)$$

Then the output signal is given by

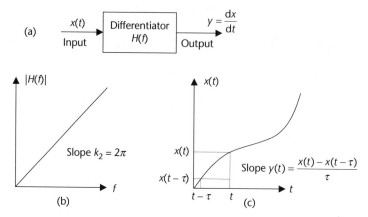

Figure 4.34 Differentiator: (a) block diagram; (b) amplitude response.

$$y = \frac{dx}{dt} = -2\pi f \sin(2\pi ft)$$
$$= 2\pi f \cos(2\pi ft + \pi/2)$$
$$\equiv |H(f)| \cos[2\pi ft + \phi_H(f)]$$

Note that, as discussed in Section 2.8, the effect of the differentiator is to change the amplitude of the input sinusoid by a factor $|H(f)|$ equal to its amplitude response, and to shift the phase of the input sinusoid by an amount $\phi_H(f)$ equal to its phase response. It follows that the frequency response of a differentiator is given by

$$H(f) \equiv |H(f)| \exp[j\phi_H(f)]$$
$$= 2\pi f \exp(j\pi/2)$$
$$= 2\pi f [\cos(\pi/2) + j\sin(\pi/2)] \tag{4.87}$$
$$= j2\pi f$$

which satisfies Eq. (4.86) with $k_1 = 0$, and $k_2 = j2\pi$. Thus, FM demodulation can be carried out by differentiating the FM signal followed by envelope demodulation. Question 4.15 addresses this further. Equation (4.87) shows that in general, if the transfer function of a circuit in a specified frequency range can be approximated by

$$H(f) = jKf$$

where K is a constant, then that circuit acts as a differentiator of gain $K/2\pi$ in that frequency band. Note that the frequency response of a differentiator (see Fig. 4.34(b)) is linear over the entire frequency axis, not just within a limited band of interest. We will consider two examples of differentiator circuits.

Delay-line differentiator The output of a differentiator is the derivative of its input signal, which, according to Fig. 4.34(c) may be approximated by

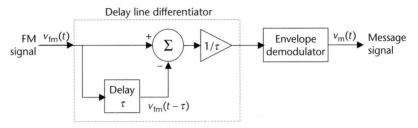

Figure 4.35   Phase shift demodulator.

$$y(t) = \frac{x(t) - x(t - \tau)}{\tau} \tag{4.88}$$

where τ is the time delay between adjacent sample values, which must be small enough to satisfy the condition

$$\tau \ll \frac{1}{2\pi f_c}$$

Equation (4.88) suggests a system known as a delay-line differentiator, which uses a delay line and a summing device to obtain the difference between adjacent input signal samples, followed by a gain factor of $1/\tau$. Since a time delay of τ (on a frequency component f) is equivalent to a phase shift of $2\pi f\tau$, the demodulator realised using a delay-line differentiator followed by an envelope demodulator is referred to as *phase shift demodulator*. This is shown in Fig. 4.35.

RC differentiator   The simple high-pass *RC* filter circuit shown in Fig. 4.36(a) has the frequency response

$$\begin{aligned}
H(f) &= \frac{R}{R + 1/(j2\pi fC)} \\
&= \frac{j2\pi fRC}{1 + j2\pi fRC} \\
&\approx j2\pi fRC, \qquad \text{for } 2\pi fRC \ll 1
\end{aligned} \tag{4.89}$$

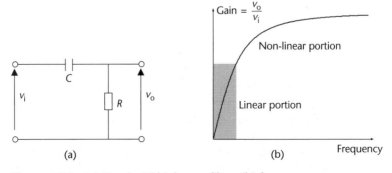

Figure 4.36   (a) Simple *RC* high-pass filter; (b) frequency response.

It therefore acts as a differentiator of gain RC at low frequencies ($f \ll 1/2\pi RC$), which is the linear portion of the frequency response shown (shaded) in Fig. 4.36(b). The RC filter will work as a discriminator for FM demodulation if the frequency band $f_c \pm f_d$ falls in this linear region. Assuming $f_c \sim 10$ MHz, and $R = 1$ kΩ, this requires a capacitance C of less than about 3.0 pF, which is a small value indeed, comparable to stray capacitances in circuits. An LC bandpass filter (BPF) is more suitable for linear frequency response approximation at the usual high values of f_c, an intermediate frequency (IF) value of 10.7 MHz being common in FM broadcast receivers.

4.6.4.2 *Tuned circuits*

A tuned (RLC) circuit can also be used as a discriminator if it is detuned such that the unmodulated carrier frequency falls in the centre of the linear portion of the circuit's gain response, as shown in Fig. 4.37. The main limitation of this simple circuit is that the linear portion of the gain response is very narrow, and not sufficient for wideband FM that has a large frequency deviation. The linear portion can be extended by using two back-to-back bandpass filters tuned to two different resonant frequencies spaced equally below and above the carrier frequency. This gives what is referred to as a *balanced discriminator* circuit, an example of which is shown in Fig. 4.38 along with the resulting frequency response. In the circuit, L and C are tuned to frequency f_c, L_1 and C_1 are tuned to frequency f_1 and L_2 and C_2 to frequency f_2. The remaining part of the circuit provides envelope demodulation.

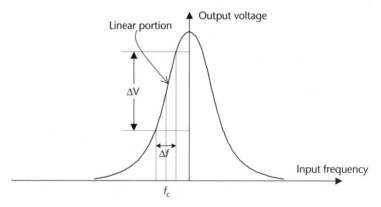

Figure 4.37 Frequency response of tuned circuit showing linear portion.

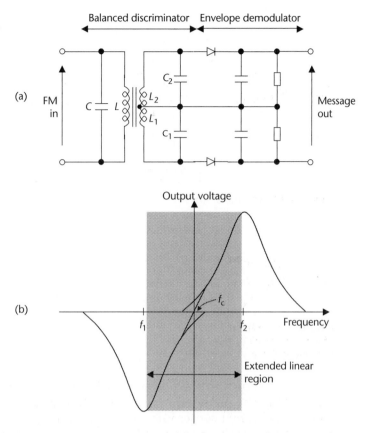

Figure 4.38 Balanced discriminator:(a) Circuit diagram; (b) frequency response.

4.7 FM transmitter and receiver

4.7.1 Transmitter

The basic elements of a broadcast FM transmitter are shown in Fig. 4.39. The output of the wideband FM modulator, the operation of which was described in connection with Fig. 4.26, is amplified into a high-power FM signal and coupled to an antenna for radiation. There is, however, a new processing block, called *pre-emphasis*, which operates on the message signal before it is applied to angle-modulate the carrier. The role of pre-emphasis is to improve the noise performance of the FM communication system as briefly discussed below.

The effect of additive noise is to alter both the amplitude and phase of the transmitted FM signal, as illustrated in Fig 4.40(a). A signal of amplitude V_{fm} is transmitted, but due to the effect of additive noise of random amplitude V_n, the demodulator receives a signal V_{fmn}, which is the sum of V_{fm} and V_n. The noise voltage V_n can have any phase relative to the FM signal

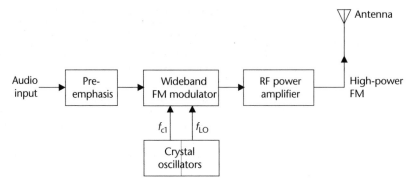

Figure 4.39 FM transmitter.

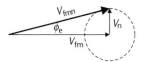

Figure 4.40 Worst-case phase error ϕ_e due to noise voltage V_n.

V_{fm}, but is shown in the phasor diagram with a phase of 90° (relative to V_{fm}), where the phase error ϕ_e is maximum for a given noise amplitude. Since an FM signal carries information in its angle, the amplitude error in V_{fmn} is of no effect and all amplitude variations are removed by a limiting circuit prior to demodulation. However, the phase error ϕ_e will somehow corrupt the received message signal since the demodulator has no way of knowing that the additional phase comes from noise.

The maximum phase error ϕ_e increases with noise amplitude up to a value of $\pi/4$ rad at $V_n = V_{fm}$. Using Eq. (4.28), we see that this phase error will lead to an error f_{dn} in the frequency deviation, which translates to an error V_{nr} in the received message signal given by

$$f_{dn} = k_f V_{nr} = \phi_e f_m \tag{4.90}$$

where f_m is the frequency of the message signal. We make two important observations:

1. The effect of the phase error increases with message signal frequency. That is, the voltage error due to noise is larger for the higher frequency components of the message signal. The problem is further compounded by the fact that the higher frequency components of the message signal are usually of small amplitudes. As a result, the signal to noise voltage ratio s/n decreases significantly with frequency. To reduce this problem, the amplitude of the high-frequency components of the message signal can be artificially boosted prior to modulation. This process is known as *pre-emphasis*, and the circuit that is used is called a pre-emphasis filter. This introduces a known distortion into

the message signal, which is readily removed at the receiver after demodulation by applying a filter whose transfer function is the exact inverse of the pre-emphasis filter. This second operation, performed at the receiver is known as *de-emphasis*.

The effect of noise, as indicated by the error voltage V_{nr} in the demodulated signal, can be reduced arbitrarily by increasing frequency sensitivity k_f. Since modulation index $\beta = k_f V_m/f_m$, this amounts to increasing modulation index, and hence transmission bandwidth. Thus, FM provides an effective means of trading bandwidth for reduced noise degradation, or improved noise performance.

4.7.2 SNR and bandwidth trade-off

We can obtain a rough calculation of the worst-case improvement in noise performance afforded by FM as follows. From Fig. 4.40, the ratio of signal-to-noise voltage at the input of the demodulator is

$$s/n_i = V_{fm}/V_n$$

If V_n is small compared with V_{fm}, i.e. $s/n_i \gg 1$, then the phase error can be approximated by

$$\tan \phi_e = \frac{V_n}{V_{fm}} = \frac{1}{s/n_i}$$
$$\approx \phi_e \tag{4.91}$$

Note that ϕ_e is the largest possible phase error due to noise of amplitude V_n, and leads to the worst-case or smallest ratio of signal-to-noise voltage at the output of the demodulator. Let us denote this ratio as s/n_o. It is clearly given by the ratio between the frequency deviation f_d due to the message signal and the frequency deviation f_{dn} due to noise, since the demodulator translates frequency variation to voltage variation. Thus,

$$s/n_o = \frac{f_d}{f_{dn}} = \frac{f_d}{\phi_e f_m} = \frac{\beta}{\phi_e}$$
$$= \beta(s/n_i) \tag{4.92}$$

where we have used Eq. (4.91). Since the square of voltage gives normalised power, we square both sides of Eq. (4.92) to obtain the relationship between the output signal-to-noise power ratio SNR_o and the input signal-to-noise power ratio SNR_i:

$$SNR_o = \beta^2 (SNR_i) \tag{4.93}$$

Equation (4.93) is an important result, which shows that FM gives an improvement in output signal-to-noise power ratio that increases as the square of modulation index β. However, this is the worst-case scenario, and the actual improvement is usually better by a constant factor. When account is taken of the random variation of the phase of the noise voltage V_n relative to V_{fm}, then the effective phase error is less than ϕ_e. The exact relationship between SNR_o and SNR_i — for large SNR_i — will be deriv̄

Chapter 9, where it will be shown that SNR_o is larger by a factor of 1.5 than the worst-case value given in Eq. (4.93). Bear in mind that Eq. (4.93) assumes a sinusoidal message signal and a large SNR_i.

4.7.3 Pre-emphasis and de-emphasis

Simple RC filters are usually employed for pre-emphasis and de-emphasis. Figure 4.41 shows the pre-emphasis and de-emphasis circuits used for standard FM broadcasting. The frequency response of the pre-emphasis filter is given by

$$H_p(f) = \frac{R_2}{R_2 + R_1/(1 + j2\pi f R_1 C)}$$
$$= K\frac{1 + jf/f_1}{1 + jf/f_2}$$
$$K = \frac{R_2}{R_1 + R_2}; \quad f_1 = \frac{1}{2\pi\tau_1} = \frac{1}{2\pi R_1 C}$$
$$f_2 = \frac{1}{2\pi\tau_2} = \frac{1}{2\pi RC}; \quad R = \frac{R_1 R_2}{R_1 + R_2}$$

(4.94)

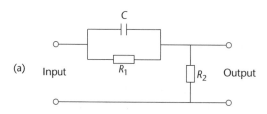

(a) Input R_1 R_2 Output

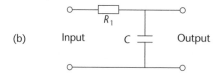

(b) Input R_1 C Output

Figure 4.41 (a) Pre-emphasis filter; (b) de-emphasis filter.

Similarly, the frequency response of the de-emphasis filter is

$$H_d(f) = \frac{1}{1 + jf/f_1}$$

(4.95)

with f_1 given as above. The two frequency responses are plotted in Fig. 4.42.

In FM audio broadcasting, the RC time constant $\tau_1 = 75\ \mu s$, so that the first corner frequency $f_1 = 2120$ Hz. The second corner frequency f_2 is chosen to be well above the maximum frequency component f_m (= 15 kHz) of the audio signal. Observe that the linearly increasing response of the pre-emphasis circuit between f_1 and f_m means that the circuit behaves as a

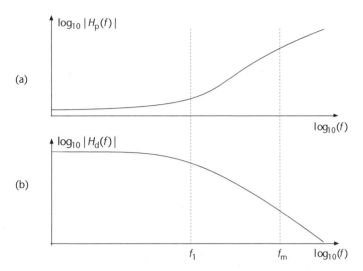

Figure 4.42 Frequency response of (a) pre-emphasis and (b) de-emphasis filters.

differentiator at these frequencies. Refer to Eq. (4.87). It follows from Fig. 4.5 that when the pre-emphasised audio signal frequency-modulates the carrier, the result will be FM for frequencies up to about 2120 Hz, and PM for higher frequencies. Thus, FM with pre-emphasis is actually a combination of FM (at lower message frequencies) and PM (at the higher message frequencies).

We have stated earlier that the de-emphasis circuit is used at the receiver after the frequency demodulator to undo the effect of pre-emphasis. However, an illuminating alternative view of the role of de-emphasis can be obtained by observing that the frequency response of the de-emphasis circuit is approximately uniform up to f_1 and linearly decreasing beyond this point. That is, this circuit acts as an integrator for frequencies above f_1. Thus, in the light of Fig. 4.33, we have FM demodulation for frequencies below f_1, and PM demodulation for frequencies above f_1, and the original message signal is accurately recovered from the received hybrid FM–PM signal. This is remarkable.

4.7.4 Receiver

Figure 4.43 shows a block diagram of a complete FM receiver system. It is based on the superheterodyne principle discussed in detail in Chapter 3 for AM reception. See Fig. 3.22. Note the following differences in Fig. 4.43. The intermediate frequency (IF) is $f_{IF} = 10.7$ MHz for audio broadcasting, and the bandwidth of the IF amplifier is 200 kHz to accommodate the received FM signal. The demodulator is usually by the direct method of Fig. 4.31, consisting of limiter, discriminator, and envelope demodulator; but it may also be by the indirect method of Fig. 4.32 involving a PLL. Note that, as discussed above, de-emphasis is carried out after FM demodulation.

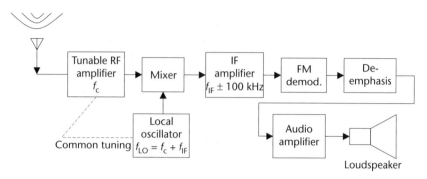

Figure 4.43 FM superheterodyne receiver.

You may wish at this point to review the discussion of the operation of an FM stereo receiver given in Chapter 3 (Section 3.7.1.4 and Fig. 3.32).

4.8 Overview of FM and PM features

Let us complete our study of angle modulation with a discussion of its merits and demerits when compared with *amplitude modulation* (studied in Chapter 3). The major applications of FM and PM are also presented.

4.8.1 Merits

1. Wideband FM gives a significant improvement in the signal-to-noise power ratio (*SNR*) at the output of the receiver. The output *SNR* is proportional to the square of modulation index. A further improvement in *SNR* of about 13 dB in sound broadcasting can be obtained using pre-emphasis (to boost the amplitude of high-frequency components of the modulating signal) and de-emphasis (to remove the pre-emphasis distortion from the demodulated signal).

2. Angle modulation is resistant to propagation-induced selective fading, since amplitude variations are unimportant and are removed at the receiver using a limiting circuit.

3. Angle modulation is very effective in rejecting interference in the same manner that it minimises the effect of noise. The receiver locks unto the wanted signal and suppresses the interfering signal, provided it is not nearer in strength to the wanted signal than the *capture ratio*. A capture ratio of, say, 5 dB means that the receiver suppresses any signal that is weaker than the wanted signal (to which it is tuned) by 5 dB or more. A small capture ratio is desirable.

4. Angle modulation allows the use of more efficient transmitters. The FM signal is generated with low-level modulation. Highly efficient non-linear Class C amplifiers are then employed to produce a high-power RF signal for radiation. These amplifiers can be optimally operated since the angle-modulated signal is of fixed amplitude. There is no need for

the high-power audio amplifiers used in high-level AM transmitters, or the inefficient linear RF amplifiers required to preserve the information-bearing RF envelope in low-level AM transmitters.

5. Angle modulation is capable of handling a greater dynamic range of modulating signal than AM without distortion, by employing sufficient frequency sensitivity to translate all message signal variations to a proportionate and significant carrier frequency variation. The penalty is an increase in transmission bandwidth.

4.8.2 Demerits

1. The most significant disadvantage of angle modulation is that it requires a transmission bandwidth that is much larger than the message signal bandwidth, depending of course on the modulation index. For example, in FM audio broadcasting, a 15 kHz audio signal requires a bandwidth of about 200 kHz. PM is even less efficient in spectrum utilisation than FM.

2. The interference rejection advantage of angle modulation can be detrimental in, for example, mobile receivers near the edge of a service area, where the wanted signal may be captured by an unwanted signal or noise voltage. If the two signals are of comparable amplitude, the receiver locks intermittently onto one signal or the other — a problem known as the *capture effect*.

3. Angle modulation generally requires more complex and expensive circuits than AM. However, with advances in IC technology this is no longer a very significant demerit.

4.8.3 Applications

1. Audio broadcasting within the VHF band at frequencies from 88 MHz to 108 MHz. The audio signal occupies the frequency band 50 Hz to 15 kHz, and the allowed transmission bandwidth is 200 kHz with a rated system deviation F_D = 75 kHz. In the USA, non-commercial stations are assigned carrier frequencies in increments of 200 kHz from 88.1 to 91.9 MHz, and commercial stations from 92.1 to 107.9 MHz. The implementation of FM stereo was discussed in Chapter 3 under applications of DSB (Section 3.7.1.4).

2. Transmission of accompanying sound in television broadcast using VHF frequencies 54–88 MHz and 174–216 MHz. An audio signal of baseband 50 Hz to 15 kHz frequency-modulates a carrier with a rated system deviation F_D = 25 kHz.

3. Two-way mobile radio systems transmitting audio signals of bandwidth 5 kHz, with rated system deviations F_D = 2.5 kHz and 5 kHz for channel bandwidths 12.5 kHz and 25 kHz, respectively. Various frequency bands have been assigned to different services, such as

amateur bands at 144–148 MHz and 420–450 MHz; and public service bands at 108 – 174 MHz.

4. Multi-channel telephony systems. Long-distance telephone traffic is carried on analogue point-to-point terrestrial and satellite links using FM. Several voice channels are stacked in frequency to form a composite frequency division multiplex (FDM) signal, which is used to frequency-modulate a carrier at an intermediate frequency of, say, 70 MHz. The resulting FM signal is then up-converted to the right UHF frequency (for terrestrial microwave links) or SHF frequency (for satellite links).

5. PM and various hybrids are used in modulated digital communication systems, such as data communication over public switched telephone networks and in digital satellite communication systems.

SUMMARY

This now completes our study of analogue signal modulation techniques begun in Chapter 3. In this chapter, we have covered in detail the principles of phase and frequency modulations, and emphasised throughout our discussions the relationships between these two angle modulation techniques. Various angle modulation and demodulation circuits were discussed. FM can be generated using a PM modulator that is preceded by a suitable low-pass filter or *integrator*, and demodulated using a PM demodulator followed by a suitable high-pass filter or *differentiator*. Similarly, PM can be obtained from an FM modulator preceded by a differentiator, and demodulated using an FM demodulator followed by an integrator. However, PM is not used for transmitting analogue message signals due to its poor bandwidth efficiency when compared to FM. The use of PM for digital signal transmission is addressed in Chapter 7.

In the next chapter, we embark on a thorough understanding of the issues involved in the sampling of analogue signals – an essential step in the process of analogue-to-digital conversion.

REVIEW QUESTIONS

4.1 The staircase waveform shown in Fig. 4.44 modulates the angle of the carrier signal $v_c(t) = V_c\cos(1000\pi t)$. Make a sketch of the angle $\theta_c(t)$ of the modulated carrier in degrees as a function of time in ms, over the entire duration of the modulating signal, for the following cases.

(a) Frequency modulation with a frequency sensitivity $k_f = 0.2$ kHz/volt.
(b) Phase modulation with phase sensitivity $k_p = \pi/4$ rad/volt.

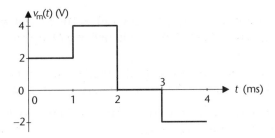

Figure 4.44 Question 4.1.

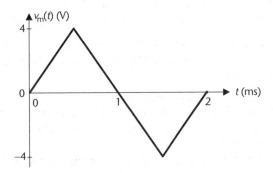

Figure 4.45 Question 4.2.

4.2   Repeat Question 4.1 for the case of the triangular modulating signal shown in Fig. 4.45. Compare the final angle (at t = 4ms) of the unmodulated carrier with that of the modulated carrier and comment on your result.

4.3   The message signal in Fig. 4.44 frequency-modulates the carrier $v_c(t) = 10\sin(4000\pi t)$ volts using a circuit of frequency sensitivity 500 Hz/volt.

(a) Sketch the FM signal waveform.
(b) Determine the frequency deviation and frequency swing of the modulated carrier.

4.4   Sketch the resulting PM waveform when the message signal in Fig. 4.44 phase-modulates the carrier $v_c(t) = 5\sin(4000\pi t)$ volts using a circuit of phase sensitivity 45°/volt.

4.5   A message signal $v_m(t) = 2\sin(10 \times 10^3\pi t)$ volt is used to frequency-modulate the carrier $v_c(t) = 10\sin(180 \times 10^6\pi t)$ volt, giving a percent modulation of 60%. Determine

(a) The frequency deviation of the modulated carrier.
(b) The frequency sensitivity of the modulator circuit.
(c) The frequency swing of the modulated carrier.
(d) The modulation index.
(e) The phase deviation of the modulated carrier.

4.6 A message signal $v_m(t) = 5\sin(20 \times 10^3 \pi t)$ volt phase-modulates the carrier $v_c(t) = 10\sin(10^6 \pi t)$ volt, giving a phase modulation factor $m = 1$. Determine

(a) The phase sensitivity of the modulating circuit.
(b) The frequency deviation of the modulated carrier.

4.7 *MATLAB exercises*: The triangular waveform shown in Fig. 4.45 modulates the carrier signal $v_c(t) = 5\sin(20 \times 10^3 \pi t)$ volts. Following the discussion and equations in Section 4.3.2, make an accurate plot of the modulated carrier waveform for each of the following cases:

(a) Frequency modulation with sensitivity 2 kHz/volt.
(b) Phase modulation with sensitivity $\pi/4$ rad/volt.

4.8 The display of a NBFM signal on a spectrum analyser shows three frequency components at 18, 20 and 22 kHz, with respective amplitudes 1 volt, 10 volts and 1 volt.

(a) What is the modulation index?
(b) Determine the minimum and maximum amplitudes of the modulated carrier and hence the percentage variation in carrier amplitude.
(c) Compare the results obtained in (b) above with the case of an AM signal that has an identical amplitude spectrum.
(d) Draw a phasor diagram — similar to Fig. 4.16, but with all sides and angles calculated — of the NBFM signal at each of the time instants t = 0, 62.5 µs, 125 µs, 250 µs and 437.5 µs.
(e) Based on the results in (d), or otherwise, make a sketch of the NBFM waveform, as would be displayed on an oscilloscope. Your sketch must be to scale and with clearly labelled axes.

4.9 Obtain Equations (4.55) and (4.56) for the Fourier series of tone-modulated FM and PM signals. To do this, you may wish to expand Eq. (4.36) using the relevant trigonometric identity and then apply the following relations:

$$\cos[\beta\sin(\omega_m t)] = J_0(\beta) + 2J_2(\beta)\cos(2\omega_m t)$$
$$+ 2J_4(\beta)\cos(4\omega_m t) + \cdots$$
$$\sin[\beta\sin(\omega_m t)] = 2J_1(\beta)\sin(\omega_m t) + 2J_3(\beta)\sin(3\omega_m t)$$
$$+ 2J_5(\beta)\sin(5\omega_m t) + \cdots$$

4.10 A message signal of baseband frequencies 300 Hz → 5 kHz is used to frequency-modulate a 60 MHz carrier, giving a frequency deviation of 25 kHz. Determine the Carson's and 1% transmission bandwidths.

4.11 When the carrier signal $v_c(t) = 10\sin(10^6 \pi t)$ volts is frequency-modulated by the message signal $v_m(t) = 2\sin(10^4 \pi t)$ volts, the carrier frequency varies within ±4% of its unmodulated value.

(a) What is the frequency sensitivity of the modulator?
(b) What is the modulation index?
(c) Determine the Carson's and 1% transmission bandwidths.

(d) Sketch the amplitude spectrum of the FM signal. Include all spectral components with an amplitude larger than 1% of the unmodulated carrier amplitude.

(e) Determine the percentage of the total power contained in the frequency band 473 kHz → 526 kHz.

4.12 Determine the percentage of total power contained within the Carson's and 1% bandwidths of a tone-modulated FM signal with the following values of modulation index:

(a) $\beta = 0.2$
(b) $\beta = 2$
(c) $\beta = 20$

4.13 The circuit of Fig. 4.25 is employed to generate a NBFM signal of modulation index $\beta = 0.2$. The message signal is a 2 kHz sinusoid. If the required frequency sensitivity is $k_f = 5$ kHz/V, give a specification of suitable component values R and C and the message signal amplitude V_m.

4.14 Fig. 4.46 is the block diagram of an Armstrong modulator involving two stages of frequency multiplication. The message signal $v_m(t)$ contains frequencies in the range 50 Hz to 15 kHz. The wideband FM output signal has a carrier frequency $f_c = 96$ MHz and a minimum frequency deviation $f_d = 75$ kHz. The NBFM modulator uses a carrier frequency $f_{c1} = 100$ kHz, with a modulation index $\beta_1 = 0.2$. Determine the frequency multiplication ratios n_1 and n_2, which will allow an oscillator frequency $f_{LO} = 8.46$ MHz to be used in the down-converter, with $f_{LO} > n_1 f_{c1}$.

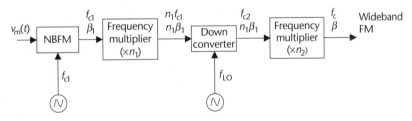

Figure 4.46 Question 4.14.

4.15 By taking the derivative of the general expression for an FM signal — Eq. (4.32) — show that frequency demodulation can be obtained using a circuit that consists of a differentiator followed by an envelope demodulator. Show the modification or addition required to use this circuit for phase demodulation.

Sampling

5.1 Introduction

This chapter lays an important foundation for the introduction of digital transmission techniques. The subject of sampling is introduced as a non-destructive elimination of the redundancy inherent in analogue signal representations. The sampling theorem is presented and terminologies such as *Nyquist frequency*, *Nyquist interval* and *aliasing* are discussed.

Using sinusoidal signals, we demonstrate how sampling at a sufficient rate duplicates (without distortion) the baseband spectrum of the sampled signal. The penalty of undersampling is also illustrated in the time and frequency domains, and the measures usually taken to minimise aliasing distortion are discussed with an example from telephone speech.

Instantaneous sampling is discussed and it is shown that although this method is highly desirable, it is impossible to realise in practice. Natural and flat-top sampling using a pulse train that has a non-zero duty cycle are discussed. The distortion due to aperture effect is presented along with practical measures to minimise this distortion.

5.2 Sampling theorem

Analogue signals are continuous in both time and amplitude, and they require exclusive use of a communication system resource for the entire duration of transmission. However, the values of an analogue signal at two sufficiently close time instants are usually related in some way and there is therefore inherent redundancy in such signals. For example, the values of a DC signal at all time instants are related as *equal*, so that only one value is required to recover the entire signal. A signal that is a linear function of time can be fully reconstructed from its values taken at only two time instants. The advantage of storing and transmitting only selected values of one signal is that the system resource can be allocated to other signals during the unused intervals.

The process of taking only a few values of an analogue signal $g(t)$ at regular time intervals is referred to as *sampling*. Thus sampling converts the *continuous-value continuous-time* signal $g(t)$ to a continuous-value *discrete-time* signal $g(nT_s)$, where $n = 0, 1, 2, 3, ...$, and T_s is the *sampling interval*. The surprise is that you can perfectly reconstruct the original signal $g(t)$ from the samples $g(0)$, $g(T_s)$, $g(2T_s)$, $g(3T_s)$, ..., provided you follow a simple rule, known as the *sampling theorem*, which may be stated as follows.

> A band-limited low pass signal that has no frequency components above f_m (Hz) may be perfectly reconstructed, using a low-pass filter, from its samples taken at regular intervals at the rate $f_s \geq 2f_m$ (samples per second, or Hz).

There are three important points to note about the sampling theorem.

1. The analogue signal must have a finite bandwidth f_m. A signal of infinite bandwidth cannot be sampled without distortion. In practice, it is necessary to artificially limit the bandwidth of the signal using a suitable low-pass filter.

2. At least two samples must be taken during each period T_m of the highest-frequency sinusoid in the signal. That is, the sampling interval T_s must be less than or equal to half T_m, which is the same as stated above that the sampling rate f_s must be at least twice f_m.

3. When the above two conditions are satisfied, the original signal $g(t)$ can be recovered from these samples $g(nT_s)$, with absolutely no degradation, by passing $g(nT_s)$ through a low-pass filter. The filter used in this way is referred to as a *reconstruction filter*.

The minimum sampling rate f_{smin} specified by the sampling theorem, equal to twice the bandwidth of the analogue signal, is called the *Nyquist rate* or *Nyquist frequency*. The reciprocal of the Nyquist rate is referred to as the *Nyquist sampling interval*, which represents the maximum sampling interval T_{smax} allowed by the sampling theorem.

$$\text{Nyquist rate} = f_{smin} = 2f_m$$

$$\text{Nyquist interval} = T_{smax} = \frac{1}{\text{Nyquist rate}} = \frac{1}{2f_m} \tag{5.1}$$

5.3 Proof of sampling theorem

Rather than attempt a formal mathematical proof of the sampling theorem, we will follow an intuitive discussion that highlights the conditions for distortion-free sampling stated in the theorem. The sampling of an arbitrary analogue signal $g(t)$ can be obtained as shown in Fig. 5.1(a). The switching signal $\delta_{T_S}(t)$ is an impulse train of period T_S, which causes the electronic switch to close and open instantaneously at intervals of T_S. The result is a sampled signal $g_\delta(t)$ that is equal to the analogue signal $g(t)$ at the instants $t = nT_S$ when the switch is closed, and is zero everywhere else. This type of sampling is therefore referred to as *instantaneous* or *ideal sampling*. The waveforms $g(t)$, $\delta_{T_S}(t)$, and $g_\delta(t)$ are shown in Figs. 5.1(b)–(d). We see that the sampled signal may be expressed as the product of the continuous-time analogue signal $g(t)$ and a switching signal $\delta_{T_S}(t)$:

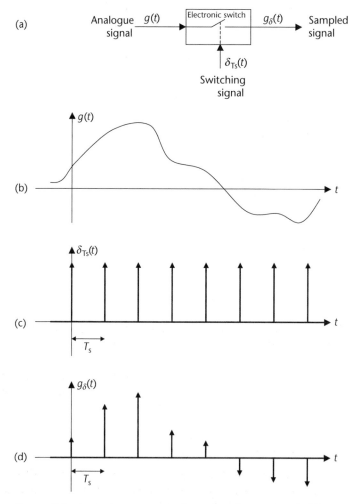

Figure 5.1 Instantaneous sampling of analogue signal: (a) switch; (b) analogue signal; (c) switching impulse train; (d) instantaneously sampled signal.

$$g_\delta(t) = g(t) \times \delta_{T_s}(t) \tag{5.2}$$

Note that the switching signal $\delta_{TS}(t)$ is a periodic rectangular pulse of infinitesimally small duty cycle d, and of period T_s. It can therefore be expressed in terms of the Fourier series

$$\begin{aligned}\delta_{T_s}(t) = A_0 &+ A_1 \cos[2\pi f_s t] + A_2 \cos[2\pi(2f_s)t] \\ &+ A_3 \cos[2\pi(3f_s)t] + A_4 \cos[2\pi(4f_s)t] + \cdots\end{aligned} \tag{5.3}$$

where $f_s = 1/T_s$ is the sampling frequency. From the discussion of the amplitude spectrum of a rectangular pulse train in Section 2.4.1, we recall that the amplitudes of the harmonic frequency components of $\delta_{TS}(t)$ are given by

$$\begin{aligned}A_0 &= Ad \\ A_n &= 2Ad\,\text{sinc}(nd), \qquad n = 1, 2, 3, \ldots\end{aligned} \tag{5.4}$$

where A is the amplitude of the pulse train, and the first null in the spectrum occurs at frequency $f = f_s/d$. Thus as $d \to 0$, the sinc envelope flattens out and the first null occurs at $f \to \infty$, so that the amplitude A_n of the harmonic frequency components becomes

$$\begin{aligned}A_0 &= Ad \\ A_n &= 2Ad, \qquad n = 1, 2, 3, \ldots\end{aligned} \tag{5.5}$$

Normalising the factor Ad to unity, and substituting Eq. (5.5) in (5.3), we obtain the normalised Fourier series of an impulse train as

$$\begin{aligned}\delta_{T_s}(t) = 1 &+ 2\cos[2\pi f_s t] + 2\cos[2\pi(2f_s)t] \\ &+ 2\cos[2\pi(3f_s)t] + 2\cos[2\pi(4f_s)t] + \cdots\end{aligned} \tag{5.6}$$

Substituting in Eq. (5.2) yields an alternative expression for the instantaneously sampled signal $g_\delta(t)$:

$$\begin{aligned}g_\delta(t) &= g(t)\{1 + 2\cos[2\pi f_s t] + 2\cos[2\pi(2f_s)t] + \cdots\} \\ &= g(t) + 2g(t)\cos[2\pi f_s t] + 2g(t)\cos[2\pi(2f_s)t] + \cdots \\ &= g(t) + 2\sum_{n=1}^{\infty} g(t)\cos(2\pi n f_s t)\end{aligned} \tag{5.7}$$

The above equation is an important result, which shows that the instantaneously sampled signal $g_\delta(t)$ is the sum of the original signal $g(t)$ and the product of $2g(t)$ and an infinite array of sinusoids of frequencies f_s, $2f_s$, $3f_s$, ... Recall that the double-sided spectrum of $2g(t)\cos(2\pi n f_s t)$ is merely the spectrum $G(f)$ of $g(t)$ shifted without modification from the location $f = 0$ along the frequency axis to the locations $f = \pm n f_s$.

5.3.1 Low-pass signals

Let the original signal $g(t)$ have the spectrum $G(f)$ shown in Fig. 5.2(a). The shape of $G(f)$ shown is merely representative and is unimportant. What matters is that $g(t)$ is bandlimited with bandwidth f_m. Therefore the double-sided spectrum of $g_\delta(t)$ is as shown in Fig. 5.2(c). The normalised spectrum of the switching impulse train is also shown in Fig. 5.2(b).

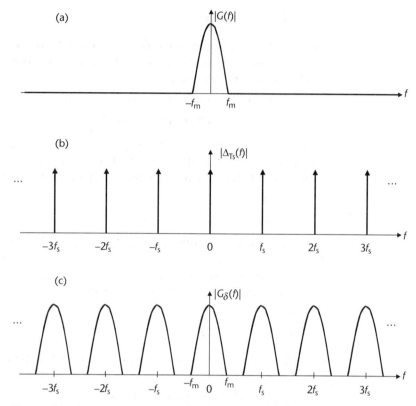

Figure 5.2 Instantaneous sampling of analogue signal. Spectra of the following signals: (a) analogue signal, (b) switching impulse train, and (c) sampled signal.

Note that (instantaneous) sampling does not destroy the spectrum $G(f)$ of a bandlimited signal $g(t)$. Rather, it duplicates $G(f)$ at intervals of the sampling frequency f_s. As long as f_s is at least twice the bandwidth of $g(t)$, i.e. $f_s \geq 2f_m$, the duplicated spectra or sidebands do not overlap, and any one of them and hence the original signal $g(t)$ can be recovered without distortion by employing a realisable filter. A low-pass filter with a cut-off frequency of f_m will recover $g(t)$ by passing the zeroth sideband or baseband in $G_\delta(f)$, corresponding to the first term in the RHS of Eq. (5.7), and blocking all other sidebands. We see therefore that a bandlimited signal of bandwidth f_m can be recovered without distortion from its samples taken at a rate $f_s \geq 2f_m$. This is a statement of the sampling theorem.

5.3.2 Bandpass signals

A low-pass signal has been assumed so far. However, the sampling theorem is also applicable to a bandpass signal $g_{bp}(t)$ of bandwidth f_m that contains positive frequencies starting at $f_c \gg 0$, as shown in Fig. 5.3(a). The highest frequency component of $g_{bp}(t)$ is $f_c + f_m$, and the original bandpass signal can obviously be recovered from samples taken at the rate $f_s \geq 2(f_c + f_m)$.

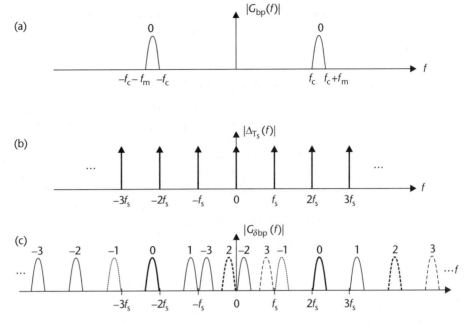

Figure 5.3 Sampling of a bandpass analogue signal of bandwidth f_m at rate $f_s \geq 2f_m$. Spectra of the following signals are shown: (a) bandpass signal with $f_c = 49$, $f_m = 10$; (b) switching impulse train with $f_s = 24$; and (c) sampled signal ($f_s = 2.4 \, f_m$).

Note:
1. For identification, the spectrum duplicated at nf_s has been labelled n.
2. To avoid spectral overlap and hence distortion, f_s must satisfy the conditions $f_s = 2(f_m + \Delta f)$ and $f_s = (2f_c - \Delta f)/N$, where N is an integer and $\Delta f \geq 0$ provides the transition band required by a realisable reconstruction bandpass filter.

This sampling rate can be unacceptably high since f_c can be very large. By definition, a bandpass signal has a bandwidth f_m that is much smaller than the highest frequency component of the signal. Figure 5.3(c) shows the result of sampling at the much lower rate $f_s \geq 2f_m$. We see that the spectrum $G_{\delta bp}(f)$ of the sampled bandpass signal $g_{\delta bp}(t)$ consists of non-overlapping duplicates of the shape of $G_{bp}(f)$ — the spectrum of $g_{bp}(t)$. The original bandpass signal $g_{bp}(t)$ can thus be recovered from $g_{\delta bp}(t)$ using a bandpass filter of passband f_c to $f_c + f_m$, which passes only the spectrum shown in bold.

In the light of Fig. 5.3, it should be emphasised that the required minimum sampling rate or Nyquist frequency f_{smin} is twice the bandwidth of the analogue signal, and not necessarily twice the maximum frequency component of the signal. In low-pass signals, *bandwidth* and *maximum frequency component* are equal, and f_{smin} may be correctly expressed as twice the maximum frequency component. However, the bandwidth of bandpass signals is typically much less than the maximum frequency component of the signal, and f_{smin} in this case must be expressed as twice the bandwidth.

In the rest of this chapter it will be assumed that the analogue signal $g(t)$ is a low-pass signal. The discussion that follows may be applied to a bandpass signal $g_{bp}(t)$ of minimum positive frequency component f_c if the signal is first transformed to a low-pass signal by a frequency translation of f_c.

5.3.3 Sampling at Nyquist rate

Figure 5.4 shows the result of sampling an analogue signal $g(t)$ of bandwidth f_m at the Nyquist rate $2f_m$. Note that the sidebands in the spectrum of the sampled signal touch but do not overlap. In order to recover the original signal a low-pass filter is required that passes the baseband spectrum containing frequencies $f = 0$ to f_m, and completely rejects the sidebands at frequencies $f = f_m$ to ∞. The filter must have the ideal brickwall frequency response of zero *transition width*, as shown by the dotted line in Fig. 5.4(c). Such a response is physically unrealisable.

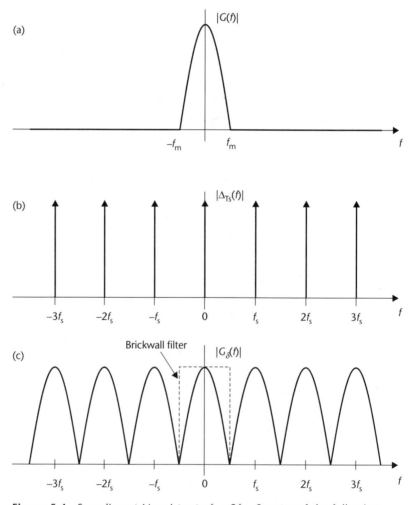

Figure 5.4 Sampling at Nyquist rate $f_s = 2f_m$. Spectra of the following signals: (a) analogue signal $g(t)$, (b) switching impulse train, and (c) sampled signal $g_\delta(t)$.

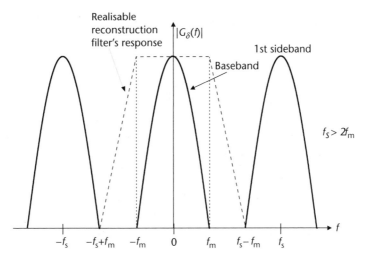

Figure 5.5 Sampling at rate f_s > Nyquist rate to allow use of realisable reconstruction filter.

Therefore in practice a sampling rate higher than the Nyquist frequency is employed to allow the use of a realisable reconstruction filter having a finite transition width. The frequency response of the reconstruction filter is shown in dashed lines in Fig. 5.5. It has the following specifications:

$$\text{Pass band: } 0 \le f \le f_m$$
$$\text{Transition band: } f_m \le f \le f_s - f_m \tag{5.8}$$
$$\text{Stop band: } f_s - f_m \le f < \infty$$

Let us now consider what happens if the sampling theorem is flouted by reducing the sampling frequency below the Nyquist rate.

5.4 Aliasing

An analogue signal $g(t)$ sampled at less than the Nyquist rate is said to be undersampled. The sidebands in the spectrum $G_\delta(f)$ of the sampled signal overlap as shown in Fig. 5.6, giving a resultant spectrum that is no longer an exact replica of the original spectrum $G(f)$. The baseband spectrum in $G_\delta(f)$ — the shaded region of Fig. 5.6(c) — is clearly distorted. The original signal $g(t)$ can no longer be recovered from the sampled signal $g_\delta(t)$ even with an ideal low-pass filter.

This distortion resulting from undersampling is known as *aliasing distortion* because every frequency component f_h in the original signal that is higher than half the sampling frequency appears in the sampled signal at a *false* or *alias frequency*

$$f_a = |f_s - f_h| \tag{5.9}$$

To understand how the alias frequency is produced, let us consider the sampling of a sinusoidal signal $g(t)$ of frequency $f_0 = 4$ kHz. Figure 5.7(a) shows samples of the sinusoid being taken at a rate $f_s = 12$ kHz, which satisfies the

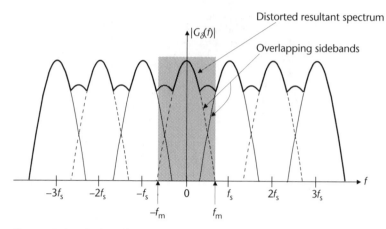

Figure 5.6 Aliasing distortion due to undersampling at rate $f_s <$ Nyquist rate.

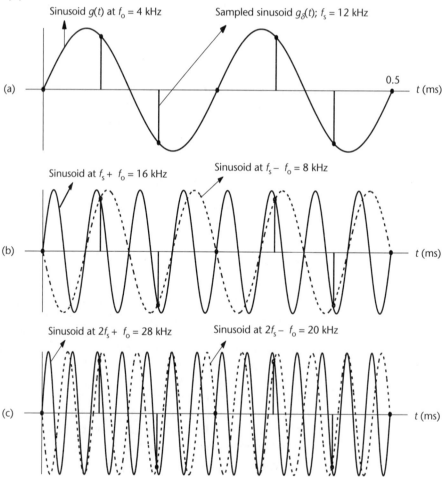

Figure 5.7 The samples $g_\delta(t)$ of a sinusoidal signal $g(t)$ of frequency f_o taken at rate $f_s >$ Nyquist rate fit (i.e. contain) an infinite set of sinusoids f_o, $f_s \pm f_o$, $2f_s \pm f_o$, $3f_s \pm f_o$, ...

sampling theorem. You may observe in Figs. 5.7(b) and (c) that this sequence of samples, denoted $g_\delta(t)$, not only fits the original sinusoid f_0, but it also exactly fits an infinite set of sinusoids at frequencies

$$f_s \pm f_0, \quad 2f_s \pm f_0, \quad 3f_s \pm f_0, \quad \ldots$$

This means that $g_\delta(t)$ contains the frequency components

$$f_0, \quad f_s - f_0, \quad f_s + f_0, \quad 2f_s - f_0, \quad 2f_s + f_0, \quad 3f_s - f_0, \quad 3f_s + f_0, \ldots$$

Thus, when $g_\delta(t)$ is passed through a low-pass reconstruction filter — specified by Eq. (5.8) with $f_m \equiv f_0$ — the lowest frequency component f_0 is extracted, thereby recovering the original sinusoid without distortion. Figure 5.8 gives a plot of the spectrum of $g_\delta(t)$ showing the above frequency components and the response of a reconstruction filter that would extract the original sinusoid from the sample values.

Consider what happens when the sinusoid is sampled as shown in Fig. 5.9(a) at the rate $f_s = 6$ kHz, which is less than the Nyquist rate (= 8 kHz). Now the sequence of samples is so widely spaced that it also exactly fits a lower-frequency sinusoid $f_a = f_s - f_0 = 2$ kHz, which is shown in Fig. 5.9(b). The sequence also fits higher-frequency sinusoids at $f_s + f_0$ and $nf_s \pm f_0$, $n = 2$, 3, 4, ..., but only the sinusoids $2f_s \pm f_0$ are shown in Fig. 5.9(c). Thus, in this case of undersampling, the sampled signal contains the frequency components

$$f_a, \quad f_0, \quad f_s + f_0, \quad 2f_s - f_0, \quad 2f_s + f_0, \quad 3f_s - f_0, \quad 3f_s + f_0, \ldots$$

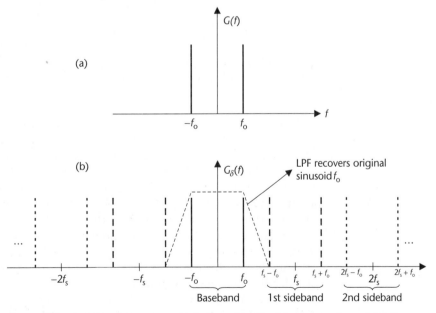

Figure 5.8 Amplitude spectra of (a) sinusoid $g(t)$ of frequency f_0 and (b) the sinusoid sampled at rate f_s.

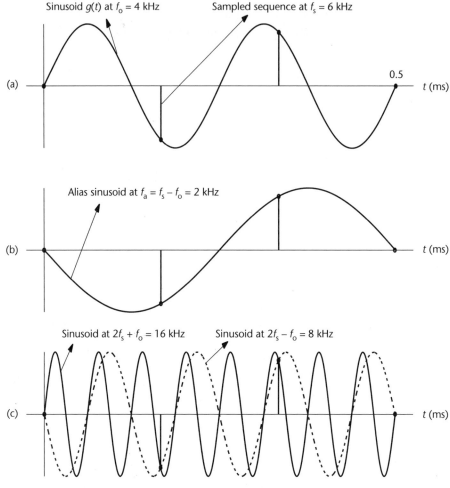

Figure 5.9 The samples of a sinusoid of frequency f_o' taken at rate $f_s <$ Nyquist rate fit (i.e contain) an infinite set of sinusoids f_a, f_o, $f_s + f_o$, $2f_s \pm f_o$, $3f_s \pm f_o$, ...

The low-pass reconstruction filter will pass two sinusoids, namely the original sinusoid f_0, and an alias sinusoid f_a, which causes distortion. This can be seen in Fig. 5.10(b), which shows the spectrum of the undersampled sinusoid. For clarity, the sidebands have been sketched using different line patterns — solid for the baseband, dashed for the 1st sideband, and dotted for the 2nd sideband. Note that the alias sinusoid of frequency f_a arises from the 1st sideband overlapping into the baseband. The overlapping of sidebands occurs because they have been duplicated too close to each other along the frequency axis at intervals of (a small value of) f_s.

It must be emphasised that only frequency components higher than half the sampling frequency produce an alias. When the sampling frequency is chosen to be at least twice the maximum frequency component of the (low-pass) analogue signal as required by the sampling theorem, then no such high-frequency component exists in the signal, and aliasing does not

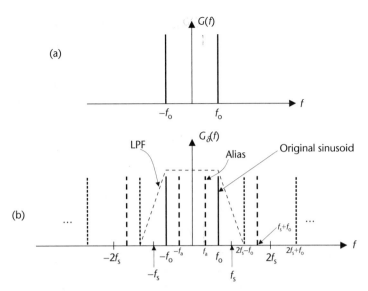

Figure 5.10 Amplitude spectrum $G_\delta(f)$ of a sinusoid of frequency f_o that is undersampled at rate $f_s <$ Nyquist rate. Spectra of (a) the sinusoid and (b) the sampled sinusoid. Note that if the LPF's stopband conforms to Eq. (5.8) then only f_a is recovered.

occur. Figure 5.10 shows that aliasing can be viewed in the frequency domain as resulting from the first sideband overlapping into the baseband of the sampled signal spectrum. This is further explained in the following worked example.

WORKED EXAMPLE   5.1

An information-bearing signal $g(t)$ has the spectrum shown in Fig. 5.11(a).

(a) What is the minimum sampling frequency f_{smin} to avoid aliasing?

(b) Sketch the spectrum of the sampled signal (in the interval ± 28kHz) when sampled at f_{smin}. Why would f_{smin} not be used in practice?

(c) Sketch the spectrum of the sampled signal over the interval ± 16 kHz when $g(t)$ is sampled at a rate $f_s = 6$ kHz, and determine the band of alias frequencies.

(a) Minimum sampling frequency f_{smin} required to avoid aliasing is twice the maximum frequency component f_m of the analogue signal. From Fig. 5.11(a), $f_m = 4$ kHz, so that

$$f_{smin} = 2f_m = 8 \text{ kHz}$$

(b) Fig. 5.11(b) shows a sketch of the spectrum of the information signal when sampled at the above rate. This minimum sampling rate is not used in practice because it would necessitate the use of an ideal brick-wall reconstruction filter to recover the original signal $g(t)$ at the receiver. A higher sampling rate is used, which allows a frequency

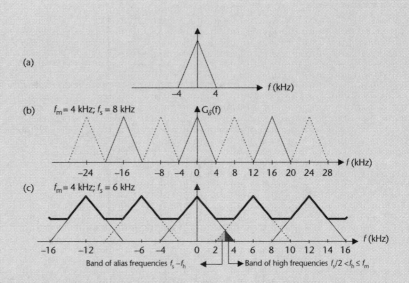

Figure 5.11 Worked example 5.1.

gap between the duplicated spectra. This gap is needed by a realisable filter to make a transition from passband to stopband.

(c) The spectrum of the sampled signal with $f_s = 6$ kHz is shown in Fig. 5.11(c). All high-frequency components f_h in the range $f_s/2 < f_h \leq f_m$, shaded dark in the diagram, introduce alias or false frequencies $f_s - f_h$. The band of alias frequencies is therefore

$$f_a = f_s - f_h$$
$$= 6 - (3 \to 4) = 2 \to 3 \text{ kHz}$$

Notice in Fig. 5.11(c) that we may also take the view that aliasing is caused by the high-frequency components in the baseband *folding back* about the frequency point $f_s/2$. Note how the spectrum is distorted by the overlapping sidebands. Under this situation, the original spectrum $G(f)$ and hence the original signal $g(t)$ cannot be recovered.

Two steps are usually employed to minimise aliasing distortion.

- Prior to sampling, the signal bandwidth is limited to a small value f_m that gives acceptable quality. The low-pass filter employed for this purpose is therefore called an *anti-alias* filter.
- The filtered signal is sampled at a rate $f_s > 2f_m$. For example, in standard telephone speech transmission using pulse code modulation (PCM), $f_m = 3.4$ kHz and $f_s = 8$ kHz.

5.5 Anti-alias filter

As stated above, the anti-alias circuit is a low-pass filter used to remove non-essential or insignificant high-frequency components in the message signal in order, ultimately, to reduce the required transmission bandwidth. The particular application and desired fidelity determine the extent to which high-frequency components are discarded. For example, in high-fidelity compact disc audio, all audible frequencies must be faithfully recorded. This means that frequency components up to $f_m = 20$ kHz are retained, and a sampling rate $f_s > 2f_m$ is employed. Usually $f_s = 44.1$ kHz.

However, in telephone speech the requirements for fidelity is much less stringent and the bandwidth of the transmission medium is very limited. Although the low frequencies (50–200 Hz) in speech signals enhance speaker recognition and naturalness, and the high frequencies (3.5–7 kHz) enhance intelligibility, good subjective speech quality is still possible in telephone systems with the baseband frequency limited to 300–3400 Hz. This frequency range has been adopted as the standard telephone speech baseband. In television signals, the eye is largely insensitive to the high-frequency components of the colour signal, so these frequencies may be suppressed without a noticeable degradation in colour quality.

An anti-alias filter is required to pass the baseband signal frequencies up to f_m, and ideally to present infinite attenuation to higher frequencies. In this way there is no overlapping of sidebands when the filtered signal is sampled at a rate $f_s > 2f_m$. In practice, we can achieve neither the infinite attenuation nor the brickwall (zero-transition-width) performance, but can only design a filter that has a specified minimum attenuation in the stopband and has a small but non-negligible transition width from passband to stopband.

Let us examine the issues involved in the specification of an anti-alias filter using the worst-case situation shown in Fig. 5.12 where a baseband information signal $g_i(t)$ has a uniform spectrum, and is to be limited in bandwidth to f_m before sampling to minimise aliasing distortion. The spectrum $G(f)$ of the filtered signal is shown in Fig. 5.12(a) along with the spectrum $G_\delta(f)$ of the signal obtained by sampling $g(t)$ at frequency f_s. Figure 5.12(b) shows a more detailed view of $G_\delta(f)$. Observe that frequency components beyond f_{sb} in the 1st sideband cross over into the message baseband $(0 \to f_m)$ and cause aliasing. Thus, we must have the following specifications for the anti-alias filter.

1. The stopband of the filter must start at frequency f_{sb} given by

$$f_{sb} = f_s - f_m \tag{5.10}$$

2. In the majority of cases, sampling is followed by quantisation to restrict the signal to a discrete set of values, as discussed in the next chapter. The process of quantisation inevitably introduces error, and it is therefore sufficient to ensure that aliasing error in the passband is maintained at a level just below the inevitable quantisation noise. So the minimum stopband attenuation A_{min} must be as indicated in Fig. 5.12(b):

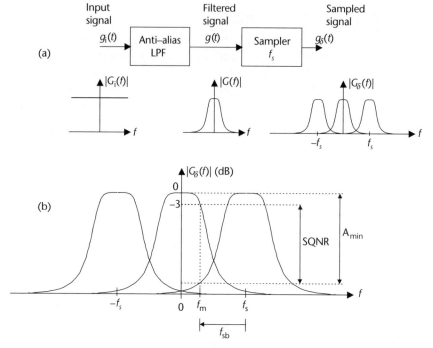

Figure 5.12 Specification of an anti-alias filter.

$$A_{\text{min}} = \text{SQNR} + 3 \text{ dB} \tag{5.11}$$

where SQNR is the signal to quantisation noise power ratio.

Let the anti-alias filter be an nth-order low-pass Butterworth filter. The attenuation A of this filter as a function of frequency f is given by

$$A = 10\log_{10}\left[1+\left(\frac{f}{f_m}\right)^{2n}\right] \text{ dB} \tag{5.12}$$

where f_m is the maximum passband frequency — the 3-dB point. Since $A = A_{\text{min}}$ at $f = f_{\text{sb}}$, we may write

$$A_{\text{min}} = 10\log_{10}[1 + (f_{\text{sb}}/f_m)^{2n}]$$

and solve for f_{sb} to obtain

$$f_{\text{sb}} = f_m[10^{(A_{\text{min}}/10)} - 1]^{1/2n}$$

Finally, using Eq. (5.10), we obtain an expression for the required sampling frequency f_s:

$$f_s = f_m\{1 + [10^{(A_{\text{min}}/10)} - 1]^{1/2n}\} \tag{5.13}$$

The above equation is an important result, which gives the minimum sampling frequency f_s required to maintain alias frequencies at a level at least A_{min} (dB) below the desired baseband frequency components.

WORKED EXAMPLE   5.2

The analogue input signal to a 12-bit uniform quantisation PCM system has a uniform spectrum that is required to be limited to the band $0 \rightarrow 4$ KHz using a 6th order Butterworth anti-alias filter. The input signal fully loads the quantiser. In designing the filter, the goal is to maintain aliasing error in the passband at a level just below quantisation noise.

(a) Determine the minimum stopband attenuation A_{min} of the anti-alias filter.
(b) Calculate the minimum sampling frequency f_s.
(c) How does f_s compare with the standard sampling rate of 8 kHz used for speech.

(a) A_{min} is given by Eq. (5.11). It will be shown in Chapter 6 that

$$SQNR = 1.76 + 6.02k \tag{5.14}$$

where k ($= 12$ in this case) is the number of bits needed to identify each of the discrete signal levels in the quantiser. Thus,

$$A_{min} = 1.76 + (6.02 \times 12) + 3 = 77 \text{ dB}$$

(b) Substituting the values $f_m = 4$ kHz, $n = 6$ and $A_{min} = 77$ dB in Eq. (5.13) gives the desired minimum sampling frequency,

$$f_s = 4\{1 + [10^{(77/10)} - 1]^{1/12}\} = 21.53 \text{ kHz}$$

(c) The required sampling frequency, $f_s = 21.53$ kHz, is rather high compared with a Nyquist rate of 8 kHz. To see why, note that a worst-case scenario was assumed in which the input analogue signal has a uniform amplitude spectrum that needs to be limited to the band $0 \rightarrow f_m$ using a realisable filter. The anti-alias filter requires sufficient transition width to reduce the signal's spectral components within the stopband by the required amount A_{min}. In practice, e.g. speech signals, the amplitude spectrum $G_i(f)$ is not uniform, and the frequency components above f_m are of very small amplitudes, requiring only a little extra attenuation by a filter to bring them down to the level of the quantisation noise voltage. Even for signals of uniform spectrum, the sampling frequency required to maintain aliasing error below quantisation noise can be reduced by using a higher-order (i.e. a steeper roll-off) filter. For example, if in the above problem we use a Butterworth filter of order $n = 12$, then f_s would be only 12.37 kHz. Note, however, that in many cases filters with a steeper roll-off introduce more phase distortion.

Question 5.6 deals with the design of an anti-alias filter for a signal of non-uniform spectrum.

5.6 Non-instantaneous sampling

We have so far discussed instantaneous sampling, which is not feasible in practice for the following reasons:

1. It requires sampling pulses of infinite amplitude to carry sufficient signal energy. This can be seen by examining Eq. (5.4) and noting that the pulse amplitude A must be infinite if the factor Ad, and hence the spectral components of the impulse train, are to be non-zero as $d \to 0$.

2. Instantaneous sampling requires a system of infinite bandwidth to sustain the pulses without distortion.

3. It requires instantaneous switching, which is not attainable using physically realisable electronic devices with their inherent capacitive and inductive elements that tend to slow down the rates of change of voltage and current, respectively.

Let us therefore consider the practical implementation of sampling using pulses of finite width, known as *non-instantaneous sampling*. We will discuss its effect on the spectrum of the sampled signal, and the distortion on the reconstructed signal. There are two types of non-instantaneous sampling, namely *natural* and *flat-top* sampling.

5.6.1 Natural sampling

If we replace the impulse train switching signal $\delta_{Ts}(t)$ in Fig. 5.1(a) with the rectangular pulse train $\Pi_{Ts}(t)$ of non-zero duty cycle $d = \tau/T_s$ shown in Fig. 5.13(b), then we obtain the sampled signal $g_{\Pi n}(t)$ shown in Fig. 5.13(c). Note how the top of each pulse follows the variation of the original analogue signal $g(t)$. This scheme, in which an input analogue signal is simply switched through to the output by a rectangular pulse train, is known as *natural sampling*. The electronic switch in this case is realisable using, for example, CMOS hardware. The output or sampled signal follows the variations of the analogue input during the fraction d of time that the switch is closed, and is zero during the fraction $(1 - d)$ of time that the switch is open. The question now is whether the original signal $g(t)$ can be recovered from this non-instantaneously sampled signal. This question is most easily addressed in the frequency domain.

Let us assume that $g(t)$ is of bandwidth f_m and that it has the amplitude spectrum shown in Fig. 5.14(a). The particular shape of the spectrum is irrelevant, however we have chosen a rectangular shape because it makes spectral distortion more easily observable. The same arguments leading to Eq. (5.2) and Eq. (5.4) apply. However, in this case $d > 0$ so that the simplification of Eq. (5.5) does not apply. With this in mind, the normalised ($Ad = 1$) Fourier series of the rectangular pulse train $\Pi_{Ts}(t)$ (of duty cycle d and amplitude A), and that of the naturally sampled signal $g_{\Pi n}(t)$ are given by

$$\Pi_{T_s}(t) = 1 + 2\operatorname{sinc}(d)\cos[2\pi f_s t] + 2\operatorname{sinc}(2d)\cos[2\pi(2f_s)t]$$
$$+ 2\operatorname{sinc}(3d)\cos[2\pi(3f_s)t] + 2\operatorname{sinc}(4d)\cos[2\pi(4f_s)t] + \cdots \tag{5.15}$$

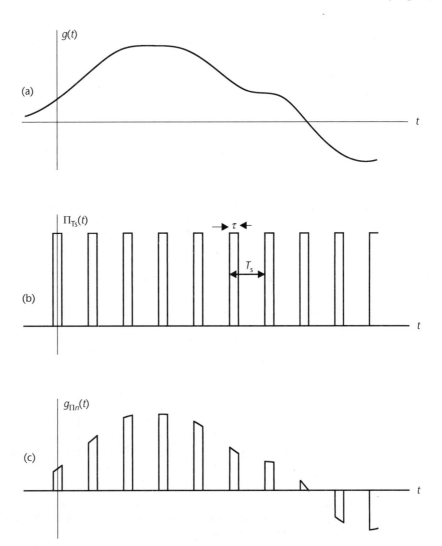

Figure 5.13 Natural sampling. (a) Analogue signal; (b) switching rectangular pulse train; (c) sampled signal.

$$g_{\Pi n}(t) = g(t) + 2\sum_{n=1}^{\infty} g(t)\,\text{sinc}(nd)\cos(2\pi n f_s t) \tag{5.16}$$

We see that the naturally sampled signal $g_{\Pi n}(t)$ is the sum of the original signal $g(t)$ and the product of $2g(t)$ and an infinite array of sinusoids of frequencies nf_s, $n = 1, 2, 3, \ldots$, each product scaled by the factor $\text{sinc}(nd)$. This is an interesting result, which shows that the only difference between natural sampling and instantaneous sampling is that the nth sideband in the sampled spectrum is reduced in size (but not distorted) by the factor $\text{sinc}(nd)$. The spectrum of $g_{\Pi n}(t)$ is shown in Fig. 5.14(c) for $d = \frac{1}{4}$.

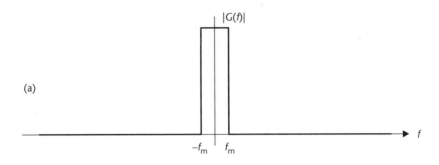

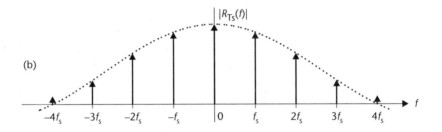

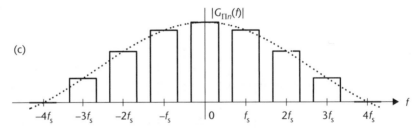

Figure 5.14 Natural sampling with rectangular pulse train of duty cycle 0.25. Spectra of the following: (a) analogue signal; (b) switching rectangular pulse train and (c) sampled signal.

You will recall from Chapter 2 that sinc(nd) = 0 whenever nd is a whole number (1, 2, 3, ...). This means that the following sidebands will be scaled by a zero factor and therefore will be missing from the spectrum of $g_{\Pi n}(t)$:

$$n = \frac{1}{d}, \quad \frac{2}{d}, \quad \frac{3}{d}, \quad \frac{4}{d}, \quad \cdots$$

In Fig. 5.14 with $d = ¼$, the missing sidebands are the 4th, 8th, 12th, ... It is clear that the original signal $g(t)$ can be recovered from $g_{\Pi n}(t)$ using a low-pass filter as discussed earlier, provided the sampling frequency $f_s \geq 2f_m$, as specified by the sampling theorem.

Natural sampling is rarely used in practice because it places a severe limitation on the maximum frequency f_m that can be accurately digitised after sampling. In Question 5.8, it will be shown that if the quantiser (that follows the natural sampler) has a conversion time τ, and the desired conversion accuracy is half the quantiser step size, then the highest frequency that can be digitised is

$$f_\mathrm{m} = \frac{1}{2^k \pi \tau} \qquad (5.17)$$

where k is the number of bits/sample of the quantiser. Note that there is a limitation on f_m whenever the conversion time τ is non-zero, as is usually the case. For example, with $\tau = 0.1\mu s$ and $k = 12$, we have $f_\mathrm{m} = 777$ Hz.

5.6.2 Flat-top sampling

If the top of each pulse is maintained constant or flat with a height equal to the instantaneous value of the analogue signal at the beginning of the pulse, then we have what is known as flat-top sampling. This is the usual method of sampling implemented by an integrated circuit referred to as *sample-and-hold*, the operation of which is shown in Fig. 5.15. At the instance of the positive-going edge of the switching rectangular pulse train $\Pi_{Ts}(t)$, the sampling switch S1 is momentarily turned on and the discharging switch S2 is turned off. The capacitor C charges up very rapidly to the value of $g(t)$ at that instant and holds this value while S1 is off. At the negative-going edge of $\Pi_{Ts}(t)$, switch S2 is turned back on and C discharges very rapidly to zero. The output signal is taken across C and gives the required flat-top sampled signal $g_\Pi(t)$.

Figure 5.16 shows the waveforms of the signals featured in the sample-and-hold block diagram. Again we must ask whether the original signal $g(t)$ can be extracted from the flat-top sampled signal $g_\Pi(t)$ in Fig. 5.16(c).

To examine this we note that the instantaneously sampled signal $g_\delta(t)$ in Fig. 5.1(d) is a train of impulse or Dirac delta functions each weighted by $g(nT_s)$, the value of the analogue signal at the sampling instant. Figure 5.17 shows that the flat-top sampled signal $g_\Pi(t)$ consists of a rectangular pulse $\Pi(t)$ replicated at the locations of the impulse functions that constitute

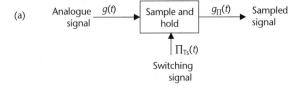

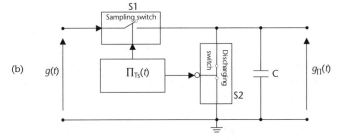

Figure 5.15 Sample-and-hold operation.

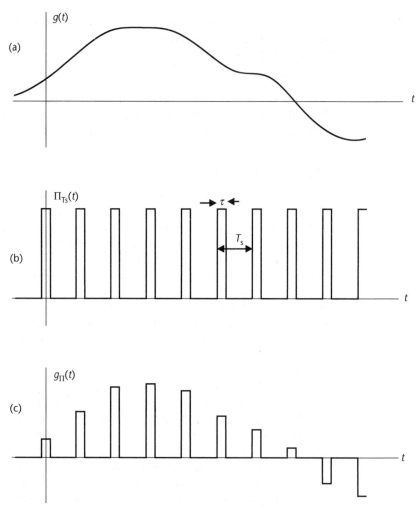

Figure 5.16 Flat-top sampling. (a) Analogue signal; (b) switching rectangular pulse train; (c) sampled signal.

$g_\delta(t)$. The height of each replicated pulse is equal to the weight of the impulse at that location. This can be recognised as a *convolution* process. That is, $g_\Pi(t)$ is obtained by convolving $g_\delta(t)$ with $\Pi(t)$, which is written as follows:

$$g_\Pi(t) = g_\delta(t) * \Pi(t) \tag{5.18}$$

Noting that convolution in the time domain translates into multiplication in the frequency domain, it follows that the spectrum $G_\Pi(f)$ of the flat-top sampled signal is given by the product of the spectrum $G_\delta(f)$ of the instantaneously sampled signal $g_\delta(t)$ and the spectrum $R(f)$ of the rectangular pulse $\Pi(t)$:

$$G_\Pi(f) = G_\delta(f)R(f) \tag{5.19}$$

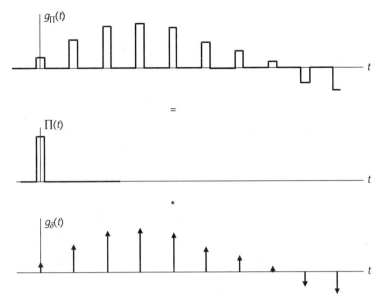

Figure 5.17 Flat-top sampling as a convolution between instantaneous sampling and a rectangular pulse.

With the spectrum $G_\delta(f)$ being a replication of $G(f)$ at intervals f_s along the frequency axis, and $R(f)$ being a sinc envelope (Fig. 2.26(c)), it follows that $G_\Pi(f)$ is as shown in Fig. 5.18(c).

We see that the spectrum of $g_\Pi(t)$ is distorted by the sinc envelope of $R(f)$ — the spectrum of the finite-width rectangular pulse. This distortion is called *aperture effect* and is similar to the distortion observed in television and facsimile arising from a finite scanning aperture size. Note, however, that the distortion to the baseband spectrum is very small, depending on the duty cycle of the sampling pulse. A low-pass filter can therefore be used to recover the spectrum $G(f)$ and hence the original signal $g(t)$ from the flat-top sampled signal, with compensation made for aperture effect, as discussed after the worked example. Again, we require that $f_s \geq 2f_m$.

WORKED EXAMPLE   **5.3**

Obtain expressions for the following spectra in terms of the spectrum $G(f)$ of the original analogue signal $g(t)$:

(a) $G_\delta(f)$, the spectrum of the instantaneously sampled signal.
(b) $G_{\Pi n}(f)$, the spectrum resulting from natural sampling.
(c) $G_\Pi(f)$, the spectrum of the flat-top sampled signal.

(a) $G_\delta(f)$ is obtained by taking the Fourier transform of both sides of Eq. (5.7). Before doing this, we first reintroduce in the RHS of (5.7) the factor Ad that was normalised to unity, and note that

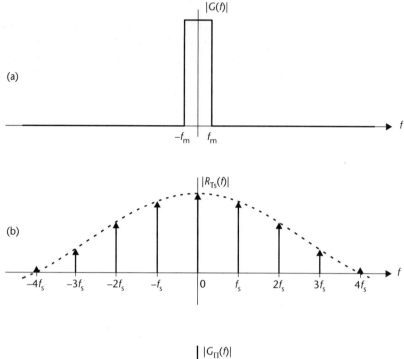

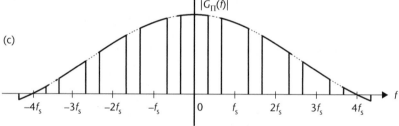

Figure 5.18 Flat-top sampling with rectangular pulse train of duty cycle 0.25. Spectra of the following: (a) analogue signal; (b) switching rectangular pulse train; and (c) sampled signal.

$$Ad = A\tau/T_s = 1/T_s$$

since $A\tau$ is the area under the impulse function and we are dealing with a unit impulse train. Therefore,

$$G_\delta(f) = \frac{1}{T_s}G(f) + F\left[\frac{2}{T_s}\sum_{n=1}^{\infty}g(t)\cos(2\pi nf_s t)\right]$$

$$= \frac{1}{T_s}\sum_{n=-\infty}^{\infty}G(f - nf_s) \qquad (5.20)$$

where we have used the fact that the spectrum of $2g(t)\cos(2\pi nf_s t)$ is $G(f \pm nf_s)$, which means the spectrum $G(f)$ shifted to the locations

$-nf_s$ and $+nf_s$ along the frequency axis. Equation (5.20) states that $G_\delta(f)$ is given by exact duplications – except for a scaling factor $1/T_s$ – of $G(f)$ at intervals of f_s along the frequency axis. This spectrum is shown in Fig. 5.2(c) for a representative $G(f)$.

(b) Let us denormalise the RHS of Eq. (5.16) by reintroducing the factor Ad, and note that usually the rectangular pulse train is of unit amplitude, so that $A = 1$. Taking the Fourier transform of Eq. (5.16) after this change yields,

$$G_{\Pi n}(f) = dG(f) + F\left[d\sum_{n=1}^{\infty} 2g(t)\,\text{sinc}(nd)\cos(2\pi nf_s t)\right]$$

$$= d\sum_{n=-\infty}^{\infty} \text{sinc}(nd)G(f - nf_s) \tag{5.21}$$

Eq. (5.21) states that $G_{\Pi n}(f)$ is obtained by replicating $G(f)$ without distortion at intervals of f_s along the frequency axis; however the duplicates located at $\pm nf_s$ are scaled down by the factor $d\,\text{sinc}(nd)$, where d is the duty cycle of the rectangular pulse train employed in sampling. The spectrum $G_{\Pi n}(f)$ is shown in Fig. 5.14(c) for a representative $G(f)$.

(c) $G_\Pi(f)$ is given by Eq. (5.19), with $G_\delta(f)$ given by Eq. (5.20) and $R(f) = \tau\,\text{sinc}(f\tau)$ — from Section 2.4.3. Thus,

$$G_\Pi(f) = [\tau\,\text{sinc}(f\tau)] \times \left[\frac{1}{T_s}\sum_{n=-\infty}^{\infty} G(f - nf_s)\right]$$

$$= d\,\text{sinc}(df/f_s)\sum_{n=-\infty}^{\infty} G(f - nf_s) \tag{5.22}$$

where we have substituted d for the factor τ/T_s, and used d/f_s instead of τ in the argument of the sinc function. Equation (5.22) states that $G_\Pi(f)$ is obtained by duplicating $G(f)$ at intervals of f_s along the frequency axis, and modifying the frequency component f within each duplicate by the factor $d\,\text{sinc}(df/f_s)$. A plot of $G_\Pi(f)$ is shown in Fig. 5.18(c) for a representative $G(f)$.

5.6.3 Aperture effect

We have observed above that neither instantaneous nor natural sampling is suitable for practical applications although they provide samples from which the original signal can be recovered without distortion. The more feasible technique of flat-top sampling, however introduces a distortion known as aperture effect, which increases with duty cycle d, as shown in Fig. 5.19 for $d = 0.1$, 0.5, and 1.0.

A measure of aperture effect is given by the attenuation A_a (in dB) of a frequency f in the baseband of $G_\Pi(f)$ relative to $f = 0$. Ignoring the factor d in

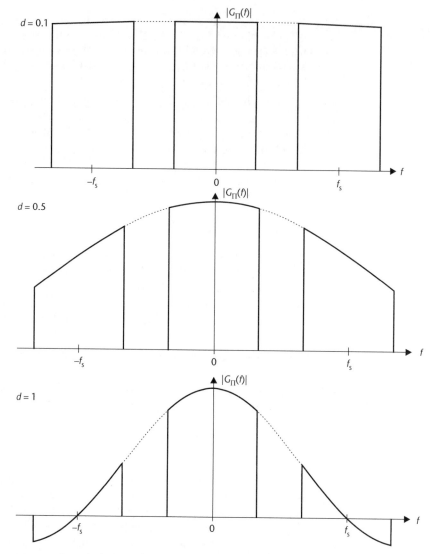

Figure 5.19 Distortion to the baseband spectrum of a flat-top sampled signal increases with the duty cycle d of sampling pulses. A representative rectangular spectrum of the original signal is assumed.

Eq. (5.22) since it represents a constant scaling factor, we see that A_a is given by

$$A_a = -20\log_{10}[\text{sinc}(df/f_s)], \quad 0 \le f \le f_s/2 \tag{5.23}$$

where the negative sign is required to make A_a positive. The indicated frequency range applies since the maximum frequency component f_m of the original signal is at most half the sampling frequency. The maximum attenuation due to aperture effect occurs at the maximum frequency component f_m. In the worst case, $f_m = f_s/2$, giving

$$A_{amax} = -20\log_{10}[\text{sinc}(d/2)] \tag{5.24}$$

Equation (5.24) yields a maximum distortion of 0.04 dB, 0.9 dB and 3.9 dB at duty cycles $d = 0.1$, 0.5 and 1.0, respectively. There is, therefore, negligible distortion for duty cycles $d \leq 0.1$, which is evident in Fig. 5.19.

There are three different ways of minimising aperture effect.

1. By using sampling pulses of small duty cycle d. As noted above, the distortion is negligible for d less than about 10%.

2. By oversampling with $f_s \gg f_m$. If this condition is satisfied, then the term f/f_s in Eq. (5.23) is much less than unity for all frequency components of the original signal, which leads to very small values of attenuation A_a. However, there is a penalty of an increased bandwidth requirement as the sampling frequency is increased.

3. By using a compensated reconstruction low-pass filter. At large values of duty cycle and a moderate sampling frequency f_s satisfying the sampling theorem, the amplitude distortion due to aperture effect is significant and must be compensated for. Since the functional form of the distortion is known, it is a straightforward matter to replace the ordinary LPF having a uniform passband response with a low-pass equaliser whose (normalised) response in the passband ($f = 0 \rightarrow f_m$) is given by

$$|H_e(f)| = \frac{1}{\text{sinc}[(d/f_s)f]} \tag{5.25}$$

In practice, the distortion can be treated as a linear effect, allowing the use of an equaliser whose gain increases linearly with frequency in the range 0 to f_m.

SUMMARY

In this chapter, we have studied in some detail the three types of sampling, namely instantaneous, natural, and flat-top. It was noted that the first two do not introduce any distortion, provided the sampling frequency is larger than twice the analogue signal bandwidth. However, instantaneous sampling is not realisable using physical circuits, and natural sampling places a limitation on the maximum frequency that can be digitised when the conversion time is non-zero. The more practical technique of flat-top sampling introduces a distortion known as aperture effect, which is, however, not a serious drawback, since it can be readily minimised.

The problem of aliasing, which arises when a signal is sampled at a rate less than twice its bandwidth, was examined in detail in both the time and frequency domains. Several measures for minimising aliasing distortion were also discussed, including the specifications of an anti-alias filter.

The samples of an analogue signal have a continuum of values, which may be transmitted by analogue means using the so-called pulse amplitude modulation (PAM), pulse duration modulation (PDM) or pulse position modulation (PPM). These techniques were discussed in Chapter 1 and their demerits were highlighted. Signal processing that goes beyond sampling is required in order to exploit the numerous advantages of digital communications.

In the next chapter, we will study the processes of quantisation and encoding, which complete the transformation of a signal from analogue to digital. In particular, we will consider the techniques of pulse code modulation (PCM) and its variants.

REVIEW QUESTIONS

5.1 Determine the Nyquist rate and Nyquist sampling interval for the following signals:

(a) $5\cos(200\pi t)$ volts
(b) $20 - \sin^2(10^4\pi t)$ volts
(c) $10\text{rect}(2 \times 10^3 t)$ volts
(d) $20\text{rect}(10^4 t)\cos(10^6\pi t)$
(e) $5\sin(10^5\pi t)\text{trian}(500t)$
(f) $10\text{sinc}^2(400t)\sin(2 \times 10^6\pi t)$

Note: The rectangular (rect) and triangular (trian) pulse functions are defined in Section 2.4.3.

5.2 A sinusoidal voltage signal $v(t) = 20\sin(2\pi \times 10^4 t)$ volts is sampled using an impulse train $\delta_{Ts}(t)$ of period $T_s = 40$ μs. Sketch the waveform and corresponding double-sided amplitude spectrum of the following signals:

(a) $v(t)$
(b) $\delta_{Ts}(t)$
(c) Sampled signal $v_\delta(t)$

Note: The spectrum of $v_\delta(t)$ should extend over three sidebands.

5.3 Repeat Question 5.2 with a sampling interval $T_s = 66\frac{2}{3}$ μs. Can $v(t)$ be recovered from $v_\delta(t)$ in this case? Explain.

5.4 Fig. 5.20 shows the single-sided spectrum of a signal $g(t)$. Sketch the spectrum of the instantaneously sampled signal $g_\delta(t)$ over the frequency range $\pm 4f_s$, for the following selections of sampling frequency f_s:

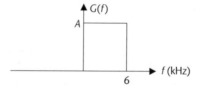

Figure 5.20 Question 5.4.

(a) f_s = Nyquist rate (i.e. f_{smin})

(b) $f_s = 2f_{smin}$

(c) $f_s = \frac{2}{3}f_{smin}$

(d) Determine the band of alias frequencies in (c)

5.5 An AM signal $g(t)$ lies in the frequency band 800 to 810 kHz. Assuming a triangular spectrum for $g(t)$, sketch the spectrum of the instantaneously sampled signal $g_\delta(t)$ obtained by sampling $g(t)$ at three times the Nyquist rate. Your sketch should extend over three sidebands. How would $g(t)$ be recovered from $g_\delta(t)$?

5.6 Let us assume that the spectrum $G(f)$ of a speech signal can be approximated as shown in Fig. 5.21, where the spectrum is constant up to 500 Hz and then decreases linearly to −52 dB at 7 kHz. The signal is to be sampled at $f_s = 8$ kHz and digitised in a uniform ADC using $k = 8$ bits/sample.

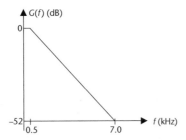

Figure 5.21 Question 5.6.

(a) Determine the order n of an anti-alias Butterworth filter of cut-off frequency $f_m = 3.4$ kHz that is required to maintain aliasing error in the passband at a level just below quantisation noise.

(b) Repeat (a) for a signal that has a uniform spectrum and compare the two results.

5.7 A sinusoidal voltage signal $v(t) = 20\sin(2\pi \times 10^4 t)$ volts is sampled using a rectangular pulse train $\Pi_{T_s}(t)$ of period $T_s = 40$ μs and duty cycle $d = 0.5$. Sketch the waveform and corresponding double-sided amplitude spectrum of the following signals: (i) $v(t)$, (ii) $\Pi_{T_s}(t)$ and (iii) the sampled signal $v_\Pi(t)$, assuming

(a) Natural sampling

(b) Flat-top sampling

Note: The spectrum of the sampled signal should extend over three sidebands.

5.8 Starting with a sinusoidal message signal of frequency f_m, show that if the quantiser has a conversion time τ, and the desired conversion accuracy is half the quantiser step size, then the highest frequency that can be digitised using natural sampling is given by Eq. (5.17).

5.9 Speech signal of baseband frequencies 300 Hz to 3400 Hz is sampled in a sample-and-hold circuit that uses a rectangular pulse train of duty cycle d and sampling frequency f_s. Determine the maximum distortion (in dB) due to aperture effect for the following cases:

(a) $f_s = 6.8$ kHz, $d = 0.8$
(b) $f_s = 8$ kHz, $d = 0.8$
(c) $f_s = 40$ kHz, $d = 0.8$
(d) $f_s = 8$ kHz, $d = 0.1$

Comment on the trends in your results.

Digital baseband transmission

6.1 Introduction

The four steps involved in converting analogue signals to digital were introduced in Section 1.5.3 and Fig. 1.27, and the first two steps of low-pass filtering and sampling were discussed in detail in Chapter 5. This chapter focuses on the remaining steps involving quantisation and encoding. Quantisation converts a sampled analogue signal $g(nT_s)$ to digital form by approximating each sample to the nearest of a set of discrete values. The result is a discrete-value discrete-time signal $g_q(nT_s)$, which can be conveyed accurately in the presence of channel noise that is less than half the spacing of quantisation levels.

However, further robustness to noise can be achieved if the N quantisation levels are numbered from 0 to $N - 1$, and each level is expressed as a binary number consisting of k binary digits (or *bits*), where $k = \log_2 N$. This encoding process in which $g_q(nT_s)$ is converted to a string of binary 0s and 1s has been traditionally called *pulse code modulation* (PCM). Note, however, that the use of the word modulation in this context is inappropriate, in view of our discussions in Chapters 3 and 4. The resulting bit stream is electrically represented as voltage values by using a suitable line code, e.g. +12 V for binary 0 and −12 V for binary 1. Binary coding gives maximum robustness against noise and is easy to regenerate. The concern at the receiver is not with the exact voltage level, but with whether the received voltage level falls in the range that represents a binary 0 or 1. Thus, the noise level has to be large in order to cause any error. The technique of line coding (first introduced in Chapter 1) will be discussed further in this chapter.

In discussing PCM, we concentrate first on uniform quantisation, which is also called *linear ADC*, in order to discuss in quantitative terms the problem of quantisation noise and various design considerations, including the noise–bandwidth trade-off in PCM. The demerits of uniform quantisation that make them unsuitable for bandwidth-limited applications are highlighted. Attention then shifts to the more practical non-uniform quantisation techniques. Encoding and decoding procedures are explained in detail for the standard A-law and μ-law PCM.

Various modifications to PCM, mainly aimed at improved spectrum efficiency, are discussed. These include differential PCM, with delta modulation (DM) and adaptive differential PCM (ADPCM) introduced as special cases. Various low-bit-rate coding techniques for speech are summarised. The chapter ends with discussions of line codes for digital signals, and the concepts of pulse shaping to minimise intersymbol interference, and the matched filter to optimise signal detection in the presence of noise.

6.2 Quantisation and encoding

The sampling process converts an analogue signal $g(t)$ into a discrete sequence of sample values $g(nT_s)$, $n = 0, 1, 2, 3, \ldots$, spaced at the sampling interval T_s. As these samples are obtained from the instantaneous values of an analogue (continuous-value) signal, they can take on any value in a range from the smallest to the largest sample value. The sampled signal $g(nT_s)$, although discrete in time, is still continuous in value and is thus not a digital signal. To convert $g(t)$ into a digital signal, the next step after sampling must be to constrain the sequence of values to a finite set of possible values. This process is known as quantisation.

We saw earlier that sampling a signal at the correct rate does not introduce any errors. That is, sampling is a reversible process. The original signal can be accurately recovered from the samples. By contrast, quantisation introduces irrecoverable errors, known as *quantisation noise*. We can make this noise as small as we wish, but at a price!

Quantisation can be either midstep or midrise, and either uniform or non-uniform, as illustrated in Fig. 6.1 for $N = 8$ intervals. Mid-step (also

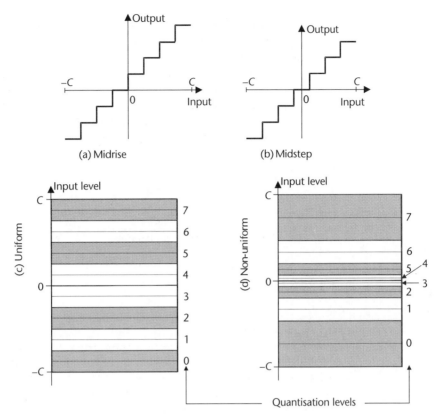

Figure 6.1 Classes of quantisation.

known as mid-tread) quantisation is used in μ-law PCM, and is thought to remove noise chatter on idle lines, while mid-rise quantisation is used in A-law PCM. A-law and μ-law PCM are based on non-uniform quantisation and will be studied in detail. We begin our discussion with the simpler scheme of uniform quantisation, which facilitates the introduction of key design parameters.

6.2.1 Uniform quantisation

The simplest method of quantisation is to divide the full range of possible signal values, from $-C$ to $+C$, into N equal intervals as shown in Fig. 6.2. The number of intervals is usually chosen to be an integer power of 2:

$$N = 2^k \tag{6.1}$$

This choice allows the k-bit binary codes to be fully utilised at the coding stage of the analogue-to-digital conversion (ADC) process to represent the intervals (numbered from 0 to $N-1$). For example, if we chose $N = 5$, then we require $k = 3$ bits to represent these five intervals; see Table 6.1. The codes 101, 110 and 111 are not used.

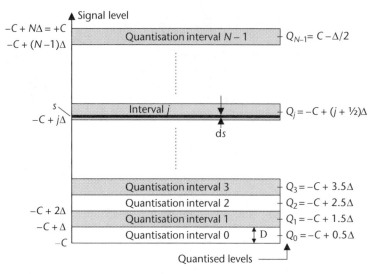

Figure 6.2 Uniform quantisation.

Table 6.1 Choosing $N = 8$ intervals uses all 3-bit binary codewords.

Quantisation interval	0	1	2	3	4	5	6	7
Binary codeword	000	001	010	011	100	101	110	111

$\leftarrow$ Not used if $N = 5$ $\rightarrow$

It is shown below that quantisation noise is reduced as N increases. In this example therefore, we can reduce quantisation noise at no extra cost (i.e. without increasing the number of bits k required to represent each quantisation interval) simply by increasing N from 5 to $2^3 = 8$.

6.2.1.1 *Quantisation noise*

In a uniform or linear quantisation, all intervals are of an equal size Δ, called the *quantiser step size*. A sample is approximated by the midpoint value of the interval in which it falls. For example, any sample of value in the range $-C$ to $-C + \Delta$ (interval 0) is quantised to Q_0, and any sample in the jth interval is quantised to Q_j. Therefore, for each sample of value s in the jth interval, quantisation produces a quantisation error given by

$$q = |s - Q_j| \tag{6.2}$$

This error has a maximum value q_{max} when s is at the top ($s = Q_j + \Delta/2$) or bottom ($s = Q_j - \Delta/2$) of the interval. Thus,

$$q_{max} = |Q_j \pm \Delta/2 - Q_j| = \Delta/2 \tag{6.3}$$

The maximum possible error incurred in each quantisation is therefore half the quantiser step size.

We found in Section 2.5 that the mean square value of a signal gives its (normalised) power. Therefore, to determine the quantisation noise power we must calculate the mean squared quantisation error (MSQE) across all the samples of the signal. To do this, we first determine the MSQE for all samples that are quantised to level Q_j. Denoting the probability that a sample falls in the interval j by P_j and assuming a small quantiser step Δ, it follows that the probability that a sample falls within the infinitesimally small interval ds shown in Fig. 6.2 is $P_j ds/\Delta$. The desired MSQE for interval j is obtained by summing the products of square quantisation error q^2 and probability over all such sub-intervals ds in j from $Q_j - \Delta/2$ to $Q_j + \Delta/2$:

$$\text{MSQE}_j = \int_{Q_j - \Delta/2}^{Q_j + \Delta/2} (s - Q_j)^2 \frac{P_j ds}{\Delta} = \frac{P_j}{\Delta} \int_{-\Delta/2}^{\Delta/2} S^2 dS = \frac{P_j \Delta^2}{12} \tag{6.4}$$

where we have used the substitution $S = s - Q_j$ in the second integral.

The total MSQE is obtained by summing the above result for all intervals from $j = 0$ to $j = N - 1$

$$\text{MSQE} = \sum_{j=0}^{j=N-1} \frac{P_j \Delta^2}{12} = \frac{\Delta^2}{12} \sum_{j=0}^{j=N-1} P_j \tag{6.5}$$

The last summation term is the probability that a sample falls in any of the N intervals. This must be equal to 1, since by definition each sample is certain to lie somewhere between $-C$ and $+C$. Therefore,

$$\text{MSQE} = \frac{\Delta^2}{12} \tag{6.6}$$

Thus the mean squared quantisation error depends only on the step size Δ. This error will appear as noise associated with the signal. The main advantage of this quantisation process is that if we can somehow convey the information about each quantised level without error, then we will introduce no further degradation to the signal. We can therefore make this quantisation noise as small as we wish by sufficiently reducing Δ. However, there is a price to pay for this improved noise performance. From Fig. 6.2 and Eq. (6.1) it follows that

$$\Delta = \frac{2C}{N} = \frac{2C}{2^k} \tag{6.7}$$

Here, k is the number of bits required to represent each quantised level, i.e. the number of *bits per sample*. Thus, Δ and hence quantisation noise can be reduced by increasing the number of bits per sample. *This increases the bit rate and hence the bandwidth required for transmission.*

6.2.1.2 *Dynamic range of a quantiser*

A sinusoidal input signal of amplitude $V_{max} = C$ will fully load the quantiser in Fig. 6.2, since it has values that cover the entire range from $-C$ to $+C$. Sinusoids of a larger amplitude would cause clipping and distortion. On the other hand, the variations of a sinusoidal input signal of amplitude $V_{min} =$

$\Delta/2$ are confined to a single interval of the quantiser. In other words, variations in this sinusoid will go undetected at the quantiser output. The ratio of the largest amplitude V_{max} of a sinusoid that avoids clipping to the largest amplitude V_{min} of a sinusoid whose variations go undetected is called the *dynamic range* of the quantiser:

$$\text{Dynamic range} = \frac{V_{max}}{V_{min}} = \frac{C}{\Delta/2} = 2^k = 6.02k \text{ dB} \tag{6.8}$$

The dynamic range therefore depends on the number of bits per sample. It increases by 6 dB for each extra bit available for representing each sample.

6.2.1.3 Signal to quantisation noise ratio (SQNR)

An important parameter for assessing the performance of the quantiser is the ratio of signal power to quantisation noise power, called the *signal to quantisation noise ratio* (SQNR). Let us define a parameter R known as the *peak-to-rms ratio* of the signal to be quantised. For a signal of rms = σ, and peak value V_p

$$R = \frac{V_p}{\sigma}; \quad \text{Signal power} = \sigma^2 = \frac{V_p^2}{R^2}$$

$$\text{SQNR} = \frac{\text{Signal power}}{\text{MSQE}} = \frac{V_p^2/R^2}{\Delta^2/12} = \frac{12 \times 2^{2k} V_p^2}{4C^2 R^2} = \frac{3V_p^2}{C^2 R^2} 2^{2k} \tag{6.9}$$

where we have made use of the expression for Δ in Eq. (6.7). Expressing Eq. (6.9) in dB,

$$\text{SQNR} = 10\log\left[\frac{3V_p^2}{C^2 R^2} 2^{2k}\right]$$

$$= 10\log(3) + 10\log(2^{2k}) \tag{6.10}$$
$$+ 10\log(R^{-2}) + 10\log(V_p^2/C^2)$$
$$= 4.77 + 6.02k - 20\log(R) + 20\log V_p/C \text{ dB}$$

If the signal fully loads the quantiser, $V_p = C$, and the SQNR improves to

$$\text{SQNR} = 4.77 + 6.02k - 20\log(R) \tag{6.11}$$

WORKED EXAMPLE 6.1

Determine the signal to quantisation noise ratio (SQNR) as a function of number of bits/sample for each of the following signals:

(a) Sinusoidal signal
(b) Signal with a uniform probability density function (pdf)
(c) Speech signal

(a) If a sinusoidal signal $g(t)$ fully loads the quantiser, then its amplitude $V_p = C$, and we may write $g(t) = C\sin(\omega t)$. The signal $g(t)$ has a period $T = 2\pi/\omega$, and a mean square value

$$\sigma^2 = \frac{1}{T}\int_0^T g^2(t)\mathrm{d}t = \frac{1}{T}\int_0^T C^2 \sin^2(\omega t)\mathrm{d}t$$

$$= \frac{C^2}{2T}\int_0^T (1 - \cos 2\omega t)\mathrm{d}t$$

$$= \frac{C^2}{2}$$

$$R = \frac{\text{Peak value}}{\sigma} = \frac{C}{C/\sqrt{2}} = \sqrt{2}$$

It follows from Eq. (6.11) that

$$\begin{aligned} \text{SQNR} &= 4.77 + 6.02k - 20\log(\sqrt{2}) \\ &= 1.76 + 6.02k \text{ dB} \end{aligned} \tag{6.12}$$

(b) The samples of this signal can take on any value between a minimum $-C$ and a maximum $+C$ with equal probability. It is assumed that the signal fully loads the quantiser. The probability that a sample of the signal lies between $s - \mathrm{d}s/2$ and $s + \mathrm{d}s/2$ is given by the shaded area $p\mathrm{d}s$ in Fig. 6.3. Since each sample must lie somewhere between $-C$ and $+C$, we must have $p \times 2C = 1$, or $p = 1/2C$. The mean square value σ^2 of the signal is obtained by summing (over the entire signal range $-C$ to $+C$) the product of the square of the sample value s and the probability $p\mathrm{d}s$ that a sample lies within the infinitesimal interval centred on s:

$$\sigma^2 = \int_{-C}^{+C} s^2 p\mathrm{d}s = \frac{1}{2C}\int_{-C}^{+C} s^2 \mathrm{d}s = \frac{C^2}{3}$$

Thus,

$$R = \frac{\text{Peak}}{\sigma} = \frac{C}{C/\sqrt{3}} = \sqrt{3}$$

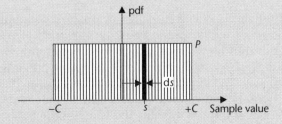

Figure 6.3 Uniform probability density function (pdf)

Eq. (6.11) then yields

$$SQNR = 6.02k \qquad (6.13)$$

(c) Measurements show that speech signals have on average $20\log(R) = 9$ dB. Thus, if the speech signal fully loads the quantiser (i.e. peak value $V_p = C$), then it follows from Eq. (6.11) that

$$SQNR = 6.02k - 4.23 \text{ dB} \qquad (6.14)$$

WORKED EXAMPLE ● **6.2**

A speech signal is to be transmitted by PCM with an output SQNR of 55 dB.

(a) What is the minimum number of bits per sample that must be used to achieve this performance, assuming that the speech signal fully loads the quantiser?

(b) If the quantiser is only half-loaded by the speech signal, what is the resulting output SQNR for the same bits/sample as above?

(a) The required bits/sample is obtained by rewriting Eq. (6.14) to make k the subject:

$$k = \frac{SQNR + 4.23}{6.02} = \frac{55 + 4.23}{6.02} = 9.84$$

The smallest integer larger than or equal to the above result gives the minimum number of bits/sample: **$k = 10$**.

(b) The full expression for SQNR in Eq. (6.10) must be used in this case, with $20\log(R) = 9$ and $V_p/C = \frac{1}{2}$:

$$\begin{aligned}
SQNR &= 4.77 + 6.02k - 9 + 20\log(\tfrac{1}{2}) \\
&= 4.77 + 6.02 \times 10 - 9 - 6.02 \\
&= 50 \text{ dB}
\end{aligned}$$

Note how the SQNR degrades when the quantiser is underloaded by a small input signal. Overloading, on the other hand, leads to clipping. Optimum performance is obtained by scaling the signal prior to quantisation to ensure that it just fully loads the quantiser.

A demonstration of a combined process of sampling and uniform quantisation of a sinusoidal signal is shown in Fig. 6.4. There are eight quantiser output levels, requiring $k = 3$ bits to represent each output level. The input signal is scaled prior to sampling in order to fully load the quantiser. The bottom plot of Fig. 6.4 shows the quantisation error, which is the difference between the quantised output and the analogue input signal. At each sampling instant the value of the analogue signal sample is approximated to the midpoint of the quantisation interval in which it lies. This quantised value is then held until the next sampling instant. The result is a staircase output signal.

Quantised levels

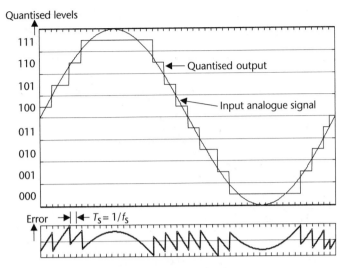

Figure 6.4 Eight-level uniform quantisation.

6.2.1.4 Design considerations

A number of important PCM system design considerations may be deduced from the relationships between the design parameters in Eqs. (6.9) and (6.10).

1. Signal to quantisation noise ratio (SQNR) increases exponentially with the number of bits per sample k, which is itself directly proportional to the bandwidth B required to transmit the PCM signal. Thus, PCM provides an exponential increase of SQNR with bandwidth. This is a better bandwidth for noise improvement trade-off than offered by FM, where signal to noise ratio increases only as the square of bandwidth. That is, if the signal-to-noise ratio is SNR_1 at bandwidth B_1, and the bandwidth is increased by a factor n to nB_1, then the signal to noise ratio increases to $n^2 \times SNR_1$ in FM, but more dramatically to SNR_1^n in PCM. More simply put, you make a gain of 6.02 dB per extra bit used for coding each sample in PCM, but you generate more bits per second as a result, and therefore require a larger transmission bandwidth. The number of bits/sample required for a desired SQNR can be determined from Fig. 6.5 for the three signals discussed in Worked example 6.1.

2. SQNR decreases as the square of the quantiser range $2C$ needed to accommodate the input signals without clipping. An improvement in SQNR can therefore be realised by reducing the range of input signal values. Some differential quantisers achieve such gains by quantising the difference between adjacent samples, rather than the samples themselves. If the sampling rate is sufficiently high, then adjacent samples are strongly correlated and the difference between them is very small, resulting in a reduced range of quantiser input values.

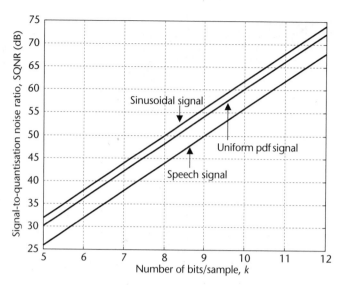

Figure 6.5 Output signal to noise ratio of a uniform quantiser as a function of number of bits/sample for various signal types.

3. A large segment of the quantisation error signal resembles a sawtooth waveform with a fundamental frequency that increases with the sampling frequency f_s. Thus, oversampling an analogue signal (i.e. choosing a much higher value of f_s than required by the sampling theorem) will have the effect of spreading out the quantisation noise power over a wider frequency band. As a result, only a significantly reduced fraction of the noise lies within the signal band at the reconstruction filter.

4. When an input signal underloads the quantiser, SQNR decreases by $20\log(r)$ dB, where r is the ratio between the quantiser range $2C$ and the peak-to-peak value of the input signal. More simply put, a signal that is at r dB below the level that fully loads the quantiser will have a SQNR that is r dB worse than the values obtained from Fig. 6.5. In speech communication, for example, this would mean a good SQNR for the loudest speakers and a significant degradation for soft speakers.

6.2.1.5 *Demerits of uniform quantisation*

We have observed that the quantisation error associated with each quantised sample can range from 0 to a maximum of $\Delta/2$, where Δ is the quantiser step size. This error must be kept small compared to the sample value. To faithfully quantise small samples, one must therefore choose a very small step size, which results in a large number of quantisation intervals and hence a large number of bits k required to code each sample. For example, speech signals are characterised by a non-uniform pdf with a preponderance of low values. To maintain fidelity, these low values must be faithfully transmitted as they mostly represent the consonants that carry intelligibility. The typical dynamic range of a speech signal is 60 dB, which means a ratio of highest to lowest sample magnitude given by

$$60 = 20 \log_{10} \left(\frac{V_H}{V_L} \right)$$

Thus,

$$\frac{V_H}{V_L} = 10^{(60/20)} = 1000$$

That is, if the peak value allowed when digitising a speech signal is $V_H = 1$ V, then the weakest passage may be as low as $V_L = 1$mV. A step size $\Delta < V_L$ is required to faithfully quantise the smallest samples. Choosing $\Delta = V_L$ results in 1000 intervals for the positive samples, and another 1000 for the negative samples, or 2000 intervals in total. The number of bits required to code up to 2000 levels is given by

$$k = \lceil \log_2(2000) \rceil = 11 \text{ bits}$$

where $\lceil x \rceil$ denotes the smallest integer larger than or equal to x.

With a sampling frequency $f_s = 8$ kHz, the bit rate that must be transmitted is 8000 samples × 11 bits/sample = 88 kbit/s. Such a high bit rate translates to an unacceptably large transmission bandwidth requirement.

Another problem with uniform quantisation may be observed by noting that the quantisation error magnitude is constant across all intervals. The signal to quantisation noise ratio (SQNR) is therefore much smaller at the lower intervals (corresponding to small signal values) than nearer the top, since

$$V_L^2/q^2 \ll V_H^2/q^2$$

In telephony in particular, it is desirable to have a constant SQNR over a wide range of input signal values so that the service quality is maintained at the same level for both quiet and loud talkers.

The above problems of large bit rate and non-constant SQNR can be alleviated by using a non-uniform quantiser in which the step size is a function of input signal value. Large input samples are coarsely quantised using larger step sizes, while the smaller input samples are more finely quantised using smaller step sizes.

6.2.2 Non-uniform quantisation

Non-uniform quantisation may be achieved through either of the schemes shown in Fig. 6.6. In Fig. 6.6(a), the analogue signal is first compressed before being quantised in a uniform quantiser. At the receiver, the decoded PCM signal is expanded in a way that perfectly reverses the compression process. The combined process of compression at the transmitter and expansion at the receiver is called *companding*. Note that companding does

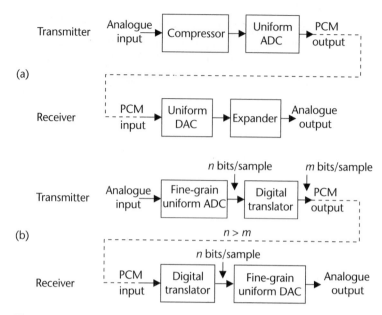

Figure 6.6 Non-uniform quantisation schemes.

not introduce any distortion, and quantisation error remains the only source of distortion in the analogue-to-digital signal conversion process.

The scheme of Fig. 6.6(b) first quantises the input signal using a fine-grain uniform quantiser of say, $n = 13$ bits/sample, corresponding to $2^{13} = 8192$ levels. A digital translator is then used to reduce the number of transmitted bits/sample to say $m = 8$, corresponding to $2^8 = 256$ levels. The reduction is achieved in compressor fashion by mapping an increasing number of fine-grain levels to the same output level as one moves from the low to high range of signal values. For example, the translation may progress from two-to-one near zero, to 128-to-one near the maximum signal value. A 128-to-one translation means that 128 fine-grain levels are equated to one output level, usually the midpoint of the 128 levels. At the receiver, a reverse translation is performed that converts from m to n bits/sample. The overall effect of this scheme is again finer quantisation of small signal samples and coarser quantisation of the larger samples.

The quantisation scheme of Fig. 6.6(b) is in practice the preferred approach, since it can be implemented using low cost DSPs. However, to understand the required compressor characteristic, we first discuss the system of Fig. 6.6(a), and then present the implementation of Fig. 6.6(b) as a piecewise linear approximation of the non-linear compression function in the system of Fig. 6.6(a).

6.2.2.1 Compressor characteristic

Figure 6.7 shows the input-output characteristic of the compressor. The input is normalised to the range $(-1, +1)$. The output (y-axis) is divided into

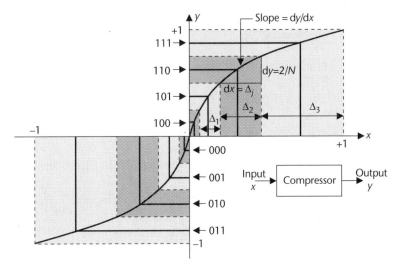

Figure 6.7 Compressor characteristic.

N uniform intervals (illustrated in Fig. 6.7 for $N = 8$), corresponding to uniform quantisation with step size $\Delta = 2/N$. The binary code of each quantised output level is indicated. Note that the uniform intervals of the compressor output y correspond to differently-sized intervals of the compressor input signal x, which are small near the origin and increase steadily for larger magnitudes of x. It is clear that this arrangement achieves finer quantisation of the smaller samples of x than the larger samples. In the example shown in Fig. 6.7, all input samples in the second positive interval are quantised to level 101 with maximum error $\Delta_1/2$, while the input samples in the fourth positive interval are quantised to level 111 with a bigger maximum error of $\Delta_3/2$.

Recall that one of the goals of non-uniform quantisation is to achieve a constant SQNR throughout the entire range of input signal x. Let us obtain the SQNR for a signal that is compressed and uniformly quantised as illustrated in Fig. 6.7. Our aim is to determine the shape of the compression curve that gives a SQNR that is independent of x.

Quantisation noise power follows from Eq. (6.4):

$$\text{MSQE} = \frac{1}{12} \sum_j P_j \Delta_j^2 \tag{6.15}$$

Assuming sufficiently small intervals, the slope of the compressor curve is constant within the space of one interval, and — from Fig. 6.7 — is given for interval j by

$$\frac{dy}{dx} = \frac{2/N}{\Delta_j}$$

It follows that the jth step size is given by

$$\Delta_j = \frac{2}{N}\frac{\mathrm{d}x}{\mathrm{d}y} \tag{6.16}$$

The probability of the input signal value falling in the jth interval (of width $\mathrm{d}x$) is

$$P_j = p(x)\mathrm{d}x \tag{6.17}$$

where $p(x)$ is the pdf of the input signal x. In the limit of a large number of quantisation levels, the summation for MSQE in Eq. (6.15) becomes an integration operation over the normalised input signal range $(-1, +1)$. Thus,

$$\mathrm{MSQE} = \frac{1}{12}\sum_j P_j \Delta_j^2 = \frac{1}{3N^2}\sum_{\text{All intervals}} p(x)\mathrm{d}x\left(\frac{\mathrm{d}x}{\mathrm{d}y}\right)^2$$

$$= \frac{1}{3N^2}\int_{-1}^{+1} p(x)\left(\frac{\mathrm{d}x}{\mathrm{d}y}\right)^2 \mathrm{d}x \tag{6.18}$$

where we have used Eqs. (6.16) and (6.17) for Δ_j and P_j, respectively.

The normalised input signal power is given by

$$\text{Signal power} = \int_{-1}^{+1} x^2 p(x)\mathrm{d}x \tag{6.19}$$

The desired SQNR is given by the ratio between Eq. (6.19) and Eq. (6.18):

$$\mathrm{SQNR} = \frac{\text{Signal power}}{\mathrm{MSQE}} = 3N^2 \frac{\int_{-1}^{+1} x^2 p(x)\mathrm{d}x}{\int_{-1}^{+1}(\mathrm{d}x/\mathrm{d}y)^2 p(x)\mathrm{d}x} \tag{6.20}$$

The RHS of Eq. (6.20) must be independent of x if SQNR is to be independent of x as desired. By examining the above equation, it is easy to see that this can be achieved by setting

$$\frac{\mathrm{d}x}{\mathrm{d}y} = Kx, \text{ where } K \text{ is a constant} \tag{6.21}$$

This leads to the result

$$\mathrm{SQNR} = 3N^2 \frac{\int_{-1}^{+1} x^2 p(x)\mathrm{d}x}{\int_{-1}^{+1} K^2 x^2 p(x)\mathrm{d}x} = \frac{3N^2}{K^2} \tag{6.22}$$

which is independent of input signal level x as desired. Thus, the correct compression characteristic is one that satisfies Eq. (6.21), or

$$\frac{\mathrm{d}y}{\mathrm{d}x} = \frac{1}{Kx}$$

Integrating,

$$y = \frac{1}{K}\ln(x) + D$$

where D is a constant that we choose in order to make $(x, y) = (1, 1)$ a point on the curve, since the normalised maximum input is compressed to the normalised maximum output. Thus $D = 1$, and the desired compressor characteristic is

$$y = \frac{1}{K}\ln(x) + 1 \tag{6.23}$$

which has a slope

$$\frac{dy}{dx} = \frac{1}{Kx} \tag{6.24}$$

What have we achieved? We now have in Eq. (6.23) the full specification of a compression curve that can be used to compress the input signal x to give an output y, which is then uniformly quantised. The result of these two steps is fine quantisation of small input values and coarse quantisation of larger input values.

However, there is a practical problem with the compression function of Eq. (6.23). The slope of the curve is infinite at $x = 0$, implying infinitesimally small quantiser steps as $x \to 0$. To circumvent this problem, the logarithmic function in Eq. (6.23) is replaced by a linear function in the region $x \to 0$. The ITU-T has standardised two such compressor characteristics, the A-law in Europe, and the μ-law in North America and Japan.

6.2.2 A-law companding

This companding law follows from Eq. (6.23) by setting the constant

$$K = 1 + \ln(A) \tag{6.25}$$

where A is a positive constant (usually $A = 87.6$). This defines the logarithmic portion of the characteristic:

$$\begin{aligned} y_{\log} &= \frac{1}{K}\ln(x) + 1 = \frac{\ln(x) + K}{K} \\ &= \frac{\ln(x) + 1 + \ln(A)}{1 + \ln(A)} \\ &= \frac{1 + \ln(Ax)}{1 + \ln(A)} \end{aligned} \tag{6.26}$$

A linear function $y_{\lin}$ is used in the region $|x| \leq 1/A$. This is the region $x \to 0$ referred to above. The linear function

$$y_{\lin} = mx + c \tag{6.27}$$

where m and c are constants, is determined by satisfying two conditions:

1. That $y_{\lin}$ passes through the origin, so that $x = 0$ is compressed to $y = 0$. This means that in Eq. (6.27), $y_{\lin} = 0$ when $x = 0$, so that the constant $c = 0$.

2. That — for continuity — the linear and logarithmic functions have the same value at $x = 1/A$. Since

$$y_{\lin}\,|_{1/A} = m(1/A)$$

and

$$y_{\log}\big|_{1/A} = \frac{1+\ln[A\times(1/A)]}{1+\ln(A)} = \frac{1}{1+\ln(A)}$$

It follows by equating both expressions that

$$m = \frac{A}{1+\ln(A)}$$

Thus,

$$y_{\text{lin}} = mx + c = \frac{Ax}{1+\ln(A)} \tag{6.28}$$

In summary, the A-law compression curve is defined by the following equations:

$$y = \begin{cases} \dfrac{Ax}{1+\ln(A)}, & 0 \le x \le 1/A \\[2mm] \dfrac{1+\ln(Ax)}{1+\ln(A)}, & 1/A \le x \le 1 \\[2mm] -y(|x|), & -1 \le x \le 0 \end{cases} \tag{6.29}$$

The last expression in Eq. (6.29) indicates that the compression curve y has odd symmetry, so that a negative input value, say, $-X$, where X is positive, is compressed to give a negative output that has the same magnitude as the output corresponding to input X.

6.2.2.3 μ-law companding

This companding function is obtained from Eq. (6.23) in two steps:

1. Set the constant
    $$K = \ln(1+\mu) \tag{6.30}$$

    where μ is a positive constant (usually $\mu = 255$), so that

    $$y = \frac{\ln(x)}{\ln(1+\mu)} + 1 = \frac{\ln(x)+\ln(1+\mu)}{\ln(1+\mu)} = \frac{\ln(x+\mu x)}{\ln(1+\mu)}$$

2. Modify the above result by replacing $x + \mu x$ in the numerator with $1 + \mu x$. This gives the μ-law compression function

    $$y = \begin{cases} \dfrac{\ln(1+\mu x)}{\ln(1+\mu)}, & x \ge 0 \\[2mm] -y(|x|), & -1 \le x \le 0 \end{cases} \tag{6.31}$$

The modification in the second step is necessary in order to satisfy the requirement for linear compression in the region $x \to 0$. To see that this is the case, note that $\ln(1 + z) \approx z$ for $z \to 0$, which means that the μ-law compression curve reduces to the following linear relation near the origin:

$$y \equiv y_{\text{lin}} = \frac{\mu x}{\ln(1+\mu)}, \qquad x \to 0 \tag{6.32}$$

Furthermore, if $\mu \gg 1$ then $1 + \mu x \approx \mu x$ for $x \to 1$. Thus, the compression is logarithmic as required for large input values:

$$y \equiv y_{\text{log}} = \frac{\ln(\mu x)}{\ln(1+\mu)}, \qquad x \to 1 \tag{6.33}$$

WORKED EXAMPLE   **6.3**

Discuss how the values of A and μ affect the relative sizes of the quantisation steps in A-law and μ-law companding.

The maximum step size occurs at $x = 1$ (normalised), and the minimum at $x = 0$. Let us denote these step sizes as Δ_{max} and Δ_{min}, respectively. Applying Eq. (6.16),

$$\Delta_{\text{min}} = \frac{2}{N} \left.\frac{dx}{dy}\right|_{x=0} = (2/N) \bigg/ \left(\left.\frac{dy}{dx}\right|_{x=0}\right)$$

$$\Delta_{\text{max}} = \frac{2}{N} \left.\frac{dx}{dy}\right|_{x=1} = (2/N) \bigg/ \left(\left.\frac{dy}{dx}\right|_{x=1}\right)$$

The ratio of maximum step size to minimum step size is therefore

$$\frac{\Delta_{\text{max}}}{\Delta_{\text{min}}} = \frac{(dy/dx)\big|_{x=0}}{(dy/dx)\big|_{x=1}}$$

For the A-law, we take the derivative of Eq. (6.29) to obtain

$$\left.\frac{dy}{dx}\right|_{x=0} = \frac{A}{1+\ln(A)}; \quad \left.\frac{dy}{dx}\right|_{x=1} = \frac{1}{1+\ln(A)}$$

Thus,

$$\frac{\Delta_{\text{max}}}{\Delta_{\text{min}}} = A \tag{6.34}$$

In the case of the μ-law, the derivative of Eq. (6.31) yields

$$\left.\frac{dy}{dx}\right|_{x=0} = \frac{\mu}{\ln(1+\mu)}; \quad \left.\frac{dy}{dx}\right|_{x=1} = \frac{\mu}{(1+\mu)\ln(1+\mu)}$$

so that

$$\frac{\Delta_{\text{max}}}{\Delta_{\text{min}}} = 1+\mu$$

or

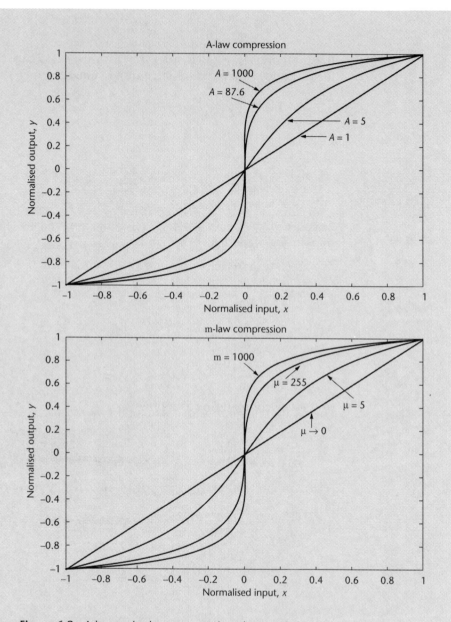

Figure 6.8 A-law and μ-law compression characteristics.

$$\mu = \frac{\Delta_{\max}}{\Delta_{\min}} - 1 \qquad\qquad (6.35)$$

We see therefore that the constant A sets the ratio between the maximum and minimum step size in A-law compression. If $A = 1$, then $\Delta_{\max} = \Delta_{\min}$ and the step sizes are all equal. This is the special case of uniform quantisation. A significant compression is achieved by choosing $A \gg 1$.

In the case of μ-law compression, $\mu = 0$ gives $\Delta_{max} = \Delta_{min}$ and corresponds to uniform quantisation. The required compression characteristic, Eq. (6.33), is obtained only by choosing a large value for the constant μ. Usually $\mu = 255$. Figure 6.8 shows the A-law and μ-law characteristics for various values of A and μ.

6.2.2.4 *Companding gain*

Companding gain G_C is defined as the improvement in SQNR for small input values in a non-uniform quantiser compared with the SQNR of the same signal type when using a uniform quantiser of the same number of bits/sample. It follows that G_C is the square of the ratio between the step size of a uniform quantiser and the smallest step size of a non-uniform quantiser of the same bits/sample and input range. Following from Fig. 6.7,

$$G_c = 10\log\left[\left(\frac{dy}{dx}\right)^2\bigg|_{x=0}\right] = 20\log\left(\frac{dy}{dx}\bigg|_{x=0}\right)$$

Using Eq. (6.28) and Eq. (6.32), we obtain the companding gain for A-law and μ-law companding as follows:

$$G_{c\,A\text{-law}} = 20\log_{10}\left[\frac{A}{1+\ln(A)}\right]\text{dB}$$

$$G_{c\,\mu\text{-law}} = 20\log_{10}\left[\frac{\mu}{\ln(1+\mu)}\right]\text{dB}$$

(6.36)

Thus, if $A = 87.6$, A-law non-uniform quantisation gives a gain of 24 dB over a uniform quantisation that uses the same number of bits/sample. A gain of 33 dB is realised with μ-law for $\mu = 255$. We will see later that in practice, a piecewise linear approximation is adopted, resulting in a slightly lower companding gain of 30 dB for μ-law. Recall that an improvement of 6 dB in SQNR is provided by each extra bit used for coding the quantised samples. A gain of 24 dB is therefore equivalent to four extra coding bits. This means that a uniform quantiser would require 12 bits/sample in order to have the same performance as A-law with 8 bits/sample. By using A-law non-uniform quantisation, we have reduced the required number of bits/sample from 12 to 8, representing a saving of 33% in bit rate and hence bandwidth. In the case of μ-law, the bit rate reduction is from 13 to 8 — a saving in bandwidth of 38.5%. Note that these figures apply only to the bandwidth required for transmitting information bits. In practice, *overhead* (non-information) bits must be added — as discussed in Chapter 8, leading to a lower saving in overall bandwidth.

6.2.2.5 Companding advantage

We noted earlier that the SQNR of a uniform (or linear) quantiser decreases with peak input signal level. SQNR in the non-uniform log-quantiser discussed above does not vary significantly over the entire input signal range. However, we fail to realise an ideal non-linear quantisation in which SQNR is strictly constant. This is because, for practical implementation, we had to replace the logarithmic curve of Eq. (6.23) with a linear curve for $|x| \le 1/A$ in the A-law. In the case of μ-law, an approximate curve was employed that becomes linear as $x \to 0$ and logarithmic as $x \to 1$ (normalised).

Consider a log quantiser and a linear quantiser that use the same number of bits/sample. Let a given SQNR be achieved in the linear quantiser at an input level S_{lin}. If the smallest input level at which the same SQNR is achieved in the log-quantiser is S_{log}, then the difference $S_{\text{lin}} - S_{\text{log}}$ is called the *companding advantage* of the log-quantiser:

$$\text{Companding advantage} = S_{\text{lin}} - S_{\text{log}} \text{ dB} \tag{6.37}$$

Note that the input levels are specified in dB relative to the maximum level C.

6.2.2.6 Practical non-linear PCM

In practice, non-linear A-law and μ-law companding are implemented using the piecewise linear approximation shown in Figs. 6.9 and 6.10 for the A-law (A = 87.6) and μ-law (μ = 255), respectively.

Details of this piecewise companding scheme are presented in Tables 6.2 and 6.3 for the two laws. Consider first the A-law scheme in Fig. 6.9 and Table 6.2.

The input signal is normalised to the range $\pm C$, where $C = 4096$ to represent all step sizes using integers. The magnitude of negative and positive input signal values is processed in exactly the same way, except that in the output code the most significant bit (MSB) is set to 1 for positive values and 0 for negative. Figure 6.9, Table 6.2 and the following discussion show how the positive input values (0 → 4096) are handled.

The A-law curve is approximated using a series of eight straight-line segments covering the input intervals (0→32), (32→64), (64→128), (128→256), (256→512), (512→1024), (1024→2048), (2048→4096). These segments are numbered from 0 to 7 in the first column of Table 6.2. Each segment is divided into 16 equal intervals, numbered from 0 to 15 in column 4 of the table. The first two segments ($s = 0, 1$) have equal intervals or step sizes — normalised to 2, whereas in the remaining six segments ($s = 2$ to 7) the step size in one segment is double that of the previous segment. The compression line for segments 0 and 1 is actually a single straight line that straddles the origin and covers the input range −64 → +64. Thus, there are 13 unique line segments in all.

The range of input values that constitute a quantisation interval in each segment is given in the 3rd column of Table 6.2, which also shows the 128 output levels available to the positive input signal, numbered from 0 to 127

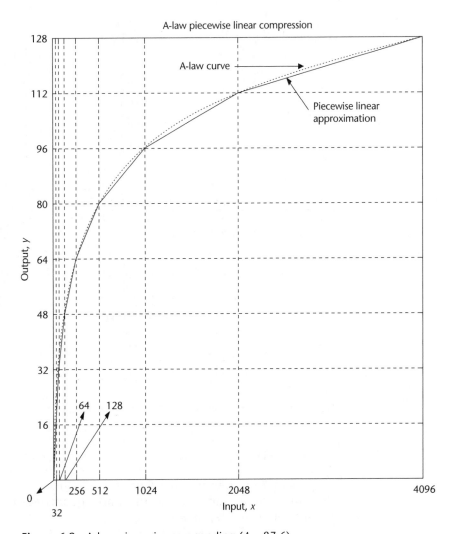

Figure 6.9 A-law piecewise companding ($A = 87.6$).

in column 5. There are a further 128 output levels, not shown, for negative input signals. This gives 256 output levels in total, which can therefore be represented using 8 bits.

Observe that segments $s = 0$ and 1 have the smallest step size $\Delta_{\min} = 2$. If the entire input range ($\pm C$) were quantised uniformly using this step size, the number of quantisation levels would be

$$N = \frac{2C}{\Delta_{\min}} = \frac{2 \times 4096}{2} = 2^{12}$$

which would require 12 bits to represent. Thus, the small input values have an equivalent of $k = 12$ bits/sample linear quantisation, which we may express as

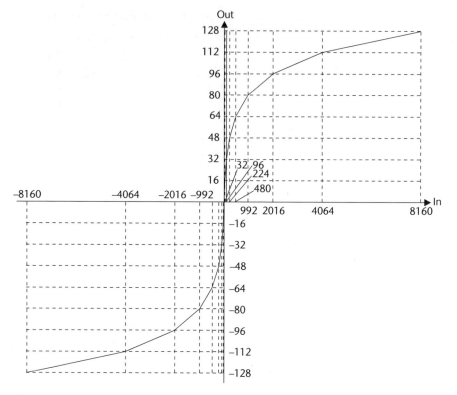

Figure 6.10 μ-law piecewise companding ($\mu = 255$).

$$k_{\max} = \left\lceil \log_2(2C/\Delta_{\min}) \right\rceil \tag{6.38}$$

Segment 7 on the other hand has the maximum step size $\Delta_{\max} = 128$. If the entire input range were uniformly quantised at this spacing, the number of output levels would be

$$N = \frac{2C}{\Delta_{\max}} = \frac{2 \times 4096}{128} = 64 = 2^6$$

Thus the large input values are coarsely quantised at a resolution equivalent to $k = 6$ bits/sample linear quantisation, or

$$k_{\min} = \left\lceil \log_2(2C/\Delta_{\max}) \right\rceil \tag{6.39}$$

The binary code $b_7 b_6 b_5 b_4 b_3 b_2 b_1 b_0$ for each of the 256 output levels is given in column 6 of Table 6.2. This code is determined as follows.

1. The most significant bit (MSB) b_7 is set to 1 for positive input values and 0 for negative input values.

2. $b_6 b_5 b_4$ is the binary number equivalent of segment s. For example, if $s = 6$, then $b_6 b_5 b_4 = 110$.

3. $b_3 b_2 b_1 b_0$ is the binary number equivalent of the interval l within a segment. For example, if $l = 13$, then $b_3 b_2 b_1 b_0 = 1101$.

Table 6.2 A-law 13-segment companding.

Segment s	Step size	Input range	Interval I	Output (256 levels)	Output code 8 bits/sample	Receiver output
0	2	0–2	0	0	1 000 0000	1
		⋮	⋮	⋮	⋮	⋮
		30–32	15	15	1 000 1111	31
1	2	32–34	0	16	1 001 0000	33
		⋮	⋮	⋮	⋮	⋮
		62–64	15	31	1 001 1111	63
2	4	64–68	0	32	1 010 0000	66
		⋮	⋮	⋮	⋮	⋮
		124–128	15	47	1 010 1111	126
3	8	128–136	0	48	1 011 0000	132
		⋮	⋮	⋮	⋮	⋮
		248–256	15	63	1 011 1111	252
4	16	256–272	0	64	1 100 0000	264
		⋮	⋮	⋮	⋮	⋮
		496–512	15	79	1 100 1111	504
5	32	512–544	0	80	1 101 0000	528
		⋮	⋮	⋮	⋮	⋮
		992–1024	15	95	1 101 1111	1008
6	64	1024–1088	0	96	1 110 0000	1056
		⋮	⋮	⋮	⋮	⋮
		1984–2048	15	111	1 110 1111	2016
7	128	2048–2176	0	112	1 111 0000	2112
		⋮	⋮	⋮	⋮	⋮
		3968–4096	15	127	1 111 1111	4032

At the receiver, this code is converted to the value shown in the last column of Table 6.2, which is the midpoint of the interval (column 3) in which the original input sample falls.

μ-law piecewise companding (Fig. 6.10 and Table 6.3) follows a similar strategy to the A-law, but with several important differences discussed below.

Note that the input signal is normalised to the range ±8160 to allow the use of integer numbers for the step sizes. Of the 16 segments, the two that straddle the origin are co-linear, giving 15 unique segments. Starting from segment 0 (for the positive signal range), the step size of each segment is double that of the previous one.

Table 6.3 μ-law 15-segment companding.

Segment s	Step size	Input range	Interval I	Output (256 levels)	Output code 8 bits/sample	Receiver output
0	2	0–2	0	0	1 000 0000	1
		⋮	⋮	⋮	⋮	⋮
		30–32	15	15	1 000 1111	31
1	4	32–36	0	16	1 001 0000	34
		⋮	⋮	⋮	⋮	⋮
		92–96	15	31	1 001 1111	94
2	8	96–104	0	32	1 010 0000	100
		⋮	⋮	⋮	⋮	⋮
		216–224	15	47	1 010 1111	220
3	16	224–240	0	48	1 011 0000	232
		⋮	⋮	⋮	⋮	⋮
		464–480	15	63	1 011 1111	472
4	32	480–512	0	64	1 100 0000	496
		⋮	⋮	⋮	⋮	⋮
		960–992	15	79	1 100 1111	976
5	64	992–1056	0	80	1 101 0000	1024
		⋮	⋮	⋮	⋮	⋮
		1952–2016	15	95	1 101 1111	1984
6	128	2016–2144	0	96	1 110 0000	2080
		⋮	⋮	⋮	⋮	⋮
		3936–4064	15	111	1 110 1111	4000
7	256	4064–4320	0	112	1 111 0000	4192
		⋮	⋮	⋮	⋮	⋮
		7904–8160	15	127	1 111 1111	8032

Following Eq. (6.38) and (6.39), we see that the μ-law scheme is equivalent to a fine linear quantisation of the smallest input values (in segment $s = 0$) using

$$k_{max} = \lceil \log_2(2C/\Delta_{min}) \rceil = \left\lceil \log_2\left(\frac{2 \times 8160}{2}\right) \right\rceil$$
$$= 13 \text{ bits/sample}$$

and a coarse linear quantisation of the largest input values (in segment $s = 7$) using

Table 6.4 Segments and step sizes in A-law and μ-law PCM.

Segment s	A-law		μ-law	
	Step size Δ	Input range $(X_{min} \to X_{max})$	Step size Δ	Input range $(X_{min} \to X_{max})$
0	2	$0 \to 32$	2	$0 \to 32$
1	2	$32 \to 64$	4	$32 \to 96$
2	4	$64 \to 128$	8	$96 \to 224$
3	8	$128 \to 256$	16	$224 \to 480$
4	16	$256 \to 512$	32	$480 \to 992$
5	32	$512 \to 1024$	64	$992 \to 2016$
6	64	$1024 \to 2048$	128	$2016 \to 4064$
7	128	$2048 \to 4096$	256	$4064 \to 8160$

$$k_{min} = \lceil \log_2(2C/\Delta_{max}) \rceil = \left\lceil \log_2\left(\frac{2 \times 8160}{256}\right) \right\rceil$$

$$= 6 \text{ bits/sample}$$

An important summary of the segments and step sizes used in A-law and μ-law PCM is provided in Table 6.4. In Worked example 6.4, we show how the information in this table is used for PCM coding and decoding.

Piecewise linear companding may be viewed as a two-step process (Fig. 6.6(b)) of fine uniform quantisation and digital translation. This view is demonstrated in Fig. 6.11 for A-law piecewise companding. Note that the results of Fig. 6.11 and Table 6.2 are the same.

Figure 6.12 provides a summary of the steps involved in converting an analogue sample to a PCM code. In the coding process, the analogue sample $x(n)$ is first scaled by a factor F in order for the input signal $x(t)$ to fully load the quantiser, which has an input range $-C$ to $+C$. In our case, in order to use Table 6.4, $C = 4096$ for A-law PCM and 8160 for μ-law. The scaled sample, denoted $X(n)$, is converted in the quantiser to a value $X_q(n)$ equal to the midpoint of the quantisation interval in which $X(n)$ lies. The encoder then converts $X_q(n)$ to a binary code according to the procedure outlined above. It is noteworthy that at every stage of Fig. 6.12 the signal is processed in a reversible manner, except at the quantiser. The original input sample $x(n)$ can be obtained from $X(n)$, and likewise $X_q(n)$ from the binary PCM code $b_7 b_6 b_5 b_4 b_3 b_2 b_1 b_0$. But once the exact sample $X(n)$ has been converted to the approximate value $X_q(n)$, knowledge of $X(n)$ is lost forever and the incurred quantisation error is a permanent degradation of the transmitted signal. It is important to keep this error at a minimum.

At the receiver, an incoming PCM code is converted to a quantised value $X_q(n)$, which is the midpoint of interval l within segment s, the values of both l and s being indicated by the code. $X_q(n)$ is de-scaled by the factor $1/F$ to yield a received signal sample $x_q(n)$, which, barring channel-induced

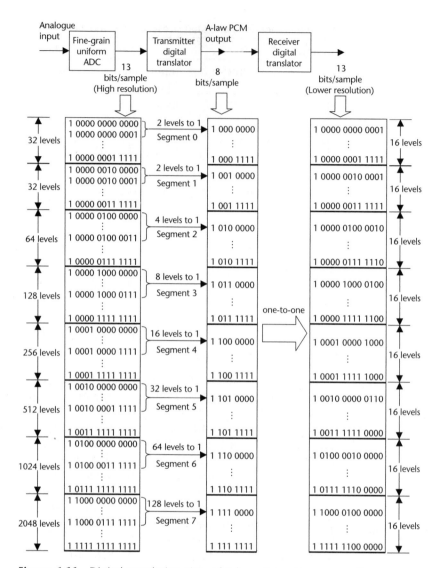

Figure 6.11 Digital translation view of A-law piecewise companding.

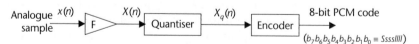

Figure 6.12 Converting analogue sample to PCM code. In the PCM code, *S* represents a sign bit; *sss* represents one of eight segments; and *llll* represents one of 16 quantisation intervals within each segment.

errors in the received PCM code, differs from the original sample $x(n)$ by a quantisation error given by

$$q = \left|x_q(n) - x(n)\right|$$
$$= \left|\frac{X_q(n) - X(n)}{F}\right| \tag{6.40}$$

The maximum value of q, denoted q_{max}, is half the step size of the segment s in which $X(n)$ lies. It follows from Table 6.4 that for A-law PCM,

$$q_{max} = \begin{cases} 1/F, & s = 0 \\ 2^{(s-1)}/F, & s = 1, 2, \ldots, 7 \end{cases} \tag{6.41}$$

and for μ-law PCM,

$$q_{max} = 2^s/F \tag{6.42}$$

Since samples of larger magnitude fall in higher segments s, we see that the maximum quantisation error increases as the sample value increases. This maintains the ratio of sample value to quantisation error and hence SQNR approximately constant over the entire input signal range.

All the coding and decoding processes discussed above, including the filtering and sample-and-hold functions discussed in Chapter 5, are usually performed by a single large scale IC unit known as a *codec*. On the transmit side the codec takes in an analogue signal and generates a serial bit stream output, being the A-law or μ-law PCM representation of the analogue signal. On the receive side it takes an incoming PCM serial bit stream and recovers the original analogue signal, subject of course to quantisation noise and any channel-induced errors in the received PCM code.

WORKED EXAMPLE   6.4

An analogue signal of values in the range $-V_p$ to $+V_p$ is to be digitised. Let $V_p = 5$ V, and assume that the signal fully loads the quantiser. Determine

(a) The A-law PCM code for the sample value –4 volts
(b) The voltage value to which the A-law code 0 101 1100 is converted at the receiver
(c) The quantisation error incurred in transmitting the sample value 3.3 V using μ-law.

(a) In order to use Table 6.4, we scale the input signal from the range $\pm V_p$ to the range $\pm C$, where $C = 4096$ (for A-law). This requires that every input sample $x(n)$ is multiplied by a factor

$$F = \begin{cases} 4096/V_p, & \text{A-law} \\ 8160/V_p, & \mu\text{-law} \end{cases} \tag{6.43}$$

In this case, with $V_p = 5$, $F = 819.2$. Ignoring for the moment the sign of the input sample $x(n) = -4$ V, since that only affects the sign bit in the PCM code, and following Fig. 6.12,

$$X(n) = Fx(n) = 819.2 \times 4 = 3276.8$$

Table 6.4 shows that $X(n)$ lies in the segment $s = 7$. The interval l in which $X(n)$ lies within this segment is given by the number of steps Δ (= 128 in segment 7) required to reach a value just below or equal to $X(n)$ starting from the lower limit ($X_{min} = 2048$) of the segment:

$$l = \left\lfloor \frac{X(n) - X_{min}}{\Delta} \right\rfloor \tag{6.44}$$

where $\lfloor y \rfloor$ denotes the integer part of y. Using the above values in Eq. (6.44) gives $l = 9$.

Thus the (negative) sample lies in the interval $s = 7$; $l = 9$; and is therefore assigned the 8-bit PCM code (= $Sssslll$)

0 111 1001

where the MSB = 0 for a negative sample. The segment s *must* be expressed as a 3-bit binary number sss, and interval l as a 4-bit binary number $llll$. This means, for example, that $s = 0$ would be expressed as $sss = 000$; and $l = 2$ as $llll = 0010$

(b) The A-law code 1 101 1100 represents a positive sample $X(n)$ in the interval $l = 1100_2 = 12$ and within segment $s = 101_2 = 5$, where the subscript 2 denotes a binary number equal to the indicated decimal equivalent. The receiver converts this sample to the mid-point $X_q(n)$ of the interval:

$$X_q(n) = X_{min} + l\Delta + \Delta/2 \tag{6.45}$$

where X_{min} is the lower limit and Δ the step size of segment s (= 5 in this case). From Table 6.4,

$$X_{min} = 512, \text{ and } \Delta = 32$$

giving

$$X_q(n) = 912$$

De-scaling yields the received sample

$$x_q(n) = X_q(n)/F = 912/819.2 = 1.11\,\text{V}$$

(c) Proceeding in a similar manner as in (a) for this μ-law case, we obtain the scaling factor $F = 1632$, and a scaled sample

$$X(n) = Fx(n) = (1632)(3.3) = 5385.6$$

We see from Table 6.4 that $X(n)$ lies in segment $s = 7$, which has X_{min} = 4064 and $\Delta = 256$. Substituting in Eq. (6.44) yields the interval $l = 5$.

The mid-point $X_q(n)$ of this interval to which $X(n)$ is quantised is given by Eq. (6.45):

$$X_q(n) = 4064 + 5 \times 256 + 256/2 = 5472$$

Thus the quantisation error incurred is, from Eq. (6.40),

$$q = \left| \frac{5472 - 5385.6}{1632} \right| = 52.9 \text{ mV}$$

You may prefer to use the following direct formulas that give the sample value $X_q(n)$ to which any received PCM code $b_7b_6b_5b_4b_3b_2b_1b_0$ is decoded:

$$s = 4b_6 + 2b_5 + b_4$$
$$l = 8b_3 + 4b_2 + 2b_1 + b_0$$

$$x_q(n) = \frac{(-1)^{b_7+1}}{F} \times \begin{cases} 2^s(l+0.5), & \text{A-law, } s = 0 \\ 2^s(l+16.5), & \text{A-law, } s = 1, 2, \ldots, 7 \\ 2^{s+1}(l+16.5) - 32, & \mu\text{-law} \end{cases} \qquad (6.46)$$

where F is the scaling factor given by Eq. (6.43). You should verify that Eq. (6.46) yields the expected result for the A-law PCM code 1 101 1100 of Worked example 6.4(b).

6.2.2.7 SQNR of practical non-linear PCM

Let us consider the SQNR characteristic of A-law and μ-law PCM as a function of the peak input signal level, and compare this with that of a linear ADC of the same number of bits per sample ($k = 8$). This important exercise allows us to examine the extent to which A-law and μ-law PCM achieve the ideal of a constant SQNR independent of the input signal level.

We noted earlier that the SQNR of a linear ADC (or uniform quantisation) decreases with signal level. This follows from Eq. (6.10), the last term of which gives the peak value V_p of the input signal expressed in dB relative to the maximum level C of the quantiser. It was shown in Worked example 6.1 that $R = \sqrt{3}$ for a uniform pdf input signal. Thus the SQNR of an 8-bit linear ADC decreases exactly as the input signal level (dB) decreases, the maximum SQNR being 48.2 dB for a uniform pdf input.

Usually, the input signal is scaled before quantisation in order that the overall peak value of the input signal just fully loads the quantiser. There will, however, be a large variation in the short-term peak value of the input signal. For example, the voice level in one conversation may vary between a whisper (with a short-term peak value much less than C) and a shout when the peak value equals C. The SQNR will be unacceptably low during the 'whisper' intervals if 8-bit linear ADC is employed.

To overcome this problem we derived a non-linear — more specifically logarithmic — PCM scheme that has a constant SQNR at all signal levels, given by Eq. (6.22). Implementing this ideal log-PCM scheme, with $N = 2^k = 256$ and $K = 5.5$ — see Eq. (6.25) and (6.30) — gives a constant SQNR:

$$SQNR = 10\log\left(\frac{3N^2}{K^2}\right) = 10\log\left(\frac{3\times256^2}{5.5^2}\right)$$
$$= 38 \text{ dB}$$

However, for practical implementation it was necessary to modify the ideal log-PCM in two ways, resulting in the A-law and μ-law PCM schemes. Firstly, small input values were uniformly quantised using a small step size, which is equivalent to using a linear compression curve in the region where the input value $x \to 0$, as discussed earlier. Secondly, the step size Δ does not decrease continuously with x as required by the ideal log-PCM. Rather, Δ only changes in discrete steps and is held constant within specified segments of the input signal, listed in Table 6.4. This corresponds to a piecewise linear approximation. How is SQNR affected by these modifications?

Obviously, the SQNR of (8-bit) A-law and μ-law PCM schemes will not be constant at 38 dB as in the ideal case. Let us obtain an expression for the SQNR of an input signal with a (scaled) peak value

$$V_p = X_{S\max}, \qquad S = 0, 1, 2, ..., 7 \tag{6.47}$$

where $X_{S\max}$ is the top level of segment S in Table 6.4. For example, $X_{2\max} = 224$ for μ-law and 128 for A-law. It follows from Worked example 6.1 that

$$\text{Signal power } = \begin{cases} X_{S\max}^2/2, & \text{Sine wave input} \\ X_{S\max}^2/3, & \text{Uniform pdf input} \end{cases} \tag{6.48}$$

Each segment s is divided into 16 quantisation intervals (numbered from $l = 0$ to 15), with a constant interval spacing or step size Δ_s. It follows from Eq. (6.5) that the MSQE of segment s is given by

$$MSQE_s = \frac{\Delta_s^2}{12}\sum_{l=0}^{15} P_{s,l} \tag{6.49}$$

where $P_{s,l}$ is the probability that the input sample lies in interval l of segment s. The total MSQE is obtained by summing Eq. (6.49) over all the segments covered by the input signal:

$$MSQE = \sum_{s=0}^{S}\left[\frac{\Delta_s^2}{12}\sum_{l=0}^{15} P_{s,l}\right] \tag{6.50}$$

The SQNR can then be obtained as the ratio (expressed in dB) between the signal power in Eq. (6.48) and the noise power in Eq. (6.50). To derive an explicit expression for SQNR, let us assume that the input signal (of peak value V_p) has a uniform pdf. Then,

$$P_{s,l} = \Delta_s/V_p$$

So that, from Eq. (6.47), (6.49) and (6.50),

$$\text{MSQE}_s = \frac{4\Delta_s^3}{3V_p}$$

$$\text{MSQE} = \frac{4}{3V_p}\sum_{s=0}^{S}\Delta_s^3 = \frac{4}{3X_{S\max}}\sum_{s=0}^{S}\Delta_s^3$$

and

$$\text{SQNR} = 10\log\left(\frac{\text{Signal power}}{\text{MSQE}}\right)$$

$$= 10\log\left(X_{S\max}^3 \bigg/ 4\sum_{s=0}^{S}\Delta_s^3\right) \qquad (6.51)$$

$$= 30\log(X_{S\max}) - 10\log\left(\sum_{s=0}^{S}\Delta_s^3\right) - 6.02\text{ dB}$$

Equation (6.51) applies to both A-law and μ-law PCM. It gives the SQNR of a signal of peak value $V_p = X_{S\max}$ — the upper boundary of segment S. Note that this result is not affected by normalisation. For example, we presented the A-law scheme based on a quantiser range of ± 4096. The above expression for SQNR holds even when the quantiser range is arbitrarily scaled to a different limit (such as ± 1), provided step sizes are also scaled by the same factor to retain the shape of the compression curve.

The result of Eq. (6.51) is presented in Tables 6.5 and 6.6 for A-law and μ-law PCM schemes and in Fig. 6.13 where the peak input levels have been extended to include values below $X_{0\max}$. The curves of SQNR versus peak input signal level for linear ADCs with $k = 8$, 12 and 13 bits/sample are also shown in Fig. 6.13, from which we make the following important observations.

Table 6.5 SQNR in A-law and linear PCMs versus input signal level.

Segment s	Peak input level (normalised)	Peak input level (dB)	SQNR (dB)	
			A-law PCM	8-bit linear PCM
7	4096	0	38.55	48.16
6	2048	−6.02	38.55	42.14
5	1024	−12.04	38.55	36.12
4	512	−18.06	38.55	30.10
3	256	−24.08	38.50	24.08
2	128	−30.10	38.17	18.06
1	64	−36.12	36.12	12.04
0	32	−42.14	30.10	6.02

Table 6.6: SQNR in μ-law and linear PCMs versus input signal level.

Segment s	Peak input level (normalised)	Peak input level (dB)	SQNR (dB)	
			μ-law PCM	8-bit linear PCM
7	8160	0	38.50	48.16
6	4064	−6.05	38.45	42.11
5	2016	−12.14	38.35	36.02
4	992	−18.30	38.14	29.86
3	480	−24.61	3,7.71	23.55
2	224	−31.23	36.82	16.93
1	96	−38.59	34.87	9.57
0	32	−48.13	30.10	0.03

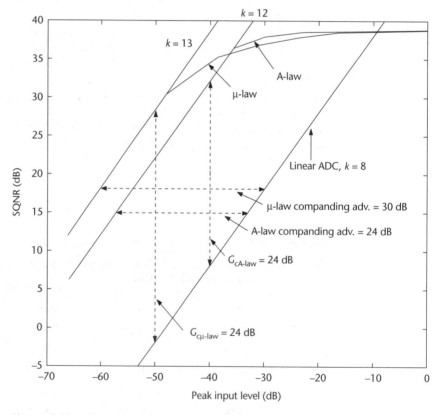

Figure 6.13 SQNR versus input signal level for A-law, μ-law and linear ADC.

- A-law PCM maintains a constant SQNR of about 38 dB over a wider range of peak input levels than μ-law PCM. It is interesting to observe that the SQNR of A-law PCM at a peak input level $V_p = -36$ dB ($= X_{1max}$) is 36 dB, which represents a drop of only 2 dB. On the other hand, the SQNR of an 8-bit linear PCM at this input level has fallen to an unacceptable value of 12 dB. The input level X_{1max} marks roughly the beginning of the linear portion of the A-law compression curve. More specifically, Eq. (6.29) shows that the A-law curve is linear in the region $x \leq 1/A$ or -38.9 dB, which corresponds to input values $X \leq 46.76$ when the normalised range ± 4096 is used, with $A = 87.6$. However, in the practical implementation of this curve using a piecewise linear approximation, the terminal linear portion starts slightly earlier at $X = 64$ or -36.12 dB.

- The SQNR of (8-bit) A-law PCM at input levels below -36 dB is the same as that of a 12-bit linear PCM. This agrees with our earlier observation that small input values are finely quantised at the equivalent of 12 bits/sample. Inputs to the A-law quantiser at levels below -36 dB effectively see a linear PCM of (normalised) step size $\Delta = 2$, and therefore the SQNR decreases linearly with the peak input level in step with that of a 12-bit linear PCM.

- In the case of a μ-law PCM, small input levels below -48 dB have the same SQNR as a 13-bit linear PCM, which again confirms our earlier observation that small input samples are quantised in μ-law at the resolution of a 13-bit linear PCM.

- The actual companding gains of A-law and μ-law PCM schemes are indicated in Fig. 6.13 as follows:

$$G_{cA\text{-law}} = 24 \text{ dB}$$
$$G_{c\mu\text{-law}} = 30 \text{ dB}$$

  As discussed earlier, every 6 dB of companding gain is exchanged for a saving of 1 bit/sample. This is the reason why, at small input levels, μ-law PCM delivers the SQNR of a 13-bits/sample linear PCM using only 8 bits/sample — a saving of 5 bits/sample. Similarly, A-law PCM achieves the SQNR of a 12-bits/sample PCM using only 8 bits/sample — a saving of 4 bits/sample.

- Companding gain and companding advantage are numerically equal in the region of small input levels.

- Improvements in the SQNR of A-law and μ-law PCM at low input levels have been achieved at a price. The larger input levels are more coarsely quantised in log-PCM, compared to linear PCM. The effect of this can be seen in Table 6.6, which shows that, for a large input signal that fully loads the quantiser, the SQNR of an 8-bit linear PCM is better by about 10 dB than that of log-PCM. However, log-PCM gives a subjectively more satisfying result, maintaining a constant SQNR over a wide input range.

6.3 Differential PCM (DPCM)

It was pointed out earlier from Eq. (6.9) that SQNR is inversely proportional to the square of the quantiser range. This means that an improvement in SQNR can be realised by reducing the range of sample values presented to the quantiser. Each 6 dB improvement in SQNR can be exchanged for a unit reduction in the number of bits/sample so that the same SQNR as in a PCM system is achieved using fewer bits/sample and hence a smaller transmission bandwidth. In fact the underlying principle in all DPCM, low bit rate speech coding and data compression techniques is to avoid the transmission of redundant information. The original signal is processed in some way at the transmitter to obtain a signal of much reduced information content that requires a proportionately lower transmission bandwidth. An acceptably close copy of the original signal is obtained at the receiver by processing the received signal to recover the full information.

In differential pulse code modulation (DPCM) the required quantiser range is reduced by encoding the difference $e(nT_s)$ between the actual signal sample $s(nT_s)$ and a predicted value $\hat{s}(nT_s)$ generated by a predictor circuit:

$$e(nT_s) = s(nT_s) - \hat{s}(nT_s) \tag{6.52}$$

In a properly designed predictor the error $e(nT_s)$ is small, allowing the number of quantiser levels 2^k and hence the number of bits/sample k to be significantly reduced. The sampling rate f_s may be chosen not just to satisfy the sampling theorem but also to be above the rate that would be used in ordinary PCM. This maintains a high correlation between adjacent samples and improves prediction accuracy, thereby keeping $e(nT_s)$ small. However, k is reduced by a larger factor than f_s is increased, so that the bit rate $R = kf_s$ is lower than that of a PCM system of the same SQNR.

Figure 6.14 shows a block diagram of a DPCM system. The low-pass filter serves to minimise aliasing by limiting the bandwidth of the input signal before it is sampled at intervals T_s in a sample-and-hold circuit. A summing device produces the difference or error $e(nT_s)$ between the sampled signal $s(nT_s)$ and the output of a predictor. It is this error signal that is quantised as $e_q(nT_s)$ and encoded to produce an output DPCM bit stream. If the analogue signal $s(t)$ changes too rapidly, the predictor will be unable to track the sequence of samples $s(nT_s)$ and the error signal $e(nT_s)$ will exceed the range expected at the quantiser input, resulting in clipping. This type of distortion is known as *slope overload*.

The variance of the error signal $e(nT_s)$ is much smaller than that of $s(nT_s)$. Thus, $e(nT_s)$ can be more accurately represented than $s(nT_s)$ using the same number of quantisation levels. This implies improved SQNR for the same bit rate. Alternatively, $e(nT_s)$ can be represented with the same accuracy as $s(nT_s)$ using fewer quantisation levels, which implies the same SQNR at a reduced bit rate. Note from the block diagram that the input of the predictor at the transmitter is the original sample plus a small quantisation error:

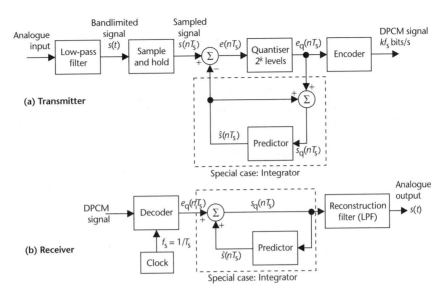

(a) Transmitter

(b) Receiver

Figure 6.14 DPCM system.

$$s_q(nT_s) = \hat{s}(nT_s) + e_q(nT_s)$$
$$= \hat{s}(nT_s) + e(nT_s) + q(nT_s)$$
$$= \hat{s}(nT_s) + s(nT_s) - \hat{s}(nT_s) + q(nT_s) \qquad (6.53)$$
$$= s(nT_s) + q(nT_s)$$

where $q(nT_s)$ is the quantisation error associated with the nth sample.

Identical predictors are used at both transmitter and receiver. At the receiver, the DPCM bit stream is passed through a decoder to recover the quantised error sequence $e_q(nT_s)$. This is added to the output of a local predictor to give a sequence of samples $s_q(nT_s)$, according to the first line of Eq. (6.53), which when passed through a low-pass reconstruction filter yields the original analogue signal $s(t)$, degraded only slightly by quantisation noise.

The predictor is a tapped-delay-line filter, as shown in Fig. 6.15. Using the quantised samples $s_q(nT_s)$, rather than the unquantised samples $s(nT_s)$, as the predictor input is important to avoid the accumulation of quantisation errors. The predictor provides an estimate or prediction of the nth sample $\hat{s}(nT_s)$ from a linear combination of p past values of $s_q(nT_s)$. It is therefore referred to as a linear prediction filter of order p:

$$\hat{s}(nT_s) = a_1 s_q(nT_s - T_s) + a_2 s_q(nT_s - 2T_s) + \cdots$$
$$= \sum_{j=1}^{p} a_j s_q(nT_s - jT_s) \qquad (6.54)$$

Note that, taking $t = nT_s$ as the current sampling instant, then $s(nT_s)$ denotes the current sample of signal $s(t)$, $s(nT_s - T_s)$ denotes the previous sample — at time $t = (n-1)T_s$, and $s(nT_s - jT_s)$ denotes a past sample at time

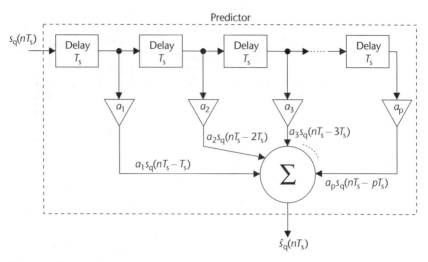

Figure 6.15 Predictor realised using a tapped-delay-line filter.

$t = (n - j)T_s$. The optimum values for the coefficients a_j (also called *tap gains*) depend on the input signal. In the simplest case, all the coefficients are equal, i.e. $a_1 = a_2 = ... = a_p$, and the predicted value is a scaled sum or integration of the last p samples. The DPCM can then be implemented using an integrator connected as indicated in dotted outline in Fig. 6.14.

With the exception of delta modulators discussed later, DPCM systems are in general more complex than PCM since they require a prediction filter in addition to all the other components of a PCM system. Furthermore, they are subject to quantisation noise as in PCM, and to *slope overload distortion*, which is not present in PCM.

However, DPCM offers an important advantage over PCM in that it requires a much lower bit rate than a PCM system of a comparable SQNR. The ITU-T has adopted a 32 kbit/s DPCM standard (identified as G.726) for voice telephony. This corresponds to using $k = 4$ bits/sample at a sampling rate $f_s = 8$ kHz. The standard provides for operations at other bit rates, namely 16, 24 and 40 kbit/s (corresponding respectively to $k = 2$, 3 and 5 bits/sample at the same sampling rate). This allows transmission to be adapted to available channel capacity. Another ITU-T standard (G.722) specifies the use of DPCM to transmit wideband audio (of bandwidth 7 kHz) at the same bit rate (64 kbit/s) employed by standard PCM for standard telephony speech (of 3.4 kHz bandwidth). In this case, $k = 4$ and $f_s = 16$ kHz. Wideband audio gives a significant improvement in the fidelity of the received sound for applications such as audio conferences and loud-speaking telephones.

There are two special cases of DPCM worth considering further, one known as *delta modulation* in which $k = 1$, and the other known as *adaptive DPCM* in which the step size is adjusted depending on the difference signal $e(nT_s)$, in order to minimise noise arising from slope overload distortion and quantisation error.

6.3.1 Adaptive differential pulse code modulation (ADPCM)

In the ITU-T standards referred to above, adaptive quantisation and adaptive prediction are employed to reduce the required number of bits/sample from $k = 8$ for standard PCM to about $k = 4$. Such a system is referred to as adaptive differential pulse code modulation (ADPCM). The speech quality of 32 kbit/s ADPCM is about the same as 64 kbit/s PCM. Ordinary DPCM (with $k = 4$, $f_s = 8$ kHz) delivers a poorer quality because the fixed step size Δ would have to be large to avoid overload distortion, or with a small step size the prediction error $e(nT_s)$ would frequently exceed the quantiser range. It is for this reason that ordinary DPCM is not used in practice.

Adaptive quantisation uses a time-varying step size Δ in the quantiser. The value of Δ is changed in proportion to the variance of the prediction error, which is the input signal of the quantiser. In this way the ratio between signal power and quantisation noise power (or SQNR) in the adaptive quantiser is maintained at an acceptable and approximately constant value.

Adaptive prediction employs samples of the quantiser output as well as past prediction errors to compute optimum values for the predictor coefficients a_j. This leads to a significant improvement in prediction accuracy, and allows fewer bits to be used to code the small prediction errors involved.

ITU standard G.721 specifies a transcoding algorithm in which the coder takes A-law or μ-law PCM bit stream as input and yields an ADPCM output bit stream. At the receiver, a decoder accepts the ADPCM format and converts it back to PCM.

6.3.2 Delta modulation

Figure 6.16 shows the block diagrams of delta modulation (DM) transmitter and receiver. By comparing Fig. 6.16 with the DPCM block diagram in Fig. 6.14, it can be seen that DM is a special case of DPCM with a number of distinctive features. There are only two quantisation levels (i.e. $N = 2$) in the quantiser, labelled as binary 0 and 1, and separated by the step size Δ as shown in Fig. 6.17. With $N = 2$, we know that $k = 1$ bit/sample. The difference signal $e(nT_s)$ is approximated to the nearer of the two levels, and at each sampling instant the encoder output is a single bit, which is a binary 1 if $e(nT_s)$ is positive and a binary 0 if $e(nT_s)$ is negative. Let us examine the quantisation error and important design parameters of the DM scheme.

6.3.2.1 Quantisation error

To address this issue we assume that there is no overload distortion, so that the difference signal e lies within the range $\pm\Delta$. Let P_1 be the probability that the difference signal is positive and P_2 the probability that it is negative. Then

$$P_1 + P_2 = 1$$

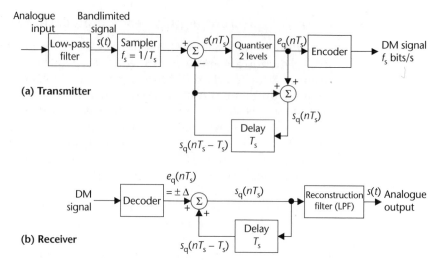

(a) Transmitter

(b) Receiver

Figure 6.16 DM transmitter and receiver.

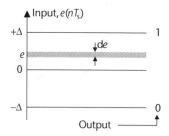

Figure 6.17 Quantisation levels in DM

Consider first the values of e in the positive range 0 to Δ. These are all quantised to output level Δ (represented as binary 1) with a quantisation error $e - \Delta$. The maximum quantisation error is Δ, which is twice that of PCM. Following the same arguments leading to Eq. (6.4), we obtain the mean square quantisation error (MSQE) for positive differences.

$$\text{MSQE}_1 = \int_0^\Delta (e - \Delta)^2 P_1 \, de/\Delta = \frac{P_1 \Delta^2}{3}$$

Similarly, the MSQE for negative differences is $\text{MSQE}_2 = P_2 \Delta^2/3$. The total quantisation noise power is therefore

$$
\begin{aligned}
\text{MSQE} &= \text{MSQE}_1 + \text{MSQE}_2 \\
&= \frac{P_1 \Delta^2}{3} + \frac{P_2 \Delta^2}{3} = \frac{\Delta^2}{3}(P_1 + P_2) \\
&= \frac{\Delta^2}{3}
\end{aligned}
\tag{6.55}
$$

Note that this is four times the noise power obtained in Eq. (6.6) for linear ADC and PCM systems. However, the noise power in this case is distributed over a frequency range from 0 to f_s, which is much wider than the receiver bandwidth B. The effective noise power is therefore a fraction B/f_s of the MSQE. Using the minimum allowed step size obtained below in Eq. (6.58) for a sinusoidal signal of peak value V_m and frequency f_m, we obtain

$$\text{SQNR} = \frac{\text{Signal power}}{\text{Effective noise power}}$$

$$= \frac{\frac{1}{2}V_m^2}{(\Delta^2/3)(B/f_s)} = \frac{3f_sV_m^2}{2B} \times \left(\frac{f_s}{2\pi f_m V_m}\right)^2 \tag{6.56}$$

$$= \frac{3f_s^3}{8\pi^2 B f_m^2}$$

It can be seen that the SQNR of a DM system increases as the cube of f_s, so that doubling the sampling frequency yields a 9 dB improvement in SQNR.

6.3.2.2 Prediction filter

A DM system uses a prediction filter of order $p = 1$, with tap gain $a_1 = 1$. It follows from Eq. (6.54) and (6.53) that the predicted sample is simply the previous sample plus a small quantisation noise:

$$\hat{s}(nT_s) = s_q(nT_s - T_s)$$
$$= s(nT_s - T_s) + q(nT_s - T_s) \tag{6.57}$$

The predictor is therefore a delay line, with delay equal to the sampling interval T_s.

6.3.2.3 Design parameters

A sampling rate f_s, much higher than Nyquist frequency, is employed in DM to reduce the difference $e(nT_s)$ between adjacent samples, thereby avoiding overload distortion and minimising quantisation noise. To see what factors influence the choice of f_s, consider a sinusoidal input signal

$$s(t) = V_m \sin(2\pi f_m t)$$

The maximum change in $s(t)$ during one sampling interval T_s is given by

$$\left|\frac{ds(t)}{dt}\right|_{\max} \times T_s = 2\pi f_m V_m T_s = \frac{2\pi f_m V_m}{f_s}$$

To avoid overload distortion, this change must not exceed the step size Δ. Thus,

$$\frac{2\pi f_m V_m}{f_s} \leq \Delta \tag{6.58}$$

Equation (6.58) is an important result, which provides the interrelationship that must be satisfied by the parameters of a DM system, namely sampling frequency, step size, message signal frequency and message signal amplitude. It is apparent that irrespective of the values of the other parameters, Eq. (6.58) can be satisfied by making f_s sufficiently large — the penalty being increased bandwidth.

6.3.2.4 Merits and demerits of DM

DM has two important advantages over standard PCM.

1. It can be realised using a very simple codec that does not require the type of quantiser and encoder found in PCM. It is therefore more reliable and more economical. The quantiser is a simple pulse generator (or comparator) that gives an output $+V$ volts (or binary 1) when its input $e(nT_s)$ is positive and $-V$ volts (or binary 0) when $e(nT_s)$ is negative. The predictor uses only a single tap gain and may be replaced by an integrator, as discussed earlier. A simple analogue RC low-pass filter could be used. The output voltage of the integrator rises or falls by one step Δ in response to each pulse input. This enables the integrator to track the input voltage. The receiver then uses a similar integrator whose output rises by Δ when its input is a binary 1 and falls by the same amount when its input is binary 0. In this way both integrators produce the same staircase waveform $s_q(nT_s)$, and a low-pass reconstruction filter will easily smooth out the integrator output at the receiver to yield the original analogue signal. Figure 6.18 shows a block diagram of the simplified DM codec, and the associated waveforms including the generated DM bit stream for an arbitrary input signal $s(t)$.

2. DM is more robust to transmission errors than PCM, and intelligibility can be maintained at bit error rates as high as one in a hundred (i.e. 10^{-2}). Every transmitted bit has the same weight and the maximum error due to one bit being received in error is equal to a quantiser step size Δ. In PCM, on the other hand, an error in the MSB can have a significant effect on the received signal, causing an error ranging in magnitude from Δ to $2^k\Delta$. This robustness to noise makes DM the preferred technique in certain military applications. The USA military and NATO have operational DM systems at 16 and 32 kbit/s.

DM has, however, the following disadvantages:

1. Oversampling with $f_s \gg 2f_m$ is required to allow the use of a small step size Δ while ensuring that the difference between adjacent samples rarely exceeds Δ. With 1 bit/sample and f_s samples per second, the bit rate of DM is f_s bits/s, which may in some cases exceed that of standard PCM and therefore require a larger bandwidth.

2. With a fixed step size, the maximum error per sample is constant at $\pm\Delta$ for all samples. However, while the quantisation noise power is fixed, the signal power varies across the range of input levels. Thus SQNR varies with input level and may fall to unacceptably small values at low signal levels. The useful dynamic range of input signals over which the SQNR does not change significantly is therefore severely limited.

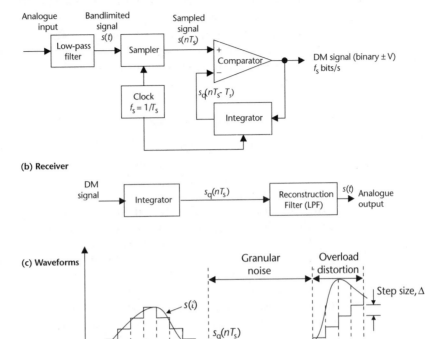

Figure 6.18 Simplified DM system and waveforms.

3. When there is a roughly constant portion of the input signal $s(t)$, the staircase approximation $s_q(nT_s)$ hunts about this level as shown in Fig. 6.18(c). This gives rise to a type of noise known as *granular noise*, which can only be minimised by making Δ as small as possible, subject to Eq. (6.58). However, a small Δ makes the system prone to overload distortion, as discussed below. Granular noise manifests itself in the DM bit stream as a string of alternating 0s and 1s.

4. Fig. 6.18(c) also shows an incidence of *overload distortion* in which the input waveform $s(t)$ changes too quickly to be tracked by $s_q(nT_s)$. To avoid overload distortion, Eq. (6.58) must be satisfied in the choice of step size and sampling frequency. This requires one of the following options:

   (a) Make f_s sufficiently large, so that $f_s \geq 2\pi f_m V_m / \Delta$. This increases transmission bandwidth requirements.

   (b) Limit the message signal amplitude to $V_m \leq \Delta f_s / 2\pi f_m$, which limits the allowable dynamic range of the input signal. Note that the allowable peak value V_m decreases with the frequency f_m of the input signal.

(c) Increase the step size to $\Delta \geq 2\pi f_m V_m / f_s$. This increases granular noise, however.

(d) Limit the input signal frequencies to $f_m \leq \Delta f_s / 2\pi V_m$. The problem here is that the range of f_m depends on the type of information signal and cannot be significantly reduced without compromising fidelity.

6.3.2.5 Adaptive delta modulation (ADM)

We have seen the conflicting requirement of a large step size Δ to combat overload distortion, and a small step size to minimise granular noise. Adaptive delta modulation (ADM) provides for the control of both types of noise by varying the step size. This technique actually belongs in the general class of adaptive PCM (ADPCM). It is introduced here to show how both overload distortion and granular noise may be reduced.

In basic ADM, the step size is changed in discrete amounts. To start with, the step size Δ is set to a very small value δ to minimise granular noise. This (the smallest) step size is maintained for as long as the DM bit stream consists of a string of alternating 1s and 0s, or two successive 1s, or two successive 0s. After encountering three successive 1s or 0s the step size is increased to $\Delta = 2\delta$, and Δ is increased even further to 4δ when four consecutive 1s or 0s occur. The larger step sizes allow the integrator output, which is the staircase approximation $s_q(nT_s)$, to catch up more quickly with the sequence of input samples $s(nT_s)$.

ADM has also been implemented with the step size continuously varied in proportion to the input signal. This variant of ADM is referred to as *continuously variable slope delta modulation* (CVSDM).

6.3.2.6 Delta sigma modulation

It was noted earlier that the amplitude of the higher frequency components in the input signal must be minimised to avoid overload distortion. This can be done by first passing the input signal through a low-pass filter whose gain decreases linearly with frequency. Recall that such a LPF is actually an integrator. At the receiver, a high-pass filter of linearly increasing gain response, which is a differentiator, must be employed to remove the spectral distortion imposed at the transmitter. However, a DM receiver already contains an integrator. The resulting receiver will consist of an integrator followed by a differentiator, and the two components can therefore be eliminated altogether. This leaves a low-pass reconstruction filter as the only component required at the receiver. The scheme described above is shown in Fig. 6.19, and is traditionally known as *delta sigma modulation* (DSM), but should more appropriately be called *sigma delta modulation* (SDM). SDM allows the use of a greatly simplified receiver, and the transmission of signals with allowable peak levels that are independent of frequency.

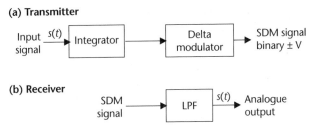

(a) Transmitter

Input signal $s(t)$ → Integrator → Delta modulator → SDM signal binary ± V

(b) Receiver

SDM signal → LPF → $s(t)$ Analogue output

Figure 6.19 Sigma delta modulation system (SDM).

6.4

6.4 Low bit rate speech coding

The purpose of low bit rate (LBR) speech coding is to achieve a digital representation of speech signals with acceptable fidelity using as few bits as possible. This is essential in bandwidth- and/or power-limited voice communication services such as mobile communications and Internet telephony, and in voice storage services such as voicemail, store-and-forward messaging and automatic voice response systems. Transmission bandwidth and storage capacity requirements increase proportionately with bit rate. For example, standard PCM with a bit rate of 64 kbit/s requires a minimum transmission bandwidth of 32 kHz, and a storage capacity of 1.44 Mbyte for a call of duration 3 minutes. If we somehow manage to reduce the bit rate to say 6.4 kbit/s, then the bandwidth and storage capacity requirements fall proportionately to 3.2 kHz (minimum) and 144 kbyte, respectively.

Figure 6.20 shows the trade-offs involved in LBR speech coding. The main characteristics against which the performance of a speech codec is judged include the following.

● *Quality*: In general, the achievable speech quality falls as the bit rate is reduced. How much degradation there is depends on the type of algorithm used to reduce the bit rate. Obviously, if a bit rate of 32 kbit/s were achieved simply by reducing the number of bits/sample from $k = 8$ to $k = 4$ in standard PCM, there would be a drop in SQNR of 24 dB and hence a significant degradation in quality. However, 32 kbit/s ADPCM and even some 16 kbit/s codecs provide speech quality that is practically indistinguishable from that of 64 kbit/s PCM.

Speech quality is usually specified using a subjective mean opinion score (MOS), which is obtained by averaging the judgement of a large number of listeners expressed in the form of a score on a scale from 1 to 5. Table 6.7 provides a classification of the scores. Note, however, that the MOS recorded for a particular speech codec can vary significantly with tests and language. A MOS < 3.0 corresponds to speech of synthetic quality, which may have high intelligibility (i.e. the speech is understandable), but sounds unnatural — lacking the attributes that allow recognition of the speaker and the speaker's emotion. Communication quality speech of MOS between 3.5 and 4.0 contains perceptible, but not annoying distortion; while speech with perceptible and

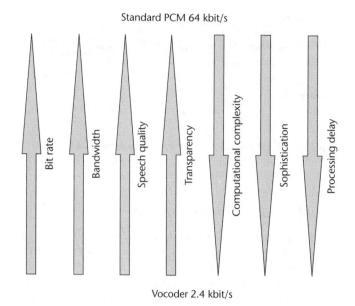

Figure 6.20 Trade-offs in low bit rate speech coding.

Table 6.7 Speech quality using mean opinion score (MOS).

MOS	Quality description	Quality class
1	Bad, unacceptable	Synthetic
2	Poor	
3	Fair	Professional Communication
4	Good	Near-transparent, toll quality
5	Excellent	

slightly annoying distortion could be classed as professional quality, with MOS between 3.0 and 3.5. MOS values in excess of 4.0 indicate high-quality and natural-sounding speech with practically imperceptible distortion. A-law and μ-law PCM produce high-quality speech with MOS of about 4.2. MOS scores of 4.0 and above are regarded as *toll quality*. A *vocoder* (discussed below) produces synthetic speech with MOS of about 2.2.

● *Transparency*: Significant reductions in bit rate are achieved by exploiting signal characteristics that are specific to speech. Such codecs will cause excessive distortion to non-voice signals such as voiceband data modem signals. It then becomes essential that non-voice signals are recognised and diverted from the codec for processing using a different algorithm. In general, a codec's transparency — its ability to handle both speech and non-speech signals — improves with bit rate.

- *Computational complexity*: The amount of computation required to maintain acceptable quality in LBR coded speech increases significantly as the bit rate is reduced. Sophisticated digital signal processing (DSP) hardware must be employed to minimise processing delay, and this increases both codec cost and operational power consumption. The latter is of concern, especially in battery-operated portable units. However, due to advances in integrated circuit technology, DSP units capable of increasingly complex operations are now available in the market at very low costs.

- *Robustness to transmission errors*: As the original speech signal is represented using fewer and fewer bits, the role of each transmitted bit becomes more crucial, and therefore the impact of transmission errors is more drastic. For example, a single bit error in a vocoder could render a 20 ms speech segment unintelligible. By contrast, the impact of a single bit error in standard PCM is restricted to one sample and will be virtually imperceptible if it involves the least significant bit (LSB). Error protection of at least some of the more crucial bits is therefore required in LBR codecs. It is for this reason that the full-rate GSM speech codec operating at 13 kbit/s devotes an additional 3 kbit/s for error protection.

- *Processing delay*: Most LBR codecs have to accumulate a statistically significant block of samples (typically over 10–25 ms) in a storage buffer, from which certain parameters are extracted. To this *buffering* or *frame delay* is added the time it takes to complete the processing of the accumulated samples. The total *processing delay* may be up to 3 times the frame delay, depending on computational complexity. An isolated delay of this magnitude may contribute to an increase in sidetone, but is otherwise imperceptible and perfectly acceptable to a user. However, if such a codec is connected to the public telephone network, or several of them are present in a long-distance link, then the total delay may lead to annoying echo, necessitating the use of echo control circuits (e.g. echo suppressors or cancellers).

In addition to the above characteristics, other important considerations include *robustness to background noise*, and the effect of *tandem operation* with other codecs. The latter arises because, in many cases, a speech codec has to operate on the output of coders located in other parts of the network. The distortion resulting from such multiple coding/decoding must not be excessive. The priority assigned to each of these characteristics is determined by the application. For example, processing delay is not crucial in applications such as voice messaging and videoconferencing. In the latter, the accompanying video signal usually has a much larger processing delay than that of speech. Extra delay would normally be inserted in the speech processing to synchronise with the processed video.

Table 6.8 provides a list of some of the most important speech codecs, with their bit rates (excluding any additional error protection bits), and a rough indication of perceived quality. Each coder is specified by the name of its processing algorithm, followed by a reference to the standard or

Table 6.8 Speech coding standards.

Speech coder	Coder class	Bit rate (kbit/s)	Quality	Year
PCM, G.711	Waveform	64	Toll	1972
ADPCM, G.726	Waveform	16, 24, 32, 40	Synthetic, professional, toll, toll	1991
Embedded ADPCM, G.727	Waveform	16, 24, 32, 40	Synthetic, professional, toll, toll	1991
SB-ADPCM, G.722, for 7-kHz speech	Waveform	48, 56, 64	Communication, toll, toll	1988
IMBE, Inmarsat-M	Vocoder	4.15	Professional	1990
LPC–10, FS1015; MELP	Vocoder; Vocoder	2.4; 2.4	Synthetic; Professional	1976; 1996
APC, Inmarsat-B	Hybrid	16	Toll	1994
MPE-LPC, BT Skyphone	Hybrid	9.6	Professional	1989
RPE-LTP, GSM full-rate	Hybrid	13	Communication	1989
CELP, FS1016	Hybrid	4.8	Professional	1991
VSELP, NA cellular	Hybrid	8	Communication	1992
LD-CELP, G.728	Hybrid	16	Toll	1992
VSELP, JDC full-rate	Hybrid	6.8	Communication	1993
PSI-CELP, JDC half-rate	Hybrid	3.45	Communication	1993
QCELP, NA CDMA	Hybrid	1, 2, 4, 8	Professional	1993
VSELP, GSM half-rate	Hybrid	5.6	Professional	1994
ACELP, GSM-EFR	Hybrid	13	Toll	1995
CSA-CELP, G.729	Hybrid	8	Toll	1995
A & MP-MLQ CELP, G.723	Hybrid	5.3 & 6.3	Communication	1995

system under which the coder has been adopted. The G.7xx series are ITU-T standards. Three broad classes of coders are indicated in the table, namely *waveform coders*, *vocoders* and *hybrid coders*.

6.4.1 Waveform coders

A waveform coder attempts an accurate digital representation of the speech waveform. If this is done directly in the time domain, the coder is described as a *predictive coder*. It is also possible to first divide the speech signal into contiguous frequency bands using bandpass filters, before coding each sub-band using a separate waveform coder. The coder is then said to be a *frequency domain coder*. The main advantage of such a sub-band (SB) coding approach is that the number of bits/sample assigned to each sub-band can be varied according to the information content of the band. Those sub-bands with negligible information content or energy can be skipped altogether. The result is that a speech quality comparable to that of predictive waveform coders can be achieved at a lower bit rate. Waveform coders are generally the least complicated of the three classes of coders. They introduce the lowest processing delays, and produce speech of high quality, but require high bit rates ≥ 16 kbit/s. The distortions at lower bit rates are excessive, and other techniques must be adopted in order to reduce the bit rate any further while maintaining acceptable quality.

The most important examples of predictive waveform coders include DM, PCM and ADPCM, which have been discussed earlier. The ITU-T G.726 standard, which effectively superseded the G.721 (32 kbit/s ADPCM) standard, provides ADPCM speech coding at variable rates, namely 40, 32, 24 and 16 kbit/s. This allows the flexibility of sacrificing speech quality inorder to maintain transmission under heavy traffic conditions. The ITU-T G.727 provides for coding at the same variable bit rates as in G.726, but uses a technique known as embedded ADPCM. This involves 32, 16, 8 or 4 uniform quantisation levels, the levels for coarse quantisation being a subset of levels in finer quantisation. Using all 32 levels, requiring 5 bits/sample, gives the best speech quality at a bit rate of 40 kbit/s. As traffic load increases, the network can adopt lower bit rates by simply discarding one, two, or three of the less significant bits. Discarding the least significant bit, for example, effects coarser quantisation using only 16 of the 32 possible levels, with the step size doubled.

The ITU-T G.722 standard for coding wideband (7 kHz) speech at rates of 64, 56 and 48 kbit/s is a good example of a sub-band waveform coder. The input speech signal, sampled at 16 kHz with a resolution of 14 bits/sample, is split into two 4 kHz bands. The lower band, which contains most of the information is sampled at 8 kHz and coded using embedded-ADPCM at 6, 5 or 4 bits/sample. This yields lower-band coding bit rates of 48, 40 or 32 kbit/s. ADPCM at a resolution of 2 bits/sample is used for the upper band, which gives a bit rate of 16 kbit/s. Thus, a total bit rate of 64, 56 or 48 kbit/s is achieved.

6.4.2 Vocoders

A *vocoder*, or *vocal tract coder*, does not code the speech waveform at all. Rather, it explicitly models the vocal tract as a filter in order to represent the speech production mechanism. At the receiver, the representation is simply animated to reproduce a close version of the original speech signal. The main source of degradation in reproduced speech quality is not quantisation error, but the use of a model that cannot accurately represent the speech production mechanism of the vocal tract. For example, each segment of speech (of duration say 20 ms) is classified as either *voiced* or *unvoiced* and reproduced at the receiver by exciting the filter with a pulse train or random noise, respectively. In practice, the speech segment will be partially voiced and unvoiced. This 'black or white' classification alone gives a vocoder a synthetic speech quality. Vocoders do give good intelligibility at very low bit rates (e.g. 2.4 and 4.15 kbit/s), and therefore are widely used in applications that require intelligibility without a strong need for speaker identity/emotion recognition. However, they involve complex processing and introduce delays above about 20 ms. The vocoders listed in Table 6.8 are briefly discussed below.

6.4.2.1 IMBE

The *improved multiband excited* (IMBE) vocoder was adopted as the speech codec in Inmarsat's satellite mobile communication system standard-M. It operates as follows. Filters are used to break the speech signal into narrow frequency bands, each spanning about three harmonics. The energy in each band is measured and a voicing decision is made that identifies each band as voiced or unvoiced. This information (namely, the energy and voice flag of each band) is coded and transmitted. At the receiver, each filter is excited at its identified energy level using a sinusoidal oscillator for a voiced band and a noise source for an unvoiced band. The synthesised speech signal is obtained as the sum of the output of all the filters.

6.4.2.2 LPC

The other type of vocoder is the *linear predictive coding* (LPC) vocoder LPC-10, which was developed by the US Department of Defense (DoD) and adopted as federal standard 1015. Figure 6.21 shows a block diagram of the speech synthesis model. LPC-10 uses a predictor (i.e. filter) of order $p = 10$ for voiced speech and $p = 4$ for unvoiced speech. At the transmitter, each 22.5 ms segment of the speech signal is analysed to obtain the following parameters:

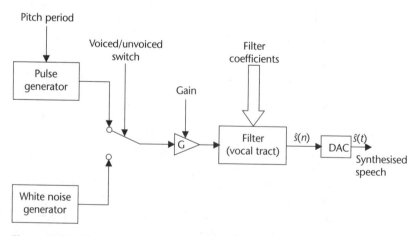

Figure 6.21 LPC speech synthesis model.

1. A voiced/unvoiced flag, which is coded with one bit.

2. A gain factor G to model the energy of the segment, which is quantised using five bits.

3. A pitch period in the range 51.3 to 400 Hz, which is quantised using six bits.

4. Ten predictor coefficients a_1 to a_{10}, which are quantised using five bits each for a_1, a_2, a_3 and a_4. If it is a voiced segment, then a further 21 bits is used to code six more coefficients, with four bits used for each of a_5 to a_8, three bits used for a_9, and two bits for a_{10}. Higher coefficients are not used in the case of an unvoiced segment, and the 21 bits are devoted to error protection.

One bit, alternating between 1 and 0, is added to each segment for synchronisation at the receiver. Thus, we have 54 bits per 22.5 ms, or a bit rate of 2400 b/s. The above parameters are used at the receiver to synthesise the speech signal, as shown in Fig. 6.21.

6.4.2.3 MELP

A new 2.4 kbit/s vocoder was adopted in 1996 to replace the FS1015 standard. It achieves professional speech quality by using *mixed excitation linear prediction* (MELP). The excitation consists of a mixture of periodic pulses and white noise, which varies across the frequency band according to an estimate of the voiced speech component within the bands.

6.4.3 Hybrid coders

This represents the class of coders with by far the greatest scope for innovation in the LBR coding of speech, and has been the focus of intense research efforts over the last 15 years. It is therefore not surprising that most of the coders listed in Table 6.8 belong to this class, which is so named because it combines the advantages of waveform coders and vocoders to achieve good reproduction of speech at low bit rates. Hybrid coders use a technique called analysis-by-synthesis. At the transmitter various combinations of the model parameters are used to synthesise the speech as would be done at the receiver, and the combination yielding the best perceptual match to the original speech signal is selected. Hybrid codecs are highly complex, and introduce processing delays at least of the same order as vocoders. Several hybrid coders are listed in Table 6.8. The differences between these hybrids lie mainly in the excitation signal pattern, the analysis procedure, and the type of information transmitted to the receiver.

6.4.3.1 APC

Adaptive predictive coding (APC) is used in the toll-quality 16 kbit/s Inmarsat-B standard codec. Here segments of the speech signal are processed to remove voice model information leaving a residual signal, a quantised version of which is scaled by various trial gains and used as the excitation signal to synthesise the speech segment. The scaled residual yielding the best perceptual match to the original speech segment is chosen, and is encoded along with the voice model parameters and transmitted. At the receiver, a good copy of the original speech signal is reproduced using the scaled residual signal as the excitation signal of a filter constituted from the voice model parameters.

6.4.3.2 MPE-LPC

Multipulse excited linear predictive coding (MPE-LPC) employs perceptual weighting to obtain an improved modelling of the excitation. This signal is constituted as a sequence of pulses with amplitude, polarity, and location determined to minimise the total weighted squared error between synthesised and original speech signals. The 9.6 kbit/s Skyphone codec, developed by British Telecommunications (BT), is based on this algorithm. It was adopted by Inmarsat and the Airlines Electronic Engineering Committee (AEEC) for aeronautical satellite communications. If in MPE the (unequal-amplitude) pulses are regularly spaced within the excitation vector, we have what is termed *regular pulse excitation* (RPE). Regular pulse spacing shortens the search procedure and hence reduces processing delay. RPE, combined with long-term prediction (LTP), is the basis of the 13 kbit/s speech codec standardised for GSM — the Pan-European digital cellular mobile system.

6.4.3.3 CELP

Code excited linear prediction (CELP) allows the use of a multi-pulse excitation (MPE) with lower bit rates. The excitation vector that gives the best perceptual match between synthesised and original speech signals is selected from a set or *codebook* of vectors. The excitation signal is usually a weighted sum of contributions from two codebooks, one codebook being adaptive and constantly updated with past excitation vectors, and the other consisting of zero-mean unit-variance random sequences. The saving in bit rate comes about because fewer bits can be used to code the addresses of the selected vectors, allowing the excitation signal to be reconstituted at the receiver from local copies of the codebooks. Several CELP-based codecs are listed in Table 6.8, including the impressive ITU-T G.729 *conjugate structure algebraic* (CSA)-CELP codec, which delivers toll-quality speech at only 8 kbit/s.

6.5 Line codes

Line codes were introduced in Chapter 1 as a means of electrically representing a bit stream in a digital baseband communication system. In this section we want to familiarise ourselves with the most commonly used line codes, and develop an appreciation of their merits and demerits in view of the desirable characteristics of line codes. You may wish to refer to Section

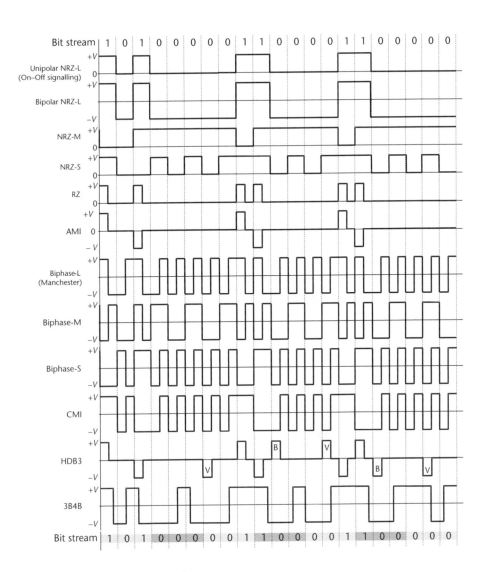

Figure 6.22 Common line codes.

1.5.3.1 for a detailed discussion of these characteristics. Figure 6.22 shows waveforms of the line codes discussed below under various classes, for a representative bit stream.

6.5.1 NRZ codes

Non-return-to-Zero-Level (NRZ-L): There are two types of NRZ-L, namely *unipolar* and *bipolar* NRZ-L. In unipolar NRZ-L, binary 1 is represented by a positive voltage pulse $+V$ volts lasting for the entire bit interval τ, and a binary 0 is represented by no pulse (0 volt) during the bit interval. For this reason unipolar NRZ-L is also referred to as *On–Off signalling*. Bipolar NRZ-L represents binary 1 with a positive voltage pulse $+V$, and binary 0 with a negative voltage pulse $-V$, each pulse lasting for the entire bit interval. Note that NRZ codes are so called because the code level remains constant within a bit interval and does not return to zero.

By considering the desirable characteristics of a good line code, you can readily convince yourself that although NRZ-L has 100% efficiency it nevertheless exhibits numerous unsatisfactory features. It is usually seen as a basic data format and referred to as *uncoded* data. It is used only for transmission over a very short distance, such as within one piece of equipment. A separate clock signal has to be used. One of the many undesirable features of this code is that a level inversion during transmission causes all symbols to be incorrectly received. A differential NRZ code overcomes this problem.

Differential NRZ: Bits are coded using voltage transitions, rather than actual voltage levels as in NRZ-L. There are two types of differential NRZ. In NRZ-Mark (NRZ-M), there is a transition at the beginning of a bit interval if the bit is 1 (called '*mark*' in the days of telegraphy), and no transition if the bit is 0. The other type is NRZ-Space (NRZ-S), which codes a binary 0, formerly called '*space*', with a transition at the beginning of the bit interval, and a binary 1 with no transition. Therefore, denoting the current input bit as $x(n)$, the current output of the coder as $y(n)$, and the previous coder output as $y(n-1)$, we may summarise the coding rule of differential NRZ as follows:

Input $x(n)$	Output, $y(n)$	
	NRZ-M	NRZ-S
0	$y(n-1)$	$\overline{y(n-1)}$
1	$\overline{y(n-1)}$	$y(n-1)$

where the overbar denotes a *complement* operation (i.e. change of state), so that $\overline{V} = 0$ and $\overline{0} = V$. Note that $x(n)$ is binary, having two possible values 0 and 1; and the code $y(n)$ is also binary, with two possible voltage levels 0 and V. In Fig. 6.22 it is assumed that the output is initially high, that is, $y = V$ before the first input bit. You may wish to verify that if y is initially at a low level (0 volt), then the resulting code waveform for NRZ-M and NRZ-S is the complement of the corresponding waveforms shown in Fig. 6.22.

A major handicap with NRZ codes is that they have very poor and non-guaranteed timing content. A long run of the same bit in NRZ-L, 0s in NRZ-M, and 1s in NRZ-S, gives rise to a transmitted waveform that is void of level transitions. It is then impossible to extract the clock signal from the received waveform at the receiver. A slight improvement in timing content is provided by the return-to-zero (RZ) code, although at the cost of doubling the bandwidth requirement compared to NRZ.

6.5.2 RZ codes

Return-to-Zero (RZ): RZ code represents binary 1 using a voltage pulse of amplitude $+V$ during the first half of the bit interval followed by 0 V (no pulse) in the remaining half of the bit interval. Binary 0 is represented as no pulse (0 V) for the entire bit interval.

Observe that a long run of 0s in RZ code will still cause timing problems at the receiver. Furthermore, the code exhibits another serious handicap in that it has a DC component (average value) that depends on the fraction of 1s in the transmitted data. Most links for long-distance data transmission incorporate transformers and series capacitors, which will effectively block any DC component in a message signal. A long run of 1s in RZ code introduces a DC offset that may result in droop and baseline wander due to charging and discharging capacitors. Another code, the alternate mark inversion (AMI), eliminates the DC offset problem, but at the expense of increased codec complexity.

Alternate Mark Inversion (AMI): This code is obtained from RZ by reversing the polarity of alternate binary 1s. As a result, three voltage levels (–V, 0 and +V) are employed, making this a three-level or *ternary* code.

AMI eliminates droop and base-line wander while keeping bandwidth requirement the same as in RZ. However, a train of data 0s still results in a transmitted waveform without transitions, which causes timing problems when the receiver tries to establish bit synchronisation. The problem of lack of transitions in some bit sequences is overcome in biphase codes, which contains a transition in each symbol whether it represents a binary 1 or 0.

6.5.3 Biphase codes

There are three types of biphase code, namely *biphase-L*, which is also called *Manchester* code, *biphase-M* and *biphase-S*. In biphase-L, a binary 1 is represented by a transition from high (+V) to low (–V) at the middle of the bit interval, while a binary 0 is represented by a transition from low (–V) to high (+V) at the middle of the bit interval. That is, to represent a binary 1, a positive pulse +V is transmitted for the first half of the bit interval followed by a negative pulse –V for the remaining half of the bit interval. A symbol of opposite polarity is used to represent a binary 0.

Manchester code finds application in the Ethernet standard IEEE 802.3 for local area networks (LAN). It has good timing content, but suffers the same inversion problem as NRZ-L, a handicap eliminated in the other biphase code types.

In biphase-M, there is always a transition at the beginning of each bit interval. Binary 1 is represented with an additional transition at the middle of the bit interval, while binary 0 has no additional transition. Biphase-S similarly always has a transition at the beginning of each bit interval, but uses an additional transition at the middle of the bit interval for a binary 0, and no additional transition for a binary 1.

6.5.4 RLL codes

Run-length-limited (RLL) codes limit the length of a run of voltage levels void of transition. One type of implementation is called *bipolar with n zeros* substituted (B*n*ZS), e.g. B3ZS, B4ZS, B6ZS and B8ZS. The case of $n = 4$ (i.e. B4ZS) is also called *high-density bipolar with 3 zero maximum* (HDB3).

Coded Mark Inversion (CMI): This is the simplest type of RLL code. It is a binary code in which binary 1 is represented by full width alternating polarity pulses, and binary 0 by $-V$ volts for the first half of the bit interval followed by $+V$ volts for the remaining half. CMI is preferred to HDB3 in high bit rate systems because of its simplicity and efficiency.

HDB3: This is actually an AMI code in which the number of successive 0s transmitted is somehow limited to three. The 4th of four adjacent 0s is represented using a *violation* (V) pulse. That is, it is represented as a 1 that violates the alternating polarity rule. In this way, a level transition is introduced and the receiver will recognise the violating pulse as representing a binary 0. A little thought will show, however, that violation pulses can cause a build-up of DC offset. To avoid this, whenever necessary, a *balancing* (B) pulse is used for the first of four adjacent zeros in order to prevent two successive violation pulses having the same polarity. To identify a B-pulse, note that whenever a V-pulse occurs after only two zeros, the previous pulse is a B-pulse, and therefore represents a binary 0. These pulses are labelled in Fig. 6.22.

Let us take a moment to understand HDB3 coding. Figure 6.23 shows the same bit stream as before, with the bit positions numbered for easy reference. The AMI waveform for this bit stream is repeated in Fig. 6.23(a). Note how binary 1s are represented using pulses of alternating polarity, so that the average value of the waveform is always approximately zero. Thus, unlike RZ code, there is no DC build-up in the waveform as binary 1s are

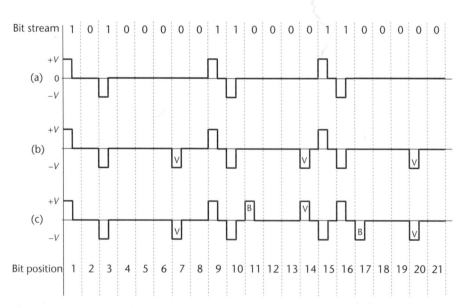

Figure 6.23 Steps leading up to HDB3 code. (a) AMI; (b) AMI with 4th zero in a 4-zero-string represented with a violation (V-) pulse; (c) Balancing (B-) pulse introduced to complete HDB3 coding.

coded. However, there is a string of 0s from bit 4 to bit 8, and the AMI waveform is void of transition during the entire interval.

To overcome this problem of poor timing content, HDB3 limits the maximum run of 0s to three by changing the 4th zero in a 4-zero-string to binary 1 and representing it with a V-pulse to enable the receiver to spot the substitution. The implementation of this idea is shown in Fig. 6.23(b). Note how positions 7, 14 and 20 are coded. These are V-pulses because each of them has the same polarity as the previous pulse, whereas the rule stipulates an alternating polarity. Now we have solved the problem of poor timing content and can guarantee that in four bit intervals there will be at least one transition in the code waveform. However, there is a new problem. The code waveform contains three positive and six negative pulses, and so contains an undesirable DC component. Observe that this has arisen because successive V-pulses have the same polarity. To eliminate this build-up of DC offset in the waveform, we make the following modification that prevents successive V-pulses from having the same polarity: Before inserting a new V-pulse we check to see if it would have the same polarity as the previous V-pulse. If so, we change the first zero in the 4-zero-string to a 1; represent this 1 with a pulse that obeys the alternating polarity rule and call it the B-pulse; and then insert the new V-pulse to violate this B-pulse.

Figure 6.23(c) shows the implementation of the above modification to obtain the desired HDB3 waveform. Let's walk through this waveform. The first V-pulse at No. 7 does not have the same polarity as the previous V-pulse (in this case simply because there is no previous V-pulse), so no modification is necessary. Next, there is a 4-zero-string from No. 11 to 14, and a V-pulse is therefore required at No. 14. This would have the same polarity as the previous V-pulse at No. 7, so a modification is needed. Therefore insert a B-pulse at No. 11 and then insert the V-pulse at No. 14 to violate this B-pulse. After this, there is a 4-zero-string from No. 17 to 20, meaning that a V-pulse is needed at No. 20. We see that this V-pulse would have to be positive (in order to violate the pulse at No. 16), and therefore would have the same polarity as the previous V-pulse at No. 14. Therefore insert a B-pulse as shown at No. 17 before inserting the V-pulse at No. 20.

Note that at the receiver it is a straightforward matter for the decoder to correctly interpret the code waveform as follows:

1. Every 0 V (for the entire bit interval) represents binary 0.
2. Every V-pulse represents binary 0.
3. Every pulse that is followed by a V-pulse after only two bit intervals is a B-pulse and hence represents binary 0.
4. Every other pulse represents binary 1.

6.5.5 Block codes

We have so far discussed line codes that work on one bit at a time to select the code symbols. In block codes on the other hand, blocks of input bits are

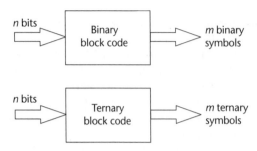

Figure 6.24 Block coding.

coded into code symbols according to rules defined in a coding table. As shown in Fig. 6.24, a ternary block code uses m ternary symbols to represent n bits, and is designated nBmT. A binary block code uses m binary symbols to represent n bits, and is designated nBmB. Usually, not all the possible symbol combinations or codewords are used in the block code output. This allows the flexibility of choosing those codewords with the desired characteristics. For example, balanced codewords containing equal amounts of positive (+) and negative (–) pulses, and hence no DC offset, are preferred to unbalanced codewords. Furthermore, codewords with more frequent transitions, such as $-+-+-+$, are preferred to those with fewer transitions, such as $---+++$.

From the definition of code efficiency in Section 1.5.3.1, it follows that the efficiencies of nBmT and nBmB codes are given, respectively, by

$$\eta_{n\text{B}m\text{T}} = \frac{n}{m\log_2(3)} \times 100\%$$

$$\eta_{n\text{B}m\text{B}} = \frac{n}{m} \times 100\%$$

(6.59)

Equation (6.59) is obtained by noting that in the nBmT code, n bits of information are carried using m ternary (i.e. three-level) symbols, each of which has a potential information content of $\log_2(3)$ bits. Similarly, in the nBmB code, m binary symbols (which have a potential information content equal to m bits) are employed to carry only n bits of information, yielding the efficiency stated above. For a given m, efficiency is maximised in a binary block code by choosing $n = m - 1$. With this relation, the coding efficiency increases with m, but at the expense of increased codec complexity and an increased length of a continuous run of like pulses.

Table 6.9 shows the coding table of three simple block codes. The last column gives the disparity, which is the *digital sum* of each codeword; a digital sum being a count of the imbalance between negative and positive pulses in a sequence of symbols. Observe that CMI and Manchester codes can be treated as a 1B2B block code, which takes one bit at a time and represents it using two binary symbols. For example, the coding table for CMI shows that binary 0 is represented by a negative pulse followed by a positive pulse. This is denoted $-+$, and was earlier presented as two half-width pulses. Binary 1 is represented using either two negative or two positive pulses, denoted $--$ and $++$, respectively and introduced earlier as a single full-width pulse.

The waveform of a 3B4B code obtained using the coding table in Table 6.9 is shown at the bottom of Fig. 6.22. To see how the 3B4B code waveform was obtained, note that the input bit stream is taken in blocks of three bits: see the demarcation of the bit stream listed below the 3B4B waveform. The encoder maintains a *running digital sum* (RDS), which is the cumulative sum of the disparity of each transmitted codeword. To code an input block that

Table 6.9 Coding table for 3B4B and 1B2B codes.

Type	Input	Output codeword			Disparity
		Negative	0	Positive	
CMI	0		− +		0
= 1B2B	1	− −		0	±2
Manchester	0		− +		0
= 1B2B	1		+ −		0
	001		− − + +		0
	010		− + − +		0
	011		− + + −		0
3B4B	100		+ − − +		0
	101		+ − + −		0
	110		+ + − −		0
	000	− − + −		+ + − +	±2
	111	− + − −		+ − + +	±2

has two codeword options, the negative-disparity option is selected if RDS is positive or zero, and the positive-disparity option is chosen if RDS is negative. Let us assume that initially RDS = 0. Then with the bit stream as in Fig. 6.22, the first input block is 101, which is represented with the codeword + − + −, according to Table 6.9. The 3B4B waveform during this interval corresponds to this code. The RDS stays at zero. The next input block is 000, which (since RDS = 0) is represented using its negative-disparity code option − − + −, according to Table 6.9. RDS is updated to −2, by adding the disparity of the new codeword. Again, the portion of the 3B4B waveform in Fig. 6.22 during this interval corresponds to the new codeword. The coding continues in this manner with the RDS being updated after each codeword until the last input block 000, which is represented with its positive-disparity code option + + − + to raise the RDS from −2 to 0.

Block codes have a number of advantageous features.

1. *Good timing content*: Codewords are selected that have sufficient transitions.

2. *No baseline wander*: DC offset is eliminated by using balanced codewords whenever possible. When an input block has to be represented using unbalanced codewords, then two options that balance out each other are provided for the block.

3. *Greater efficiency*: This means that a lower signalling rate can be used to provide the desired bit rate, which allows a greater spacing between repeaters without excessive degradation of transmitted symbols.

However, block codes have the demerit of increased codec complexity, which translates to higher costs. They are typically used on long-distance transmission links where savings in number of repeaters justify the higher complexity.

WORKED EXAMPLE 6.5

Determine the code efficiency, signalling rate and symbol period for the following baseband transmission systems:

(a) 139 264 kbit/s transmitted using CMI
(b) 139 264 kbit/s transmitted using 6B4T

(a) CMI is a 1B2B code. Its efficiency therefore follows from Eq. (6.59):

$$\eta_{CMI} = \frac{1}{2} \times 100\% = 50\%$$

Signalling rate R_s is the number of symbols transmitted each second. In this case (1B2B), two binary symbols are used for each bit, and since 139 264 000 bits are transmitted each second, it follows that

$$R_s = 2 \times 139\,264\,000$$
$$= 278\,528\,000 \text{ symbols/second}$$
$$= 278.53 \text{ Mbaud}$$

We have used the word *baud* for symbols/second, as is common practice. The symbol period T_s is the reciprocal of R_s. Thus,

$$T_s = \frac{1}{R_s} = \frac{1}{278\,528\,000} = 3.59 \text{ ns}$$

(b) 6B4T is a ternary code with $n = 6$, $m = 4$. Equation (6.59) gives

$$\eta_{6B4T} = \frac{6}{4\log_2(3)} \times 100\% = 94.64\%$$

In this case, four ternary symbols are used to carry six bits. With 139 264 000 bits transmitted each second, the number of ternary symbols transmitted per second (i.e. the signalling rate) is

$$R_s = \frac{139\,264\,000}{6} \times 4$$
$$= 92.84 \text{ Mbaud}$$

The symbol period $T_s = 1/R_s = 10.77$ ns.

Observe that the more efficient ternary system uses a lower signalling rate to accommodate the same information transmission rate as the less efficient CMI. However, CMI has the advantage of simplicity. The decision on which code is used will be dictated by the priorities of the particular application.

6.6   Pulse shaping

So far, we have represented the transmitted symbols as rectangular pulses. However, as was discussed in Chapter 2, rectangular pulses — because of their sharp transitions — contain high-frequency components, which would be attenuated in practical finite-bandwidth baseband systems. This causes a (formerly) rectangular pulse to spread out beyond its bit interval, so that it contributes significant energy to one or more adjacent bit intervals. The phenomenon is known as *intersymbol interference* (ISI) and, if not addressed, will be a source of bit errors, as the receiver cannot discriminate between energy in the current symbol and left over energy from previous symbols. To eliminate ISI, each received pulse $p(t)$ must be shaped in such a way that, although it spreads out significantly into subsequent bit intervals, it always has zero value at the crucial sampling instants of those bit intervals. Therefore, an outline of the required pulse shape is as shown in Fig. 6.25 for the nth pulse. That is, at the decision point in the receiver where incoming pulses are sampled at intervals T_s, the waveform of $p(t)$ should pass through the points marked with an asterisk on the diagram. We don't care much about the values of $p(t)$ at non-sampling time instants, as long as we get the timing correct at the receiver.

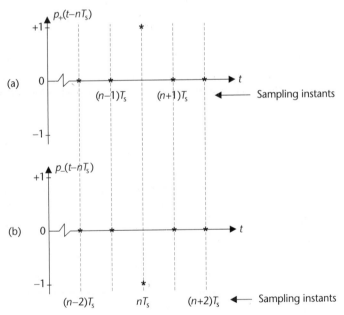

Figure 6.25   Outline of pulse shape to avoid ISI. (a) Positive symbol; (b) negative symbol.

6.6.1   Ideal filtering

One pulse waveform that fits the above description is the sinc function shown in Fig. 6.26. Thus,

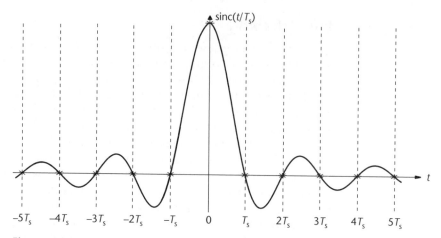

Figure 6.26 A sinc pulse satisfies zero ISI requirement.

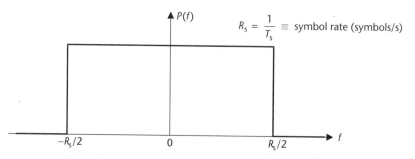

Figure 6.27 Spectrum of the zero-ISI sinc pulse of Fig. 6.26.

$$p(t) = \text{sinc}(t/T_s) \tag{6.60}$$

It is informative to look at this pulse in the frequency domain in order to understand the overall frequency response that is required of the filters that lie in the path of the pulse from the transmitter to the decision (i.e. sampling) point within the receiver. Recall, from Chapter 2, that $p(t)$ has the rectangular spectrum shown in Fig. 6.27 and given by

$$P(f) = T_s \, \text{rect}(fT_s)$$

$$= \frac{1}{R_s} \text{rect}\left(\frac{f}{R_s}\right) \tag{6.61}$$

where $R_s = 1/T_s$ is the symbol rate in *baud*. Note in Fig. 6.27 that the bandwidth of the pulse is half the symbol rate:

$$B_N = R_s/2$$

$$= \frac{1}{2} \times \text{Symbol rate} \tag{6.62}$$

This means that the pulse will be transmitted without distortion through a system of bandwidth given by Eq. (6.62). Equivalently, we can state that using sinc pulses allows us to transmit (without ISI) at a symbol rate that is twice the available bandwidth. This is a notable result. But there are two practical problems — one impossible to overcome, and the other simply challenging:

1. The amplitude spectrum $P(f)$ has an abrupt drop to zero at $f = R_s/2$. This requires the action of an ideal low-pass filter, which is physically unrealisable. That is, to shape our originally impulse-like binary symbols into sinc pulses at the detection point, we require (overall) an ideal low-pass frequency response in the channel between the symbol output point at the transmitter and the sampling point at the receiver. Such a channel is known as an *ideal Nyquist channel* and cannot be achieved in practice. Our perfect pulse that eliminates ISI and requires a minimum transmission bandwidth is merely an unrealisable dream.

2. The sinc pulse deviates rapidly from zero outside the sampling instants, 0, T_s, $2T_s$, ... ISI is therefore actually eliminated only if we get the timing precisely right at the receiver. In practice, there will be some timing error, and therefore significant residual energy from previous and *future* (!) sinc pulses at each mistimed sampling instant. That the future affects the present only serves to highlight that a sinc pulse is not of this world.

6.6.2 Raised cosine filtering

To make the filtering requirement of a zero-ISI pulse achievable, thus making the pulse realisable, let us modify the spectrum of $P(f)$ in Eq. (6.61) by giving it a gradual roll-off towards zero as shown in Fig. 6.28. What we have done is to make $P(f)$ decrease gradually towards zero, starting at a

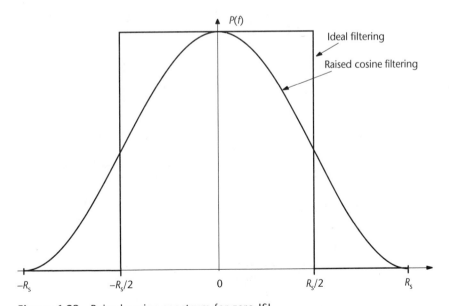

Figure 6.28 Raised cosine spectrum for zero-ISI

maximum at $f = 0$ and following a cosine function. The spectrum is therefore called a *raised cosine* spectrum — *raised* because the number 1 is added to limit it to non-negative values — and is given by

$$P(f) = \frac{1}{2R_s}\begin{cases}1 + \cos(\pi |f|/R_s), & |f| \le R_s \\ 0, & |f| > R_s\end{cases} \qquad (6.63)$$

where, as before, $R_s = 1/T_s$. You may wish to ignore the scale factor $1/2R_s$ in Eq. (6.63) in order to appreciate better the simplicity of the expression. It can be seen that $P(f)$ has a bandwidth

$$\begin{aligned}B_{RC} &= R_s \\ &\equiv \text{Symbol rate}\end{aligned} \qquad (6.64)$$

Comparing Eq. (6.62) and (6.64), we see that the bandwidth requirement of the realisable raised cosine filtered pulse is double that of the ideal Nyquist channel. To confirm that it actually does lead to zero ISI, let us consider the waveform $p(t)$ of this pulse, which is obtained by taking the inverse Fourier transform of $P(f)$:

$$p(t) = \left[\frac{\cos(\pi t/T_s)}{1 - 4(t/T_s)^2}\right]\text{sinc}(t/T_s) \equiv A_p\,\text{sinc}(t/T_s) \qquad (6.65)$$

This pulse is plotted in Fig. 6.29. What have we achieved?

The raised cosine filtered pulse is essentially a sinc pulse whose amplitude A_p is a rapidly decreasing function of time given by the term in square bracket. We see in Fig. 6.29 that the pulse value is zero at the sampling instants of neighbouring symbols as required for zero ISI. Apart from requiring a realisable filter, there is another important improvement on the ideal Nyquist channel. The effect of A_p is to force the pulse to decay very rapidly to zero outside the main lobe so that it contributes negligible residual energy into adjacent symbol intervals. This makes the transmission system

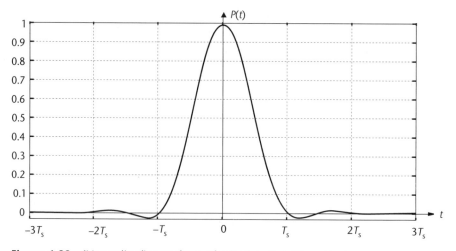

Figure 6.29 (Normalised) waveform of raised-cosine-filtered pulse.

practically insensitive to small timing errors. Thus, we have eliminated ISI in a practicable manner, but at a price! The raised cosine spectrum requires twice the bandwidth of the ideal Nyquist channel for the same symbol rate. However, the raised cosine filter is realisable and can be approximated to any degree of accuracy using DSP hardware.

In Fig. 6.28 and Eq. (6.63) we modified the ideal filter by making its response roll off gradually in a manner that is asymmetric about $R_s/2$. Starting from a value $P(f) = 1$ at $f = 0$, the response decreases to $P(f) = 0$ at $f = R_s$. This is the most gradual roll-off that can be achieved using the cosine function. It results in the widest possible transition band, and expectedly the most rapid pulse decay. Equation (6.63) is in fact a special case of a general class of raised cosine filtering in which the roll-off from unity (normalised) does not start until a frequency $f = f_1$, and is completed at frequency $f = f_2$, the two frequencies f_1 and f_2 being equally displaced to the left and right of $f = R_s/2$. Modifying Eq. (6.63) with this in mind yields the general case of raised cosine filtering:

$$P(f) = \frac{1}{R_s} \times \begin{cases} 1, & |f| \leq f \\ \frac{1}{2}\left[1 + \cos\left(\pi\frac{|f| - f_1}{f_2 - f_1}\right)\right], & f_1 \leq |f| \leq f_2 \\ 0, & |f| > f_2 \end{cases} \tag{6.66}$$

Once we choose the starting point of the roll-off by selecting f_1, the endpoint (where $P(f)$ just reaches zero) is automatically fixed at a frequency f_2 by the asymmetry of the roll-off, where

$$\begin{aligned} f_1 &= \frac{R_s}{2} - \Delta f \equiv \frac{R_s}{2} - \alpha\frac{R_s}{2} = (1 - \alpha)\frac{R_s}{2} \\ f_2 &= \frac{R_s}{2} + \Delta f \equiv \frac{R_s}{2} + \alpha\frac{R_s}{2} = (1 + \alpha)\frac{R_s}{2} \end{aligned} \tag{6.67}$$

We have given f_1 and f_2 in terms of a frequency shift from $R_s/2$, and expressed this frequency shift as a fraction α of $R_s/2$. The parameter α is called the *roll-off factor* and can take on values between 0 and 1. Using Eq. (6.67), we see that when $\alpha = 0$, $f_1 = f_2 = R_s/2$, giving the abrupt transition case that requires ideal filtering. When $\alpha = 1$, then $f_1 = 0$ and $f_2 = R_s$. This is the special case presented in Fig. 6.28 and Eq. (6.63), which gives the most gradual roll-off, and is known as the *full-cosine roll-off characteristic*.

The bandwidth of a raised cosine spectrum with a roll-off factor α follows from Eq. (6.66) and (6.67):

$$\begin{aligned} B_{RC} &= f_2 = (1 + \alpha)\frac{R_s}{2} \\ &\equiv \frac{1 + \alpha}{2} \times \text{Symbol rate} \end{aligned} \tag{6.68}$$

The pulse waveform $p(t)$ in this general case is obtained by taking the inverse Fourier transform of Eq. (6.66):

$$p(t) = \left[\frac{\cos(\pi \alpha t/T_s)}{1 - 4(\alpha t/T_s)^2} \right] \text{sinc}(t/T_s) \equiv A_p \, \text{sinc}(t/T_s) \tag{6.69}$$

You may wish to verify that Eq. (6.68) and (6.69) yield the expected results for $\alpha = 0$ and 1. Clearly, the above pulse achieves zero ISI. However, as α is reduced from 1 — to minimise bandwidth requirements — the amplitude factor A_p decreases less rapidly with time. The pulse then has significant values outside the main lobe, and timing accuracy becomes more critical to avoid ISI. Furthermore, the order, and hence processing delay of the DSP filter implementation increases as α is decreased.

WORKED EXAMPLE **6.6**

(a) Determine the bandwidth of the system in Worked example 6.5(b), given that pulses with a full-cosine roll-off characteristic are used for transmission.

(b) If the bandwidth requirement is to be reduced to 60 MHz, calculate the roll-off factor of the raised cosine filter.

(c) Suggest how the same bit rate may be transmitted using less than the bandwidth of the ideal Nyquist channel.

(a) The symbol rate for this system is $R_s = 92.84$ Mbaud. Using pulses with a full-cosine roll-off characteristic, the bandwidth required equals the symbol rate; see Eq. (6.64). Thus,

Bandwidth = 92.84 MHz

(b) Making α the subject of Eq. (6.68) and putting $B_{RC} = 60$ MHz and $R_s = 92.84$ Mbaud, we obtain

$$\alpha = \frac{2B_{RC}}{R_s} - 1 = \frac{2 \times 60}{92.84} - 1$$
$$= 0.293$$

(c) If an ideal Nyquist channel ($\alpha = 0$) is used, then the bandwidth can be reduced to $R_s/2 = 46.42$ MHz. This is the minimum bandwidth required to transmit at $R_s = 92.84$ Mbaud. The only way to reduce the bandwidth any further is by reducing the symbol rate, and this would require changing the coding scheme if the same bit rate R_b is to be maintained. In the 6B4T system, each ternary symbol carries 6/4 = 1.5 bits. We must adopt a scheme in which each symbol carries more bits k. That is, we represent a block of k bits using one code symbol. Clearly, we require $M = 2^k$ unique symbols to cover all possible unique input blocks. Following our naming convention for block codes, this coding scheme may be identified as kB1M, where M denotes *M-ary* (just as T denotes ternary in, e.g., 6B4T). In general, M unique symbols (sometimes called levels) allows us to represent $k = \log_2(M)$ bits per symbol, which gives a symbol rate

$$R_s = \frac{\text{Bit rate}}{k} \equiv \frac{R_b}{k} \qquad (6.70)$$

For example, if $M = 16$, we have $k = 4$, and a symbol rate $R_s = R_b/4 = 139\ 264\ 000/4 = 34.82$ Mbaud can be used in this example. With this coding scheme, we can (ideally) transmit at 139 264 kbit/s using a transmission bandwidth of only 17.41 MHz. In fact we can reduce transmission bandwidth indefinitely by correspondingly increasing k. So why, you must be asking, are kB1M block codes (called M-ary modulation in modulated systems) not used in baseband systems? There are two main reasons. Codec complexity increases dramatically, and the unique code symbols become so close in identity that it is difficult to correctly detect them at the receiver in the presence of noise. As a result, symbol error becomes frequent. The impact is even more severe because each symbol error potentially affects not just one bit, but up to k bits.

6.6.3 Information capacity theorem

We saw in Section 6.6.1 that the maximum rate at which symbols can be transmitted through a channel of bandwidth B is $R_{smax} = 2B$. As discussed in the above worked example, we may maximise the bit rate R_b by sending the symbols with M possible levels so that each symbol conveys $\log_2 M$ bits. Thus,

$$R_b = 2B \log_2 M \qquad (6.71)$$

This equation suggests that we can increase bit rate indefinitely simply by increasing M. For example, a baseband channel of bandwidth $B = 3.1$ kHz can be made to support a bit rate of 62 kbit/s by using $M = 32\ 768$ symbol levels. The bit rate can even be doubled to $R_b = 124$ kbit/s in the same channel by increasing M to 1 048 576. You are right to wonder whether there is no restriction on the maximum value of M.

The above argument does not take account of noise effects. It assumes that the symbol levels can be distinguished at the receiver no matter how closely spaced they are. We may use the following intuitive argument in order to include the limiting effect of noise on bit rate. With a noise power N at the receiver, the spacing of symbol levels cannot be less than the rms noise voltage $\sqrt{N}$. Otherwise, adjacent symbols will be indistinguishable due to noise. The received signal (of power S) and noise (of power N) are uncorrelated, so their powers add to give a range of symbol levels equal to $\sqrt{N + S}$. With the noise-imposed minimum spacing given above, the maximum number of distinguishable symbol levels is therefore

$$M = \sqrt{\frac{N+S}{N}} = \sqrt{1 + S/N}$$

Substituting this expression for M in Eq. (6.71) yields the maximum rate (in bits per second) at which information may be transmitted through a channel without error. This maximum rate is known as the *information capacity* C of the system. Thus,

$$C = 2B\log_2(1 + S/N)^{1/2}$$
$$= B\log_2(1 + S/N) \text{ bits/second} \tag{6.72}$$

Equation (6.72) is Shannon's *information capacity theorem*. It lays down the rule that governs how bandwidth and signal-to-noise ratio may be exchanged in the design of a communication system. Note some of the implications of the theorem:

1. By increasing bandwidth, the transmission rate can be proportionately increased without degrading noise performance or raising signal power.

2. By exponentially increasing signal power, the transmission rate can also be increased without increasing bandwidth or degrading noise performance. For example, with $B = 4$ kHz and $S/N = 63$, we obtain $C = 24$ kbit/s. To double the bit rate to 48 kbit/s at the same bandwidth, we must increase the signal-to-noise ratio to $(S/N)_2 = 4095$. Note that $(S/N)_2 = [S/N + 1]^2 - 1$. In general, to increase the bit rate by a factor n without increasing bandwidth, the signal-to-noise ratio must be increased exponentially from S/N to a new value $[S/N + 1]^n - 1$.

3. As bandwidth B is increased, the signal power required for error-free transmission decreases. Letting E_b denote the average signal energy per bit and N_0 the noise power spectral density, then $S = E_bC$ and $N = N_0B$. Equation (6.72) may then be written in the equivalent form

$$\frac{C}{B} = \log_2\left(1 + \frac{E_b}{N_0}\frac{C}{B}\right) \text{ bits/second/Hz} \tag{6.73}$$

The ratio C/B is the *bandwidth efficiency* of the system, while E_b/N_0 gives a measure of the *power efficiency* of the system. The information capacity theorem therefore shows us how to trade bandwidth efficiency for power efficiency. The latter is an important consideration for example in portable transceivers where battery life must be preserved. In fact, Eq. (6.73) shows that we may have error free transmission and detection with E_b/N_0 reduced down to the limiting value 0.69315 or −1.592 dB if bandwidth is increased indefinitely. You can determine this limiting value most easily by rewriting Eq. (6.73) in the form

$$\frac{E_b}{N_0} = \frac{2^{C/B} - 1}{C/B} = \frac{2^\eta - 1}{\eta} \tag{6.74}$$

and noting the value of E_b/N_0 as $\eta \equiv C/B$ tends to zero. You can do this either graphically or analytically. For the analytic approach,

$$\frac{E_b}{N_0}\bigg|_{B\to\infty} = \lim_{\eta\to 0}\frac{2^\eta - 1}{\eta}$$

$$= 2^\eta \ln 2\big|_{\eta=0}$$

$$= \ln 2 = 0.69315$$

In the above, the second line is obtained by taking the derivatives (with respect to η) of the numerator and denominator of the expression under the limit operator. This limiting value of E_b/N_0 is referred to as the *Shannon limit*.

4. Finally, we must point out that the theorem merely tells us that it is possible to have error-free transmission at the channel capacity, but does not show us how to design such a system. In practice, all digital transmission systems — both modulated and baseband — fall short of achieving the specified maximum data rate for a given bandwidth and *S/N*. The theorem is nevertheless a useful yardstick against which the performance of practical systems can be measured.

6.7 Digital baseband receiver

We have established that at the decision point in the receiver the pulse must have a raised cosine spectrum in order to avoid ISI. Let us now trace the path of a pulse through a digital baseband system and comment on the required filtering characteristics (or transfer function) of the components of this system, as shown in Fig. 6.30.

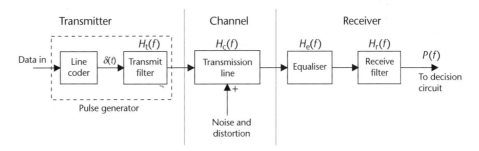

Figure 6.30 Filtering operations in digital baseband system.

6.7.1 Adaptive equalisation

The transmission medium or channel distorts the transmitted pulses in a manner fully described by the channel transfer function $H_c(f)$. In nearly every case, this channel effect is undesirable and, as discussed in Section 2.9.2, a filter known as an *equaliser* is needed at the receiver to remove the channel distortion. That is, we must have

$$H_c(f)H_e(f) = 1 \text{ (normalised)} \tag{6.75}$$

where $H_e(f)$ is the transfer function of the equaliser. Note that Eq. (6.75) specifically excludes propagation delay τ, which can be accounted for by inserting the factor $\exp(-j2\pi f\tau)$ in the RHS.

In most cases, as in the PSTN, the channel characteristic and hence $H_c(f)$ is time-varying in a non-deterministic way. The equalisation then has to be adaptive, with $H_e(f)$ constantly and automatically adjusting itself to satisfy Eq. (6.75). One way of achieving this is by using a tapped-delay-line filter. See Fig. 6.15. In this case, however, the tap gains are constantly adjusted to minimise the mean square error between expected and received pulse shapes averaged over a number of sampling instants. This can be done with the help of a training sequence of bits transmitted prior to the information bits. The optimum values computed for the tap gains are then maintained for the duration of the call on the assumption that the channel does not change significantly during this (short) period.

6.7.2 Matched filter

Let us now consider the effect of noise in order to correctly specify the transfer function $H_r(f)$ of the receiver filter. Note in Fig. 6.30 that the channel also introduces noise and this includes noise from the front end of the receiver. We will assume that this noise is *additive white Gaussian noise* (AWGN). The noise is described as *additive* because it is present in the same amount regardless of signal value. It is *white* because it contains all frequency components at the same amplitude (i.e. it has a uniform amplitude spectrum, or equivalently, a uniform power spectral density), just as *white light* contains equal amounts of all colours. Finally, it is described as *Gaussian* because it has a normal (i.e. Gaussian) probability density function.

The receive filter must be designed to minimise the effect of noise. This is accomplished by maximising the ratio between receiver output signal power and noise power (SNR) at the decision instant T_s. We can obtain the transfer function $H_r(f)$ of a receive filter that gives such optimum performance by making three increasingly specific observations.

1. The bandwidth of the receiver must be just enough to pass the incoming pulse. If it is too wide, noise power is unnecessarily added, and if it is too narrow then some pulse energy is cut out. Denoting the pulse as $g(t)$ and its spectrum as $G(f)$, we see that $G(f)$ and $H_r(f)$ must span exactly the same frequency band. How should their shapes compare?

2. The gain response $|H_r(f)|$ of the filter should not necessarily be flat within its passband. Rather, it should be such that the filter attenuates the white noise significantly at those frequencies where $G(f)$ is small — since these frequencies contribute little to the pulse energy. And the filter should boost those frequencies at which $G(f)$ is large in order to maximise the output pulse energy. We see then that the filter should be tailored to the incoming pulse, with a gain response that is small where $G(f)$ is small and large where $G(f)$ is large. The perfect way of doing this

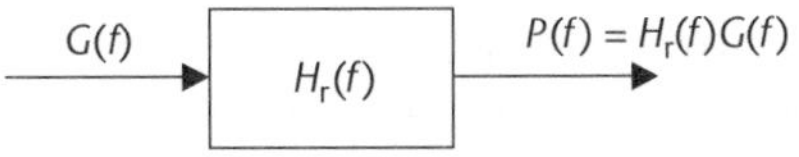

Figure 6.31 Filter action.

is by making the (normalised) gain response of the filter identical with the amplitude spectrum of the pulse. That is,

$$|H_r(f)| = |G(f)| \qquad (6.76)$$

3. We complete the filter specification by considering phase requirements. The instantaneous signal power at the decision instant $t = T_s$ (equal to the pulse duration) will be maximum if all frequency components in the pulse have been delayed by the same amount. This means that the only complex term in the spectrum of the filter output $P(f)$ must be the factor $\exp(-j2\pi fT_s)$, since this ensures the same delay T_s for all frequencies. See our discussion of distortionless transmission in Section 2.9.1 if in doubt. Therefore, in view of Fig. 6.31, we may write

$$P(f) = G(f)H_r(f) \equiv R(f)\exp(-j2\pi fT_s)$$

where $R(f)$ is a real function of frequency. Making $R(f)$ the subject of this equation yields,

$$R(f) = [G(f)\exp(j2\pi fT_s)]H_r(f)$$

The left-hand side (LHS) of this equation is real, and so must be the RHS, which is the product of two complex functions — one of them in square brackets. Since the product of two complex functions is real if and only if the two functions are related as complex conjugates, it follows that

$$H_r(f) = G^*(f)\exp(-j2\pi fT_s) \qquad (6.77)$$

The asterisk denotes complex conjugation, which is performed by replacing j with –j wherever it occurs in $G(f)$. A filter that satisfies Eq. (6.77) is called a *matched filter*, since it has been matched to the pulse signal.

It is informative to consider the impulse response $h_r(t)$ of this filter. Recall that $h_r(t)$ is the inverse Fourier transform of the transfer function $H_r(f)$. Since complex conjugation of the Fourier transform of a real signal corresponds to time reversal in the time domain, and the exponential term corresponds to a delay of T_s, it follows that

$$h_r(t) = g(T_s - t) \qquad (6.78)$$

That is, the impulse response of the matched filter is a time-reversed and delayed version of the pulse $g(t)$.

This is a good point to study Section 6.7.6 where we employ several worked examples to introduce important concepts, including the convolution integral, the irrelevance of pulse shapes to a matched filter and the correlation receiver. Wherever possible, the simplicity of a graphical approach is employed in these worked examples. You are encouraged to work through them with care. Doing this will pay future dividends.

6.7.3 Root raised cosine filter

Consider again the baseband system in Fig. 6.30 and assume for simplicity that the line coder generates impulses, which are shaped by a transmit filter to give the transmitted pulses. This approximation is entirely adequate for narrow-width rectangular pulses. Note then that the Fourier transform of a normalised positive output pulse from the line coder is $F[\delta(t)] = 1$. The frequency response of the transmit filter is given by its transfer function $H_t(f)$. It follows in Fig. 6.30 that the spectrum $P(f)$ of the pulse at the output of the receive filter is given by

$$
\begin{aligned}
P(f) &= F[\delta(t)]H_t(f)H_c(f)H_e(f)H_r(f) \\
&= H_t(f)H_r(f)
\end{aligned}
\tag{6.79}
$$

where $H_r(f)$ is the transfer function of the receive filter and we require $P(f)$ to be a raised cosine spectrum. Equation (6.79) is an important result, which shows that to minimise ISI the transmit and receive filters must be designed so that the product of their transfer functions is a raised cosine spectrum. To satisfy this requirement as well as that of matched filtering for optimum performance in the presence of white noise, we must have

$$
\begin{aligned}
|H_t(f)| = |H_r(f)| &= \sqrt{\text{raised cosine spectrum}} \\
&= \begin{cases} 1, & |f| \le f_1 \\ \sqrt{\dfrac{1}{2}\left[1 + \cos\left(\pi \dfrac{|f| - f_1}{f_2 - f_1}\right)\right]}, & f_1 \le |f| \le f_2 \\ 0 & |f| > f_2 \end{cases}
\end{aligned}
\tag{6.80}
$$

where f_1 and f_2 are given as before by Eq. (6.67). Note that a scale factor $\sqrt{1/R_s}$ has been ignored in the transfer function. This means that using a pair of *root raised cosine filters*, one located at the transmitter and the other at the receiver, allows us to eliminate ISI and at the same time obtain optimum performance in the presence of white noise. This is a notable achievement!

One final observation that must be made concerns the effect of the equaliser on our specification of the receive filter. In general, channel attenuation increases with frequency. The equaliser must therefore have a gain that increases with frequency in keeping with Eq. (6.75). The result is that the noise reaching the receive filter, having passed through the equaliser, is no longer white but 'coloured' — with an amplitude spectrum that increases with frequency. Under this condition, SNR can be maximised by arranging for the receiver to attenuate the higher frequencies in order to reduce noise. This also unavoidably attenuates the desired pulse energy at these frequencies. So we compensate for this by designing the transmit filter to proportionately boost the high-frequency components of the pulse. RZ codes serve the same aim by reducing the pulse widths by a factor of two, which boosts the high-frequency components in keeping with the inverse relationship between time and frequency (Section 2.4.5). In this way, Eq. (6.79) holds and we still have a raised cosine spectrum $P(f)$ at the decision point, implying zero ISI. There is also optimum performance in the presence of noise. However, the gain responses of the transmit and receive filters are no longer identical root raised cosine, as specified in Eq. (6.80).

6.7.4 Clock extraction

Decision instants at the receiver must be accurately spaced at intervals of the transmitted symbol period T_s. This allows the matched filter output to be sampled at the optimum instants, for negligible ISI and maximum $(S/N)_0$. Small short-term deviations from the optimum timing instants are known as *timing jitter*. If this is unchecked, especially in long-distance high data rate systems with many intermediate repeaters, it may accumulate sufficiently so that the timing error exceeds half the symbol period, causing the decision instant to be set at the wrong symbol interval, entirely missing out one or more intervals. This problem is known as *symbol slip*. It causes subsequent symbols to be in error until there is a realignment.

Clock or timing extraction is a process that seeks to derive from the incoming symbol stream a sinusoidal signal of the correct phase and of a frequency equal to the symbol rate ($R_s = 1/T_s$). This sinusoid may then be passed through a comparator — a zero-crossing detector — to give a square wave clock signal of period T_s. The incoming symbol stream is then decoded by arranging for the matched filter output to be sampled at every rising (or falling) edge of the clock signal.

The need for the transmitted symbol stream to contain frequent voltage transitions (e.g. between $\pm V$ volts for binary coding) was emphasised in our discussion of line coding. When this is the case, the symbol stream may contain a significant component at the sampling frequency f_s ($= R_s$), which can be directly filtered out using a narrow bandpass filter tuned to f_s. However, some symbol patterns may only contain a fraction or multiple of the desired frequency component. Therefore, in general, the incoming symbol stream is passed through a suitable non-linear device, such as a square-law device or a full-wave rectifier. From our discussion of non-linear distortion (Section 2.9.3), it is clear that the output of such a device will contain the desired frequency component f_s, which may then be filtered out. Figure 6.32 shows one possible arrangement for clock extraction. A phase-locked loop (PLL), discussed in Sections 3.5.2 and 4.6.2, may be used in place of the narrowband filter to improve the phase match between the clock signal used at the transmitter and that extracted at the receiver.

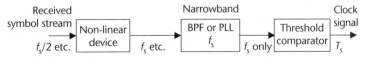

Figure 6.32 Clock extraction.

6.7.5 Eye diagrams

An indication of the likelihood of decision error at the receiver due to the corruption of the incoming symbol stream by undesirable noise and filtering can be readily displayed using eye diagrams. Figure 6.33(a) shows a corrupted bipolar NRZ symbol stream, with adjacent symbol elements identified by different line patterns. If all the incoming symbol elements are superimposed in one symbol interval, the result is the plot shown in Fig. 6.33(b), which is called an *eye diagram* because it resembles the human eye. The eye diagram of an actual transmission can easily be displayed on an oscilloscope. The symbols in successive intervals will be automatically superimposed on the screen when the oscilloscope is triggered using the receiver's clock signal. Useful performance information provided by the eye diagram include:

1. The width of the eye opening gives the timing error that can be tolerated in the sampling instants at the receiver. The best sampling instant is at the centre of the eye opening.

2. The slope of the opening gives an indication of the sensitivity of the baseband system to timing error.

3. The height of the eye opening gives the noise margin of the system.

It is therefore obvious that the larger the eye opening the lower will be the symbol error rate of the system. Figure 6.34 demonstrates the impact of noise and timing error on the eye diagram of a binary system that uses raised cosine-filtered pulses. A narrowing of the eye opening by these effects clearly indicates an increased probability of error. The eye diagram is indeed a very useful diagnostic tool for checking for the presence of timing error, noise and pulse distortion in a digital baseband system.

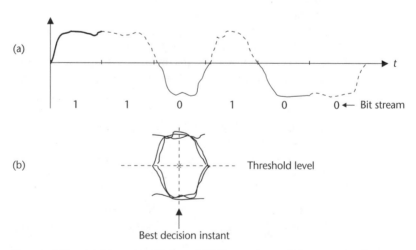

Figure 6.33 (a) Incoming distorted NRZ waveform; (b) corresponding eye diagram.

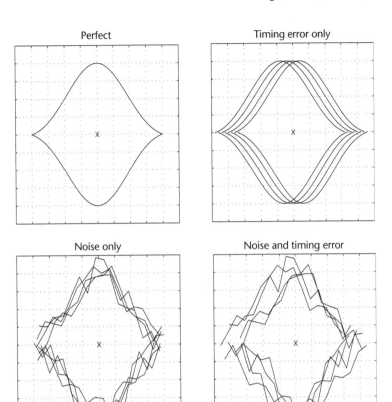

Figure 6.34 Effects of noise and timing error on eye diagram.

6.7.6 Matched filter worked examples

WORKED EXAMPLE 6.7 _____

Time-reversal and delay

Sketch the impulse response of a matched filter for receiving the pulse $g(t)$ shown in Fig. 6.35(a), where the pulse duration $T_s = 5$ μs.

The required impulse response is given by Eq. (6.78) and can be obtained in two steps. First, the pulse $g(t)$ is time-reversed to give $g(-t)$. Then, $g(-t)$ is delayed by T_s to give $g(T_s - t)$, which is the required impulse response. The waveforms $g(-t)$ and $g(T_s - t)$ are sketched in Figs. 6.35(b) and (c). It is important to understand how these two waveforms are obtained. Observe that the waveform of $g(-t)$ may be obtained simply by flipping

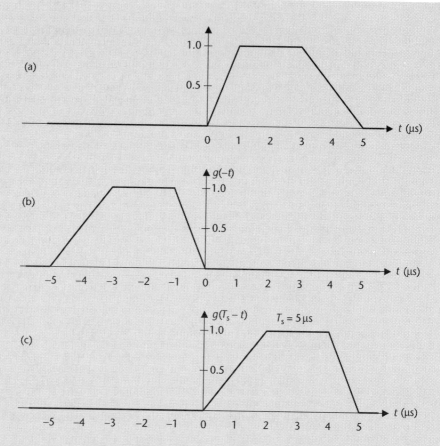

Figure 6.35 Worked example 6.7.

$g(t)$ horizontally about $t = 0$, and that the waveform $g(T_s - t)$ results from delaying $g(-t)$ by a time T_s. In this case, since $g(-t)$ 'starts' at the time $t = -5$ µs, it follows that $g(T_s - t)$ must 'start' at a time T_s (= 5 µs) later, which is therefore the time $t = 0$.

Table 6.10 provides verification of the above procedures. Noting that $g(t_i)$ is the value of the pulse $g(t)$ at $t = t_i$, it follows by definition of $g(t)$ in Fig. 6.35(a) that $g(-10) = 0$, $g(-5) = 0$, $g(1) = 1$, $g(4) = 0.5$, $g(10) = 0$ and so on, where t is in µs. Table 6.10 gives values of the waveforms $g(t)$, $g(-t)$ and $g(T_s - t)$ at various values of t. For example, at $t = 4$, $g(t) = g(4) = 0.5$ (by definition); $g(-t) = g(-4) = 0$ (by definition); and $g(T_s - t) = g(5-4) = g(1) = 1$ (by definition). Plotting the entries of this table leads to Fig. 6.35, with column 3 plotted against column 1 to give Fig. 6.35(b) and column 4 plotted against column 1 to give Fig. 6.35(c).

Table 6.10 Worked example 6.7. Entries plotted in Fig. 6.35. Note that $T_s = 5\ \mu s$.

$t\ (\mu s)$	$g(t)$	$g(-t)$	$h_r(t) = g(T_s - t)$
−10	0	$= g(10) = 0$	$= g(5 - -10) = g(15) = 0$
−5	0	$= g(5) = 0$	$= g(5 - -5) = g(10) = 0$
−4	0	$= g(4) = 0.5$	$= g(5 - -4) = g(9) = 0$
−3	0	$= g(3) = 1$	$= g(5 - -3) = g(8) = 0$
−2	0	$= g(2) = 1$	$= g(5 - -2) = g(7) = 0$
−1	0	$= g(1) = 1$	$= g(5 - -1) = g(6) = 0$
0	0	$= g(0) = 0$	$= g(5 - 0) = g(5) = 0$
1	1	$= g(-1) = 0$	$= g(5 - 1) = g(4) = 0.5$
2	1	$= g(-2) = 0$	$= g(5 - 2) = g(3) = 1$
3	1	$= g(-3) = 0$	$= g(5 - 3) = g(2) = 1$
4	0.5	$= g(-4) = 0$	$= g(5 - 4) = g(1) = 1$
5	0	$= g(-5) = 0$	$= g(5 - 5) = g(0) = 0$
10	0	$= g(-10) = 0$	$= g(5 - 10) = g(-5) = 0$

WORKED EXAMPLE   6.8

Convolution integral

Determine the output pulse $g_0(t)$ that is obtained at the receiver when the transmitted pulse $g(t)$ in the previous Example (Fig. 6.35a) is detected using a matched filter.

We know (from Section 2.8 and Fig. 6.31) that a filter of transfer function $H(f)$ and corresponding impulse response $h(t)$ processes an input signal $g(t)$ — with spectrum $G(f)$ — to give an output signal $g_0(t)$ whose spectrum is given by

$$G_o(f) = G(f)H(f)$$

To obtain the time domain relationship, we take the inverse Fourier transform of this equation, noting that the frequency domain multiplication (on the RHS) becomes a convolution operation — denoted using the star operator ($\star$) — in the time domain. Thus,

$$g_0(t) = g(t) \star h(t)$$

$$= \int_{-\infty}^{\infty} g(\tau)h(t - \tau)\,d\tau \tag{6.81}$$

Eq. (6.81) defines the *convolution integral*, which states that $g_0(t)$ is given at each time instant t by the total area under the function $g(\tau)h(t - \tau)$, which is the product of the input waveform and a time-reversed and delayed (by t) version of the impulse response. It is worth noting that an equivalent definition may be written as follows:

$$g_0(t) = h(t) \star g(t)$$

$$= \int_{-\infty}^{\infty} h(\tau)g(t-\tau)d\tau$$

We will however follow Eq. (6.81) in this discussion. For convenience, the input pulse $g(\tau)$ and the impulse response $h(\tau)$ of the matched filter (obtained in the previous example) are sketched again in Figs. 6.36(a) and (b). When both $g(t)$ and $h(t)$ are of finite duration as in this case, then it is easier, and indeed very illuminating, to evaluate the convolution integral graphically as follows.

1. Obtain the waveform $h(t - \tau)$ using the procedure described in the previous Example. In Fig. 6.36(c), a few examples of $h(t - \tau)$ are shown for $t = -2, 0, 2, 5, 7$ and 10 μs.

2. Multiply together the waveforms $h(t - \tau)$ and $g(\tau)$ to obtain the integrand $g(\tau)h(t - \tau)$ in Eq. (6.81). Note that this integrand is identically zero for those values of t that lead to a $h(t - \tau)$, which does not overlap $g(\tau)$. It can be seen in Fig. 6.36 that this happens for $t \le 0$, and $t \ge 10$, which means that the output pulse $g_0(t)$ is zero in this region of time. Example curves of $g(\tau)h(t - \tau)$ are shown in Fig. 6.36(d), for $t = 2, 5$ and 7 μs.

3. The value of the output pulse $g_0(t)$ at a time t is the area under the curve of $g(\tau)h(t - \tau)$. For example, it can be seen in Fig. 6.36(d) that the area under the curve of $g(\tau)h(7 - \tau)$ is 1.5, which means that $g_0(t) = 1.5$ at $t = 7$ μs.

4. Repeat the above steps for a sufficient number of different values of t to obtain the output $g_0(t)$ sketched in Fig. 6.37.

Note that the matched filter has distorted the transmitted pulse $g(t)$ in such a way that the maximum value of the output pulse $g_0(t)$ occurs at the decision instant $t = T_s$. It can be seen in Fig. 6.36(c) that $h(T_s - \tau) = g(\tau)$. Since the pulse $g(t)$ is a real signal, it follows from Eq. (6.81) that,

$$g_0(T_s) = \int_{-\infty}^{\infty} g(\tau)h(T_s - \tau)d\tau = \int_{-\infty}^{\infty} g(\tau)g(\tau)d\tau$$

$$= \int_{-\infty}^{\infty} |g(\tau)|^2 \, d\tau \qquad (6.82)$$

$$\equiv E \equiv \text{Energy of signal } g(t)$$

Thus $g_0(T_s)$ is the energy of the transmitted pulse $g(t)$, assuming of course that the gain of the matched filter is normalised to unity and the effect of the transmission channel has been equalised according to Eq. (6.75). The matched filter in this example can be approximated using an *integrate-*

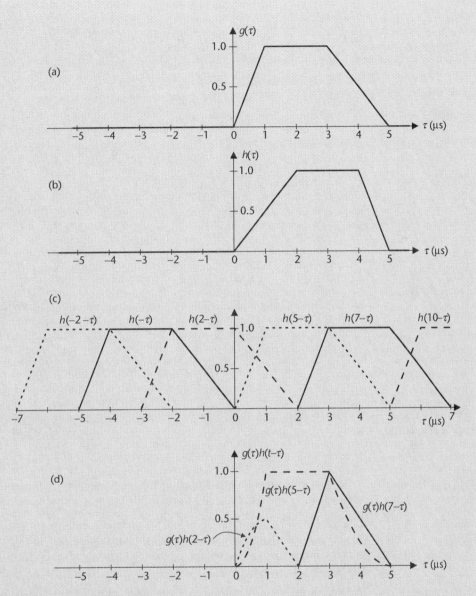

Figure 6.36 Worked example 6.8. (a) Input pulse; (b) impulse response of matched filter; (c) time-reversed and delayed versions of $h(\tau)$; (d) Curves of $g(\tau)h(t - \tau)$, for $t = 2$, 5 and 7 μs.

and-dump filter, which consists of an integrator followed by a sample-and-hold (S/H) circuit. The input pulse is integrated over its duration T_s, and the output is sampled and the integrator reset at the end of each integration period. This technique yields an exact matched filter realisation if the transmitted pulse is rectangular.

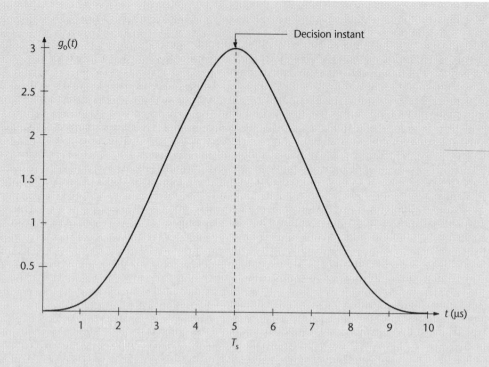

Figure 6.37 Worked example 6.8: Output $g_o(t)$ of matched filter.

WORKED EXAMPLE 6.9

Irrelevance of pulse shapes

Show that the signal-to-noise ratio $(S/N)_o$ at the output of a matched filter depends only on the ratio between input pulse energy E and noise power density, and not on the particular shape of the pulse.

It is clear from the last worked example, and more specifically Eq. (6.82), that the signal at the output of a matched filter has a maximum value E at the decision instant $t = T_s$, where E is the transmitted pulse energy. Therefore, the instantaneous output signal power at the decision instant is

$$P_s = [g_0(T_s)]^2 = E^2 \tag{6.83}$$

Let the amplitude of the uniform (double-sided) spectrum of white noise $w(t)$ at the input of the matched filter be $\sqrt{N_0/2}$, where N_0 is a constant. The filter processes this noise to give a coloured noise $c(t)$ at its output, with a spectrum

$$|C(f)| = |W(f)||H(f)|$$
$$= \sqrt{N_0/2}\,|G(f)| \tag{6.84}$$

where $G(f)$ is the spectrum of the transmitted pulse, and we have used the matched filter transfer function given by Eq. (6.77). The square of $|C(f)|$ gives the output noise *power spectral density*, and hence the average output noise power as

$$P_n = \int_{-\infty}^{\infty} |C(f)|^2 \, df = \frac{N_0}{2} \int_{-\infty}^{\infty} |G(f)|^2 \, df$$

$$= \frac{N_0}{2} E \tag{6.85}$$

where we took the last step by applying *Rayleigh's energy theorem*

$$E = \int_{-\infty}^{\infty} |G(f)|^2 \, df \tag{6.86}$$

Thus,

$$(S/N)_o = \frac{P_s}{P_n} = \frac{E^2}{(N_0/2)E}$$

$$= \frac{2E}{N_0} \tag{6.87}$$

Eq. (6.87) is the desired result. Note that $N_0/2$ is the power spectral density of the input (white) noise. It is interesting that the shape or waveform of the transmitted pulse $g(t)$ does not feature in the achievable signal-to-noise ratio. All that matters is the pulse energy, which may be increased to improve $(S/N)_o$ by increasing the amplitude and/or duration of the pulse. The latter option however would reduce the symbol rate. In summary then, *provided a matched filter is used at the receiver*, all pulses of the same energy are equally detected in the presence of white noise irrespective of the pulse shapes. We must therefore emphasise that pulse shaping (studied in Section 6.6) is required for ISI minimisation and has no bearing whatsoever on the impact of white noise.

WORKED EXAMPLE **6.10**

Correlation receiver

Show that the matched filter may be implemented as a correlation receiver.

Fig. 6.38 shows a *correlation receiver* and a matched filter for detecting a known pulse $g(t)$. The correlation receiver consists of a multiplier followed by an integrator, which integrates the product of the known pulse $g(t)$ and the received pulse $g'(t)$ over the duration T_s of the known pulse. The received pulse is a noise-corrupted version of $g(t)$. The output of the correlation receiver follows from the block diagram:

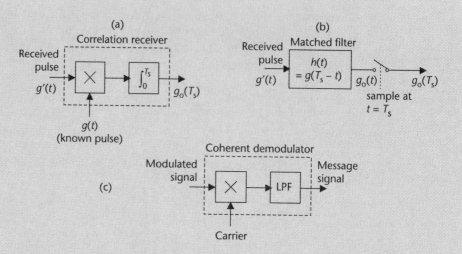

Figure 6.38 Worked example 6.9: Equivalence between (a) correlation receiver, (b) matched filter and (c) coherent demodulator.

$$g_0(T_s) = \int_0^{T_s} g'(\tau)g(\tau)\mathrm{d}\tau \tag{6.88}$$

Thus, in the absence of noise, the output of the correlation receiver is exactly equal to the energy of the transmitted pulse. Now consider the output of the matched receiver,

$$g_0(t) = \int_{-\infty}^{\infty} g'(\tau)h(t-\tau)\mathrm{d}\tau$$

$$= \int_0^{T_s} g'(\tau)g(T_s-t+\tau)\mathrm{d}\tau \tag{6.89}$$

where we have used our knowledge that the pulse has a finite duration T_s, and also substituted the expression for the impulse response of the matched filter $h(t) = g(T_s - t)$, which, when t is replaced by $t - \tau$ on both sides of the expression, leads to the above result. Sampling $g_0(t)$ in Eq. (6.89) at $t = T_s$ gives

$$g_0(T_s) = \int_0^{T_s} g'(\tau)g(T_s-T_s+\tau)\mathrm{d}\tau$$

$$= \int_0^{T_s} g'(\tau)g(\tau)\mathrm{d}\tau$$

which is identical to Eq. (6.88). Thus the correlation receiver and the matched filter give identical results, provided of course that the matched filter output is sampled at $t = T_s$.

We will see in the next chapter that a digital modulated system may transmit *orthogonal* bandpass symbols to represent groups of 0s and 1s. Therefore, a matched filter may be implemented in such a system as a bank of *correlators*. Each correlator is fed with one of the symbols. When the received symbol is applied to all the correlators, the largest output is obtained at the correlator corresponding to the transmitted symbol.

Note that real symbols or waveforms $g_1(t)$, $g_2(t)$, $g_3(t)$, ..., $g_N(t)$, each of duration T_s, are said to be orthogonal with respect to each other if

$$\int_0^{T_s} g_i(t)g_j(t)\,dt = \begin{cases} 0, & i \neq j \\ E_i, & i = j \end{cases} \tag{6.90}$$

where E_i, the energy of $g_i(t)$, is non-zero and positive.

It is worth noting that when two symbols (also referred to as *energy signals*) $g_1(t)$ and $g_2(t)$ are orthogonal, then their energies add independently. That is, the energy E of the sum signal $g(t) = g_1(t) + g_2(t)$ is given by the sum of the energies E_1 and E_2 of $g_1(t)$ and $g_2(t)$, respectively. This is the case since, from Eq. (6.90),

$$\begin{aligned}
E &= \int_0^{T_s} g^2(t)\,dt \\
&= \int_0^{T_s} [g_1(t) + g_2(t)]^2\,dt \\
&= \int_0^{T_s} g_1^2(t)\,dt + \int_0^{T_s} g_2^2(t)\,dt + 2\int_0^{T_s} g_1(t)g_2(t)\,dt \\
&= E_1 + E_2 + 0
\end{aligned} \tag{6.91}$$

If in Eq. (6.90), $E_i = 1$, for $i = 1, 2, 3, ..., N$, then the waveforms $g_1(t)$, $g_2(t)$, $g_3(t)$, ..., $g_N(t)$ are said to be *orthonormal*.

A little thought will show that the correlation receiver is not an entirely new concept. An integrator is just a special low-pass filter — with a gain response that decreases linearly with frequency. The correlation receiver is therefore a special case of the *coherent demodulator*, which was discussed at length in Chapter 3 (e.g. see Fig. 3.20(a)) and is repeated in block diagram form in Fig. 6.38(c) for comparison.

SUMMARY

This now completes our study of digital baseband transmission. We have acquired a thorough grounding in the principles of uniform and non-uniform quantisation and encoding of analogue signals for digital transmission, and a basic understanding of low bit rate speech coding. We also studied how such digitised signals, and indeed all types of digital data, are electrically represented and transmitted in digital baseband systems. The design of the baseband system for optimum and ISI-free performance in noise was examined with emphasis on raised cosine pulse shaping, channel equalisation and matched reception.

Baseband transmission is limited to fixed wire-line channels. To exploit the huge bandwidth of optical fibre in addition to the broadcast and mobility capabilities of radio channels (albeit with smaller bandwidths), we must modulate a suitable carrier with the digital data before transmission. The next chapter therefore deals with digital modulation, which allows us to apply the principles learnt in Chapters 3 and 4 to digital signals, and to further explore the application of matched receivers in modulated systems.

REVIEW QUESTIONS

6.1   The output of a midrise uniform quantiser of input range ±5 V is coded using 8 bits/sample. Determine

   (a) the maximum quantisation error.
   (b) The quantisation error associated with an input sample of value −2.3 V.
   (c) The quantisation noise power.
   (d) The dynamic range of the system.
   (e) The SQNR when the input is a speech signal that fully loads the quantiser.
   (f) The SQNR during a weak passage when the peak value of the input speech signal is only 0.5 V.

6.2   Determine the SQNR of a linear ADC as a function of number of bits/sample for an input signal that has a Gaussian probability density function with zero mean. Ignore sample values that occur on average less than 0.1% of the time. How does your result compare with Eq. (6.14), which gives the SQNR for a speech input signal?

6.3   Determine the values of A and μ that yield a companding gain of 48 dB in A-law and μ-law PCM, respectively. Why aren't such (or even larger) values of A and μ used in practical PCM systems to realise more companding gain and hence greater savings in bandwidth?

6.4   Produce a diagram similar to Fig. 6.11 for a digital translation view of μ-law PCM.

6.5   An analogue input signal of values in the range ±2 V fully loads the quantiser of a μ-law PCM system. Determine

   (a) the quantisation error incurred in transmitting the sample value −1.13 V.
   (b) The PCM code for the sample value −1.9 V.
   (c) The voltage value to which the code 10011110 is converted at the receiver.

     (d) The maximum quantisation error in the recovered sample in (c).

     (e) The minimum and maximum quantisation errors of the whole process.

6.6   Determine the maximum SQNR in the following non-linear PCM systems, and comment on the trend of your results.

     (a) A-law with $A = 1$ and $k = 8$ bits/sample.
     (b) A-law with $A = 100$ and $k = 8$ bits/sample.
     (c) A-law with $A = 1000$ and $k = 8$ bits/sample.
     (d) A-law with $A = 100$ and $k = 6$ bits/sample.
     (e) A-law with $A = 100$ and $k = 10$ bits/sample.

6.7   The message signal $v_m(t) = 5\cos(2000\pi t)$ is coded using delta modulation and a sampling frequency of 10 kHz. Determine

     (a) The minimum step size to avoid overload distortion.
     (b) The quantisation noise power when the minimum step size is used.
     (c) The SQNR. How does this compare with the maximum SQNR realisable using a linear PCM of the same bit rate?

6.8   Sketch the HDB3 and 3B4B waveforms for the following bit stream:

     1 1 1 0 1 1 0 0 0 1 0 0 0 0 0 1 1 0 0 0 0 1 1 1

6.9   Determine the code efficiency, signalling rate and symbol period of a baseband transmission operating at 140 Mbit/s and employing the 4B3T line code.

6.10   A wideband audio signal of baseband frequencies 50 Hz to 7 kHz is processed in a 10-bit linear ADC at a sampling rate of 1.5 times the Nyquist rate. The resulting bit stream is conveyed in a noiseless channel using

     (a) Binary ($M = 2$) signalling.
     (b) Quaternary ($M = 4$) signalling.

     In each case, determine (i) the minimum required transmission bandwidth, and (ii) the transmission bandwidth when the channel has a raised cosine response with $\alpha = 0.5$

6.11   Determine the minimum SNR and hence signal power required for error-free transmission of the signal in Question 6.10 over an AWGN channel of noise power spectral density 10^{-15} W/Hz and bandwidth

     (a) 10 kHz.
     (b) 20 kHz.
     (c) 200 kHz.

     Comment on the trend of your results.

6.12   Sketch the impulse response of a matched filter for detecting each of the pulses shown in Fig. 6.39.

6.13   Determine and sketch the matched filter output for each of the pulses in Question 6.12. What is the maximum value of each output pulse?

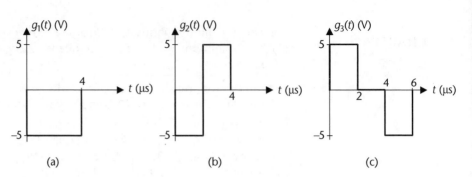

Figure 6.39 Question 6.12.

6.14 Repeat Questions 6.12 and 6.13 for a triangular pulse of amplitude A and duration T_s.

Digital modulated transmission

IN THIS CHAPTER

- Why digital modulated transmission.

- Two views of digital modulated transmission: (1) Frequency, phase or amplitude modulation of a sinusoidal carrier with a digital signal; (2) coding of binary data using sinusoidal (i.e. bandpass) pulses.

- Signal space: You will learn this simple yet powerful tool for analysing both baseband and modulated digital systems.

- Noise effects and bit error rate. You will be able to evaluate the impact of noise on all types of binary modulated and baseband systems. You will also have the foundation needed later to extend the analysis to multilevel digital systems.

- Binary modulation and coherent detection: How ASK, PSK and FSK signals are generated at a transmitter and detected at a receiver. You will also learn the effect of frequency spacing on the bandwidth and bit error rate of FSK.

- Non-coherent detection: This avoids the complexity of phase synchronisation in coherent detectors, but suffers from an inferior noise performance.

- *M*-ary transmission: A detailed and clear presentation of the generation, detection and bit error rates of multilevel ASK, PSK, FSK and hybrid systems.

- *Design considerations*: A lucid discussion that gives you an excellent insight into the interplay of various design parameters, namely bandwidth, signal power, bit rate and bit error rate.

7.1 Introduction

Digital baseband transmission, discussed at length in Chapter 6, conveys information using symbols (or pulses) that contain significant frequency components down to, or near, DC. This technique is impracticable in a number of important situations:

1. When it is required to confine the transmitted frequencies in a digital system within a passband centred at a frequency $f_c \gg 0$. This situation arises in the exploitation of radio and optical fibre transmission media whose useable passband is naturally limited to frequencies well above DC. Radio is the only type of medium that allows broadcast and mobility capabilities, while optical fibre is preferred to coaxial cable for high-capacity fixed telecommunication links. These two media, radio and optical fibre, are involved at some stage in the vast majority of modern transmissions.

2. When the available bandwidth of the transmission medium is insufficient to convey the baseband pulses at the desired symbol rate without significant distortion. An important example here is the global wireline telephone network, which was optimised in the early days for the transmission of analogue voice signals, containing frequencies between 300 and 3400 Hz. However, with digital transmission becoming the preferred method of communication, a means had to be devised to transmit digital signals over these voice-optimised channels in order to exploit the huge financial investment that they represent. This limited-bandwidth situation also arises in radio where separate frequency bands have to be allocated to different users to allow simultaneous transmission by many users on the same link.

The means of utilising the above media for digital communication is by digital modulated transmission in which one or more parameters of a sinusoidal carrier are varied by the information-bearing digital signal. An introduction to the basic techniques of digital modulated transmission, namely amplitude shift keying (ASK), frequency shift keying (FSK) and phase shift keying (PSK) was presented in Section 1.5.3.2, which is worthwhile reviewing at this point.

An important clarification of terminology is in order here. Throughout this chapter, we will use ASK, FSK and PSK to refer to their binary implementation. Multilevel transmission will be explicitly identified with terms such as QPSK, 4-ASK, 4-FSK, M-ary etc. Furthermore, ASK is treated as On–Off Keying (OOK) in which one of the two amplitude levels of the transmitted sinusoid is zero. There is nothing to be gained from making both levels non-zero, except a poorer noise performance for a given transmitted power.

We may approach the subject of digital modulated transmission in two ways.

1. The more obvious approach is to treat the technique as that of sinusoidal carrier modulation involving digital signals. The theories of

amplitude and angle modulations presented in Chapters 3 and 4 can then be applied, but with the modulating signal $v_m(t)$ being digital. Thus ASK, for example, is obtained using an AM modulator with modulation factor $m = 1$, and the (digital) message signal is recovered at the receiver by AM demodulation using an envelope detector. The circuit components in this case are very similar to those of analogue modulation, except that the recovered message signal will be applied to a regenerator to obtain a pure digital signal free from accumulated noise effects.

2. A less obvious but greatly simplifying approach is to treat the technique as an adaptation of baseband transmission to passband channels. The basis of this approach is that the modulated sinusoidal carrier can only take on a discrete number of states in line with the discrete values of the digital modulating signal. Thus we simply treat the modulated carrier transmitted during each sampling interval as a 'bandpass' pulse or symbol. Under this approach, the process of modulation simplifies to symbol *generation*. More importantly, the receiver does not need to reproduce the transmitted waveform, but merely to determine which symbol was transmitted during each interval. Demodulation therefore simplifies to symbol *detection* and subsequent digital baseband signal *regeneration*. Binary ASK, FSK and PSK each involve the transmission of two distinct symbols, shown in Fig. 7.1; while, in general, *M*-ary modulated transmission involves *M* distinct bandpass symbols, as shown in Fig. 7.2 for *M* = 4. To understand why these *sinusoidal symbols* are bandpass, we may consider the case of binary ASK shown in Fig. 7.1. Here, a symbol $g(t)$ is transmitted for the bit duration T_s if the bit is a 1, and no symbol is transmitted if the bit is a 0. We see from Fig. 7.3 that the symbol $g(t)$ can be written as the product of a rectangular pulse of duration T_s and a sinusoidal function (of limitless duration). That is,

$$g(t) = V \operatorname{rect}(t/T_s) \cos(2\pi f_c t) \tag{7.1}$$

Recall (Fig. 2.26) that a rectangular pulse $\operatorname{rect}(t/T_s)$ has a sinc spectrum of null bandwidth $1/T_s$, and that the effect of multiplication by $\cos(2\pi f_c t)$ is to shift this spectrum from its baseband (centred at $f = 0$), to a passband centred at $\pm f_c$. Therefore the spectrum $G(f)$ of $g(t)$ is as shown in Fig. 7.3, which is clearly a bandpass spectrum, of bandwidth $2/T_s$, having significant (positive) frequencies centred around f_c:

$$G(f) = \frac{VT_s}{2} \{ \operatorname{sinc}[(f - f_c)T_s] + \operatorname{sinc}[(f + f_c)T_s] \} \tag{7.2}$$

Our presentation in this chapter follows the second approach. This will allow us to apply the important concepts related to matched filtering, which we learnt in Section 6.7. You will recall that the matched filter can be realised using a correlation receiver or a coherent detector. The main task at the receiver is to determine (in the presence of noise) which symbol was sent during each interval of duration T_s. As long as a matched filter is employed, then what matters is not the symbol shape but the symbol

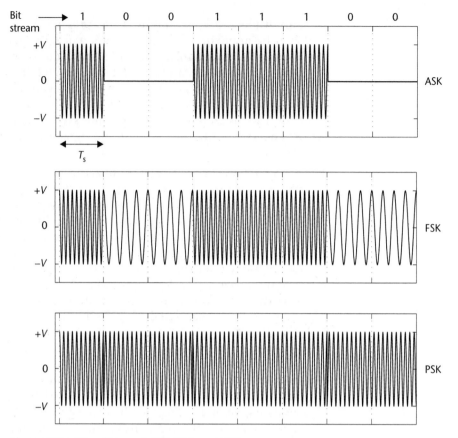

Figure 7.1 Waveforms of ASK, FSK and PSK.

energy E compared to noise power. In the case of sinusoidal symbols used in digital modulated transmission, the symbol energy is given by

$$E = \text{Symbol power} \times \text{Symbol duration}$$
$$= A_c^2 T_s / 2 \tag{7.3}$$

where A_c is the sinusoidal symbol amplitude, and we have assumed (as is usual) a unit load resistance in the computation of power.

Each modulated carrier state or symbol can therefore be fully represented by a point on a *signal space* or *constellation* diagram, the distance of the point from the origin being related to the symbol energy.

In the sequel, we first discuss important general concepts that are applicable to both baseband and modulated digital systems. These include *signal space*, *digital transmission model*, *noise effects* and *bit error rate*. Working carefully through these sections will give you a sound understanding of vital principles, and equip you to easily deal with the special cases of digital modulated transmission discussed in the remaining sections of the chapter. These special cases are briefly discussed under the headings *binary*

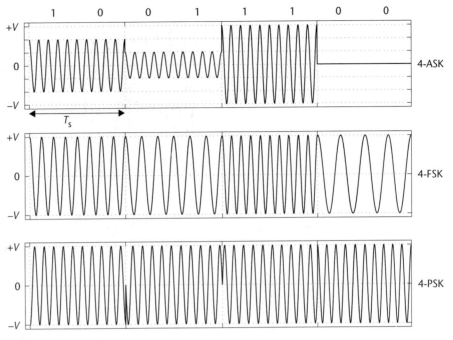

Figure 7.2 Waveforms of 4-ASK, 4-FSK and 4-PSK.

modulation, coherent binary detection, non-coherent binary detection and *M-ary transmission.* The chapter ends with a brief comparison of various digital modulation techniques in terms of the important system design parameters, namely bit rate, required bandwidth, transmitted power and bit error rate.

7.2 Signal space

In digital transmission, information is conveyed using a finite set of M distinct symbols $g_0(t), g_1(t), ..., g_{M-1}(t)$, where $M = 2$ for binary, and $M > 2$ for multilevel or M-ary transmissions. The transmitted symbols are rectangular or shaped pulses in the baseband systems studied in Chapter 6. However, systems involving bandpass transmission media require sinusoidal symbols, which lead to digital modulated transmissions — the subject of this chapter. Each symbol $g_i(t)$ is an energy signal, being of finite duration T_s and of finite amplitude A_c, and hence of finite energy E_i, given by Eq (7.3) for a sinusoidal symbol.

We wish to adopt a *geometric representation* of the set of symbols $\{g_i(t)\}$, which is an excellent tool for visualising the corresponding transmitted states $\{S_i\}$ of a system and their energies and closeness to each other, and for evaluating the impact of additive white Gaussian noise (AWGN) on the system. Orthonormal functions were defined in Section 6.7.6 (Worked

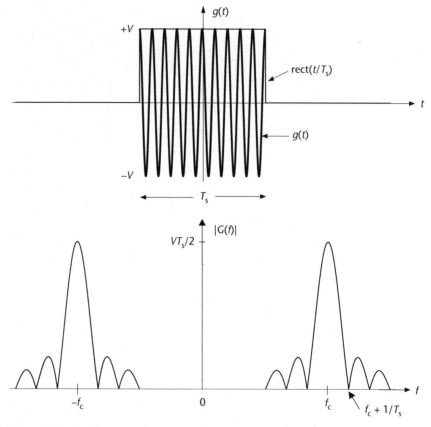

Figure 7.3 Bandpass symbol $g(t)$ and spectrum $G(f)$.

Example 6.10). We may express each of the M energy signals as a linear combination of N *orthonormal basis functions* $\phi_0(t), \phi_1(t), ..., \phi_{N-1}(t)$, where $N \le M$ and $0 \le t \le T_s$:

$$g_i(t) = s_{i0}\phi_0(t) + s_{i1}\phi_1(t) + \cdots + s_{iN-1}\phi_{N-1}(t)$$
$$= \sum_{j=0}^{N-1} s_{ij}\phi_j(t), \qquad \text{for } i = 0, 1, ..., M-1 \tag{7.4}$$

You may recall that by *orthonormal* we mean that the set of functions $\{\phi_i(t)\}$ are mutually orthogonal, and each function in the set is of unit energy. That is,

$$\int_0^{T_s} \phi_i(t)\phi_j(t)dt = \begin{cases} 0, & i \ne j \\ 1, & i = j \end{cases} \tag{7.5}$$

It follows that the energy of $g_i(t)$ is given by

$$E_i = \int_0^{T_s} g_i^2(t)dt$$

$$= \int_0^{T_s} [s_{i0}\phi_0(t) + s_{i1}\phi_1(t) + \cdots + s_{iN-1}\phi_{N-1}(t)]^2\, dt$$

$$= s_{i0}^2 \int_0^{T_s} \phi_0^2(t)dt + s_{i1}^2 \int_0^{T_s} \phi_1^2(t)dt + \cdots + s_{iN-1}^2 \int_0^{T_s} \phi_{N-1}^2(t)dt \qquad (7.6)$$

$$+ 2\sum_{k=1}^{N-1} s_{ik} \sum_{j=0}^{k-1} s_{ij} \int_0^{T_s} \phi_j(t)\phi_k(t)dt$$

$$= s_{i0}^2 + s_{i1}^2 + \cdots + s_{iN-1}^2 = \sum_{j=0}^{N-1} s_{ij}^2$$

Therefore, by analogy with Pythagoras' theorem, we represent the ith transmitted state S_i as a point in *N-dimensional Euclidean space*, which consists of N mutually perpendicular axes $\phi_0, \phi_1, ..., \phi_{N-1}$, and is called the *signal space*. Signal spaces with $N > 3$ cannot be visualised or sketched in real-life space which is limited to three dimensions, but they remain an important mathematical concept. Distances in this space represent the *square root of energy*. In particular, the distance of a point from the origin gives the square root of the energy of the transmitted state that the point represents.

We show signal space examples in Fig. 7.4, with $N = 1$, $M = 2$ in (a); $N = 2$, $M = 8$ in (b); and $N = 3$, $M = 4$ in (c). Let us take a moment to understand what these diagrams tell us about the transmission systems that they represent.

1. *Number of transmitted states*: Information (in the form of a string of 0s and 1s, or bit stream) is conveyed using 2, 8 and 4 distinct symbols or transmitted signal states in (a), (b) and (c), respectively. The assignment of states may be as follows. In Fig. 7.4(a), state S_0 represents bit 0, and S_1 represents bit 1. In Fig. 7.4(b), each state represents a block of three bits; for example, S_0 represents 000, S_1 represents 001, ... and S_7 represents 111. Similarly, each state in Fig. 7.4(c) represents a block of two bits, with S_0 representing 00, S_1 representing 01, and so on. Generally, in a signal space of M states, each state represents $\log_2(M)$ bits.

2. *Energy E_i of each transmitted state S_i*: The energy of each state equals the square of its distance from the origin. Using arbitrary energy units for the moment, we have in Fig. 7.4(a),

$$E_0 = 0$$
$$E_1 = 3^2 = 9$$

In Fig. 7.4(b),

$$E_0 = 1^2 + 1^2 = 2$$
$$E_1 = 1^2 = 1, \text{ and so on}$$

and in Fig. 7.4(c),

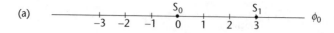

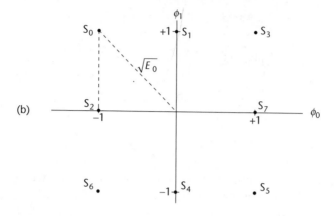

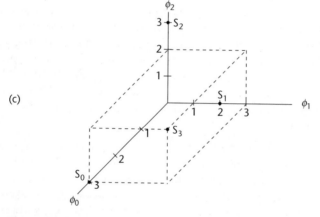

Figure 7.4 Signal space diagrams: (a) $N = 1$, $M = 2$; (b) $N = 2$, $M = 8$; (c) $N = 3$, $M = 4$.

$$E_1 = 2^2 = 4$$
$$E_3 = 3^2 + 3^2 + 2^2 = 22, \text{ and so on}$$

3. *Transmitted symbols*: The symbol $g_i(t)$ transmitted for each state S_i follows from Eq. (7.4), with the coefficients equal to the distance moved along (or parallel to) each axis in order to get to point S_i starting from the origin. Thus, in Fig. 7.4(a),

$$g_0(t) \equiv s_{00}\phi_0(t) = 0$$
$$g_1(t) \equiv s_{10}\phi_0(t) = 3\phi_0(t)$$

In Fig. 7.4(b),

$$g_0(t) \equiv s_{00}\phi_0(t) + s_{01}\phi_1(t)$$
$$= -\phi_0(t) + \phi_1(t)$$
$$g_1(t) \equiv s_{10}\phi_0(t) + s_{11}\phi_1(t)$$
$$= \phi_1(t)$$

and in Fig. 7.4(c),

$$g_1(t) \equiv s_{10}\phi_0(t) + s_{11}\phi_1(t) + s_{12}\phi_2(t)$$
$$= 2\phi_1(t)$$
$$g_3(t) \equiv s_{30}\phi_0(t) + s_{31}\phi_1(t) + s_{32}\phi_2(t)$$
$$= 3\phi_0(t) + 3\phi_1(t) + 2\phi_2(t)$$

Note that the transmitted symbols are of duration T_S and are given in terms of the orthonormal basis functions $\{\phi_i(t)\}$. The form of these basis functions determines whether the system is baseband or modulated. Baseband systems use rectangular (or shaped) basis functions, whereas modulated systems use sinusoidal basis functions. The following worked examples provide a more detailed discussion and further insight.

WORKED EXAMPLE 7.1

Baseband system

A baseband transmission system conveys information using the symbols $g_0(t)$, $g_1(t)$ and $g_2(t)$ shown in Fig. 7.5(a).

(a) Determine a suitable set of two basis functions $\phi_0(t)$ and $\phi_1(t)$.
(b) Sketch the signal space or constellation diagram for this system.

(a) The form of the transmitted symbols suggests that a suitable set of basis functions would be two half-width rectangular pulses $\phi_0(t)$ and $\phi_1(t)$, one occupying the interval $0 \leq t \leq T_S/2$, and the other the interval $T_S/2 \leq t \leq T_S$, as shown in Fig. 7.5(b). A general method for selecting basis functions will be given shortly. We know that $\phi_0(t)$ and $\phi_1(t)$ must be orthogonal, and that their height V_ϕ must be such that each basis function has unit energy. Recall from Worked example 6.10 that two pulses are orthogonal if the energy of their sum equals the sum of the energy of each pulse. In this case the sum pulse $\phi(t)$ is shown in Fig. 7.5(c) and has energy

$$E_\phi = V_\phi^2 T_s$$

But the individual pulses $\phi_0(t)$ and $\phi_1(t)$ have energies

$$E_{\phi 0} = E_{\phi 1} = V_\phi^2 T_s/2 \tag{7.7}$$

It follows that

$$E_\phi = E_{\phi 0} + E_{\phi 1}$$

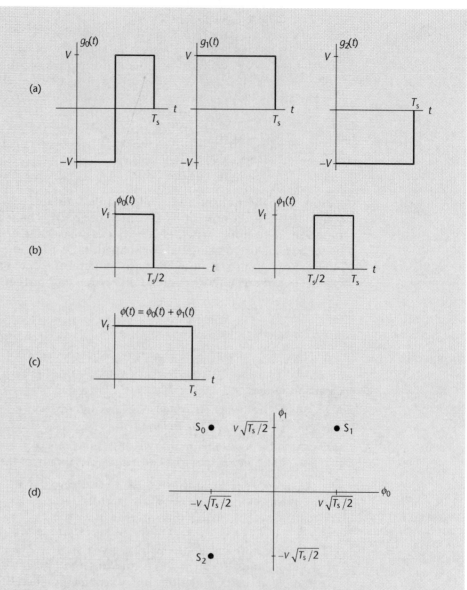

Figure 7.5 Worked example 7.1: (a) transmitted symbols; (b) orthonormal basis functions; (c) sum pulse; and (d) signal space diagram.

and we conclude that $\phi_0(t)$ and $\phi_1(t)$ are orthogonal. In general, pulses that occupy non-overlapping time intervals are orthogonal. Basis functions in baseband systems therefore consist of fractional-width rectangular (or shaped) pulses, one for each interval between transitions in the voltage level of transmitted symbols. In this example, we have two separate time instants at which voltage level transitions occur, one at $t = T_s/2$ in $g_0(t)$ only, and the other at $t = T_s$ in all three transmitted symbols. Thus, we require two basis functions as shown in Fig. 7.5(b). One important exception to this rule is when there are only two opposite polarity (or *antipodal*) symbols $g_0(t)$ and $g_1(t)$, as in Manchester code. In this case only one basis function $\phi_0(t)$ is required, which is the symbol $g_0(t)$ appropriately scaled to unit energy. The two symbols are then given by $g_0(t) = K\phi_0(t)$ and $g_1(t) = -K\phi_0(t)$, where K is a constant.

Finally, we complete the specification of the basis functions by determining the height V_ϕ that gives them unit energy. Thus, from Eq. (7.7),

$$V_\phi = \sqrt{2/T_s} \qquad (7.8)$$

(b) It is clear from Fig. 7.5(a) and (b) that we can now write the transmitted symbols in terms of $\phi_0(t)$ and $\phi_1(t)$:

$$g_0(t) = -\frac{V}{V_\phi}\phi_0(t) + \frac{V}{V_\phi}\phi_1(t)$$

$$= V\sqrt{T_s/2}[-\phi_0(t) + \phi_1(t)] \qquad (7.9)$$

$$g_1(t) = V\sqrt{T_s/2}[\phi_0(t) + \phi_1(t)]$$

$$g_2(t) = -V\sqrt{T_s/2}[\phi_0(t) + \phi_1(t)]$$

The signal space diagram is therefore as shown in Fig. 7.5(d). Note that the transmitted symbols have equal energy

$$E_0 = E_1 = E_2 = V^2 T_s \qquad (7.10)$$

If you have studied Chapter 6, you might have observed by now that the coding used in this baseband system is the *coded mark inversion* (CMI) in which bit 0 is conveyed by $g_0(t)$ and bit 1 is conveyed alternately by $g_1(t)$ and $g_2(t)$.

WORKED EXAMPLE 7.2 _____

Modulated system

In the following problems, a sinusoidal pulse is defined as a signal of duration T_s that has a sinusoidal variation with an integer number of cycles within the interval $0 \leq t \leq T_s$, and is zero elsewhere.

(a) Show that the sinusoidal pulses $g_0(t) = V_0\sin(2\pi f_c t)$ and $g_1(t) = V_1\cos(2\pi f_c t)$ are orthogonal, where $f_c = n/T_s$ and $n = 1, 2, 3, \ldots$.

(b) Show that the set of sinusoidal pulses $\cos(2\pi f_s t)$, $\cos(2\pi 2 f_s t)$, ..., $\cos(2\pi n f_s t)$, ..., where $f_s = 1/T_s$, are mutually orthogonal.

(c) Sketch the signal space diagrams of 4-ASK, 4-PSK, and 4-FSK.

(a) From Eq. (7.3), the energy of each pulse is given by

$$E_0 = V_0^2 T_s/2$$

$$E_1 = V_1^2 T_s/2 \qquad (7.11)$$

The sum pulse $g(t) = g_0(t) + g_1(t)$ is also of duration T_s and is given in the interval $0 \leq t \leq T_s$ by

$$
\begin{aligned}
g(t) &= V_0 \sin(2\pi f_c t) + V_1 \cos(2\pi f_c t) \\
&= V_0 \cos(2\pi f_c t - \pi/2) + V_1 \cos(2\pi f_c t) \\
&= \sqrt{V_0^2 + V_1^2} \cos(2\pi f_c t - \alpha) \\
&\equiv V \cos(2\pi f_c t - \alpha)
\end{aligned}
$$

where $\alpha = \arctan(V_0/V_1)$. Note that we applied the technique of sinusoidal signal addition learnt in Chapter 2. The energy of $g(t)$ is therefore,

$$
\begin{aligned}
E &= V^2 \frac{T_s}{2} = (V_0^2 + V_1^2) \frac{T_s}{2} \\
&= V_0^2 T_s/2 + V_1^2 T_s/2 \\
&= E_0 + E_1
\end{aligned}
$$

We therefore conclude that $g_0(t)$ and $g_1(t)$ are orthogonal since their energies add independently. Note from Eq. (7.11) that $g_0(t)$ and $g_1(t)$ will have unit energy, and hence become a set of two orthonormal basis functions $\phi_0(t)$ and $\phi_1(t)$, if we set their amplitudes to

$$
V_0 = V_1 = \sqrt{2/T_s} \tag{7.12}
$$

In general, the orthonormal basis functions of modulated systems are sinusoidal signals of duration T_s, with frequency f_c equal to an integer multiple of $1/T_s$, and amplitude given by Eq. (7.12).

(b) There is no general rule for adding sinusoids of different frequencies, so in this case we apply Eq. (7.5) to prove orthogonality. Consider two different functions, $g_m(t) = \cos(2\pi m f_s t)$ and $g_n(t) = \cos(2\pi n f_s t)$, in the given set. We have

$$
\begin{aligned}
\int_0^{T_s} g_m(t) g_n(t) \mathrm{d}t &= \int_0^{T_s} \cos(2\pi m f_s t) \cos(2\pi n f_s t) \mathrm{d}t \\
&= \frac{1}{2} \int_0^{T_s} \cos[2\pi (m + n) f_s t] \mathrm{d}t \\
&\quad + \frac{1}{2} \int_0^{T_s} \cos[2\pi (m - n) f_s t] \mathrm{d}t \\
&= 0
\end{aligned}
$$

where we expanded the first integrand on the RHS using the trigonometric identity for the product of cosines. The resulting integrals evaluate to zero since each is the area under a sinusoidal curve over a time interval T_s in which the sinusoid completes an integer number of cycles. Over this interval, there is exactly the same amount of positive and negative area, giving a total area or integral of zero.

Now for $m = n$, we have

$$\int_0^{T_s} g_m(t)g_m(t)dt = \int_0^{T_s} \cos^2(2\pi mf_s t)dt$$

$$= \frac{T_s}{2}$$

where we evaluated the integral by noting that it is the energy of a unit-amplitude sinusoidal pulse, which allows us to apply Eq. (7.3) with $V = 1$. From the foregoing, it follows that

$$\int_0^{T_s} \cos(2\pi mf_s t)\cos(2\pi nf_s t)dt = \begin{cases} 0, & m \neq n \\ T_s/2, & m = n \end{cases} \tag{7.13}$$

where $f_s = 1/T_s$. Therefore the set of sinusoidal pulses with frequencies at integer multiples of $1/T_s$ are mutually orthogonal over the interval $0 \leq t \leq T_s$.

The set of orthonormal basis functions in FSK modulation consists of these sinusoidal pulses with amplitude given by (7.12). M-ary FSK requires M basis functions giving rise to an M-dimensional signal space. On the contrary, M-ary ASK is one-dimensional requiring only one basis function, while M-ary PSK is two-dimensional, requiring two basis functions, albeit of the same frequency. Hybrid modulation techniques, which combine ASK and PSK are also two-dimensional and are realised using a linear combination of the same basis functions as in PSK.

(c) *4-ASK*: This has a one-dimensional signal space with four states S_0, S_1, S_2 and S_3. Only one basis function is involved:

$$\phi_0(t) = \begin{cases} \sqrt{2/T_s}\cos(2\pi nf_s t), & 0 \leq t \leq T_s \\ 0, & \text{elsewhere} \end{cases} \tag{7.14}$$

where n is an integer, and $f_s = 1/T_s$. Transmitted symbols differ only in amplitude, which, if equally spaced in the range from 0 to V, leads to the following symbols:

$$g_0(t) = 0;$$

$$g_1(t) = \frac{V}{3}\sqrt{\frac{T_s}{2}}\phi_0(t)$$

$$g_3(t) = \frac{2V}{3}\sqrt{\frac{T_s}{2}}\phi_0(t) \tag{7.15}$$

$$g_2(t) = V\sqrt{\frac{T_s}{2}}\phi_0(t)$$

4-PSK: The signal space is two-dimensional with the four states represented using a linear combination of two basis functions:

$$\phi_0(t) = \begin{cases} \sqrt{2/T_s}\,\cos(2\pi nf_s t), & 0 \le t \le T_s \\ 0, & \text{elsewhere} \end{cases}$$

$$\phi_1(t) = \begin{cases} \sqrt{2/T_s}\,\sin(2\pi nf_s t), & 0 \le t \le T_s \\ 0, & \text{elsewhere} \end{cases} \tag{7.16}$$

Transmitted symbols have the same amplitude V and frequency nf_s, differing only in phase. One implementation could be

$$g_0(t) = V\sqrt{\frac{T_s}{4}}[\phi_0(t) + \phi_1(t)]$$

$$g_1(t) = V\sqrt{\frac{T_s}{4}}[-\phi_0(t) + \phi_1(t)]$$

$$g_3(t) = V\sqrt{\frac{T_s}{4}}[-\phi_0(t) - \phi_1(t)] \tag{7.17}$$

$$g_2(t) = V\sqrt{\frac{T_s}{4}}[\phi_0(t) - \phi_1(t)]$$

4-FSK: Four basis functions are needed, one for each of the four states S_0, S_1, S_2 and S_3:

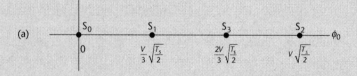

$$\phi_i(t) = \begin{cases} \sqrt{2/T_s}\,\cos[2\pi(n + ki)f_s t], & 0 \le t \le T_s \\ 0, & \text{elsewhere} \end{cases} \tag{7.18}$$

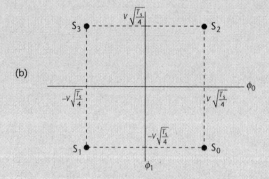

Figure 7.6 Worked example 7.2: Signal space diagrams of (a) 4-ASK and (b) 4-PSK.

where $i = 0, 1, 2, 3$; n and k are integers, with k determining the spacing of the frequencies of the transmitted sinusoidal symbols $g_i(t)$, which are of equal amplitude V, but different frequencies:

$$g_i(t) = V\sqrt{\frac{T_s}{2}}\phi_i(t), \quad i = 0, 1, 2, 3 \tag{7.19}$$

Fig. 7.6 shows the signal space diagrams of the 4-ASK and 4-PSK discussed above. The orientation of the ϕ_1 and ϕ_0 axes in Fig. 7.6(b) is consistent with our definition (Eq. (7.16)) of $\phi_1(t)$ as the sine pulse and $\phi_0(t)$ as the cosine pulse, and the fact that the cosine function leads the sine function by 90°. We have omitted to sketch the signal space diagram of 4-FSK because it is impossible to illustrate four mutually perpendicular axes.

7.3 Digital transmission model

The discussion so far leads us to adopt the simplified model for digital transmission shown in Fig. 7.7. It consists of a symbol generator capable of generating M distinct transmitted symbols $\{g_i(t), i = 0, 1, ..., M-1\}$, a transmission medium that accounts for noise $w(t)$ — including contributions from the receiver, and a symbol detector that determines which of the M symbols is most likely to have been sent given the (noise-corrupted) received signal $r(t)$.

The transmission system is fully described by a set of N orthonormal basis functions $\phi_0(t)$, $\phi_1(t)$, ..., $\phi_{N-1}(t)$, and its signal space diagram. The signal space diagram provides a lucid summary of the adopted coding procedure that maps each distinct input block of $\log_2 M$ bits to a distinct point in N-dimensional space. There are M such input blocks, and therefore M (message) points S_0, S_1, S_{M-1} in the signal space diagram, which corresponds respectively to the M transmitted symbols $g_0(t)$, $g_1(t)$, ..., $g_{M-1}(t)$. Point S_i is identified by a vector s_i called the *signal vector* with N elements s_{i0}, s_{i1}, ..., s_{iN-1}, which are the components of the point along the N mutually perpendicular axis. In a commonly used arrangement, known as *Gray coding*, adjacent message points represent blocks of bits that differ in only one bit position. Figure 7.4(b) is an example of Gray coding. Unless otherwise stated, we employ a notation in which S_i represents a block of bits whose decimal equivalent is i. For example, with $M = 8$, S_0 represents 000, S_5 represents 101, etc.

We may summarise the processes performed at the transmit end of the simplified model in Fig. 7.7 as follows:

1. During each symbol interval, a block of $\log_2 M$ input bits is read and mapped to point S_i according to the agreed coding procedure. Equivalently, we say that signal vector s_i is generated.

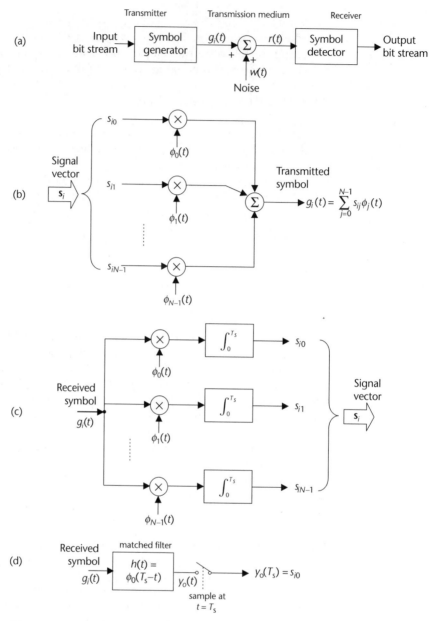

Figure 7.7 (a) Digital transmission model; (b) symbol generation; (c) symbol detection; (d) matched filter equivalent of correlator $j = 0$.

2. Using the basis functions (which characterise the transmission system), and the signal vector $\mathbf{s}_i$, the transmitted symbol $g_i(t)$ is generated according to the block diagram shown in Fig. 7.7(b). Note that this diagram is an implementation of Eq. (7.4).

    Ignoring noise effects for the moment, the receiver has the task of extracting the signal vector $\mathbf{s}_i$ from the symbol $g_i(t)$ received during each symbol interval. Once s_i has been extracted, the corresponding bit block is obtained by mapping from message point S_i to a block of $\log_2 M$ bits according to the coding procedure used at the transmitter. To see how this symbol detection may be carried out, consider the output of a correlation receiver (discussed in Section 6.7.6) which is fed with the received symbol $g_i(t)$ and the jth basis function $\phi_j(t)$:

$$\int_0^{T_s} g_i(t)\phi_j(t)\mathrm{d}t$$

$$= \int_0^{T_s} [s_{i0}\phi_0(t) + s_{i1}\phi_1(t) + \cdots + s_{ij}\phi_j(t) + \cdots + s_{iN-1}\phi_{N-1}(t)]\phi_j(t)\mathrm{d}t$$

$$= s_{ij}\int_0^{T_s} \phi_j^2(t)\mathrm{d}t + s_{i0}\int_0^{T_s} \phi_0(t)\phi_j(t)\mathrm{d}t + \cdots + s_{ij-1}\int_0^{T_s} \phi_{j-1}(t)\phi_j(t)\mathrm{d}t \qquad (7.20)$$

$$+ s_{ij+1}\int_0^{T_s} \phi_{j+1}(t)\phi_j(t)\mathrm{d}t + \cdots + s_{iN-1}\int_0^{T_s} \phi_{N-1}(t)\phi_j(t)\mathrm{d}t$$

$$= s_{ij}$$

In the above, we obtained the second line by expanding $g_i(t)$ according to Eq. (7.4), and the last line by invoking the orthonormality property of the basis functions — Eq. (7.5). We see that the operation yields the jth element s_{ij} of the desired vector $\mathbf{s}_i$. Thus, to determine the entire vector $\mathbf{s}_i$, we feed the received symbol $g_i(t)$ as a common input to a bank of N correlators each of which is supplied with its own basis function. The N outputs of this arrangement, which is shown in Fig. 7.7(c), are the N elements of the vector $\mathbf{s}_i$. You may recall from Section 6.7.6 that the correlator supplied with function $\phi_j(t)$ is equivalent to a matched filter that gives optimum detection (in the presence of white noise) of a symbol of the same waveform as $\phi_j(t)$. Thus each correlator in the bank may be replaced by the matched filter equivalent shown in Fig. 7.7(d).

7.4 Noise effects

In practice, the transmitted symbol is corrupted by noise before it reaches the detection point at the receiver, and the input to the bank of correlators discussed above is the signal

$$r(t) = g_i(t) + w(t) \qquad (7.21)$$

In most practical situations it is adequate to assume that $w(t)$ is additive white Gaussian noise. The output of the jth correlator is

$$\int_0^{T_s} r(t)\phi_j(t)\mathrm{d}t = \int_0^{T_s} [g_i(t) + w(t)]\phi_j(t)\mathrm{d}t$$

$$= \int_0^{T_s} g_i(t)\phi_j(t)\mathrm{d}t + \int_0^{T_s} w(t)\phi_j(t)\mathrm{d}t \qquad (7.22)$$

$$= s_{ij} + w_j$$

Comparing Eq. (7.20) and (7.22), we see that the effect of noise is to shift the output of the jth correlator by a random amount

$$w_j = \int_0^{T_s} w(t)\phi_j(t)\mathrm{d}t \qquad (7.23)$$

In other words, rather than the desired vector s_i (which corresponds to a precise message point S_i), we now have at the output of Fig. 7.7(c) an output vector

$$\mathbf{r} = \mathbf{s}_i + \mathbf{w} \qquad (7.24)$$

where $\mathbf{w}$ is a random vector with components $w_0, w_1, ..., w_{N-1}$, given by Eq. (7.23) with $j = 0, 1, ..., N - 1$, respectively. The received vector $\mathbf{r}$ corresponds to a received signal point R in signal space. This point is displaced from the message point S_i by a distance $|\mathbf{w}|$. The displacement can be in any direction with equal likelihood, but smaller displacements are more likely than large ones, in line with the probability density function (pdf) of a Gaussian random variable. The picture is as shown in Fig. 7.8 for two adjacent message points S_1 and S_2 separated by a distance $\sqrt{E}$. The level of shading at a point gives an indication of the likelihood of the received signal point R to be around that point.

Two important tasks must now be performed at the receiver in order to recover an output bit stream from the received signal $r(t)$. First, a bank of correlators (as in Fig. 7.7(c)) is used to extract the received vector $\mathbf{r}$. Next, given vector $\mathbf{r}$, or equivalently point R, which in general does not coincide exactly with any of the message points $\{S_i, i = 0, 1, ..., M - 1\}$, the receiver has to make a decision on which message point is most likely to have been transmitted. On the assumption that all M message points are transmitted with equal probability, the *maximum likelihood rule* leads to a decision in favour of the message point that is closest to the received signal point. The decision boundary for message points S_1 and S_2 (in Fig. 7.8) is the perpendicular bisector of the line joining S_1 and S_2. Therefore, a symbol error will occur whenever noise effects shift the received point R across this decision boundary.

Clearly, the likelihood of such an error increases as the spacing $\sqrt{E}$ between signal points is reduced. Because of the random nature of noise, we can only talk of the probability P_e that a symbol error will occur, but cannot predict with certainty the interval when this error will occur. For example, a *probability of symbol error* $P_e = 0.01$ means that on average one symbol in a hundred will be incorrectly received. Note that this does not imply that there will always be one error in every 100 transmitted symbols. In fact, there may well be some periods of time during which a thousand or more symbols are received without a single error, and others in which there are two or more errors in 100 symbols. What this statement means is that if we observe the transmission over *a sufficiently long time*, then we will find

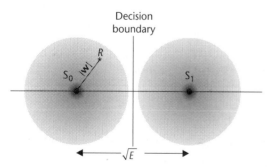

Figure 7.8 Effect of noise.

that the ratio of the number of symbols in error to the total number of symbols transmitted is $P_e = 0.01$. This probability is therefore also referred to as *symbol error rate*, which we determine below for a binary transmission system.

7.5 Symbol and bit error rates

To obtain a more quantitative expression of the effect of noise, consider a binary system with two message points S_0 and S_1 that are separated by distance $\sqrt{E}$ in signal space. This is shown in Fig. 7.9, where the origin has been chosen to be at the message point S_0 and the axis is orientated to pass through S_0 and S_1. Given that S_0 was sent, we wish to determine the probability that S_1 is received — i.e. that the receiver erroneously decides in favour of S_1. This error (denoted P_{e0}) occurs whenever the root energy ($\xi = $ voltage $\times \sqrt{T_s}$) of noise at the decision point exceeds $\sqrt{E}/2$, causing the received signal point to be nearer S_1 than S_0. The probability of this event is equal to the shaded area in Fig. 7.9:

$$P_{e0} = \int_{\sqrt{E}/2}^{\infty} p(\xi)d\xi \tag{7.25}$$

ξ has a Gaussian probability density function (pdf) with zero mean and variance σ^2, so that

$$p(\xi) = \frac{1}{\sqrt{2\sigma^2\pi}} \exp\left(-\frac{\xi^2}{2\sigma^2}\right) \tag{7.26}$$

The mean square value of ξ is the noise energy E_n during one symbol interval. That is,

$$E_n = \int_{-\infty}^{\infty} \xi^2 p(\xi)d\xi \tag{7.27}$$
$$= \sigma^2$$

The last line in the above is obtained by noting that the variance σ^2 of the (zero-mean) distribution is by definition equal to the integral. To obtain E_n we note that the minimum required transmission bandwidth is half the

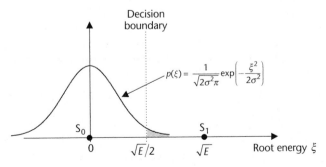

Figure 7.9 Shaded area gives the probability that S_0 is received in error.

symbol rate, or $1/2T_s$ in this case. With a white noise power spectral density N_0 at the receiver input, the total noise power is $P_n = N_0/2T_s$, so that over one symbol interval T_s the noise energy is

$$E_n = P_n T_s = N_0/2 \tag{7.28}$$

It follows from Eq. (7.27) that the variance of ξ is $N_0/2$, and Eq. (7.26) becomes,

$$p(\xi) = \frac{1}{\sqrt{\pi N_0}} \exp\left(-\frac{\xi^2}{N_0}\right)$$

which, when substituted in Eq. (7.25), yields the desired probability,

$$
\begin{aligned}
P_{e0} &= \int_{\sqrt{E}/2}^{\infty} \frac{1}{\sqrt{\pi N_0}} \exp\left(-\frac{\xi^2}{N_0}\right) d\xi \\
&= \frac{1}{2} \frac{2}{\sqrt{\pi}} \int_{\frac{1}{2}\sqrt{E/N_0}}^{\infty} \exp(-y^2) dy \\
&= \frac{1}{2} \operatorname{erfc}\left(\frac{1}{2}\sqrt{\frac{E}{N_0}}\right)
\end{aligned}
\tag{7.29}
$$

In the above, we used the substitution $\xi = \sqrt{N_0} y$ to get to the second line, and obtained the last line by using the following definition of the *complementary error function*:

$$\operatorname{erfc}(x) = \frac{2}{\sqrt{\pi}} \int_x^{\infty} \exp(-y^2) dy$$

Values of this error function are available from standard statistical tables. The graph of Fig. 7.10 will prove useful for obtaining $\operatorname{erfc}(x)$ for values of the argument x in the practical range between 0 and 5. However, for $x > 1.5$, the following approximation may be used:

$$\operatorname{erfc}(x) \simeq \frac{\exp(-x^2)}{\sqrt{\pi}x} \tag{7.30}$$

Let us point out straight away two characteristics of the complementary error function, which have important implications on the interplay between the signal-to-noise ratio (SNR) and the bit error rate (BER) of a transmission system. It will become clear in due course that the first characteristic means that we can always improve (i.e. reduce) BER by increasing SNR, while the second implies that the improvement in BER per dB increase in SNR is larger at higher values of SNR:

1. $\operatorname{erfc}(x)$ decreases monotonically as x increases.
2. The rate of decrease of $\operatorname{erfc}(x)$ is higher at large x.

From the symmetry of the problem in Fig. 7.9, it is clear that the probability P_{e1} of an error in S_1 is the same as P_{e0}. A transmission channel that satisfies this condition, $P_{e1} = P_{e0}$, is referred to as a *binary symmetric channel*. Therefore the probability of error in any symbol is given by

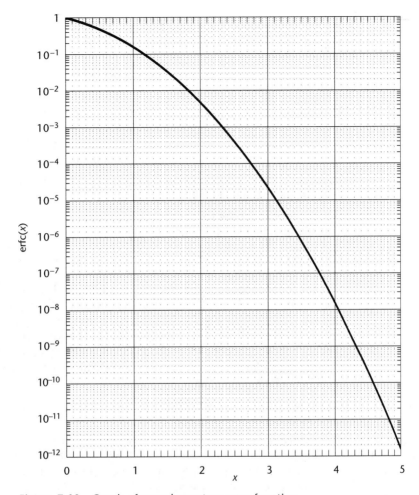

Figure 7.10   Graph of complementary error function.

$$P_{\mathrm{e}} = \frac{1}{2}\,\mathrm{erfc}\!\left(\frac{1}{2}\sqrt{\frac{E}{N_0}}\right) \tag{7.31}$$

To reiterate, Eq. (7.31) gives the symbol error rate (SER) in a binary transmission system where (1) white noise of power spectral density N_0 is the only source of degradation and (2) the two transmitted states are separated by a distance $\sqrt{E}$ in signal space. As the following worked example shows, this important result is directly applicable to the following digital transmission systems:

1. *Unipolar baseband systems*, e.g. all variants of the NRZ line code in Fig. 6.22 (except bipolar) and the RZ code.

2. *Bipolar baseband systems*, e.g. bipolar NRZ and Manchester codes.

3. *All binary modulated systems*, including ASK, PSK and FSK.

We will also show with a specific example of 4-PSK how Eq. (7.31) may be applied to obtain the bit error rate of M-ary systems.

7.5.1 Special cases

WORKED EXAMPLE 7.3

Apply Eq. (7.31) to obtain expressions for the bit error rate (BER) of the following systems in terms of the average energy per bit E_b and the noise power spectral density N_0:

(a) Unipolar baseband transmission and ASK.
(b) Bipolar baseband transmission and PSK.
(c) FSK.
(d) 4-PSK.

Symbol error rate and bit error rate are identical in binary systems, since each transmitted symbol conveys one bit. Equation (7.31) will therefore give the desired expression when E is expressed in terms of E_b. In the following we sketch the signal space diagram of each system with their two states S_0 and S_1 separated by distance $\sqrt{E}$, write out the implied relationship between E and E_b, and substitute this relationship into Eq. (7.31) to obtain the BER.

(a) Unipolar baseband (UBB) transmission and ASK have the one-dimensional signal space shown in Fig. 7.11(a). Note that, in practice, ASK is always implemented as On–Off Keying (OOK). State S_0 represents, say, bit 0 and is sent with zero energy, which means that there is no signalling during the symbol interval T_s. State S_1 has energy E_s and represents, say, bit 1. It is clear from the diagram that $E_s = E$. Thus, Eq. (7.31) yields

$$\text{BER} = \frac{1}{2}\text{erfc}\left(\frac{1}{2}\sqrt{\frac{E_s}{N_0}}\right)$$

E_s is actually the peak symbol energy, which is contained in state S_1, whereas state S_0 contains zero energy. Assuming that both states are equally likely, then the average energy per symbol is $E_{sav} = E_s/2$. In fact, E_{sav} is also the average energy per bit E_b. Thus, substituting $2E_b$ for E_s in the above expression yields the desired formula,

$$\text{BER} = \frac{1}{2}\text{erfc}\left(\sqrt{\frac{E_b}{2N_0}}\right) \quad \text{for UBB and ASK}$$

(b) Fig. 7.11(b) shows the signal space diagram of bipolar baseband (BBB) and (binary) PSK systems. S_0 and S_1 have equal energy E_s, but opposite polarity. Clearly, $\sqrt{E} = 2\sqrt{E_s}$, and in this case E_s is also the average energy per bit E_b. Thus, Eq. (7.31) becomes

(a)

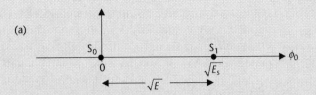

(b)

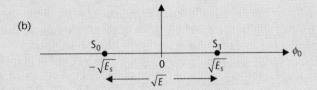

(c)

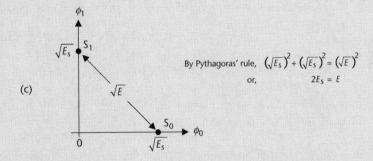

Figure 7.11 Signal space diagrams for Worked example 7.3.
(a) Unipolar baseband systems and ASK (usually OOK); (b) bipolar
baseband and PSK; (c) FSK.

$$\text{BER} = \frac{1}{2}\text{erfc}\left(\sqrt{\frac{E_b}{N_0}}\right) \quad \text{for BBB and PSK}$$

(c) The signal space diagram of a (binary) FSK system is two-dimensional, as shown in Fig. 7.11(c). The two states S_0 and S_1 have equal energy E_s (which is also the average energy per bit E_b), but different frequencies represented by the orthogonal basis functions $\phi_0(t)$ and $\phi_1(t)$. These states are shown separated by distance $\sqrt{E}$, as required for using Eq. (7.31). Applying Pythagoras' rule to the diagram, we see that $E = 2E_s$ (or $2E_b$). Equation (7.31) therefore yields

$$\text{BER} = \frac{1}{2}\text{erfc}\left(\sqrt{\frac{E_b}{2N_0}}\right) \quad \text{for FSK}$$

(d) 4-PSK, also referred to as *quadriphase shift keying* (QPSK), has a two-dimensional signal space diagram, which was sketched in Fig. 7.6(b), but is repeated in Fig. 7.12(a) using a labelling that is appropriate to the following discussion. There are four states, each with energy E_s.

By Pythagoras' rule, the distance between S_0 and S_1 is $\sqrt{2E_s}$, and so is the distance between S_0 and S_2. The separation between S_0 and S_3 is obviously $2\sqrt{E_s}$. Let us determine the probability P_{e0} that there is an error given that S_0 was transmitted. Clearly, an error will occur if S_0 is sent whereas the received point R lies in quadrant 2, 3 or 4 – the shaded region in Fig. 7.12(b).

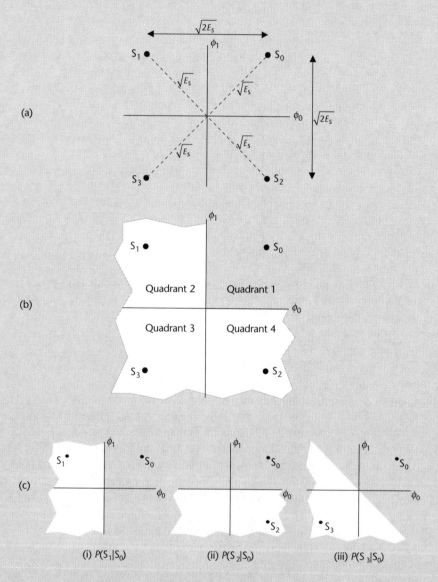

Figure 7.12 QPSK. (a) Signal space diagram; (b) error occurs if S_0 is sent but received point lies in shaded region; (c) taking two states at a time, error occurs if the received point falls in the shaded region.

In order to apply Eq. (7.31), we take two states at a time, as shown in Fig. 7.12(c). Consider Fig. 7.12(c)(i). All points in the shaded region are nearer to S_1 than S_0, and the receiver will therefore decide in favour of S_1 whenever the received point lies in this region. So an error occurs if S_0 is sent but the received state lies in the shaded area. The probability of this error, denoted $P(S_1|S_0)$ and read 'probability S_1 received given S_0 sent', is given by Eq. (7.31) with $\sqrt{E} = \sqrt{2E_s}$:

$$P(S_1 \mid S_0) = \frac{1}{2}\operatorname{erfc}\left(\sqrt{\frac{E_s}{2N_0}}\right)$$

Similarly, in (c)(ii) and (c)(iii),

$$P(S_2 \mid S_0) = \frac{1}{2}\operatorname{erfc}\left(\sqrt{\frac{E_s}{2N_0}}\right)$$

$$P(S_3 \mid S_0) = \frac{1}{2}\operatorname{erfc}\left(\sqrt{\frac{E_s}{N_0}}\right)$$

Observe that the shaded area of Fig. 7.12(b) is given by the sum of the shaded areas in Figs. 7.12(c)(i) and (ii) less half the shaded area in (c)(iii) – to correct for quadrant 3 being included twice in the summation. Therefore, the probability P_{e0} that R is in the shaded region of Fig. 7.12(b) is given by

$$P_{e0} = P(S_1 \mid S_0) + P(S_2 \mid S_0) - \frac{1}{2}P(S_3 \mid S_0)$$

$$= \operatorname{erfc}\left(\sqrt{\frac{E_s}{2N_0}}\right) - \frac{1}{4}\operatorname{erfc}\left(\sqrt{\frac{E_s}{N_0}}\right)$$

$$\simeq \operatorname{erfc}\left(\sqrt{\frac{E_s}{2N_0}}\right)$$

where the approximation holds because the second term in the previous line is negligible compared to the first term for practical values of E_s/N_0. For example, the ratio between the two terms is 25 at $E_s/N_0 = 5$ dB, increasing rapidly to 809 at $E_s/N_0 = 10$ dB. An important implication of this observation is that when E_s/N_0 is large, then $P(S_3|S_0)$ is small compared to $P(S_1|S_0)$ and $P(S_2|S_0)$. In other words, it can be assumed that errors involve the mistaking of one symbol for its nearest neighbours only. From the symmetry of the signal space diagram, it follows that the probability of error in any of the other symbols is the same as obtained above for S_0. Thus, the probability of error in any symbol is given by

$$P_{es} \equiv \mathrm{SER} = \operatorname{erfc}\left(\sqrt{\frac{E_s}{2N_0}}\right) = \operatorname{erfc}\left(\sqrt{\frac{E_b}{N_0}}\right) \tag{7.32}$$

since each symbol conveys two bits, so that $E_s = 2E_b$. Finally, to obtain bit error rate (BER), we observe that in M-ary transmission with Gray coding, neighbouring states differ in only one bit position. An error in one symbol, which represents $\log_2 M$ bits, gives rise to one bit error. Thus,

$$BER = \frac{\text{Symbol error rate}}{\log_2 M} \tag{7.33}$$

In this case, with $M = 4$ and symbol error rate given by Eq. (7.32) we obtain the desired result:

$$BER = \frac{1}{2}\text{erfc}\left(\sqrt{\frac{E_b}{N_0}}\right) \quad \text{for QPSK} \tag{7.34}$$

From the above worked example, we summarise the following important results, which are also plotted in Fig. 7.13 with E_b/N_0 expressed in dB. An important word of caution is in order here: Before using any of the formulas for BER presented in this Chapter, the quantity E_b/N_0 must first be computed as the (non-dB) ratio between E_b in joules ($\equiv$ watt seconds) and N_0 in watts/hertz ($\equiv$ watt seconds).

$$BER = \begin{cases} \dfrac{1}{2}\text{erfc}\left(\sqrt{\dfrac{E_b}{2N_0}}\right), & \text{ASK, FSK \& UBB} \\[3mm] \dfrac{1}{2}\text{erfc}\left(\sqrt{\dfrac{E_b}{N_0}}\right), & \text{PSK, QPSK \& BBB} \end{cases} \tag{7.35}$$

7.5.2 Arbitrary binary transmission

Equation (7.31) may be expressed in a very useful form that gives the BER of any type of binary transmission system directly in terms of the average energy per bit E_b. To do this, let us first define an important parameter known as the *correlation coefficient* ρ of two energy signals $g_0(t)$ and $g_1(t)$ of duration T_s and respective energies E_0 and E_1 as follows:

$$\rho = \frac{\int_0^{T_s} g_0(t)g_1(t)dt}{\text{Average energy}} = \frac{2\int_0^{T_s} g_0(t)g_1(t)dt}{E_0 + E_1} \tag{7.36}$$

Note from this definition, and the definition of orthogonality in Eq. (7.5), that the correlation coefficient of two orthogonal energy signals is zero.

Next, consider the general signal space diagram shown in Fig. 7.14. This diagram applies to all binary systems with an appropriate choice of coefficient values (s_{00}, s_{01}, s_{10}, s_{11}) and basis functions $\phi_0(t)$ and $\phi_1(t)$. We also know that the BER is given by Eq. (7.31) with $\sqrt{E}$ the distance between points S_0 and S_1, and that this system employs two symbols,

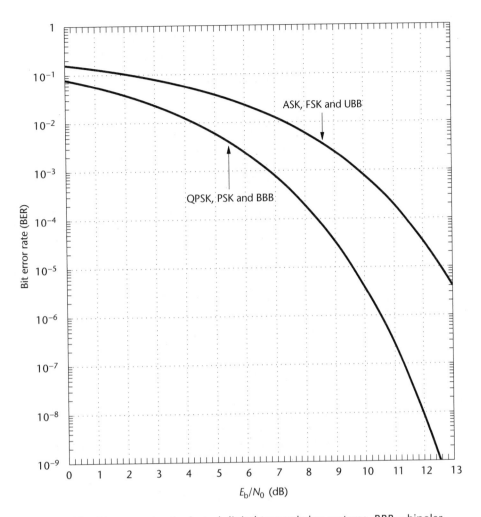

Figure 7.13 Bit error rate of selected digital transmission systems. BBB = bipolar baseband; UBB = unipolar baseband.

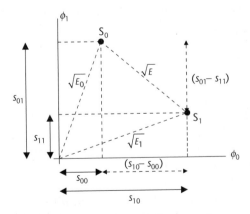

Figure 7.14 Signal space diagram of an arbitrary binary transmission system

$$g_0(t) = s_{00}\phi_0(t) + s_{01}\phi_1(t), \quad \text{for binary } 0$$
$$g_1(t) = s_{10}\phi_0(t) + s_{11}\phi_1(t), \quad \text{for binary } 1$$

The respective energies of the symbols are

$$E_0 = s_{00}^2 + s_{01}^2$$
$$E_1 = s_{10}^2 + s_{11}^2 \tag{7.37}$$

The average energy per bit E_b is given by

$$E_b = \frac{E_0 + E_1}{2} \tag{7.38}$$

and the correlation coefficient of the two symbols follows from Eq. (7.36):

$$
\begin{aligned}
\rho &= \frac{1}{E_b} \int_0^{T_s} g_0(t)g_1(t)dt \\
&= \frac{1}{E_b} \int_0^{T_s} [s_{00}\phi_0(t) + s_{01}\phi_1(t)][s_{10}\phi_0(t) + s_{11}\phi_1(t)]dt \\
&= \frac{1}{E_b} \left\{ s_{00}s_{10} \int_0^{T_s} \phi_0^2(t)dt + s_{01}s_{11} \int_0^{T_s} \phi_1^2(t)dt \right\} \\
&= \frac{s_{00}s_{10} + s_{01}s_{11}}{E_b}
\end{aligned}
\tag{7.39}
$$

In the above, we obtained the third line by ignoring the integrals involving the product $\phi_0(t)\phi_1(t)$ since they evaluate to zero — in view of the orthogonality property; and the last line by noting that $\phi_0(t)$ and $\phi_1(t)$ are unit-energy basis functions.

Finally, applying Pythagoras' rule in Fig. 7.14 allows us to express the energy E in terms of E_b and ρ as follows:

$$
\begin{aligned}
(\sqrt{E})^2 &= (s_{01} - s_{11})^2 + (s_{10} - s_{00})^2 \\
&= (s_{00}^2 + s_{01}^2) + (s_{10}^2 + s_{11}^2) - 2(s_{00}s_{10} + s_{01}s_{11})
\end{aligned}
$$

Replacing each term on the RHS with its equivalent from Eq. (7.37) to (7.39) yields the following important relation,

$$
\begin{aligned}
E &= E_0 + E_1 - 2\rho E_b \\
&= 2E_b - 2\rho E_b \\
&= 2E_b(1 - \rho)
\end{aligned}
\tag{7.40}
$$

Substituting this relation in Eq. (7.31) gives the BER of *any* binary transmission system (assumed to have binary symmetry):

$$\text{BER} = \frac{1}{2}\text{erfc}\left(\sqrt{\frac{E_b(1 - \rho)}{2N_0}}\right) \tag{7.41}$$

It is worth emphasising that Eq. (7.41) applies to all binary symmetric systems, whether modulated or baseband. A few special cases will help to demonstrate the utility of this important equation.

1. *Identical symbols*: if $g_0(t) = g_1(t)$, then $\rho = 1$, and Eq. (7.41) gives BER = $0.5\mathrm{erfc}(0) = 0.5$. It would be ridiculous to use the same symbol to convey both binary 1 and 0. The BER is the same as would be obtained by basing each decision entirely on the result of flipping a fair coin. The receiver does not gain any information from detecting the incoming symbols, and should not even bother.

2. *PSK and BBB*: two antipodal symbols are used. With $g_0(t) = -g_1(t)$, we obtain $\rho = -1$. Equation (7.41) then reduces to Eq. (7.35).

3. *FSK*: two orthogonal symbols are used, giving $\rho = 0$. Equation (7.41) then reduces to (7.35).

4. *ASK and UBB*: two symbols are used that differ only in their amplitudes A_0 and A_1, which are of course positive numbers. You may wish to verify that in this case $\rho \geq 0$. Specifically,

$$\rho = \frac{2A_0 A_1}{A_0^2 + A_1^2} \qquad (7.42)$$

We see from Eq. (7.41) that for a given E_b, the lowest BER is obtained when $A_0 = 0$, giving $\rho = 0$. For all other values of A_0, the correlation coefficient ρ has a positive value between 0 and unity. This reduces the argument of the complementary error function and leads to a larger BER. Setting $A_0 = 0$ gives what is known as On–Off Keying (OOK). It is therefore clear that OOK gives ASK its best (i.e. lowest) possible BER. Assigning non-zero values to both A_0 and A_1 always results in a poorer BER compared to an OOK of the same energy per bit. Note that setting A_0 and A_1 to the same non-zero value yields $\rho = 1$, and BER = 0.5. This, and the case of $A_0 = A_1 = 0$, correspond to the identical-symbol system discussed earlier.

From the foregoing we have a very clear picture of the BER performance of the three types of binary modulation. We see that PSK gives a lower BER than either ASK or FSK for a given received signal power, which is measured in terms of the average energy per bit E_b. To achieve the same error rates in the three systems, twice as much symbol energy (i.e. 3 dB increase) is required in ASK and FSK. The increase is more worthwhile at higher values of E_b/N_0. For example, when E_b/N_0 is 12 dB, then a 3dB increase in E_b improves the BER of ASK and FSK dramatically from 3.4×10^{-5} to 9×10^{-9}. On the other hand, at $E_b/N_0 = 2$ dB, a similar increase in E_b only yields a modest improvement in BER from 0.1 to 0.04. Furthermore, for the same channel bandwidth (proportional to symbol rate) and transmitted power (proportional to E_b), QPSK has exactly the same BER as PSK, but it allows transmission at twice the bit rate.

WORKED EXAMPLE ⬤ **7.4**

A binary PSK system transmits at 140 Mbit/s. The power spectral density of (Gaussian) noise at the receiver input is 5×10^{-21} W/Hz, and the received signal power is –82 dBm.

(a) Determine the bit error rate (BER).

(b) Show how BER may be improved to 1×10^{-8} if the modulation technique and noise level remain unchanged.

(a) To determine BER we need the average energy per bit E_b, which equals the product of received power and bit duration. The received power P (in watts) is

$$P = [10^{(-82/10)}] \times 10^{-3} = 6.31 \times 10^{-12} \text{ W}$$

The duration of one bit is given by

$$T_s = \frac{1}{\text{Bit rate}} = \frac{1}{140 \times 10^6} = 7.143 \times 10^{-9} \text{ s}$$

Therefore energy per bit is

$$E_b = PT_s = 4.507 \times 10^{-20} \text{ J}$$

With $N_0 = 5 \times 10^{-21}$, the ratio $E_b/N_0 = 9.0137$ or 9.55 dB. There are now several options for obtaining the BER. From the curve labelled 'PSK and BBB' in Fig. 7.13, we see that at $E_b/N_0 = 9.55$ dB, the BER is 1.1×10^{-5}. Alternatively, using Eq. (7.35), with $E_b/N_0 = 9.0137$ we obtain:

$$\text{BER} = 0.5 \text{erfc}(\sqrt{9.0137}) = 0.5 \text{erfc}(3)$$

Now we may read the value erfc(3) from Fig. 7.10, or (with 5% error) calculate it using the approximation in Eq. (7.30). Whichever way, the result is BER $\approx 1.1 \times 10^{-5}$.

(b) Fig. 7.13 shows that in binary PSK a BER of 1×10^{-8} requires $E_b/N_0 = 12$ dB. Therefore with N_0 unchanged, we must increase E_b by 2.45 dB (i.e 12 – 9.55) or a factor of 1.758 to achieve this lower BER. Since $E_b = PT_s$, it is clear that E_b may be increased either by increasing the transmitted power (and hence received power P) or increasing the symbol duration T_s. Note that increasing T_s is equivalent to reducing bit rate by the same factor. Therefore we may maintain the bit rate at 140 Mbit/s but raise the transmitted power to give a received power level of 11.1 pW. Alternatively, we maintain the previous power level but reduce the bit rate to 79.64 Mbit/s. Transmitted power level is often restricted in order to minimise the interference to other systems, or to reduce radiation hazards to users of handheld transmitters, or to prolong battery life in portable systems. However, with E_b determined by both transmitted power level and bit rate, acceptable values of these two parameters can always be selected to match the noisiness of the transmission system and deliver a desired BER.

7.6 Binary modulation

In binary modulation one symbol is transmitted to represent each bit in the information-bearing bit stream. There are therefore two distinct symbols, namely $g_0(t)$ representing binary 0, and $g_1(t)$ representing binary 1. Clearly then, binary modulation is the simplest special case of our discussion in previous sections with

Number of states in signal space $M = 2$
Symbol duration $T_s =$ Bit duration T_b
Symbol rate $R_s =$ Bit rate R_b $\qquad$ (7.43)
Symbol energy $E_s =$ Bit energy E_b

Binary modulation has already been discussed to some extent in this chapter, especially in the worked examples. This section is devoted to a brief discussion of the generation and bandwidth of the three types of binary modulated signals, namely ASK, FSK and PSK. Each generator in the following discussion involves a product modulator, which is represented as a multiplier. A detailed description of the operation of a product modulator was presented in Section 3.7.1.2.

7.6.1 ASK

Amplitude shift keying (ASK) signal $g(t)$ may be generated using the circuit shown in block diagram form in Fig. 7.15(a). The bit stream is first represented as a unipolar non-return-to-zero (UNRZ) waveform. At the output of the UNRZ coder, binary 1 is represented by a pulse of height $+V$ and duration spanning the entire bit interval T_b, and binary 0 by the absence of a pulse in the bit interval. The pulse shape is shown as rectangular, but may be shaped (using for example the root raised cosine filter discussed in Chapter 6) in order to reduce the frequency components outside the main lobe of Fig. 7.3. The UNRZ waveform and a sinusoidal signal $\phi_0(t)$ — the basis function of the system, are applied to a product modulator. The resulting output is the desired ASK signal. This consists of a sinusoidal pulse during the bit interval for a binary 1 and no pulse for a binary 0:

$$v_{ask}(t) = \begin{cases} g_1(t), & \text{Binary 1} \\ 0, & \text{Binary 0} \end{cases}$$

$$g_1(t) = \begin{cases} A_c \cos(2\pi f_c t), & 0 \leq t \leq T_b \\ 0, & \text{elsewhere} \end{cases} \qquad (7.44)$$

$$f_c = n/T_b = nR_b, \qquad n = 1, 2, 3, \ldots$$

The frequency f_c of the sinusoidal symbol is an integer multiple of the bit rate R_b, and the amplitude A_c has a value that gives the required *average energy per bit* E_b. If binary 1 and 0 are equally likely in the input bit stream, it follows from Eq. (7.3) that

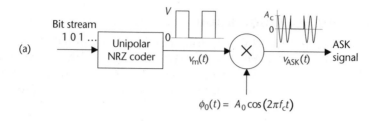

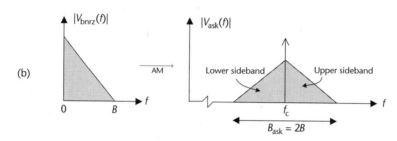

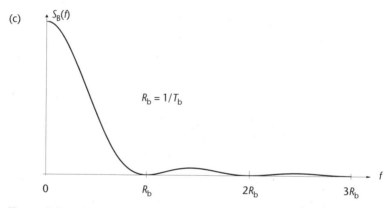

Figure 7.15 ASK. (a) Modulator; (b) Single-sided amplitude spectrum based on a triangular shape for the spectrum of a BNRZ waveform; (c) Actual power spectral density of a BNRZ waveform for a random bit stream.

$$E_b = \frac{1}{2}\left(\frac{A_c^2}{2}T_b + 0\right) = \frac{A_c^2 T_b}{4}$$

$$\text{or} \quad A_c = 2\sqrt{E_b/T_b}$$

(7.45)

To examine the spectrum of ASK, let us rewrite $v_{ask}(t)$ in the form

$$v_{ask}(t) = \frac{A_c}{2}[1 \pm m]\cos(2\pi f_c t), \qquad m = 1$$

(7.46)

where the positive sign holds during an interval of binary 1 and the negative sign during binary 0. In this form, we see that ASK is a double sideband transmitted carrier amplitude modulation signal, with modulation factor $m = 1$. A little thought and, if need be, reference to Chapter 3 will show that in this view, the modulating signal $v_m(t)$ is a *bipolar* NRZ waveform of value $A_c/2$ during binary 1, and $-A_c/2$ during binary 0; and the unmodulated carrier amplitude is $A_c/2$. The spectrum of the ASK signal then consists of an upper sideband, a lower sideband, and an impulse (of weight $A_c/2$) at the carrier frequency, as shown in Fig. 7.15(b) for a symbolic spectrum of $v_m(t)$. The bandwidth of ASK is therefore twice the bandwidth of the baseband bipolar NRZ waveform. We have assumed that the input bit stream is completely random, 1s and 0s occurring with equal likelihood. Under this condition the power spectral density $S_B(f)$ of the bipolar NRZ waveform equals the square of the amplitude spectrum of the constituent pulse. Thus, assuming a rectangular pulse shape,

$$S_B(f) = \text{sinc}^2(fT_b), \qquad \text{Normalised} \qquad (7.47)$$

Figure 7.15(c) shows a plot of $S_B(f)$, which decreases rapidly as the square of frequency, and has a null bandwidth equal to the bit rate R_b (= $1/T_b$). Setting the baseband signal bandwidth equal to this null bandwidth, it follows that the bandwidth of ASK is given by

$$B_{ask} = 2R_b \qquad (7.48)$$

7.6.2 PSK

A block diagram for the generation of PSK is shown in Fig. 7.16. The bit stream is first coded as a bipolar non-return-to-zero (BNRZ) waveform. At the output of the BNRZ coder, binary 1 is represented by a pulse of height $+V$ and duration spanning the entire bit interval T_b, and binary 0 is represented by a similar pulse but of opposite polarity. Pulse shaping may be included prior to modulation by following the coder with a suitable filter, or making the filter an integral part of the coder. The BNRZ waveform is applied to a product modulator along with a sinusoidal signal $\phi_0(t)$, which serves as the basis function of the system. The resulting output is the desired PSK signal. This consists of two distinct sinusoidal pulses of duration T_b that have the same frequency f_c and amplitude A_c, but differ in phase by 180°. The generation process shown in Fig. 7.16(a) leads to a sinusoidal pulse with 0° phase during intervals of binary 1, and an opposite polarity pulse (i.e. 180° phase) during intervals of binary 0. That is,

$$v_{psk}(t) = \begin{cases} g_1(t), & \text{Binary 1} \\ -g_1(t), & \text{Binary 0} \end{cases}$$

$$g_1(t) = \begin{cases} A_c \cos(2\pi f_c t), & 0 \le t \le T_b \\ 0, & \text{elsewhere} \end{cases} \qquad (7.49)$$

$$f_c = n/T_b = nR_b, \qquad n = 1, 2, 3, \ldots$$

Both transmitted symbols have the same energy. In this case the energy per bit E_b is given by

$$E_b = A_c^2 T_b/2$$
$$\text{or} \quad A_c = \sqrt{2E_b/T_b} \qquad (7.50)$$

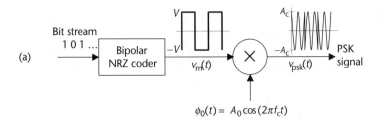

(a)

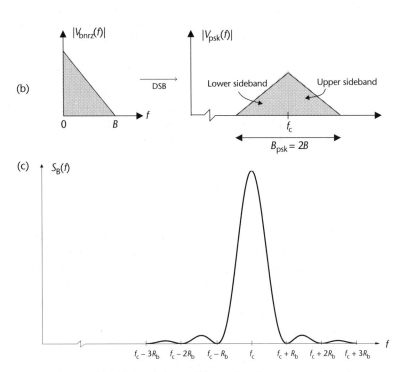

(b)

(c)

Figure 7.16 PSK. (a) Modulator; (b) amplitude spectrum based on a triangular shape for the spectrum of a BNRZ waveform; (c) power spectral density, assuming a random bit stream.

We may obtain the spectrum of PSK by noting that Fig. 7.16(a) represents a double sideband suppressed carrier amplitude modulation. PSK will therefore have a spectrum similar to that of ASK, except that there is no impulse at the frequency point f_c, which reflects the absence or suppression of the carrier. Figs. 7.16(b) and (c) show, respectively, a representative amplitude spectrum of PSK and the power spectral density of a PSK signal when the input bit stream is completely random. Clearly, PSK has the same bandwidth as ASK, which is twice the bandwidth of the baseband bipolar waveform:

$$B_{psk} = 2R_b \tag{7.51}$$

7.6.3 FSK

7.6.3.1 Generation

In frequency shift keying (FSK), two orthogonal sinusoidal symbols are employed, one of frequency f_1 to represent binary 1, and the other of frequency f_0 to represent binary 0. FSK can therefore be generated by combining (i.e. interleaving) two ASK signals as shown in Fig. 7.17(a). The bit stream is first represented using a UNRZ waveform. The output of the UNRZ coder is fed directly into the top product modulator, which is also supplied with a sinusoidal signal of frequency f_1. The output of the top modulator is therefore an ASK signal that has a sinusoidal pulse of frequency f_1 during intervals of binary 1, and no pulse during intervals of binary 0. The UNRZ coder output is also fed into the lower product modu-lator but is first passed through an inverter. The lower modulator is supplied with another sinusoidal signal of frequency f_0. The inverter produces a UNRZ waveform, which has a value $+V$ during intervals of binary 0, and a value 0 for binary 1. As a result, the output of the lower modulator is another ASK signal, but one which contains a sinusoidal pulse of frequency f_0 during intervals of binary 0 and no pulse during intervals of binary 1. It is easy to see that by combining the outputs of the two modula-tors in a summing device, we obtain a signal that contains a sinusoidal

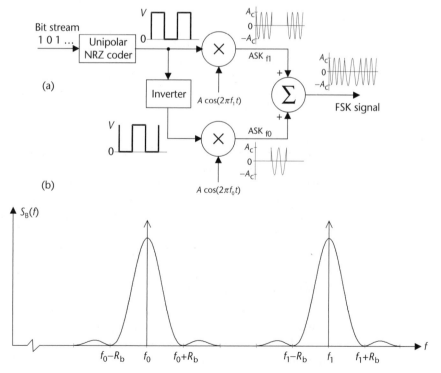

Figure 7.17 FSK. (a) Modulator; (b) power spectral density, assuming a random bit stream.

pulse of frequency f_1 for binary 1, and another sinusoidal pulse of frequency f_0 for binary 0. This is the desired FSK signal, and we may write,

$$v_{fsk}(t) = \begin{cases} g_1(t), & \text{Binary 1} \\ g_0(t), & \text{Binary 0} \end{cases}$$

$$g_1(t) = \begin{cases} A_c \cos(2\pi f_1 t), & 0 \le t \le T_b \\ 0, & \text{elsewhere} \end{cases} \tag{7.52}$$

$$g_0(t) = \begin{cases} A_c \cos(2\pi f_0 t), & 0 \le t \le T_b \\ 0, & \text{elsewhere} \end{cases}$$

$$f_1 = n_1/T_b; \quad f_0 = n_0/T_b; \quad n_1 \ne n_0 = 1, 2, 3, \dots$$

It is important that the two transmitted symbols $g_1(t)$ and $g_0(t)$ are orthogonal. This requires that the sinusoidal signals supplied to the pair of modulators in Fig. 7.17(a) should have exactly the same phase at all times. There is an implicit assumption of this phase synchronisation in Fig. 7.17(a) where the sinusoidal signals both have the same phase (0°). Phase synchronisation coupled with the use of sinusoids whose frequencies are integer multiples of the bit rate ensures that there is phase continuity between symbols. The FSK is then described as *continuous phase frequency shift keying* (CPFSK). Note that both symbols have the same energy. The average energy per bit is the same as in PSK and is given by Eq. (7.50).

7.6.3.2 Spectrum

The view of FSK as two interleaved ASK signals leads logically to the power spectral density of FSK shown in Fig. 7.17(b). Each constituent ASK power spectrum has an impulse of weight $A_c^2/4$ at its respective carrier frequency, as explained earlier. It follows from this power spectrum that the bandwidth of FSK is given by

$$B_{fsk} = (f_1 - f_0) + 2R_b \tag{7.53}$$

The bandwidth increases as the frequency spacing $f_1 - f_0$ between the two orthogonal symbols $g_1(t)$ and $g_0(t)$. In Eq. (7.52), f_1 and f_0 are expressed as integer multiples of $1/T_b$. This means that they are selected from the set of orthogonal sinusoidal pulses discussed in Worked example 7.2(b). The minimum frequency spacing in this set is $f_1 - f_0 = 1/T_b$, which is obtained by setting $n_1 = n_0 + 1$ in Eq. (7.52).

7.6.3.3 Frequency spacing and MSK

You may wonder whether it is possible to have two orthogonal sinusoidal pulses that are more closely spaced than $1/T_b$. We can gain excellent insight into this issue by considering two unit-energy pulses $g_1(t)$ and $g_0(t)$ with a frequency separation Δf:

$$g_0(t) = \begin{cases} \sqrt{2/T_b} \cos(2\pi f_0 t), & 0 \le t \le T_b \\ 0, & \text{elsewhere} \end{cases}$$

$$g_1(t) = \begin{cases} \sqrt{2/T_b} \cos[2\pi(f_0 + \Delta f)t], & 0 \le t \le T_b \\ 0, & \text{elsewhere} \end{cases}$$

From Eq. (7.36), the correlation coefficient of the two pulses is given by

$$
\begin{aligned}
\rho &= \frac{2}{T_b} \int_0^{T_b} \cos(2\pi f_0 t)\cos[2\pi(f_0 + \Delta f)t]dt \\
&= \frac{1}{T_b} \int_0^{T_b} \cos(2\pi\Delta f t)dt + \frac{1}{T_b} \int_0^{T_b} \cos[2\pi(2f_0 + \Delta f)t]dt \\
&= \frac{\sin(2\pi\Delta f T_b)}{2\pi T_b \Delta f} + \frac{\sin[2\pi(2f_0 + \Delta f)T_b]}{2\pi T_b(2f_0 + \Delta f)} \\
&= \text{sinc}(2\Delta f T_b) + \text{sinc}[2(2f_0 + \Delta f)T_b]
\end{aligned}
\tag{7.54}
$$

Don't worry much about the derivation of this equation, but concentrate rather on the simplicity of its graphical presentation in Fig. 7.18. There are several important observations based on this graph.

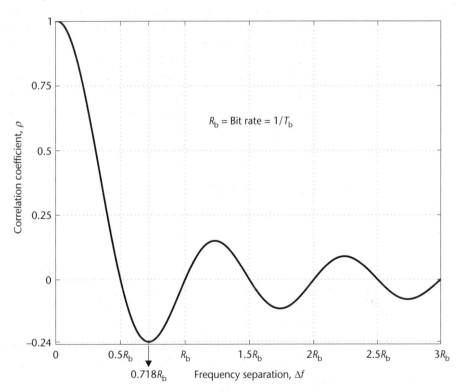

Figure 7.18 Correlation coefficient of two sinusoidal pulses of frequencies f_0 and $f_0 + \Delta f$, as a function of their frequency separation Δf. Here $f_0 = 3R_b$.

1. The correlation coefficient $\rho = 0$ at integer multiples of bit rate R_b ($= 1/T_b$). That is, the two sinusoidal pulses are orthogonal when their frequencies differ by an integer multiple of R_b. This agrees with the result obtained in Worked example 7.2(b).

2. The correlation coefficient is in fact zero at all integer multiples of half the bit rate, e.g. $1 \times 0.5R_b$, $2 \times 0.5R_b$, $3 \times 0.5R_b$, etc. In particular, we see that two sinusoidal pulses are orthogonal when they differ in frequency by only *half the bit rate*. This is the smallest frequency separation at which two sinusoidal pulses can be orthogonal. Below this separation, the pulses become increasingly positively correlated. An FSK scheme that uses this minimum frequency separation as well as having continuous phase is given the special name *minimum shift keying* (MSK). It follows from Eq. (7.53) that the bandwidth of MSK is

$$B_{msk} = 2.5R_b \qquad\qquad (7.55)$$

3. ρ has a minimum value of -0.24 at $\Delta f = 0.718R_b$. In view of Eq. (7.41), this frequency separation gives FSK the largest possible immunity to noise. To appreciate this, recall that PSK has the lowest BER for a given E_b, because it uses symbols that have a correlation coefficient $\rho = -1$. And it follows from Eq. (7.41) that the 'effective' E_b is increased by 100%. In the case of FSK that employs two sinusoidal pulses separated in frequency by $0.718R_b$, the effective E_b is increased by about 25% compared to that of orthogonal-symbol FSK. It is for this reason that all FSK modems operate with a frequency separation that lies in the first region of negative correlation, between $R_b/2$ and R_b. A commonly used separation is two-thirds the bit rate.

4. Fig. 7.18 was plotted with $f_0 = 3R_b$. The above observations hold for other values of f_0, with only a minor variation in the minimum value of ρ. At one extreme when $f_0 \to \infty$, the second term of Eq. (7.54) becomes negligible, and we have $\rho_{min} = -0.217$ at $\Delta f = 0.715R_b$. At the other extreme, when $f_0 = R_b$, we have $\rho_{min} = -0.275$ at $\Delta f = 0.721R_b$.

7.6.4 Minimum transmission bandwidth

It is important to bear in mind the assumptions involved in obtaining the bandwidths of ASK, PSK, FSK and MSK given by Eqs. (7.48), (7.51), (7.53) and (7.55).

1. A completely random bit stream with equally likely 1s and 0s.

2. A baseband waveform representation of the bit stream that is either rectangular, or shaped using a realisable raised cosine filter with roll-off factor $\alpha = 1$.

These assumptions lead to a baseband waveform (which serves as the modulating signal) that has bandwidth $B = R_b$, and hence the above results for B_{ask}, B_{psk} and B_{fsk}.

The minimum transmission bandwidth requirement of these binary modulation systems may be specified using two alternative arguments that

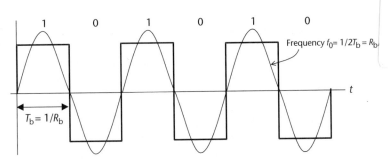

Figure 7.19 Bipolar waveform and fundamental-frequency sinusoid for the most rapidly changing bit sequence.

lead to the same result. Firstly, if the rectangular pulses of the baseband waveform are shaped using an ideal Nyquist filter, then, as discussed in Section 6.6.1, the baseband waveform will have a bandwidth $B = R_b/2$.

Alternatively, consider the fastest changing bit sequence 101010.... The corresponding baseband waveform is a periodic signal of period $2T_b$, and the fundamental frequency $f_0 = 1/2T_b = R_b/2$. Figure 7.19 shows how this sequence is clearly identifiable from a waveform that contains only the fundamental frequency $R_b/2$. The minimum bandwidth of the sequence is therefore $R_b/2$. All other sequences will change more slowly and hence have a lower fundamental frequency. So the minimum bandwidth of the modulating baseband waveform is $R_b/2$.

Correspondingly, the minimum transmission bandwidth of a binary modulated system is given by

$$B_{ask\,min} = B_{psk\,min} = R_b$$
$$B_{fsk\,min} = (f_1 - f_0) + R_b = \Delta f + R_b \quad\quad (7.56)$$
$$B_{msk\,min} = 1.5R_b$$

7.7 Coherent binary detection

Coherent demodulation was discussed at length in Chapter 3 as a technique for receiving analogue signals transmitted by amplitude modulation of a sinusoidal carrier. In Chapter 6, we developed the matched filter for the detection of rectangular or shaped pulses in digital baseband systems and sinusoidal pulses in digital modulated systems. We also showed that a matched filter is realisable as a correlation receiver, which consists of a product modulator followed by an integrator. We also made an important observation that all three techniques, namely coherent demodulation, correlation receiver and matched filter, are in fact equivalent. You may wish to review Sections 6.7.2 and 6.7.6 if in doubt. Note, however, that coherent demodulators used in analogue systems differ in a subtle way from those in digital systems. In the former, we want the output signal to be a faithful reproduction of the original modulating (i.e. message) signal. In the latter, the main aim is that the output has a form that gives the most reliable indication of whether or not a matched pulse is present at a given decision instant. It is then more appropriate to use the terms *coherent demodulation* when referring to analogue receivers and *coherent detection* in reference to digital receivers.

With this clarification in mind, we may now briefly discuss the coherent detection of ASK, PSK and FSK signals. We present the receiver as a matched filter of impulse response $h(t)$ followed by a decision device. The output $y(t)$ of the matched filter is given by the convolution of the received input signal $r(t)$ and $h(t)$. See Section 6.7.6 for a detailed discussion of the computation of this convolution. For simplicity and clarity, we will concentrate on a graphical presentation of the output signal for various input signals. This will serve to clarify the criteria used by the decision device to decide in favour of a binary 1 or 0 in each interval of duration T_b.

Equation (7.41) gives the probability of error or bit error rate (BER) in each of the coherent detectors discussed below. You may wish to refer to the important discussion accompanying that equation. The BER may also be conveniently read from the graph of Fig. 7.13.

7.7.1 ASK detector

Figure 7.20 shows the block diagram of a coherent ASK receiver. The filter is matched to $A_c\cos(2\pi f_c t)$. The output of the filter for each of the two symbols $g_1(t)$ and $g_0(t)$ transmitted for binary 1 and 0 respectively, is shown in Fig. 7.21. It can be seen that the output $y(t)$, taken at $t = T_b$ and denoted $y(T_b)$, equals $2E_b$ for binary 1 and 0 for binary 0, where E_b is related to the amplitude A_c of the sinusoidal pulse by Eq. (7.45). Figure 7.21 represents an ideal situation of noiseless transmission in which $y(T_b)$ is exactly $2E_b$ for binary 1, and is 0 for binary 0. In practice, the symbols are corrupted by noise as shown in Fig. 7.22. The inputs $r_1(t)$ and $r_0(t)$ in this particular diagram results from adding Gaussian noise $w(t)$ of variance $10E_b$ to $g_1(t)$ and $g_0(t)$. Note that the exact shape of the output $y_1(t)$ and $y_0(t)$ will depend on the particular sequence of values in $w(t)$, which is in general not identical for two noise functions — even of the same variance. To demonstrate this, Fig. 7.23 shows the outputs $y_1(t)$ and $y_0(t)$ in six different observation intervals with the same noise variance. Note that in the second interval, binary 1 would be erroneously detected as binary 0, as is made clear below.

It is interesting to observe the similarity between the output $y_1(t)$ in Figs. 7.21 and 7.22. The matched filter effectively pulls the sinusoidal pulse $g_1(t)$

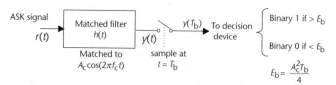

Figure 7.20   Coherent ASK receiver.

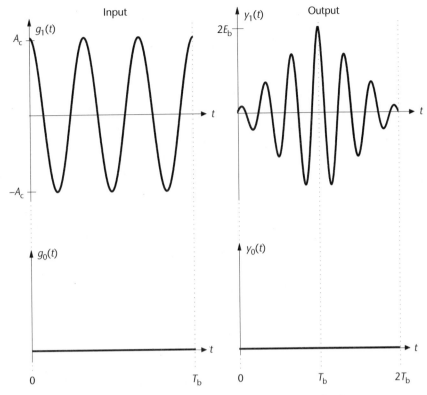

Figure 7.21 Matched filter output for noiseless inputs in ASK detector.

(to which it is matched) out of noise. However in the presence of noise, $y_1(T_b) \neq 2E_b$ and $y_0(T_b) \neq 0$. The decision threshold is therefore set halfway between $2E_b$ and 0, and binary 1 is chosen if $y(T_b) > E_b$ and binary 0 if $y(T_b) < E_b$. In the rare event of $y(T_b)$ being exactly equal to E_b, a random choice is made between 1 and 0.

7.7.2 PSK detector

A coherent PSK detector is shown in Fig. 7.24(a). The filter is matched to the pulse $g_1(t) = A_c\cos(2\pi f_c t)$ that represents binary 1. Recall that binary 0 is represented using a pulse of opposite polarity, $g_0(t) = -g_1(t)$. The output of the filter with $g_1(t)$ and $g_0(t)$ as input is shown in Fig. 7.24(b). The output is sampled at $t = T_b$. It can be seen that $y(T_b) = E_b$ for binary 1 and $-E_b$ for binary 0, where E_b is related to the pulse amplitude A_c by Eq. (7.50). The effect of noise is to shift $y(T_b)$ from $+E_b$ during the interval of binary 1, and from $-E_b$ during binary 0. See the discussion of Figs. 7.22 and 7.23. The decision threshold is set halfway between $+E_b$ and $-E_b$, so that the decision device chooses binary 1 if $y(T_b) > 0$, and binary 0 if $y(T_b) < 0$. In the rare event of $y(T_b) = 0$, the receiver makes a random guess of 1 or 0.

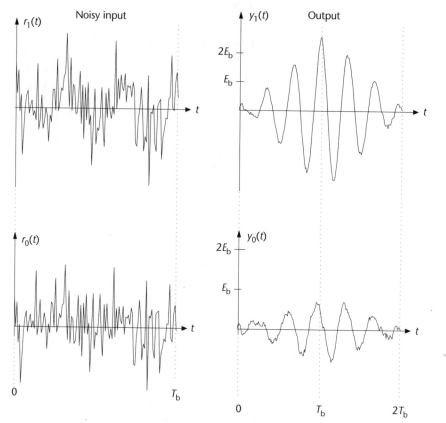

Figure 7.22 Matched filter output for noisy inputs in ASK detector.

7.7.3 FSK detector

Figure 7.25(a) shows the block diagram of a coherent FSK detector. Two matched filters are employed. The upper filter has an impulse response $h_U(t)$ which is matched to the sinusoidal pulse $g_1(t) = A_c\cos(2\pi f_1 t)$ that represents binary 1, while the lower filter's impulse response $h_L(t)$ is matched to the sinusoidal pulse $g_0(t) = A_c\cos(2\pi f_0 t)$ that represents binary 0. Figure 7.25(b) shows the output of the two filters, denoted $y_U(t)$ and $y_L(t)$ respectively, when the received input signal $r(t)$ is either $g_1(t)$ or $g_0(t)$. The outputs of both filters are sampled at $t = T_b$ and subtracted in a summing device to give a value $y(T_b)$ that is fed into the decision device. It can be seen that when the input is the binary 1 pulse $g_1(t)$, then $y_U(T_b) = E_b$ and $y_L(T_b) = 0$, so that $y(T_b) = E_b$. On the other hand, when the input is the binary 0 pulse $g_0(t)$, then $y_U(T_b) = 0$ and $y_L(T_b) = E_b$, giving $y(T_b) = -E_b$. With $y(T_b)$ obtained in this manner, the situation in the decision device is similar to that of PSK detection. Therefore the decision threshold is set halfway between $+E_b$ and $-E_b$, and the decision device chooses binary 1 if $y(T_b) > 0$, and binary 0 if $y(T_b) < 0$, and a random guess of 1 or 0 if $y(T_b) = 0$.

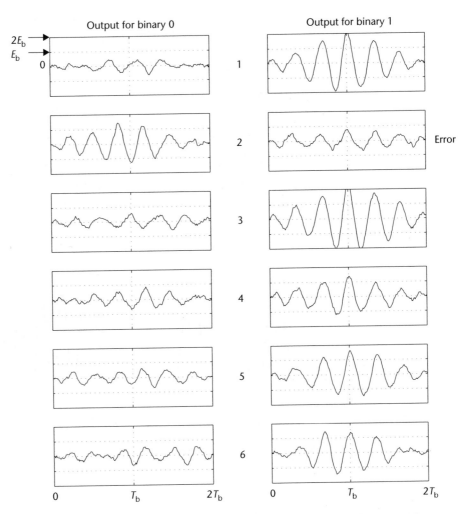

Figure 7.23 Output of matched filter in 6 different observation intervals with Gaussian noise of the same variance.

The values of $y(T_b)$ quoted above apply only when the symbols $g_1(t)$ and $g_0(t)$ are orthogonal. Specifically, Fig. 7.25(b) is based on the frequency values $f_0 = 3R_b$, and $f_1 = f_0 + R_b$. If the frequency spacing $\Delta f = f_1 - f_0$ has a value between $0.5R_b$ and R_b then, as discussed in Section 7.6.3.3, the two symbols are negatively correlated. In this case, $y(T_b) > +E_b$ for binary 1, and $y(T_b) < -E_b$ for binary 0. The decision threshold is still halfway at $y(T_b) = 0$, but there is increased immunity to noise due to the larger spacing between the nominal values of $y(T_b)$ corresponding to binary 1 and binary 0. If on the other hand Δf is less than $0.5R_b$, or between R_b and $1.5R_b$, etc, then the two symbols are positively correlated, and $y(T_b) < +E_b$ for binary 1, and $> -E_b$ for binary 0. The reduced spacing of these nominal values increases the susceptibility of the system to noise.

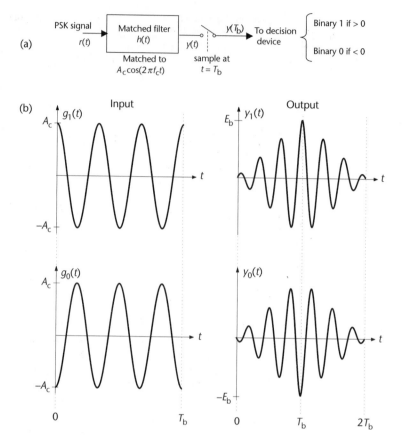

Figure 7.24 Coherent PSK detector. (a) Receiver; (b) output of matched filter.

To further demonstrate the importance of frequency spacing, we show in Fig. 7.26 the difference signal $y(t) = y_U(t) - y_L(t)$ of the two matched filters, for three different values of frequency spacing $\Delta f = R_b$, $0.718R_b$ and $0.25R_b$. With $\Delta f = R_b$, we have the orthogonal pulses scenario plotted earlier in Fig. 7.25, and you can see that $y(T_b) = \pm E_b$ for binary 1 and binary 0, respectively, giving a gap of $2E_b$ between these nominal values of difference signal. The case $\Delta f = 0.718R_b$ corresponds to the most negative correlation between the two pulses, and we have an increased gap of $2.49E_b$. Finally, the pulses separated in frequency by $\Delta f = 0.25R_b$ are positively correlated, giving a reduced gap of $0.68E_b$. In the extreme case of $\Delta f = 0$, both matched filters are identical, and so are the transmitted symbols $g_1(t)$ and $g_0(t)$. The difference signal $y(t)$ is then zero at all times, and the decision device chooses between 1 and 0 each time by a random guess. Clearly, this is the identical-symbol system discussed earlier in connection with Eq. (7.41). You can see that the probability of a wrong guess is 0.5, which agrees with the BER obtained earlier for such a system.

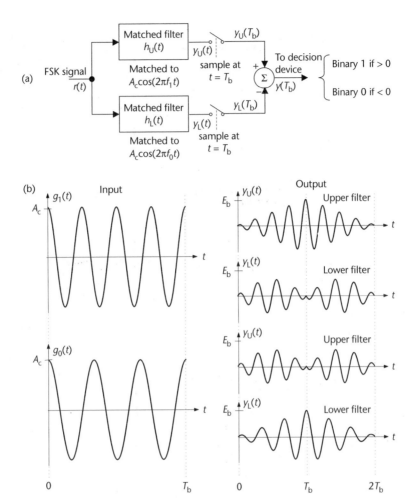

Figure 7.25 Coherent FSK detector. (a) Block diagram; (b) response of the two matched filters to transmitted symbols $g_0(t)$ and $g_1(t)$.

7.8 Non-coherent binary detection

Coherent detection gives a high immunity to noise, but poses two major problems in its implementation.

1. We must have complete knowledge of the phase of the incoming pulses in order to have a perfectly matched filter. Put another way, the locally generated pulse used in the correlation receiver must match the incoming pulse exactly in phase. In practice, variations in the transmission medium will cause the incoming pulse to arrive with a variable phase. This gives rise to a non-zero and variable phase difference between the incoming pulse and a local pulse generated with fixed initial phase. This phase error will significantly degrade the detection process, and increase the probability of error. Figure 7.27 shows the

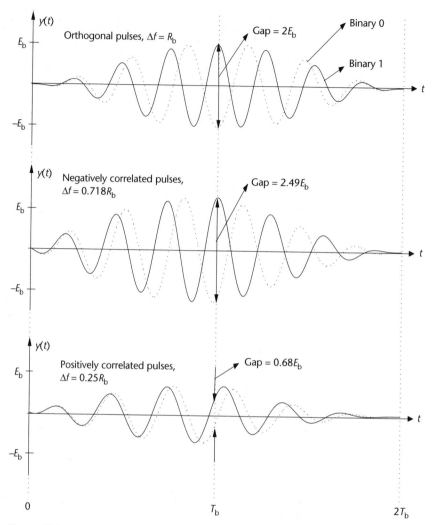

Figure 7.26 Difference signal $y(t) = y_U(t) - y_L(t)$ in a coherent FSK detector using orthogonal, negatively-correlated and positively-correlated pulses.

effect of phase errors of 45° and 120° in a coherent ASK detector. Note that in the former, the output of the filter at $t = T_b$ is $y(T_b) = 1.414E_b$, rather than the value $2E_b$ that is obtained in the absence of phase error. Since the decision threshold is at $y(T_b) = E_b$, it means that noise margin has been lowered by 58.6%. In the second example, $y(T_b) = -E_b$ leading to outright error — the decision device would mistake the binary 1 for 0.

2. We must sample the output of the matched filter at the correct instants $t = T_b$. By examining, for example, Fig. 7.24(b), you can see that the filter output changes very rapidly away from the sampling instant $t = T_b$. There is therefore little tolerance for timing error, the effect of which is to reduce the noise margin or (beyond a small fraction) give rise to outright error. This problem is much less crucial in baseband

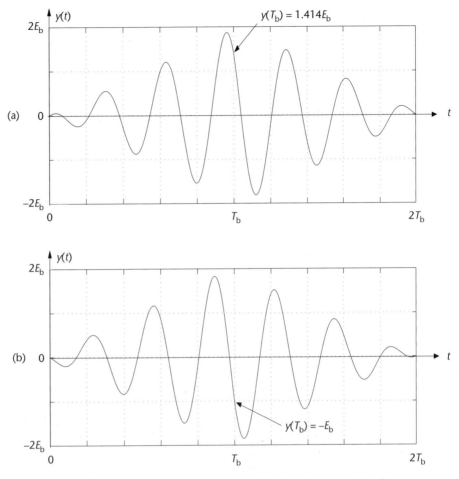

Figure 7.27 Effect of phase error in coherent ASK. The filter is matched to $A_c\cos(2\pi f_c t)$. Graphs show output when the input is (a) $A_c\cos(2\pi f_c t + 45°)$; (b) $A_c\cos(2\pi f_c t + 120°)$.

transmission systems, where a matched filter output decreases more slowly away from the sampling instant, as is evident in Fig. 6.37.

We can minimise the first problem by extracting the desired pulse frequency from the incoming signal and using this to provide the locally generated pulse. ASK and FSK contain impulses at the pulse frequency, which can therefore be extracted using a bandpass filter or, more accurately, a phase-locked loop. See Section 3.5.2 for a more detailed discussion of this carrier extraction process.

A PSK signal does not, however, contain an impulse at the carrier frequency f_c, but this may be obtained by full-wave rectifying the PSK signal to create a component at $2f_c$, extracting this component using a bandpass filter, and dividing by 2 to obtain the desired pulse frequency. This process is explained in Fig. 7.28. There is a phase uncertainty of 180° in the generated carrier, depending on the phase of the division. This makes it

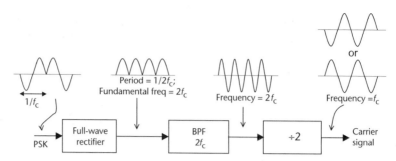

Figure 7.28 Generating a carrier signal from incoming PSK.

impossible to be certain that the receiver is matched to $g_1(t)$ — the symbol for binary 1, and not to $g_0(t)$ — the symbol for binary 0, which would cause the output bit stream to be an inverted copy of the transmitted bit stream. To resolve this phase ambiguity of the locally generated carrier, a known *training sequence* of bits or *preamble* is first transmitted to the receiver. By comparing the receiver output to the expected output the carrier phase is correctly set.

The arrangement discussed above achieves phase synchronisation at the cost of increased complexity of the coherent binary detector. The effect of phase errors can be completely eradicated if we ignore phase information in the incoming binary modulated signal. The receiver is then described as a *non-coherent detector*. Obviously this method is not applicable to PSK since it is the phase that conveys information. But the need for generating a phase-synchronised carrier at the receiver can also be eliminated in PSK by using a variant technique known as *differential phase shift keying* (DPSK). These non-coherent receivers are briefly discussed below.

7.8.1 Non-coherent ASK detector

Figure 7.29 shows the outputs of a matched filter in a coherent ASK receiver with inputs of phase error 0°, 90° and 180°. Note that all three outputs have a common envelope, which is shown by dotted lines. It is true in general that the envelope of the output of a matched filter is independent of the particular phase of the input signal. Therefore we may follow a matched filter with an envelope detector. When the output of the envelope detector is sampled at $t = T_b$, it will have a value $y(T_b) = 2E_b$ for binary 1 irrespective of the phase error in the incoming sinusoidal pulse $g_1(t)$. For binary 0 the sample value will of course be $y(T_b) = 0$. For a discussion of the operation and design of envelope detectors, see Section 3.5.1.

The receiver just described is a non-coherent ASK detector, and is shown in Fig. 7.30. Note that the matched filter is just a (special-response) bandpass filter centred at f_c, and is frequently indicated as such in some literature. Non-coherent detection has two main advantages over coherent detection.

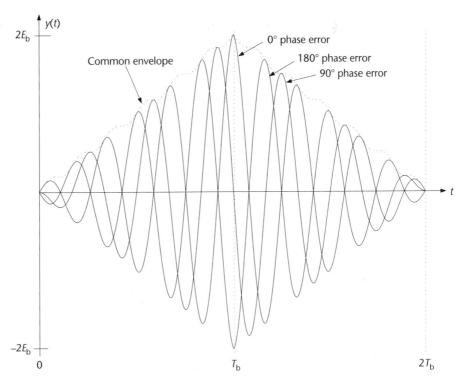

Figure 7.29 Output of a matched filter in a coherent ASK receiver for inputs with different phase errors.

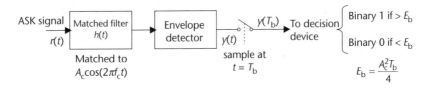

Figure 7.30 Non-coherent ASK detector.

1. The output is independent of phase error, making it unnecessary to provide phase synchronisation at the receiver. This greatly simplifies receiver design.

2. The envelope does not decrease rapidly away from the sampling instant T_b. Therefore the system is much more tolerant of timing errors at the receiver.

The main drawback of a non-coherent receiver is that it is more susceptible to noise. By ignoring phase information, the receiver inadvertently admits contributions from noise of all phases. A coherent receiver, on the other hand, is not affected by noise components that are 90° out of phase with the incoming signal to which the receiver is matched. Eqs. (7.35) and (7.41) therefore do not apply to non-coherent reception. We will not derive this here, but assuming that (1) $E_b \gg N_o$, and (2) the bandwidth of the bandpass filter (shown as a matched filter in Fig. 7.30) is the minimum required to pass the ASK signal — see Eq. (7.56) — then the probability of error of a non-coherent ASK receiver is given by the expression

$$\text{BER} = \frac{1}{4}\text{erfc}\left(\sqrt{\frac{E_b}{2N_0}}\right) + \frac{1}{2}\exp\left(-\frac{E_b}{2N_0}\right) \qquad (7.57)$$

where E_b is the average energy per bit given by Eq. (7.45) and N_o is the noise power spectral density. Note that the BER expression in Eq. (7.57) is dominated by the second term on the RHS.

7.8.2 Non-coherent FSK detector

From the foregoing discussion, a non-coherent FSK detector is obtained by inserting an envelope detector after each of the matched filters in a coherent FSK detector. Figure 7.31 is a block diagram of the resulting non-coherent FSK detector. In this diagram, it is helpful to view the upper matched filter as a bandpass filter that passes the pulse of frequency f_1 while completely rejecting the other pulse of frequency f_0. The lower matched filter similarly serves as a bandpass filter that passes f_0 and rejects f_1. To help you understand the operation of this receiver, the waveforms at various points of the circuit are plotted in Fig. 7.32. The upper half of Fig. 7.32 gives the outputs when the incoming pulse is $g_1(t) = A_c\cos(2\pi f_1 t + \phi_e)$, which represents a binary 1, while the lower half of the figure gives outputs for input $g_0(t) = A_c\cos(2\pi f_0 t + \phi_e)$, which represents binary 0. The parameter ϕ_e is a phase error, which has no effect on the output, as shown earlier.

It can be seen that the input to the decision device is $y(T_b) = E_b$ for binary 1 and $y(T_b) = -E_b$ for binary 0. Therefore the decision threshold is set halfway at $y(T_b) = 0$. Figure 7.32 assumes that $g_1(t)$ and $g_0(t)$ are orthogonal pulses. For correlated pulses, the value of $y(T_b)$ changes in the manner discussed in Section 7.7.3. On the same assumptions as in the previous section, we find that the BER of a non-coherent FSK receiver is given by

$$\text{BER} = \frac{1}{2}\exp\left(-\frac{E_b}{2N_0}\right) \qquad (7.58)$$

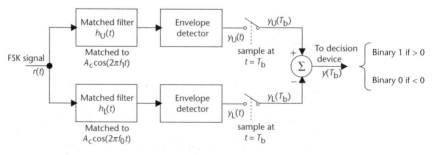

Figure 7.31 Non-coherent FSK detector.

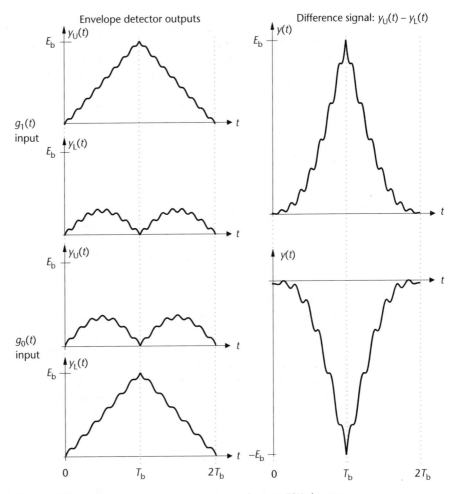

Figure 7.32 Output waveforms in a non-coherent FSK detector.

In this case, the energy per bit E_b is calculated from the received pulse amplitude A_c and pulse duration T_b using Eq. (7.50). By comparing Eq. (7.57) and (7.58), you can see that for the same average E_b/N_0 ratio, non-coherent FSK has a slightly better noise performance (in terms of lower BER) than non-coherent ASK. However, the ASK system would have double the peak energy of FSK, since it is only on for half the time (during binary 1) and off during every interval of binary 0.

7.8.3 DPSK

We have noted that it is impossible to distinguish the two pulses used in PSK by observing the envelope of an incoming PSK signal. Therefore, strictly speaking, incoherent PSK detection does not exist. However, we can obviate the need for phase synchronisation at the receiver if information (i.e. binary 1 and 0) is coded at the transmitter as *changes* in phase, rather than as absolute phase values. This means that we keep the sinusoidal pulse amplitude and frequency constant at A_c and f_c, respectively, but we transmit the pulse with its phase incremented by (say) 180° to represent binary 0, and the phase left unchanged to represent binary 1. This technique is known as *differential phase shift keying* (DPSK). We may write

$$v_{dpsk}(t) = \begin{cases} g_1(t), & \text{Binary 1} \\ g_0(t), & \text{Binary 0} \end{cases}$$

$$g_1(t) = \begin{cases} A_c \cos(2\pi f_c t + \phi_{n-1}), & 0 \leq t \leq T_b \\ 0, & \text{elsewhere} \end{cases} \qquad (7.59)$$

$$g_0(t) = \begin{cases} A_c \cos(2\pi f_c t + \phi_{n-1} + \pi), & 0 \leq t \leq T_b \\ 0, & \text{elsewhere} \end{cases}$$

In the above, f_c is an integer multiple of bit rate, and ϕ_{n-1} is the phase of the sinusoidal pulse transmitted during the previous bit interval, which will always be either 0 or π radians. Note that $\phi_{n-1} = 0$ in the first bit interval.

Figure 7.33(a) shows the block diagram of a DPSK modulator. Comparing this with the block diagram of a PSK modulator in Fig. 7.16(a), we see that the only difference is in the type of baseband coder that precedes the product modulator. A bipolar NRZ-S coder is used in a DPSK modulator, whereas a PSK modulator uses a bipolar NRZ coder. These line codes were discussed in Section 6.5.1. For a random bit stream consisting of equally likely 1s and 0s, DPSK and PSK will therefore have identical power spectra, and hence bandwidth.

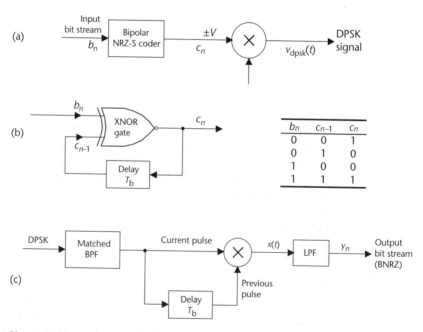

Figure 7.33 DPSK. (a) Modulator; (b) NRZ-S coder and truth table of XNOR gate; (c) detector.

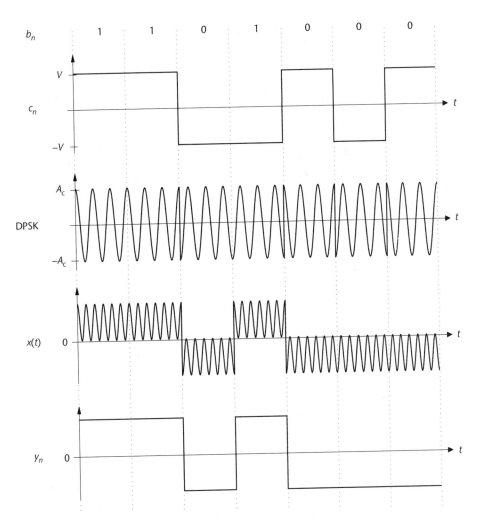

Figure 7.34 Waveforms in DPSK modulator and detector.

The bipolar NRZ-S coder is implemented using an inverted exclusive-OR (XNOR) gate and a one-bit delay device (e.g. a clocked flip-flop) connected as shown in Fig. 7.33(b). Note the accompanying truth table, where b_n denotes current input, c_n denotes current output, and c_{n-1} denotes previous output. What is entered as binary 1 in the truth table is represented electrically in the circuit as $+V$ volts, and binary 0 is represented as $-V$ volts. The output of the XNOR gate is the bipolar NRZ-S waveform c_n, which is shown in Fig. 7.34 for a selected input bit stream b_n. The easiest way to remember the coding strategy of NRZ-S is that the waveform makes a transition between $\pm V$ at the beginning of the bit interval if the bit is binary 0, and makes no transition if the bit is binary 1. Note that the c_n waveform shown corresponds to an initially high ($+V$) state of the XNOR gate output.

When this NRZ-S waveform is multiplied by a carrier $[A_c/V]\cos(2\pi f_c t)$ in a product modulator, the result is the DPSK waveform given by Eq. (7.59) and also shown in Fig. 7.34.

Detection is performed at the receiver by comparing the phase of the current pulse with that of the previous pulse. A significant phase difference indicates that the current interval is binary 0, while a negligible difference indicates binary 1. It is assumed that phase variations due to the transmission medium are negligible over the short period of one bit interval T_b. That is, the only significant change in phase from one bit interval to the next is due entirely to the action of the DPSK modulator. To make this phase comparison, the current and previous pulses are multiplied together, which yields the signal $x(t)$ shown in Fig. 7.34. Note that in the very first bit interval, the previous pulse used has zero phase. It is easy to see that when the two pulses are antipodal their product is negative, whereas when the pulses have the same phase the product is positive. Passing $x(t)$ through a low-pass filter gives an output voltage y_n, which is positive for binary 1 and negative for binary 0, as shown in Fig. 7.34. You will no doubt recognise y_n as a bipolar NRZ representation of the transmitted bit stream b_n. So the DPSK signal has been successfully demodulated.

A block diagram of a DPSK detector that operates as described above is shown in Fig. 7.33(c). For optimum detection, the bandpass filter is matched to the sinusoidal pulse $A_c\cos(2\pi f_c t)$ of duration T_b. The BER of this optimum DPSK detector is given by the expression

$$\text{BER} = \frac{1}{2}\exp\left(-\frac{E_b}{N_0}\right)$$

(7.60)

You can see that DPSK — our 'non-coherent PSK' — has a better noise performance than either non-coherent ASK or non-coherent FSK, but is inferior in this respect to coherent PSK. However, the main advantage of DPSK compared with PSK is the simplicity of its receiver circuit, which does not require phase synchronisation with the transmitter.

7.9 *M*-ary transmission

It is only in a limited number of situations, e.g. optical fibre communication that employs (binary) ASK, that the available channel bandwidth is sufficient to allow the use of binary modulated transmission to achieve the required bit rate. In communication systems involving radio and copper-wired telephone channels, *bandwidth efficiency* is an important design parameter, and multilevel or *M*-ary transmission must therefore be considered.

7.9.1 Bandwidth efficiency

Bandwidth efficiency η was introduced in Section 6.6.3, where it was defined as the ratio between the bit rate R_b (in bits per second) and the channel bandwidth B (in Hz). Each symbol in M-ary transmission conveys $\log_2 M$ bits. Thus the bit rate is related to the symbol rate R_s by

$$R_b = R_s \log_2 M \tag{7.61}$$

From Section 7.6.4, the minimum bandwidth required for transmitting in ASK and PSK at a symbol rate R_s is $B = R_s$. The bandwidth efficiency of M-ary ASK and M-ary PSK is therefore

$$\eta = \frac{\text{Bit rate}}{\text{Bandwidth}} = \frac{R_s \log_2 M}{R_s}$$
$$= \log_2 M, \quad M\text{-ary ASK and } M\text{-ary PSK} \tag{7.62}$$

In the case of M-ary FSK, we require M orthogonal sinusoidal pulses of frequencies $f_0, f_1, f_2, ..., f_{M-1}$. The minimum frequency spacing required for the pulses to be mutually orthogonal is $R_s/2$; see Section 7.6.3.3. Thus,

$$f_1 = f_0 + R_s/2$$
$$f_2 = f_0 + 2R_s/2$$
$$\vdots$$
$$f_{M-1} = f_0 + (M-1)R_s/2$$

The minimum bandwidth of M-ary FSK then follows from Eq. (7.56) with R_b replaced by R_s, and

$$\Delta f = f_{M-1} - f_0 = (M-1)R_s/2$$

That is,

$$B = \Delta f + R_s = (M-1)R_s/2 + R_s$$
$$= \frac{R_s}{2}(M+1), \quad M\text{-ary FSK} \tag{7.63}$$

It follows that

$$\eta = \frac{R_s \log_2 M}{(R_s/2)(M+1)}$$
$$= \frac{2\log_2 M}{M+1}, \quad M\text{-ary FSK} \tag{7.64}$$

Figure 7.35 provides a comparison of the results of Eq. (7.62) and (7.64) for the bandwidth efficiencies of M-ary transmissions. You can see that M-ary FSK has a maximum bandwidth efficiency of $\eta = 0.8$ when $M = 4$. Beyond this value of M, η decreases steadily and is, for example, 0.02 for $M = 1024$. On the other hand, the bandwidth efficiency of M-ary ASK and M-ary PSK increases steadily with M from a minimum of $\eta = 1$ at $M = 2$, reaching $\eta = 10$ at $M = 1024$. ASK and PSK therefore have a significantly superior spectral efficiency compared with FSK. However, as we will see shortly, what FSK lacks in spectral efficiency it makes up for in noise immunity. M-ary FSK is therefore the preferred modulation technique in applications, e.g. deep space communication, that involve very weak received signals, making noise immunity a prime design consideration.

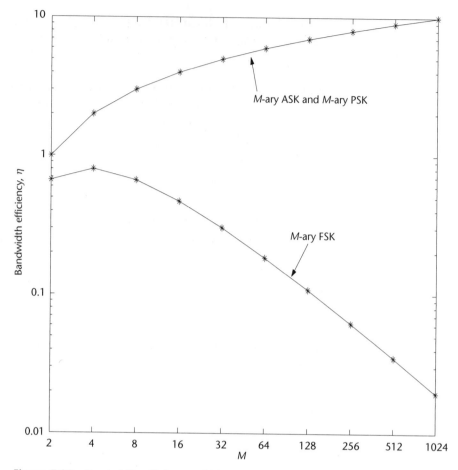

Figure 7.35 Bandwidth efficiency of *M*-ary transmissions.

7.9.2 *M*-ary ASK

The general principles of *M*-ary modulation and detection were presented in Section 7.3. We now apply these ideas to *M*-ary ASK.

7.9.2.1 *Modulator*

Figure 7.36(a) shows a block diagram of an *M*-ary modulator. A serial-to-parallel converter, implemented using a shift register, converts the serial input bit stream to a parallel block B_i consisting of $\log_2 M$ bits. A Gray code converter then maps each of the *M* distinct states of B_i to a unique state consisting of the same number of bits.

Table 7.1 shows the mapping rule for $M = 16$. Column 3 is the 4-bit output of the Gray code converter, and is the binary equivalent of the decimal numbers from 0 to 15 (column 2). Notice the pattern in this binary number sequence. Going down column 3 and considering the first (i.e. rightmost or

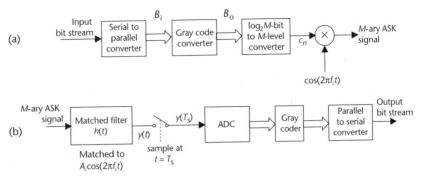

Figure 7.36 *M*-ary ASK. (a) Modulator; (b) detector.

Table 7.1 Step-by-step mapping of 4-bit input sequence B_i into a transmitted symbol $g_i(t)$ in 16-ASK modulator.

B_i (Gray code)	Decimal equivalent	B_0	Normalised DAC output, c_n	Transmitted symbol
0000	0	0000	0	$g_0(t)$
0001	1	0001	1/15	$g_1(t)$
0011	2	0010	2/15	$g_3(t)$
0010	3	0011	3/15	$g_2(t)$
0110	4	0100	4/15	$g_6(t)$
0111	5	0101	5/15	$g_7(t)$
0101	6	0110	6/15	$g_5(t)$
0100	7	0111	7/15	$g_4(t)$
1100	8	1000	8/15	$g_{12}(t)$
1101	9	1001	9/15	$g_{13}(t)$
1111	10	1010	10/15	$g_{15}(t)$
1110	11	1011	11/15	$g_{14}(t)$
1010	12	1100	12/15	$g_{10}(t)$
1011	13	1101	13/15	$g_{11}(t)$
1001	14	1110	14/15	$g_9(t)$
1000	15	1111	1	$g_8(t)$

LSB) bit position only, we see that it consists of the two-element repeating pattern 01, which we will call the *fundamental pattern*. Similarly, the second bit position consists of the 4-element repeating pattern 0011, obtained by repeating each element of the fundamental pattern. The third bit position consists of the pattern 00001111 obtained by using each element of the fundamental pattern four times. In this way, the *k*th bit position of a binary number sequence (representing the decimal numbers 0, 1, 2, 3, ...) is generated from a pattern obtained by using each element of the fundamental pattern 2^{k-1} times.

There is also a pattern in the Gray code B_i of column 1, only in this case the fundamental pattern is 0110. Thus the first bit position of the Gray code consists of the sequence 0110... From the above discussion, we therefore expect the second bit position to consist of the sequence 00111100..., the third bit position to consist of the sequence 0000111111110000..., and so on. The importance of Gray coding lies in the fact that adjacent codewords (in this case consisting of 4 bits) differ in only one bit position. Thus Table 7.1 shows that the Gray code for decimal number 2 is 0011, rather than the usual 0010. The latter requires a change in two bit positions from the adjacent codeword 0001, which violates the Gray code rule.

The Gray code converter in Fig. 7.36(a) is a logic circuit that maps column 1 to column 3 in Table 7.1. So for example, the 4-bit sequence 1010 is converted to 1100. The output of the converter is then processed in a $\log_2M$-bit to M-level converter to yield the normalised output shown in column 4 of Table 7.1. This output consists of M distinct and uniformly spaced levels from 0 to 1, and is multiplied by a sinusoidal carrier of frequency f_c to produce the desired M-ary ASK signal. Make sure you can see that the overall result of the whole process is that adjacent states in the signal space diagram of this M-ary ASK represent a block of $\log_2M$ input bits that differ in only one bit position. This means that Eq. (7.33) applies in relating bit and symbol error rates. Refer to Fig. 7.6(a) for the signal space diagram of M-ary ASK with $M = 4$.

The M-ary ASK signal consists of one of the following M sinusoidal pulses in each symbol interval of duration $T_s = T_b\log_2M$. The pulses differ only in amplitude, which is determined by the output of the M-level converter during the interval:

$$g_i(t) = \left[\frac{A_c i}{M-1}\right]\cos(2\pi f_c t), \quad i = 0, 1, 2, ..., M-1 \tag{7.65}$$

7.9.2.2 Detector

An M-ary ASK detector operates on the principle shown in block diagram form in Fig. 7.36(b). The incoming signal is passed through a bandpass filter that is matched to the sinusoidal pulse $A_c\cos(2\pi f_c t)$ of duration T_s. The output of the filter is sampled at $t = T_s$ and fed into an ADC, which quantises the sample $y(T_s)$ to the nearest of M levels and provides a binary number representation of the level at its output. The M levels are

$$0, \frac{E_{s\,max}}{M-1}, \frac{2E_{s\,max}}{M-1}, \frac{3E_{s\,max}}{M-1}, ..., E_{s\,max}$$

where E_{smax} is the maximum pulse energy given by

$$E_{s\,max} = \frac{A_c^2 T_s}{2} \tag{7.66}$$

Note that the output of the ADC is given by column 3 in Table 7.1. To recover the original bit stream, the ADC output is fed into a Gray coder, which effectively maps from column 3 to column 1.

7.9.2.3 Bit error rate

The main handicap of M-ary ASK is its very poor bit error rate caused by the use of strongly correlated sinusoidal pulses. You will have the opportunity in Question 7.16 to show that the correlation coefficient of adjacent pulses $g_i(t)$ and $g_{i+1}(t)$ in Eq. (7.65) is given by

$$\rho = \frac{2i(i+1)}{2i(i+1)+1}, \quad i = 0, 1, 2, \ldots, M-2 \tag{7.67}$$

This result is shown in Fig. 7.37 for M = 8. It shows that only $g_0(t)$ is orthogonal to the other pulses. The rest of the pulses are strongly correlated, with ρ increasing rapidly towards unity as i increases. For example, the correlation coefficient between $g_6(t)$ and $g_7(t)$ is 0.99. In view of Eq. (7.41), the consequence of such high correlation coefficients is a high bit error rate, which we now determine.

Figure 7.38 shows the signal space diagram of an M-ary ASK with message states S_i corresponding to the transmitted symbols $g_i(t)$ given by Eq. (7.65). Consider the probability of error P_{esi} in symbol S_i. In Worked example 7.3 we justified the fact that P_{esi} is dominated by the event of S_i being mistaken

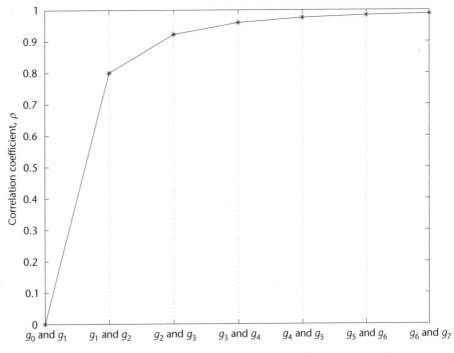

Figure 7.37 Correlation coefficient between adjacent pulses in M-ary ASK, M = 8.

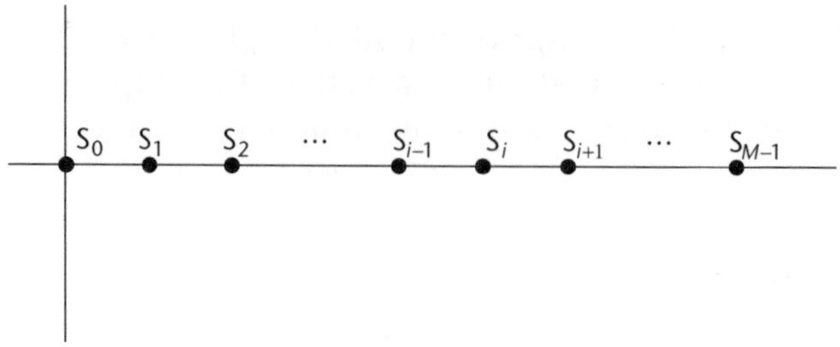

Figure 7.38 Signal space diagram of *M*-ary ASK.

either for S_{i-1} or for S_{i+1}. Denoting the probability that S_i is mistaken for S_{i-1} as P_{esi-} and the probability that it is mistaken for S_{i+1} as P_{esi+}, we may write

$$P_{esi} = P_{esi-} + P_{esi+} \tag{7.68}$$

P_{esi+} follows from Eq. (7.41) with E_b replaced by E_{si+} — the average energy of S_i and S_{i+1}, and ρ given by Eq. (7.67). Using the pulse amplitudes given by Eq. (7.65) and the expression for pulse energy given by Eq. (7.3) we obtain

$$
\begin{aligned}
E_{si+} &= \frac{1}{2}\left[\frac{A_c^2 i^2}{(M-1)^2} \frac{T_s}{2} + \frac{A_c^2 (i+1)^2}{(M-1)^2} \frac{T_s}{2} \right] \\
&= \frac{A_c^2 T_s}{4(M-1)^2}[2i(i+1)+1]
\end{aligned}
\tag{7.69}
$$

Furthermore,

$$
\begin{aligned}
1 - \rho &= 1 - \frac{2i(i+1)}{2i(i+1)+1} \\
&= \frac{1}{2i(i+1)+1}
\end{aligned}
$$

so that Eq. (7.41) yields

$$
\begin{aligned}
P_{esi+} &= \frac{1}{2}\operatorname{erfc}\left(\sqrt{\frac{E_{si+}(1-\rho)}{2N_0}} \right) \\
&= \frac{1}{2}\operatorname{erfc}\left(\sqrt{\frac{A_c^2 T_s}{8(M-1)^2 N_0}} \right) \equiv P_{esa}
\end{aligned}
\tag{7.70}
$$

We see that the result is independent of *i*, and therefore is the probability (denoted P_{esa}) of mistaking any symbol for an adjacent symbol. It follows from Eq. (7.68) that the probability of error in S_i is $P_{esi} = 2P_{esa}$, and this applies for all $i = 1, 2, 3, ..., M - 2$. Symbols S_0 and S_{M-1}, however, have only one immediate neighbour, and hence $P_{es0} = P_{esM-1} = P_{esa}$. The desired probability of symbol error P_{es} in the *M*-ary ASK detector is obtained by averaging these errors over all symbols. Thus,

$$P_{es} = \frac{1}{M}\left[P_{esa} + \sum_{i=1}^{M-2} 2P_{esa} + P_{esa} \right]$$

$$= \frac{2(M-1)}{M} P_{esa} \tag{7.71}$$

$$= \frac{(M-1)}{M}\, \mathrm{erfc}\left(\sqrt{\frac{A_c^2 T_s}{8(M-1)^2 N_0}} \right)$$

It is more useful to express this equation in terms of the average energy per bit E_b in the M-ary system. Now the average energy per symbol is

$$E_s = \frac{1}{M}\sum_{i=0}^{M-1}\left[\frac{A_c^2 i^2}{(M-1)^2}\frac{T_s}{2} \right]$$

$$= \frac{A_c^2 T_s}{2M(M-1)^2}\sum_{i=0}^{M-1} i^2$$

$$= \frac{A_c^2 T_s}{2M(M-1)^2}\frac{(M-1)M(2M-1)}{6}$$

$$= \frac{A_c^2 T_s(2M-1)}{12(M-1)}$$

We obtained the third line by using the standard expression for the sum of squares:

$$1^2 + 2^2 + 3^2 + \cdots + n^2 = \frac{1}{6}n(n+1)(2n+1) \tag{7.72}$$

Since each symbol represents $\log_2 M$ bits, the average energy per bit is therefore

$$E_b = \frac{E_s}{\log_2 M}$$

$$= \frac{A_c^2 T_s(2M-1)}{12(M-1)\log_2 M} \tag{7.73}$$

We can now use this relationship to eliminate $A_c^2 T_s$ from Eq. (7.71). Thus

$$P_{es} = \frac{(M-1)}{M}\,\mathrm{erfc}\left(\sqrt{\frac{3E_b \log_2 M}{2N_0(2M-1)(M-1)}} \right)$$

Finally, with Gray coding, Eq. (7.33) applies, and we obtain the bit error rate of M-ary ASK as

$$\mathrm{BER} = \frac{(M-1)}{M\log_2 M}\,\mathrm{erfc}\left(\sqrt{\frac{3E_b \log_2 M}{2N_0(2M-1)(M-1)}} \right) \tag{7.74}$$

This is a remarkable equation. It gives the BER of M-ary ASK explicitly in terms of M and our now familiar E_b/N_0. Note that when $M = 2$ this equation reduces nicely to Eq. (7.35) for (binary) ASK, as expected. Figure 7.39 shows a plot of BER against E_b/N_0 for various values of M. We see that the BER increases rapidly with M. For example, at $E_b/N_0 = 14$ dB, the BER is 2.7×10^{-7}

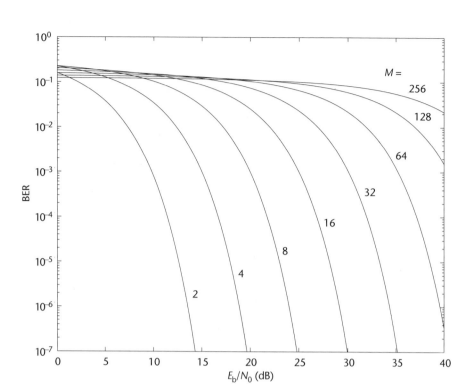

Figure 7.39 BER of coherent *M*-ary ASK systems.

for $M = 2$, but increases dramatically to 2.8×10^{-3} for $M = 4$. To put it in another way, we need to increase transmitted signal power very significantly in order to obtain the same BER in multilevel ASK as in binary ASK. For example, to obtain the same BER of 1×10^{-7} in both binary ASK and 32-ASK the transmitted power in the 32-ASK system must be increased by 20.7 dB — a factor of 117. This finding is, however, not at all surprising. 32-ASK would increase transmission bit rate by a factor of 5 while operating with the same bandwidth as binary ASK. The information capacity theorem (Section 6.6.3) stipulates that signal power must be increased if the same error performance is to be maintained.

Therefore, in spite of the excellent bandwidth efficiency of *M*-ary ASK, its poor noise performance makes multilevel ASK unsuitable for most applications. Binary ASK is, however, widely used, especially on optical fibre links. Note that Eq. (7.74) is the optimum noise performance attainable with a coherent detector. A poorer noise performance will be obtained if an envelope (non-coherent) detector is used at the receiver.

7.9.3 *M*-ary PSK

An *M*-ary PSK signal is made up of one of the following *M* sinusoidal pulses in each symbol interval of duration T_s. The pulses have the same amplitude and frequency, differing only in phase.

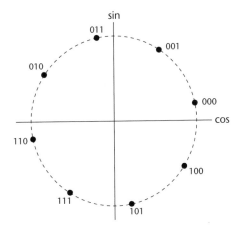

Figure 7.40 8-PSK constellation.

$$g_i(t) = A_c \cos(2\pi f_c t + \alpha i + \phi), \quad i = 0, 1, 2, \ldots, M-1$$
$$\alpha = 2\pi/M; \qquad\qquad f_c = n/2T_s, \quad n = 1, 2, 3, \ldots \tag{7.75}$$

The constant ϕ is an additional phase shift, which is common to all the pulses and is not necessarily zero. Clearly therefore, the signal space diagram of M-ary PSK consists of message points uniformly spaced along a circle that is centred at the origin. The angular spacing is $\alpha = 2\pi/M$. An example is shown in Fig. 7.40 for 8-PSK. The special case $M = 2$ (binary) has already been discussed at length, and the case $M = 4$ (QPSK) was introduced in Worked Examples 7.2 and 7.3. We will briefly consider the generation and detection of QPSK before presenting a general discussion of BER in M-ary PSK systems.

7.9.3.1 QPSK

Figure 7.41 shows the block diagram of a QPSK modulator and detector. Consider first the modulator. The bit splitter is a 2-bit shift register that effectively implements serial-to-parallel conversion. It takes in two serial bits $b_1 b_0$ during one symbol interval $T_s = 2T_b$, and makes b_1 available to the upper modulator and b_0 to the lower modulator. The sinusoidal carrier supplied to each of the two product modulators comes from a common source, but the carrier is passed through a 90° phase shifting network before being fed to the lower modulator. Bits b_1 and b_0 are represented in the circuit as bipolar voltages of normalised value +1 volt (for binary 1) and –1 volt (for binary 0). Thus, when the input is $b_1 b_0 = 00$ the output pulse is

$$g_{00}(t) = -\frac{A_c}{\sqrt{2}}\cos(2\pi f_c t) - \frac{A_c}{\sqrt{2}}\sin(2\pi f_c t)$$
$$= A_c \cos(2\pi f_c t + 135°) \tag{7.76}$$

Similarly for the remaining 2-bit inputs 01, 10 and 11, we obtain

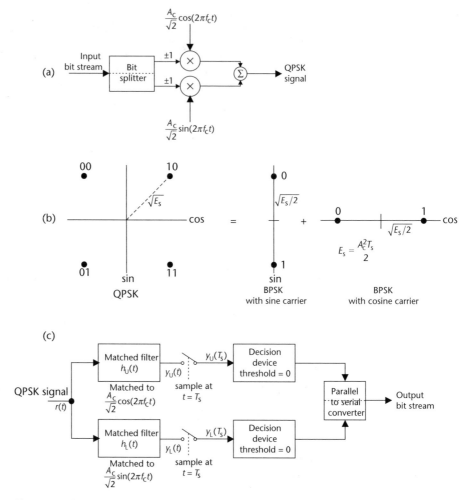

Figure 7.41 QPSK (a) modulator; (b) signal space diagram; (c) coherent detector.

$$g_{01}(t) = -\frac{A_c}{\sqrt{2}}\cos(2\pi f_c t) + \frac{A_c}{\sqrt{2}}\sin(2\pi f_c t) = A_c\cos(2\pi f_c t + 225°)$$

$$g_{10}(t) = \frac{A_c}{\sqrt{2}}\cos(2\pi f_c t) - \frac{A_c}{\sqrt{2}}\sin(2\pi f_c t) = A_c\cos(2\pi f_c t + 45°) \qquad (7.77)$$

$$g_{11}(t) = \frac{A_c}{\sqrt{2}}\cos(2\pi f_c t) + \frac{A_c}{\sqrt{2}}\sin(2\pi f_c t) = A_c\cos(2\pi f_c t + 315°)$$

The signal space diagram of the generated QPSK signal is therefore as shown in Fig. 7.41(b). Comparing with Eq. (7.75) we see that the modulator is characterised by an additional phase shift $\phi = 45°$. By examining the block diagram we also see that QPSK consists of the simultaneous transmission of two binary PSK (BPSK) signals, one on a cosine carrier and the other on an orthogonal sine carrier of the same frequency. This means that the QPSK signal space diagram can be realised by combining two BPSK constellations, as shown in Fig. 7.41(b).

QPSK detection is accomplished using two matched filters, as shown in Fig. 7.41(c). The task is to detect the two bits $b_1 b_0$ transmitted during each symbol interval T_s. The upper filter is matched to the cosine pulse and detects b_1, while the lower filter is matched to the sine pulse and detects b_0. It is clear from Eq. (7.76) and (7.77) that the cosine component in the transmitted pulse is positive for $b_1 = 1$ and negative for $b_1 = 0$. Similarly, the sine component is positive for $b_0 = 1$ and negative for $b_0 = 0$. Thus, $y_U(T_s)$, the output of the upper filter sampled at $t = T_s$, equals $+E_s/2$ for $b_1 = 1$, and $-E_s/2$ for $b_1 = 0$. In the same way, $y_L(T_s) = +E_s/2$ for $b_0 = 1$, and $y_L(T_s) = -E_s/2$ for $b_0 = 0$. So the sampled output of each filter is passed through a decision device with a threshold of zero, which gives a binary 1 output when its input is positive and a binary 0 output for a negative input. You may wish to review our detailed discussion of matched filter operation in Section 7.7 if you are in any doubt. The parallel-to-serial converter is a 2-bit shift register that takes the bits generated by the two decision devices in each interval T_s and clocks them out serially, b_1 first followed by b_0.

7.9.3.2 BER

The task of determining the BER of M-ary PSK is simplified by the symmetry in the signal space diagram; e.g. see Fig. 7.40. Every transmitted state has the same probability of error, which is therefore the probability of symbol error P_{es} of the system. We will continue with our justified assumption that symbol errors arise from the mistaking of a message state for its immediate neighbour.

In Fig. 7.42, the probability P_{esi+} of mistaking a message state S_i for its immediate anticlockwise neighbour S_{i+1} is given by Eq. (7.41), with E_b replaced by E_s ($=A_c^2 T_s/2$), and ρ the correlation coefficient of the pulses $g_i(t)$ and $g_{i+1}(t)$ in Eq. (7.75). By definition, see Eq. (7.36),

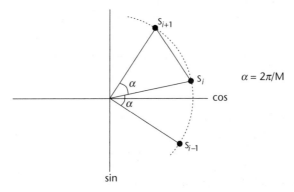

Figure 7.42 Computation of BER in M-ary PSK.

$$\rho = \frac{\int_0^{T_s} g_i(t)g_{i+1}(t)dt}{E_s}$$

$$= \frac{A_c^2 \int_0^{T_s} \cos[2\pi f_c t + \alpha i + \phi]\cos[2\pi f_c t + \alpha(i+1) + \phi]dt}{A_c^2 T_s/2} \tag{7.78}$$

$$= \frac{1}{T_s}\left\{\int_0^{T_s} \cos(\alpha)dt + \int_0^{T_s} \cos[4\pi f_c t + 2(\alpha i + \phi) + \alpha]dt\right\}$$

$$= \cos\alpha$$

Note that the second integral in the third line is zero, being the integration of a sinusoidal function of frequency $2f_c \ (= n/T_s)$ over an interval T_s that is an integer number of its period. Equation (7.78) is an interesting result that confirms what we already know in the following special cases.

1. Two states separated by $\alpha = 90°$ are orthogonal: ($\rho = \cos 90° = 0$), e.g. QPSK.

2. Two states separated by $\alpha = 180°$ are antipodal: ($\rho = \cos 180° = -1$), e.g. BPSK. Note, therefore, that the two message states in a BPSK system do not have to lie on (opposite sides of) the cosine axis. All that is required is that they differ in phase by 180°.

3. Two (equal-energy) states separated by $\alpha = 0°$ are identical: ($\rho = \cos 0° = 1$).

Armed with this result, we return to the problem at hand and obtain

$$P_{esi+} = \frac{1}{2}\text{erfc}\left(\sqrt{\frac{E_s(1-\cos\alpha)}{2N_0}}\right)$$

$$= \frac{1}{2}\text{erfc}\left(\sqrt{\frac{E_b(1-\cos\alpha)\log_2 M}{2N_0}}\right)$$

where E_b is the energy per bit. P_{esi+} obtained above would be the probability of symbol error in an M-ary system with $M = 2$. You may wish to verify that this result agrees with Eq. (7.35). However, for $M > 2$, there is also an immediate clockwise neighbour S_{i-1} for which S_i can be mistaken with equal probability. Thus the probability of symbol error $P_{es} = 2P_{esi+}$, and BER $= P_{es}/\log_2 M$. Thus, for an M-ary PSK system (with coherent detection and $M > 2$) we have

$$\text{BER} = \frac{1}{\log_2 M}\text{erfc}\left(\sqrt{\frac{E_b[1-\cos(2\pi/M)]\log_2 M}{2N_0}}\right) \tag{7.79}$$

As expected, when $M = 4$ this equation reduces to Eq. (7.35) for the BER of a QPSK system. It should be emphasised that to apply Eq. (7.79) to the binary case ($M = 2$) a factor of ½ is required to account for the absence of a second immediate neighbour in the signal space diagram. Figure 7.43 gives a plot of Eq. (7.79) for various values of M. The BER of M-ary ASK is also shown in dotted lines for comparison.

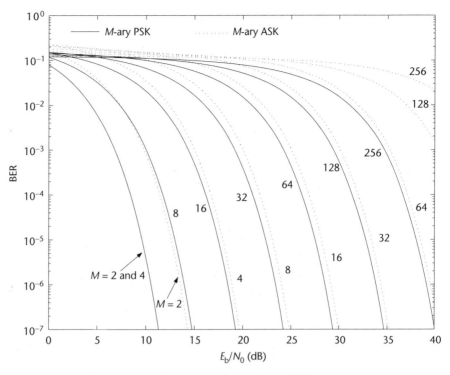

Figure 7.43 BER of M-ary PSK compared with *M*-ary ASK.

We see that beyond $M = 4$, the average energy per bit E_b in an *M*-ary PSK system must be increased in order to maintain the error rate obtainable with BPSK and QPSK. Recall, however, that bandwidth is reduced by a factor of $\log_2 M$. So this is a case of trading power for bandwidth. The noise performance of *M*-ary PSK is clearly superior to that of *M*-ary ASK. In fact 8-PSK has about the same BER as a binary ASK (i.e. OOK) system that transmits the same average energy per bit. You would, for example, have to increase the transmitted power in a 4-ASK system by a factor of 7 (or 8.5 dB) to achieve the same BER as in a 4-PSK system. Since *M*-ary ASK and *M*-ary PSK require the same bandwidth, there is no reason to choose multilevel ASK, except for the simplicity of its modulation and detection circuits.

The complexity of *M*-ary PSK detection can be greatly simplified if the modulator represents message state *i* by a shift αi in the carrier phase of the previous interval, rather than by an absolute phase value. The receiver then performs detection by comparing the phase of the sinusoidal pulse received in the current interval to that of the previous interval. This implementation is known as *M-ary DPSK*, the binary case of which was discussed in Section 7.8.3. *M*-ary DPSK however has the disadvantage of an inferior noise performance compared to coherent *M*-ary PSK.

7.9.4 *M-ary FSK*

An *M*-ary FSK signal consists of one of the following *M* orthogonal sinusoidal pulses in each symbol interval of duration T_s. The pulses differ only in frequency, which are spaced at half the symbol rate to achieve mutual orthogonality of the transmitted symbols with a minimum required bandwidth.

$$g_i(t) = A_c \cos[2\pi(f_0 + i\Delta f)t], \qquad i = 0, 1, 2, ..., M-1$$
$$\Delta f = 1/2T_s = R_s/2 \tag{7.80}$$

The frequency f_0 is chosen to place the transmission in the desired or allocated frequency band.

7.9.4.1 *Generation and detection*

A simple arrangement for generating *M*-ary FSK is shown in Fig. 7.44(a). During each symbol interval (of duration T_s) the $\log_2 M$-bit to *M*-level converter takes $\log_2 M$ bits from the input bit stream and converts them to a normalised output equal to their decimal equivalent, 0, 1, 2, ..., *M* − 1. The output of the *M*-level converter drives a voltage-controlled oscillator (VCO). If the normalised frequency sensitivity of the VCO is Δf and its free-running frequency is f_0, then its output is the *M*-ary FSK signal given by Eq. (7.80).

Detection of *M*-ary FSK requires *M* matched filters connected as shown in Fig. 7.44(b). Only one orthogonal pulse is present in the received signal during each symbol interval. Thus, during each interval only one filter (the

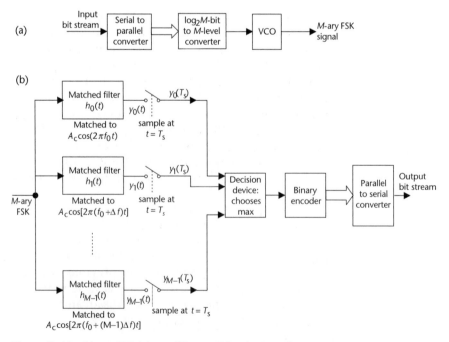

Figure 7.44 *M*-ary FSK (a) modulator; (b) coherent detector.

one matched to the transmitted pulse) will have a significant output while the output of the other filters will be negligible. So the output of all M filters are sampled simultaneously at $t = T_s$ and fed into a decision device, which generates a normalised output equal to the serial number (0, 1, 2, ..., $M - 1$) of the input port with the maximum sample. A binary encoder then produces the corresponding group of $\log_2 M$ bits, which may be clocked out in a serial fashion using a parallel-to-serial converter.

7.9.4.2 BER performance

We can obtain an upper bound, referred to as the *union bound*, for the bit error rate of M-ary FSK in a straightforward manner if we make three important observations.

1. M-ary FSK has an M-dimensional signal space with all message points at the same distance from each other. Thus every message point has $M - 1$ adjacent (or nearest) neighbours. This observation is illustrated in Fig. 7.45 for $M = 3$. In fact, the distance between any pair of message points in the signal space of M-ary FSK (for all M) is $\sqrt{2E_s}$, where E_s is the energy per symbol.

2. All message points are mutually orthogonal, which yields $\rho = 0$ in Eq. (7.41).

3. Gray coding is not applicable. By averaging the number of bit errors incurred when a message state is mistaken for each of its $M - 1$ neighbours we find that

$$\text{BER} = \frac{M/2}{M-1} \times \text{Symbol error rate} \tag{7.81}$$

With these observations, the probability P_{es1} of mistaking a message point for one other message point follows from Eq. (7.41) with E_b replaced by E_s (the energy per symbol), and $\rho = 0$. Thus,

$$\begin{aligned} P_{es1} &= \frac{1}{2}\,\text{erfc}\left(\sqrt{\frac{E_s}{2N_0}}\right) \\ &= \frac{1}{2}\,\text{erfc}\left(\sqrt{\frac{E_b \log_2 M}{2N_0}}\right) \end{aligned} \tag{7.82}$$

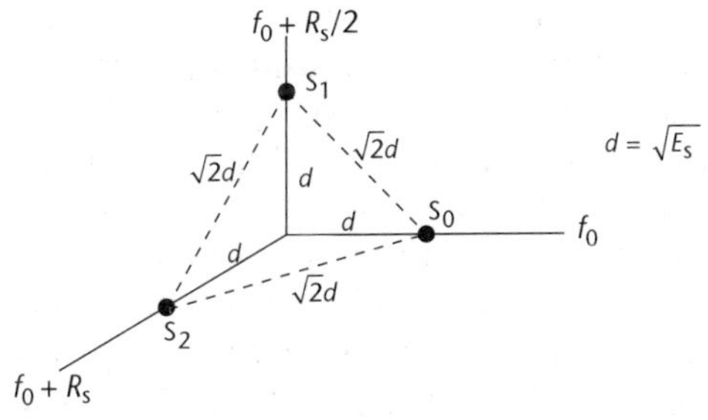

Figure 7.45 Distances in M-ary FSK signal space, $M = 3$.

where E_b is the energy per bit. The maximum probability of symbol error P_{esmax} is the sum of the probabilities (all equal to P_{es1}) of mistaking a message state for each of its $M - 1$ neighbours. That is,

$$P_{es\,max} = (M - 1)P_{es1} \tag{7.83}$$

This is an upper bound on P_{es}, because summing the individual probabilities implicitly assumes independence of each of the events. That is, it assumes that when an error occurs, the received state is nearer to only one other state than to the transmitted state. In reality, there will be some situations in which a received state is nearer to two or more other states than the transmitted state. In this case, summing the probabilities needlessly increases the overall probability of error by including regions of intersection more than once. It follows from Eqs. (7.81), (7.82) and (7.83) that the upper bound on bit error rate in an M-ary FSK system (with coherent detection) is given by

$$\text{BER} \le \frac{M}{4}\,\text{erfc}\left(\sqrt{\frac{E_b \log_2 M}{2N_0}}\,\right) \tag{7.84}$$

For $M = 2$ the bound becomes an equality and Eq. (7.84) reduces to the result obtained earlier for binary FSK.

7.9.4.3 Noise–bandwidth trade-off

Equation (7.84) is plotted in Fig. 7.46 for selected values of M. Note that in contrast to M-ary ASK and M-ary PSK, the BER performance improves as M increases. It is very important that you understand why this is the case.

M-ary ASK and M-ary PSK transmit different amplitudes and phases of the same carrier frequency. In so doing, bandwidth is conserved, but the transmitted sinusoidal pulses become increasingly positively correlated as M is increased. As a result, it becomes more and more difficult to distinguish the pulses at the receiver and the system becomes increasingly vulnerable to noise. In M-ary FSK, on the other hand, mutually orthogonal pulses are transmitted at all values of M, making them perfectly distinguishable at the receiver. However, this is achieved at the expense of bandwidth since each of the M pulses must have a different frequency, with a separation equal to half the symbol rate or $1/2T_s$. Increasing M increases T_s and allows closer spacing of the frequencies. But the spacing reduces proportionately to $\log_2 M$, while the number of frequencies required increases with M. So on the whole the bandwidth increases roughly proportionately to $M/\log_2 M$. As M is increased, the symbol interval T_s ($= T_b \log_2 M$) increases. Since the receiver performs detection by integrating over an interval T_s, the contribution of random noise is significantly reduced as the integration interval increases, leading to improved BER performance.

You can see how an increase in T_s reduces noise effects by noting that if random noise is observed over a sufficiently long time, then the amount of positive and negative samples will be equal, giving a sum of zero. The action of integration is equivalent to summing these samples and including a scaling factor. Of course the effect of noise is also reduced in M-ary ASK

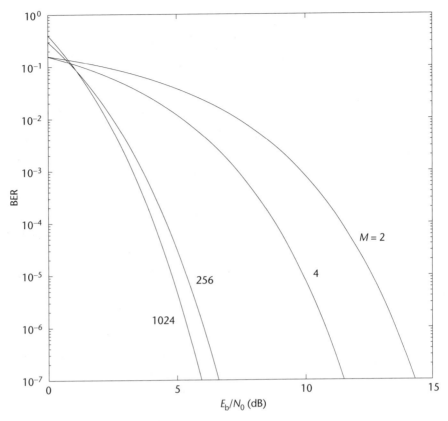

Figure 7.46 BER of *M*-ary FSK.

and *M*-ary PSK as *M* and hence T_s increases, but the benefit to the receiver of this reduction is more than cancelled out by the increased correlation of the transmitted pulses. Therefore *M*-ary FSK gives us the ability to trade bandwidth for an improved noise performance in a way that is not possible with *M*-ary PSK and *M*-ary ASK.

7.9.5 *M*-ary QAM

M-ary PSK constrains all *M* message states to a circle centred about the origin in signal space. BER performance improvement can be achieved if the message states are spaced more freely and widely in the two-dimensional signal space. This requires combining two quadrature (sine and cosine) carriers that are modulated in both amplitude and phase. This is therefore a *hybrid modulation* technique and is referred to as *M-ary quadrature amplitude modulation* (QAM). There are different implementations of QAM, leading to *square*, *circular* and *star* constellations as shown in Fig. 7.47 for *M* = 16. The star QAM for *M* = 16 is also known as 16-APK (*amplitude and phase keying*). It has a minimum phase difference of 90° between message points of the same energy and is therefore thought to perform better than square QAM in transmission media with a predominance of phase distortion.

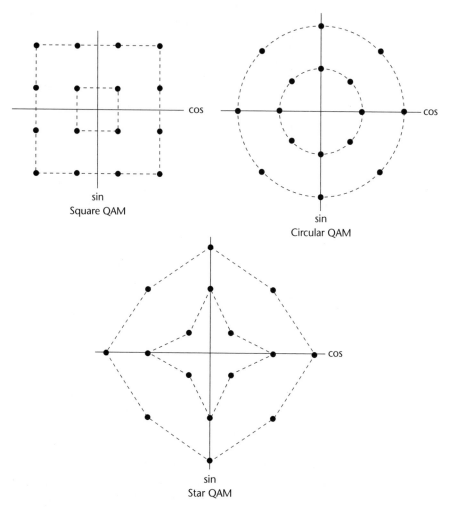

Figure 7.47 Various QAM constellations.

Our discussion will be focussed on square QAM and its BER performance, with 16-QAM modulation and detection presented in detail. The same principles can be applied to other types of QAM. In general, QAM involves sinusoidal pulses of duration T_s and of the form

$$g_i(t) = A_i \cos(2\pi f_c t + \phi_i) \tag{7.85}$$

The amplitude A_i and phase ϕ_i take on a discrete set of values, which depend on the particular implementation.

7.9.5.1 16-QAM

An illustration of the combination of two quadrature carriers to form M-ary QAM is shown in Fig. 7.48 for $M = 16$. A sine pulse (of frequency f_c and duration T_s) codes two bits using two phases (0 and 180°) and two (normalised) amplitudes 1 and 3. An orthogonal cosine pulse also codes two bits in a similar

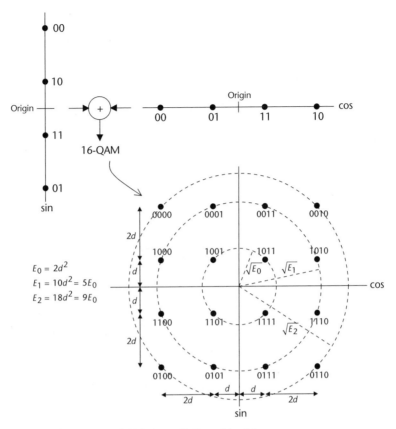

Figure 7.48 *M*-ary QAM constellation, *M* = 16.

manner. The two pulses are added, with the result that four bits are conveyed in each symbol interval using a sinusoidal pulse (of frequency f_c and duration T_s) that can take on three different amplitudes (indicated by the dotted circles) and a number of phase angles. Thus, whereas all transmitted pulses in 16-PSK have the same energy E_s, in 16-QAM four symbols are transmitted with minimum energy E_0, eight symbols with energy $E_1 = 5E_0$, and four with peak energy $E_2 = 9E_0$. The average energy per symbol in 16-QAM is therefore

$$E_s = \frac{4E_0 + 8(5E_0) + 4(9E_0)}{16}$$

$$= 5E_0 = 5A_c^2 T_s$$

(7.86)

where A_c is the amplitude of each quadrature carrier.

Figure 7.49(a) shows the block diagram of a 16-QAM modulator. The two-bit Gray code converter (GCC) performs the following conversions

$$
\begin{aligned}
00 &\rightarrow -3 \\
01 &\rightarrow -1 \\
11 &\rightarrow +1 \\
10 &\rightarrow +3
\end{aligned}
$$

(7.87)

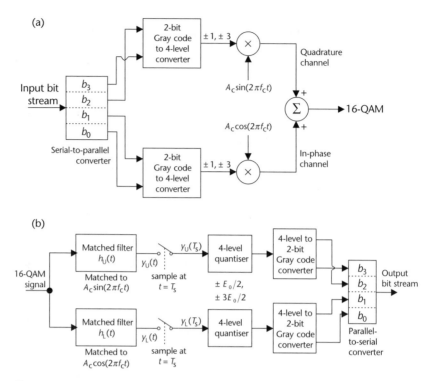

Figure 7.49 16-QAM. (a) Modulator; (b) detector.

During each symbol interval $T_s = 4T_b$, the serial-to-parallel converter takes four bits $b_3b_2b_1b_0$ of the input bit stream and presents b_1b_0 to the lower GCC and b_2b_3 to the upper GCC. Note the flipping of bit order in the latter. The output of the upper GCC multiplies a carrier $A_c\sin(2\pi f_c t)$ to give the quadrature component of the 16-QAM signal, while the output of the lower GCC multiplies a carrier $A_c\cos(2\pi f_c t)$ to give the in-phase component. Both carriers are derived from a common source and have exactly the same amplitude A_c and frequency f_c, but differ in phase by 90°. The desired 16-QAM signal is obtained by summing the in-phase and quadrature channels.

As an example, assume an input $b_3b_2b_1b_0 = 0111$. Following the Gray code conversion in Eq. (7.87), the in-phase channel output is

$$y_{i11}(t) = A_c \cos(2\pi f_c t)$$

and the quadrature channel output is

$$y_{q01}(t) = 3A_c \sin(2\pi f_c t)$$

Note that the swapping of bits at the input to the upper GCC causes b_3b_2 to be received as b_2b_3, and hence the above result for $b_3b_2 = 01$. The resulting 16-QAM pulse is therefore

$$g_{0111}(t) = A_c \cos(2\pi f_c t) + 3A_c \sin(2\pi f_c t)$$
$$= \sqrt{10}A_c \cos(2\pi f_c t - 71.6°) \tag{7.88}$$

Note that this pulse (of duration T_s) has energy $5A_c^2 T_s$, and phase $-71.6°$, which is in agreement with the location of 0111 on the 16-QAM constellation diagram of Fig. 7.48. By proceeding in the same manner, you may verify that the block diagram of Fig. 7.49(a) does generate the array of message points in Fig. 7.48. It is noteworthy that all adjacent points on the 16-QAM constellation differ in only one bit position, even for points (like 1111) with up to four immediate neighbours. This is important for BER minimisation, as discussed earlier, and results from the use of a Gray code in each channel.

A 16-QAM detector is shown in Fig. 7.49(b). The four-level quantiser approximates each matched filter output to the nearest of four levels $-3E_0/2$, $-E_0/2$, $+E_0/2$, and $+3E_0/2$. A four-level to 2-bit Gray code converter then generates the bits in each channel according to the conversions

$$
\begin{aligned}
-3E_0/2 &\rightarrow 00 \\
-E_0/2 &\rightarrow 01 \\
E_0/2 &\rightarrow 11 \\
3E_0/2 &\rightarrow 10
\end{aligned}
\tag{7.89}
$$

The two bits from each channel are combined as shown in a parallel-to-serial converter to produce a serial output bit stream.

7.9.5.2 BER

Let us consider a square QAM that carries an equal number of bits in the quadrature and in-phase channels. This applies to 16-QAM discussed above, with two bits per channel during each symbol interval. It also applies to 4-QAM — one bit per channel, 64-QAM (three bits per channel), 256-QAM (four bits per channel), and so on. We will show in Section 7.11 that the bit error rate of such M-ary QAM is given by the expression

$$
\text{BER} = \frac{2}{\log_2 M}\left(1 - \frac{1}{\sqrt{M}}\right)\text{erfc}\left(\sqrt{\frac{3E_b \log_2 M}{2(M-1)N_0}}\right)
\tag{7.90}
$$

Note that when $M = 4$, this equation reduces to Eq. (7.35) for the BER of a QPSK system. This is to be expected since 4-QAM and QPSK are of course identical. Figure 7.50 shows the BER of M-ary QAM versus E_b/N_0 (expressed in dB) for $M = 4, 16, 64$ and 256. For comparison, the BER of the corresponding M-ary PSK is also shown in dotted lines. We can see that M-ary QAM provides a significant improvement in BER and allows a lower value of E_b/N_0 to be used for a given error performance. For example, there is a gain of 9.5 dB in the signal power required by 64-QAM for a BER of 10^{-7} compared to a 64-PSK system of the same BER. However, unlike M-ary PSK, the performance of M-ary QAM is sensitive to channel non-linearity. The superior noise performance shown in Fig. 7.50 assumes that there are no significant amplitude distortions in the transmission system.

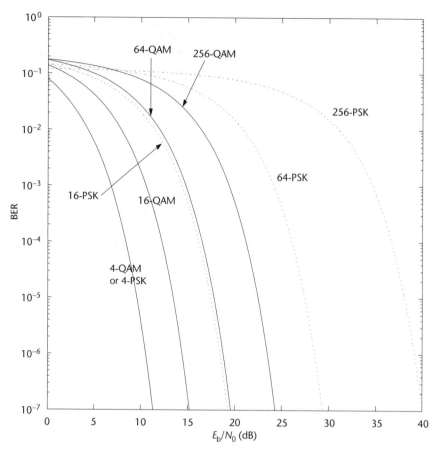

Figure 7.50 BER of M-ary QAM compared with M-ary PSK.

7.10 Design considerations

Designers of digital transmission systems have the following important parameters at their disposal.

- *Transmission bandwidth*: This is a scarce resource that must be used judiciously to maximise the number of users or services.

- *Signal power*: This is an expensive resource that has a direct bearing on component sizes, battery life, radiation safety and potential interference to other systems. Note that system performance is determined not just by signal power, but actually by the ratio E_b/N_0 between the average energy per bit and the noise power spectral density at the receiver. Therefore, the system designer must think beyond simply increasing the transmitted signal power and explore ways of reducing overall signal loss as well as the noisiness of the transmission medium and the receiver.

- *Bit rate*: Some services, such as interactive digital television require a minimum transmission bit rate for proper operation. The time (and cost) of transmitting data over the telephone network decreases proportionately with bit rate.
- *Bit error rate*: Most services specify a maximum BER that can be tolerated, for example 10^{-4} for voice and 10^{-7} for data.

Let us bring together in one place the expressions, which we have obtained in this chapter that relate the above design parameters in each of the digital modulated systems that we have studied.

The relationship between bit rate R_b and transmission bandwidth B is conveniently expressed in terms of bandwidth efficiency η (in bits/s/Hz), which is given by

$$\eta = R_b/B$$
$$= \begin{cases} \log_2 M, & \text{ASK, PSK \& QAM} \\ 2\log_2 M/(M+1), & \text{FSK} \\ \log_2(1+\eta E_b/N_0), & \text{Shannon limit (Section 6.6.3)} \end{cases} \tag{7.91}$$

Bit error rate (BER) and E_b/N_0 are related as follows:

$$\text{BER} = \begin{cases} \dfrac{(M-1)}{M\log_2 M}\operatorname{erfc}\left(\sqrt{\dfrac{3E_b\log_2 M}{2N_0(2M-1)(M-1)}}\right), & \text{ASK} \\[3ex] \dfrac{1}{\log_2 M}\operatorname{erfc}\left(\sqrt{\dfrac{E_b[1-\cos(2\pi/M)]\log_2 M}{2N_0}}\right), & \text{PSK} \atop (M>2) \\[3ex] \dfrac{2}{\log_2 M}\left(1-\dfrac{1}{\sqrt{M}}\right)\operatorname{erfc}\left(\sqrt{\dfrac{3E_b\log_2 M}{2(M-1)N_0}}\right), & \text{QAM} \\[3ex] \leq \dfrac{M}{4}\operatorname{erfc}\left(\sqrt{\dfrac{E_b\log_2 M}{2N_0}}\right), & \text{FSK} \end{cases} \tag{7.92}$$

Recall that the BER for binary PSK ($M = 2$) is the same as for QPSK ($M = 4$), and is also given as half the above PSK expression with $M = 2$. Recall also that for binary FSK, the BER is exactly equal to the upper bound given above.

A useful comparison of the performance of the systems in Eqs. (7.91) and (7.92) can be obtained by determining the value of E_b/N_0 required to achieve a BER = 10^{-4} for various values of M, and plotting this against bandwidth efficiency η. This has been done in Fig. 7.51, where the Shannon limit is also shown. The following example will serve to demonstrate the information provided by this graph. To transmit information at a rate of 60 kbit/s over a bandwidth $B = 10$ kHz, we may use 64-ASK, 64-PSK or 64-QAM, since each of these systems has a bandwidth efficiency $\eta = 6$. However, in order for the transmission to have a BER of 10^{-4}, different power levels are required in each system. 64-ASK requires $E_b/N_0 = 37.2$ dB; 64-PSK requires 26.1 dB; while 64-QAM requires only 16.5 dB. The minimum E_b/N_0 required for error-free transmission at 60 kbit/s over a 10 kHz bandwidth is the Shannon limit, equal to 10.2 dB. In conclusion, we note the following important points:

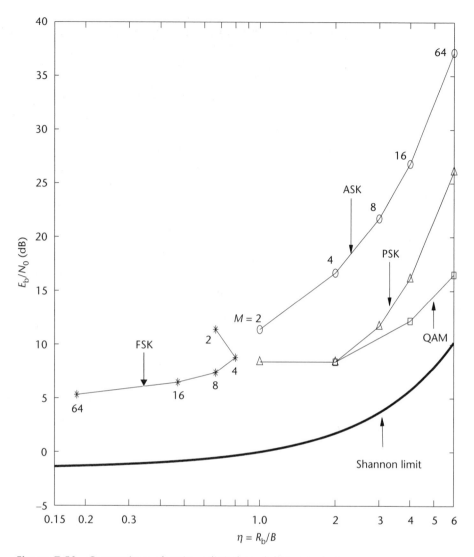

Figure 7.51   Comparison of various digital modulation techniques.

- All the *M*-ary systems fall short of the performance predicted by Shannon's information capacity theorem.

- ASK, PSK and QAM have the same bandwidth efficiency, but the most power-efficient system is QAM, followed by PSK. ASK is by far the most wasteful in transmitted power requirement.

- QPSK or 4-QAM doubles bandwidth efficiency — allowing transmission at twice the bit rate of BPSK (*M* = 2) without any increase in bit error rate.

- Binary FSK requires the same E_b/N_o as binary ASK but is less efficient in bandwidth utilisation.
- FSK allows us to exchange bandwidth for power efficiency. As M is increased and hence bandwidth, the value of E_b/N_o required to maintain a given bit error rate decreases. Viewed another way, we obtain an improved BER at the same E_b/N_o as M is increased. In this case, FSK allows the exchange of bandwidth for improved noise performance.

7.11 BER derivation for *M*-ary QAM

You may skip this section without any loss of continuity. Figure 7.52 shows the generation of M-ary QAM from the sum of two quadrature channels. The in-phase channel uses L distinct states (marked S_0 to S_{L-1}) of a cosine carrier of frequency f_c to convey $\log_2 L$ bits per state. The quadrature channel similarly employs a sine carrier of the same frequency. The symbols of the two channels are summed to give an M-ary symbol that conveys $\log_2 L + \log_2 L = \log_2 M$ bits. Clearly,

$$\log_2 M = 2\log_2 L = \log_2 L^2$$

or

$$L = \sqrt{M} \tag{7.93}$$

It follows from the signal space diagram of each channel that the transmitted symbols (of duration T_s) are given by the expressions

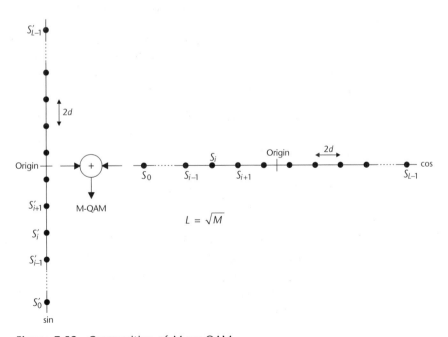

Figure 7.52 Composition of *M*-ary QAM.

$$g_i(t) = \begin{cases} A(L-1-2i)\cos(2\pi f_c t), & \text{In-phase channel} \\ A(L-1-2i)\sin(2\pi f_c t), & \text{Quadrature channel} \end{cases}$$
$$i = 0, 1, 2, ..., L-1$$

(7.94)

Here, A is a constant that depends on the separation $2d$ between adjacent states in signal space:

$$A = d\sqrt{2/T_s}$$

The two channels clearly have an identical distribution of states, which means that the probability P_{es} of symbol error is the same in either channel. An M-ary QAM symbol will be correctly detected in a given interval when there is no error in the in-phase channel *and* no error in the quadrature channel. The independence of the two channels allows us to write:

$$1 - P_{esQAM} = (1 - P_{es}) \times (1 - P_{es})$$

where P_{esQAM} is the probability of symbol error in the M-ary QAM transmission and the LHS is therefore the probability of correct detection (i.e. no error). This equation simplifies to

$$\begin{aligned} P_{esQAM} &= 2P_{es} - P_{es}^2 \\ &\simeq 2P_{es} \end{aligned}$$

(7.95)

The approximation holds with negligible error, since typically $P_{es} \ll 1$. Equation (7.95) shows that obtaining the symbol error rate of an M-ary QAM reduces to the less complicated task of calculating the symbol error rate P_{es} of a one-dimensional signal space.

To determine P_{es}, we confine our attention as before to errors involving adjacent states. Consider then, in Fig. 7.52, the adjacent states S_i and S_{i+1}. To apply Eq. (7.41) to obtain the probability P_{esi+} that the receiver decides in favour of S_{i+1} even though S_i was sent, we need the average symbol energy E_{si+} and correlation coefficient ρ of the two states. It follows from Eq. (7.94) that

$$\begin{aligned} E_{si+} &= \frac{1}{2}\left[\frac{A^2(L-1-2i)^2 T_s}{2} + \frac{A^2(L-1-2i-2)^2 T_s}{2}\right] \\ &= \frac{A^2 T_s}{2}(p^2 - 2p + 2); \quad p \equiv L-1-2i \end{aligned}$$

(7.96)

and from Eq. (7.42),

$$\begin{aligned} \rho &= \frac{2A^2(L-1-2i)(L-1-2i-2)}{A^2(L-1-2i)^2 + A^2(L-1-2i-2)^2} \\ &= \frac{p^2 - 2p}{p^2 - 2p + 2} \end{aligned}$$

or

$$1 - \rho = \frac{2}{p^2 - 2p + 2}$$

(7.97)

Therefore,

$$P_{esi+} = \frac{1}{2}\text{erfc}\left(\sqrt{\frac{E_{si+}(1-\rho)}{2N_0}}\right)$$

$$= \frac{1}{2}\text{erfc}\left(\sqrt{\frac{A^2 T_s}{2N_0}}\right) \tag{7.98}$$

Note that the result is independent of the signal state i and is therefore applicable between any two neighbouring states. It can be seen in Fig. 7.52 that two states ($i = 0$ and $L - 1$) have one neighbour each and therefore a probability of error equal to P_{esi+}. The remaining $L - 2$ states ($i = 1, 2, ..., L - 2$) each has two neighbours and therefore a probability of error equal to $2P_{esi+}$. Assuming that all symbols are equally likely to be transmitted, the probability of symbol error in the channel is given by the average of these errors:

$$P_{es} = \frac{1}{L}[P_{esi+} + 2P_{esi+} \times (L - 2) + P_{esi+}]$$

$$= \frac{2(L-1)}{L} P_{esi+} \tag{7.99}$$

$$= \frac{(L-1)}{L}\text{erfc}\left(\sqrt{\frac{A^2 T_s}{2N_0}}\right)$$

It is more useful to express P_{es} in terms of the average energy per symbol E_s. Taking the average of the energies of the L signal states in the channel, we obtain:

$$E_s = \frac{1}{L}\sum_{i=0}^{L-1}\left[\frac{A^2(L-1-2i)^2 T_s}{2}\right]$$

$$= \frac{A^2 T_s}{2L}\sum_{i=0}^{x}[x^2 - 4xi + 4i^2]; \qquad x \equiv L - 1$$

$$= \frac{A^2 T_s}{2L}\left\{(x+1)x^2 - 4x\sum_{i=0}^{x} i + 4\sum_{i=0}^{x} i^2\right\} \tag{7.100}$$

$$= \frac{A^2 T_s}{6}x(x+2) = \frac{A^2 T_s}{6}(L-1)(L+1)$$

Note that, to simplify the third line in the above derivation, we made use of the standard relations

$$\sum_{i=0}^{x} i = \frac{1}{2}x(x+1)$$

$$\sum_{i=0}^{x} i^2 = \frac{1}{6}x(x+1)(2x+1) \tag{7.101}$$

Equation (7.100) gives the result

$$A^2 T_s = \frac{6E_s}{L^2 - 1}$$

which when substituted in Eq. (7.99) yields

$$P_{es} = \frac{(L-1)}{L} \text{erfc}\left(\sqrt{\frac{3E_s}{N_0(L^2-1)}}\right)$$

$$= \frac{(L-1)}{L} \text{erfc}\left(\sqrt{\frac{3E_b \log_2 L}{N_0(L^2-1)}}\right) \tag{7.102}$$

where E_b is the average energy per bit.

With P_{es} determined, we return to Eq. (7.95) for P_{esQAM}, replacing L by $\sqrt{M}$ in Eq. (7.102) to obtain

$$P_{esQAM} = 2\left(1 - \frac{1}{\sqrt{M}}\right)\text{erfc}\left(\sqrt{\frac{3E_b \log_2 M}{2N_0(M-1)}}\right) \tag{7.103}$$

Finally, the use of Gray coding leads to a bit error rate

$$\text{BER} = P_{esQAM}/\log_2 M$$

$$= \frac{2}{\log_2 M}\left(1 - \frac{1}{\sqrt{M}}\right)\text{erfc}\left(\sqrt{\frac{3E_b \log_2 M}{2N_0(M-1)}}\right) \tag{7.104}$$

This important result gives the bit error rate of M-ary QAM systems operating with an average received energy per bit E_b and a noise power spectral density N_0. It must be emphasised that Eq. (7.104) is applicable only when M is an even power of 2, e.g. $M = 2^2$, 2^4, 2^6 and 2^8. This condition is not as restrictive as it may first appear. There is nothing to be gained from choosing a value of M that is an odd power of 2, which would result in one of the quadrature channels carrying more bits than the other. Practical M-ary QAM systems for high bit rate operations, however, usually include extra signal states for forward error correction, resulting in values of M that may not even be a power of 2.

SUMMARY

We have now come to the end of our study of digital modulated transmission, which featured a lucid and in-depth instruction in the analysis, design and operation of the major digital modulation schemes. It must be emphasised that our discussion was not exhaustive. However, the solid foundation and thorough understanding which you have now acquired in the *principles* should give you plenty of confidence and all the skills required for dealing with the *many* novel applications and variant techniques in this rapidly developing field.

Binary and M-ary ASK offer the advantages of bandwidth efficiency and simple modulation and demodulation circuits. However, this class of techniques suffer from a poor bit error rate and require, comparatively, the largest signal power for an acceptable BER.

Binary and M-ary PSK have the same high bandwidth efficiency as the corresponding ASK system as well as the added advantage of good (i.e. low) bit error rates. However, they require complex modulation and demodulation circuits and, beyond $M = 4$, they are significantly inferior to M-ary QAM in BER performance.

Binary and *M*-ary FSK have the poorest bandwidth efficiency of all the digital modulation techniques, with a peak at $M = 4$. The BER performance is the same as in ASK for $M = 2$, but *M*-ary FSK allows a unique and subtle exchange between bandwidth, signal power and bit error rate, as has been extensively discussed. The circuit complexity of FSK systems lies somewhere between that of ASK and PSK.

M-ary QAM, with its less restricted distribution of signal states in a two-dimensional signal space, provides the closest approach to the Shannon limit on the required signal power. It has the same bandwidth efficiency as the corresponding ASK and PSK systems, but a better BER than both of these systems. However, it has the disadvantage of high circuit complexity, comparable to PSK.

Binary ASK, implemented as OOK and in some cases combined with wavelength division multiplexing (Chapter 8), is currently the only modulation technique employed for transmission in optical fibre. Early low-speed modems used for data transmission over the PSTN employed FSK. Many ITU standards have been specified. For example, the V.21 specifies a full duplex modem operating at 300 bit/s. Sinusoids at frequencies $f_0 = 980$ Hz and $f_1 = 1180$ Hz are used in the forward direction, and $f_0 = 1650$ Hz and $f_1 = 1850$ Hz in the return direction. The V.23 modem provides a half duplex operation at 1.2 kbit/s using frequencies $f_0 = 1300$ Hz and $f_2 = 2100$ Hz. There is provision in this standard for a 75 bit/s back channel that uses tones at 390 Hz and 450 Hz. FSK is also employed for teletype transmission via HF and VHF radio, and in deep space communications where its unique features can be exploited to enhance the reliable detection of extremely weak signals.

Many variants of PSK are used in high-speed full-duplex modems for data transmission over the PSTN. For example, QPSK is used in the V.22 and V.26 modems, which, respectively, operate at carrier frequencies of 1.2 kHz and 1.8 kHz, and bit rates of 1.2 kbit/s and 2.4 kbit/s. The V.29 modem uses 16-APK to achieve a bit rate of 9.6 kbit/s, while the V.32 achieves the same bit rate using 16-QAM. The V.32 can also operate with a 32-state signal space (or 32-QAM), where extra bits are included for forward error correction, using a technique known as *trellis coding*. This allows the same BER to be achieved with 4 dB less signal power than in 16-QAM. Such a saving in signal power at the same BER and transmission bandwidth is referred to as a *coding gain*. There is of course necessarily a higher circuit complexity. The V.33 modem operates at a carrier frequency of 1.8 kHz and delivers a maximum bit rate of 14.4 kbit/s using 128-QAM, and 12 kbit/s using 64-QAM. Both include trellis coding. The V.34 modem delivers various bit rates up to a maximum of 33.6 kbit/s using trellis coding and subsets of a 1664-QAM constellation. The new V.90 modem also employs QAM, with a constellation in excess of 1024 states, to achieve a bit rate of 56 kbit/s.

In the next chapter, we undertake a step-by-step and comprehensive study of multiplexing strategies for multi-user communication systems, which will include up-to-date information on various international telecommunications standards.

REVIEW QUESTIONS

7.1 (a) Determine the duration, energy, centre frequency and bandwidth of the bandpass pulse

$$v(t) = 20\,\text{rect}(2 \times 10^3 t)\sin(4\pi \times 10^4 t)\ \text{volts}$$

(b) Sketch the waveform of the above pulse.

7.2 Figure 7.53 shows the orthonormal basis functions and constellation diagram of a baseband transmission system.

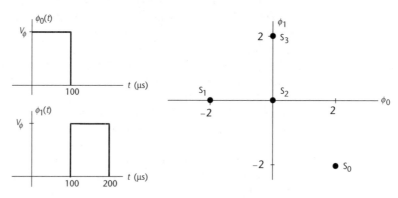

Figure 7.53 Question 7.2.

(a) Determine the amplitude V_ϕ of the basis functions.
(b) Sketch a clearly labelled waveform of each transmitted symbol.
(c) Calculate the energy of each transmitted symbol.

7.3 A transmission system conveys information using the symbols shown in Fig. 7.54.

(a) Determine and sketch the orthonormal basis functions of the system.
(b) Calculate the energy of each of the transmitted symbols.
(c) Express each symbol as a linear combination of the basis functions.
(d) Sketch the constellation diagram of the transmission system.

7.4 Sketch the constellation diagram of a transmission system that employs the symbols $g_0(t)$ to $g_7(t)$ shown in Fig. 7.55. Calculate the energy of each symbol.

7.5 Determine and sketch the orthonormal basis function(s) of a transmission system that uses the following pulses:

(a) $g_2(t)$ and $g_5(t)$ in Fig. 7.55.
(b) $g_0(t)$ and $g_1(t)$ in Fig. 7.54.
(c) $g_3(t)$ and $g_8(t)$ in Fig. 7.54.

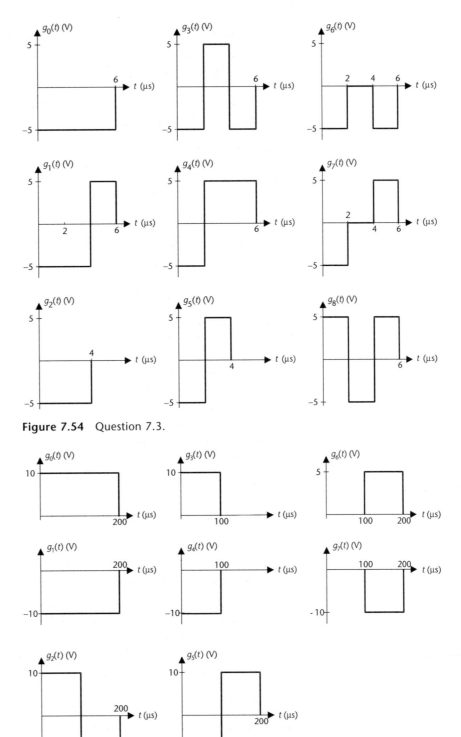

Figure 7.54 Question 7.3.

Figure 7.55 Question 7.4.

7.6 A digital modulated system transmits the following symbols:

$$g_k(t) = \begin{cases} 10(1+j)\cos\left[8000\pi t + \dfrac{\pi}{4}(2i+1)\right], & 0 \le t \le 1\,\text{ms} \\ 0, & \text{elsewhere} \end{cases}$$

where $i = 0, 1, 2, 3$; $j = 0, 1$; $k = i + 4j$

(a) What is the dimension N of the system's signal space?
(b) Sketch the constellation diagram. What are the values of symbol energies used?
(c) Determine the system's orthonormal basis functions.
(d) Express each transmitted symbol as a linear combination of the orthonormal basis functions.
(e) What is the name of the modulation technique employed?

7.7 Calculate the correlation coefficient of the following energy signals:

(a) $g_4(t)$ and $g_5(t)$ in Fig. 7.55.
(b) $g_1(t)$ and $g_2(t)$ in Fig. 7.55.
(c) $g_4(t)$ and $g_6(t)$ in Fig. 7.55.
(d) $g_1(t)$ and $g_4(t)$ in Fig. 7.54.
(e) $g_3(t)$ and $g_8(t)$ in Fig. 7.54.

7.8 A binary ASK system uses two sinusoidal pulses of duration T_s and amplitudes A_0 and $A_1 = \alpha A_0$, where $A_0 > 0$ and $\alpha \ge 0$. Determine

(a) An expression for the average energy per bit E_b.
(b) An expression for the BER of the system in terms of α and E_b/N_o only, where N_o is the noise power spectral density.
(c) The value of α that yields the lowest BER for a given E_b.

7.9 A binary PSK system uses two sinusoidal pulses of phases θ_0 and $\theta_1 = \theta_0 + \phi$. Determine

(a) An expression for the BER of the system in terms of ϕ and E_b/N_0, where N_0 is the noise power spectral density and E_b is the energy per bit.
(b) The value of ϕ that yields the lowest BER for a given E_b.
(c) Comment on the significance of θ_0 and ϕ on BER.

7.10 A binary modulated system transmits at 8448 kbit/s. The power spectral density of noise at the receiver input is 10^{-19} W/Hz and each received sinusoidal pulse has amplitude $A_c = 5.2\ \mu\text{V}$. What are the transmission bandwidth and BER when the following schemes are used?

(a) Coherent PSK.
(b) Coherent FSK.
(c) Coherent OOK, assuming that 1s and 0s are equally likely.

7.11 A binary baseband system transmits the following pulses, shown in Fig. 7.55:

(a) $g_5(t)$ and $g_1(t)$ for binary 0 and binary 1, respectively.
(b) $g_5(t)$ and $g_2(t)$ for binary 0 and binary 1, respectively.

The pulses experience an attenuation of 140 dB up to the detection point where the noise power spectral density is 10^{-20} W/Hz. Calculate the bit rate and BER of each transmission. Comment on the difference in BER.

7.12 A data transmission system operates at a bit rate of 4 kbit/s using an 11 kHz tone to convey binary 1 and an 8 kHz tone for binary 0. The noise power spectral density at the receiver is 83.33 nW/Hz. The transmitted tones are of amplitude one volt and they suffer a net loss of 20 dB along the path leading to the detection point. Determine

(a) the transmission bandwidth.
(b) The bit error rate.

7.13 The noise power spectral density at the receiver of a 140 Mbit/s data transmission system is 10^{-19} W/Hz. Determine the minimum received average signal power in dBm that is required to achieve a maximum BER of 10^{-7} using the following modulation techniques:

(a) Coherent ASK
(b) QPSK.
(c) DPSK.
(d) Non-coherent FSK.

7.14 A transmission system is to have a maximum BER of 10^{-4}. The average received signal power is −60 dBm and the noise power spectral density is 4.2×10^{-18} W/Hz. Determine the maximum bit rate that is possible with the following modulation schemes:

(a) Coherent ASK.
(b) PSK.
(c) QPSK.
(d) DPSK.

7.15 Derive an expression for the bit error rate of the following systems when there is a phase error ϕ in the incoming signal:

(a) PSK.
(b) Coherent ASK.

Hence, determine the extra signal power required to make up for a phase error of 10° and prevent an increase in BER.

7.16 By making use of Eq. (7.42), show that the correlation coefficient of adjacent pulses $g_i(t)$ and $g_{i+1}(t)$ in Eq. (7.65) is as given in Eq. (7.67).

7.17 Repeat Question 7.13 for the following modulation schemes

(a) 16-FSK.
(b) 16-PSK.
(c) 16-ASK.
(d) 16-QAM.

7.18 A transmission system is to have a maximum BER of 10^{-7}. The average received signal power is −60 dBm and the noise power spectral density is

4.2×10^{-18} W/Hz. Determine the maximum bit rate that is possible with the following modulation schemes:

(a) 64-ASK.
(b) 64-PSK.
(c) 64-FSK.
(d) 64-QAM.

Multiplexing strategies

IN THIS CHAPTER

- A non-mathematical introduction of four classes of techniques for simultaneously accommodating multiple users in a communication system.

- Frequency division multiplexing (FDM): You will see that FDM is indispensable to radio communication services, and learn various standardised hierarchical implementations of FDM telephony.

- Time division multiplexing (TDM): A step-by-step and detailed discussion of this increasingly prevalent technique, including the plesiochronous and synchronous digital hierarchies, and an introduction to ATM (asynchronous transfer mode).

- Code division multiplexing (CDM): A lucid discussion of spread spectrum techniques, including a detailed step-by-step graphical description of signal processing in CDM. You will learn the simplicity of this 'free-for-all' sharing strategy.

- Space division multiplexing (SDM): This indispensable strategy for global telecommunications and cellular mobile communications is discussed in the introductory section.

8.1 Introduction

The discussion in previous chapters concentrated mainly on the processing of a telecommunication signal emanating from a single source. There are a number of reasons why a communication system must be able to simultaneously handle signals from multiple and independent sources without mutual interference.

1. To satisfy the communication needs of a larger number of people. The modern lifestyle has become very dependent on telecommunication, so that at any given time in an average city there will be a large number of people needing to make a phone call, send a fax, access the Internet, hold a teleconference etc. If the communication system could only handle one signal at a time, and each user occupied the system continuously for an average duration of three minutes, then only 480 users per day could be serviced, assuming inconvenient times (such as 2.00 a.m.) are not rejected. If such a communication system served a city of one million people, then at this rate it would take nearly 6 years for every person to have just one 3-minute access. Clearly, you couldn't rely on such a system to call an ambulance in a health emergency. By the time it reached your turn on the service queue, you would either have fully recovered or be dead and buried.

2. To reduce the cost of the service to each user. This important consideration can be demonstrated by assuming a satellite communication system built exclusively for telephony at a total cost of £300m, which includes design, construction, launching and maintenance costs over a projected satellite lifetime of 10 years. Allowing a 16% profit margin, the operator must earn (by charging users of the service) a total sum of £348m during a period of 10 years or 5.22 million minutes. Excluding system idle time of 8 hours per day — you would not normally like to make or receive a phone call during sleeping hours — leaves us with 3.48 million income-yielding minutes over which to recover £348m. It is easy to see that if the system could only handle one call at a time then the charge for each call would have to be £100 per minute. However, if we can somehow design the system to handle up to 24 000 simultaneous calls, then assuming on average 20 000 users every minute, the operator's required earning could be spread out over this number of users, bringing down the charge per user to a mere halfpenny per minute.

3. To allow the coexistence of a multiplicity of telecommunication services in a given geographical area or city. Audio broadcast, television broadcast and mobile communication, to name but a few radio services, must operate simultaneously and independently without mutual interference.

4. To improve the exploitation of the available bandwidth of a transmission medium. For example, if a coaxial cable of bandwidth 10 MHz is used to carry one voice signal (of bandwidth 4 kHz), only 0.04% of the cable capacity is being utilised. As the communication distance and hence link cost increases it becomes more and more important to dramatically increase the utilisation of the cable capacity by somehow packing many voice signals onto the cable medium.

5. To allow the use of identical radio systems for the provision of localised broadcast and communication services in different geographical regions. For example, FM radio broadcasts can be provided in two different cities using exactly the same carrier frequency of say 98.5 MHz.

To realise the above benefits, there are *four* multiplexing strategies that may be used separately, but frequently in combination, to simultaneously accommodate multiple users and services in a common transmission medium. Figure 8.1 provides an illustration of these resource-sharing techniques for N

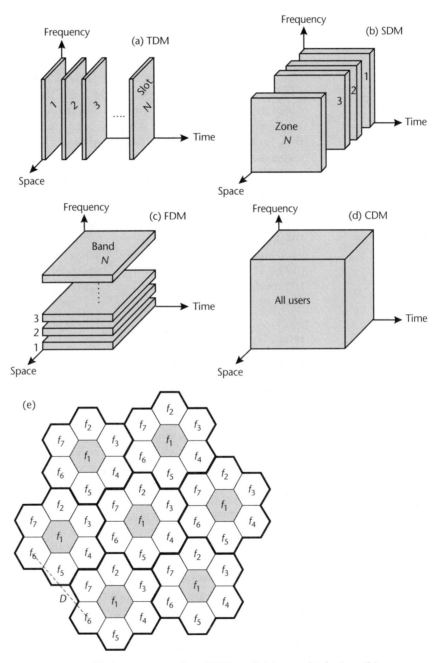

Figure 8.1 Multiplexing strategies. (a) Time division multiplexing; (b) space division multiplexing; (c) frequency division multiplexing; (d) code division multiplexing; (e) SDM in cellular telephony.

users. Three axes are used, namely frequency, which represents the available bandwidth of the transmission medium; time, which represents the instants of usage of the medium; and space, which represents the physical location of the medium.

1. In *time division multiplexing* (TDM) the duration of usage of the transmission medium is divided into time slots each of which is allocated to a single user. Thus each of the N signals has exclusive use of the entire transmission medium during the time slot allocated to it. TDM was briefly introduced in Section 1.5.3.1, which you may wish to review at this point. A useful analogy to TDM is the sharing of the use of a lecture room by four different groups of students, each needing the room for a total period of one hour. We may draw up a roster dividing the room usage into one-hour time slots so that each group occupies the entire room once in turn; or we may allocate 20-minute time slots so that it takes three slots for each group to complete their business; etc. There is, however, an important difference between this analogy and the way TDM is implemented in communication systems. Here there is a noticeable sense of queuing and waiting for one's turn, whereas in real TDM the time slots are extremely short and are used to convey samples of each signal taken at regular and sufficiently short intervals. Thus users of the TDM system are totally oblivious of the time-sharing roster and the receiver is able to reconstruct (without distortion) each of the original signals from their samples. See Chapter 5 if you are in any doubt.

2. *Frequency division multiplexing* (FDM) gives each user exclusive use of a separate frequency band (often referred to as a *channel*) for the whole time. Ideally then, with an average channel bandwidth B_c, and total available bandwidth B_t in the transmission medium, the maximum number of users that can be accommodated is

$$N = B_t/B_c \qquad\qquad (8.1)$$

3. *Space division multiplexing* (SDM) allocates the same frequency band or all the available bandwidth to more than one user for all time, but user signals of the same frequency are confined to physically separate regions or zones. In closed transmission media it means that each user has exclusive use of a separate line-pair, whereas in open media it requires that the radiated strength of each signal be negligible outside the signal's geographical region. In our lecture room analogy, we may apply SDM by allowing all four groups simultaneous use of the room, but with each group seated sufficiently far apart at different corners of the room. As long as the students follow a simple SDM rule of speaking softly, then all groups can coexist with little mutual disturbance.

An important area of application of SDM is in cellular mobile communications where the same frequency bands are reused many times. In this way a limited radio spectrum allocation is very efficiently utilised to meet a huge communications demand in a given *serving area* such as a city. For example, in the North American advanced mobile phone system (AMPS) only 25 MHz in the UHF band is available to one operator in a serving area. Of this, 12.5 MHz is for transmission in the forward direction from base station to mobile, and a further 12.5 MHz for transmission in the reverse direction. With 30 kHz per channel and making provision for control channels it follows that only about 400 users can be accommodated simultaneously in the available bandwidth. This is grossly inadequate to meet the demand for mobile services. The use of SDM dramatically increases capacity, enabling the operator to handle tens of thousands of simultaneous calls.

A typical SDM or *frequency reuse* plan is shown in Fig. 8.1(e). The serving area is divided into small zones called *cells*, each of which has one base station for communication with mobile units. A group of cells (enclosed in bold lines in the diagram) across which the entire bandwidth allocation is used up is called a *cluster*. Figure 8.1(e) shows a cluster size of 7, but it can also be 3, 4, 9, 12 or multiples of these. The available channels are shared amongst the cells in each cluster. We identify the sets of channels as f_1, f_2, f_3 etc. A mobile unit wanting to make a call is assigned an available channel from the set allocated to its cell. Notice how the frequencies are reused in cells separated by a distance D, meaning for example that calls can be made at the same time in each of the shaded cells using exactly the same set of frequency bands. Obviously, radiated power in each cell must be limited to minimise *co-channel interference*, i.e. interference between cells that use the same frequency. The choice of cell diameter and cluster size is influenced by many factors such required capacity, acceptable carrier-to-interference ratio (typically ≥ 18 dB) etc. A smaller cell size allows a particular frequency band to be reused more times in the serving area, thus increasing capacity; but *handover* — the process of a mobile unit's transmission being changed from one channel to another as the mobile crosses a cell boundary — occurs more frequently.

4. *Code division multiplexing* (CDM) is a kind of free-for-all sharing strategy in which multiple users transmit in the *same frequency* band at the *same time* and in the *same physical medium*. The secret is that each user is assigned a unique pseudo-random code sequence with which their signal is spread over a wide bandwidth giving it a noise-like appearance. A target receiver equipped with exactly the same code sequence is able to extract the wanted signal from the received mix of signals and to effectively block out the unwanted signals from other users. Returning to our lecture room analogy, the four groups of students may simultaneously share the entire room in CDM fashion, with one group speaking say in *German*, another in *Swahili*, another in *Ibo* and the remaining in *Chinese*. So long as the students understand only the language of their group, then secure and effective communication can take place, with only a slight inconvenience of background noise in each group.

It should be noted that these multiplexing strategies are rarely used in isolation. In fact by taking a broad interpretation of FDM we see that it is inherent in all radio communication systems to allow a multiplicity of services in a given locality. See for example Table 1.6, which gives an indication of the allocation of radio frequency bands to different services. Similarly, to allow the reuse of the same radio band in different regions (or localities in some cases) of the world, SDM is inherent in nearly all radio systems, except, for example, international broadcasting at HF. Thus, if TDM is used on a satellite link at say 6 GHz, then we could describe the system as employing SDM/FDM/TDM. However, we will henceforth define multiplexing more restrictively in terms of how multiple signals are combined for transmission on a *common link*. Therefore the satellite system in this example is regarded simply as a TDM system.

In the remaining sections of this chapter we will consider FDM, TDM and CDM in detail, and study the implementation of various standard FDM and TDM hierarchies.

8.2 Frequency division multiplexing

8.2.1 General concepts

Frequency division multiplexing stacks a number of narrowband signals in non-overlapping frequency bands and transmits them simultaneously in a common transmission medium. The required frequency translation of each baseband signal can be achieved using any of the modulation techniques studied in Chapters 3 and 4, such as AM, DSB, SSB, FM or PM. The use of a single sideband suppressed carrier (SSB) modulation minimises bandwidth and power requirements and hence the cost of high-capacity long-distance transmission systems. However, for low-capacity short-haul systems (e.g. in rural telephony) the use of AM with its simple modulation and demodulation circuits may yield a more cost-effective FDM implementation. The following discussion will be confined to the use of SSB, a much more prevalent choice for which international standards exist in FDM telephony. It is a straightforward matter to extend the principle to other modulation techniques. A detailed discussion of SSB modulation and demodulation was presented in Section 3.7.2. For convenience, Fig. 8.2 shows a block diagram of an SSB modulator. Note that it contains pre- and post-modulation filters with the indicated passbands. The roles of these filters will become clear in the following discussion.

Figure 8.3(a) shows an FDM multiplexer that combines N independent input signals $v_1(t)$, $v_2(t)$, ..., $v_N(t)$ to give a composite (FDM) signal $v_{fdm}(t)$. Each input signal occupies the baseband spectrum with frequencies in the

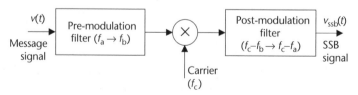

Figure 8.2 (Lower sideband) SSB modulator.

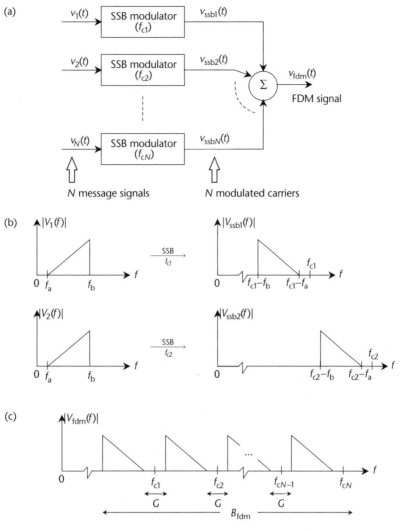

Figure 8.3 FDM. (a) Multiplexer; (b) frequency translation effect of SSB modulation; (c) spectrum of FDM signal.

range f_a to f_b. Clearly, combining these signals in their baseband form would result in an unacceptable state of complete mutual interference. To avoid this, each signal $v_i(t)$, $i = 1, 2, ..., N$, is first passed through a lower-sideband SSB modulator supplied with a unique carrier f_{ci}. The resulting modulation converts $v_i(t)$ to the signal $v_{ssbi}(t)$, which occupies an exclusive frequency band or channel $f_{ci} - f_b \rightarrow f_{ci} - f_a$. This frequency translation process is illustrated in Fig. 8.3(b) for $i = 1, 2$. A symbolic baseband spectral shape — a triangle by convention — is used for the illustration. Note that the spectrum of $v_{ssbi}(t)$ is *inverted* relative to that of $v_i(t)$ because it is the lower sideband that is taken by the post-modulation filter from the product of $v_i(t)$ and the carrier. An *erect* spectrum of $v_{ssbi}(t)$ in the frequency band

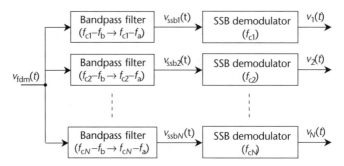

Figure 8.4 FDM demultiplexer.

$f_{ci} + f_a \to f_{ci} + f_b$ would be obtained if the upper sideband were taken. Following this modulation, the SSB signals are added together in a summing device to yield the desired FDM signal:

$$v_{fdm}(t) = v_{ssb1}(t) + v_{ssb2}(t) + \cdots + v_{ssbN}(t) \tag{8.2}$$

The remarkable outcome of this multiplexing process is that $v_{fdm}(t)$ is a composite signal containing N independent signals each of which can be extracted at the receiver without mutual interference. Figure 8.3(c) shows the spectrum of $v_{fdm}(t)$. An arrangement for *de-multiplexing* $v_{fdm}(t)$ is shown in Fig. 8.4. The FDM signal is connected as shown to a bank of N bandpass filters. Clearly, the filter with passband $f_{ci} - f_b \to f_{ci} - f_a$ passes the ith component $v_{ssbi}(t)$ in Eq. (8.2) and blocks all others. The signal $v_{ssbi}(t)$ so extracted is demodulated in an SSB demodulator which is supplied with a carrier of frequency f_{ci}. This yields the original signal $v_i(t)$. In this way, all the multiplexed signals are successfully recovered.

There are a number of conditions that must be satisfied for the above implementation of FDM to be free of interference in any of the channels.

1. Each of the N input signals to the multiplexer must be bandlimited, with frequency components in the range $f_a \to f_b$, where

$$0 < f_a < f_b < \infty \tag{8.3}$$

If this condition is not satisfied and f_b is infinite then the signals cannot be confined within exclusive bands. On the other hand, if $f_a = 0$ then SSB cannot be used for frequency translation since it becomes impossible to separate the sidebands using a realisable filter. To satisfy the condition of Eq. (8.3), a pre-modulation filter is employed to remove all non-essential frequency components below f_a and above f_b in each input signal. In speech telephony for example, $f_a = 300$ Hz and $f_b = 3400$ Hz. Video signals contain essential components down to DC. This means that $f_a = 0$. It is for this reason that SSB cannot be used for obtaining the FDM of television signals.

2. The carrier frequencies $f_{c1}, f_{c2}, ..., f_{cN}$ used by the bank of SSB modulators in the multiplexer must be sufficiently spaced to allow a frequency gap, called *guard band*, between adjacent spectra of the SSB signals that

constitute the FDM signal. Without such a gap, a non-realisable brick-wall bandpass filter would be required at the receiver to extract each of the SSB signals. In Fig. 8.3(c) a guard band G is shown. Thus, the bandwidth of each signal, and hence the spacing of the carrier frequencies, is given by

$$B = f_b - f_a + G \tag{8.4}$$

With the bank of carrier frequencies starting at f_{c1} for the lowest channel, it follows that the value of the ith carrier is

$$f_{ci} = f_{c1} + B(i-1) \tag{8.5}$$

and the bandwidth of the composite FDM signal is

$$\begin{aligned} B_{fdm} &= NB \\ &= N(f_b - f_a + G) \end{aligned} \tag{8.6}$$

A guard band of 900 Hz is used in speech telephony, with f_b and f_a as given above, so that the channel bandwidth $B = 4$ kHz.

3. Amplifiers in the transmission system must be operated in the linear region of their transfer (i.e. input to output) characteristic. Any non-linearity causes harmonic and intermodulation products to be generated in one channel that may fall in the frequency interval of some other channel, giving rise to noise. See Section 2.9.3 for a discussion of this effect.

4. The post-modulation filter must suppress the upper sideband (USB), otherwise any remnants will interfere with the next higher channel causing *unintelligible crosstalk* — since the interfering USB is inverted relative to the wanted lower sideband (LSB) of the next channel. In practice, perfect elimination of the USB is not possible, and it is sufficient for the post-modulation filter to reduce the USB by 60 dB or more relative to the LSB.

8.2.2 Demerits of flat-level FDM

We have so far presented a flat-level FDM in which N signals are frequency-translated in one step using N carriers uniformly spaced in frequency from f_{c1} to $f_{c1} + B(N-1)$. This approach has a number of serious drawbacks when used in the implementation of high capacity systems where N may be very large, e.g. up to 10 800 for FDM telephony.

First, consider the design of the post-modulation filter, which is required to suppress one of the sidebands at the output of the product modulator. Figure 8.5 shows a piecewise linear approximation of the response of this filter (for the ith channel, $i = 1, 2, ..., N$), indicating the passband for the LSB, the transition width and the stopband to block the USB. A standard measure of the selectivity of a filter is its *quality factor Q*, which is defined by

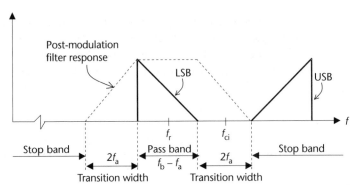

Figure 8.5 Post-modulation filter response – a piecewise linear approximation.

$$Q = \frac{\text{Filter centre frequency}}{\text{Filter bandwidth}} = \frac{f_r}{f_b - f_a}$$

$$= \frac{f_{ci} - \frac{1}{2}(f_a + f_b)}{f_b - f_a}$$

$$= \frac{f_{c1} + (i-1)B - \frac{1}{2}(f_a + f_b)}{f_b - f_a} \qquad (8.7)$$

A related measure of filter performance is the required steepness in the roll-off of the filter's response in order to block the unwanted sideband while passing the wanted sideband. This measure is best given by the ratio between the centre frequency of the transition band and the transition width, which we will call the *slope factor* $\mathbb{Z}$:

$$\mathbb{Z} = \frac{\text{Transition centre frequency}}{\text{Transition width}} = \frac{f_{ci}}{2f_a}$$

$$= \frac{f_{c1} + (i-1)B}{2f_a} \qquad (8.8)$$

Note that a brickwall filter — an unrealisable ideal device — has zero transition width and hence $\mathbb{Z} = \infty$. Equation (8.7) and (8.8) show that both Q and $\mathbb{Z}$ increase with i, the channel number. For example, consider the post-modulation filters required for the 10th and 10 000th channels of a high capacity FDM telephony system, with $f_{c1} = 64$ kHz, $f_a = 0.3$ kHz, $f_b = 3.4$ kHz and $B = 4$ kHz. Substituting these values in the above equations yields

$$Q = 32, \qquad \mathbb{Z} = 167; \qquad \text{for } i = 10$$
$$Q = 12\,922, \qquad \mathbb{Z} = 66\,767; \qquad \text{for } i = 10\,000$$

Note that the channel $i = 10\,000$ requires a filter with very high values of quality and slope factors, which is both expensive and difficult to achieve. So we see that in a flat-level FDM it is difficult to realise post-modulation filters for the higher-frequency channels. The same argument holds for the bandpass filters required in the demultiplexer at the receiver. The other problems posed by flat-level FDM implementation include the following.

- Provision would have to be made for generating N different carrier frequencies at the transmitter, and the same number at the receiver. Considering that the carrier frequencies are required to be highly stable (to guarantee distortionless transmission of especially non-voice signals), it is obvious that such a system would be very complex for large N.

- The required Q and $\mathbb{Z}$ factors of the filter in each channel depend on the channel number, according to Eq. (8.7) and (8.8). So no two filters are identical, leading to N different filter designs. Building and maintaining a system with say 10 800 unique filters is, to say the least, very cumbersome.

- The structure of each FDM system depends on the number of channels. Standardisation is therefore lacking, which would make it easier to set up systems of various capacities by using a small set of standardised equipment obtainable from various manufacturers.

- The summing device at the multiplexer is fed by N different sources, while at the receiver the incoming FDM signal is connected to N different bandpass circuits. As N increases the problem of loading becomes significant, necessitating for example a much higher signal level to drive the bandpass filters.

- We require N different pairs of wires to carry the signals to the single multiplexing point. This can be very expensive (and unsightly if carried on overhead poles) for providing telephone services to, say, N different homes. Preferably, we would like to perform the multiplexing in stages and use a single wire-pair to carry signals from a small cluster of homes.

To overcome the above problems FDM is implemented in a hierarchy. Hierarchical arrangements have been standardised for FDM telephony, which we now consider. The manner in which non-voice signals are accommodated within these plans is also briefly addressed.

8.2.3 FDM hierarchies

There are three different hierarchical implementations of FDM in the world, namely the UK system, the European system and the Bell system (used in North America). These schemes are identical at the first two levels of the hierarchy and differ only at the higher levels. It is important to bear this in mind as we initially discuss these first two levels, which achieve the multiplexing of 60 voice channels into an FDM signal known as the *supergroup* signal. The three FDM standards are realised by multiplexing supergroup signals in different ways, which we discuss in the relevant sections below.

Figure 8.6 shows how a supergroup signal is generated using two stages or levels of multiplexing. A notation $f_{ci,j}$ has been used to identify the carrier frequencies in the SSB modulators. It denotes the carrier frequency used in the ith level of the FDM hierarchy to translate the jth signal combined at that level. In the first multiplexing level, 12 voice signals, each of which contains frequency components from $f_a = 0.3$ kHz to $f_b = 3.4$ kHz are

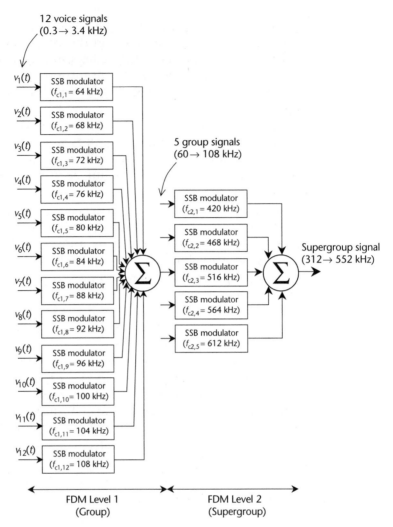

Figure 8.6 First two levels of FDM hierarchy: generation of supergroup signal.

frequency-translated and summed to give an FDM signal known as a *group* signal. The 12 carriers used are spaced at 4 kHz with frequencies 64, 68, 72, ..., 108 kHz. This carrier spacing allows a 900 Hz guard band between the translated voice signals, and gives a nominal voice channel bandwidth of 4 kHz. Since it is the LSB that is selected, it follows that the first voice signal is translated by the 64 kHz carrier to the band 60→64 kHz. Note that this band includes the 900 Hz guard band, made up of two gaps of 600 Hz and 300 Hz on either side of the voice spectrum. The second voice signal is translated by the 68 kHz carrier to the band 64→68 kHz, and so on until the 12th voice signal, which is translated by the 108 kHz carrier to the band 104→108 kHz. Thus the group signal, which comprises 12 independent and non-interfering voice signals, lies in the frequency band 60→108 kHz, and has a bandwidth of 48 kHz. The spectrum of a group signal is shown in Fig. 8.7(a).

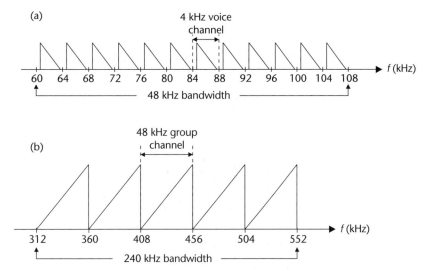

Figure 8.7 (a) Spectrum of group signal; (b) spectrum of supergroup signal.

It is worth mentioning at this point that a standard exists that allows a 33% increase in system capacity with the same transmission bandwidth by packing 16 voice channels into the 48 kHz group signal. To do this, each voice signal is restricted to the frequencies $0.25 \rightarrow 3.05$ kHz, and the frequency translation is performed in a manner that allows a guard band of 0.2 kHz between each of the translated voice bands. The voice channel bandwidth is therefore 3 kHz. The use of a 16-channel group signal (i.e. 3 kHz voice channels) is restricted mostly to submarine cable installations where equipment cost is very high. We will henceforth concentrate on the more prevalent 4 kHz voice channel, but will consider further details of the 3 kHz channel in Question 8.1.

In the second level, five group signals are frequency-translated and summed to give a *supergroup* signal. The carriers used to effect these translations are spaced apart by 48 kHz and have frequencies 420, 468, 516, 564 and 612 kHz. Clearly, the first group signal (of frequencies $f_a = 60$ kHz to $f_b = 108$ kHz) is translated by the carrier of frequency $f_{c2,1} = 420$ kHz to the band $f_{c2,1} - f_b \rightarrow f_{c2,1} - f_a$, which is $312 \rightarrow 360$ kHz. The other group signals are similarly translated, and in particular the 5th group signal is translated to the band $504 \rightarrow 552$ kHz. Thus the supergroup signal occupies the frequency band $312 \rightarrow 552$ kHz, has a bandwidth of 240 kHz, and contains 60 voice channels. The spectrum of this supergroup signal is shown in Fig. 8.7(b). Note in particular that the spectrum is erect, having undergone double inversion in the two multiplexing stages.

The advantages of this two-level hierarchical multiplexing are immediately obvious. The most stringent filter performance required is for the 12th voice channel at the first multiplexing level, and has a quality factor of 34. Using flat-level FDM to combine 60 voice signals would require a filter with $Q = 96$ for the 60th channel. Secondly, standardised equipment can be used

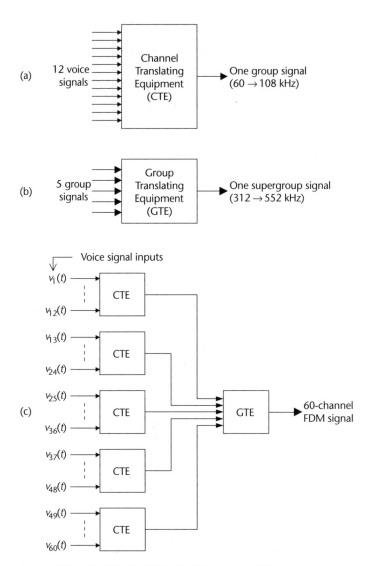

Figure 8.8   (a) CTE; (b) GTE; (c) 60-channel FDM.

for the hierarchical implementation. A group signal is generated using a *channel translating equipment* (CTE) shown in Fig. 8.8(a), and a supergroup signal by a *group translating equipment* (GTE) in Fig. 8.8(b). This means that a 60-channel FDM system can be set up very quickly using only five CTEs and one GTE, connected as shown in Fig. 8.8(c).

To build systems of higher capacity, we must go to higher levels in the FDM hierarchy, and this is where the adopted standards differ. The ITU recommends two procedures. The European system corresponds to ITU Procedure 1 and the UK system to ITU Procedure 2, while the Bell system used in North America does not conform to any of the two recommendations.

8.2.3.1 UK system

Figure 8.9 shows a self-explanatory block diagram of the supergroup translating equipment (STE) in the UK system. Fifteen supergroup (SG) signals $v_{sg1}(t)$, $v_{sg2}(t)$, ..., $v_{sg15}(t)$ are multiplexed to give one *hypergroup* (HG) signal $v_{hg}(t)$. Clearly, $v_{hg}(t)$ contains $60 \times 15 = 900$ independent and non-interfering voice channels. Examining Fig. 8.9, we can make the following observations on the operation of the STE in this system.

- The first SG signal $v_{sg1}(t)$ is connected directly to the summing point without any frequency translation. It will therefore have an erect spec-

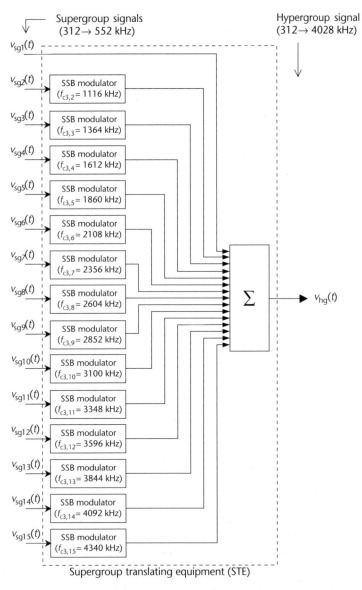

Figure 8.9 UK system: generation of hypergroup (HG) signal.

trum in the range $312 \rightarrow 552$ kHz within the spectrum of the hypergroup signal $v_{hg}(t)$. The remaining SGs, namely $v_{sgi}(t)$, $i = 2, 3, ...,$ 15, all have inverted spectra at the output since they are frequency-translated using a carrier of frequency $f_{c3,i}$. Thus $v_{sgi}(t)$ occupies the frequency range $f_{c3,i} - 552 \rightarrow f_{c3,i} - 312$ kHz within the spectrum of $v_{hg}(t)$.

- The carriers used for the frequency translation of $v_{sg2}(t)$, $v_{sg3}(t)$, ..., $v_{sg15}(t)$ have frequencies spaced apart by 248 kHz and starting from 1116 kHz to 4340 kHz. Since the SGs have a bandwidth of 240 kHz, it follows that the spectrum of the composite HG signal includes a guard band of 8 kHz between each of the component spectra, except between the first and second component spectra, which are separated by 12 kHz. You should be able to see that $v_{sg2}(t)$ is translated to the band $564 \rightarrow 804$ kHz, whereas $v_{sg1}(t)$ of frequency range $312 \rightarrow 552$ kHz is directly added, hence the separation of 12 kHz (i.e. $564 - 552$) between the two bands.

- Following the above observations, the spectrum of the HG signal can be easily sketched, as was done in Fig. 8.7(a) for a group signal. This is left as an exercise in Question 8.2, which you may wish to tackle at this point. Note that the last SG signal $v_{sg15}(t)$ is translated using a 4340 kHz carrier from its baseband at $312 \rightarrow 552$ kHz to the band $3728 \rightarrow 4028$ kHz. Thus, reckoning from the location of $v_{sg1}(t)$, we see that the hypergroup signal occupies the band $312 \rightarrow 4028$ kHz. It therefore carries 900 voice signals in a bandwidth of 3716 kHz.

The hypergroup signal is used in a 4th level of the FDM hierarchy as a building block to assemble more voice channels depending on the required capacity. A few examples are given below.

- Multiplexing two HG signals as shown in Fig. 8.10(a) to obtain an 1800-channel FDM signal with frequencies in the range $312 \rightarrow 8120$ kHz and a bandwidth of 7.808 MHz. This FDM signal is used to frequency-modulate a suitable high-frequency carrier and transmitted by radio.

- Multiplexing three HG signals as shown in Fig. 8.10(b) to obtain a 2700-channel FDM signal with frequencies in the range $312 \rightarrow 12336$ kHz, and a bandwidth of 12.024 MHz. This signal may be conveyed as is on a coaxial cable system, or by radio using frequency modulation.

- A 3600-channel FDM signal with frequencies in the range $312 \rightarrow 16\ 612$ kHz and a bandwidth of 16.3 MHz, which is obtained by multiplexing four HG signals. It is suitable for transmission on 18 MHz coaxial cable systems.

- A 10 800-channel FDM signal occupying the frequency band $4404 \rightarrow 59580$ kHz and resulting from the multiplexing of 12 HG signals. This is recommended for transmission on 60 MHz coaxial cable systems. Figure 8.10(c) shows in a self-explanatory manner how the system is assembled. You will have an opportunity in Question 8.3 to determine the most stringent filter performance (in terms of Q- and $\mathbb{Z}$-factors)

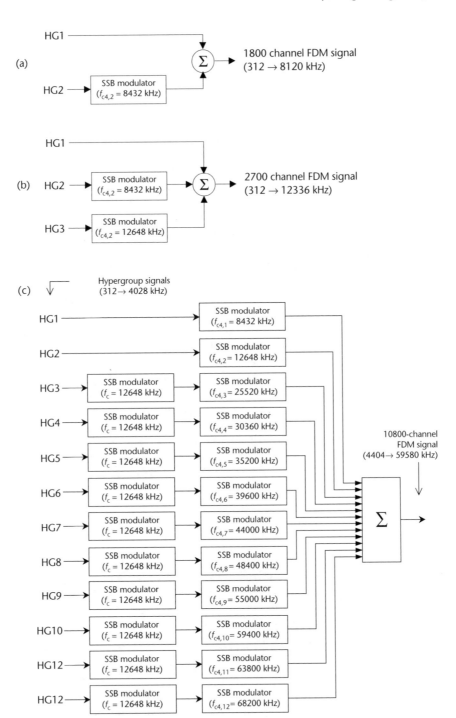

Figure 8.10 Examples of UK system high-capacity FDM built using hypergroup (HG) signals as building blocks. (a) 1800-channel system; (b) 2700-channel system; (c) 10800-channel system.

required in the entire 10 800-channel hierarchical FDM system, and to compare this with the case of flat-level FDM.

8.2.3.2 European system

In the European system, a two-stage multiplexing procedure is employed to assemble (starting from SG signals) a 900-channel FDM signal, called *supermastergroup* (SMG). Figure 8.11 shows a block diagram of a SMG generator. In the first stage, which corresponds to level 3 of the overall FDM hierarchy, five SG signals are translated and combined to give one *mastergroup* (MG) signal occupying the band $812 \rightarrow 2044$ kHz. The translation uses carriers at frequencies 1364, 1612, 1860, 2108 and 2356 kHz. Thus an MG signal has bandwidth 1232 kHz, contains 300 voice channels, and includes a guard band of 8 kHz between its component translated SG signals.

In the second stage, which corresponds to level 4 in the overall FDM hierarchy, three MG signals are translated and combined into a supermastergroup (SMG) signal occupying the band $8516 \rightarrow 12388$ kHz. The translation uses carriers at frequencies 10 560, 11 880 and 13 200 kHz. Thus an SMG signal has bandwidth 3872 kHz, contains 900 voice channels, and includes a guard band of 88 kHz between the spectra of the translated MG signals that form it.

Higher capacity systems are realised by multiplexing various combinations of the MG and SMG signals at level 5 of the overall FDM hierarchy. For example, four MGs are combined to give a 1200-channel signal in the band $312 \rightarrow 5564$ kHz. Two SMGs are combined to give an 1800-channel signal in the band $316 \rightarrow 8204$ kHz. A 2700-channel system of baseband $316 \rightarrow 12388$ kHz is realised by combining three SMG signals; a 3600-channel system of baseband $316 \rightarrow 17004$ kHz is realised by combining four SMG

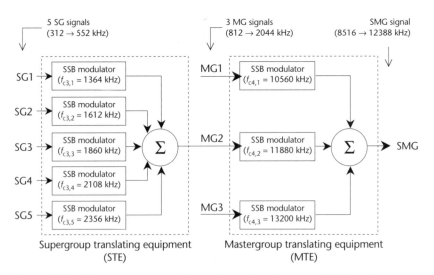

Figure 8.11 European system. Generation of mastergroup (MG) and supermastergroup (SMG) signals.

signals; and a 10 800-channel system of baseband $4332 \rightarrow 59684$ kHz is realised by combining 12 SMG signals.

8.2.3.3 *Bell system*

Figure 8.12 shows the implementation of level 3 of the overall FDM hierarchy in the Bell system. Ten SG signals are translated and combined into one mastergroup signal occupying the band $564 \rightarrow 3084$ kHz, and referred to as the U600 mastergroup (UMG) signal. The carrier frequencies used for the translation are as indicated in the diagram, and are spaced at 248 kHz, except at the 7th carrier where the frequency increment is 296 kHz. The UMG signal therefore has a bandwidth of 2520 kHz, contains 600 voice channels, and includes a guard band of 8 kHz between the constituent supergroups, except between the 6th and 7th where the gap is 56 kHz.

Systems of various capacities can be built using mainly the UMG. For example, six MG signals may be multiplexed to form what is referred to as a *jumbogroup* (JG), which contains 3600 voice channels and occupies the band $564 \rightarrow 17\,548$ kHz. To form the JG, one UMG is connected directly to the summing point without frequency translation, while the other five

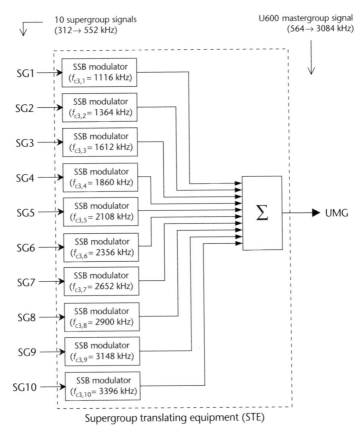

Figure 8.12 Bell system. Generation of Bell U600 mastergroup (UMG) signal.

UMGs are added after being frequency-translated using carriers at frequencies 6336, 9088, 11 968, 14 976 and 18 112 kHz. A 10 800-channel system in the band 3124 → 51 532 kHz may be realised by multiplexing 18 UMGs or three JGs.

8.2.3.4 Non-voice signals

Only telephony speech signals have been considered thus far. However, the following non-voice signals are also transmitted in the hierarchical FDM systems discussed above.

Pilot tones The translating equipment at the transmitter inserts a reference pilot sinusoid into the composite signal at its output. This signal can be monitored at various points in the transmission system for fault location — a missing pilot indicates a malfunctioning of the relevant translating equipment. The pilot signal is also used at repeater stations and receivers for automatic gain control to compensate for variations in the attenuation along the cable path due especially to seasonal temperature changes. A CTE adds a *group reference pilot* at 84.080 kHz; a GTE adds a *supergroup reference pilot* at 411.920 kHz; an STE adds a *hypergroup* or *mastergroup reference pilot* at 1552 kHz; and an MTE adds a *supermastergroup reference pilot* at 11 092 kHz. Note that the group and supergroup reference pilots lie in the 0.9 kHz gaps between translated voice bands, while the 1552 and 11 092 kHz pilots are in the guard bands between translated supergroup and hypergroup/ mastergroup assemblies, respectively.

Cable transmission systems also include regulation pilots with frequencies (shown in Table 8.1) at the top end of the passband of the cable, where the unwanted variation in path attenuation is at a maximum. The gain of each repeater along the transmission system is adjusted to maintain a constant level of the regulation pilot signal. In addition, the frequency comparison pilots (FCP) shown in Table 8.1 are included at the bottom end of the cable passband, where phase error is at a minimum. The FCP is employed at frequency translation points to maintain the frequency stability of the master oscillator from which all carrier frequencies are derived.

Table 8.1 Regulation and frequency comparison pilots of various cable transmission systems.

Cable system				Ref. pilot (kHz)	FCP (kHz)
Bandwidth (MHz)	No. of channels	Cable size (mm)	Repeater spacing (km)		
1.3	300	1.2/2.4	8	1364	60
4	960	1.2/2.4	4	4092	60
12	2700	1.2/2.4	2	12435	308
18	3600	2.6/9.5	4	18480	564
60	10800	2.6/9.5	1.5	61160	564

Data The individual 4 kHz voice channels have been extensively used to carry data signals. First, the bit stream of the data signal is used to modulate a voice-frequency carrier in a modem. The technique of digital modulation was covered in Chapter 7. Early modems (e.g. Bell 202 standard) achieved bit rates of 1.2 kbit/s using FSK. Bit rates up to 56 kbit/s can now be achieved (e.g. in ITU V.90 standard) using QAM modulation formats. You will recall from Chapter 7 that transmission bandwidth is proportional to bit rate. To achieve higher bit rates, an entire group channel of bandwidth 48 kHz or supergroup channel of bandwidth 240 kHz may be used to transmit data, which is of course again carried using a suitable carrier frequency. Data transmission is particularly sensitive to phase distortion and it is necessary to employ an adaptive equaliser at the receiver (discussed in Chapter 6) to compensate for group-delay distortion.

Wideband audio The band of several adjacent voice channels may be used for transmitting a single wideband audio or sound programme signal. The three standards specified by the ITU include:

1. Two voice channels for 50 Hz → 6.4 kHz audio.
2. Three voice channels for 50 Hz → 10 kHz audio.
3. Six voice channels for 30 Hz → 15 kHz audio.

Note that the lower frequency limit of the above audio signals is lower than the value of 300 Hz allowed for voice signals. This gives rise to a more stringent filter requirement, increasing $\mathbb{Z}$ by a factor of about 6 and 10 for the 50 Hz and 30 Hz limits, respectively. An entire group channel may also be used for the transmission of stereophonic sound.

Television Television signals can also be carried in high-capacity FDM systems. Because of the significant low-frequency content, which makes frequency translation by SSB impracticable, and the large video signal bandwidth (~6.0 MHz), a modulation technique known as *vestigial sideband* (VSB) is employed to place the television signal in the desired frequency band. VSB was discussed at length in Chapter 3. One television signal (in the upper band) and up to 1200 voice channels (in the lower band) can be accommodated in a 12 MHz coaxial cable system. In the 18 MHz and 60 MHz coaxial cable systems, one television signal may be carried in two adjacent hypergroup or supermastergroup bands. Thus the 18 MHz system can carry a maximum of two television signals, and the 60 MHz system can carry six. Alternatively, 1800 voice channels + one television signal may be carried simultaneously in the 18 MHz system. And the 60 MHz system can carry 9000 voice channels + one television signal, or 7200 voice channels + two television signals.

8.2.4 Wavelength division multiplexing

FDM is used in some high-capacity optical fibre communication systems, but is referred to as *wavelength division multiplexing* (WDM). The reason for

this needless change of nomenclature is that above the radio band (3 kHz →
3000 GHz), physicists have traditionally identified electromagnetic radiation by its wavelength, rather than frequency. And since the electromagnetic radiation that can propagate in a fibre transmission medium with
minimum attenuation lies in the infrared band, we follow physicists to
identify the carrier signal by its wavelength. WDM then results when
multiple carrier signals, each carrying an independent bit stream, are transmitted simultaneously along one fibre.

Figure 8.13(a) shows a basic implementation of WDM in which N independent bit streams are multiplexed onto a single fibre transmission
medium. Each bit stream is a TDM signal (see Section 8.3), for example the
OC-48 signal, which carries 32 256 voice channels, or the OC-192 carrying
129 024 voice channels. The bit streams are represented as non-return-to-
zero (NRZ) voltage waveforms, and each modulates (by on–off keying) the
optical emission of a separate laser source of respective wavelengths λ_1, λ_2,
..., λ_N. There are three transmission windows where the attenuation of the
fibre per kilometre is at a minimum. These windows lie in the infrared
region and are given in Table 8.2 along with an approximate attenuation
value.

A separation of 2 nm between the wavelengths of the optical emissions
(i.e. carrier signals) from the laser sources would allow up to $N = 50$ WDM
channels in the 1550 nm band, and $N = 40$ channels in the 1330 nm band.

The optical multiplexer is a passive coupler, which may be realised by
butting all N laser diodes to a large-diameter fibre or 'mixing rod' of short
length. A single fibre butted to the other end of the rod collects the
composite signal, which is a well-diffused mixture of the emissions from all

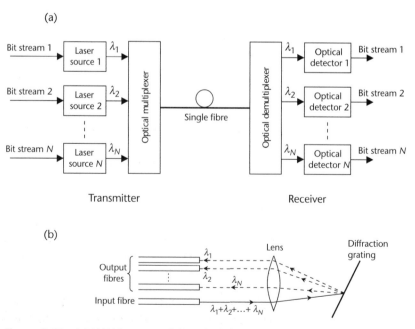

Figure 8.13 (a) WDM system; (b) optical demultiplexer.

Table 8.2 Transmission windows of optical fibre.

Wavelength band (nm)	Nominal wavelength (nm)	Attenuation (dB/km)
810–850	820	~2
1260–1340	1330	~0.5
1510–1610	1550	~0.2

the diodes. Not surprisingly, there is a significant insertion loss penalty in this simple multiplexer realisation. Demultiplexing is based on the spatial dispersion of the mixture of wavelengths by a prism or diffraction grating, as shown in Fig. 8.13(b). The incoming optical signal consisting of N wavelengths is focused by a lens onto a diffraction grating, which returns the incident beam back to the lens with the different wavelengths separated at different angles. The lens focuses the separated optical signals onto different output fibres so that each fibre carries one of the originally multiplexed signals to an optical detector (e.g. a PIN diode or avalance photodiode), which extracts the corresponding bit stream.

A 16-channel WDM of OC-48 TDM signals enables a single fibre to carry 16 × 32 256 or 516 096 voice channels. Applying the same multiplexing strategy to OC-192 TDM signals allows one fibre to handle a massive 2 064 384 voice channels. Note that this is an example of *hybrid multiplexing* in which independent signals are packed into a common transmission medium using more than one multiplexing strategy. In this case, the OC-48 or OC-192 signal is assembled by time division multiplexing of a number of digitised voice signals. These TDM signals are then stacked in different frequency bands of the fibre transmission medium using frequency (sorry, wavelength) division multiplexing.

8.2.5 The future of FDM

FDM, seen in the restrictive context of hierarchical FDM telephony discussed earlier, is an analogue technology that has a severely limited future in the light of the ongoing digital revolution. However, it must be noted that the future of frequency division multiplexing in general is assured. As long as radio communication endures, there will always be the need to allocate different frequency bands to different services (e.g. Table 1.6) and users (as in two-way radio systems and mobile cellular telephony). These are all instances of FDM. Furthermore, the hybrid TDM/WDM multiplexing strategy discussed above is an application of FDM in optical fibre communication that has a very promising future. FDM also appears set to continue to be an important multiple access technique in satellite communications. A satellite transponder is partitioned into frequency bands, which are assigned to users, and can support both analogue and digital transmissions.

The deployment of FDM telephony reached its peak in the mid-1970s. Since then, developments in digital transmission techniques with all their advantages have led to a rapid digitalisation of the telephone network, and a replacement of FDM telephony with time division multiplexing. The telephone network in many countries is now nearly 100% digital. There is a period of transition from analogue to digital transmission, which is likely to last for a few more years in some countries because of the huge investment already made in analogue transmission technology.

The ITU has specified some transition equipment namely *transmultiplexers*, FDM *codecs* and *transition modems*, that allow the interconnection of digital and analogue systems during this transition period. The transmultiplexer (TMUX) transforms an FDM signal to TDM in one direction of transmission, and performs the opposite conversion in the other direction. For example, a 60-channel TMUX transforms a supergroup signal to two 2048 kbit/s TDM signal and vice versa, while a 24-channel TMUX converts between two group signals and one 1544 kbit/s TDM signal. The FDM codec is used for digitising an FDM signal before transmission over a digital link. At the other end of the link, the codec converts the incoming bit stream back into the original FDM signal. The ITU recommends two types of transition modem for high-speed data transfer over an analogue link, namely the *data-in-voice* (DIV) modem and the *data-over-voice* (DOV) modem. A suitable carrier is modulated by the digital signal in both modems, but the DIV modem displaces several FDM channel assemblies, while the DOV modem places the signal above the frequency band occupied by these voice signals and so does not replace them.

8.3 Time division multiplexing

8.3.1 General concepts

We saw in Chapter 5 that an analogue signal can be perfectly reconstructed from its samples taken at intervals of T_s (= $1/f_s$), provided the sampling frequency f_s is at least equal to the bandwidth of the analogue signal. Based on this (sampling) theorem, all bandlimited analogue signals can be digitised (e.g. converted to a PCM signal), as was discussed in detail in Chapter 6. The signal is sampled at a suitable frequency f_s and each sample is represented using k bits, referred to as a *word*. The case k = 8 is called a *byte* or *octet*. This yields an information-bearing bit stream that occurs at the rate

$$R_c = kf_s \text{ bits/second} \tag{8.9}$$

Equation (8.9) gives the bit rate of one signal, which in this context is also referred to as a channel or *tributary*. We wish to examine how N such tributaries may be combined into one composite bit stream by *time division multiplexing* (TDM) and the steps necessary to ensure accurate recovery of each channel at the receiver.

An analogue TDM system was discussed in Chapter 1 using Figs. 1.24 and 1.25, which you may wish to refer to at this point. In particular, Fig. 1.25 shows a TDM signal (for N = 3) obtained by interleaving samples from each of the N channels. Here we are dealing with a digital system in which the samples have been digitised and each is represented with k bits. Thus, for

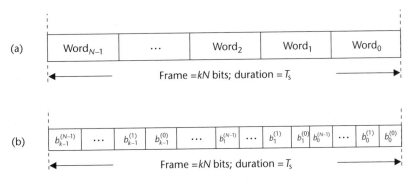

Figure 8.14 Frame organisation. (a) Word-interleaving; (b) bit-interleaving.

correct reconstruction at the receiver, each of the N channels must have k bits in time slots of duration T_s. This time interval over which one word has been taken from each of the N channels is known as a *frame*. There are two types of frame organisation.

- *Word-interleaved frame*: The frame (of duration T_s) is filled by an interleaver, which visits each of the N channel ports once during the interval T_s, and at each visit takes one word (of k bits) from the storage dedicated to that channel. These bits are clocked out serially to give the TDM signal. The result is the frame structure shown in Fig. 8.14(a), and we see that a frame contains kN message bits. In this diagram, Word_j is the k-bit code $b_{k-1}...b_2b_1b_0$ of the sample taken from the jth channel during the interval T_s, where b_{k-1} is the most significant bit of the word, b_0 the least significant bit (LSB) etc.

- *Bit-interleaved frame*: A bit-interleaved frame is formed by taking one bit at a time from each of the N channel ports visited by the interleaver in a cyclic order (i.e. 0, 1, 2, ..., $N-1$, 0, 1, 2, ...). The bits are clocked out in a serial fashion to give the output TDM signal. Since each channel requires a word of k bits to be sent in each interval of T_s, the interleaver must visit each port k times during this interval. The structure of the bit-interleaved frame is therefore as shown in Fig. 8.14(b), where $b_0^{(j)}$ is the LSB of the sample from the jth channel, etc. Note that both types of frames (bit- and word-interleaved) are of the same duration T_s and contain the same number of message bits kN. However, bit-interleaving does not require storage at the channel ports, as does word-interleaving, to hold each message word until it is read by the interleaver. We will see that TDM is obtained at the first level of the plesiochronous digital hierarchy (PDH) by word-interleaving, whereas bit-interleaving is used at the higher levels.

Synchronisation between transmitter and receiver is crucial to the correct operation of any digital transmission system. In Section 6.7.4 we discussed clock extraction, which enables the receiver to achieve *bit synchronisation* with the transmitter and hence to use precisely correct decision instants for detecting the incoming bit stream. However, the packaging of bits from N tributaries into frames introduces a further synchronisation requirement, known as *frame alignment* or *frame synchronisation*. This is needed to give the receiver a precise knowledge of the start of each frame so that the bits in the TDM signal can be correctly distributed to their respective channels without the need for additional address information. To this end, the multiplexer inserts at regular intervals a special pattern of bits known as a *frame alignment word* (FAW). This serves as a marker onto which the demultiplexer is synchronised at the receiver. Two different arrangements of the framing bits are in common use.

1. *Grouped or bunched FAW*: Here the FAW occupies a number of consecutive bit positions in each frame.

2. *Distributed FAW*: A distributed FAW consists of several bits spread over one frame, or one bit per frame spread over several adjacent frames called a *multiframe* or *superframe*.

Grouped FAW is employed in the European E1 TDM system, while the T1 system of North America uses a distributed FAW. There is a chance that a FAW can occur within the message bits leading to wrong alignment, and that a transmitted FAW can be corrupted by one or more bit errors. To minimise the problems posed by these two events, alignment is declared only after a correct FAW is detected at the same relative position within a number of (say 3) consecutive time intervals. This interval is that over which a complete FAW was inserted at the transmitter, which could be a frame (for a bunched FAW) or a multiframe (for some distributed FAWs). Secondly, a loss of alignment is declared (and a free search for the FAW thereby initiated) only after a number of (say 4) incorrect FAWs are received in consecutive intervals. Thirdly, the FAW is chosen to be of an intermediate length. Too long and it is more readily corrupted by noise; too short and it is more frequently imitated in the message bits. Furthermore, the FAW must be a sequence of bits that cannot be reproduced when a part of the FAW is concatenated with adjacent message bits (with or without bit errors), or when several FAWs are bit-interleaved.

The control of switching and execution of other network management functions require the transmission of *signalling information* in addition to the message and FAW bits discussed above. This is accomplished by inserting a few auxiliary bits in various ways.

- *Bit robbing*: A signalling bit periodically replaces the LSB of a message word. This is done in every 6th frame in the T1 system that employs this technique. The resulting degradation is imperceptible for voice messages, but is clearly totally unacceptable for data (e.g. ASCII-coded) messages. For this reason, in a TDM system that uses bit-robbed signalling the LSB of message words in all frames is left unused when carrying data.

- *Out-of-word signalling*: Within the sampling interval T_s, the message word from each channel is accompanied by one signalling bit, which gives a signalling rate of f_s bits/second per channel. Alternatively, a time slot of k bits in every sampling interval is dedicated as a signalling channel whose bits are assigned in turn to each of the N channels. The signalling rate in this case is therefore kf_s/N bits/second per channel. We will see that the E1 system uses this type of signalling.

- *Common signalling*: One slot of k bits is dedicated in each time interval T_s to signalling, which leads to an overall signalling rate of kf_s bits/second. The entire signalling slot is assigned to one message channel at a time according to need. Some of the bits are, however, used to provide a label that identifies which channel the signalling belongs to.

From the foregoing discussion we see that the bit rate of an N-channel TDM signal exceeds N times the bit rate of each tributary because of the insertion of *overhead bits* for frame alignment and signalling. There are kN message bits in each frame of duration T_s. Thus, f_s $(= 1/T_s)$ is the frame rate. If we denote the total number of framing and signalling bits in each frame by c (for control bits), it follows that the bit rate of the TDM signal is given by

$$
\begin{aligned}
R &= \frac{Nk + c}{T_s} \\
&= Nkf_s + cf_s \\
&= NR_c + cf_s
\end{aligned}
\tag{8.10}
$$

where R_c is the tributary bit rate stated earlier in Eq. (8.9). Considering the fraction of message bits in the TDM signal, we may define the data transmission *efficiency* as

$$
\begin{aligned}
\eta &= \frac{\text{Number of message bits}}{\text{Total number of bits}} \\
&= \frac{NR_c}{R}
\end{aligned}
\tag{8.11}
$$

It is important to note the significance of the parameters on the RHS of Eq. (8.11). N is the number of message channels at the input of the non-hierarchical or flat-level TDM multiplexer; R_c is the message bit rate emanating from each channel; and R is the output bit rate of the multiplexer. Equation (8.11) can be applied to a TDM signal obtained after several hierarchical levels of multiplexing, with NR_c being the total number of message bits per second in the TDM signal, which includes bits added ahead of the multiplexer to each of the tributary bit streams for error control.

We have so far discussed in very general terms what is actually a flat-level TDM. To allow the building of high-capacity TDM systems using standardised equipment, a hierarchical multiplexing procedure was adopted.

8.3.2 Plesiochronous digital hierarchy

The basic building block of the plesiochronous digital hierarchy (PDH) is the 64 kbit/s channel, which results from the digitisation of analogue speech in the following manner. Analogue speech signal is first filtered to limit its frequency content to a maximum value of 3400 Hz. It is then sampled at the rate $f_s = 8$ kHz, meaning that the sampling interval is $T_s = 1/f_s$ = 125 μs, which constitutes a frame. Each sample is quantised and represented using $k = 8$ bits. The coding scheme follows a non-uniform quantisation procedure, which is either A-law (in Europe) or μ-law (in North America). Thus each voice signal is converted to a bit stream generated at the rate 8000 samples/second × 8 bits/sample = 64 kbit/s. This is the bit rate of each input channel or tributary at the very first level of the multiplexing hierarchy. This brief summary of sampling and digitisation is adequate for our treatment here, but you should feel free to consult Chapters 5 and 6 for a more detailed discussion.

There are three different procedures for hierarchical multiplexing of these 64 kbit/s channels, namely the E1 system in Europe, the T1 system in North America, and the (non-ITU standardised) J1 system in Japan.

8.3.2.1 *E1 system*

The first level of multiplexing combines 30 digitised speech signals, each of bit rate 64 kbit/s, to give the Order-1 TDM signal or simply E1. The equipment used for this purpose is known as a *primary muldex* (for multiplexer and demultiplexer), a block diagram of which is shown in Fig. 8.15 with emphasis on the multiplexing operation. Note that the PCM *codec* (for *co*der and *dec*oder) is the A-law type. The E1 frame is often described as CEPT PCM-30, where CEPT refers to Conference of European Posts and Telecommunications and 30 signifies the number of voice channels.

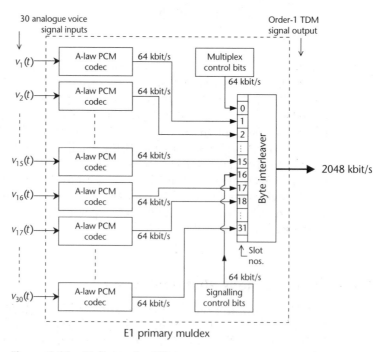

Figure 8.15 E1 first-order TDM.

E1 frame structure A frame of duration $T_s = 125$ μs is divided into 32 time slots, and 8 bits are placed in each slot. These bits are clocked out serially to give the E1 signal, which therefore has a bit rate

$$R_1 = \frac{32 \times 8 \text{ bits}}{125 \times 10^{-6} \text{ seconds}} = 2048 \text{ kbit/s} \tag{8.12}$$

Of the 32 slots or channels C0 to C31 in each frame, 30 carry message bits, which will vary from frame to frame according to the samples of the respective message signals. Two of the channels (C0 and C16) carry overhead bits for managing the multiplexing operation and signalling. The efficiency of the E1 signal therefore follows from Eq. (8.11), with $N = 30$, $R_c = 64$ kbit/s and $R = 2048$ kbit/s,

$$\eta_1 = \frac{30 \times 64}{2048} \times 100\% = 93.75\%$$

Out-of-word signalling is employed with channel C16 providing the signalling needs of two of the message channels at a time, four bits to each channel. It therefore takes 15 adjacent frames to cover the signalling of the 30 message channels. Dedicating channel C16 in the first frame for marking the beginning of this group of frames, we have what is known as a *multiframe* that consists of 16 adjacent frames, and is of duration 16×125 μs $= 2$ ms. The complete content of channels C0 and C16 can be seen over an entire multiframe consisting of frames F1 to F16, as shown in Fig. 8.16. In considering this multiframe, we

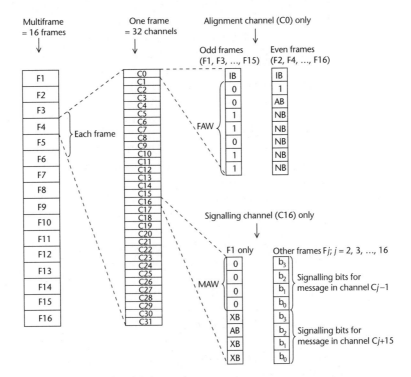

Figure 8.16 E1 level-1 frame format.

ignore the contents of channels C1 to C15 and C17 to C31 in each frame since these are message bits. We note the following.

- *Signalling channel C16*:
  In the first frame F1, the first four bits of the channel (C16) are used to carry a *multiframe alignment word* (MAW) = 0000, which marks the beginning of a multiframe and allows correct numbering of the component frames. Three bits are unassigned extra bits (XB) and one bit is used as an alarm bit (AB) to signal the loss of multiframe alignment. AB is binary 0 during normal operation.

  In all other frames Fj (for j = 2, 3, ..., 16), four bits of the channel carry signalling data (on or off hook, dialling digits, call progress etc.) for channel Cj–1, and the remaining four bits carry the signalling for channel Cj+15. What this means is that channel C16 in frame F2 carries the signalling bits for message-carrying channels C1 and C17. In frame F3, the signalling channel C16 carries signalling bits for channels C2 and C18, and so on until in the last frame F16 of the multiframe it carries signalling bits for channels C15 and C31. In this way, each one of the message channels uses four signalling bits in every multiframe of duration 2 ms, which gives a channel signalling bit rate of

  $$R_{\text{signalling}} = \frac{4 \text{ bits}}{2 \text{ ms}} = 2 \text{ kbit/s}$$

- *Alignment channel C0*:
  The first bit of this channel in all frames is an international bit (IB), which is now used to provide a check sequence for error detection as follows. A 4 bit cyclic redundancy check (CRC-4) code is computed using all 2048 bits in frames F1 to F8, referred to as the first *submultiframe* (SMF). This code is conveyed in the first bit (IB) of frames F9, F11, F13 and F15 (i.e. within the next SMF). Another CRC-4 code is computed on the bits in the second SMF (i.e. frames F9 to F16), and conveyed in the first bit of frames F1, F3, F5 and F7 in the next SMF. At the receiver the same computation is repeated and the result is compared with the received CRC-4 code. Any discrepancy is an indication of error in one or more bits of the relevant SMF.

  In the odd frames F1, F3, ..., F15, the last seven bits of channel C0 carry a frame alignment word (FAW) = 0011011.

  In the even frames F2, F4, ..., F16, the second bit is always set to binary 1 to avoid a chance imitation of the FAW within these even frames. The third bit is used as an alarm bit (AB), which is set to 1 to indicate the loss of frame alignment, and is 0 during normal operation. The last five bits are designated as national bits (NB), which are set to 1 when an international boundary is crossed.

E1 hierarchy A digital multiplexing hierarchy, shown in Fig. 8.17, is used to build TDM systems of the required capacity, which allows a better exploitation of the bandwidth available on the transmission medium. Five levels of multiplexing are shown.

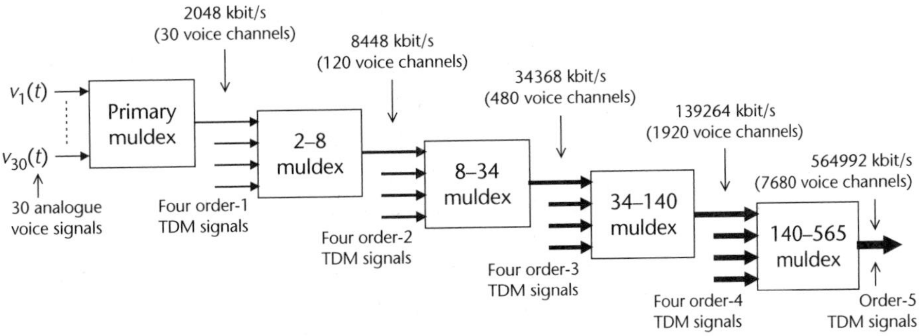

Figure 8.17 CEPT plesiochronous digital hierarchy.

1. In level 1, referred to as the primary level and discussed in detail above, 30 voice channels are multiplexed by byte-interleaving in a primary muldex to yield an Order-1 TDM or E1 signal of bit rate 2048 kbit/s. This rate is often identified simply as 2 Mbit/s.

2. Four Order-1 TDM signals are combined in a muldex, more specifically identified as a 2-8 muldex. The output is an Order-2 TDM or E2 signal of bit rate 8448 kbit/s (a rate often referred to as 8 Mbit/s), which contains $4 \times 30 = 120$ voice channels. The multiplexing is by bit-interleaving in this and higher levels of the hierarchy. From Eq. (8.11), the efficiency η_2 of this Order-2 TDM signal is given by

$$\eta_2 = \frac{120 \times 64 \text{ kbit/s}}{8448 \text{ kbit/s}} = 90.91\%$$

3. Four Order-2 TDM signals are combined in an 8-34 muldex. The output is an Order-3 TDM or E3 signal of bit rate 34368 kbit/s — often abbreviated to 34 Mbit/s. This signal contains $4 \times 120 = 480$ voice channels, and has an efficiency $\eta_3 = 89.39\%$.

4. Four Order-3 TDM signals are multiplexed in a 34–140 muldex to give an Order-4 TDM or E4 signal of bit rate 139264 kbit/s — often referred to simply as 140 Mbit/s, which contains $4 \times 480 = 1920$ voice channels, and has an efficiency $\eta_4 = 88.24\%$.

5. Finally, four Order-4 TDM signals are multiplexed in a 140-565 muldex to give an Order-5 TDM or E5 signal of bit rate 564 992 kbit/s — referred to simply as 565 Mbit/s, which contains $4 \times 1920 = 7680$ voice channels, and has an efficiency $\eta_5 = 87.00\%$. A further multiplexing level is possible that combines four Order-5 TDM signals to yield a 2.5 Gbit/s TDM signal carrying 30 720 voice channels.

We observe that at each level of the hierarchy the bit rate of the output TDM signal is more than the sum of the bit rates of the input tributaries. The efficiency of the TDM signals therefore decreases monotonically as we go up the hierarchy. The reason for this is the insertion of control bits into the TDM frame produced by each muldex in the hierarchy. It is worthwhile to examine this further.

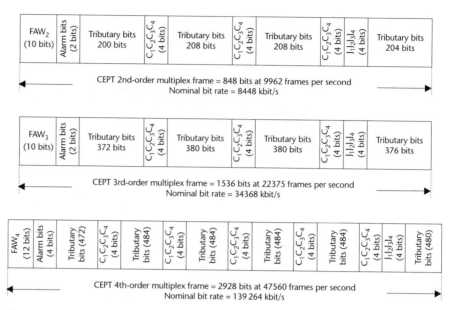

Figure 8.18 CEPT higher level frame formats.

Higher-level frames structure The frame format of the primary muldex has already been discussed in detail. The frame structure at the other levels of the hierarchy is shown in Fig. 8.18. We note the following.

- A bunched FAW is inserted at the beginning of each frame, with

  $$FAW_2 = FAW_3 = 1111010000$$
  $$FAW_4 = 111110100000$$

  This enables the demultiplexer to recognise the start of each frame and therefore to correctly route the bits to their tributaries.

- The tributary bits are filled by taking one bit at a time in order from each of the four (input) tributaries. That is, bit-interleaving is used.

- J_i is a justification bit for the ith tributary, i.e. J_1 for tributary 1, J_2 for tributary 2, and so on. It is either a dummy bit or a legitimate bit taken from the tributary. The basis of this decision and the purpose of the J bit are explained below. The role of the J bits is to allow correct multiplexing of four tributaries whose bit rates, although nominally equal, may drift slightly apart. In fact this is why the hierarchy is referred to as *plesiochronous*, which means nearly synchronous. Each tributary bit stream is written into a buffer under the control of a clock frequency extracted from the bit stream. The buffer is then read by the interleaver under the control of a common clock of slightly higher frequency. Occasionally, to prevent buffer i (for tributary i) from emptying, a dummy bit J_i is given to the interleaver rather than a bit being read from the buffer. This is known as *positive justification* or *bit stuffing*. Thus, J_i will be either a legitimate bit from the ith tributary or a dummy bit that must be discarded at the demultiplexer. The demultiplexer must therefore have a way of knowing which one is the case.

- C_i is a control bit that is set to 1 to indicate that J_i is a dummy bit. $C_i = 0$ thus indicates that J_i is a legitimate bit from the ith tributary. To protect this important control bit from error, it is sent more than once at different locations within the frame. The demultiplexer decides on the value of C_i based on *majority voting*. For example, in the third-order multiplex frame, C_i is taken to be a 1 if up to two of its three repeated transmissions are 1s. Note that a wrong decision about C_i and hence about whether J_i is a dummy bit would lead to a very serious problem of *bit slip* in subsequent bit intervals of the frame.

8.3.2.2 T1 and J1 systems

The T1 system (in North America) and J1 system (in Japan) both have identical first-order or primary multiplexing. 24 analogue voice signals are each digitised to 64 kbit/s using μ-law PCM, and multiplexed by byte-interleaving to yield a TDM signal, which is referred to as DS1. The DS1 frame, of duration $T_s = 125$ μs, contains 24 time slots of 8 bits per slot, plus one extra bit used for framing. Thus, the bit rate R_1 and efficiency η_1 of the DS1 signal are given by

$$R_1 = \frac{(24 \times 8) + 1 \text{ bits}}{125 \times 10^{-6} \text{ seconds}} = 1544 \text{ kbit/s}$$

$$\eta_1 = \frac{24 \times 64 \text{ kbit/s}}{1544 \text{ kbit/s}} \times 100\% = 99.48\%$$

T1 hierarchy Figure 8.19(a) shows the North American plesiochronous digital hierarchy, which features four levels of multiplexing that are used to build systems of the required capacity. The first level of multiplexing generates the DS1 signal referred to above and discussed further shortly. Subsequent levels of multiplexing are based on bit-interleaving of the input tributaries, with extra bits inserted for distributed frame alignment, justification and justification control, and other services such as alarm. The second level of multiplexing combines four DS1 signals into a 96-channel 6312 kbit/s DS2 signal of efficiency 97.34%. At the third level, seven DS2 signals are multiplexed into a 672-channel 44736 kbit/s DS3 signal of efficiency 96.14%. There are three options at the 4th level of multiplexing. In the old procedure, six DS3 signals were multiplexed into a 4032-channel 274 176 kbit/s DS4 signal of efficiency 94.12%. A new standard involves the multiplexing of three DS3 signals into a 2016-channel 139 264 kbit/s DS4 signal of efficiency 92.65%. Another procedure (not standardised by ITU) combines 12 DS3 signals into an 8064-channel 564 992 kbit/s DS4 signal of efficiency 91.35%. Observe that the last two procedures yield signals of the same bit rates as the Order-4 and Order-5 TDM signals in the CEPT hierarchy, but the DS4 signals have a higher efficiency by about 4.4%.

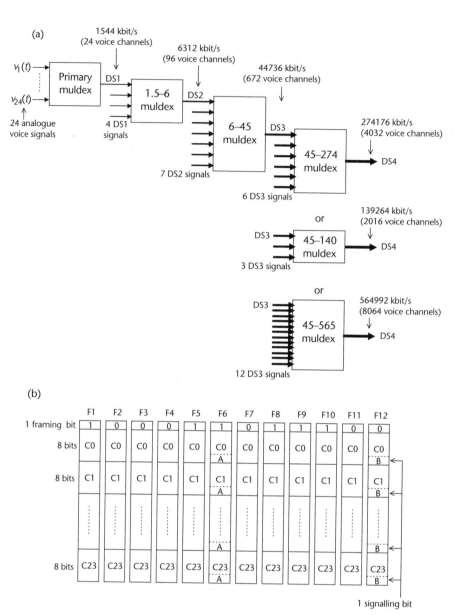

Figure 8.19 (a) North American PDH; (b) DS1 superframe.

T1 frame structure Let us consider the constitution of the DS1 frame in more detail. Figure 8.19(b) shows what is referred to as a *superframe*, which consists of 12 adjacent DS1 frames numbered F1 to F12. We note that each frame (of duration 125 μs) contains 193 bits, which are assigned as follows.

- The first bit of each frame in the superframe is used to provide a distributed 12-bit FAW = 100011011100.

- The remaining 192 bits are message bits taken 8 bits at a time from 24 input channels numbered C0 to C23.

- Every six frames — the 6th and 12th frames of the superframe — the bit interval of the LSB of each channel is used to send a signalling bit, which we have identified as A-bit for the 6th frame, and B-bit for the 12th frame. The distortion is imperceptible for voice signals, but totally unacceptable for data. Two different approaches may be adopted to get around this problem. (1) The 8th bit is not used at all in all channels of every frame. This restricts each channel to 7 bits per frame at 8000 frames per second, which gives a clear channel capability of only 56 kbit/s. Efficiency of the output TDM signal drops significantly from 99.48% to 87.05%. (2) The 24th channel (C23) is devoted as a common signalling channel, called the D-channel. In this case efficiency equals 95.34%. This is the technique employed in the North American primary rate integrated services digital network (PRI), termed 23B+D service, in which there are 23 bearer channels each of bit rate 64 kbit/s, and one 64 kbit/s data channel. The corresponding European PRI is 30B+D, providing 30 bearer channels and one data channel. These ISDN services are carried over wire pairs, and offer bit rates up to 2.048 Mbit/s (in multiples of 64 kbit/s). They are termed *narrowband* to distinguish them from *broadband ISDN* (B-ISDN), which is provided over optical fibre and offers data rates in excess of 45 Mbit/s, possibly up to 9.95 Gbit/s.

- There exists a different signalling procedure for the T1 system in which 24 frames are grouped into what is known as an *extended superframe* (ESF). The first bit of each member-frame, formerly dedicated to framing only, are then used to perform various control functions. These 24 bits are assigned as follows. Six bits provide a distributed FAW = 001001; six bits are used for CRC error checking; and the remaining 12 bits are used to provide a management channel known as the *facilities data link* (FDL). However, signalling is still performed by bit-robbing the LSB of all message channels in every 6th frame.

J1 hierarchy The Japanese PDH is shown in Fig. 8.20. The first two levels of multiplexing are identical with the North American hierarchy. Beyond this, at the third multiplexing, 5 DS2 signals are combined to give a 480-channel 32064 kbit/s TDM signal of efficiency 95.81%. We call this signal J3. At the 4th level, three J3 signals are multiplexed to obtain a 1440-channel 97728 kbit/s J4 signal of efficiency 94.30%.

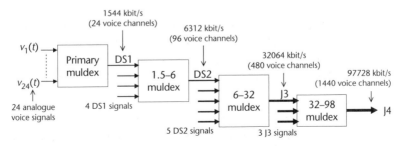

Figure 8.20 Japanese PDH.

8.3.2.3 PDH problems

1. It is clear from the above discussions that the plesiochronous digital hierarchies used in North America (T1), Japan (J1) and the rest of the world (E1) are not compatible. The interconnection of PDH systems originating from different parts of the world thus requires proprietary conversion equipment, which maps 8-bit time slots (at the 1.5 Mbit/s and 2 Mbit/s levels) from one hierarchy into slots in the other hierarchy, a process known as *timeslot interchange*. When converting between E1 and T1 or J1 systems that carry voice traffic, it is necessary to re-code each 8-bit word between A-law and μ-law PCM.

2. The PDH was designed to cater for the basic 64 kbit/s telephony rate. It is therefore unsuitable for the transmission of video traffic, which (even with the use of compression) requires much higher bit rates. Inherent limitations in PDH make it impossible to realise a well-managed system having the required video rates simply by concatenating several 64 kbit/s channels. Furthermore, multiple stages of multiplexing are needed to realise higher capacity systems for data and voice traffic. There is a small problem here in that control bits must be inserted at each stage to manage the multiplexing process. This leads to lower efficiencies at the higher levels of the hierarchy. For example, the T1 system has an efficiency of 99.48% at the first multiplexing stage that produces the 1544 kbit/s 24-channel signal, but an efficiency of only 92.65% for the 139 264 kbit/s 2016-channel signal generated at the 4th multiplexing stage.

3. Beyond the first level of the hierarchy, PDH involves the multiplexing of plesiochronous tributaries, which requires occasional insertion of dummy bits into the TDM signal, as earlier explained. This leads to two problems, one minor and the other major. When the dummy bits are removed at the receiver, gaps are left in the extracted bit stream, which causes severe *jitter* that must be smoothed using a process that involves extra buffering. More seriously, the presence of these dummy bits and framing bits makes it impossible to drop and insert a lower rate tributary without completely demultiplexing (i.e. unpacking) the TDM signal down to its component tributaries at the desired rate. Thus a *multiplexing mountain* is required at the drop and insert point, an example of which is shown in Fig. 8.21 for the case where a 2 Mbit/s bit stream is extracted from a 140 Mbit/s system. PDH-based networks are therefore expensive, inflexible and cumbersome to build with provision for *cross-connect* points. Such points are needed in modern networks to allow lower-rate tributaries to be dropped and inserted at intermediate points, channels to be provided for private networks, and sub-networks to be interconnected to provide alternative paths through a larger network as a backup against the failure of a particular link.

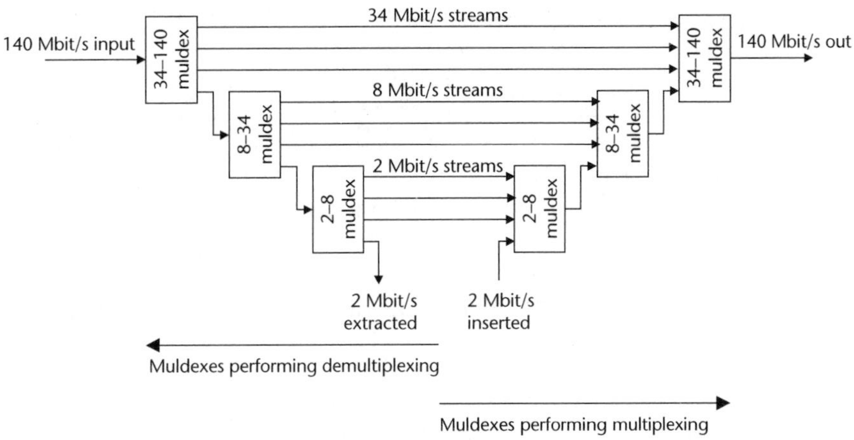

Figure 8.21 PDH multiplex mountain required to access one of the 2 Mbit/s channels within a 140 Mbit/s signal.

8.3.3. Synchronous digital hierarchy

The synchronous digital hierarchy (SDH) is a new multiplexing technique designed to operate in synchronism with the digital switches now used at network nodes. It allows individual tributaries (down to 64 kbit/s) to be readily accessed, and it very conveniently accommodates the standardised PDH signals presented above, as well as being well suited for carrying ATM payloads (discussed later). Moreover, SDH makes ample provision of channel capacity to meet all the requirements of advanced network management and maintenance for the foreseeable future.

8.3.3.1 SDH rates

You will recall that the E1 frame (in Fig. 8.16) contains 32 bytes in a 125 µs duration, which gives it a bit rate of 2048 kbit/s. The basic SDH frame is called *synchronous transport module at level 1* (STM-1) and contains 2430 bytes. It has the same duration $T_s = 125$ µs, which means that 8000 STM-1 frames are transmitted each second, i.e. frame rate = 8 kHz. Thus the basic SDH bit rate is

$$R_1 = \frac{2430 \times 8}{125 \times 10^{-6}} = 155.52 \text{ Mbit/s}$$

The STM-1 frame can therefore accommodate all the American and European PDH multiplex signals up to the 4th level of the plesiochronous hierarchy, namely 1.5, 2, 6, 8, 34, 45 and 140 Mbit/s.

Higher SDH rates are obtained by multiplexing, through *byte-interleaving*, a number (N) of STM-1 frames to give what is referred to as the STM-N frame. The ITU has standardised those rates in which N is a power of 4. For example, the STM-4 and STM-16 frames have duration $T_s = 125$ µs, contain 2430×4 and 2430×16 bytes respectively, and have bit rates

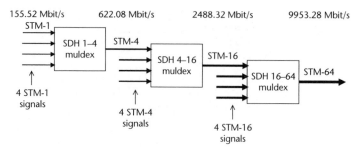

Figure 8.22 Higher-capacity synchronous transport modules.

$$R_4 = \frac{2430 \times 4 \times 8}{125 \times 10^{-6}} = 622.08 \text{ Mbit/s}$$

$$R_{16} = \frac{2430 \times 16 \times 8}{125 \times 10^{-6}} = 2488.32 \text{ Mbit/s}$$

Figure 8.22 shows the assembly of higher-capacity transport modules up to STM-64. It can be seen that the output bit rate at each level is the sum of the bit rates of the input tributaries. This is because of the synchronous operation of these inputs, which makes *bit-stuffing* unnecessary. Note that although we have depicted a hierarchical assembly in Fig. 8.22, an STM-N frame, whatever the value of N, can also be obtained by byte-multiplexing N STM-1 frames in a $1 - N$ SDH muldex.

8.3.3.2 *SDH frame structure*

Figure 8.23 shows the structure of the STM-1 and STM-N frames. It is sufficient that we consider only the STM-1 frame structure in detail, since the structure of the STM-N frame follows straightforwardly from a byte-by-byte interleaving of N STM-1 frames.

We have shown the 2430 bytes of the STM-1 frame arranged in nine rows of 270 bytes each. However, it must be emphasised that the frame is transmitted serially one bit at a time starting from row 1, then row 2, and so on to row 9. The MSB of each byte is transmitted first. One STM-1 frame is sent in an interval of 125 µs, followed by the next frame in the next 125 µs interval, and so on. Note that there are 2430 (= 270 × 9) cells in our rectangular-matrix representation of the STM-1 frame. Each cell corresponds to 8 bits transmitted in 125 µs, which represents a 64 kbit/s channel capacity. Similarly, each column represents a channel capacity of 64 × 9 = 576 kbit/s. Clearly then, one cell of the STM-1 frame can carry one PCM voice signal. Three columns can carry one DS1 signal (of bit rate 1544 kbit/s), with some bits to spare. Four columns can carry one E1 signal (of bit rate 2048 kbit/s) etc. We will have more to say on this when considering how the STM-1 frame is assembled.

The STM-1 frame is divided into two parts. The first part is the *frame header* and consists of a 9-byte *pointer field* and a 72-byte *section overhead*

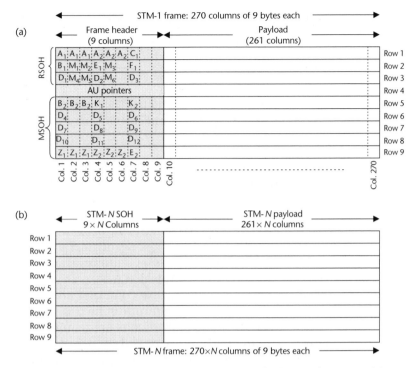

Figure 8.23 SDH frame structure. (a) STM-1; (b) STM-*N* for *N* = 4, 16, 64, ...

(SOH). The frame header covers the first nine columns of the frame, which corresponds to a channel capacity of 5.184 Mbit/s. It is used for carrying control bits, such as frame alignment, error monitoring, multiplex and network management, etc. The remaining part of the frame is the *payload*, which consists of 261 columns or a channel capacity of 150.336 Mbit/s. This area is used for carrying a variety of signals, and is therefore referred to as a *virtual container* (VC). More specifically, it is identified as VC-4, to distinguish it from smaller-sized virtual containers, since it is large enough to contain the 140 Mbit/s PDH signal at the 4th level of the plesiochronous hierarchy. In general, the payload area provides virtual containers of various sizes identified as VC-*j*, which is large enough to accommodate the PDH signal at the *j*th level of the plesiochronous hierarchy, but too small for the signal at the next higher level. At lower levels *j* < 4, a second digit is appended to the identification to distinguish between the American (1) and European (2) signals. Thus, VC-11 (pronounced veecee-one-one) is a virtual container adequate for the American DS1 signal (of bit rate 1544 kbit/s). Similarly, VC-12 is for the European E1 signal (of bit rate 2048 kbit/s), VC-21 is for the American DS2 signal (of bit rate 6312 kbit/s), VC-22 is for the European E2 signal (of bit rate 8448 kbit/s) etc. VC-1 and VC-2 are described as *lower-order* virtual containers, while VC-3 and VC-4 are *higher-order*.

VCs include bits for a *path overhead* (POH), which is added at the point that the tributary signal is incorporated into the SDH system, and is used to manage the transmission of the signal and ensure its integrity. The process of adding a POH is known as *mapping*. A VC without its POH is known simply as a *container* (C), which is therefore the maximum *information payload* available to a user in the VC. The entire first column (9 bytes) of a VC-4 is used for the path overhead. Thus a C-4 has 260 × 9 bytes or a capacity of 149.76 Mbit/s, which is the maximum information rate in a VC-4 — more than enough for the 140 Mbit/s PDH signal. As a reminder we may write,

$$\text{Virtual container} = \text{Container} + \text{POH} \tag{8.13}$$

When a tributary signal is inserted into the SDH system, we say that it has been incorporated in a container. This process requires single-bit or *asynchronous* justification if the tributary and SDH clocks are not locked in frequency. Justification has already been discussed in Section 8.3.2 in connection with the multiplexing of nearly synchronous tributaries in PDH. The capacity of a container is always larger than that required by the tributary signal for which it is defined. So as part of the mapping process, the spare byte positions in the container are filled with a defined filler pattern of *stuffing bits* to synchronise the tributary signal with the payload capacity. The POH and stuffing bits are removed at the drop point in the network where the tributary is demultiplexed.

Before leaving this issue, it is worth pointing out that the maximum efficiency of an SDH system can be obtained as follows:

$$\eta_{max} = \frac{\text{Max no. of information cells in frame}}{\text{Total no. of cells in frame}} \times 100\%$$
$$= \frac{260 \times 9}{2430} \times 100\% = 96.30\% \tag{8.14}$$

Actually a VC need not start at the first byte of the frame payload. Typically it begins in one frame and ends in the next. The starting point of a VC (i.e. the location of its first byte) in an STM frame is indicated by a *pointer*, which keeps track of the phase offset between the two. There is therefore no need for delay-causing re-timing buffers at network nodes, which may be controlled by slightly different clock rates. A higher-order VC and its pointer constitute an *administrative unit* (AU). The pointer is called an *AU pointer*. It is 3 bytes long and located in the header part of the STM frame.

The scenario just described actually applies to the simple case where no intervening multiplexing is required because the input tributary is large enough (e.g. the 140 Mbit/s signal) to use up the available information capacity of the STM-1 frame. In this case a VC-4 is formed, followed by the addition of a pointer to give an AU-4. Finally, a section overhead is added to the AU-4 to complete the STM-1 frame. A more general case involving the multiplexing — always through byte-interleaving — of several lower-rate signals to fill the STM-1 frame will be considered under frame multiplexing.

Frame header Returning to Fig. 8.23(a) we see that the 81-byte frame header consists of 27 bytes for a *regenerator section overhead* (RSOH), 9 bytes for administrative unit (AU) pointers, and 45 bytes for a *multiplex section* *overhead* (MSOH). The RSOH is interpreted at regenerators along the transmission path, while the MSOH remains intact and is interpreted only at multiplexing points.

- *RSOH*: The regenerative SOH consists of the following elements.

  (i) A 48-bit frame alignment word (FAW) $A_1A_1A_1A_2A_2A_2$, composed using two bytes A_1 and A_2 only. This marks the start of the STM-1 frame.

  (ii) A label C_1 that identifies the order of appearance of this frame in the STM-N frame, $N = 4, 16, ...$

  (iii) A byte B_1 used for error detection by *bit interleaved parity* (BIP). In general, a BIP-n code provides error protection for a specified section of a transmitted bit stream. The jth bit of the code gives an even parity check on the jth bit in all blocks of n bits in the section. For example, you should verify that the BIP-3 code for protecting the bit stream

  $$1\ 0\ 0\ 0\ 1\ 0\ 1\ 1\ 0\ 1\ 1\ 1\ 0\ 1\ 1\ 0\ 0\ 0\ 1\ 0\ 1$$

  is given by

  $$\text{BIP-3 code} = 0\ 0\ 1$$

  (iv) Medium-specific bytes M_1–M_6, the use of which depends on the type of transmission medium — radio, coaxial cable or optical fibre.

  (v) A 64 kbit/s voice channel E_1, for use by system maintenance personnel. This communication channel is usually referred to as *engineer's orderwire* (EOW).

  (vi) A 64 kbit/s user channel F_1.

  (vii) Data communication channels (DCC) D_1, D_2 and D_3, providing a 192 kbit/s capacity for network management.

- *AU pointers*: the AU pointer field consists of 9 bytes, three of which indicate the exact location of one virtual container (VC) in the STM-1 frame. The frame may either carry one VC-4, in which case only three AU pointer bytes are used, or it may carry up to three VC-3s.

- *MSOH*: the assignments of the multiplex SOH are as follows.

  (i) Byte B_2 is used for error monitoring.

  (ii) Bytes K_1 and K_2 are used for automatic protection switching (APS) in line transmission.

  (iii) Bytes D_4 to D_{12} provide a 576 kbit/s data communication channel for network management.

  (iv) Bytes Z_1 and Z_2 are reserved for future functions.

  (v) Byte E_2 provides a 64 kbit/s orderwire.

Path overhead (POH) We indicated earlier that the frame payload may consist of only one virtual container VC-4, or several smaller-sized VCs. An

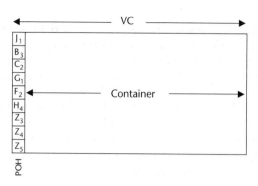

J_1 = Path trace. A unique identifier for verifying the VC-n connection

B_3 = BIP-8 code. Computed over all bits of the previous container
  and used for monitoring error.

C_2 = Signal label. Shows the composition of the VC.

G_1 = Path status. Indicates received signal status

F_2 = Path user channel. For network operator communication between path equipment

H_4 = Multiframe indicator. Gives multiframe indication or cell start for ATM

Z_3, Z_4, Z_5 = Three bytes reserved for use by national network operator

Figure 8.24 Composition of path overhead (POH) for VC-3 and VC-4.

important part of a VC is its path overhead (POH), which is used to support and maintain the transport of the VC between its entry and exit path terminations. The POH of a VC-4 as well as that of a VC-3 is 9 bytes long and occupies the entire first column of the VC. Figure 8.24 shows the composition of this 9-byte POH. On the other hand, VC-1 and VC-2 each has a shorter POH that is only one byte long. The bits $b_7 b_6 b_5 b_4 b_3 b_2 b_1 b_0$ of this one-byte POH are assigned as follows.

1. $b_7 b_6$ = BIP-2 for error monitoring.
2. b_5 = Far end block error (FEBE) to indicate receipt of a BIP error.
3. b_4 = Unused.
4. $b_3 b_2 b_1$ = Signal label (L1, L2, L3) to indicate type of VC payload.
5. b_0 = remote alarm to indicate receiving failure.

Frame assembly   The process of constituting an STM-1 frame starting from a C-4, which may carry for example the 140 Mbit/s PDH signal, was described earlier and is illustrated in Fig. 8.25. The STM-1 frame may also be constituted using lower-rate tributaries in smaller-sized containers. An illustration of this procedure for C-12, which carries one 2.048 Mbit/s E1 signal, is shown in Fig. 8.26(a). The result of this multiplexing procedure is that the STM-1 frame has been employed to convey 63 E1 signals, each of which can be easily extracted at a network node using a simple add/drop muldex (ADM) without having to unpack the entire frame. For this to be possible, the starting point of every lower-order VC must be indicated by a pointer known as a *tributary unit* (TU) *pointer*. Other multiplexing possibilities are shown in the ITU-defined basic SDH multiplexing structure of Fig.

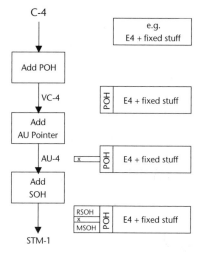

Figure 8.25 Assembly of STM-1 frame from C-4.

8.26(b). Note that Figs. 8.25 and 8.26(a) were obtained by following two different routes in Fig. 8.26(b). Taking a moment to identify these routes will help you understand how to interpret Fig. 8.26(b). The following discussion explains the new SDH terms that appear in these figures.

A lower-order VC together with its TU pointer constitutes what is known as a *tributary unit*, which occupies a certain number of columns in the STM-1 payload area. For example, it is shown in Fig. 8.27 that TU-11 has three columns, TU-12 has four columns, and TU-21 and TU-22 both have 12 columns. An assembly of identical-rate TUs, obtained using byte-interleaving, is known as a *tributary unit group* (TUG). A TUG-2 consists of one TU-2, or three TU-12s, or four TU-11s, and a TUG-3 consists of one TU-3 or seven TUG-2s. Similarly, an assembly of identical-rate administrative units is known as an *administrative unit group* (AUG). Only two realisations of an AUG have been defined, namely one AU-4 or three AU-3s. Finally, adding an SOH to an AUG yields an STM-1 frame, and N of these frames may be multiplexed to obtain the higher-capacity transport module STM-N.

8.3.3.3 SONET

The *synchronous optical network* (SONET) transmission standard was developed in 1988 by the T1X1 committee of the American National Standards Institute (ANSI). It is the forerunner of SDH. Both SONET and SDH are based on the same principles, the most noticeable differences between them being in terminology and the standardised transmission rates. The basic SONET frame is called the *synchronous transport system level 1* (STS-1) or *optical carrier level 1* (OC-1). This frame has duration 125 μs and contains 810 bytes, which corresponds to a rate of 51.84 Mbit/s. The structure of the frame may be represented similarly to Fig. 8.23 as a rectangular matrix of 90 columns of 9 bytes each. The first three columns (equivalent to 1.728 Mbit/s) serve as the header, while the remaining 87 columns (or 50.112 Mbit/s) are the payload. Thus the STS-1 frame can contain one DS3 signal (of bit rate 44.736 Mbit/s) or 28 DS1 signals or 28 × 24 = 672 voice channels. Based on the SDH considerations discussed earlier, individual DS1 signals in the STS-1 frame can be extracted without having to disassemble the entire frame.

Higher-capacity frames, called STS-N or OC-N, are obtained by multiplexing N basic frames. In particular, $N = 3$ gives the STS-3 frame, which has exactly the same capacity (155.52 Mbit/s) as the basic SDH frame, namely STM-1. The other standardised SONET and SDH rates that are identical include OC-12 and STM-4 with a line rate of 622.08 Mbit/s, OC-48 and STM-16 with a line rate of 2488.32 Mbit/s, and OC-192 and STM-64 with line rate 9953.28 Mbit/s.

International transmission is based on SDH, with the required conversions performed at North American gateways. SONET has, however, been

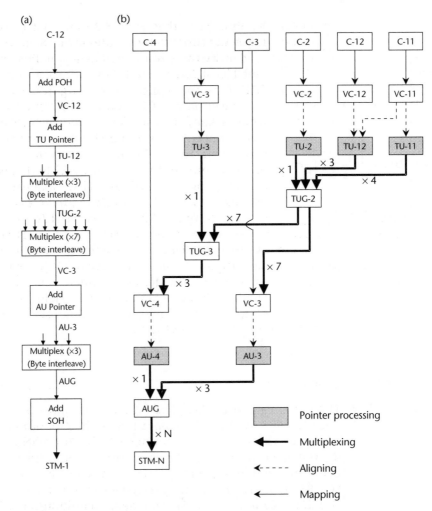

Figure 8.26 (a) Assembly of STM-1 frame from C-12. (b) Basic SDH multiplexing structure.

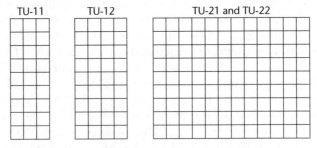

Figure 8.27 Tributary units. Each cell represents 64 kbit/s, i.e. 8 bits per frame duration $T_s = 125$ µs.

around longer than SDH and is currently more widely implemented in North America than SDH is in the rest of the world. As the name suggests, optical fibre is the transmission medium for which SONET was designed. The PDH-based T1 carrier systems in North America are gradually being replaced by SONET technology. Offices in a metropolitan area can be linked together in an optical fibre ring network that runs the OC-48 system carrying $48 \times 672 = 32\,256$ channels. An add/drop muldex at each office allows desired channels to be efficiently extracted and inserted.

8.3.4 ATM

You may have observed that PDH and SDH techniques are optimised for voice transmission, their basic frame duration of 125 µs being the sampling interval of a voice signal. Non-voice traffic of diverse bit rates cannot be simultaneously accommodated in a flexible and efficient manner. Asynchronous transfer mode (ATM) is a flexible transmission scheme that efficiently accomplishes the following.

1. Accommodation of multiple users by *statistical time division multiplexing*, as demonstrated in Fig. 8.28. Time slot allocation is not regular as in the (*non-statistical*) TDM techniques discussed hitherto. Rather, each user is allocated time slots (and hence bandwidth) as demanded by their bit rate. A time slot contains a group of bits known as a *cell* or *packet*, which consists of user data plus identification and control bits called a *header*. If in any time slot there are no bits to send then an *idle* cell is inserted to maintain a constant bit rate in the transmission medium.

2. Provision of multiple services such as transmission of voice, text, data, image, video and high-definition television, and connections to LANs, including LAN and WAN interconnections.

3. Support of multiple transmission speeds or bit rates (ranging from 2 to 622 Mbit/s) according to the requirements of each service.

ATM is more efficient than PDH and SDH because it dynamically and optimally allocates available network resources (e.g. bandwidth) via *cell relay switching*. It is the transfer mode or protocol adopted for broadband

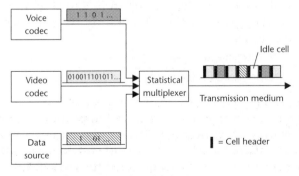

Figure 8.28 Statistical multiplexing.

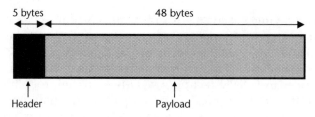

Figure 8.29 ATM cell.

integrated services digital network (B-ISDN), which supports all types of interactive point-to-point and distributive point-to-multipoint communication services. These include voice and video telephony, video-conferencing, high-speed data connection, email messaging, information retrieval, multimedia communication, video-on-demand, pay-per-view TV, digital audio broadcast, digital TV broadcast and high-definition TV (HDTV). In the following, we briefly discuss the features, structure, and network components and interfaces of ATM.

ATM breaks the information bit stream, whatever its origin — voice, video, text etc. — into *small packets* of fixed length. A *header* is attached to each data packet to enable correct routing of the packets and reassembling of the bit stream at the desired destination. The fixed-length combination of service (or other) data and header is known as an ATM *cell*, which is shown in Fig. 8.29. It is 53 bytes long, with a 48-byte *payload* that carries service data, and a 5-byte *header* that carries identification, control, and routing information. The maximum transmission efficiency of ATM is therefore

$$\eta_{\text{ATM}} = \frac{48}{53} \times 100\% = 90.57\%$$

The size of the cell is a compromise between the conflicting requirements of high transmission efficiency and low transmission delay and delay variation. To see this, imagine that the header is maintained at 5 bytes and the cell size is increased to 50 000 bytes. The efficiency would increase to 99.99%, but so would the delay if two sources A and B attempted to send data simultaneously, and the cell from say source A had (inevitably) to wait temporarily in a buffer for the cell from B to go first. The waiting time is a *switching delay* given by the cell duration — in this simple case of waiting for only one cell:

$$\tau_{\text{d}} = \frac{\text{Cell size (in bits)}}{\text{Line speed (in bits/second)}}$$

Thus, at a typical linespeed of 2 Mbit/s and the above cell size, we have τ_{d} = 200 ms. It is important to see the implication of this result. A received signal would have to be assembled at a destination from cells some of which were not buffered at all, and some of which were buffered for 200 ms or even longer in the event of a queue at the switch. This amounts to a variation in propagation time or *cell delay variation* of at least 200 ms, which is unacceptable for delay-sensitive traffic such as voice and video. On top of this, there is also another cell-size-dependent delay known as *packetisation delay* τ_p. This occurs at the source of real-time signals and is the time it takes to accumulate enough bits to fill one cell.

$$\tau_p = \frac{\text{Cell payload size (in bits)}}{\text{Source bit rate (in bits/second)}} \tag{8.16}$$

Thus, for a voice signal (of source bit rate 64 kbit/s) and a 50 000-byte cell (with a 5-byte header as above), $\tau_p = 6.25$ s. Some samples of the signal would be more than six seconds old before even beginning the journey from transmitter to receiver, and this is clearly unacceptable in interactive communication.

At the other extreme, if we make the cell size very small, say 6 bytes, then the efficiency is only 16.67%, but the packetisation delay and cell delay variation are also drastically reduced, with $\tau_p = 125$ μs and $\tau_d = 24$ μs, which are practically imperceptible.

8.3.4.1 ATM layered architecture

The functions performed in an ATM system can be organised hierarchically into layers with clearly defined interfaces; see Fig. 8.30.

Physical layer The *physical layer* is divided into two sub-layers: the *physical medium* (PM) *sub-layer* and the *transmission convergence* (TC) sub-layer. The PM sub-layer defines (1) the electrical/optical interface, (2) the line code, i.e. the voltage waveforms used for representing binary 1s and 0s, (3) the insertion and extraction of bit timing information, and (4) the transmission medium, e.g. optical fibre, coaxial cable or wire pair.

The TC sub-layer performs the following cell functions.

1. Transmission frame (e.g. STM-1) *generation* at the transmitter and *recovery* at destination.

2. *Transmission frame adaptation*: This is the process of adapting the flow of cells to match the capacity and structure of the transmission frame.

3. Generation of *header error correction* (HEC) at sending node and verification at destination. Any cell arriving at a network node with an error in the header that cannot be corrected is discarded. Note that the ATM network does not perform error monitoring on bits in the payload.

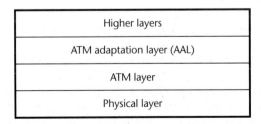

Higher layers
ATM adaptation layer (AAL)
ATM layer
Physical layer

Figure 8.30 ATM layered architecture.

4. *Cell delineation*: This is a process of identifying the cell boundaries in a stream of bits arriving at the destination. Assuming that byte boundaries are known — this will be the case if ATM cells are transported using SDH frames — then the process is as follows. In the HUNT state, the receiver (using a 5-byte-long window) takes the first five bytes, performs HEC calculation on the first four and compares the result to the 5th. If they match, then those five bytes are probably the header, and the receiver skips the next 48 (supposedly payload) bytes and repeats the process on the five bytes that follow. If a match is obtained several times (typically six) in a row then it is concluded that the cell boundaries have been found, and the receiver enters the SYNCH state. However, if the specified number of consecutive matches is not obtained the receiver simply slides the window before starting all over in the HUNT state. While in the SYNCH state, cell delineation is assumed lost, and the HUNT state is initiated if the HEC calculation fails a certain number of times (typically seven) in a row.

5. *Cell rate decoupling*: A constant cell rate is maintained by inserting idle cells (as necessary) for transmission, and removing them at the destination. Idle cells are indicated by the following standardised bit pattern in the cell header, listed from the 1st to the 5th byte:

> 00000000   00000000   00000000   00000001   01010010

All (48) bytes of the idle cell payload are filled with the bit pattern 01101010.

ATM layer   The ATM layer provides the functionality of a basic ATM network and controls the transport of cells through the network of ATM switches. Specific functions performed include the following.

1. Generation and extraction of cell header, excluding HEC calculation.

2. Multiplexing and demultiplexing of cells. Services are allocated bandwidth on demand by assigning to them only the number of cells they require. This is clearly a more efficient utilisation of transmission system resource than in non-statistical TDM (e.g. PDH), which allocates a fixed time slot and hence system bandwidth to each service.

3. Translation of values of virtual path identifier (VPI) and virtual channel identifier (VCI) at switches and cross-connect nodes. See later.

4. Generic Flow Control (GFC). This controls the rate at which user equipment submits cells to the ATM network.

ATM adaptation layer   The ATM adaptation layer (AAL) defines how the higher layer information bits are bundled into the ATM cell payload. It is divided into two sub-layers, namely the segmentation and reassembly (SAR) sub-layer and the convergence sub-layer (CS). The functions of these sub-layers depend on the class of service, of which ITU has defined four. Generally, the CS divides the higher-level information into suitable sizes, while the SAR sub-layer segments them into 48-byte chunks, and at the destination reassembles the payloads into data units for the higher layers. The ITU-defined classes of service are as follows.

- Class A service has a constant bit rate (CBR), is connection-oriented (CO), and requires end-to-end timing relation (TR). Examples of a class A service include voice and CBR video. The applicable protocol is identified as AAL1. One byte of the 48-byte payload is used as a header, which performs various functions such as cell loss detection. If a cell is lost the receiver inserts a substitute cell to maintain the timing relation between transmitter and receiver. Numbering of the cells by the SAR sub-layer enables the detection of cell loss.

- Class B service, like Class A, is both CO and TR, but unlike Class A has a *variable bit rate* (VBR). A variable bit rate arises in compressed video and audio where the compression ratio and hence bit rate at any time depends on the detailed content of the signal segment.

- Class C service, like Class B, is both CO and VBR, but unlike Class B does not require timing relation (TRN). An example of this service is connection-oriented data transfer.

- Class D service, like Class C is both VBR and TRN, but unlike any of the other services is connectionless (CL). An example is connectionless data transfer.

Two different AAL protocols have been defined for data transfer (Classes C and D). In AAL3/4 the first two bytes of the 48-byte payload are used as a header, which gives a *message identifier* (MID) that allows the multiplexing of several packets onto a single virtual channel. The last two bytes provide a trailer for a cyclic redundancy check (CRC) to monitor bit errors. Thus, only 44 bytes of the 53-byte ATM cell carry data bits, giving an efficiency of only 83%.

AAL5 is for those data transfer services that do not require shared media support and protection against mis-sequencing, e.g. point-to-point ATM links. A block of bits is formed in the convergence sub-layer consisting of the following: (1) data payload ranging from 0 to 65 536 bytes, (2) a padding ranging from 0 to 47 bytes to make the block an integer number of 48-byte segments, (3) a length field, and (iv) a CRC-32 field for error detection. This block is then broken into 48-byte cells in the SAR sub-layer and sent sequentially. A payload type identifier (PTI) bit in the ATM cell header is set to 1 to indicate the last cell. Thus AAL5 makes (almost) the entire 48-byte ATM cell payload available for data. This yields an efficiency value approaching the maximum 90.57%.

Higher layers There are three types of higher layer information, usually identified as the *user plane*, the *control plane* and the *management plane*. The user plane involves all types of user application information — voice, video etc. The control plane deals with control information for setting up or clearing calls, and for providing switched services. The management plane provides network management information for monitoring and configuring network elements and for communication between network management staff.

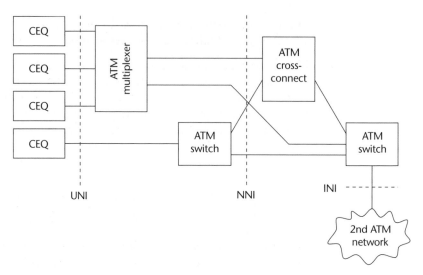

Figure 8.31 ATM network and interfaces.

8.3.4.2 *ATM network components*

Figure 8.31 shows a network reference model for ATM made up of four types of equipment and three standard interfaces.

- The *customer equipment* (CEQ) or *B-ISDN terminal equipment* (B-TE) communicates across the network, serving as a source and sink for the video, audio, and data bit streams carried by ATM. These streams are referred to as *virtual channels* (VC). The interface between a CEQ and the network is known as the *user network interface* (UNI), and is stand-ardised to allow interoperability of equipment and network from different manufacturers.

- The *ATM multiplexer* enables a number of *virtual channels* (VC) from different UNI ports to be carried over a single transmission line. In ATM parlance we say that the virtual channels have been bundled into a container, called a *virtual path* (VP), just as several letters are bundled into a postal sack in the postal system for easier transportation to a depot or sorting office. Note, however, that a VP is not synonymous with the physical link, and there may be several VPs on one link, just as there may be a number of postal sacks in one van.

- The ATM *cross-connect* routes a virtual path from an input port to an output port according to a routing table, leaving the contents of each VP (i.e. their VCs) undisturbed. In this respect a cross-connect is analo-gous to a postal depot where sacks may be moved unopened from one van to another.

- An ATM *switch* is the most complicated equipment of the ATM network, able not only to cross-connect VPs but also to sort and switch their VC contents. This is like a postal sorting office where some sacks are opened and the letters are re-sorted into new sacks that contain letters with a narrower range of destinations. Other sacks may be switched, i.e. loaded onto a designated van, with all their contents intact.

● The *network node interface* (NNI) is the interface between network nodes or sub-networks, while the *inter-network interface* (INI) is the interface between two ATM networks. INI includes features for security, control and administration of connections between networks belonging to different operators.

8.3.4.3 *ATM cell header*

The structure of the ATM cell header is shown in Fig. 8.32. The header consists of 5 bytes or 40 bits in all with the following designations.

● 28 bits (at NNI) or 24 (at UNI) are virtual path identifier (VPI) and virtual channel identifier (VCI) fields used for routing.

● At UNI, the first four bits provide a generic flow control (GFC) field, which is used to control cell transmission between CEQ and network. The GFC field is only of local significance and is usually set to the *uncontrolled access* mode with a value 0000 where it has no effect on the CEQ. Any other value in this field will correspond to the *controlled access* mode, where the rate of transmission from the CEQ is expected to be modified in some (yet to be specified) manner.

● The *payload type identifier* (PTI) field has three bits $b_4b_3b_2$. Bit b_4 is set to 0 to indicate that the cell is carrying user information. A maintenance/operation information cell is identified with $b_4 = 1$. Bit b_3 is a congestion experience bit, which is set to 1 if the cell passes a point of network congestion, to allow a (yet unspecified) reaction. Bit b_2 is carried trans-

(a)

8	7	6	5	4	3	2	1	bit ← ↓byte
GFC				VPI				1
VPI				VCI				2
VCI								3
VCI				PTI			CLP	4
HEC								5

(b)

8	7	6	5	4	3	2	1	bit ← ↓byte
VPI								1
VPI				VCI				2
VCI								3
VCI				PTI			CLP	4
HEC								5

Figure 8.32 Structure of ATM cell header. (a) At UNI; (b) at NNI.

parently by the network, and is currently used by AAL5 (as explained earlier) to indicate the last cell in a block of bits.

- One bit serves as the cell loss priority (CLP) field. When set (i.e. CLP = 1), it indicates that the cell is of lower priority and should be discarded (if need be) before cells with CLP = 0.

- The header error control (HEC) field has 8 bits, which are used in one of two modes to provide error protection for the cell header. This is especially important to prevent an error in the VPI/VCI values causing a cell to be delivered to the wrong address. In the correction mode, one-bit errors can be corrected. The detection mode on the other hand only allows errors to be detected. The corrupted cell is then simply discarded. Using the correction mode may be appropriate in an optical fibre transmission medium where errors are rare and isolated. The detection mode is however preferred in copper transmission media where error bursts are not uncommon. This avoids the risk of a multiple-bit error being mistaken for a single-bit error and erroneously 'corrected'. The VPI/VCI values change at each network node, necessitating a re-calculation of the HEC field.

8.3.4.4 ATM features summary

In concluding our brief discussion of ATM let us summarise some of the most important features of this emerging transmission technique.

- ATM is the transmission technique adopted for B-ISDN. It may not handle voice signals as well as PDH and SDH systems, and may not be as efficient for data transmission as the packet switching protocols (e.g. the X.25 whose efficiency approaches 99.93%), but it is an excellent compromise for handling *all types* of services.

- Bits to be transmitted are packaged in fixed-length cells of 53 bytes, which include a 5-byte header. The cells are transported at regular intervals, with idle periods carrying idle (i.e. unassigned) cells.

- Cell sequence integrity is maintained. There is a non-zero cell delay variation and occasional loss of cells, but cells are delivered to their destinations in the right order.

- ATM provides a connection establishment contract whereby the bit-rate and quality of service (QOS) are specified by the end-user device at call setup and guaranteed by the network for the duration of the call. QOS parameters include maximum permissible delay, delay variation and cell loss ratio.

- Network overload control is implemented. In the event of network congestion, new connections are prevented and available capacity is allocated to delay-sensitive services, namely voice and video.

- ATM functionality follows a layered architecture with a physical layer that is nearly equivalent to the physical layer of the open systems interconnection (OSI) model. This is followed by an ATM layer, which implements a basic ATM network. Finally, there is an ATM adaptation layer (AAL), which interfaces various user, control and management information to ATM.

8.4 Code division multiplexing

Code division multiplexing (CDM) is based on *spread spectrum modulation*, a technique that was developed in the 1940s for military communications. The message signal of (unspread) bandwidth B_m, is spread in a pseudo-random manner over a bandwidth $B_c \gg B_m$. The bandwidth ratio

$$G = \frac{B_c}{B_m} \tag{8.17}$$

represents a processing gain, which accounts for an increase in the *signal-to-noise ratio* at the output of a spread spectrum receiver. Transmitting a signal by spread spectrum modulation yields important benefits.

1. The signal is immune to intentional interference, called *jamming*. A high-power jamming signal is necessarily narrowband and will fail to drown the information signal since only a small fraction of the signal energy is corrupted. More accurately, the process of spread spectrum demodulation at the receiver involves the use of a pseudo-random code that de-spreads the wanted signal back into a narrow band B_m. Interestingly, the effect of this process on the jamming signal is to spread it over a wide band B_c. In this way, the jamming signal energy is rendered insignificant within the narrow band occupied by the recovered wanted signal.

2. By a similar consideration, spread spectrum signals are immune to frequency-selective fading arising from multipath propagation.

3. An unauthorised receiver cannot recover the information signal from the transmitted spread spectrum signal. Simply put, you must have knowledge of the carrier frequency in order to tune into a transmission. And if, as in an equivalent view of spread spectrum, the carrier frequency is not fixed but changes pseudo-randomly, then the oscillator frequency at the receiver must change exactly in step for demodulation to be possible. Only authorised receivers will know precisely the pseudo-random sequence of carrier frequencies used at the transmitter.

4. Spread spectrum signals have a noise-like appearance to other (unauthorised) receivers. Thus multiple user transmissions can simultaneously occupy the same frequency band with guaranteed message privacy, provided each user's signal has been spread using a unique pseudo-random code, also referred to as *pseudo-noise* (PN) sequence. This is CDM, which is finding increased non-military applications especially in satellite and mobile cellular communications. Clearly, as the number of users increases a point is reached where the 'background noise' at each receiver becomes excessive, leading to unacceptable bit error rates. However, through a careful selection of PN sequences to

minimise their cross-correlation, more users can be accommodated in a given frequency band by CDM than is possible with FDM and TDM.

8.4.1 Types of spread spectrum modulation

There are various types of spread spectrum (SS) modulation depending on the method employed to spread the message signal over a wider bandwidth.

- *Time-hopping* (TH): The message signal is transmitted in bursts during pseudo-randomly selected time slots. Figure 8.33(a) shows the block diagram of a TH transmitter. Let R_m denote the bit rate of the encoded message signal — giving a bit interval $T_m = 1/R_m$, and a message bandwidth $B_m = R_m$. Each time interval $T \gg T_m$ is divided into L equal time slots, and one of these slots is selected pseudo-randomly (by opening the gate for this duration) for transmission. To keep up with the message rate, we must take from the buffer an average of R_m bits per second, or $R_m T$ bits in each interval T, which must all be sent during the one time slot (of duration T/L) when the gate is open. Thus, the burst bit rate is

$$R_s = \frac{R_m T}{T/L} = LR_m$$

  With PSK modulation, the transmission bandwidth is $B_c = LR_m$, which gives processing gain $G = L$.

  A TH receiver is shown in Fig. 8.33(b). The gate must be opened in precise synchronism with the transmitter, which requires that (1) the gate is controlled by the same PN code used at the transmitter, and (2) both codes are in phase. This synchronisation is very stringent and becomes more difficult to achieve as L increases. Note that the role of

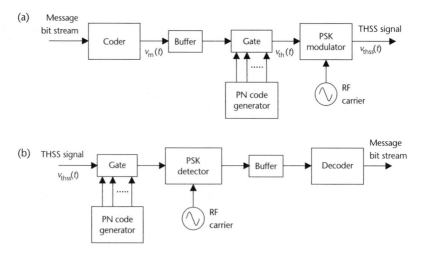

Figure 8.33 Time-hopping spread spectrum (THSS). (a) Transmitter; (b) receiver.

the buffer at the receiver is to play out the demodulated bursty bit stream at the uniform rate of the coded message signal.

● *Frequency hopping* (FH): The message signal is conveyed on a carrier, which hops pseudo-randomly from one frequency to another, making R_h hops per second. Figure 8.34(a) shows a block diagram of a FHSS transmitter. A coded message bit stream first FSK-modulates a carrier signal, which is then multiplied in a mixer by a digital frequency synthesiser output, and the sum frequency is selected. The output frequency f_0 of the synthesiser is controlled by a PN sequence taken k bits at a time. Noting that an all-zero combination does not occur in a PN sequence, we see that there are $L = 2^k - 1$ different values over which f_0 hops. The FSK modulator generates symbols at a rate R_s — one symbol per bit for binary FSK, or per $\log_2 M$ bits for M-ary FSK. If the hop rate R_h is an integer multiple of the symbol rate R_s, several frequency hops occur during each symbol interval. This type of FHSS is known as *fast-frequency hopping*. If, however, $R_h \leq R_s$, then one or more symbols are transmitted on each hop, and we have *slow-frequency hopping*.

At the receiver (Fig. 8.34(b)), exactly the same pseudo-random sequence of frequencies f_0 is generated and used in a mixer to remove the frequency hopping imposed on the FSK signal. It is extremely difficult for frequency synthesisers to maintain phase coherence between

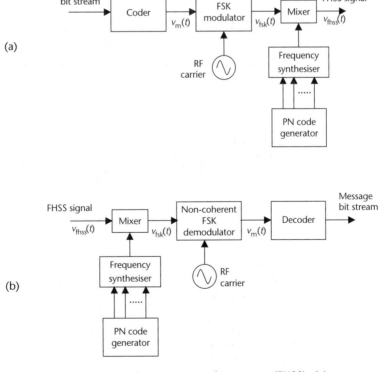

Figure 8.34 Frequency-hopping spread spectrum (FHSS). (a) Transmitter; (b) receiver.

hops, which means that a non-coherent FSK demodulator has to be used at the receiver. The main advantages of FHSS are that synchronisation requirements are less stringent, and larger spread spectrum bandwidths can be more easily achieved to realise higher processing gains $G \approx 2^k - 1$.

- *Direct sequence* (DS): The coded message signal, of bit duration T_m, is multiplied by a PN bit stream of much shorter bit duration T_c, referred to as *chip duration*. This pseudo-randomises the message bit stream and spreads its (null) bandwidth from $B_m = 1/T_m$ to $1/T_c$, which yields a processing gain

$$G = T_m/T_c \tag{8.18}$$

This highly spread product signal is then used to modulate a carrier by BPSK, QPSK or M-ary QAM. DSSS is the type of spread spectrum modulation employed in CDM-based mobile cellular communication (standard IS-95), and our discussion of CDM will be restricted to this method. One disadvantage of DSSS (compared to FHSS) is that the processing gain that can be achieved is limited by current device technology as T_m decreases (in high information rate systems), since the required low values of T_c become difficult to implement. Timing requirements in DSSS are also more stringent than in FHSS but less than in THSS.

- *Hybrid methods*: Hybrid SS techniques are possible that combine TH, FH and DS. The most common hybrid technique is DS/FH, which combines the large processing gain possible in FH with the advantage of coherent detection in DS. Each frequency hop carries a DS spread spectrum signal and is coherently detected, but the signals from different hops have to be incoherently combined because of their lack of phase coherence.

8.4.2 CDM transmitter

Figure 8.35(a) shows the block diagram of a CDM transmitter based on DS spread spectrum modulation. The waveforms associated with this transmitter are shown in Fig. 8.35(b). Unit-amplitude bipolar waveforms are assumed for convenience. The coded message waveform $v_m(t)$ has the indicated bit duration T_m, while the PN waveform $v_{pn}(t)$ has a chip duration T_c. Note that the waveforms correspond to the case $T_m = 15T_c$. More than one user (say N) can be accommodated, with each assigned a unique PN code $v_{pn1}(t)$, $v_{pn2}(t)$, ..., $v_{pnN}(t)$, or a unique time-shift in a common PN code $v_{pn}(t - \tau_1)$, $v_{pn}(t - \tau_2)$, ..., $v_{pn}(t - \tau_N)$.

The PN code generator is in general a linear feedback shift register. Figure 8.36(a) shows the circuit connection that produces the PN sequence $v_{pn}(t)$ used in Fig. 8.35(b). The shift register consists of four flip-flops (FF1 to FF4), which are controlled by a common clock. Clock pulses occur at intervals of T_c, and at each clock pulse the input state of each flip-flop is shifted to its output. The outputs of FF1 and FF4 are added in an EX-OR gate and fed back

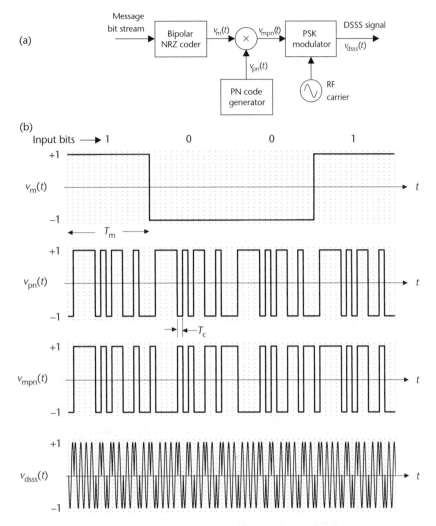

Figure 8.35 Direct sequence spread spectrum. (a) Transmitter; (b) waveforms.

as input to the shift register. This gate performs a *modulo*-2 addition defined as follows

$$0 \oplus 0 = 0$$
$$0 \oplus 1 = 1$$
$$1 \oplus 0 = 1$$
$$1 \oplus 1 = 0$$

(8.19)

Because the feedback taps are located at the outputs of the 4th and 1st flip-flops, we have what is known as a [4, 1] code generator. In general, a linear feedback shift register that consists of m flip-flops and has feedback taps at the outputs of flip-flops $m, i, j, \ldots$ is identified as $[m, i, j, \ldots]$. The serial PN code generated is of course the sequence of states of the mth flip-flop. As an

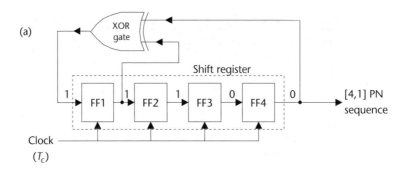

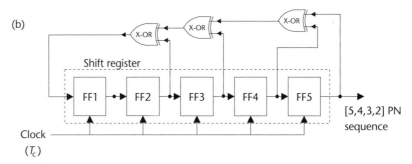

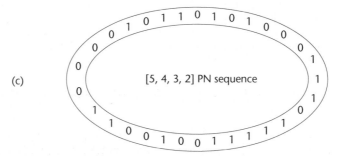

Figure 8.36 Maximum-length PN sequence. (a) Generator of the [4, 1] code listed in Table 8.3; (b) [5, 4, 3, 2] code generator; (c) [5, 4, 3, 2] code.

example, Fig. 8.36(b) shows the connection of a [5, 4, 3, 2] PN code generator, which gives the cyclic pseudo-random sequence shown in (c). The following discussion clarifies how this sequence is obtained.

Let us assume that the [4, 1] PN code generator in Fig. 8.36(a) has the indicated *initial* register state (FF1, FF2, FF3, FF4) = (1, 1, 0, 0). This is the state before the first clock pulse occurs at time $t = 0$. The initial feedback input is therefore FF1 $\oplus$ FF4 = 1. Table 8.3 lists the sequence of flip-flop outputs. After the first clock pulse at $t = 0$, the initial feedback state is shifted to become the FF1 output, the initial FF1 output becomes FF2 output etc. Thus, the register state just after $t = 0$ is (1, 1, 1, 0), and the feedback state is $1 \oplus 0 = 1$. This gives the entry 1, 1, 1, 1, 0 in row $t = 0$ of the table. You may wish to carry on in this way and verify the remaining entries of Table 8.3, and then skip to Question 8.13 for more practice.

Table 8.3 Sequence of flip-flop outputs in [4,1] PN code generator.

Time	Input to shift register (feedback)	Flip-flop output			
		FF1	FF2	FF3	FF4 (PN sequence)
< 0	1	1	1	0	0
0	1	1	1	1	0
T_c	0	1	1	1	1
$2T_c$	1	0	1	1	1
$3T_c$	0	1	0	1	1
$4T_c$	1	0	1	0	1
$5T_c$	1	1	0	1	0
$6T_c$	0	1	1	0	1
$7T_c$	0	0	1	1	0
$8T_c$	1	0	0	1	1
$9T_c$	0	1	0	0	1
$10T_c$	0	0	1	0	0
$11T_c$	0	0	0	1	0
$12T_c$	1	0	0	0	1
$13T_c$	1	1	0	0	0
$14T_c$	1	1	1	0	0
$15T_c$	1	1	1	1	0

Note in Table 8.3 that the register goes through all possible 2^4 states, except the all-zero state (0,0,0,0), before starting all over again at $t = 15T_c$. In general, a PN sequence (generated by a linear feedback register of m flip-flops) that has the maximum period

$$L = (2^m - 1) \text{ clock cycles} \qquad (8.20)$$

is called a *maximum length sequence*, or simply *m-sequence*. The all-zero state is forbidden and in fact cannot be entered except from an all-zero initial state, which would then cause the register to remain permanently in this state, and the PN sequence to be a train of 0s. Note further that the periodic code sequence generated by a linear feedback shift register is fixed entirely by the number of flip-flops m and the feedback tap locations. The initial state of the register merely determines the starting point of the cycle.

8.4.3 CDM receiver

A CDM receiver is shown in Fig. 8.37(a). There are two stages of processing. First, the spread signal $v_{mpn}(t)$ is extracted by coherent PSK detection. The PSK detector consists of a product modulator followed by a low-pass filter of

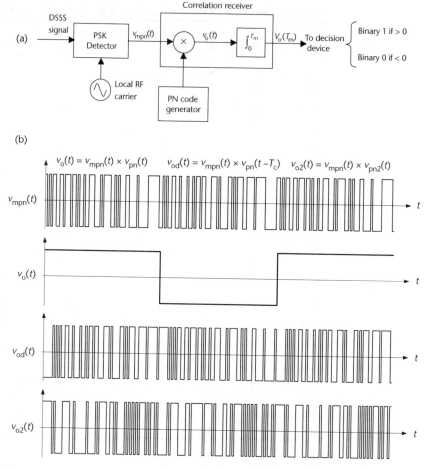

Figure 8.37 Direct sequence spread spectrum. (a) Receiver; (b) waveforms of indicated signals. *Note*: $v_{mpn}(t)$ corresponds to message signal segment 101 spread using $v_{pn}(t)$ = Code [6,1]; and $v_o(t)$, $v_{od}(t)$, and $v_{o2}(t)$ are the results of de-spreading using locally generated codes, where $v_{pn2}(t)$ = Code [6,5,2,1].

bandwidth equal to that of $v_{mpn}(t)$. Further details of PSK detection are given in Chapter 7, but are not required for this discussion. The second stage of processing involves a correlation receiver (discussed in Chapter 6). This multiplies $v_{mpn}(t)$ by a locally generated code, which must be identical to and exactly in step with the code $v_{pn}(t)$ used at the transmitter. The multiplication yields a de-spread signal $v_0(t)$, which is then integrated over an interval of one message bit duration T_m. A decision device compares the integration result $V_0(T_m)$ to a zero threshold. The (message) bit interval is declared to contain a binary 1 if $V_0(T_m)$ exceeds zero. A decision in favour of binary 0 is taken if $V_0(T_m)$ is less than zero, and a random guess of 1 or 0 is made if $V_0(T_m)$ is exactly equal to zero.

An illustration of the operation of the receiver is given in Fig. 8.37(b). The waveform $v_{mpn}(t)$ corresponds to a message bit stream segment $v_m(t) \equiv 101$ that was spread at the transmitter using $v_{pn}(t)$ = Code [6,1]. Multiplying

$v_{mpn}(t)$ with a perfectly synchronised Code [6,1] yields $v_0(t)$. Clearly, this process has somehow extracted the original waveform $v_m(t)$ from a signal $v_{mpn}(t)$ that is in appearance noise. You can see that this is the case by noting that $v_{pn}(t) = \pm 1$, so that

$$v_{pn}^2(t) = 1 \qquad (8.21)$$

Hence,

$$\begin{aligned} v_o(t) &= v_{mpn}(t)v_{pn}(t) \\ &= [v_m(t)v_{pn}(t)]v_{pn}(t) \\ &= v_m(t)[v_{pn}^2(t)] \\ &= v_m(t) \end{aligned} \qquad (8.22)$$

The importance of synchronisation is illustrated in the waveform $v_{od}(t)$, which is the result of using the right code [6,1] but with a misalignment of one chip duration T_c. In addition, we illustrate in $v_{o2}(t)$ the effect of using a wrong code $v_{pn2}(t) = $ Code [6,5,2,1]. Proceeding as in Eq. (8.22), we write

$$\begin{aligned} v_{od}(t) &= v_m(t)[v_{pn}(t)v_{pn}(t - T_c)] \\ v_{o2}(t) &= v_m(t)[v_{pn}(t)v_{pn2}(t)] \end{aligned} \qquad (8.23)$$

You can see that in these two cases we have failed to de-spread $v_{mpn}(t)$ since the term in bracket is not a constant. The input to the integrator is therefore a randomised version of the original signal $v_m(t)$, the spreading signal being the term in bracket. It means that $v_m(t)$ remains hidden, and the integrator sees only noise-like signals $v_{od}(t)$ and $v_{o2}(t)$. By examining these two waveforms you can see that the decision device will make random guesses of 1 or 0, since the average of these waveforms in intervals of T_m is approximately zero. Note that the process of integration is equivalent to averaging except for a scaling factor.

Figure 8.38 illustrates the code misalignment problem more clearly. Here the output $V_0(T_m)$ of the correlation receiver is plotted against misalignment

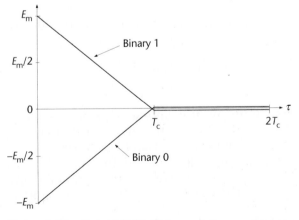

Figure 8.38 Output $V_0(T_m)$ of correlation receiver as a function of PN code misalignment.

τ. With perfect synchronisation between transmitter and receiver codes, $\tau = 0$ and $V_0(T_m) = E_m$ for binary 1 and $-E_m$ for binary 0, where E_m is the energy per message bit. We see that the noise margin (*i.e.* difference between the output levels of the correlation receiver for binary 1 and 0 in the absence of noise) is $2E_m$. As τ increases, the noise margin decreases steadily, causing increased bit error rate (BER) and reaching zero — with $V_0(T_m) = 0$ and BER = 0.5 — at

$$\tau_o = \frac{L}{L+1} T_c \tag{8.24}$$

Here $L = 2^m - 1$ is the length of the PN code, and m is the length of the linear feedback register that generates the code. For a misalignment of T_c or larger — but less than $(L - 1)T_c$ beyond which the two codes begin to approach perfect alignment at $\tau = LT_c$ due to their cyclic sequence — we have

$$V_o(T_m) = \begin{cases} -E_b/L, & \text{Binary 1} \\ +E_b/L, & \text{Binary 0} \end{cases} \tag{8.25}$$

That is, in an ideal noiseless receiver, a binary 1 would always be mistaken for binary 0 and vice versa, and the error rate is 100%. However, in a practical (noisy) receiver with large L, the value of $V_0(T_m)$ is negligible compared to noise, and the BER is ~50%, which is what you get in the long run from random guesses in a binary sample space.

We have demonstrated above that a message signal can only be recovered from a spread spectrum signal in a receiver equipped with a synchronised correct PN code. We now demonstrate with the aid of Fig. 8.39 that a receiver will also correctly extract its desired signal from a multitude of spread spectrum signals. We show two message waveforms $v_{m1}(t) \equiv 101$, and $v_{m2}(t) \equiv 001$, which have been spread using different PN codes $v_{pn1}(t)$ and $v_{pn2}(t)$ assigned to users 1 and 2, respectively. Thus the signal at the receiver of each user (at the output of the PSK detector) is a composite signal given by

$$v_{mpn}(t) = v_{m1}(t)v_{pn1}(t) + v_{m2}(t)v_{pn2}(t) \tag{8.26}$$

Receiver 1 multiplies $V_{mpn}(t)$ by its unique code $v_{pn1}(t)$, while receiver 2 multiplies by $v_{pn2}(t)$ to obtain

$$v_{01}(t) = v_{m1}(t) + v_{m2}(t)v_{pn2}(t)v_{pn1}(t)$$
$$v_{02}(t) = v_{m2}(t) + v_{m1}(t)v_{pn1}(t)v_{pn2}(t) \tag{8.27}$$

These waveforms are also plotted in Fig. 8.38, and it is clear that integrating each one over the message bit interval leads to correct decisions regarding the transmitted bit streams. That is, each receiver successfully extracts only the bit stream intended for it from the mix of bit streams contained in the CDM signal $V_{mpn}(t)$. This is a remarkable result. In general, the signal at the input of a receiver in a CDM system with N simultaneous transmissions is given by

$$v_{mpn}(t) = v_{m1}(t)v_{pn1}(t) + v_{m2}(t)v_{pn2}(t) + \cdots + v_{mN}(t)v_{pnN}(t) \tag{8.28}$$

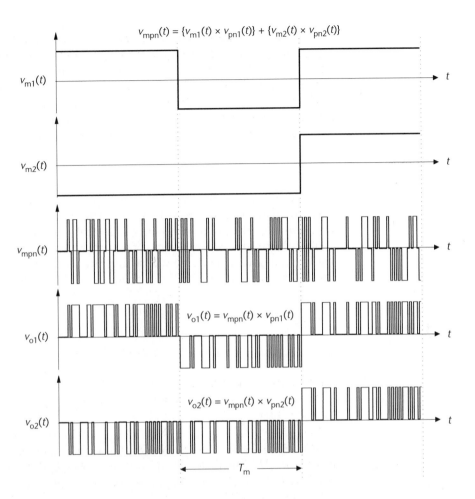

Figure 8.39 User data waveforms $v_{m1}(t)$ and $v_{m2}(t)$, and received signal waveforms in a two-user CDM scenario.

The de-spread signal of say receiver 1 is therefore

$$v_o(t) = v_{mpn}(t)v_{pn1}(t)$$
$$= v_{m1}(t) + v_{m2}(t)v_{pn2}(t)v_{pn1}(t) + \cdots + v_{mN}(t)v_{pnN}(t)v_{pn1}(t) \qquad (8.29)$$
$$= v_{m1}(t) + \text{Noise}$$

Similar results apply to every one of the N receivers, and we have the familiar — Chapter 7 — problem of digital signal detection in noise. As the number of users N goes up, the noise term in Eq. (8.29) becomes larger, and the probability of error, or bit error rate (BER), increases. So there is a limit N_{max} on the number of users in order to guarantee a specified BER. However, QUALCOM, a pioneer of CDMA-based cellular telephony indicate that CDM can allow up to 10–20 times more subscribers than FDM, and up to three times more than TDM. Furthermore, unlike FDM and TDM, the number of subscribers can be easily increased beyond the maximum, with a small penalty of degraded BER in the unlikely event that more than N_{max} subscribers are simultaneously active.

8.4.4 Crucial features of CDM

Let us conclude our discussion of CDM by emphasising those features that are crucial to the smooth operation of this multiplexing strategy.

8.4.4.1 Synchronisation

The PN code generated at the receiver must be identical to and synchronised with the spreading code used at the transmitter. There is usually no problem with the two codes being identical — unless of course the receiver is unauthorised — so we concentrate on the synchronisation requirement. Let the transmitter code be $v_{pn}(t)$, and the receiver code $v_{pn}(t - \tau)$ — with a misalignment τ. It follows from the receiver block diagram that

$$
\begin{aligned}
V_o(T_m) &= \int_0^{T_m} v_{mpn}(t)v_{pn}(t - \tau)dt \\
&= \int_0^{T_m} v_m(t)v_{pn}(t)v_{pn}(t - \tau)dt \\
&= \pm\frac{E_m}{T_m} \int_0^{T_m} v_{pn}(t)v_{pn}(t - \tau)dt \\
&= \pm E_m R_p(\tau)
\end{aligned}
\tag{8.30}
$$

In the above we have used the fact that $v_m(t)$ is a constant $\pm E_m/T_m$ over the integration interval, the positive sign applying to a binary 1. $R_p(\tau)$ is the *autocorrelation* function of a periodic signal — in this case $v_{pn}(t)$ — of period T_m and is defined by

$$
R_p(\tau) = \frac{1}{T_m} \int_0^{T_m} v_{pn}(t)v_{pn}(t - \tau)dt
\tag{8.31}
$$

The autocorrelation function of a signal has a number of interesting properties, which we will not digress to consider. However, Eq. (8.31) has been evaluated for a normalised unit-amplitude maximum-length PN sequence of length L and chip duration T_c, and is shown in Fig. 8.40. By examining this figure, we see the importance of synchronisation. Equation (8.30) states that the output of the correlation receiver is proportional to $R_p(\tau)$, which from Fig. 8.40 is clearly maximum at $\tau = 0$ and decreases rapidly to $-1/L$ at $\tau = T_c$. You may wish to look back at Fig. 8.39 and note that it is actually a plot of Eq. (8.30).

In practice synchronisation is accomplished at the receiver in two stages. First is the *acquisition* stage, also known as *coarse synchronisation*, which is performed at the start of signal reception, or after loss of synchronisation, by sliding the timing of the locally generated PN code until a peak output is obtained. To do this the PN code first modulates a carrier, as was done in the transmitter. The resulting signal is then correlated with the incoming

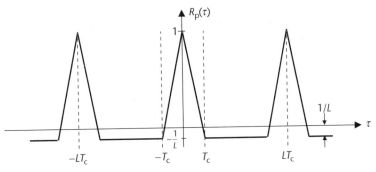

Figure 8.40 Autocorrelation of a maximum-length PN sequence of length L and chip interval T_c.

spread spectrum signal, and the code alignment is shifted until maximum correlation is achieved. Next follows the *tracking* stage or *fine synchronisation* in which a phase-locked loop is used to keep the locally generated PN code in step with the transmitter code.

8.4.4.2 Cross-correlation of PN codes

Returning to Eq. (8.29), which deals with the detection of a spread spectrum signal in a multi-user environment, we see that the correlation output of receiver 1 may be written as

$$
\begin{aligned}
V_{o1}(T_m) &= \int_0^{T_m} v_{mpn}(t)v_{pn1}(t)\,dt \\
&= \int_0^{T_m} [v_{m1}(t)v_{pn1}(t) + v_{m2}(t)v_{pn2}(t-\tau_2) + \cdots \\
&\quad + v_{mN}(t)v_{pnN}(t-\tau_N)]v_{pn1}(t)\,dt \\
&= \pm E_{m1} \pm \frac{E_{m2}}{T_m}\int_0^{T_m} v_{pn1}(t)v_{pn2}(t-\tau_2)\,dt \pm \cdots \\
&\quad \pm \frac{E_{mN}}{T_m}\int_0^{T_m} v_{pn1}(t)v_{pnN}(t-\tau_N)\,dt \\
&= \pm E_{m1} \pm E_{m2}R_{12}(\tau_2) \pm \cdots \pm E_{mN}R_{1N}(\tau_N)
\end{aligned}
\tag{8.32}
$$

Here, τ_k (for $k = 2, 3, \ldots, N$) is the misalignment between receiver 1 and the PN code of the kth user transmission, and $R_{1k}(\tau)$ is the cross-correlation function of the PN sequences $v_{pn1}(t)$ and $v_{pnk}(t)$, defined by

$$
R_{1k}(\tau) = \frac{1}{T_m}\int_0^{T_m} v_{pn1}(t)v_{pnk}(t-\tau)\,dt
\tag{8.33}
$$

Equation (8.32) shows that for there to be no interference between users in a CDM system, the cross-correlation of any two PN codes in the system must be zero. Equivalently, we say that the PN sequences should be mutually *orthogonal*. This requirement is impossible to meet in practice, and we can only search for classes of PN codes that give acceptably small (i.e. good)

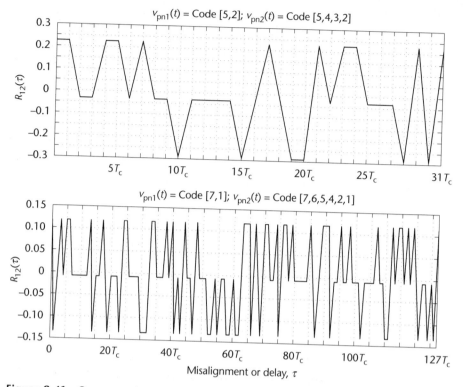

Figure 8.41 Cross-correlation $R_{12}(\tau)$ of maximum-length PN sequences.

cross-correlation. Figure 8.41 shows the cross-correlation of maximum-length PN sequences [5,2] versus [5,4,3,2], and [7,1] versus [7,6,5,4,2,1]. A class of codes known as *Gold sequences* gives better cross-correlation properties. A Gold sequence results from an EX-OR combination of two carefully selected *m*-sequences. For example, Fig. 8.42 shows the cross-correlation of two gold sequences $v_{pn1}(t)$ and $v_{pn2}(t)$. The first sequence $v_{pn1}(t)$ results from combining *m*-sequences [6,1] and [6,5,2,1] with no cyclic shift between them, while $v_{pn2}(t)$ is obtained by shifting one *m*-sequence by $3T_c$ relative to the other before combination. It can be seen that, for the majority (70% in this case) of delay values τ, the cross-correlation of the two gold sequences is only $-1/L$. It is apparent here and in Fig. 8.41 that the larger the sequence length L the smaller is the cross-correlation, which leads to reduced mutual interference. However, processing delay (for example during coarse synchronisation) increases with L.

8.4.4.3 *Power control*

By examining Eq. (8.32) we see that our failure to find a class of PN codes with zero cross-correlation leads to stringent power control requirements in order to minimise mutual interference in a multi-user CDM system. To be more specific, consider a receiver such as a base station in CDM-based

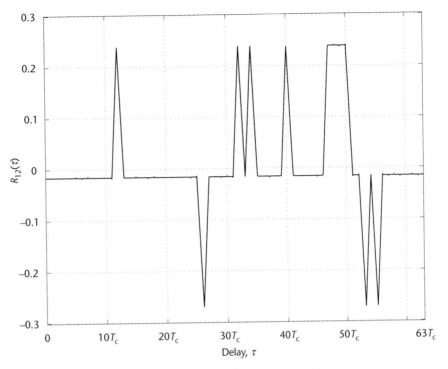

Figure 8.42 Cross-correlation $R_{12}(\tau)$ of length $L = 63$ gold sequences.

cellular telephony or a satellite transponder that employs a CDM-based multiple access. This receiver is equipped with N correlators, one for each of the N user transmissions. Let $V_{oj}(T_m)$ denote the output of correlator j, and E_{mj} the energy per message bit reaching the receiver from the jth user. It is clear that the unwanted contribution to $V_{o1}(T_m)$ from the other user transmissions will depend on $E_{m2}, E_{m3}, \ldots E_{mN}$ according to Eq. (8.32). Similarly, the unwanted contribution to $V_{o2}(T_m)$ depends on $E_{m1}, E_{m3}, \ldots, E_{mN}$, and so on. You can therefore see that the condition for minimum mutual interference is that

$$E_{m1} = E_{m2} = E_{m3} = \ldots = E_{mN} \tag{8.34}$$

That is, the transmission from each of the N users must reach the receiver at the same power level. As the radio link from each user to the receiver is typically of a different length and subject to different propagation conditions, we must implement some form of power control in order to achieve Eq. (8.34).

One way of implementing power control is by each user terminal monitoring the level of a *pilot signal* from the base station, and adjusting its transmitted power level accordingly. A low pilot level indicates high path loss between terminal and base station, perhaps because the two are far apart, and causes the terminal to increase its transmitted power level. A high pilot level on the other hand indicates low path loss, perhaps due to increased proximity between user terminal and base station, and causes the terminal to reduce its transmitted power. This technique is known as *open loop power control*. It assumes identical propagation conditions in the two directions of transmission between terminal and base station, which will often not be the case for a mobile terminal or if the pilot signal is at a different frequency from the user transmission. For example, if the monitored pilot signal undergoes a frequency-selective fade, the user terminal would overestimate the path loss experienced by its transmissions to the base station. As a result this terminal would increase its transmitted power excessively. Figure 8.43 illustrates this concern for a pilot signal at 890 MHz and a user terminal transmitting at 825 MHz. Note that at a relative location of 3.7 m the pilot signal frequency is in a deep fade, whereas the user terminal frequency is not. You can also see that there will be times (e.g. relative locations 0.65 and 7.5 m) when the user terminal grossly underestimates the attenuation on its transmissions to the base station.

Closed loop power control solves the above problem but requires a higher operational overhead. Here, the base station monitors the transmission from each terminal and regularly issues a command that causes the terminal to increase or decrease its transmitted power. For example, in the IS-95 standard for CDM-based cellular telephony a one-bit command is issued every 1.25 ms. A 1 indicates that the power transmitted by the terminal is too high, the terminal responding by decreasing its power by 1 dB. A 0 indicates that the power reaching the base station from the

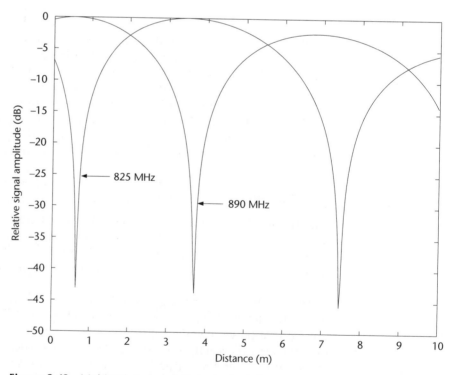

Figure 8.43 Multipath-induced frequency-selective fade.

terminal is too low, and in response the terminal increases its radiated power by 1 dB. The power transmitted by a base station is also controlled based on *power measurement reports* received from user terminals, which indicate the signal strength reaching each terminal and the number of detected bit errors.

8.4.4.4 Processing gain

It is illuminating to examine PN codes in the frequency domain in order to make important observations on their signal processing roles. The autocorrelation function $R_p(\tau)$ of an m-sequence $v_{pn}(t)$ was sketched in Fig. 8.40. The Fourier transform of $R_p(\tau)$ gives the power spectral density $S_p(f)$ of $v_{pn}(t)$, which furnishes complete information on the frequency content of the PN sequence. We obtain $S_p(f)$ easily from the waveform of $R_p(\tau)$ by making the following observations.

1. The value of $S_p(f)$ at $f = 0$ is the DC value of $R_p(\tau)$, i.e. its average value. To calculate this average we add an offset of $1/L$ to $R_p(\tau)$ in Fig. 8.40 so that the only non-zero area in one cycle is a triangle of height $1 + 1/L$ and base $2T_c$. Dividing this area by the period LT_c and then removing the offset yields the desired average

$$S_p(0) = \frac{\frac{1}{2}(1+1/L) \times 2T_c}{LT_c} - \frac{1}{L} = \frac{1}{L^2} \tag{8.35}$$

2. $R_p(\tau)$ is a periodic waveform of period $T = LT_c$, therefore it contains only frequencies that are harmonics of $f_0 = 1/T$. That is, $R_p(\tau)$ has a line spectrum $S_p(f)$ with components spaced at $1/LT_c$.

3. $R_p(\tau)$ is actually a triangular pulse train, each pulse being of width $2T_c$. We know from Section 2.4.3 (see in particular Fig. 2.26(d)) that the spectrum $S_p(f)$ will therefore follow a square sinc envelope with nulls at intervals of $1/T_c$.

4. Our determination of $S_p(f)$, the power spectral density (PSD) of m-sequences is now complete, and a sketch is shown in Fig. 8.44. This spectrum provides valuable information.

A PN sequence $v_{pn}(t)$ therefore contains sinusoidal components of frequencies up to a (null) bandwidth equal to the reciprocal of the chip duration T_c. From Chapter 3, recall that the effect of multiplying a baseband signal by a sinusoid of (carrier) frequency f_c is to shift the baseband spectrum to be centred at f_c. Recall furthermore that the frequency translation can be removed without distortion to the baseband spectrum simply by performing the multiplication a second time using a carrier of the same frequency and phase. Thus multiplying a message bit stream $v_m(t)$ by a PN sequence will duplicate (in other words spread) the spectrum of $v_m(t)$ at intervals of $1/LT_c$ over a bandwidth of $1/T_c$. A little thought will show that the duplicated spectra are diminished in amplitude in proportion to T_c, and that they overlap each other. The composite spread spectrum is therefore roughly uniform (somewhat like that of white noise) and bears little

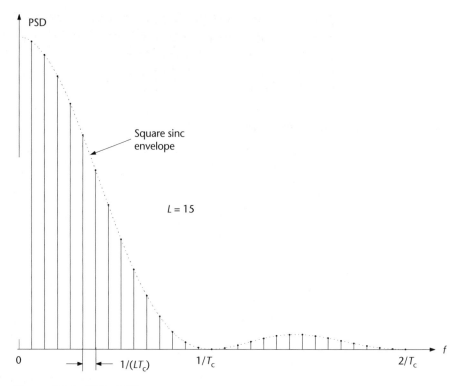

Figure 8.44 PSD of PN sequence.

resemblance to the baseband spectrum, which means that the signal has been successfully hidden. Overlapping of the duplicated spectra is important, otherwise the situation reduces to the straightforward process of sampling where the spectra are distinguishable and the 'spreading' can be removed by low-pass filtering. We ensure overlapping by using a spreading sequence that has a dense spectrum — implying a small value of $1/LT_c$. For a given chip duration T_c, this requires that we make the sequence length L very large.

A second multiplication by $v_{pn}(t)$ at the receiver has the 'magical' effect of reconstructing the message signal spectrum, because the spectra originally translated to $f = j/LT_c, j = 1, 2, 3, ..., L$, are simply thrown back to $f = 0$, and these all add to give the original baseband spectrum. This is provided the 'carrier frequencies' j/LT_c have exactly the same phases at transmitter and receiver, which is another way of saying that the two PN codes are synchronised. You will recall that a time shift of τ on $v_{pn}(t)$ has the effect of altering the phases of its frequency components by $2\pi f \tau$. Yes, the multiplication also creates new spectra at $2j/LT_c$, but these are filtered out.

Herein lies the spread spectrum processing gain. For interference signals entering the receiver along with the wanted signal, this is their first multiplication with this code, which therefore spreads them over a bandwidth $1/T_c$. However, for the wanted signal it is the second multiplication, and this returns its frequency components back to the (null) bandwidth $1/T_m$, where T_m is the message bit interval. Clearly then, the signal-to-noise ratio at the output of the spread spectrum receiver, denoted SNR_O, is larger than the signal-to-noise ratio at the input (SNR_I) by the amount

$$
\begin{aligned}
\text{Processing gain} &= 10\log_{10}\left(\frac{T_m}{T_c}\right), \text{dB} \\
&= 10\log_{10}\left[\frac{\text{Spread bandwidth (Hz)}}{\text{Message bit rate (bits/s)}}\right], \text{dB}
\end{aligned}
\tag{8.36}
$$

For example, the QUALCOM system uses a spread bandwidth of 1.23 MHz to transmit at a message bit rate of 9.6 kbit/s, giving a processing gain of 21.1 dB. For a given message bit rate, processing gain can be increased to realise improved performance in the presence of noise and interference by using a larger spread bandwidth $1/T_c$. But allocated radio bandwidths are limited, and device technology places a limit on how small we can make the chip duration T_c.

SUMMARY

This now completes our study of multiplexing strategies. We started by giving a number of compelling reasons for multiplexing in modern telecommunications and then presented a non-mathematical discussion of the four strategies of SDM, FDM, TDM, and CDM. This was followed by a more detailed discussion of the last three techniques.

FDM is truly indispensable to radio communications, and has a very long list of applications. It allows the existence of a number of audio and TV broadcast houses in one locality, and the simultaneous provision of a large variety of communication services. Capacity enhancement in cellular telephony and satellite communication relies heavily on FDM. Closed media applications of FDM include the so-called wavelength division multiplexing (WDM) in optical fibre, which allows literally millions of toll-quality digital voice signals to be transmitted in one fibre, and FDM telephony that allows up to 10 800 analogue voice signals to be transmitted in one coaxial cable. FDM implementation is very straightforward. A frequency band is allocated to a user, and the user's signal is applied to modulate a suitable carrier thereby translating the signal into its allocated band. The type of modulation technique depends on the communication system, with typically SSB used in FDM telephony, OOK in optical fibre, FM in first generation cellular telephony and analogue satellite communication, and M-ary QAM in digital satellite communications etc. Each of these modulation techniques was covered in previous chapters. Our discussion of FDM concentrated on its application in telephony where a complete set of standards exists for hierarchical implementation.

TDM fits in very well with the techniques of digital switching in modern networks and is ideally suited for transmitting digital signals or bit streams from multiple sources. It allows the advantages of digital communications to be extended to a larger number of simultaneous users in a common transmission medium than would be possible with FDM. We presented a detailed discussion of (non-statistical) TDM optimised for digital transmission of voice, and which results in the plesiochronous and synchronous digital hierarchies. To show how the requirements of broadband integrated services are satisfied, we presented the statistical TDM technique of ATM, which satisfactorily multiplexes all types of digital signal, including voice, data and video.

Finally, we discussed various spread spectrum modulation techniques, including time-hopping, frequency-hopping and direct sequence. In studying CDM, we clearly demonstrated the importance of a number of factors, including code synchronisation and cross-correlation, power control, processing gain and the length of the code sequence.

We are now ready to conclude our studies in this book with the final chapter, in which we bring together in one place a detailed analysis of signal attenuation and noise, and their effects in communication systems.

REVIEW QUESTIONS

8.1 Higher line utilisation may be realised by multiplexing 16 voice signals into one 48 kHz group signal. The following procedure has been specified by the ITU for doing this. Each voice signal is limited to frequencies 0.25 to 3.05 kHz. Frequency translation of each voice signal to an exclusive passband is accomplished for the odd-numbered channels using 8 LSB-modulated carriers at frequencies (kHz) 63.15, 69.15, 75.15, ... The even-numbered channels are translated using 8 USB-modulated carriers at frequencies (kHz) 62.85, 68.85, 74.85, ...

(a) Draw detailed block diagrams of the multiplexer and demultiplexer for this 16-channel FDM system.
(b) Sketch a clearly labelled spectrum (similar to Fig. 8.7(a)) of the 16-channel group signal.
(c) Determine the nominal bandwidth and guard band of each voice channel.
(d) Determine the Q and $\mathbb{Z}$ factors of the most stringent filter used in this FDM system.
(e) Compare your result in (d) to that of a standard 12-channel group signal.

8.2 (a) Sketch a clearly labelled spectrum of the hypergroup signal in the UK FDM system.
(b) Determine the Q-factor of the most stringent filter in the STE of Fig. 8.9.

8.3 Determine the Q and $\mathbb{Z}$ factors of the most stringent filter in a 10 800-channel UK hierarchical FDM system. How does this compare with a flat-level assembly of the same number of voice channels using sub-carriers of 4 kHz spacing starting at 1 MHz?

8.4 Determine the number of CTE, GTE and STE required to set up a 600-channel Bell FDM system. Draw a block diagram showing the connection of these devices from the second multiplexing stage.

8.5 Frequency gaps or guard bands are necessary in FDM signals to allow the use of realisable filters and the transmission of control tones in the gaps. The efficiency of an FDM signal is the percentage of total bandwidth that actually contains voice frequencies. Determine the efficiency of a 10 800-channel FDM signal in each of the three hierarchical standards, namely UK, Europe and Bell, discussed in this chapter.

8.6 Determine the number of signals multiplexed and the guard bands involved when a group signal (60–108 kHz) is built, according to ITU standards, exclusively from each of the following types of wideband audio signals.

(a) 50–6400 Hz
(b) 50–10 000 Hz
(c) 30–15 000 Hz

If each baseband audio signal is translated by LSB modulation so that half of the guard band is on either side of the translated spectrum, determine the set of carrier frequencies required in (a)–(c).

8.7 Examine the frame structures of the E1 and T1 signals shown in Figs. 8.16 and 8.19(b), and calculate the rate of each of the following types of bits for the indicated frame.

(a) Framing bits in E1 and T1
(b) Signalling bits in E1 and T1
(c) Signalling bits per channel in E1 and T1
(d) CRC-4 error checking using IB bit in E1
(e) Message bits in T1

8.8 Justification bits are used in PDH frames to accommodate slight variations in the rates of input tributaries. For example, the E1 signal may vary slightly from its nominal 2048 kbit/s rate without hindering the operation of the 2-8 muldex. Examine the frame structures given in Fig. 8.18, and determine the allowable range of bit rate variation in the following CEPT PDH signals.

(a) E1
(b) E2
(c) E3

8.9 We showed that the maximum efficiency of SDH is $\eta_{max} = 96.30\%$. Considering the conveyed PDH signals to be the message bits, determine the actual efficiency of the following STM-1 frames.

(a) STM-1 assembled as shown in Fig. 8.25.
(b) STM-1 assembled as shown in Fig. 8.26(a).
(c) Why is actual efficiency significantly lower than η_{max}?
(d) Give reasons for the discrepancy between your answers in (a) and (b).

(e) In what situation would the assembly procedure of Fig. 8.26(a) be preferred to that of Fig. 8.25?

8.10 Determine the rates of the following types of bits in the STM-1 frame of Fig. 8.26(a).

(a) Filler pattern bits
(b) POH bits
(c) TU pointer bits
(d) AU pointer bits
(e) SOH bits

8.11 Repeat all of Question 8.10, except (c), for the STM-1 frame of Fig. 8.25.

8.12 The fixed-length ATM cell is a compromise between the requirements of high efficiency in data transmission and low delay in voice and video transmission. Determine the following.

(a) The ATM packetisation delay for 64 kbit/s voice signals.
(b) The ATM cell duration in a transmission medium operating at (i) 2 Mbit/s and (ii) 140 Mbit/s.
(c) The efficiency of an AAL1 ATM cell.

Comment on your results in (b) and the impact of line rate on cell delay variation.

8.13 Using a table similar to Table 8.3, show that the PN sequence of the code generator of Fig. 8.36(b) is as given in Fig. 8.36(c). You may assume any initial register state, except of course all-zero.

8.14 Draw the block diagram of a [4,2] PN sequence generator. Determine the PN sequence. Is this an m-sequence? Repeat your analysis for a [4,3] code, and determine whether it is an m-sequence.

8.15 Determine the processing gain of a CDM system that uses BPSK modulation and an m-sequence spreading code generated by a linear feedback shift register of length 12. Note that the spreading code is periodic, with period equal to the bit interval of the coded message signal.

Noise in communication systems

IN THIS CHAPTER

- A brief review of signal attenuation in various transmission media including copper lines, optical fibre and radio.

- A lucid discussion of Gaussian noise, white noise and narrowband noise.

- Sources of random noise: A detailed review of the physical sources of random noise in communication systems.

- Random noise calculations: A very clear and comprehensive treatment of the quantification of random noise in single and cascaded systems, including satellite communication Earth stations.

- Noise effects: You will be able to evaluate the impact of noise in various analogue and digital communication systems, and to design systems that meet a specified noise performance.

9.1 Introduction

The purpose of a communication system is to convey information from a source point to a destination point, which may be separated by a few metres or by thousands of kilometres. Using various (modulation or baseband transmission) techniques discussed in previous chapters, the information is transformed into a suitable electrical signal of sufficient power level (i.e. strength) and transmitted towards the destination. However, as the signal propagates in the transmission medium linking source and destination points, its strength is gradually reduced. The causes of this *attenuation* are briefly reviewed in Section 9.2.

So the signal reaching the receiver will in general be very weak. For example, the signal power at the output of a receiving Earth station antenna in a satellite communication system could be just –120 dBW (= 1 pW). There would be no problem whatsoever with detecting such small signal levels if we were dealing with an ideal communication system in which only the wanted signal is present. However, problems arise in practice because of the (unavoidable) presence of one or more of the following *unwanted* signals.

- Random signals or *noise*: these have a variety of sources (discussed in Section 9.3) and are added to the signal in the transmission medium and within the receiver system itself.

- *Interference* signals: the type of interference signal and its significance depend largely on the communication system. A few examples will suffice.

  (i) *Crosstalk* may occur in which intelligible information is coupled by inductance or capacitance from one communication channel (e.g. a wire-pair) to another.

  (ii) Two separately located radio systems that intercept a common volume in the atmosphere may become coupled by *scattering*, the signal in one link being scattered into the antenna of the other link.

  (iii) Two radio systems that transmit on the same frequency using orthogonal polarisation may interfere with each other as a result of *cross-polarisation*, whereby a portion of the energy in one polarisation is converted to the other in an *anisotropic* medium.

  (iv) An interference signal may be produced in one communication channel due to insufficient *guard bands* in multiplexed systems, or due to insufficient *filtering*. For example, *hum noise* at 50 Hz and its harmonics may result from insufficient rectification and smoothing of the public power supply. Furthermore, hum noise is in the air as electromagnetic radiation from power lines and can be picked up along with the desired signal.

  (v) Interference voltages may be induced in aerials and metallic lines by lightning and by sparks (e.g. ignition) at electrical contacts.

Most interference signals can be eliminated by careful system design, although the cost of doing this may sometimes be prohibitive. However, random noise is always present.

The ability of a receiver system to correctly detect an incoming signal is not determined by the signal strength only. A reasonably strong signal can be obscured in a noisy receiver, while a much weaker signal may be accurately recovered using a low-noise system. The principal consideration is therefore not just the signal power, but how the signal and noise powers compare, which is expressed in the parameter known as the *signal-to-noise ratio* (SNR). The SNR at a given point in a communication system is defined as the ratio of average signal power at that point to the average noise power at the same point. That is,

$$\text{SNR} = \frac{\text{Average signal power}}{\text{Average noise power}} = \frac{P_s}{P_n}$$

$$= P_s|_{dBW} - P_n|_{dBW} \text{ (dB)} \tag{9.1}$$

In this chapter, we will learn how to determine signal strength, noise power and SNR at various points in a communication system. You will acquire the important skills needed to assess the impact of noise on communication systems, and to design systems that perform satisfactorily in the presence of noise. A good understanding of the characterisation of random noise is required, and this we consider in some detail.

We begin with a brief review of signal attenuation in various transmission media. This is followed by a detailed discussion of the physical sources of noise, which includes (where suitable) quantitative estimates of noise level. After laying a solid foundation in the important concepts of Gaussian noise, white noise, narrowband noise and noise equivalent bandwidth, we then proceed to a lucid treatment of system noise calculations, including noise power, noise temperature and noise factor in single and cascaded systems. The impact of noise in various analogue and digital systems is discussed, which equips us to make an informed choice of modulation technique in a given situation.

9.2 Signal attenuation

9.2.1 Metallic lines

In metallic lines, some of the signal energy is converted to heat dissipated in the conducting material of non-zero resistance R (ohm), and in the insulating material of non-zero conductance G (mho). In a perfect conductor $R = 0$, and in a perfect insulator $G = 0$, so that there is no attenuation. But in practice both R and G have small values, which results in signal energy loss at a rate (in J/s or watts):

$$P = \begin{cases} I^2R, & \text{Conductor} \\ V^2G, & \text{Insulation} \end{cases} \tag{9.2}$$

$$R = \rho l/A; \qquad G = \sigma A/l$$

Here, I is the rms current flowing in the conductor of resistivity ρ (Ω m) and length l (m), V is the root-mean-square (rms) voltage across the insulation separating the conductor-pair, and σ is the conductivity (mho/m) of the insulating material.

High-frequency current tends to flow on the outer skin of a wire conductor rather than being uniformly distributed over the entire cross-section. This phenomenon is known as *skin effect*. It reduces the cross-sectional area used by the high-frequency components of the current flow, making them see a higher line resistance, thereby experiencing a larger attenuation.

Every metallic line has a *series conductance L* due to the *magnetic field* associated with current-carrying conductors, and a *parallel capacitance C* associated with a separation of positive and negative charge whenever there is a *potential difference* between two conductors, which creates an *electric field*. These two fields store some of the signal energy in transit, the amount stored increasing with signal frequency. Thus the signal energy reaching the intended destination is reduced.

Metallic lines are also subject to *radiation loss*, which increases at higher signal frequencies, as some of the signal energy is carried away in the electromagnetic wave that is inevitably generated by the time-varying current in the conductor-pair. In this respect the metallic line behaves as a poorly designed *antenna*. Its time-varying current induces a time-varying magnetic field in its immediate vicinity, which then induces a time-varying electric field in its surrounding, which also induces a time-varying magnetic field, and so on. The result is a pair of electric and magnetic fields, known as *electromagnetic waves*, travelling outwards in space at the speed of light.

Finally, the propagation delay of a metallic line is in general frequency-dependent, a phenomenon known as *dispersion*. This causes pulse broadening in digital communications as the pulse energy carried in different frequency components reach the receiver at slightly different instants. As the receiver employs an observation interval equal to the transmitted pulse duration, this dispersion will cause the receiver to find a pulse of reduced energy. There is, however, a more serious problem associated with dispersion, known as *inter-symbol interference* (ISI), which we studied in Chapter 6. ISI places a limitation on bit rate.

The total attenuation in metallic lines therefore increases rapidly with frequency and depends on conductor size, material (usually *copper*) and temperature. For example, at 20 °C and 10 MHz, a twisted wire pair of diameter 0.63 mm attenuates the signal by 49 dB/km. A normal-core coaxial cable of inner/outer conductor diameters 2.6/9.5 mm, on the other hand, attenuates the signal by 7.5 dB/km at the same frequency and temperature.

At this point you may wish to consider Questions 9.1–9.3, which extend our discussion here. Further discussion of cable attenuation and applications may also be found in Section 1.4.5.

9.2.2 Optical fibre

A number of factors contribute to attenuation in optical fibre. First, there is *absorption loss* as a small portion of the signal energy is absorbed (and dissipated as heat) by impurities in the fibre. The main contributors are traces of transition metal ions and hydroxyl ions, the latter causing absorption peaks at wavelengths λ = 950, 1240 and 1390 nm.

Secondly, *scattering loss* occurs due to the scattering of signal energy at points of refractive index irregularity in the fibre. The irregularities arise from the amorphous structure of silica material and are of a scale less than the wavelength of the light signal. On such a scale, the resulting scattering is known as *Rayleigh scattering*, which causes the signal power to be attenuated by $8.686\alpha l$ dB over a fibre length l, where α is called the *attenuation coefficient* and decreases as the 4th power of wavelength. The combination of Rayleigh scattering and absorption by impurities gives an *intrinsic* fibre loss, which has a minimum value of 0.2 dB/km at a wavelength of 1550 nm.

Optical fibre is also subject to external sources of attenuation known as *extrinsic* losses, which may sometimes account for the bulk of the total attenuation.

Considerable *bending loss* will occur if the fibre is bent at some point into an arc of a few millimetres in radius, which allows some of the light energy to escape into the fibre cladding. The escape at sharp bends is by refraction in multimode fibre, and by radiation in single mode fibre.

Losses are also incurred at joints between two fibre lengths. For a permanent joint by means of a *fusion splice* the loss is small, typically < 0.1 dB. But for a non-permanent *butt join*, accomplished by holding the two fibre lengths in very close proximity, the loss can range from about 0.3 dB for perfect alignment to a few dB due to a significant misalignment.

Finally, *coupling losses* occur at the interface between the fibre and optical source/detector, as well as in a fibre coupler, which couples the signal from one input fibre to several output fibres, or from several input fibres to one or more outputs.

9.2.3 Radio

In *line-of-sight microwave* (also called *radio relay*) links as well as *Earth–space slant paths* that link an Earth station and a satellite, the signal experiences *spreading* (or *free space*) loss. This occurs because the (unguided) radio energy is spread over the surface of an imaginary sphere of radius equal to the distance d from the transmitter. And as d increases, the signal power per unit area or *flux density* decreases in proportion to d^2. In the absence of spreading — the radio transmission being confined within an imaginary and lossless waveguide — the signal power P_r received by an antenna of gain G_r (dB) from a source of power P_t (dBW), which is connected by a transmission line of loss L_l (dB) to a transmit antenna of gain G_t (dB) is given by

$$P_r\big|_{\text{No spreading}} = P_t - L_l + G_t + G_r \quad \text{(dBW)} \tag{9.3}$$

The term

$$\text{EIRP} = P_t - L_l + G_t \text{ (dBW)} \tag{9.4}$$

is called the *effective isotropically radiated power* (*EIRP*). The gain of an antenna is the ratio between the maximum power flux density radiated by the antenna and the maximum power flux density radiated by a *reference antenna* that is fed with the same input power. The reference is usually a fictitious antenna known as an *isotropic antenna* or *isotrope*, which radiates uniformly in all directions in free space. Occasionally, a *dipole antenna* may be used as the reference. To explicitly identify the reference, antenna gain is often expressed in dBi for an isotrope reference and in dBd for a dipole reference. However, an isotrope is universally the most common reference, because of its convenience. Therefore, antenna gain is often expressed (as above) simply in dB, with the understanding that an isotrope is the reference antenna. Since a dipole antenna has a gain of 2.15 dBi, we can convert antenna gain expressed in dBd to gain in dBi by adding 2.15 to the dBd value.

Spreading loss L_s is inevitable in unguided radio transmission and the received signal power is given by

$$P_r = \text{EIRP} + G_r - L_s \quad \text{(dBW)}$$
$$L_s = 10\log_{10}(4\pi d/\lambda)^2 \quad \text{(dB)}$$
$$= 92.44 + 20\log_{10}(d_{\text{km}}) + 20\log_{10}(f_{\text{GHz}}) \tag{9.5}$$

Note that to obtain the last line above, we made use of Eq. 2.43 in Section 2.6, and the relation f (in GHz) $= 0.3/\lambda$, where λ is the wavelength in metres. We see that free-space loss (as a ratio) increases as the square of distance and as the square of frequency, which leads to an increase in attenuation by 6 dB every time the distance or frequency is doubled.

In addition to the above free-space loss, there are losses associated with transmit and receive antennas (e.g. *mispointing*), and attenuation due to absorption in the atmosphere and scattering at atmospheric refractive index irregularities. The magnitude of this attenuation and its contributing factors depend primarily on frequency. A more detailed discussion of these propagation issues is beyond our scope. But we show the attenuation of radio waves due to gaseous absorption as a function of frequency in Fig. 9.1. Rain attenuation becomes very significant above 10 GHz and requires measures (e.g. extra transmitted power) to ensure link availability for a specified percentage of the year, such as 99.9%.

Equation (9.5) only applies to line-of-sight links where there is sufficient clearance to ensure the absence of multipath. In a mobile communication environment the signal strength decreases more rapidly with distance than in the free-space situation of Eq. (9.5), due to the destructive contribution of multipath propagation. For transmitter height h_t, receiver height h_r, and distance d between the transmitter and receiver, where d is much larger than h_r and h_t, the mobile propagation path loss is given approximately by

$$L_p = 40\log_{10}(d) - 20\log_{10}(h_t) - 20\log_{10}(h_r) \quad \text{(dB)} \tag{9.6}$$

The path loss (ratio) therefore increases as the 4th power of distance, which gives an extra 12 dB of attenuation every time the distance is doubled. Equation (9.6) assumes plane Earth propagation. In practice, additional losses are incurred, depending on the physical environment, due to the presence of *surface roughness*, *shadowing* (i.e. absence of a direct ray from the transmitter to the receiver), and the effects of buildings, trees and other terrain features.

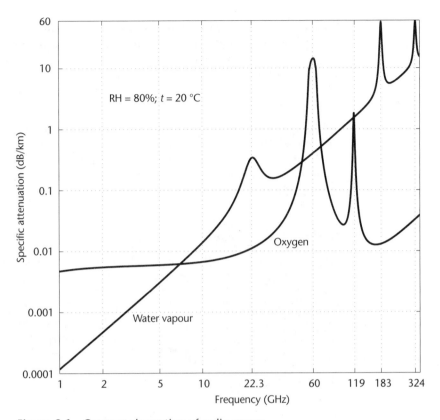

Figure 9.1 Gaseous absorption of radio waves.

9.3 Physical sources of random noise

9.3.1 Thermal or Johnson noise

Thermal agitation of electrons in conductors produces random voltage fluctuations across the conductor. The mean square value of thermal noise voltage measured across the terminals of a conductor is given by

$$\overline{v_n^2} = 4kTBR \tag{9.7}$$

Here, k is Boltzmann's constant ($= 1.38 \times 10^{-23}$ J/K); R is the resistance of the conductor in ohm; T is the absolute temperature of the conductor in kelvin (K); and B is the bandwidth of the measurement in Hz.

9.3.2 Quantisation noise

The process of converting an analogue signal to digital (Section 6.2) inevitably introduces a quantisation error in every digitised sample. For small quantisation step sizes and at sampling rates sufficient to avoid aliasing, the errors are random and have the same effect as thermal noise on the reconstructed analogue signal, hence the name *quantisation noise*. In the simple case of uniform quantisation, the mean square value of quantisation noise voltage is given by

$$\overline{v_q^2} = \frac{A_{p-p}^2}{12} \exp(-1.3863n) \tag{9.8}$$

Here, A_{p-p} is the peak-to-peak amplitude of the analogue signal required to completely fill the quantiser without clipping, and n is the number of bits per sample. Note that quantisation noise is entirely under the control of the system designer (as discussed in Section 6.2) through the two parameters A_{p-p} and n.

9.3.3 Radio or sky noise

Under thermal equilibrium, an absorbing medium re-radiates the radio wave energy that it absorbs. This re-radiation constitutes noise for a receive antenna. The *brightness temperature* or *effective noise temperature* of a source gives a measure of the power radiated in a given frequency band in the direction of a receive antenna. This is the physical temperature T of a blackbody that emits the same power P_n in that frequency band, as given by Planck's law:

$$P_n = \frac{hfB}{\exp(hf/kT) - 1} \tag{9.9}$$

where B is the bandwidth (Hz), f is the centre frequency (Hz), and h is Planck's constant = 6.626×10^{-34} Js. At radio frequencies, $hf/kT \ll 1$, and $\exp(hf/kT) \approx 1 + hf/kT$, so that

$$P_n = \frac{hfB}{1 + hf/kT - 1}$$
$$= kTB \tag{9.10}$$

This noise power will be delivered in its entirety only to a device that is matched (as discussed later) to the noise source. Mismatched devices will absorb only a fraction of this power and reject (i.e. reflect) the rest. Unfortunately, we cannot resort to using mismatched antennas in order to suppress radio noise power, since this would also cause a significant portion of the wanted signal to be rejected. Noise power is often quantified using noise temperature T, rather than P_n, where

$$T = \frac{P_n}{kB} \tag{9.11}$$

P_n depends strongly on the frequency of operation, among other factors, and includes contributions from one or more of the following.

1. *Extra-terrestrial noise* T_{xn}, including galactic noise, solar noise, noise from the surface of the Moon, and a cosmic background noise of 2.7 K. Galactic noise decreases rapidly with frequency from more than 1000 K at 100 MHz to a negligible level above about 2 GHz. The Sun is a strong

source of noise at all radio frequencies and if it fully illuminates the antenna main beam, its noise temperature will range from 10^6 K at 100 MHz to about 10^4 K at frequencies above 10 GHz under quiet Sun conditions. Direct viewing of the Sun by a receiving antenna will therefore cause a weak received signal (especially in satellite communications) to be swamped by noise, resulting in a link outage.

2. *Atmospheric noise* T_{an}, including noise radiated by hydrometeors (i.e. rain, ice, snow and cloud water droplets), aerosols and atmospheric gases. This is given by the expression

$$T_{an} = T_m \left[1 - \frac{1}{L} \right]$$

$$L = 10^{(A/10)}; \quad T_m = 1.12 T_{surf} - 50$$

(9.12)

where A (dB) is the total attenuation due to absorption in the atmosphere, L is the resulting loss factor, T_m represents a mean radiating temperature, and T_{surf} is the surface temperature. Note that on a satellite communication link the total attenuation and hence T_{an} depend on path elevation angle θ, increasing as θ decreases. In the absence of attenuation (i.e. $A = 0$ dB), we have $L = 1$, and $T_{an} = 0$.

3. Noise from the *surface of the Earth*, given by

$$T_{en} = \varepsilon_\phi T_{surf}$$

(9.13)

where T_{surf} is the surface temperature as above, and ε_ϕ is the emissivity of the surface, defined as the ratio of the absorbed power to the incident power at an angle ϕ to the horizontal. Land surfaces have a higher emissivity than water surfaces, and hence a higher brightness temperature T_{en}. If the Earth is considered a blackbody, then $\varepsilon_\phi = 1$, and $T_{en} = T_{surf} \approx 290$ K. However, radiation from the surface of the Earth usually enters a directional antenna through its sidelobe, which is typically at least a factor of $L_{sl} = 100$ (or 20 dB) below the main lobe gain. Thus, even in the worst case of a blackbody Earth, the contribution of T_{en} to the system noise temperature is reduced by this factor to at most ~3 K.

By analogy with thermal noise — Eq. (9.7) — the mean square sky noise voltage at the terminals of an antenna is given by

$$\overline{v_s^2} = 4k T_a B R_r$$

(9.14)

where T_r is the *radiation resistance* of the antenna, and T_a is the *antenna noise temperature*. The radiation resistance of an antenna is a fictitious resistance that would dissipate as much power as the antenna radiates (in transmit mode) if the resistor were connected to the same transmission line. Thus an antenna radiating P watts when drawing rms current I has a radiation resistance $R_r = P/I^2$. In satellite communications, the noise temperature of an Earth station antenna is the result of contributions from all the classes of radio noise introduced above and is given by

$$T_a = \frac{T_{xn}}{L} + T_{an} + \frac{T_{en}}{L_{sl}}$$

(9.15)

The first term represents extra-terrestrial radio noise T_{xn} — ≈ 3 K for frequencies above about 2 GHz — reduced by the atmospheric loss factor L. The third term is the radio noise from the warm Earth ($T_{en} \approx 290$ K) reduced by the factor L_{sl}, which is the loss factor (relative to the main lobe) of the antenna sidelobe that points towards the Earth. In the worst case of an omnidirectional antenna, $L_{sl} = 1$, and the third term on the RHS of Eq. (9.15) contributes about 290 K. The second term T_{an} is negligible below about 1 GHz, but the first term increases rapidly below 1 GHz, as earlier indicated. For frequencies between 1 and 50 GHz on a satellite link under clear-sky conditions, T_{an} can be obtained from Fig. 9.2, which applies to a path elevation angle $\theta = 90°$. For other elevations $\theta \geq 10°$, the value obtained from Fig. 9.2 should be multiplied by the factor $1/\sin\theta$. For non-clear weather (e.g. during rain), the total attenuation should be used in Eq. (9.12) to determine T_{an}.

It should be emphasised that the above discussion of Eq. (9.15) applies to a satellite *downlink* only, i.e. an Earth-based antenna receiving transmissions

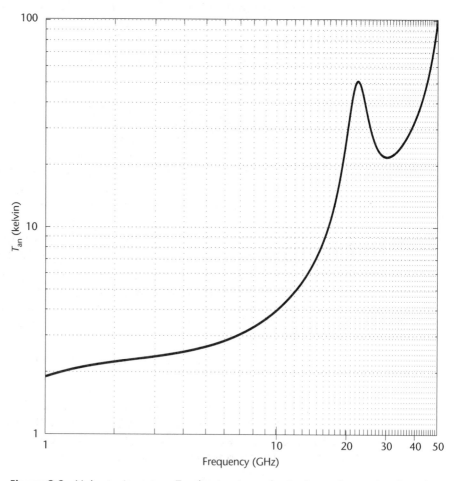

Figure 9.2 Noise temperature T_{an} due to atmospheric absorption under clear-sky conditions on a satellite link. Elevation angle = 90°.

from a satellite. For transmissions in the opposite direction, called *uplink*, the noise temperature T_a of the satellite antenna is dominated by the third term, with $L_{sl} = 1$ (since the satellite antenna must be pointed towards the warm Earth). Thus, under clear-weather conditions $T_a \approx 290$ K.

9.3.4 Shot noise

Current flow in electronic devices is not continuous but discrete, being the result of the motion of a large number of charged particles, of smallest charge $q_e = 1.602 \times 10^{-19}$ coulomb. Random fluctuations in the number of these particles — electrons emitted by a cathode in vacuum tubes, and minority carriers in semiconductor devices (e.g. diodes and transistors) — give rise to *shot noise*. The mean square value of shot noise current is given by

$$\overline{i_s^2} = 2q_e IB \tag{9.16}$$

where I is the average anode or emitter current and q_e is electronic charge, as given above.

9.3.5 Partition noise

This results from fluctuations in the recombination of minority charge carriers in the base region of bipolar junction transistors (BJT). Partition noise also occurs in multigrid valves, such as tetrodes, due to fluctuations in the sharing of current between the electrodes.

9.3.6 Quantum noise

Light signals in optical fibre consist of discrete amounts of energy particles known as *photons*. Fluctuations in photon flow in fibre give rise to quantum noise, which places a fundamental limit on the sensitivity of OOK detectors. An error occurs if, due to fluctuations in arrival rate, no photon is received during a binary 1 interval. We must therefore ensure that each transmitted light pulse contains a certain minimum average number of photons so that the required bit error rate is satisfied in spite of random fluctuations occasionally resulting in no photons being received. This consideration (see Question 9.8) leads to a required mean received power given by

$$P_r = 10\log_{10}\left[-\frac{R_s \ln(2 \times \text{BER})}{\lambda}\right] - 70 \text{ dBm} \tag{9.17}$$

where λ is the wavelength in nm; R_s is the symbol rate in Mbaud; and BER is the stipulated bit error rate of the OOK transmission system.

9.3.7 Flicker or 1/f noise

Flicker noise is observed at very low frequencies, and is thought to be due to fluctuations in the conductivity of semiconductor materials as well as the slow drift of an electronic device (e.g. an amplifier) from its operating point. The power spectral density of this noise is inversely proportional to frequency; hence it is also called $1/f$ noise. Flicker noise is negligible at high frequencies and can be ignored.

WORKED EXAMPLE 9.1

Quantisation noise

Determine the rms quantisation noise voltage in a 12-bit uniform quantiser of peak-to-peak voltage 10 V.

From Eq. (9.8), with $n = 12$ and $A_{p\text{-}p} = 10$, we obtain the mean square quantisation noise voltage, the square root of which is the desired rms voltage. Thus,

$$\overline{v_q^2} = \frac{10^2}{12}\exp(-1.3863 \times 12)$$

$$= 0.497 \text{ square millivolts}$$

$$v_{q\text{rms}} = \sqrt{\overline{v_q^2}} = 0.7 \text{ mV}$$

WORKED EXAMPLE 9.2

Sky noise power

A domestic television receive antenna delivers a sky noise power of –105 dBm to a matched coaxial feeder in a radio frequency bandwidth of 8 MHz. Determine the antenna noise temperature.

Given: $P_n = -105$ dBm $= 3.1623 \times 10^{-14}$ W. See the discussion of logarithmic units in Section 2.6 if in any doubt regarding this conversion. It follows from Eq. (9.11) that antenna noise temperature is given by

$$T_a = \frac{P_n}{kB} = \frac{3.1623 \times 10^{-14}}{(1.38 \times 10^{-23})(8 \times 10^6)}$$

$$= 286.4 \text{ K}$$

WORKED EXAMPLE 9.3

Antenna noise temperature

An Earth station antenna receives a satellite transmission at 20 GHz on a path elevation of 30°. Noise from the Earth's surface enters the antenna via its first sidelobe level at –16 dB. Determine the antenna noise temperature T_a.

(a) During clear-sky conditions.
(b) During rain, when the total atmospheric attenuation (assumed absorptive) is 12 dB.

We will determine T_a using Eq. (9.15):

$$T_a = T_{xn}/L + T_{an} + T_{en}/L_s$$

At 20 GHz, extra-terrestrial noise $T_{xn} \approx 3$ K.
The Earth's brightness temperature $T_{en} = \varepsilon T_{surf} \approx 290$ K.
The sidelobe loss factor $L_{sl} = 10^{(16/10)} = 39.8$.

(a) Clear-sky attenuation is small, and we set $L \approx 1$ with little loss of accuracy. Figure 9.2 gives $T_{an} = 26$ K at 20 GHz. But this is for zenith elevation ($\theta = 90°$). For $\theta = 30°$, we multiply by $1/\sin(30°)$ to obtain $T_{an} = 52$ K. Finally, Eq. (9.15) yields

$$T_a = 3/1 + 52 + 290/39.8 = 62.3 \text{ K}$$

(b) A 12 dB attenuation corresponds to a loss factor

$$L = 10^{(12/10)} = 15.85$$

The noise temperature T_{an} due to this atmospheric attenuation is calculated using Eq. (9.12), with $T_m = (1.12)(290) - 50 = 274.8$ K:

$$T_{an} = T_m(1 - 1/L) = 274.8(1 - 1/15.85)$$
$$= 257.5 \text{ K}$$

Eq. (9.15) then yields the desired antenna noise temperature

$$T_a = 3/15.85 + 257.5 + 290/39.8 = 265 \text{ K}$$

It is important to observe that antenna noise temperature increases significantly during atmospheric attenuation. This represents a double degradation in carrier-to-noise ratio (CNR). First, the carrier signal level is reduced by 12 dB. Second, the noise power delivered by the antenna increases by $10\log_{10}(265/62.3) = 6.3$ dB. Thus, the total reduction in CNR compared to clear-sky conditions is 18.3 dB.

WORKED EXAMPLE   **9.4**

Quantum noise

An optical fibre transmission system uses OOK at 2592 Mbaud and a light wavelength of 1.55 μm. If a bit error rate of at most 10^{-9} is to be satisfied, determine the minimum average received power P_r (in μW) imposed by quantum noise.

By a straightforward substitution in Eq. (9.17), we obtain

$$P_r = 10\log_{10}\left[-\frac{2592\ln(2 \times 10^{-9})}{1550}\right] - 70 \text{ dBm}$$
$$= 10\log_{10}(33.5) - 70 \text{ dBm}$$
$$= -54.75 \text{ dBm}$$
$$= 3.35 \text{ nW}$$

In practice, other noise sources at the receiver, e.g. thermal and shot noise, make a much higher level of P_r necessary to achieve a specified BER.

9.4 Gaussian noise

Each noise type discussed above (except flicker noise) is the result of a large number of statistically independent and random contributions. For example, thermal noise results from the contribution of a large number of electrons, each moving randomly under thermal agitation about an equilibrium position. There is no general drift of electrons in a single direction within the conductor, this requiring some externally applied voltage. If we observe the conductor over a significant period of time, we will find that at some instants the random motions lead to a slight depletion of electrons in the upper half of the conductor, which gives a positive noise voltage. At other instants there is a slight surplus of electrons in the upper half of the conductor, giving a negative noise voltage. The average or mean of the noise voltage samples measured in the observation interval is zero, since there is no reason for either a surplus or depletion of electrons to be preferred.

An important theorem, known as the *central limit theorem*, indicates that under the above circumstances the noise voltage samples follow a Gaussian distribution with zero mean, as shown in Fig. 9.3. The curve is the zero-mean Gaussian probability density function (pdf)

$$p(v_n) = \frac{1}{\sigma\sqrt{2\pi}} \exp\left(-\frac{v_n^2}{2\sigma^2}\right)$$

(9.18)

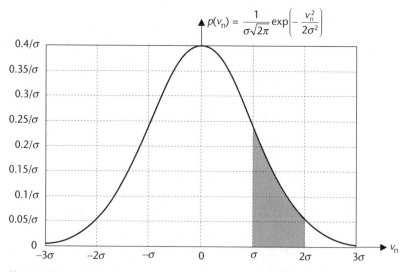

Figure 9.3 Gaussian probability density function (pdf) of zero mean and standard deviation σ.

where σ^2 is the *variance* of the noise voltage v_n and, in this case of zero mean, also gives the mean square noise voltage $\overline{v_n^2}$ or *normalised noise power* P_n — obtained by averaging the squares of the noise voltage samples taken over a sufficiently long observation interval. The square root of the variance is called the *standard deviation* σ, which gives an indication of the spread of v_n about its mean. So we may write

$$P_n = \overline{v_n^2} = \sigma^2 \equiv \text{Square of standard deviation} \tag{9.19}$$

We cannot say with certainty what the value of the next sample of v_n will be, but we can express how likely it is that v_n will lie in a certain range from z_1 to z_2. The likelihood is expressed as a probability, which is given by the area under the curve of $p(v_n)$ between z_1 and z_2. This area is written mathematically as

$$\text{Area} = \int_{z_1}^{z_2} p(v_n) dv_n \tag{9.20}$$

For example, the probability that v_n lies between σ and 2σ is given by the shaded area of Fig. 9.3. In particular, the probability that v_n exceeds a certain value z is given by

$$\begin{aligned}
\Pr(v_n \geq z) &= \int_z^\infty p(v_n) dv_n \\
&= \int_z^\infty \frac{1}{\sigma\sqrt{2\pi}} \exp\left(-\frac{v_n^2}{2\sigma^2}\right) dv_n \\
&= \frac{1}{\sqrt{\pi}} \int_{z/\sigma\sqrt{2}}^\infty \exp(-y^2) dy \\
&= \frac{1}{2} \text{erfc}\left(\frac{z}{\sigma\sqrt{2}}\right)
\end{aligned} \tag{9.21}$$

where we have invoked the complementary error function, which was defined in Section 7.5 in connection with Eq. 7.29, and was plotted in Fig. 7.10. Using Eq. (9.21) along with Fig. 7.10, we can calculate the probability that v_n lies in any given range. The following special relations are useful in this respect.

$$\Pr(v_n \geq -\infty) = 1 \tag{9.22}$$

Equation (9.22) holds because it is *certain* that v_n will have some value. Thus, by definition of probability as the area under the pdf curve — see Eq. (9.20) — it follows that the total area under the pdf curve is unity.

$$\Pr(v_n \geq 0) = \Pr(v_n \leq 0) = \frac{1}{2} \tag{9.23}$$

This follows from Eq. (9.22) and from the even symmetry of the pdf curve about zero, with half the area lying to the left and half to the right of $v_n = 0$. Thus, the noise voltage is as likely to be positive as it is to be negative.

$$\Pr(v_n \leq z) = 1 - \Pr(v_n \geq z) \tag{9.24}$$

You can see that Eq. (9.24) holds by noting that the total area (= 1) of the pdf curve is made of two portions, namely $\Pr(v_n \leq z)$, which is the area to the left of $v_n = z$, and $\Pr(v_n \geq z)$ the area to the right of the same point.

$$\Pr(v_n \geq -z) = 1 - \Pr(v_n \geq z) \tag{9.25}$$

The relation of Eq. (9.25) follows from the symmetry of the pdf function and allows us to determine probabilities involving negative sample values using Fig. 7.10, which covers positive values only. Finally, we have

$$\Pr(z_1 \leq v_n \leq z_2) = \Pr(v_n \geq z_1) - \Pr(v_n \geq z_2) \tag{9.26}$$

WORKED EXAMPLE 9.5

Gaussian noise

Determine the following for a Gaussian noise voltage $v_n(t)$ of standard deviation $\sigma = 2.5$ mV:

(a) Normalised noise power P_n in dBm.
(b) The probability that a sample of $v_n(t)$ lies between σ and 2σ.
(c) The probability that a sample of $v_n(t)$ exceeds -3.0 mV.

(a) $P_n = \sigma^2 = (2.5 \times 10^{-3})^2 = 6.25\,\mu\text{W} = -22$ dBm

(b) The required probability is the shaded area in Fig. 9.3:

$$\Pr(\sigma \leq v_n \leq 2\sigma) = \Pr(v_n \geq \sigma) - \Pr(v_n \geq 2\sigma)$$

$$= \frac{1}{2}\text{erfc}\left(\frac{\sigma}{\sigma\sqrt{2}}\right) - \frac{1}{2}\text{erfc}\left(\frac{2\sigma}{\sigma\sqrt{2}}\right)$$

$$= 0.5[\text{erfc}(1/\sqrt{2}) - \text{erfc}(\sqrt{2})]$$

$$= 0.5(0.3173 - 0.0455) = 0.136$$

(c) We apply Eq. (9.25) to obtain

$$\Pr(v_n \geq -3.0) = 1 - \Pr(v_n \geq 3.0)$$

$$= 1 - \frac{1}{2}\text{erfc}\left(\frac{3.0}{2.5\sqrt{2}}\right)$$

$$= 1 - 0.5\,\text{erfc}(0.85)$$

$$= 1 - 0.5 \times 0.23$$

$$= 0.885$$

9.5 White noise

To determine with confidence whether there is any correlation between two samples of noise voltage that are observed at time instants separated by τ, we would proceed as follows. We measure the noise voltage $v_n(t)$ over a long observation interval $T \rightarrow \infty$. Then starting from $t = 0$, we take the recorded samples in pairs $v_n(t)$ and $v_n(t + \tau)$, form the product $v_n(t)v_n(t + \tau)$,

Table 9.1 Sign of the product of two samples of noise voltage.

$v_n(t)$	$v_n(t+\tau)$	$v_n(t)v_n(t+\tau)$
Negative	Negative	Positive
Negative	Positive	Negative
Positive	Negative	Negative
Positive	Positive	Positive

and obtain the average of these products over the observation interval. This corresponds to the computation

$$R_v(\tau) = \lim_{T\to\infty} \frac{1}{T} \int_0^T v_n(t)v_n(t+\tau)dt \tag{9.27}$$

which is called the *time-averaged autocorrelation function* of the noise voltage. If $\tau = 0$, then we are pairing each sample with itself, and the computation is simply the mean square value of $v_n(t)$, otherwise known as the normalised noise power P_n given by Eq. (9.19). If, on the other hand, $\tau \neq 0$, then we are dealing with two different samples, and the sign of the product will be as shown in Table 9.1.

We have earlier shown that $v_n(t)$ is equally likely to be positive or negative. Let us make the following assumptions.

1. That $v_n(t+\tau)$ is a random value that does not depend on $v_n(t)$.

2. That the above condition holds no matter how small τ is, provided τ is not zero.

The first assumption is valid for noise resulting from a large number of statistically independent contributions. The second is an idealisation, which implies that the noise-generating mechanism has zero recovery time. That is, it can change in no time from one value to any other value within its range. For reasons that will become clear shortly, we call this type of noise *white noise* $w(t)$. We must emphasise that such perfect randomness cannot be attained in real systems because of inherent inertia. The rate of change of current in real devices is slowed down by inductance, which is always present even if extremely small. Similarly, the rate of change of voltage is impeded by capacitance, this also being always present.

Under the conditions outlined above, the product term in Table 9.1 is equally likely to be positive or negative and has zero mean, so that the integral of Eq. (9.27) is zero. It follows that for white noise,

$$R_w(\tau) = \begin{cases} P_n & \tau = 0 \\ 0 & \tau \neq 0 \end{cases} \tag{9.28}$$

We see that the $R_w(\tau)$ is a zero-width pulse of height P_n. Let the area under this pulse be $N_0/2$. Clearly, N_0 is non-zero if and only if P_n is infinite. As you decrease the width of a pulse towards zero, you must increase its height towards infinity in order to maintain a non-zero area. Thus $R_w(\tau)$ is an

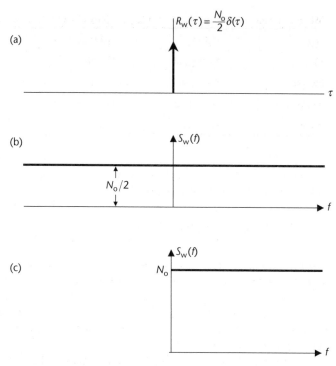

Figure 9.4 White noise: (a) autocorrelation function, (b) double-sided power spectral density (psd) and (c) single-sided psd.

impulse function (Section 2.4.3) of weight $N_o/2$, with a uniform Fourier transform $S_w(f) = N_o/2$, which gives the power spectral density (Section 8.4.4.4) of white noise; see Fig. 9.4. Thus,

$$R_w(\tau) = \frac{N_o}{2} \delta(t)$$
$$S_w(f) = \frac{N_o}{2}$$

(9.29)

We make the following important observations.

1. $w(t)$ contains the same amplitude of all frequencies from $f = 0$ to ∞. It is therefore called *white noise*, by analogy with white light, which contains equal amounts of all wavelengths in the visible spectrum.

2. The value of $N_o/2$ for the uniform psd applies to a double-sided spectrum, which represents a sinusoidal component by a pair of (positive and negative) frequencies, each sharing half of the amplitude. The height of a single-sided psd of white noise is therefore N_o, and the total noise power within a bandwidth B is given by

$$P_{nB} = N_o B$$

(9.30)

3. From our comments on Eq. (9.28), white noise has infinite average power P_n, and is not realisable in practice. Nevertheless, the concept of

white noise is a simplifying idealisation that satisfactorily models real noise in (finite-bandwidth) real systems. Within the limited bandwidth of interest, the spectrum of real noise looks flat and hence white. And we are not concerned with the inevitable tailing off of the spectrum of real noise as $f \to \infty$, since the passband of our real system does not extend to those frequencies. As an analogy, a person running on a football pitch can safely ignore the Earth's curvature and assume a flat Earth. Such an assumption incurs practically no errors because of the limited range (in our case bandwidth) involved. The flat-Earth idealisation would, however, fail where the range is significantly extended to include flying from, say, Tokyo to New York.

It is therefore clearly justifiable to assume that the random noise types encountered in communication systems (except flicker noise) and introduced in Section 9.3.1 are both *Gaussian* and *white*.

9.6 Narrowband noise

We should make an important point that white noise exists only at the input of a communication receiver. As this noise passes through the system it is inevitably filtered and limited in bandwidth. Following an argument similar to Section 2.8, it can be shown that when a signal $x(t)$ of psd $S_x(f)$ is transmitted through a linear time invariant system (e.g. a filter) of transfer function $H(f)$ then the psd $S_y(f)$ of the output signal $y(t)$ is given by

$$S_y(f) = S_x(f)\,|H(f)|^2 \qquad (9.31)$$

Equation (9.31) states that the output psd is modified — in other words *coloured* — by the square of the filter's frequency (or gain) response $|H(f)|$. Figure 9.5 shows three cases of white noise filtering. The input signal is white noise, so that

$$\text{Input psd } S_x(f) \equiv S_w(f) = N_o$$

Note that we are using single-sided spectra. Figs. 9.5(a) and (b) show transmission through normalised ideal filters, with $|H(f)| = 1$ (i.e. unit gain) in the passband of width B, and $|H(f)| = 0$ outside the passband. Thus

$$\text{Output psd } S_v(f) = \begin{cases} N_o & \text{passband} \\ 0 & \text{elsewhere} \end{cases}$$

This type of noise, having a uniform psd within a finite bandwidth is known as *bandlimited white noise*. It has a finite power P_n given by Eq. (9.30), which you should note is the total area under its psd curve. A realisable filter of normalised transfer function $H(f)$ is used in Fig. 9.5(c). Normalisation is important here, and simply means that the maximum gain of the filter $|H(f)|_{max} = 1$. For example, if the (maximum) numeric gain of a filter at its centre frequency is G, then we obtain the filter's normalised transfer function by dividing the actual transfer function by G. The psd $S_v(f)$ of the output noise $v_n(t)$ in Fig. 9.5(c) follows from Eq. (9.31):

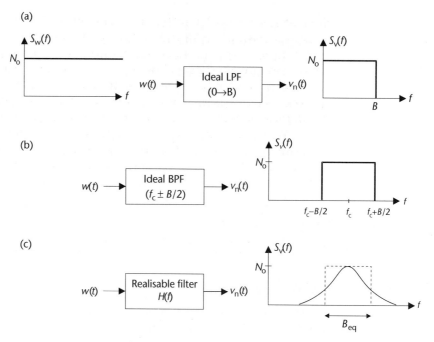

Figure 9.5 Filtering of white noise.

$$S_v(f) = N_o |H(f)|^2 \tag{9.32}$$

Noise of this kind that has a non-uniform psd within a finite bandwidth is known as *coloured noise*. Both bandlimited white noise and coloured noise are commonly referred to simply as *narrowband noise*. Note that the narrowband noise obtained in this manner, by a linear processing of white Gaussian noise, is also itself Gaussian.

9.6.1 Noise equivalent bandwidth

The power P_n of the coloured noise $v_n(t)$ in Fig. 9.5(c) is given by the area under its (single-sided) psd, which we equate to the area of a rectangle of height N_o and width B_{eq}, centred in the passband as shown (dotted) in the figure. Thus we may write

$$P_n = \int_0^\infty S_v(f)df = \int_0^\infty N_o |H(f)|^2 \, df \equiv N_o B_{eq} \tag{9.33}$$

Equating the last two terms yields

$$B_{eq} = \int_0^\infty |H(f)|^2 \, df \tag{9.34}$$

B_{eq} defines the *noise equivalent bandwidth* of the filter. This is a very useful concept, which allows us to work with the much more convenient ideal filter, as far as noise is concerned. In other words, we replace the realisable filter of frequency-dependent gain response $|H(f)|$ with a unit-gain ideal brickwall filter of bandwidth B_{eq}, given by Eq. (9.34). This converts coloured noise to a bandlimited white noise, whose power can be more easily computed using Eq. (9.30) with absolutely no error, provided that the equivalent bandwidth is used in the computation. We will adopt this approach in all system noise calculations, and it will be taken for granted that B (except where otherwise indicated) refers to noise equivalent bandwidth. When B_{eq} is not known, then the 3 dB bandwidth of the system may be used in its place. This substitution underestimates noise power, but the error is small if the filter response has steep sides with a small transition width.

WORKED EXAMPLE   **9.6**

RC low-pass filter

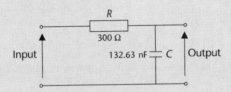

Figure 9.6   *RC low-pass filter.*

Fig. 9.6 shows a simple *RC* low-pass filter.
(a) What is the noise equivalent bandwidth B_{eq} of the filter?
(b) What is the 3 dB bandwidth B of the filter?
(c) Assuming the filter is noiseless, calculate the noise power at its output when connected to a matched antenna of noise temperature $T_a = 80$ K?
(d) How much error is incurred in noise power computation by using the 3 dB bandwidth in place of B_{eq}?

The gain response of this filter was obtained in Section 2.8 (Worked example 2.11) as follows:

$$|H(f)| = \frac{1}{\sqrt{1 + (2\pi RC)^2 f^2}} \equiv \frac{1}{\sqrt{1 + a^2 f^2}} \tag{9.35}$$

(a) We note that $|H(f)|_{max} = 1$ at $f = 0$, so the gain response is normalised and we apply Eq. (9.34) to obtain B_{eq}:

$$B_{eq} = \int_0^\infty |H(f)|^2 \, df = \int_0^\infty \frac{1}{1 + a^2 f^2} \, df$$

The form of the integrand suggests the use of the substitution $af = \tan\theta$. This transforms the integral as follows:

$$1 + a^2 f^2 = 1 + \tan^2 \theta = \sec^2 \theta = 1/\cos^2 \theta$$

$$df = d\left(\frac{\tan \theta}{a}\right) = \frac{d\theta}{a \cos^2 \theta}$$

Limits $f = 0 \to \infty$ become $\theta = 0 \to \pi/2$

Thus,

$$B_{eq} = \int_0^{\pi/2} \cos^2 \theta \frac{d\theta}{a \cos^2 \theta} = \int_0^{\pi/2} \frac{d\theta}{a} = \frac{\pi}{2a}$$

$$= \frac{\pi}{2 \times 2\pi RC} = \frac{1}{4RC}$$

$$= \frac{1}{4 \times 300 \times 132.63 \times 10^{-9}}$$

$$= 6283 \text{ Hz}$$

(b) The 3 dB bandwidth of this LPF is the range from $f = 0$ to the value of f at which the denominator of $|H(f)|$ in Eq. (9.35) equals $\sqrt{2}$. Thus

$$B = \frac{1}{a} = \frac{1}{2\pi RC}$$

$$= 4000 \text{ Hz}$$

(c) Noise power delivered by the antenna is given by

$$P_n = kT_a B_{eq}$$

$$= 1.38 \times 10^{-23} \times 80 \times 6283 \text{ W}$$

$$= 6.936 \times 10^{-18} \text{ W} = -141.6 \text{ dBm}$$

(d) It can be seen that

$$\frac{B_{eq}}{B} = \frac{\pi}{2} = 1.96 \text{ dB}$$

Use of the 3 dB bandwidth in place of B_{eq} therefore causes noise power to be underestimated by 1.96 dB.

9.6.2 Canonical representation

A communication receiver usually consists of several stages of processing, as discussed for example in Section 3.5.3, but the simple receiver model shown in Fig. 9.7(a) will serve our purpose here of noise analysis in bandpass (i.e. modulated) systems. The bandpass filter is designed to pass the wanted signal, which is a modulated carrier of frequency f_c, and to prevent (unwanted) signals at other frequencies from reaching the demodulator. The quality of the output signal depends on the signal-to-noise ratio at the input of the demodulator. As earlier established, we have white noise $w(t)$ at the input of the receiver and bandlimited white noise $v_n(t)$ at the demodulator input. Since the wanted signal is represented in terms of the

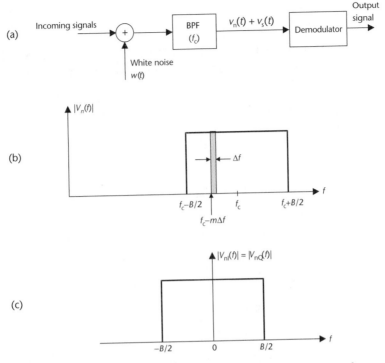

Figure 9.7 (a) Simple receiver model; (b) amplitude spectrum of bandlimited white noise $v_n(t)$ at demodulator input; (c) amplitude spectrum of in-phase and quadrature components of $v_n(t)$.

carrier frequency f_c, we wish to express $v_n(t)$ in a similar form, which will be used later to analyse the effect of noise on the system.

Figure 9.7(b) shows the (continuous) amplitude spectrum $V_n(f)$ of the bandlimited white noise $v_n(t)$. Let us approximate $v_n(t)$ using a discrete Fourier series by dividing $V_n(f)$ into infinitesimally small frequency intervals Δf, and placing in each interval a sinusoid of power equal to the noise power $N_0 \Delta f$ of that interval. Thus each sinusoid has amplitude

$$A = \sqrt{2N_0 \Delta f} \tag{9.36}$$

Using f_c as reference, the spectral line of the mth sinusoid is shown in Fig. 9.7(b) and has random phase $\phi_m(t)$ and frequency

$$f_m = f_c - m\Delta f \tag{9.37}$$

So we may express $v_n(t)$ as a Fourier series

$$v_n(t) = \sum_{m=-M/2}^{M/2} A \cos[2\pi f_m t + \phi_m(t)] \tag{9.38}$$

The summation involves M sinusoids (for $m = -M/2, -M/2 + 1, ..., -2, -1, 1, 2, ..., M/2 - 1, M/2$) in the bandwidth B, where

$$\Delta f = \frac{B}{M} \tag{9.39}$$

Note in particular that $m \neq 0$. The approximation of Eq. (9.38) becomes exact as $M \to \infty$ and $\Delta f \to 0$. Substituting Eq. (9.37) in (9.38) and expanding yields,

$$
\begin{aligned}
v_n(t) &= \sum_m A\cos[2\pi(f_c - m\Delta f)t + \phi_m(t)] \\
&= \left[\sum_{m=-M/2}^{M/2} A\cos(-2\pi m\Delta f t + \phi_m) \right]\cos(2\pi f_c t) \\
&\quad - \left[\sum_{m=-M/2}^{M/2} A\sin(-2\pi m\Delta f t + \phi_m) \right]\sin(2\pi f_c t)
\end{aligned}
\tag{9.40}
$$

This equation has the following *canonical* form,

$$v_n(t) = v_{nI}(t)\cos(2\pi f_c t) - v_{nQ}(t)\sin(2\pi f_c t) \tag{9.41}$$

where

$$
\begin{aligned}
v_{nI}(t) &= \sum_{m=-M/2}^{M/2} A\cos(-2\pi m\Delta f t + \phi_m) \\
v_{nQ}(t) &= \sum_{m=-M/2}^{M/2} A\sin(-2\pi m\Delta f t + \phi_m)
\end{aligned}
\tag{9.42}
$$

Thus we have represented the bandpass noise voltage $v_n(t)$ as the sum of two *quadrature amplitude modulated* carriers. We call $v_{nI}(t)$ the *in-phase* component of $v_n(t)$, and refer to $v_{nQ}(t)$ as the *quadrature* component. In this form, it is clear that the bandpass noise $v_n(t)$ is a modulated carrier that carries two baseband signals $v_{nI}(t)$ and $v_{nQ}(t)$ in quadrature. Figure 9.8(a) shows an arrangement suggested by Eq. (9.41) for combining $v_{nI}(t)$ and $v_{nQ}(t)$ to produce $v_n(t)$. Given $v_n(t)$, we can recover $v_{nI}(t)$ and $v_{nQ}(t)$ as shown in Fig. 9.8(b). First, $v_n(t)$ is multiplied by a cosine and a sine carrier, respectively, and then each balanced modulator output is passed through a low-pass filter. You may wish to perform the operations indicated in this block diagram in order to verify the outputs.

The random signals $v_{nI}(t)$ and $v_{nQ}(t)$ have a number of important properties, a few of which we mention below.

- Both $v_{nI}(t)$ and $v_{nQ}(t)$ have zero mean. You can see that Eq. (9.42) is a Fourier series having no DC component.
- From their Fourier series approximation, we see that $v_{nI}(t)$ and $v_{nQ}(t)$ have the same amplitude spectrum, shown in Fig. 9.7(c), which is simply the amplitude spectrum of the bandpass noise $v_n(t)$ translated from f_c to baseband. However, the phase spectra of these quadrature components, as the name implies, differ by 90°.
- $v_{nI}(t)$ and $v_{nQ}(t)$ have the same power P_n (= variance σ^2) as the bandpass noise $v_n(t)$. You can see this by noting that their Fourier series representations contain M sinusoids each of amplitude A. Thus,

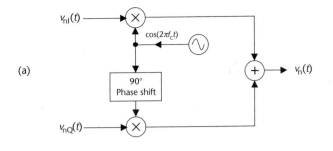

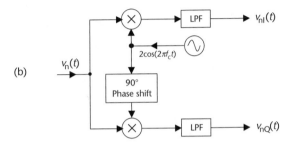

Figure 9.8 Bandpass noise: (a) construction from quadrature components; (b) extraction of quadrature components.

$$P_{nI} = P_{nQ} = \frac{A^2}{2} M$$

$$\Pi_o = \frac{2N_o \Delta f}{2} M$$

$$= N_o B$$

$$= P_n = \sigma^2$$

$$I_o = N_o \Delta f \, M$$

(9.43)

where we have made use of Eq. (9.36) and (9.39).

● The narrowband noise $v_n(t)$ is assumed to be Gaussian with zero mean, and so are $v_{nI}(t)$ and $v_{nQ}(t)$, these being obtainable from $v_n(t)$ by linear processing — Fig. 9.8(b).

9.6.3 Envelope representation

By phasor addition, we can rewrite Eq. (9.41) in the alternative form

$$v_n(t) = r(t)\cos[2\pi f_c t + \psi(t)]$$ (9.44)

where

$$r(t) = \sqrt{v_{nI}^2(t) + v_{nQ}^2(t)}$$

$$\psi(t) = \tan^{-1}\left[\frac{v_{nQ}(t)}{v_{nI}(t)}\right]$$ (9.45)

The random function $r(t)$ is called the *envelope* of the bandpass noise $v_n(t)$. Equation (9.45) specifies non-linear operations on two independent zero-

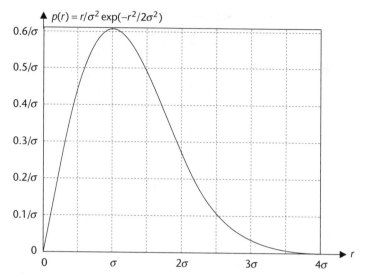

Figure 9.9 Rayleigh pdf of mean square value $2\sigma^2$.

mean Gaussian random signals of variance $\sigma^2 = N_0B$. The result of each processing is a new random signal that follows a non-Gaussian distribution. The probability density function (pdf) of $r(t)$ is given by

$$p(r) = \begin{cases} \dfrac{r}{\sigma^2}\exp\left(-\dfrac{r^2}{2\sigma^2}\right), & r \geq 0 \\ 0, & \text{elsewhere} \end{cases} \tag{9.46}$$

This equation defines what is known as a *Rayleigh* probability density function, which is plotted in Fig. 9.9. The envelope of $v_n(t)$ is said to be Rayleigh-distributed.

The function $\psi(t)$ appearing in Eq. (9.44) and (9.45) is the *phase* of $v_n(t)$. It is uniformly distributed between 0 and 2π radians. That is, the phase of narrowband noise $v_n(t)$ has the *uniform* pdf given by

$$p(\psi) = \begin{cases} \dfrac{1}{2\pi}, & 0 \leq \psi \leq 2\pi \\ 0, & \text{elsewhere} \end{cases} \tag{9.47}$$

9.7 System noise calculations

Let us now consider various ways of specifying the noisiness of communication systems, and learn how to arrange system components to minimise the effects of noise.

9.7.1 Available noise power

A noisy resistor R can be modelled as shown in Fig. 9.10. We replace the practical resistor by an ideal noiseless resistor of the same resistance. A

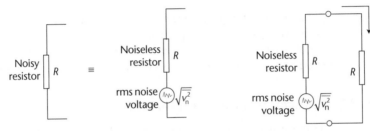

Figure 9.10 Model of a noisy resistor.

Figure 9.11 Condition for maximum noise power transfer

noise generator of root mean square (rms) voltage $\sqrt{\overline{v_n^2}}$ is connected in series, and accounts for the noise generated by the practical resistor. With this model, a resistor R is clearly depicted as a noise voltage source. The *maximum power transfer theorem* states that a signal source, of internal resistance R, delivers maximum power to a load that is *matched* to the source. Matching means that the load resistance $R_l = R$. Thus the maximum noise power, also called *available noise power* P_n, is obtained from resistor R under the condition shown in Fig. 9.11. It follows that the rms noise current delivered to the load resistance is given by

$$i_n = \frac{\sqrt{\overline{v_n^2}}}{2R} \tag{9.48}$$

and the (maximum) noise power delivered to the load is therefore

$$
\begin{aligned}
P_n &= i_n^2 R \\
&= \frac{\overline{v_n^2}}{4R^2} R \\
&= \frac{4kTBR}{4R^2} R \\
&= kTB \\
&= -198.6 + 10\log_{10} T + 10\log_{10} B \ \text{dBm}
\end{aligned}
\tag{9.49}
$$

Here, we substituted Eq. (9.48) for i_n, and Eq. (9.7) for the mean square noise voltage. Temperature T is in kelvins (K) and bandwidth B in Hz. Equation (9.49) is an important result, which states that the available thermal noise power of a resistor depends only on the physical temperature T of the resistor and the bandwidth B of the receiving system or load. That P_n does not depend on R may at first seem surprising. But note that although a larger resistance generates more noise according to Eq. (9.7), it also delivers proportionately less noise current to a matched load, according to Eq. (9.48), by virtue of its increased resistance to current flow. Comparing Eq. (9.49) and (9.30), we see that the noise power per unit bandwidth (in W/Hz) is given by

$$N_o = kT \tag{9.50}$$

Equation (9.49) was obtained for the case of thermal noise, where T represents the physical temperature of the noise source. We now extend this result to apply to all types of random noise encountered in communication systems by introducing the concept of *equivalent noise temperature T_e*.

9.7.2 Equivalent noise temperature

The equivalent noise temperature T_e of a system is the absolute temperature at which a noisy resistor has to be maintained so that when it is connected to the *input* of a noiseless version of the system the available noise power observed at the output of the system is exactly the same as that produced by all the noise sources in the actual system. Equivalent noise temperature is a very important concept that allows us to quantify the noisiness of devices. The following step-by-step procedure helps to fully explain the concept.

1. Consider a noisy system (Fig. 9.12(a)) of input resistance R_i and output resistance R_o.

2. Measure the available noise power P_n at the output of the system, as shown in Fig. 9.12(b).

3. Replace the system with its noiseless version (Fig. 9.12(c)). This gives a reading of zero on the noise power meter at the output.

4. Connect a noisy resistor R_i at the input (Fig. 9.12(d)) and vary the temperature of R_i until the output noise power is again P_n. The absolute temperature of R_i at this instant is the equivalent noise temperature T_e of the noisy system.

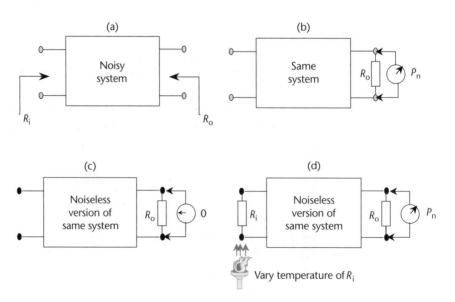

Figure 9.12 Definition of equivalent noise temperature T_e.

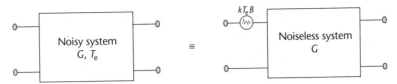

Figure 9.13 Model of a noisy linear system of gain G and equivalent noise temperature T_e.

What this means is that a resistor would have to be at a physical temperature T_e in order to generate the same amount of *thermal* noise power as the *total* noise power produced by a device of equivalent noise temperature T_e. Equivalent noise temperature is *always* referred to the input of the device. Thus the noise model of a noisy device of (numeric) gain G and equivalent noise temperature T_e is as shown in Fig. 9.13. It is important to note that the noise power kT_eB generated by the device according to Eq. (9.49) is at the device input. Clearly then, the available noise power at the device output is given by

$$P_n = GkT_eB \qquad (9.51)$$

A unit-gain device with an equivalent noise temperature $T_e = 290$ K is called a *standard noise source*. Note that 290 K is a reference temperature, which is universally taken to represent room temperature, and is denoted by T_0. The only exception is in Japan, where $T_0 = 293$ K.

9.7.3 Noise figure of a single system

Another important parameter for quantifying the noisiness of a device is its *noise factor*, which when expressed in dB is called the *noise figure*. We will give two equivalent definitions of noise factor and demonstrate that both lead to the same result.

● *Definition 1*: the noise factor F of a system is the ratio of actual noise power output when the input is a standard noise source to the noise power output that exists under the same conditions if the system is noiseless.

● *Definition 2*: the noise factor F of a system is the ratio between input and output *SNR* with the system input being a standard noise source T_0. That is,

$$F = SNR_i/SNR_o \qquad (9.52)$$

Figure 9.14 shows a linear system with a standard noise source at its input terminals 1–1'. To obtain an expression for the noise factor based on definition 1, we need the noise power P_{na} at the output terminals 2-2' of the actual noisy system (Fig. 9.14(a)), and the noise power P_{nnv} at the output of a noiseless version of the same system (Fig. 9.14(b)). Clearly,

$$P_{na} = GkT_oB + GkT_eB$$
$$P_{nnv} = GkT_oB$$

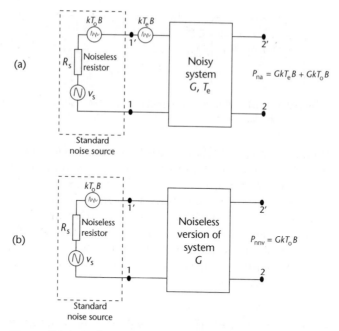

Figure 9.14 Definition of noise factor of a linear system of gain G and equivalent noise temperature T_e.

It follows from definition 1 that

$$
\begin{aligned}
F &= \frac{P_{na}}{P_{nnv}} \\
&= \frac{GkT_oB + GkT_eB}{GkT_oB} \\
&= 1 + \frac{T_e}{T_o}
\end{aligned}
\tag{9.53}
$$

Equation (9.53) relates two important parameters, namely the noise factor F and the equivalent noise temperature T_e. Bearing in mind that both T_e and T_0 (= 290 K) are positive constants, we see that in practical systems F always exceeds unity. F gives the factor by which the proportion of the noise content of a signal is increased as the signal is passed through a system. The signal-to-noise ratio therefore drops by this factor, hence the equivalence of the two definitions. In an ideal noiseless system, $T_e = 0$, and $F = 1$. We may rearrange Eq. (9.53) into the following useful form:

$$
T_e = T_o(F - 1) = 290(F - 1)
\tag{9.54}
$$

And for later use, we also note that

$$
\frac{T_e}{T_o} = F - 1
\tag{9.55}
$$

That is, the ratio between the equivalent noise temperature of a device and the reference temperature gives the noise factor of the device less one.

Let us now return to Fig. 9.14(a) and apply the second definition of F given in Eq. (9.52). Let S_i denote the signal power at the input terminal 1–1'. Note that the input noise power associated with S_i comes from the standard noise source only. Thus we may write

$$\text{Input signal power} = S_i$$
$$\text{Input noise power} = kT_oB$$
$$\text{Output signal power} = GS_i$$
$$\text{Output noise power} = GkT_oB + GkT_eB$$

and from Eq. (9.52),

$$F = \frac{SNR_i}{SNR_o} = \frac{S_i/kT_oB}{GS_i/(GkT_oB + GkT_eB)}$$
$$= 1 + T_e/T_o \tag{9.56}$$

This is the same result as Eq. (9.53), and shows that the two definitions of noise factor are equivalent. The second definition, in terms of the signal-to-noise ratio, is, however, more informative, allowing us to determine the change in SNR between the input and the output of a linear system of known noise factor. In fact, since $F > 1$, it is clear that SNR_i always exceeds SNR_o in practical linear systems — see exception below. In other words, the highest level of SNR is obtained at the signal source. From that point onwards, SNR decreases each time the signal is processed in an amplifier, which not only boosts the signal and noise at its input by the same factor, but also inevitably adds its own internally generated noise.

It should be noted however that an improvement in SNR can be realised in a signal-processing device, such as some demodulators, in which the input signal bandwidth is significantly larger than the output bandwidth. The improvement is known as *processing gain* and comes about because of the use of a modulation technique that trades bandwidth for SNR. We discussed the application of this technique in spread spectrum communication (Section 8.4.4.4), but it also applies to some other modulation techniques, such as wideband FM (Section 9.8.4).

WORKED EXAMPLE   9.7

Noise figure

An amplifier is quoted as having a noise figure of 3.5 dB. Determine its noise factor, noise temperature and noise power density.

The relation between noise figure (dB) and noise factor (numeric) is

$$\text{Noise factor} = 10^{(\text{Noise figure}/10)} \tag{9.57}$$

Thus,

$$F = 10^{(3.5/10)} = 2.24$$

and the noise temperature follows from Eq. (9.54):

$$T_e = 290(2.24 - 1)$$
$$= 360 \text{ K}$$

Finally, Eq. (9.50) gives the noise power density as

$$N_o = kT_e = 1.38 \times 10^{-23} \times 360$$
$$= 4.97 \times 10^{-21} \text{ W/Hz}$$

9.7.4 Noise figure of cascaded systems

A communication system such as a receiver usually consists of several stages of noisy devices. If the stages are matched so that there is maximum power transfer from one stage to the next, then the system is referred to as a *cascade* connection. We wish to quantify the noisiness of a cascaded system using one equivalent noise temperature — and the corresponding noise factor. Figure 9.15 shows the problem at hand for the case of three stages. Each stage has gain, noise factor, and equivalent noise temperature identified by subscripts 1, 2 and 3. The cascaded system (of gain $G = G_1G_2G_3$) is enclosed in dotted rectangle, and we wish to determine its equivalent noise temperature T_e, and hence noise factor F.

As required by the definition, we connect a standard noise source of noise power kT_0B at the input of the cascaded system, and determine the noise power at its output. First we obtain the output P_{na} for the actual system, and then the output P_{nnv} when each stage is replaced by a noiseless version. The ratio of the two noise powers is the required noise factor F of the cascaded system. You should walk through the cascade connection stage by stage to verify how P_{na} is obtained at the final stage. Each stage produces an output noise power that consists of the noise power at its input multiplied

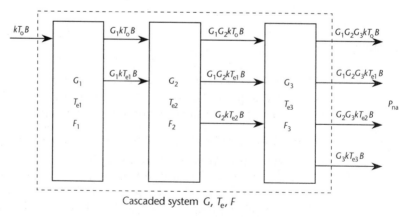

Cascaded system G, T_e, F

Figure 9.15 Cascade connection of noisy devices.

by its gain, plus the noise internally generated in that stage. For noiseless stages, the only noise output is the input noise power multiplied by the gain of the cascade connection. Thus,

$$P_{na} = G_1G_2G_3kT_0B + G_1G_2G_3kT_1B + G_2G_3kT_2B + G_3kT_3B$$
$$P_{nnv} = G_1G_2G_3kT_0B$$

and it follows that

$$F = \frac{G_1G_2G_3kT_0B + G_1G_2G_3kT_{e1}B + G_2G_3kT_{e2}B + G_3kT_{e3}B}{G_1G_2G_3kT_0B}$$

$$= 1 + \frac{T_{e1}}{T_0} + \frac{T_{e2}}{G_1T_0} + \frac{T_{e3}}{G_1G_2T_0} \qquad (9.58)$$

$$= F_1 + \frac{F_2 - 1}{G_1} + \frac{F_3 - 1}{G_1G_2}$$

Here we have used Eq. (9.55) in the last step so that $T_{e1}/T_0 = F_1 - 1$, $T_{e2}/T_0 = F_2 - 1$, and $T_{e3}/T_0 = F_3 - 1$. Equation (9.58) gives the noise factor of the cascaded system in terms of the noise factor and gain of each stage. We can obtain a similar expression for the equivalent noise temperature T_e of the system by rearranging the second line of the above equation and making use of the relation between T_e and F given in Eq. (9.54):

$$T_e = T_0(F - 1)$$
$$= T_{e1} + \frac{T_{e2}}{G_1} + \frac{T_{e3}}{G_1G_2} \qquad (9.59)$$

It is clear from the above discussion that in the general case of a cascade connection of n noisy devices, the system noise factor and equivalent noise temperature are given by

$$T_e = T_{e1} + \frac{T_{e2}}{G_1} + \frac{T_{e3}}{G_1G_2} + \frac{T_{e4}}{G_1G_2G_3} + \cdots + \frac{T_{en}}{G_1G_2G_3 \cdots G_{n-1}}$$

$$F = F_1 + \frac{F_2 - 1}{G_1} + \frac{F_3 - 1}{G_1G_2} + \frac{F_4 - 1}{G_1G_2G_3} + \cdots + \frac{F_n - 1}{G_1G_2G_3 \cdots G_{n-1}} \qquad (9.60)$$

Let us take a moment to understand the implication of this important result on the design of communication receivers to minimise their noisiness. The noise factor of the receiver is dominated by the contribution of the first stage — the first device seen by the incoming signal. The contribution from each subsequent stage is reduced by the gains of all preceding stages. Therefore, to minimise the noise factor (or noise temperature) of a receiver, we must place a low-noise high-gain amplifier at the front end or first stage of the receiver, hence the ubiquitous front-end *low-noise amplifier* (LNA). In fact, if the gain G_1 of the amplifier is high enough, then $F \approx F_1$ and the receiver is practically immune to the effect of noisy components, such as mixers, that follow the first stage.

WORKED EXAMPLE   9.8

Arrangement of receiver stages

Fig. 9.16 shows three different arrangements of the same stages of a receiver. We wish to examine the noise figure and noise temperature of the receiver under each arrangement.

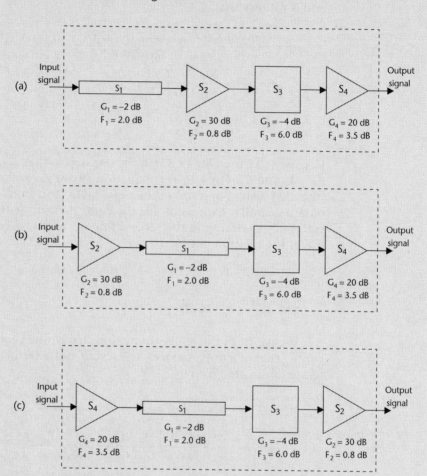

Figure 9.16   Arrangement of receiver stages.

The gain and noise figure of the receiver stages are expressed in dB in Fig. 9.16. Before applying Eq. (9.60), we must express these values as ratios, as follows.

$$F_1 = 2 \text{ dB} = 1.585; \quad G_1 = -2 \text{ dB} = 0.631$$
$$F_2 = 0.8 \text{ dB} = 1.202; \quad G_2 = 30 \text{ dB} = 1000$$
$$F_3 = 6 \text{ dB} = 3.981; \quad G_3 = -4 \text{ dB} = 0.398$$
$$F_4 = 3.5 \text{ dB} = 2.239; \quad G_4 = 20 \text{ dB} = 100$$

(a) For the $S_1S_2S_3S_4$ arrangement we obtain

$$F = F_1 + \frac{F_2 - 1}{G_1} + \frac{F_3 - 1}{G_1 G_2} + \frac{F_4 - 1}{G_1 G_2 G_3}$$

$$= 1.585 + \frac{1.202 - 1}{0.631} + \frac{3.981 - 1}{0.631 \times 1000} + \frac{2.239 - 1}{0.631 \times 1000 \times 0.398}$$

$$= 1.915 = 2.82 \text{ dB}$$

and $T_e = 290(F - 1) = 265$ K.

(b) For the $S_2S_1S_3S_4$ arrangement we obtain

$$F = F_2 + \frac{F_1 - 1}{G_2} + \frac{F_3 - 1}{G_2 G_1} + \frac{F_4 - 1}{G_2 G_1 G_3}$$

$$= 1.202 + \frac{1.585 - 1}{1000} + \frac{3.981 - 1}{1000 \times 0.631} + \frac{2.239 - 1}{1000 \times 0.631 \times 0.398}$$

$$= 1.213 = 0.84 \text{ dB}$$

and $T_e = 290(F - 1) = 62$ K.

(c) Finally, for the $S_4S_1S_3S_2$ arrangement we obtain

$$F = F_4 + \frac{F_1 - 1}{G_4} + \frac{F_3 - 1}{G_4 G_1} + \frac{F_2 - 1}{G_4 G_1 G_3}$$

$$= 2.239 + \frac{1.585 - 1}{100} + \frac{3.981 - 1}{100 \times 0.631} + \frac{1.202 - 1}{100 \times 0.631 \times 0.398}$$

$$= 2.30 = 3.62 \text{ dB}$$

and $T_e = 290(F - 1) = 377$ K.

The above results show that the equivalent noise temperature T_e of the receiver depends crucially on the arrangement of the stages. Typically, S_1 would be a lossy waveguide or coaxial cable connecting an outdoor antenna to the rest of the receiver block located indoors; S_2 would be a low-noise amplifier (LNA), S_3 a mixer, and S_4 another (more noisy) amplifier.

If the LNA is the very first stage seen by the input signal (from the antenna) — achieved by locating it outdoors with the antenna — then we have the $S_2S_1S_3S_4$ arrangement and the lowest possible noise temperature (62 K in this case). Note, as discussed earlier, that the noise figure of the receiver (0.84 dB) is only marginally worse than that of the LNA (0.8 dB).

If the lossy feed run precedes the LNA (the $S_1S_2S_3S_4$ arrangement), we have a higher noise temperature — 265 K in this case, which is an increase of $10\log_{10}(265/62) = 6.3$ dB in noise power compared to the previous arrangement.

The situation is worse still with the $S_4S_1S_3S_2$ arrangement shown in Fig. 9.16(c). Here the LNA is relegated to the last stage. As a result, $T_e = 377$ K, and the noise power is about 8 dB higher than could be achieved using a different arrangement of exactly the same set of receiver stages.

An increase in noise power leads to a reduction in signal-to-noise ratio by the same amount. Thus, in the design of communication receivers, a high-gain LNA must be used at the front end, and every effort must be made to keep losses preceding the LNA to a minimum. Losses and noise in devices that follow a high-gain LNA have a negligible effect on the noise temperature of the receiver.

9.7.5 Overall system noise temperature

We are now in a position to determine the noise temperature T_{sys} of the overall receiver system. This allows us to place a single noise source of temperature T_{sys} at a reference point in the overall system. The system is then replaced by its noiseless version for all purposes, e.g. determining the carrier-to-noise ratio at the demodulator input. The overall system noise temperature T_{sys} accounts for all noise in the receiver. This includes

1. Antenna noise, represented by the noise temperature T_a computed using Eq. (9.15).

2. Noise from a lossy feed run (a coaxial cable or waveguide) that connects the antenna to a low noise amplifier (LNA).

3. Receiver noise, represented by the noise temperature T_e computed using Eq. (9.60). The receiver is usually a cascade connection of several stages starting from the LNA.

Figure 9.17 shows the overall receiver system. It is standard practice to set the reference point at the LNA input, as indicated. Therefore, unless otherwise specified, you may safely assume that a given value of T_{sys} refers to this point. However, provided there is consistency, exactly the same SNR will be obtained using some other point as a reference (e.g. the antenna output port just before the feed run). To determine T_{sys}, we calculate the total noise power P_n at the reference point and equate this to $kT_{sys}B$.

A self-explanatory noise model of the overall system is shown in Fig. 9.17(b). It is assumed that all stages are matched so that the available noise power is delivered at every point. However, the value of SNR will be the same under unmatched conditions, since the signal and noise power are reduced by the same factor at every mismatch point. The noise temperature of the feed run depends on its physical or ambient temperature T_{amb} (usually taken to be 290 K) and its numeric loss L (≥ 1):

$$T_f = T_{amb}(L-1)$$

(9.61)

The feed run passes noise from its input to its output, reduced by the factor L. At the reference point, the total noise power is therefore

$$\frac{kT_aB}{L} + \frac{kT_fB}{L} + kT_eB \equiv kT_{sys}B$$

This gives the desired overall system noise temperature

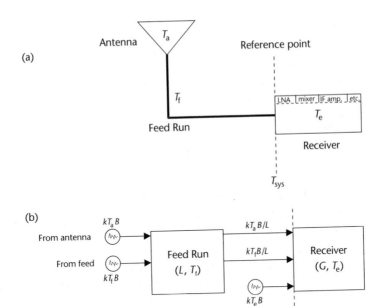

Figure 9.17 Overall noise temperature T_{sys} of receiver system: (a) overall receiver system; (b) boise model.

$$T_{sys} = T_e + (T_a + T_f)/L \qquad (9.62)$$
$$= T_e + T_a/L + 290(1 - 1/L)$$

where we have used Eq. (9.61) with $T_{amb} = 290$ K.

If there is no loss between the antenna and the receiver, $L = 1$, and

$$T_{sys} = T_e + T_a \qquad (9.63)$$

Equation (9.63) holds, for example, where the LNA is mounted in a unit just under the antenna so that the feed length is negligible. In this case, there is a cable leading from the output of the LNA to the remaining sections of the receiver inside a building. The noise effect of this cable run is included in the computation of T_e using Eq. (9.60), with the cable serving as the second stage of the cascade connection and $T_{e2} = T_f$, and $G_2 = 1/L$.

WORKED EXAMPLE 9.9

Overall system noise temperature

Determine the overall system noise temperature T_{sys} of the satellite communication Earth station in Fig. 9.18.

The noise temperature T_e of the receiver block enclosed in a dotted rectangle is obtained as follows using Eq. (9.60).

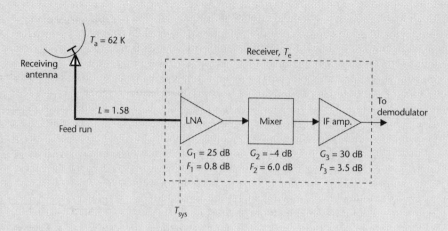

Figure 9.18 Earth station receiver.

$$F = F_1 + \frac{F_2 - 1}{G_1} + \frac{F_3 - 1}{G_1 G_2}$$

$$= 1.202 + \frac{3.981 - 1}{316.23} + \frac{2.239 - 1}{316.23 \times 0.3981}$$

$$= 1.222$$

$$T_e = 290(F - 1) = 64 \text{ K}$$

The overall system noise temperature then follows from Eq. (9.62):

$$T_{sys} = T_e + T_a/L + 290(1 - 1/L)$$

$$= 64 + 62/1.58 + 290(1 - 1/1.58)$$

$$= 210 \text{ K}$$

Note that by co-locating the LNA with the antenna, the overall system noise temperature would be reduced to about 126 K (= 64 + 62), providing a reduction of 2.2 dB in noise power.

9.7.6 Signal-to-noise ratio

We now have all the information required to determine the ratio between the power in the received signal at the input of the demodulator and the noise power at the same point. For a fixed-link line-of-sight transmission system, such as in microwave relay and satellite communications, the received signal power P_r at the reference point in the receiver is given by an extension of Eq. (9.5) to include the following extra losses:

1. Attenuation in the atmosphere, L_{atm}.

2. All losses in the receiver before the reference point, L_r. The reference point will usually be at the LNA input. We include in L_r, losses due to antenna mispointing and polarisation, antenna feed losses, waveguide or coaxial cable losses, etc.

Thus, at the reference point

$$P_r = EIRP - L_s - L_{atm} + G_r - L_r \quad (dBW)$$
$$= EIRP - L_s - L_{atm} + G \quad (dBW) \tag{9.64}$$

where $G = G_r - L_r$ represents the net gain of the receive antenna. The noise power P_n at this point is given by

$$P_n = kT_{sys}B = -228.6 + 10\log_{10}(T_{sys}) + 10\log_{10}(B) \quad dBW \tag{9.65}$$

Subtracting Eq. (9.65) from (9.64) yields the signal-to-noise ratio of the entire receiver system up to the demodulator input, also denoted C/N — for carrier-to-noise ratio:

$$C/N = EIRP - L_s - L_{atm} + 228.6 + 10\log\left(\frac{G}{T_{sys}}\right) - 10\log B$$
$$C/N_o = EIRP - L_s - L_{atm} + 228.6 + 10\log\left(\frac{G}{T_{sys}}\right) \tag{9.66}$$

This is an important result, which should be well understood. C/N_o is the ratio between received signal power and the noise power density. $EIRP$ is the transmit power (dBW) plus net transmit antenna gain (dB). L_s is the spreading loss given by Eq. (9.5). G is the net gain of the receive antenna (expressed as a ratio). The ratio between G and the system noise temperature T_{sys} is a *figure of merit* that gives some indication of a receiving system's ability to handle weak signals.

We emphasise that the signal-to-noise ratio calculated as above at the reference point is maintained at every point in the receiver up to the demodulator input, since all noise have been accounted for in T_{sys} and the receiver stages are therefore treated as noiseless. Furthermore, most transmission systems employ frequency or phase modulation in which the modulated carrier amplitude remains constant. In this case the received signal power is synonymous with received carrier power.

9.8 Noise effects in analogue communication systems

The performance of an analogue communication system is measured by the signal-to-noise ratio $(SNR)_o$ at the demodulator output, which may be expressed as

$$(SNR)_o = (SNR)_i + G_p \tag{9.67}$$

Here, $(SNR)_i$ is the signal-to-noise ratio at the demodulator input given by Eq. (9.66), where it is denoted as (C/N), and G_p is the processing gain of the demodulator. Analogue systems can be compared based on the processing gain that they afford. Is it less or greater than 0 dB? Can it be increased to improve $(SNR)_0$ or is it fixed? If it can be increased, what is the cost? These issues are now briefly considered. But first we must make an important distinction between the signal powers involved in Eq. (9.67). At the demodulator input the signal power is the total power in the received modulated carrier, whereas at the demodulator output it refers to the power in the recovered message signal.

The analogue modulation systems considered below were discussed extensively in Chapters 3 and 4, and you may wish to refer to the relevant sections of these chapters if in need of further information. Here we take the approach of walking through a model receiver for each system in order to determine their processing gain G_p. For simplicity, we assume a sinusoidal message signal. By virtue of the superposition principle, the results are applicable to a general message signal, which is simply a discrete or continuous sum of sinusoids.

9.8.1 DSB

Figure 9.19 shows a double-sideband (DSB) receiver model. The signal $v_a(t)$ at point a in the receiver consists of the wanted DSB signal $v_{dsb}(t)$, and a narrowband noise signal $v_n(t)$, which we represent in the canonical form of Eq. (9.41):

$$v_a(t) = v_{dsb}(t) + v_n(t)$$
$$v_{dsb}(t) = A\cos[2\pi(f_c + f_m)t] + A\cos[2\pi(f_c - f_m)t]$$
$$v_n(t) = v_{nI}(t)\cos(2\pi f_c t) - v_{nQ}(t)\sin(2\pi f_c t)$$
$$(9.68)$$

Thus the received signal power P_s and noise power P_n at this point, and hence $(SNR)_i$ are given by

$$P_s = A^2$$
$$P_n = N_o B$$
$$(SNR)_i = A^2/N_o B$$
$$(9.69)$$

At point b we have

$$\begin{aligned}
v_b(t) &= v_a(t) \times 2\cos(2\pi f_c t) \\
&= 2A\cos(2\pi f_m t) + v_{nI}(t) \quad \} \qquad \text{Passed by LPF} \\
&\quad + A\cos[2\pi(2f_c + f_m)t] \\
&\quad + A\cos[2\pi(2f_c - f_m)t] \\
&\quad + v_{nI}(t)\cos[2\pi(2f_c)t] \qquad \text{Rejected by LPF} \\
&\quad - v_{nQ}(t)\sin[2\pi(2f_c)t]
\end{aligned}$$
$$(9.70)$$

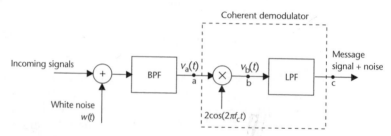

Figure 9.19 Model receiver for coherent demodulation of DSB, SSB, and AM.

It follows that after the LPF, at point c, the (message) signal power P_s and noise power P_n, and hence $(SNR)_o$ are given by

$$P_s = 2A^2$$
$$P_n = N_oB$$
$$(SNR)_o = 2A^2/N_oB$$

(9.71)

Dividing Eq. (9.71) by (9.69) yields the processing gain of the DSB receiver

$$G_p = (SNR)_o/(SNR)_i$$
$$= 2 = 3 \text{ dB}$$

(9.72)

This is an important result, which shows that a coherent DSB receiver delivers a 3 dB improvement in SNR. This comes about because there are two message sidebands in $v_{dsb}(t)$, which are translated down to baseband and added coherently. This doubles the message signal power within the message bandwidth. Noise power, on the other hand, is not doubled since the quadrature component is rejected.

9.8.2 SSB

To determine the processing gain of a single-sideband (SSB) demodulator, we again employ the receiver model of Fig. 9.19, and proceed as before, but with single-sideband transmission. At point a,

$$v_a(t) = v_{ssb}(t) + v_n(t)$$
$$= A\cos[2\pi(f_c + f_m)t] + v_{nI}(t)\cos(2\pi f_c t) - v_{nQ}(t)\sin(2\pi f_c t)$$
$$P_s = A^2/2$$
$$P_n = N_oB$$
$$(SNR)_i = A^2/2N_oB$$

(9.73)

and at point b,

$$v_b(t) = v_a(t) \times 2\cos(2\pi f_c t)$$
$$= A\cos(2\pi f_m t) + v_{nI}(t) \quad \} \quad \text{Passed by LPF}$$
$$+A\cos[2\pi(2f_c + f_m)t]$$
$$+v_{nI}(t)\cos[2\pi(2f_c)t] \quad \Big\} \quad \text{Rejected by LPF}$$
$$-v_{nQ}(t)\sin[2\pi(2f_c)t]$$

(9.74)

Thus the (message) signal power P_s, noise power P_n, and hence $(SNR)_o$ are given by

$$P_s = A^2/2$$
$$P_n = N_oB$$
$$(SNR)_o = A^2/2N_oB$$

(9.75)

The processing gain of an SSB receiver then follows from the ratio between Eq. (9.75) and (9.73):

$$G_p = (SNR)_o/(SNR)_i$$
$$= 1 = 0 \text{ dB} \tag{9.76}$$

We see that SNR is unchanged in an SSB receiver. An important point must be made here regarding the noise performance of SSB and DSB receivers. The noise power at the input of a DSB demodulator is higher than that at the input of an SSB demodulator by 3 dB, since DSB operates at twice the transmission bandwidth. Thus, for the same signal power, $(SNR)_i$ for DSB transmission is 3 dB lower than that of SSB. And with a 3 dB processing gain in the DSB case, it is clear that equal-power DSB and SSB transmissions have exactly the same output SNR. However, as discussed in Chapter 3, DSB is more susceptible to distortions due to selective fading.

9.8.3 AM

The received signal in double-sideband transmitted-carrier amplitude modulation (AM) is given by

$$v_{am}(t) = V_c \cos(2\pi f_c t)$$
$$+ \frac{mV_c}{2} \cos[2\pi(f_c - f_m)t]$$
$$+ \frac{mV_c}{2} \cos[2\pi(f_c + f_m)t] \tag{9.77}$$

where m is the modulation factor. You may wish to consult Section 3.3 if in any doubt. For coherent demodulation, we may again walk through Fig. 9.19 to obtain the following results.

At point a,

$$v_a(t) = v_{am}(t) + v_n(t)$$
$$P_s = \frac{V_c^2}{2}(1 + m^2/2)$$
$$P_n = N_o B$$
$$(SNR)_i = V_c^2(1 + m^2/2)/2N_o B \tag{9.78}$$

(handwritten: $5000 = \frac{Vc^2}{2}(1 + 0.3^2/2)$)

At point b,

$$v_b(t) = v_a(t) \times 2\cos(2\pi f_c t)$$

$$= mV_c \cos(2\pi f_m t) + v_{nI}(t) \quad \} \quad \text{Accepted}$$

$$\left. \begin{aligned} &+ \frac{mV_c}{2} \cos[2\pi(2f_c + f_m)t] \\ &+ \frac{mV_c}{2} \cos[2\pi(2f_c - f_m)t] \\ &+ V_c + V_c \cos[2\pi(2f_c)t] \\ &+ v_{nI}(t) \cos[2\pi(2f_c)t] \\ &- v_{nQ}(t) \sin[2\pi(2f_c)t] \end{aligned} \right\} \quad \text{Rejected} \tag{9.79}$$

Note in the above expression for $v_b(t)$ that V_c is a DC term, which does not contribute to information and is rejected. Thus the (message) signal power P_s, noise power P_n, and hence $(SNR)_o$ are given by

$$P_s = m^2 V_c^2 / 2$$
$$P_n = N_o B \tag{9.80}$$
$$(\text{SNR})_o = m^2 V_c^2 / 2 N_o B$$

The processing gain of a coherent AM receiver then follows from Eq. (9.80) and (9.78):

$$G_p = (\text{SNR})_o / (\text{SNR})_i$$
$$= \frac{2m^2}{2 + m^2} \tag{9.81}$$

The maximum processing gain of a coherent AM demodulator occurs at 100% modulation ($m = 1$), and is only –1.76 dB. The demodulator has a negative processing gain, and the signal-to-noise ratio is degraded in the demodulator by an amount that increases rapidly as the modulation factor m decreases. Thus, the noise performance of AM is inferior to that of SSB and DSB.

Equation (9.81) was derived for coherent AM demodulation. However, it is also applicable to the more commonly used technique of envelope demodulation under conditions of a large $(\text{SNR})_i$. On the other hand, if $(\text{SNR})_i \ll 1$, the noise performance deteriorates much more rapidly than given by Eq. (9.81). This is referred to as the *threshold effect*.

9.8.4 FM

Consider the simple FM receiver model shown in Fig. 9.20. The signal $v_a(t)$ at point 'a' consists of a frequency-modulated carrier $v_{fm}(t)$ and narrowband noise $v_n(t)$, which we represent using the envelope form of Eq. (9.44). Thus,

$$v_a(t) = v_{fm}(t) + v_n(t)$$
$$v_{fm}(t) = A \cos[2\pi f_c t + \phi(t)]$$
$$v_n(t) = r(t) \cos[2\pi f_c t + \psi(t)] \tag{9.82}$$
$$P_s = A^2 / 2; \quad P_n = N_o f_m; \quad \text{SNR}_i = A^2 / (2 N_o f_m)$$

Here, P_n is the noise power in the message bandwidth f_m, and $\phi(t)$ contains the message signal in the manner discussed in Chapter 4. In particular, for a sinusoidal message signal of frequency f_m,

$$\phi(t) = \beta \sin(2\pi f_m t) \tag{9.83}$$

where β is the modulation index.

The signal $v_a(t)$ is given in amplitude and phase $\theta(t)$ by the resultant of the phasor addition shown in Fig. 9.21. The limiter eliminates all amplitude

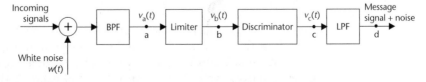

Figure 9.20 Model of FM receiver.

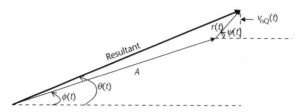

Figure 9.21 Phasor addition.

fluctuations in $v_a(t)$ caused by the noise component, while the discriminator (discussed in Chapter 4) produces an output $v_c(t)$ that is proportional to the rate of change of the angle $\theta(t)$ of its input signal:

$$v_c(t) = \frac{1}{2\pi} \frac{d\theta(t)}{dt} \qquad (9.84)$$

To simplify the evaluation of this equation, we will assume that the noise component $r(t)$ is much smaller (most of the time) than the carrier amplitude A, so that

$$\theta(t) \approx \phi(t) + \frac{r(t)}{A} \sin[\psi(t) - \phi(t)]$$

$$\approx \phi(t) + \frac{r(t)}{A} \sin[\psi(t)] \qquad (9.85)$$

$$= \phi(t) + \frac{v_{nQ}(t)}{A}$$

In the above, the second approximation is valid because the second term represents the effect of noise, and we may discard the shift of $\phi(t)$ in the argument of the sine function in that term without fundamentally altering its uniform distribution. The last step in Eq. (9.85) follows from the definition of $r(t)$, and is indicated on the phasor diagram. Equations (9.83), (9.84) and (9.85) then yield a discriminator output

$$v_c(t) = \beta f_m \cos(2\pi f_m t) + \frac{1}{2\pi A} \frac{dv_{nQ}(t)}{dt} \qquad (9.86)$$

$$= \beta f_m \cos(2\pi f_m t) + v_{nd}(t)$$

The first term represents the output message signal, while the second term represents the noise term. The amount of noise that accompanies the message signal is limited in the low-pass filter to the noise power within the message bandwidth f_m. Thus, the output (message) signal power is

$$P_s = \beta^2 f_m^2 / 2 \qquad (9.87)$$

To determine the output noise power, recall from Chapter 4 that the process of differentiation performed in Eq. (9.86) on $v_{nQ}(t)$ is equivalent to passing the quadrature noise component through a high-pass filter of transfer function $j2\pi f$. Thus, the noise signal $v_{nd}(t)$ is the result of passing $v_{nQ}(t)$ through a filter of transfer function

$$H(f) = \frac{j2\pi f}{2\pi A} = \frac{jf}{A} \tag{9.88}$$

The power spectral density $S_{nd}(f)$ of $v_{nd}(t)$ follows from Eq. (9.31) and the spectrum of $v_{nQ}(t)$ plotted in Fig. 9.7(c):

$$S_{nd}(f) = \begin{cases} N_o f^2 / A^2, & |f| \le B/2 \\ 0, & \text{elsewhere} \end{cases} \tag{9.89}$$

We see that $v_{nd}(t)$ is coloured noise, and its power P_n within the message bandwidth f_m — which is usually less than half the transmission bandwidth — is obtained by integration:

$$\begin{aligned} P_n &= \int_{-f_m}^{f_m} \frac{N_o f^2}{A^2} \, df \\ &= \frac{2 N_o f_m^3}{3A^2} \end{aligned} \tag{9.90}$$

Dividing Eq. (9.87) by (9.90) gives the output signal-to-noise ratio as follows:

$$\text{SNR}_o = \frac{3\beta^2 A^2}{4 N_o f_m} \tag{9.91}$$

Finally, the processing gain of the FM receiver follows from this equation and Eq. (9.82):

$$G_p = \frac{(\text{SNR})_o}{(\text{SNR})_i} = \frac{3}{2}\beta^2 \tag{9.92}$$

This is an important result. It tells us that the signal-to-noise ratio at the FM demodulator output increases as the square of the modulation index. Recall that the required transmission bandwidth increases with β according to the relation

$$B = 2(\beta + 1)f_m \tag{9.93}$$

Thus, unlike AM and its variant techniques, FM provides a bandwidth for SNR improvement trade-off, with SNR increasing as the square of bandwidth. Note however, that this result — Eq. (9.92) — was obtained on the assumption that $(\text{SNR})_i \gg 1$. As $(\text{SNR})_i$ decreases, e.g. by excessive increase in transmission bandwidth B and hence noise power, a point is reached when the actual $(\text{SNR})_o$ is significantly less than predicted by this result. This is the *threshold effect*.

Before leaving the subject of noise effects in FM systems, it is worth noting that the spectral shape of the coloured noise $v_{nd}(t)$ at the discriminator output suggests a means of further improving the signal-to-noise ratio. The psd of $v_{nd}(t)$ increases as the square of frequency, so we can reduce output noise power by using a low-pass filter of transfer function $H_d(f)$ to attenuate the high-frequency components of $v_{nd}(t)$. This would distort the message signal. To prevent this, we boost the high-frequency components of the message signal at the transmitter using a special high-pass filter of transfer function $H_p(f)$, where

$$H_p(f) = \frac{1}{H_d(f)} \tag{9.94}$$

The filtering operation at the transmitter is known as *pre-emphasis*, while the inverse operation at the receiver is known as *de-emphasis*. See Section 4.7.3 for circuit diagrams and further discussion of these operations.

9.9 Noise effects in digital communication systems

The performance of a digital communication system is measured by the bit error rate (BER), which depends crucially on the carrier-to-noise ratio at the demodulator input. The exact nature of this dependence was developed in detail in Chapter 7 for various baseband and modulated systems. A summary of this discussion is given in Section 7.10, which you may wish to consult at this point. There we related BER to E_b/N_o, rather than (C/N), where E_b is the energy per bit. The two quantities are related as follows. The amount of signal energy received per second is P_r, the average signal power. And the number of bits received in the same time of one second is R_b, the bit rate. It is clear then that R_b bits share P_r joules of energy, giving the following energy per bit:

$$E_b = \frac{P_r}{R_b} \tag{9.95}$$

Therefore,

$$\begin{aligned}
\frac{E_b}{N_o} &= \frac{P_r}{N_o R_b} \\
&= \frac{1}{R_b}(C/N_o) \\
&= \frac{B}{R_b}(C/N)
\end{aligned} \tag{9.96}$$

We may also express the second line above in dB units (noting that $N_o = kT_{sys}$) as follows:

$$\begin{aligned}
\frac{E_b}{N_o} &= \text{Received signal level (dBW)} + 228.6 \\
&\quad - 10\log_{10}(\text{Bit rate}) - 10\log_{10}(T_{sys})
\end{aligned} \tag{9.97}$$

The procedure for assessing the performance of a digital communication receiver in noise is therefore as follows.

1. Determine C/N_o at the demodulator input using Eq. (9.66).
2. Determine E_b/N_o using Eq. (9.96).
3. Calculate the BER corresponding to the above E_b/N_o using one of the equations developed in Chapter 7. The BER expressions applicable to binary transmission — including unipolar baseband (UBB) and bipolar baseband (BBB) are reproduced below for convenience

$$\text{BER} = \begin{cases} \dfrac{1}{2}\,\text{erfc}\!\left(\sqrt{\dfrac{E_b}{2N_o}}\right), & \text{ASK, FSK and UBB} \\[3ex] \dfrac{1}{2}\,\text{erfc}\!\left(\sqrt{\dfrac{E_b}{N_o}}\right), & \text{PSK, QPSK and BBB} \end{cases} \tag{9.98}$$

See Section 7.10 for the case of multilevel modulation.

4. If the BER exceeds the level specified for the particular application (e.g. 10^{-4} for voice and 10^{-7} for data), then there are several options to correct the situation. There will be a number of constraints in considering these options, and the final decision will depend on the priorities of the particular application:

   (a) Increase C/N using the *link budget* parameters in Eq. (9.66). For example, increase *EIRP*, or increase the net gain G of the receive antenna, or reduce the receiver system noise temperature T_{sys}.

   (b) Keep C/N at the original level, but reduce bit rate R_b, which increases E_b/N_o according to Eq. (9.96) or (9.97).

   (c) Choose a different modulation technique, which yields a lower BER at the original E_b/N_o, according to the equations in Section 7.10.

SUMMARY

Our study of noise in communication systems is now complete. You have acquired a thorough grounding in the quantification of random noise and the assessment of their impact on digital and analogue communication systems. Most importantly, you are well acquainted with the design parameters that affect SNR in analogue systems and BER in digital systems.

Some modulation techniques provide more options for SNR improvement beyond the obvious solutions of increasing received signal power or reducing receiving system noise power. For example, in FM transmission, bandwidth can be increased to realise a quadratic increase in SNR. However, a bandwidth–SNR trade-off is non-existent in amplitude modulation and all its variants, including SSB and DSB. Digital transmission, with the possibility of multilevel modulation, allows a greater flexibility than analogue FM in the exchange between transmission bandwidth, transmitted power, BER and transmission capacity or bit rate.

REVIEW QUESTIONS

9.1 A metallic line attenuates a radio frequency signal at the rate 8.686α dB/km, where α is the attenuation coefficient of the line (in neper/km) given by

$$\alpha = \frac{R}{2}\sqrt{\frac{C}{L}} + \frac{G}{2}\sqrt{\frac{L}{C}}$$

Here, R, G, L and C are the primary line constants given for a particular coaxial cable at a frequency of 10 MHz by $L = 234$ µH/km, $C = 93.5$ nF/km, $R = 77.7$ ohm/km, $G = 3450$ µmho/m.

(a) If a 10 V rms signal at 10 MHz is transmitted on this line, determine the rms value of the signal after a distance of 5 km on the line.

(b) The above cable is used for long-distance transmission of a wideband FDM signal that contains frequency components up to 10 MHz. If the signal on the line must be detected before the attenuation of the 10 MHz component exceeds 30 dB, determine the maximum repeater spacing that can be tolerated.

9.2   At audio frequencies (such as on local telephone lines), the conditions $R \gg 2\pi f L$, and $2\pi f C \gg G$ are satisfied. The attenuation constant of a metallic line is then given as a function of frequency f by the approximate expression

$$\alpha = \sqrt{\pi R C f}$$

By how much does a 5 km length of the cable in the previous problem (Question 9.1) attenuate a 1 kHz signal? How does your result compare with the attenuation of the cable at 10 MHz calculated previously?

9.3   The last two questions give expressions for attenuation that apply at radio frequencies (Question 9.1) and at audio frequencies (Question 9.2). The latter has an explicit frequency dependence, whereas the former does not. Does this mean that cable loss is not a function of radio frequency? Discuss fully.

9.4   Attenuation in optical fibre due to Rayleigh scattering is given by the expression

$$L_{sc} = 3.591 \times 10^5 \frac{n^8 p^2 \beta k T_F}{\lambda^4} \text{ dB/km}$$

where

$k \equiv$ Boltzmann's constant $= 1.38 \times 10^{-23}$ J/K
$\lambda \equiv$ Free space wavelength of the light signal
$n \equiv$ Refractive index of the fibre material
$p \equiv$ Photoelastic coefficient
$\beta \equiv$ Isothermal compressibility at temperature T_F
$T_F \equiv$ Freezing temperature at which the irregularities become frozen into the fibre structure.

(a) Determine L_{sc} for transmission over a 200 km distance in the three absorption windows, of nominal wavelengths $\lambda = 820$, 1330 and 1550 nm. The fibre material has the following parameters: $n = 1.45$, $p = 0.286$, $\beta = 7 \times 10^{-11}$ m²/N and $T_F = 1400$ K.

(b) Consider the transmission at 1550 nm. With L_{sc} having such a small value, would regenerators be needed along this link? Give a rough estimate of the total attenuation that would be encountered on this link in practice.

9.5 A satellite has an *EIRP* of 35 dBW and transmits to an Earth station of gain $G_r = 40$ dB over a 38 800 km slant path. Neglecting all other link losses except free-space loss, determine the output power of the Earth station receive antenna in µW for a transmission frequency of

(a) 20 GHz

(b) 12 GHz

(c) 3820 MHz

9.6 The gain of a parabolic antenna of diameter *D* is given by the expression

$$G_r = 9.943 + 10\log_{10}(\eta D^2) - 20\log_{10}(\lambda) \text{ dB}$$

where η is the antenna efficiency and λ, the signal wavelength, is expressed in the same units as *D*. Assuming $\eta = 0.6$,

(a) Determine the diameters of the parabolic antennas used in Question 9.5(a)–(c).

(b) If the three frequencies in Question 9.5 were received using antennas of the same size, how would the outputs compare?

(c) Comment on your results in (a) and (b).

9.7 A transmission at 890 MHz and EIRP = 12 dBW from a base station antenna of height 20 m is received at a distance of 2 km by a mobile unit of height 1.8 m.

(a) Determine the signal power at the output of the receive antenna of gain 3 dB, assuming plane Earth propagation.

(b) What would the output power be under conditions of free-space propagation?

9.8 The arrival of photons at a receiver in an optical fibre communication system is governed by Poisson statistics. This means that if the average number of photons received during a binary 1 interval is µ, then the probability $p(k)$ of detecting *k* photons during any binary 1 interval is given by

$$p(k) = \frac{\mu^k \exp(-\mu)}{k!}$$

Clearly, in an OOK system, an error occurs if no photon is received during a binary 1 interval.

(a) Assuming that binary 1s and 0s are equally likely, derive Eq. (9.17) for the minimum average received power P_r to ensure a specified BER. [*Note*: Energy of one photon = *hf*, where $h (= 6.626 \times 10^{-34}$ Js) is Planck's constant and *f* is the light signal frequency (Hz).]

(b) Determine P_r required for a bit error rate of 10^{-9} in a 1310 nm system operating at 296 Mbaud.

9.9 An Earth station antenna receives a satellite transmission at 40 GHz on a path elevation of 15°. Noise from the Earth's surface enters the antenna via its first sidelobe level at –20 dB.

(a) Determine the antenna noise temperature T_a during a rain event when the total attenuation is 15 dB.

(b) What is the total degradation in carrier-to-noise ratio (CNR) during the above rain event?

(c) What is the noise power delivered by the antenna to a matched waveguide feed in a bandwidth of 6 MHz?

9.10 The thermal noise voltage v_n observed in a certain resistor has a standard deviation $\sigma = 200$ mV.

(a) What is the mean of v_n?

(b) What is the probability that v_n is equal to its mean?

(c) Can v_n have a sample value that exceeds 10 V? Explain.

(d) Determine $Pr(v_n \geq -300$ mV)

(e) If a large number of samples of the noise voltage is taken, what percentage will lie within a range $\pm 3\sigma$ of the mean?

9.11 Determine the noise equivalent bandwidth of the following filters, and compare with their 3 dB bandwidths.

(a) A bandpass filter whose gain response is shown in Fig. 9.22.

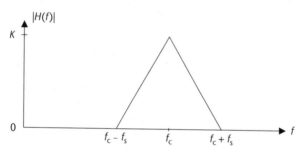

Figure 9.22 Question 9.11(a).

(b) An *n*th order *Butterworth* low-pass filter, with gain response given by

$$|H(f)| = \frac{K}{\sqrt{1+(f/f_o)^{2n}}}$$

where K is a constant.

(c) A *Gaussian* filter whose frequency response is given by

$$H(f) = \exp(-4a\pi^2 f^2 - j2\pi f t_o)$$

where a and t_0 are constants.

(d) The RLC bandpass filter shown in Fig. 9.23.

9.12 (a) Calculate the noise figure and equivalent noise temperature of a cascade connection of an amplifier and a mixer. The amplifier has a noise figure of 5 dB and a gain of 20 dB, while the mixer stage has a noise figure of 12 dB and a gain of –2 dB.

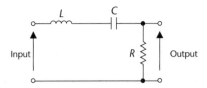

Figure 9.23 Question 9.11(d).

(b) Calculate the signal to noise ratio at the output of the mixer if the signal to noise ratio at the input of the amplifier is 30 dB.

9.13 A satellite receiving Earth station has the following parameters:

(i) Antenna noise temperature (in clear weather) = 70 K.
(ii) Antenna gain = 40 dB.
(iii) Total ohmic losses from antenna feed to LNA input = 3 dB.
(iv) LNA gain = 30 dB, and noise figure = 1.0 dB.
(v) Mixer gain = –3.5 dB, and noise figure = 8.0 dB.
(vi) IF amplifier gain = 25 dB, and noise figure = 4.0 dB.

The satellite transmits at a frequency of 20 GHz with an EIRP of 42 dBW, and the slant path length from the Earth station to the satellite is 40 000 km.

(a) What is the (figure of merit) G/T of the Earth station?
(b) What is E_b/N_0 at a bit rate of 1 Mbit/s?
(c) Determine the maximum bit rate R_{bmax} that can be achieved in clear weather using QPSK if the BER must not exceed 10^{-4}.
(d) If there is a total atmospheric attenuation of 5 dB during rain and the bit rate is maintained at the value obtained in (c), determine the BER. Comment on this result, and specify the maximum bit rate that can be supported during this rain event without exceeding the BER limit of 10^{-4}, if the other transmission parameters, including satellite EIRP and Earth station system noise and gains, are unchanged.
(e) Repeat (c) for a BER of 10^{-7}.

9.14 A 100 MHz carrier is frequency modulated by a 15 kHz sinusoidal signal. The (numeric) ratio between the received carrier amplitude and the rms noise voltage at the demodulator input is 28.3. Determine the output SNR of the demodulated signal for the following values of frequency deviation f_d in the FM transmission. Comment on the trend of your results.

(a) f_d = 15 kHz
(b) f_d = 30 kHz
(c) f_d = 75 kHz

Trigonometric identities

Let us start from the following compound angle relations, which can be readily obtained from the solution of triangles:

$$\sin(A + B) = \sin A \cos B + \cos A \sin B \tag{A.1}$$

$$\sin(A - B) = \sin A \cos B - \cos A \sin B \tag{A.2}$$

$$\cos(A + B) = \cos A \cos B - \sin A \sin B \tag{A.3}$$

$$\cos(A - B) = \cos A \cos B + \sin A \sin B \tag{A.4}$$

We obtain identities for the multiplication of sinusoids as follows:

1. Subtract Eq. (A.3) from Eq. (A.4) to obtain (A.5).
2. Add Eqs. (A.3) and (A.4) to obtain (A.6).
3. Add Eqs. (A.1) and (A.2) to obtain (A.7).

Thus,

$$\sin A \sin B = \tfrac{1}{2}[\cos(A - B) - \cos(A + B)] \tag{A.5}$$

$$\cos A \cos B = \tfrac{1}{2}[\cos(A + B) + \cos(A - B)] \tag{A.6}$$

$$\sin A \cos B = \tfrac{1}{2}[\sin(A + B) + \sin(A - B)] \tag{A.7}$$

Noting that Eqs. (A.1)–(A.7) hold for all values of A and B, we can obtain other very useful identities as follows:

1. Replace B with A in Eqs. (A.1), (A.3), (A.5), (A.6) and (A.4) to obtain Eqs. (A.8) to (A.12), respectively.
2. Substitute $B = 180°$ and $B = 90°$, in Eqs. (A.1) to (A.4) to obtain Eqs. (A.13) to (A.16), respectively.
3. Finally, substitute $A = 0°$ in Eqs. (A.2) and (A.4) to obtain Eqs. (A.17) and (A.18), respectively.

Thus,

$$\sin 2A = 2 \sin A \cos A \tag{A.8}$$

$$\cos 2A = \cos^2 A - \sin^2 A \qquad\qquad (A.9)$$

$$\sin^2 A = \tfrac{1}{2}(1 - \cos 2A) \qquad\qquad (A.10)$$

$$\cos^2 A = \tfrac{1}{2}(1 + \cos 2A) \qquad\qquad (A.11)$$

$$\sin^2 A + \cos^2 A = 1 \qquad\qquad (A.12)$$

$$\sin(A \pm 180°) = -\sin A \qquad\qquad (A.13)$$

$$\cos(A \pm 180°) = -\cos A \qquad\qquad (A.14)$$

$$\sin(A \pm 90°) = \pm\cos A \qquad\qquad (A.15)$$

$$\cos(A \pm 90°) = \mp\sin A \qquad\qquad (A.16)$$

$$\sin(-B) = -\sin B \qquad\qquad (A.17)$$

$$\cos(-B) = \cos B \qquad\qquad (A.18)$$

Transmission of ASCII-coded data

B.1 Asynchronous transmission

Data are transmitted one character (or byte) at a time. Each byte consists of a 7-bit ASCII codeword plus a parity bit for error detection. The data byte is carried in a *frame* consisting of one start bit, the byte and one or two stop bits. The asynchronous transmission of letter M is shown in Fig. B.1. The start bit is signalled as a transition from idle state (binary 1) to a binary 0 state, while the stop bit is signalled as a return to the idle state. The main disadvantage of asynchronous transmission is its poor efficiency. To transmit seven information bits, it incurs an overhead of four bits — comprising one parity bit, one start bit and two stop bits. The data transmission efficiency η of this technique is therefore

$$\eta = \frac{\text{Number of information bits}}{\text{Number of transmitted bits}} = \frac{7}{11} = 63.6\% \qquad \text{(B.1)}$$

Asynchronous transmission is not suitable for quick transmission of large volumes of data and is used mostly for transmission of keyboard inputs on ASCII-encoded terminals.

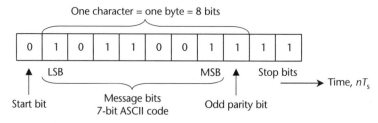

Figure B.1 Frame format for asynchronous transmission of the character M. The ASCII code for this is 1001101. Note that the LSB is transmitted first.

B.2 Synchronous transmission

Synchronous transmission provides a vastly improved efficiency and supports higher data rates. Information or message bits are segmented into blocks and each block is carried in a frame or *protocol data unit* (PDU) consisting of a *frame header*, message block and *frame trailer*, as shown in Fig. B.2. The header and trailer constitute a *protocol overhead*. This provides a flag for marking the start and end of frames, a frame (or block) check sequence (FCS) for error detection, a byte or more for frame addressing and a control byte for automatically requesting the retransmission of any faulty data blocks.

For a frame containing a message block of 128 bytes and having a 3-byte header and a 3-byte trailer, the efficiency, following Eq. (B.1), is

$$\eta = \frac{128}{134} = 95.5\% \tag{B.2}$$

A common clock is required at both the transmitter and receiver. This is accomplished by utilising a suitable line code that combines the clock and data signals into one signal at the transmitter. A clock extraction circuit is then employed at the receiver to recover the clock signal from transitions in the transmitted signal.

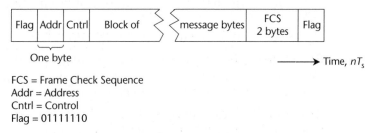

FCS = Frame Check Sequence
Addr = Address
Cntrl = Control
Flag = 01111110

Figure B.2 High-level data link control (HDLC) frame format for synchronous transmission.

Further reading and tables

C.1 Further reading

For a detailed study of the Fourier Transform, see
> Brigham, E. O. (1988) *The Fast Fourier Transform and its Applications*. Englewood Cliffs, NJ: Prentice Hall.

For a more mathematical treatment of communication systems principles, see
> Haykin, S. (2001) *Communication Systems*, 4th edn. New York: Wiley.

For a study of the propagation and system aspects of mobile communications, see
> Steele, R. (1999) *Mobile Radio Communications*, 2nd edn. New York: Wiley.

For an in-depth study of optical communication systems, see
> Agrawal, G. P. (1997) *Fiber-Optic Communication Systems*, 2nd edn. New York: Wiley.

For a readable and detailed presentation of the principles of satellite communications, see
> Pratt, T. and Bostian, C. W. (1986) *Satellite Communications*. New York: Wiley.

For a practical and comprehensive treatment of the technology of satellite communications, see
> Evans, B. G. (1999) *Satellite Communication Systems*, 3rd edn. London: IEE.

For a detailed discussion of the video and audio aspects of analogue and digital television, see
> Robin, M. and Poulin M. (1998) *Digital Television Fundamentals*. New York: McGraw-Hill.

For a study of modern telecommunication networks that includes switching principles, see
> Flood, J. E. (1997) *Telecommunication Networks*, 2nd edn. London: IEE.

For an authoritative and thorough treatment of antennas, see
Kraus, J. D. (1988) *Antennas*, 2nd edn. New York: McGraw-Hill.

For a practical discussion of a wide range of radio wave propagation issues, see
Hall, M. P. M., Barclay L. W. and Hewitt, M. T. (1996) *Propagation of Radiowaves*. London: IEE.

For an extensive collection of mathematical formulas, see
Abramowitz, M. and Stegun, I. A. (1967) *Handbook of Mathematical Functions with Formulas, Graphs, and Mathematical Tables*. New York: Dover.

C.2 Abbreviations used in the text

AAL	ATM adaptation layer
AC	Alternating current
ADC	Analogue to digital conversion (or converter)
ADM	Adaptive delta modulation. *Also* Add/Drop Muldex
ADPCM	Adaptive differential pulse code modulation
ADSL	Asymmetric digital subscriber line
AFC	Automatic frequency control
AM	Amplitude modulation
AMI	Alternate mark inversion
AMPS	Advanced mobile phone system
ANSI	American National Standards Institute
APC	Adaptive predictive coding
APD	Avalanche photodiode
APK	Amplitude and phase keying
APS	Automatic protection switching
ARPANET	Advanced Research Project Agency Network
ARQ	Automatic repeat request
ASCII	American Standard Code for Information Interchange
ASK	Amplitude shift keying
ATM	Asynchronous transfer mode
AU	Administrative unit
AUG	Administrative unit group
AWGN	Additive white Gaussian noise
BBB	Bipolar baseband
BBC	British Broadcasting Corporation
BCD	Binary coded decimal
BER	Bit error rate
BIP	Bit interleaved parity
BJT	Bipolar junction transistor
BNRZ	Bipolar non-return-to-zero
BnZS	Bipolar with n zeros substituted
BPF	Band pass filter
BPSK	Binary phase shift keying
BSF	Band stop filter

B-TE	B-ISDN terminal equipment
CBR	Constant bit rate
CCD	Charge coupled device
CCIR	International radiocommunication consultative committee. Now ITU-R
CCTV	Closed circuit television
CD	Compact disc
CD-R	Recordable compact disc
CDM	Code division multiplexing
CELP	Code excited linear prediction
CEQ	Customer equipment
CLP	Cell loss priority
CMI	Coded mark inversion
CO	Connection oriented
CPFSK	Continuous phase frequency shift keying
CRC	Cyclic redundancy check
CRT	Cathode ray tube
CS	Convergence sub-layer
CSA-CELP	Conjugate structure algebraic code excited linear prediction
CTE	Channel translation equipment
CVSDM	Continuously variable slope delta modulation
DAC	Digital to analogue conversion (or converter)
DC	Direct current
DCC	Data communication channel
DIV	Data-in-voice
DM	Delta modulation
DOV	Data-over-voice
DPCM	Differential pulse code modulation
DPSK	Differential phase shift keying
DS	Direct sequence
DSB	Double sideband suppressed carrier amplitude modulation
DSL	Digital subscriber line
DSM	Delta sigma modulation
DSP	Digital signal processing
DSS	Double sided spectrum
DTE	Data terminal equipment
DVD	Digital versatile disc
EBCDIC	Extended binary coded decimal interchange code
EHF	Extra high frequency
EOW	Engineer's orderwire
ESF	Extended superframe
FAW	Frame alignment word
FCC	Federal Communications Commission
FCP	Frequency comparison pilot
FDL	Facilities data link
FDM	Frequency division multiplexing
FDX	Full duplex
FEBE	Far end block error

FEC	Forward error correction
FET	Field effect transistor
FM	Frequency modulation
FSK	Frequency shift keying
FTTB	Fibre to the building
FTTC	Fibre to the curb
FTTH	Fibre to the home
GCC	Gray code converter
GFC	Generic flow control
GSM	Global System for Mobile communication
GTE	Group translation equipment
HDB3	High density bipolar with three zero maximum
HDSL	High-speed digital subscriber line
HDTV	High-definition television
HDX	Half duplex
HEC	Header error correction
HF	High frequency
HPF	High-pass filter
IA	International alphabet
IBM	International Business Machines Corporation
IC	Integrated circuit
IF	Intermediate frequency
ILD	Injection laser diode
IMBE	Improved multiband excitation
IMP	Inter-modulation product
INI	Inter-network interface
ISB	Independent sideband amplitude modulation
ISDN	Integrated services digital network
ISI	Inter-symbol interference
ISO	International Organisation for Standardisation
ITU	International Telecommunication Union
ITU-D	Development Sector of the ITU
ITU-R	Radio communications Sector of the ITU
ITU-T	Telecommunications standardisation Sector of the ITU
JG	Jumbogroup
LAN	Local area network
LBR	Low bit rate
LCC	Liquid crystal compound
LCO	Inductor–capacitor oscillator
LD	Laser diode
LED	Light-emitting diode
LEO	Low Earth orbit
LF	Low frequency
LHS	Left-hand side
LOS	Line of sight
LPC	Linear predictive coding
LPF	Low-pass filter
lpi	Lines per inch

LSB	Least significant bit. *Also* Lower sideband
LSF	Lower side frequency
LTI	Linear time-invariant
LTP	Long-term prediction
MAN	Metropolitan area network
MAW	Multiframe alignment word
MELP	Mixed excitation linear prediction
MEO	Medium Earth orbit
MF	Medium frequency
MG	Mastergroup
MID	Message identifier
MIDI	Musical instruments' digital interface
MOS	Mean opinion score
MPE	Multipulse excitation
MPE-LPC	Multipulse excited linear predictive coding
MSB	Most significant bit
MSK	Minimum shift keying
MSOH	Multiplex section overhead
MSQE	Mean square quantisation error
NBFM	Narrowband frequency modulation
NBPM	Narrowband phase modulation
NNI	Network node interface
NRZ	Non-return-to-zero
NSP	Network service provider
NTSC	National Television System Committee
OC	Optical carrier
OOK	On–off keying
OSI	Open systems interconnection
PAL	Phase-alternating line
PAM	Pulse amplitude modulation
PC	Personal computer
PCM	Pulse code modulation
PCS	Personal communications system
pdf	Probability density function
PDH	Plesiochronous digital hierarchy
PDM	Pulse duration modulation (= PWM)
PLL	Phase locked loop
PM	Phase modulation
PN	Pseudo-noise
POH	Path overhead
POTS	Plain old telephone service
PPM	Pulse position modulation
PRI	Primary rate ISDN
psd	Power spectral density
PSK	Phase shift keying
PSTN	Public switched telephone network
PTI	Payload type identifier
PWM	Pulse width modulation (= PDM)

QAM	Quadrature amplitude modulation
QOS	Quality of Service
QPSK	Quadri-phase shift keying
RAM	Random access memory
RDS	Running digital sum
RF	Radio frequency
RHS	Right hand side
RLL	Run length limited
rms	Root mean square
RPE	Regular pulse excitation
RSOH	Regenerator section overhead
RZ	Return-to-zero
SAR	Segmentation and re-assembly sub-layer
SB	Sub-band
SDH	Synchronous digital hierarchy
SDM	Space division multiplexing. *Also* Sigma delta modulation
SDSL	Single-line digital subscriber line
SER	Symbol error rate
SG	Supergroup
SHF	Super high frequency
SMF	Sub-multiframe
SMG	Supermastergroup
SNR	Signal-to-noise ratio
SOH	Section overhead
SONET	Synchronous optical network
SPL	Sound pressure level
SQNR	Signal to quantisation noise ratio
SS	Spread spectrum
SSB	Single sideband suppressed carrier amplitude modulation
SSS	Single-sided spectrum
STE	Supergroup translation equipment
STM	Synchronous transport module
STP	Screened twisted pair
STS	Synchronous transport system
SX	Simplex
TAT	Transatlantic telephone cable
TC	Transmission convergence
TDM	Time division multiplexing
TMUX	Transmultiplexer
TRF	Tuned radio frequency
TU	Tributary unit
TUG	Tributary unit group
UBB	Unipolar baseband
UHF	Ultra-high frequency
UMG	U600 mastergroup
UNI	User network interface
UNRZ	Unipolar non-return-to-zero
USB	Upper sideband

USF	Upper side frequency
UTP	Unscreened twisted pair
VBR	Variable bit rate
VC	Virtual container. *Also* Virtual channel
VCI	Virtual channel identifier
VCO	Voltage controlled oscillator
VCR	Video cassette recorder
VDSL	Very high-speed digital subscriber line
VF	Voice frequency
VHF	Very high frequency
VLF	Very low frequency
VLSI	Very-large-scale integrated circuit
VPI	Virtual path identifier
VSB	Vestigial sideband amplitude modulation
WDM	Wavelength division multiplexing
WLL	Wireless local loop
xDSL	Digital subscriber line ¾ various standards
ZRP	Zero-level reference point

C.3 Fourier transforms

Signal	Fourier transform
Unit impulse $\delta(t)$, defined by $$\delta(t) = 0, \quad t \neq 0$$ $$\int_{-\infty}^{\infty} \delta(t)\mathrm{d}t = 1$$	1
A constant (DC) signal of value K	$K\delta(f)$
$\delta(t - t_0)$	$\exp(-\mathrm{j}2\pi f t_0)$
$\exp(\mathrm{j}2\pi f_c t)$	$\delta(f - f_c)$
Signum function $\mathrm{sgn}(t)$, defined by $$\mathrm{sgn}(t) = \begin{cases} 1, & t > 0 \\ 0, & t = 0 \\ -1, & t < 0 \end{cases}$$	$\dfrac{1}{\mathrm{j}\pi f}$
$\dfrac{1}{\pi t}$	$-\mathrm{j}\,\mathrm{sgn}(f)$
Unit step function $u(t)$, defined by $$u(t) = \begin{cases} 1, & t > 0 \\ 0, & t < 0 \end{cases}$$	$\dfrac{1}{2}\delta(f) + \dfrac{1}{\mathrm{j}2\pi f}$

Signal	Fourier transform
Rectangular pulse $\text{rect}(t/\tau)$, defined by $$\text{rect}\left(\frac{t}{\tau}\right) = \begin{cases} 1, & -\frac{\tau}{2} \le t \le \frac{\tau}{2} \\ 0, & |t| > \frac{\tau}{2} \end{cases}$$	$\tau\,\text{sinc}(f\tau)$
Sinc function $\text{sinc}(2t/\tau)$ defined by $$\text{sinc}\left(\frac{2t}{\tau}\right) = \frac{\sin(2\pi t/\tau)}{2\pi t/\tau}$$	$\dfrac{\tau}{2}\text{rect}\left(f\dfrac{\tau}{2}\right)$
Triangular pulse $\text{trian}(t/\tau)$, defined by $$\text{trian}\left(\frac{t}{\tau}\right) = \begin{cases} 1 - |2/\tau|t, & -\tau/2 \le t \le \tau/2 \\ 0, & |t| > \tau/2 \end{cases}$$	$\dfrac{\tau}{2}\text{sinc}^2\left(f\dfrac{\tau}{2}\right)$
$\cos(2\pi f_c t)$	$\frac{1}{2}\delta(f - f_c) + \frac{1}{2}\delta(f + f_c)$
$\sin(2\pi f_c t)$	$\dfrac{1}{2j}\delta(f - f_c) - \dfrac{1}{2j}\delta(f + f_c)$
$\exp(-\pi t^2)$	$\exp(-\pi f^2)$
$\exp(-at)u(t), \quad a > 0$	$\dfrac{1}{a + j2\pi f}$
$\exp(-a|t|), \quad a > 0$	$\dfrac{2a}{a^2 + (2\pi f)^2}$

C.4 Constants

Acceleration due to gravity g	9.80665 m/s^2
Avogadro's number N	6.023×10^{26}/(kg mol)
Base of natural logarithm e	2.7182818285
Bohr magneton β	9.27×10^{-24} Am^2
Boltzmann's constant k	1.38×10^{-23} J/K
Characteristic impedance of free space Z_0	120π Ω
Electron charge q_e	1.602×10^{-19} C
Electron rest mass m_e	9.109×10^{-31} kg
Faraday constant F	9.65×10^7 C/(kg mol)
Permeability of free space μ_0	$4\pi \times 10^{-7}$ H/m
Permittivity of free space ε_0	8.85×10^{-12} F/m

Pi π	3.1415926536
Planck's constant h	6.626×10^{-34} J s
Proton mass m_p	1.672×10^{-27} kg
Speed of light in vacuum c	2.9979×10^8 m/s
Stefan–Boltzmann constant σ	5.67×10^{-8} W/(m²K⁴)
Universal constant of gravitation G	6.67×10^{-11} Nm²/kg²
Universal gas constant R_0	8314 J/(kg mol K)

C.5　SI units

	Quantity	Unit	Symbol	Equivalent
Basic units	Area	square metre	m²	—
	Electric current	ampere	A	—
	Length	metre	m	—
	Luminous intensity	candela	cd	—
	Mass	kilogram	kg	—
	Plane angle	radian	rad	—
	Temperature	kelvin	K	—
	Time	second	s	—
	Volume	cubic metre	m³	—
Derived units	Capacitance	farad	F	A s/V
	Charge	coulomb	C	A s
	Electric field strength	—	—	V/m
	Electric flux density	—	—	C/m²
	Electric potential	volt	V	W/A
	Energy, work or heat	joule	J	N m
	Force	newton	N	kg m/s²
	Frequency	hertz	Hz	s⁻¹
	Inductance	henry	H	V s/A = N m/A²
	Magnetic field strength	—	—	A/m
	Magnetic flux	weber	Wb	V s = N m/A
	Magnetic flux density	tesla	T	Wb/m²
	Power	watt	W	J/s
	Pressure or stress	pascal	Pa	N/m²
	Resistance	ohm	W	V/A

Index